THE RISE OF WESTERN CHRISTENDOM

The Making of Europe
Series Editor: Jacques Le Goff

The Making of Europe series is the result of a unique collaboration between five European publishers – Beck in Germany, Blackwell in Great Britain and the United States, Critica in Spain, Laterza in Italy and Le Seuil in France. Each book will be published in all five languages. The scope of the series is broad, encompassing the history of ideas as well as of societies, nations, and states to produce informative, readable, and provocative treatments of central themes in the history of the European peoples and their cultures.

Also available in this series

The European City*
Leonardo Benevolo

Women in European History
Gisela Bock

The Rise of Western Christendom: Triumph and Diversity, A.D. 200–1000
Second Edition
Peter Brown

The European Renaissance
Peter Burke

Europe and Islam
Franco Cardini

The Search for the Perfect Language
Umberto Eco

The Distorted Past: A Reinterpretation of Europe
Josep Fontana

The European Family
Jack Goody

The Origins of European Individualism
Aaron Gurevich

The Enlightenment
Ulrich Im Hof

The Population of Europe
Massimo Livi Bacci

Europe and the Sea*
Michel Mollat du Jourdin

The Culture of Food*
Massimo Montanari

The First European Revolution, 900–1200
R. I. Moore

Religion and Society in Modern Europe
Réne Rémond

The Peasantry of Europe*
Werner Rösener

The Birth of Modern Science
Paolo Rossi

States, Nations and Nationalism
Hagen Schulze

European Revolutions 1492–1992
Charles Tilly

* Title out of print

The Rise of Western Christendom

Triumph and Diversity, A.D. 200–1000

SECOND EDITION

Peter Brown

Blackwell Publishing

350 Main Street, Malden, MA 02148-5020, USA
108 Cowley Road, Oxford OX4 1JF, UK
550 Swanston Street, Carlton, Victoria 3053, Australia

First edition published 1996
Paperback edition published 1997
Second edition published 2003 by Blackwell Publishing Ltd
Reprinted 2003 (twice)

Library of Congress Cataloguing-in-Publication Data

Brown, Peter Robert Lamont.
    The rise of Western Christendom: triumph and diversity, A.D. 200–1000 / Peter Brown. — 2nd ed.
        p. cm. — (The making of Europe)
    Includes bibliographical references and index.
    ISBN 0–631–22137–9 (alk. paper) — ISBN 0–631–22138–7 (pbk. : alk. paper)
    1. Church history—Primitive and early church, ca.30–600. 2. Church history—Middle Ages, 600–1500. 3. Civilization, Medieval. I. Title.
II. Series.
BR162.3 .B76 2002
274—dc21

2002003526

A catalogue record for this title is available from the British Library.

Set in 10 on 12.5 pt Sabon
by Ace Filmsetting Ltd, Frome, Somerset
Printed and bound in the United Kingdom
by MPG Books Ltd, Bodmin, Cornwall

For further information on
Blackwell Publishing, visit our website:
http://www.blackwellpublishing.com

For Betsy

Contents

List of Maps   ix

Preface   x

Introduction   1

Part I: Empire and Aftermath: A.D. 200–500   35

1. "The Laws of Countries": Prologue and Overview   37
2. Christianity and Empire   54
3. *Tempora Christiana*: Christian Times   72
4. *Virtutes sanctorum . . . strages gentium*: "Deeds of Saints . . . Slaughter of Nations'   93
5. On the Frontiers: Noricum, Ireland, and Francia   123

Part II: Divergent Legacies: A.D. 500–600   143

6. *Reverentia, rusticitas*: Caesarius of Arles to Gregory of Tours   145
7. Bishops, City, and Desert: East Rome   166
8. *Regimen animarum*: Gregory the Great   190

Part III: The End of Ancient Christianity: A.D. 600–750   217

9. Powerhouses of Prayer: Monasticism in Western Europe   219
10. The Making of a *Sapiens*: Religion and Culture in Continental Europe and in Ireland   232
11. *Medicamenta paenitentiae*: Columbanus   248
12. Christianity in Asia and the Rise of Islam   267
13. "The Changing of the Kingdoms": Christians under Islam   295
14. Christianities of the North: Ireland   321
15. Christianities of the North: The Saxons of Britain   340
16. Micro-Christendoms   355

Part IV: New Christendoms: A.D. 750–1000

Part IV: New Christendoms: A.D. 750–1000   381

17. The Crisis of the Image: The Byzantine Iconoclast
    Controversy   383
18. The Closing of the Frontier: Frisia and Germany   408
19. "To Rule the Christian People": Charlemagne   434
20. *In geār dagum*, "In Days of Yore": Northern Christendom
    and its Past   463

Notes   489
Coordinated Chronological Tables   549
Bibliography   554
  Primary Sources   554
  Secondary Sources   564
Index   599

Maps

1. The world ca.350: the Roman and Sasanian empires   38
2. The territories of the Roman empire   53
3. Western Europe   94–5
4. Western Europe, excluding the British Isles   144
5. The Middle East, from Constantinople to Iran   268
6. Christianity in Asia   269
7. The British Isles and the North Sea   322
8. A new world, 800: the Carolingian, Byzantine, and Abbasid empires   384
9. Continental Europe   407
10. The Atlantic world   462

Preface

I must point out that my gratitude to those who have helped and encouraged me in this task of rewriting is implicit in almost every note of this book. For years now, the books of friends and colleagues have been my constant companions, my educators, and my delight. I trust that they will recognize themselves in all that is good in this book – and not in its errors, which are mine. But some have done far more. Julia Smith, in particular, has read many of its chapters. She has prompted me as much by her example as a historian of the early Middle Ages as by her generosity in offering advice and access to recent publications concerning almost every topic touched upon in the later parts of this book. Lisa Bailey (herself a student of the "applied Christianity" of the age) has performed a truly "Cassiodoran" labor in preparing the bibliographies and in helping to make the maps and chronological tables as "user-friendly" as possible. Above all, my wife Betsy has not only accompanied me undismayed on the travels which led, in part, to the writing of this book. She has read all of it with an eye to clarity and to presentation. But more than that: she has inspired all of it by her presence and by her rare joy in knowledge. It is dedicated to her.

Princeton,
January 12, 2002.

Introduction

This book was first published in 1995 in the series *The Making of Europe*. I have now substantially revised and rewritten it. The reason for this decision has been the veritable "dam burst" in the study of late antiquity and of the early Middle Ages which has taken place within the last five years. It would now be imprudent in the extreme to undertake to write a history of this period without allowing one's judgment to be influenced by these many studies, and without ensuring that readers knew that they now existed. A reader need only note the dates of so many of the books cited in the bibliography to realize the extent to which the study of what used to be known as the period of the Decline and Fall of the Roman Empire and of the "Dark Ages" has entered upon a new phase of creativity.[1]

Any work of synthesis such as this one involves the author in innumerable decisions and renunciations – which themes to concentrate on and which to disregard, which traditions of scholarship to adhere to, and which to leave to one side as irrelevant, unhelpful, or out of date. Experts in the field will readily recognize the choices on which this particular survey is based. The general reader, however, may benefit from knowing a little more than the narrative text itself can communicate, about what drew me to this theme in the first place and about the traditions of scholarship to which I have turned when writing about the rise of Christianity in western Europe in the way that I have done. To know how this book took on its present shape may help readers to read it with greater understanding.

Western Europe in a Wider World

One thing should be obvious to a reader. This is a book which attempts to set Western Europe itself against a wider world. It is most important that this should be so. As I hope to make plain in my very first chapter, throughout this period the Christianity of what we now call Europe was only the westernmost variant of a far wider Christian world, whose center of gravity lay, rather, in the eastern Mediterranean and in the Middle East.

Throughout this period, the east Roman empire – what we now call the "Byzantine" empire – did not remain a remote and unchanging presence, of little relevance to the emergence of Latin Catholic Christianity. Chapters 7 and 8 make plain that, for centuries after the fall of the Roman empire of the west, the eastern empire remained a constant military presence in the western Mediterranean, as was shown by the conquest of the emperor Justinian and by the subsequent tenacity of the Byzantine holdings in Italy, in Africa, and even, for a shorter period, in Spain.

For the entire period between A.D. 535 and 800, Rome was a frontier city. It lay on the western periphery of a great, eastern empire. Every document which the popes issued, at that time, was dated according to the reigns of East Roman rulers who rose and fell over 1,300 miles away, in Constantinople (modern Istanbul), and whose careers were determined not by events in western Europe, but by what happened along the eastern stretches of the Danube, on the steppes of the Ukraine, in Iran, and in the Arabian peninsula.

But the continued relevance of the eastern empire for the Christianity of the West was more than a matter of political geography. The eastern empire (and not Rome) lay at the hub of a worldwide Christianity, which stretched as far into Asia as it did into Europe. As in a great echo chamber, the theological issues which were debated most fiercely in Constantinople, Alexandria, and Antioch in the fifth and sixth centuries (as we shall see at the end of chapter 4 and in chapter 7) resounded for centuries in the West. They resounded, indeed, wherever Christians had occasion to think about the relation between God and humankind, whether this was in the monasteries of Ireland and southern Scotland, in the Caucasus, in Mesopotamia, or even in the western capital of the Chinese empire at Hsian-fu.

And it is important to realize that the Christianity of the eastern empire was not a static matter. It was in a state of constant change. As we shall see in chapter 17, Greek Christianity changed as drastically, under the impact of the Muslim invasions of the late seventh and eighth centuries, as the Christianity of the West had changed in the centuries after the fall of the Roman empire. A new "Byzantine" empire emerged from the eighth-century crisis known to scholars as the "Iconoclastic Controversy." This crisis was accompanied by an urgent effort to reform Christian practice and to redefine the Christian past which was similar to the efforts at reform and renewal made, at the same time, in the Frankish empire of Charlemagne.

Last but not least, the rise of Islam and the consequent conquest and conversion to the new faith of most of the Middle East, of North Africa, and even, for half a millennium, of southern Spain, seems to place an insuperable imaginative barrier between ourselves and an ancient Christian world where north Africa, Egypt, and Syria had been the most populous and creative regions of the Christian world. But Islam did not come from nowhere. Nor did it instantly blot out all that had come before it. As we will see in chapter 12, Islam emerged in an Arabian environment thoroughly penetrated by Christian and Jewish ideas. Far from bringing the ancient world to an abrupt end, Islamic culture and Islamic theology developed in constant, mute debate with Jews and with Christians who remained in the majority among the inhabitants of the Middle East for centuries after the Arab conquests.

As we will see in chapter 13, Christian communities formed in the time of the great theological controversies of the reign of Justinian continued for centuries largely unaffected by the great Arab empire which now arched above them. The cultural achievements of the Syriac-speaking Christians of Syria and Mesopotamia in this period are all too easily overlooked. Yet Syriac translations of Greek works, often completed at a time when the war zone between Muslim and Byzantine armies swung disastrously backwards and forwards across northern Syria and Anatolia, built up a "water table" of knowledge of classical Greek thought in Syriac versions which would be tapped, with such success, by Islamic philosophers, doctors, and mathematicians in succeeding centuries.[2]

Altogether, the shape of this book has been determined, in large part, by a conviction that students of Christianity in western Europe will be rewarded by making the effort to understand how, at the same time, other variants of the Christian faith, in other regions, faced problems which were often more similar than we might think to those which faced their western coreligionists. At that time, eastern Christianity was not an alien world. Often, its problems affected western Europe directly. But even when this was not the case, much can be learned about the particularity of Latin Christianity itself from comparison with its Christian neighbors.

The Making of Europe: "A History of European Unity"?

But the reader should know that I was led to offer a book with this particular shape because of my own rethinking, in the light of modern scholarship, of how best to write a history of western Europe itself in the period between the rise of Christianity in the Roman empire, from around A.D. 200, and the conversion of the Scandinavian world in A.D. 1000. For in the past decades I have come to realize that a series of decisive publications now suggest that much of the conventional Grand Narrative of that period might be wrong. The story of the spread of Christianity in late antique and early medieval western Europe could be told in a very different, and altogether more interesting, manner. It might help the reader of this book if I summarize briefly the principal features of the Grand Narrative of European history from which I have departed in this book.

The most striking, and decisive, feature of conventional narratives of the end of the Roman empire and the early Middle Ages has been the insistence that the history of western Europe has always been characterized by a natural unity. This unity was regarded as the ideal. Departures from it were held to be a sign of decay and of aimless anarchy. It was assumed that the unity of western Europe had first come into existence under the Roman empire. From the north of Britain to North Africa, the charmed world enclosed within the Roman frontiers was the first Europe. In 1912, the author of a study of the Romanization of Roman Britain could write: "The safety of Rome was the safety of all civilization.Outside roared the wild chaos of barbarism."[3] After the year A.D. 400 – so the Grand Narrative continues – the frontiers of the empire collapsed, and "the wild chaos of barbarism" flooded into the empire from across the North Sea, the Rhine, and the Danube. The period of the "Barbarian Invasions" effectively destroyed the first unity of Europe.

But all was not lost. Christianity had already spread widely in Continental western Europe. It was through the insubstantial but tenacious bonds created by the Catholic Church that the broken unity of Roman Europe was re-created. All roads came to lead, yet again, to Rome, as the papacy established itself as the undisputed center of a new, Catholic West. After A.D. 600, "The Age of the Barbarian Invasions" was followed by "The Age of the Missionaries." In textbooks of the period, maps of the "Barbarian Invasions" showed western Europe crisscrossed by ominous arrows as barbarian tribes appeared to sweep triumphantly from north to south, seeking out the heart of Rome. But on the very next page, a map of "The Age of the Missionaries" would show the arrows moving in a more benign direction – from Rome all the way to the furthest edges of northwest Europe. The arrows would reach the British Isles, through the famous mission of pope Gregory the Great to the pagan Saxons of Britain, in 597. Then they would bounce, like beams of light reflected from a distant source, as missionaries from Ireland and Anglo-Saxon England brought a Christianity renewed by contact with its source in Rome, first to a decadent northern Gaul (in the person of the great Irishman, Columbanus, in 590) and then, in the eighth century (in the persons of the Anglo-Saxon missionaries, Willibrord and Boniface) to pagan Holland and, eventually, into the dark woods of Germany.

After A.D. 800, the stridently Catholic Frankish empire founded by Charlemagne seemed, for a moment, to have brought to an end the four centuries of aimless fragmentation which characterized Europe's loss of its first unity. The hopes inspired by Charlemagne in early twentieth-century scholars are summed up by Christopher Dawson, a deeply humane and learned exponent of a specifically Catholic vision of the history of Europe, in a book entitled, significantly, *The Making of Europe: An Introduction to the History of European Unity*. For Dawson, the coronation of Charlemagne as "emperor" at Rome on Christmas Day 800, marked

> the full acceptance by the Western barbarians of the ideal of unity for which the Roman Empire and the Catholic Church alike stood.

But Charlemagne's Catholic Empire of Europe did not last:

> It was a premature synthesis, since the forces of barbarism both within and without the Empire were still far too strong to be completely assimilated.[4]

The disintegration of Charlemagne's empire marked a definitive failure to realize in western Europe

> the passionate longing of better minds for a formal unity of government [over and against] the instinct of separation, disorder and anarchy caused by the impulses and barbarous ignorance of the great bulk of mankind.[5]

The history of the Dark Ages, therefore, ended on a dying fall. Christianity had re-created the unity of Europe on a spiritual level. This spiritual unity would, indeed, be fully realized, in the ensuing centuries, in a Latin Christendom dominated by the medieval papacy. But it would no longer be found, as in the glory days of Rome, in the creation of a single, civilized, political community. One thing was certain: between A.D. 400 and 1000, "the instinct of separation, disorder and anarchy, caused by ungoverned impulses and barbarous ignorance" seemed – except for a few fragile moments – to hold center stage.

Barbarians and Missionaries

It is not surprising, then, that the teaching of the Dark Ages in the first part of the twentieth century was a somewhat depressing business. It appeared

that Edward Gibbon had been right in his magisterial summary of the period, *The Decline and Fall of the Roman Empire*: the fall of the Roman
empire coincided with the "triumph of religion and barbarism" throughout
western Europe.[6] No high culture could be expected to survive such violent
disorder. In the opinion of Gibbon and of his later readers, none worth the
name did survive. Yet only the Christian religion, precisely because it was a
cruder force than was the refined culture of Rome, could hope to rein in the
barbarians of the North. The "Rise of Western Christendom" amounted to
little more than a salvage operation – the preservation, within Christian monasteries, of what little remained of the culture of Rome and the slow renewal
of a sense of community around a "Roman" Catholic Church. And in the
period between 400 and 1000, this salvage operation had been, at best, a
messy business, unredeemed by flashes of genius, and frequently thwarted
by outbursts of "barbarism."

But at least everyone agreed that the "barbarians," rough fellows though
they were, could be treated as the direct ancestors of the modern nation-
states. No one in the nineteenth century doubted that England came from
the Anglo-Saxons and that Catholic France had been founded by the Franks
of Clovis. The Germans insisted on claiming Charlemagne for themselves.
Under similar, romantically "archaic" kings, the Irish managed to remain
Irish (just as they always had been and always should be) until their golden
age of independence ended with the Norman intrusion of the twelfth century. Even the most Mediterranean of Spaniards have been known to look
back with nostalgia to an imagined and distinctive "Visigothic" heritage.

Statues in public places made very clear to everyone what these rude ancestors of the modern nations must have looked like. They were Wagnerian
figures with winged helmets, scale-mail breast-plates, cloaks trimmed with
fur, and baggy trousers bound up with thongs. They carried heavy weapons
and sported impressive moustaches. Furthermore, there are few cities in western Europe whose museums and art galleries do not exhibit a nineteenth-
century painting of a Christian missionary at work among such ancestors. In
such paintings, a figure of a Christian missionary with an ethereal expression and markedly "Roman" features addresses the court of a barbarian
king. The king, a bearded figure with crown and furrowed brow, dressed in
full "barbarian" splendor and surrounded by brawny counsellors armed to
the teeth, sits on his throne and listens intently. Often, as in the case of
Clovis, king of the Franks, the ruler is shown humbly approaching the baptismal font in full warrior gear, accompanied by his fur-clad retinue, to bow
before a clergyman dressed in a strange cross between a "Roman" toga and
the later, Gothic vestments associated with a Catholic bishop.[7] These are
elevating scenes. Needless to say, they place a severe strain on a modern

historian's sense of the probable. But they are deeply embedded in the visual imagination of most Europeans. It is part of the purpose of this book to remove them from our minds, and to substitute a more truthful and complex image of what happened at this time.

Plainly, two central elements of this picture have changed irrevocably – the image of the barbarian and the image of the missionary. This change has decisively affected the manner in which I deal, in chapters 1, 4, and 5, with the relation between Romans and "barbarians" along the frontiers of the empire, from the first to the fourth centuries; with the nature of the so-called "barbarian settlements" within the empire, in the fifth century; and with the implications of the final taking over by "barbarians" of the Roman frontier zones as far apart as northern Britain, northern Gaul, Austria, and Morocco, in the late fifth century.

A similar revision of standard opinions lies behind my presentation (in chapter 6) of the sixth-century Gaul of Gregory of Tours. For once we remove the screen set up by Gregory's heartfelt but idiosyncratic narrative of his own times, we can come closer to seeing what it was really like to live in a "low-pressure" but none the less stable post-Roman society. Frankish Gaul had by no means sunk into aimless barbarism.

As for the northern barbarians at their most seemingly exotic and intractable – that is, those perched in the Atlantic and North Sea world of Ireland, Britain, and, later, of Scandinavia – I trust that what I write in chapter 14 and, again, in chapter 20, may open up a different view from the image of puzzled but well-meaning warlords, straining to catch, from the mouth of a foreign missionary, the elevated message of the Gospels. One point needs to be stressed in modern revisions of the "age of the missionaries." In coming to the British Isles, Christianity did not encounter isolated societies, each happily locked in the immemorial traditions of their tribe. Rather, when dealing with Ireland and with the Saxons of Britain, I have taken to heart the warning of an archaeologist noted for his contributions on the mysterious Anglo-Saxon burial ship discovered at Sutton Hoo in East Anglia. "The key concepts to *abandon*," he writes, sternly underlining the word "abandon," "are those of ethnicity and tradition."[8]

The worlds of the "barbarians" of the northern seas were fluid worlds. They managed to be both distinctive and, at the same time, highly adaptable to foreign influence if brought to them in the right way. Hence my account emphasizes the inner tensions and the adaptability of the barbarian host societies who welcomed Christianity. Such an emphasis differs from the former stereotype of the encounter of high-minded foreigners with the immovable mass of a tradition-bound "barbarian" society. It may help to explain the rapidity and the precise path along which Christianity spread both in Ireland, and, a little later, in Saxon Britain in the course of the late sixth and seventh centuries.

Such an approach also helps to direct attention to what is now rightly seen as one of the great triumphs of Dark Age culture: the gradual creation, by the barbarians, of a sense of their own past. It had long been taken for granted by scholars that the "barbarian" societies of Frankish Gaul, of Celtic Ireland, and Saxon Britain, and, later, of Germany and Scandinavia, were societies characterized by traditional customs which reached back into the immemorial past. Each group was thought of as encrusted with a distinctive, "ethnic" past, which was so tenacious that it would endure to become that nation's "national" past in modern Europe. As long as this assumption was made, the actual writers of the histories and the transcribers of poems, sagas, and legends who had made this "barbarian" past available to us were figures of little interest. For we assumed that they did no more than record (often in a Latin as "barbarous" as the subjects of their discourse) a barbarian past which was really there and had always been there.

What modern scholarship has recovered, precisely through eroding that sense of an impervious, "barbarian" past which waited only to be recorded, is the sheer excitement of men of the pen of the sixth, seventh, and eighth centuries as they set about to create for themselves an orderly and "usable" view of the origins of their own tribes. The tools with which they did this were, of course, provided largely by the new religion. Not only did Christian intellectuals bring the skills of writing to previously nonliterate societies. They brought ways of writing historical narratives which derived from the Old Testament and from the historical traditions of the Roman world which Christians had already adapted to their own needs in earlier centuries. We owe almost all that we know of the history and literature of pre-Christian northern Europe to learned clergymen who set to work with urgency and with great intelligence to make their own, for their own needs, large sections of the pre-Christian past. As a result, the seventh, eighth, and ninth centuries, which saw the triumph of Christianity, can also be seen as the last great age of myth-making in northern Europe.

When approaching this highly original synthesis of pagan past and Christian present, it is not easy to reach a firm conclusion as to how much of the original texture of pre-Christian society actually made it into written form. In parts of chapter 14 and, finally, in chapter 20, I have tried to communicate some of the more fruitful ways in which modern scholars have grappled with this problem. What matters most is what such an attempt at synthesis meant to those who undertook it. The creation of a "usable past" happened all over the Christian world. Here it is important to look again outside the narrow boundaries of western Europe. We now know, from recent studies of the highest quality, that without the robust sense of unity under God conveyed in Bede's *Ecclesiastical History of the English Nation* the notion of an "English nation," indeed of "England" itself, would never have been imposed, in later centuries, on the untidy patchwork of Saxon adventurers, acculturated Britons, and Celtic kingdoms on which Bede looked out in his own day. But we do not so often think of the late fifth-century Armenian *Epic Histories* of P'awst'os Buzand and the works of his successors, Elishe the Vardapet and Lazarus of P'arp, as doing the same, and with similar, millennium-long consequences for a distinctive Armenian sense of national identity, as we see in chapter 12. Nor do we appreciate that the Irish lawyers, poets, and writers of legends who have preserved for us the richest vernacular heritage of all to emerge from Dark Age western Europe were the exact contemporaries of the first collectors of the poetry and historical traditions of the Arabs. I hope, in chapter 13, to guide readers to recent literature which has done justice to the sheer verve and sense of urgency with which the Muslims of the late seventh century strove to preserve their own identity in a world which could so easily have swamped them. They did so by creating a memory of the Prophet Muhammad lovingly rooted in a purely Arabian environment, in such a way that the landscape of the seventh-century Hijâz has dominated the imagination of the Islamic world from that time until the present.

A Mediterranean Unity? The "Pirenne Thesis"

So much for the "barbarians" and their "missionaries." But what about the overall theme of the "unity" of western Europe? It is here that I suspect that scholarship has changed most decisively in recent years. It is these changes of opinion as to what constituted the "unity" of Europe at this time which have caused me to rethink the issue of the nature of Christianity itself and the implications of its expansion in western Europe. Bluntly: what do we mean by the subtitle of this book, "Triumph *and* Diversity?"

In this matter, I was challenged to rethink my own views by the slow realization, in the course of the 1980s, that I could no longer rely on the most brilliant interpretation ever written of the course of European history from the end of the Roman empire to Charlemagne – Henri Pirenne's *Mohammed and Charlemagne*. No discussion of the nature of "Dark Age" Europe can be complete without a mention of "the Pirenne thesis." This was because, in his *Mahommed and Charlemagne* (which appeared in English translation in 1937) and in a series of articles which had appeared 15 years earlier, Pirenne had looked straight through the traditional narrative of the early medieval period – a narrative in which barbarians and missionaries had predominated – to the central issue: the unity of Europe. He propounded an explanation of that unity which virtually ignored the barbarians and which offered a robustly "laicized" explanation for the success of the missionaries.[9]

Put very briefly, Pirenne's argument was as follows. The unity created by the Roman empire had not been broken by the "barbarian invasions." For the barbarian invasions were a non-event. Their long-term destructive impact had been exaggerated by shocked contemporaries. Not only this. The barbarians themselves had brought nothing new. Pirenne's "barbarians" were utterly stripped of the solidity and the magical aura with which they had been surrounded by previous generations of German nationalist historians. Their laws, their social structure, their worldview had nothing to contribute to the Roman world into which they had moved. They settled into the structures of a still-Roman world like impoverished squatters taking up residence in an ancient *palazzo*.

For Pirenne, then, in dismembering the Roman empire, the "barbarians" had not broken the unity of Europe. For the unity of Europe rested on something more substantial than a mere political system. It rested on commerce and on the life of cities sustained by commerce. This meant, in fact, that it rested on the Mediterranean. The Mediterranean was the "all-nourishing sea" along which the wealth of the Levant (an eastern Mediterranean still firmly controlled by the east Roman empire) continued to flow into Merovingian Gaul and even beyond. Hence it was possible for a Roman way of life to survive in western Europe (and especially in its Mediterranean regions) for centuries after the Roman empire itself had succumbed to barbarian invasion. Only when the Arab conquests destroyed the unity of the Mediterranean in the course of the seventh century, by placing a hostile power along its eastern and southern shores, was the "Roman" unity of Europe destroyed. It was with the Arab conquest of Carthage, in 698, and not in A.D. 400, that western Europe finally ceased to be "Roman." Only then did the balance of power and of culture shift drastically to the North. The progress of the Arab armies along the Mediterranean coastline of North Africa – and no surge of creativity from the obscure woods of Germany – was what set the pace for the rise to dominance of the family of Charlemagne, which led to the creation of a northern, Catholic empire based on Aachen. Hence the provocative title of Pirenne's book, *Mohammed and Charlemagne*: "It is therefore strictly correct to say that without Mohammed, Charlemagne would have been inconceivable."[10]

One can see at once why such a thesis was especially attractive to those of us who studied the late antique period. It did nothing less than add a quarter of a millennium to the life span of the ancient world. It was possible to study the long-term development of late Roman culture and of a "Mediterranean" style of Christianity long after the political "fall" of the Roman empire of the West. A Mediterranean-wide Christianity, in which west and east still mingled through the benign vigor of mercantile exchange, lay, like a well-installed central heating system, at the southern base of Europe. Through commerce and, a little later, even through "Roman" missionaries, it continued to blow regular gusts of warm, late classical air into the cold regions of the North.

Pirenne had given us what his younger contemporary, Christopher Dawson, had tried to give us in his characteristically Catholic insistence on the primacy of Rome – a clue to the unity of Europe. It was commerce, not Catholicism, which had held western Europe together for centuries after the so-called "barbarian invasions." In making this claim, Pirenne provided western Europe with a center of unequalled solidity. And when it came to solidity, nothing could have seemed more solid than the landscape of the pre-industrial Mediterranean, as this was conjured up (only a decade after the appearance of Pirenne's *Mohammed and Charlemagne*) by the great French exponent of the relationship between history and geography, Fernand Braudel.

Although written about the sixteenth century, Braudel's *The Mediterranean and the Mediterranean World in the Age of Philip II* quickly became the vade mecum of late antique historians. For this great book gave an inimitably concrete face to a Mediterranean whose decisive role in pre-Carolingian western Europe Pirenne had posited but never, in fact, examined. Braudel's lovingly circumstantial vision of the essential unity of the Mediterranean world provided the ballast for the brilliant but somewhat frail hypothesis of Pirenne. Historians of late antiquity could now agree that, from A.D. 200 to at least 700, the Mediterranean itself, a clearly defined landscape, encrusted with millennia of experience of human habitation and sharply distinguished from its northern and southern neighbors by a unique ecology and lifestyle, provided a center to western Europe which was notably more palpable than was the somewhat disembodied notion of a spiritual unity realized by the Catholic Church.[11]

By providing an apparently incontrovertible center to early medieval Europe, Pirenne also defined its periphery. Here, Dawson and Pirenne converged. Europe had a center. If this was not the Rome of the early medieval popes, it was, at least, the Mediterranean zone in which Rome was included, and on whose commercial and cultural vigor the popes based their spiritual claims to centrality within the Latin Church. It also had a periphery. These were the wild, non-Mediterranean lands beyond the immediate reach of the "Roman" south – the Rhine estuary, Britain and Ireland – to whom missionaries came in the course of the sixth and seventh centuries. According to Pirenne's vision (which, again, he shared with Dawson) they came to the barbarians as the representatives of a benign form of cultural diffusion from an undisputed "center" of "higher civilization" situated in the rich South.

After Empire: A World without a Center

One can imagine the combination of disquiet and excitement when it slowly became plain that this cogent model was no longer acceptable. By the middle of the 1980s, the patient work of the archaeologists had left very little to support Pirenne's thesis of the continuing commercial vigor of the Mediterranean and of the cities of Merovingian Gaul which had supposedly been nourished by this commerce. The verdict of the archaeologists is clear: by the year 600, much of western Europe was in a state of almost total economic "involution." Large areas of the hinterland of Italy, Gaul, and Spain had closed in on themselves. Even in what had once been a highly urbanized region, such as Italy, city life had shrunk dramatically.[12]

It is a bleak view of the western economy. It implies, furthermore, that we may have exaggerated the overall wealth and sophistication of western Europe under the Roman empire. It was not as highly developed a society as we might conclude from its surviving monuments. Even in classical times the apparent prosperity of the Roman cities could not be explained by commerce alone. There had never been a commercial unity to be destroyed. Fragile in the first place, the Roman unity of the West seems to have evaporated more rapidly than we had thought after A.D. 400.

How had this state of affairs come about? The fault lay with the weakening of the late Roman state. This state had been built up to an unparalleled level in order to survive the crisis of the third century (as we shall see in chapter 2). The "downsizing" of this state, in the course of the fifth century, destroyed the "command economy" on which the provinces had become dependent. As we will see in chapter 5, the total reversion of the economy of post-imperial Britain to a condition more crude, in many aspects, than in pre-Roman times, was not due to the inroads of barbarian invaders. Barbarian raiding was secondary. The truly chilling discontinuity in Britain was caused by the withdrawal of the late Roman state.

The fate of post-imperial Britain is a reminder that the long-term cost of having created an entire social order geared to supporting a world empire may have been more destructive for the inhabitants of a Roman province, once the empire which supported this social order had withdrawn, than were the imagined ravages of barbarian invaders. With its insistent gathering of wealth and goods through taxes and their distribution for the maintenance of large armies, of privileged cities, of imperial palaces, and of an entire ruling class implicated in the imperial system, the late Roman state was the crude but vigorous pump which had ensured the circulation of goods in an otherwise primitive economy. Once this pump was removed (as in Britain) or had lost the will to tax (as in Merovingian Gaul and in other "barbarian" kingdoms) the Roman-style economy collapsed. In the absence of a powerful state, no commercial activity, such as Pirenne had posited, was at hand to keep the economies of Europe from sliding into a state of acute regionalism. "Low-pressure" states and sluggish economies were the order of the day. From A.D. 400 onwards, diversity, not unity, was the hallmark of an age without empire.[13]

"Micro-Christendoms": Center and Periphery in Christian Europe

A historian of the Christian Church in early medieval western Europe must take seriously the state of modern views on the society and economy against which this Church developed. I trust that I have made available in my footnotes much of the literature on which this picture of the depleted state of post-imperial Europe depends. What concerns us here, however, is the stark fact that we are left with a western Europe without a center. Loyalty to memories of the Roman empire were not enough to provide such a center. Nor was the desire to transfer such loyalties to the popes of Rome sufficiently widespread, in a world characterized by strong regional churches, to bring about a centering of the western world on papal Rome, such as would later occur in the high Middle Ages. Now that the notion of the commercial vigor of the Mediterranean as a unifying force in the first centuries of early medieval western Europe has been removed, through careful study of the circulation of goods and of the fate of former Roman cities, we are left with a world with neither a clearly defined center nor a clearly defined periphery. It looks very much as if post-imperial western Europe was like Oakland, California, as described by Gertrude Stein: "There is no *there* there."

Nothing could pose a greater challenge to a religious historian than such a situation. For the fact remains that Pirenne saw one feature of early medieval Europe clearly, even if he explained it wrongly. Christopher Dawson saw the same feature, although he, also, was content to explain it in terms of his warm vision of the emergence of a "Roman" Catholic Europe. This feature which both Pirenne and Dawson saw was the remarkable "inter-connectivity" of the Christianity of this time.

Such inter-connectivity marked the arrival in western Europe of a cultural and religious force which had not existed in the time of the many gods. Christianity was a universal religion. As chapter 1 makes plain, this was already apparent to an intellectual writing in Edessa (Urfa, eastern Turkey) at the beginning of the third century. Christians might not convert everybody; but they could, at least, be everywhere. The possession of sacred Scriptures made of them a potentially worldwide "textual community." The reader should meditate (as I have often done) on the implications of those humble fragments which show the same book of the Psalms being copied out, at the same time, as a writing exercise by Christian children, both in Panjikent near Samarkand and in northern Ireland. The basic modules of Christianity, also, were remarkably stable and easy to transfer – a bishop, a clergy, a congregation (called in Greek a *laos*, a "people": our word for "laity") and a place in which to worship. Such a basic structure could be subjected to many local variations, but, in one form or another, it travelled well. It formed a basic "cell," which could be transferred to any region of the known world. Above all, Christians worshipped a God who, in many of his aspects, was above space and time. God and his saints could always be thought of as fully "present" to the believer, wherever he or she happened to be. In God's high world, there was no distinction between "center" and "periphery." In the words of the modern inhabitants of Joazeira, a cult site perched in a remote corner of northwest Brazil, Christian believers could be sure that, even if they lived at the notional end of the world (which, in western Europe in this period, happened, quite concretely, to be the west coast of Ireland) they had "Heaven above their heads and Hell below their feet."

Both Pirenne, the economic historian, and Dawson, the Catholic, saw very clearly the strange "inter-connectivity" of the web of Christian belief and practice which had come to cover much of western Europe by the year 500 and which would cover even more by the year 1000. Where they may have erred is in a premature attempt to ascribe the weaving of such a web to a single, pre-eminent center, whether this center was provided by the effects of a Mediterranean-wide economy or by the draw of a post-imperial, papal Rome.

For the notion of Christianity itself, shared by Pirenne and Dawson, may have misled them. Christianity was a remarkably universal religion, endowed with common codes which could spring up in many different environments. But, at this particular time, it was not necessarily a unitary, still less a uniform religion. Here, I think, it is something of an advantage to be a late antique historian, and to have spent much time, in the past years, studying the Christianities of the eastern Mediterranean and of the Middle East. Such study develops, in the scholar, a healthy taste for diversity. What has to be explained in the history of the Greek, the Coptic, the Syrian, and the Armenian Churches of the East (to name only a few) is the remarkable manner in which their Christianity remained both universal and, at the same time, highly local. As long as we think of the "localization" of Christianity as a failure to achieve some ideal of unity, we seriously misunderstand this phenomenon. Distressing though the fact may be to theologians (today as in the days of Justinian), what strikes the historian about the competing regional Churches of the east was the robust confidence of each of them that they possessed a sufficiently full measure of universal truth to allow each one of them to stand on its own.

The history of western Europe at this time was not marked by the rise of rival Churches, set against each other by differences of doctrine, as was the history of the Churches of the East. But the issue of how to reconcile a universal Christianity with the conditions of a highly regionalized world were similar. Hence my attempt, in chapter 16, to understand the particular combination of local autonomy with loyalty to the idea of a wider Christendom which characterized the Churches of seventh-century Ireland and of Saxon Britain. The title of this chapter, "Micro-Christendoms," represents a search on my part for a formula with which to express this intriguing phenomenon.

My point is that we should not think of Ireland and Britain simply as distant "peripheries" being drawn, ineluctably, into uniformity with a "center" placed in Rome. Many Irishmen and Saxons carried with them "a Rome in the Mind."[14] These "Romans" (as they called themselves) often strove to bring that distant Rome to their own region. They did this through the transfer of relics, through styles of art and building, and through following distinctive ecclesiastical customs. But they did this very much on their own terms. Their efforts were perceived as having brought to their own region a "microcosm" which reflected, with satisfactory completeness, the "macrocosm" of a worldwide Christianity. They did not aim to subject the "periphery" of the local Christianities of the British Isles to a "center" situated in Rome, as would happen in a later period under the ambitious popes of the eleventh and twelfth centuries. Rather, they strove to cancel out the hiatus between "center" and "periphery" by making "little Romes" available on their home ground.

Those who study the circulation of what have been called "symbolic goods" both in prehistoric and in living tribal societies know what this means. The arrival of objects or persons charged with the charisma of distant places did not carry with it the modern sense of dependence on a distant and "superior" center. Rather, such objects and persons could be seen as coming, in a sense, from heaven. They were welcomed because they were thought of as having enabled the local society to establish a "vertical" link with an overarching cosmos, which was shared by center and periphery alike.[15]

Even in societies considerably less developed than those of Dark Age Europe, extensive cultural "empires" can be created through such a flow of "symbolic goods." We are dealing throughout this period with a phenomenon well known to students of the relations between pre-Conquest Mesoamerica and the Anasazi societies of the American southwest. Despite the difficulties of long-distance communication and the overall poverty of the societies involved, a "symbolic system" can come to be established over surprisingly wide areas. Much fruitful study has been devoted to this process: "symbolic systems [are] maintained by the constant circulation of specialists . . . and by exchanges of women and goods and knowledge."[16]

This is as good and as value-free a definition as any that I know of the cultural processes which lay behind the "age of the missionaries" in early medieval Europe. The unusual vibrancy of the exchange of "symbolic goods" from one region to another, despite the "involution" of the local economies, goes a long way to explain the "inter-connectivity" of the western Christianity of this time. This was not an exchange between one, overwhelming "center" and its "periphery." Rather, it occurred among a loosely spread constellation of centers. Entire new cultural zones were created in northwestern Europe through such exchanges of symbolic goods between local centers. We need only think of the manner in which the Irish Sea became a "Celtic Mediterranean" in the course of the sixth century, crisscrossed by travelling scholars (as we will see in chapter 10), or the manner in which an entire cultural zone emerged in northwestern Europe in the seventh century, embracing Ireland, Britain, and Frankish Neustria in a way which compels us to think away all modern political and ethnic boundaries (as we will see, mainly, in chapters 11 and 14).

Constant inter-regional exchanges of this kind were quite as important in building up the cultural resources of northern Europe as were the occasional widely publicized moments of contact with the distant "center" at Rome. At this time, the "unity" of Western Christendom was like a geodesic dome, made up of interlocking modules. It was not like a great tent, upheld by a single tent-pole fixed in Rome or, more widely, in a still "Roman" Mediterranean. Its history, therefore, was not the sad tale of unity destroyed and then postponed, but rather, it can be read as a tale of not altogether dishonorable diversity.

This view, of course, imposes its own shape upon my narrative. Readers must be prepared to skip around a large area marked by significant diversities. I regret the inconvenience which this complex itinerary must impose on readers. I would recommend, most warmly, that they orient themselves by turning to the maps and chronological tables which are attached to each significant section of the book, and to turn to the end of the book, to consult the table of principal events placed side by side, region by region, for the full extent of the Christian world. But, alas, I can find no other way to communicate the nature of a Christianity whose principal feature, whose interest to the historian, and, perhaps, whose creativity itself, resided in its very diversity.

Early Medieval Christianity: A "Barbarized" Religion?

Last but not least, the reader is entitled to ask the blunt question: what, then, was the achievement of the Christianity of this age? He or she has usually received, in return, a blunt answer: not much. For, in the words of a fine recent essay on the subject, "Early medieval Christianity has a bad odor in modern historiography."[17] Our notion of the quality of early medieval Christianity in the centuries after A.D. 400 suffers heavily from the interstitial position which has afflicted the "Dark Age" period as a whole in most modern histories of Europe. This is a Christianity which stands somewhat awkwardly between the acclaimed Golden Age of the Fathers of the Church, who still wrote within the secure and rich cultural environment of the Roman empire (as we will see in chapter 3), and the burst of creativity and sophistication associated with the renaissance of the twelfth century and the subsequent Gothic age. Placed between two such high points, the level of European culture appears to have sagged depressingly in between. Indeed, scholars write as if it was almost necessary for the Christianity of the West to pass through a minor Ice Age of the spirit so that the achievements of later centuries should stand out in greater contrast. It is as if medievalists, having proved to their own satisfaction that their own, "Gothic" age was not nearly as dark as admirers of the Italian Renaissance used to say that it was, needed to defend their notion of a "medieval renaissance" by looking round to find a period of European history which could be treated as authentically "dark." They fixed on the Christianity of the period between 400 and 1000. "Dark Age" Christianity provided them with "a somber backdrop for the success story of western culture."[18] Even as fine a survey as Richard Southern's *Western Society and the Church in the Middle Ages* begins with a chapter entitled, bluntly, "The Primitive Age *c.*700–*c.*1050."[19]

Yet it is important to wrest ourselves free of this powerful stereotype. There is no denying that the Christianity of that time developed in a social and economic climate which was distinctly chilly. It may, indeed, have been literally a chilly time: there is evidence for a period of unusually cold and rainy climate over all of northern Europe in the sixth century.[20] Given such unprepossessing conditions, it was usual to say that the only notable achievement of which the Christian Church in this age was capable was the conversion of the northern barbarians. Scholars of the nineteenth and early twentieth centuries thought of the "barbarians" as singularly mindless creatures. In their view, the task of absorbing the rough populations of the north led to a fatal coarsening of the texture of Christianity itself.

It is often said that, after around A.D. 400, Dark Age Christianity came to differ significantly from its previous late antique forms. It is thought of as having "regressed" into an "archaic" phase.[20] The "archaic" features of this phase consisted in the merging of the individual into the community and in a consequent lack of interest in subjective experience; in the manner in which the life of the believer came to be hedged around with a complex system of taboos by which the clean was separated from the unclean and the sacred from the profane; in the wholesale adoption of the Old Testament, rather than the Gospels, as the model for Christian piety and as the basis of a Christian community; and in a thoroughly "barbaric" joy in the sheer opulence and mindless exactitude of mighty rituals. Opinions vary as to whether this state of affairs was brought about by a widespread collapse of Roman urban culture and of the "enlightened" intellectual traditions associated with it, or by direct contact with the barbarians. One thing was certain: Christianity had triumphed in Europe at the cost of losing its ancient purity and spiritual refinement.[21]

One need not accept such a view. To begin with, as a historian of the Early Church and of the late antique period, I never cease to wonder at the confidence with which scholars, Christians and non-Christians alike, declare that they somehow know for certain that such and such a feature of the Christian Church is not a manifestation of "true" Christianity – that it marked a decline from some more "pure" state of belief. This seems to me to amount to importing into the lay discipline of history a version of the potent religious myth of the pristine purity of the Primitive Church. This myth began to be formed around the end of the fourth century. It has been wielded with great effect by ecclesiastical reformers from the age of Augustine and John Cassian up to and beyond the Reformation. It has often been used for polemical purposes, to criticize many forms of Christianity through comparing them with an imagined, more perfect time. The Early Christians, however, seem to have regarded their own Church as far from perfect. Rather, I suspect that we are applying to the Christians of a distant age the basically well-bred and highly "spiritualized" notion of Christianity which we, as modern Europeans, Catholics and Protestants alike, still carry in the back of our minds.

Late antique Christianity had never been like this. If it seems more "elevated" than that of early medieval Europe, this may simply be due to a trick of perspective, caused by the changing nature of our evidence. In the third and fourth centuries, we know a lot about the writings of an undoubtedly sophisticated elite and surprisingly little about the day-to-day practice of the average Christian. To mistake the views of the Fathers of the Church for the texture of Christianity as whole in the Roman world is like taking the grandiose and elegant façade of a surviving Roman building for the sum total of life in a Roman city. Majestically balanced, such a façade was intended to project and still projects a highly sanitized image of classical antiquity. It makes us forget the levels of poverty, malnutrition, and disease which characterized the Roman world as a whole. In the same way, we should not be misled by the writings of the Fathers of the Church into mistaking their elevated views for the rougher texture of life as really lived by Christians. We should not expect to find a modern "sanitized" Christianity in the Early Church any more than we would find it in the early Middle Ages.

To take one obvious example: the more we study a phenomenon such as the cult of the saints, which swept across barbarian Europe in the sixth and seventh centuries, the more we realize that most of what we have been content to condemn as the "archaic," the "physical," and the seemingly "superstitious" features associated with its practice in barbarian lands grew directly out of its late antique Mediterranean background.[22] Such features were not the result of a later "contamination" of Christianity by a so-called "archaic" mentality.

The cult of the saints may mean nothing to us. But we have to understand how much it did mean, and had meant for so long, to late antique Christians. It was part of the religious common sense of the age. Christians of all levels of culture and ethnic background had tended to take for granted that the saints could be "present" on earth. Christians worshipped the one high God; but, unlike modern, post-Enlightenment Christians, who are wary of the notion of a universe crowded with intermediary beings, they positively gloried in the closeness of invisible guides and protectors (as we will see, especially, in chapters 3, 6, and 17). They did not carry around in their heads "the empty skies of [modern European] missionary Christianity."[23]

It is the same with the issue of taboos. As we will see in chapter 10, we happen to know a lot about restrictions on "impure" foods, on "impure" substances, and on "impure" acts from the *Penitential* books produced first in western Britain and Ireland in the sixth century. We may not like what we read. But we cannot say that such concerns were an entirely novel departure, due to the transplantation of a more "elevated" Christianity into barbarian lands. Such taboos, in fact, had also been more widespread than we think around the Mediterranean. But, in the Mediterranean, they were taken for granted and were little talked about. As a consequence, they have left little trace in the written evidence for late antique Christianity. What made Ireland different was not that its inhabitants were somehow locked in an "archaic" mentality. What was unique about Ireland was the vigor with which the *sapientes*, the Christian learned men of the island, codified and applied to every aspect of life a system of taboos which previously had been based upon the tacit agreement of local communities. The drawing up of the *Penitentials* did not represent the corruption of a more "enlightened" Christianity. Rather, it marked a startling victory of the men of the pen who turned a widespread, almost nonverbal, sense of the distinction between the sacred and the profane, and between the pure and the impure (shared alike by barbarian and by Mediterranean Christians) into a finely calibrated system to be used for the guidance of souls.

"Background Noise": Dark Age Christian Culture

Early medieval Christianity, in the forms which it took after A.D. 400, cannot be treated as a "fallen" religion: it did not represent a regression from the more elevated standards of its own Early Christian and late antique past into "archaic" modes of thinking. But how did western Christianity continue to elaborate the religious and cultural heritage which it had accumulated in the days of the Roman empire in the very different world of post-imperial Europe?

Here it is important to look carefully, once again, at the overall social and economic conditions of the Roman and post-Roman West. There is a danger that we may exaggerate the height and stability of the Roman achievement, and, as a result, that we may exaggerate the depths to which Europe fell once the empire had been removed. A drastic "downsizing" of many aspects of life cannot be denied for this period. What is not so certain is that such a "downsizing" led to the total destruction or to the fatal depletion of the religious heritage of the Christian Church.

In re-thinking this matter I have been greatly helped by one of the most important studies of the ancient and medieval world to appear in recent years – *The Corrupting Sea: A Study of Mediterranean History* by Peregrine Horden and Nicholas Purcell.[24] Though limited to the Mediterranean, the book has much to say about historical processes which are relevant also to the cultural history of the post-imperial West as a whole. Among its many cogent arguments, this study of the social and ecological history of the Mediterranean world in pre-industrial times reminds us that change was the essence of Mediterranean life. The ecology of the region ensured that, throughout its history, the Mediterranean has always been crisscrossed by patterns of movement, causing goods, ideas, and persons to flow from point to point. These frequently coagulate at one nodal point or another. But they just as frequently shift away from ancient and apparently unchallengeable centers of "superior" civilization. The pace and mass of the flow of wealth and culture toward any given center or constellation of centers can fluctuate dramatically. A period of "intensification" (marked by the pulling together of resources from widely separated regions) is followed, just as often, by drastic periods of "abatement" – of letting go.

The network of Roman cities which had once covered western Europe was no exception to this rule. In the fifth and sixth centuries, these spectacular "arguments in stone," the product of centuries of "intensification" which had rested heavily upon the landscape (as we will see in chapters 1 and 2), simply underwent a period of drastic "abatement." They lost the high visibility which they had once enjoyed all over Europe. For Horden and Purcell, therefore, it comes as no surprise that Rome should empty out after A.D. 450, so that its population dropped from 500,000 to 50,000 within a century. But neither are they surprised that, at the same time, Constantinople, "New Rome," emerged at the other end of the Mediterranean as a boom city – possibly as the largest human settlement west of China. What we are tempted to describe as the "decline and fall" of an entire civilization is never quite the end of the world. It may be no more than the result of a regional shift in the patterns of "intensification."

The advantage of this image of change is the fluidity to which it draws attention. The end of the Roman order in the west was not like the crash of a single mighty building. It is more like the shifting contours of a mudbank in an ever-flowing stream: certain prominent ridges are washed away, other, hitherto mute landscapes gain in eminence. But the shifting mud of day-to-day social, economic, and cultural activity remains, to be piled up, once again, in yet another pattern. For certain features of an economy or a culture to lose high visibility does not mean that they have vanished entirely.

This way of seeing change in the ancient and medieval worlds is important for our consideration of the cultural as well as of the economic resources of the West, both within and outside the Mediterranean itself. For it makes it possible to see two developments occurring at one and the same time in this period. The critics of Pirenne cannot be gainsaid: the Roman cities and the patterns of "intensification" on which they had been based suffered from a period of drastic "abatement." But, at the same time, as we see both in sixth-century Syria (in chapters 7 and 12) and in the seventh-century valley of the Seine (in chapter 11), the effect of the evaporation of the post-Roman cities on the Christian culture of the age was "cushioned" by extensive relocation to the countryside. The production and circulation of the "symbolic goods" associated with Christianity did not come to a halt with the decay of the post-Roman cities. These simply came to travel along different networks, which now linked great rural monasteries to the hunting lodges of kings and to the country houses of a largely nonurban aristocracy. In much of Europe, it was in a largely rural environment that one would find the "goods" which maintained a Europe-wide "symbolic system": the texts, the relics, the spiritual guides, and the skilled practitioners of teaching, music, art, and architecture.

Furthermore, the economic developments studied in *The Corrupting Sea* may provide us with an apt analogy for the fate of the culture of the post-imperial West in the sixth and seventh centuries. Discussing the apparent disappearance of a high level of trade throughout the Mediterranean which occurred at this time, Horden and Purcell warn the reader not to conclude from the absence of "glamorous manifestations of high-prestige trade" that the once "all-nourishing" sea lay empty. The little ships were still there. The historian should not neglect "the 'background noise' of coast-wise movement which we have found in supposed dark ages."[25]

Nor should the historian of post-Roman Christian culture neglect the constant "background noise" of cultural activity. The more we study the production and circulation of manuscripts in this period, the more we are impressed by the number of "little ships" that are still to be found. As we will see in chapter 10, practical literacy (connected with legal practice and with the secular needs of royal courts) was more extensive in many regions of Europe than we had once thought. We are also increasingly struck by the multiplicity of low-profile centers of book production. These were more elusive but more numerous than were the few great *scriptoria* on which we had once focused our attention. They ensured that the supposed "nadir" of writing associated with the "Dark Ages" was never as deep as we had thought.

Speaking of the achievements of the many centers of learning in seventh-century Ireland, a scholar has concluded that

> it would be appropriate to think in terms of an archipelago: a number of small islands are surfacing above the level of the water, but under the surface lies the extensive shelf which gives the islands their stability.[26]

The same could be said of many other regions of Europe. The moment of self-congratulatory achievement, which we now call "the Carolingian Renaissance," depended on the existence of that "extensive shelf" of texts, built up in previous centuries. As with trade, so with literature. The "glamorous manifestation" of the literature of the Patristic Age in the fourth and fifth centuries – the product of a quite unusual moment of "intensification" in Christian culture – should not dazzle us to such an extent that we see only a black depth in subsequent centuries.

For if we look carefully, we will not see darkness, but rather, a world which is slowly but surely becoming more like our own. To illustrate this development, let me ask the reader to consider for a moment this book which he or she is now reading. There was nothing like it in the Roman world. Only around A.D. 300 (in chapter 2) did the bound *codex*, which is the format of this book, replace the unwieldy scroll. Only around 600 (that is, by chapter 10) did the writing in this book become legible as it is here: for the individual words came to be written separately instead of being run together. This change, which is associated with Ireland, marked "the great divide in the history of reading."[27] By the time of the Carolingian Renaissance, around A.D. 800, (in chapter 19) these texts came to be punctuated and divided up into paragraphs, and were written in a uniform script as they are in this book. Last but not least, the system of "A.D." dates which we now take for granted in any European historical narrative began to appear only around the year A.D. 700 (in chapter 18).[28] Altogether, slowly over the centuries, the format and even the meaning of the book itself had changed. The Roman world still speaks to us. But we must remember that it speaks to us now only through books whose shape came into being through the silent labor of generations of "technicians of the word" – lawyers, bureaucrats, and monks – in the centuries of Dark Age Christian Europe.

"Directly Ancestral": The End of Ancient Christianity

It is important to remember that this was not the first time that western Europe had experienced a shift of "intensification" into "abatement" such as accompanied the end of the Roman empire. The megalithic culture of the Atlantic regions, which had produced Stonehenge in southern Britain, the *menhirs* of Brittany, and New Grange in Ireland, had produced "arguments in stone" quite as impressive, in their own age, as were Roman cities. The degree of "intensification" involved in the mobilization of collective labor which went toward their construction was truly awesome. Their successors, in the "Urnfield Period" of around 1300 B.C., had less to show for themselves. They left "no great stone monuments to visit." Yet prehistorians realize that, through the quiet increments of their technological advances and in their social formations, it is they, and not the spectacular builders of Stonehenge, who are "directly ancestral."[29]

Taking place as it did in the silent depths of prehistory, the shift from the

Megalithic to the Urnfield culture does not elicit the passion and disquiet which are still evoked by thoughts of the fall of Rome. But it could also be said that the Christians of the early medieval West also made the shift from an impressive but distant civilization to one which is "directly ancestral" to us. It was not only the slow emergence of the book which makes us realize that, much as we may admire the Fathers of the Church as representatives of the last, spectacular flowering of ancient culture, it is the contemporaries of Gregory the Great, Columbanus, and Charlemagne who are "directly ancestral" to the Christianity of the European Middle Ages and so of modern times. Whether we like it or not, it is their blood, and not the blood of the Early Church, which runs in our veins.

For it was in the early Middle Ages, and not earlier, that the Christian imagination took on its peculiarly western shape. We are dealing with a series of irrevocable "precipitations" of ideas which had existed in diffuse form in late antique Christianity, but which had never been brought together with such decisive clarity of focus until the seventh and eighth centuries. These novel "precipitations" of ideas did not occur in late antiquity but in the period between 550 and 750. They mark the true "End of Ancient Christianity," to which I devote an entire section of this book.

To take a few examples: the minute calibration of sins and the development of the techniques of confession go back to this time. As we will see in chapter 10, by the sheer act of writing their *Penitentials*, the *sapientes*, the men of the pen of sixth-century Ireland, transformed into a comprehensive tool of pastoral care an ancient monastic system of spiritual guidance, which they had read of in texts concerning the Desert Fathers of Egypt. Thereby they opened a way which would lead, eventually, to the establishment of auricular confession as a principal feature of medieval and modern Catholic Christianity. As we shall see in chapter 11, the first steps were also taken at this time toward a notion of purgatory, with all that such a notion implies for the idea of the continuing particularity of every soul and for the creation of permanent imaginative bonds between the living and the dead.

These changes are not associated with dramatic changes in doctrine. They are considerably more important than that. They represent nothing less than a slow reorientation of the Christian imagination of the West as mute, but as irrevocable, as the change from the alien scroll to the "modern" book. It is as if, having travelled all day through a landscape, we looked out the window to find that we had, indeed, entered a different region. Old landmarks are no longer to be seen. New ones dominate the horizon. There are now large monasteries, pastoral systems devoted to confession and to the saying of Mass for the relief of souls in the other world. We can even detect the first, tentative outlines of the "Christian" cemetery, after centuries where such an institution had been strikingly absent.[30] It is only by looking back to the beginning of our journey that we realize that these new landmarks (landmarks which we now take for granted as part and parcel of Christianity) had simply not been there when we started out. On issues which intimately affect the Christian view of the afterlife and the day-to-day practice of all believers, we have left behind an ancient Christianity.

The Christians of the East, co-inheritors of the same ancient Christianity, would also come, for the first time, to look strange to the Latin world. As we shall see at the end of chapter 19, the reactions of intellectuals at the court of Charlemagne to the cult of icons in the Greek Church show the beginnings of a lasting parting of the ways in the Christian imagination. For (as we shall see in chapter 17) the Greek theologians who fostered and refined the cult of icons in the ninth century were themselves also "directly ancestral" to their own tradition. Though appealing to the immemorial traditions of the Fathers of the Greek Church, they, in fact, made their own "precipitate" of that tradition. They struck out on a new path which leads directly to a piety still common to the entire Orthodox world, from Greece to Vladivostok. Having created to their own satisfaction their own, distinctive "precipitate" from the Fathers of their own Latin past, Western Christians refused to follow them, with consequences which have lasted up to this day.

An Applied Christianity

It is important to end, therefore, by attempting to recapture something of the momentum which enabled so many discreet but surprisingly irrevocable changes in the Christian heritage to take place at this time. Let us concentrate, first, on the agendas of the elite. For them, I would suggest, the early Middle Ages represented the age *par excellence* of "applied Christianity." In East and West alike, we are dealing with persons who were deeply committed to bringing the Early Christian past into the present. They wished to make it available in the condensed form of digests, anthologies, and encyclopedic compilations; to turn the recommendations of ancient Christian authors and the rules of former Christian councils into a finely calibrated system of rules, adjusted to the needs of pastoral guidance; and to ensure that even the material aspects of Christianity – and, most especially, its visual impact – should be discreetly disciplined so as to communicate a correct and salutary message.

The care which went into the material production of texts so as to make them increasingly "reader-friendly" (to which we have referred) was only one aspect of a drive to catch an entire world in the web of inherited Christian words. No subject was too humble – whether this was what to do when a mouse fell into one's beer – nor too magnificent – such as a glimpse of the dim outlines of heaven and hell – not to be caught by the pen. Paradoxically, as literacy appears to have receded in western Europe, the religion of the elites of both the Latin and the Greek Churches became, if anything, more "textualized": it drew its guidelines and its sustenance from the texts of former authors. The notion of the "Fathers of the Church" was created in this time. Latins were proud to look back to Ambrose, Jerome, and Augustine, and Greeks to Athanasius, the Cappadocian Fathers, John Chrysostom, and Cyril of Alexandria.

After the death of Augustine, in 430, Latin Christians took comfort in the fact that they possessed a Latin Christian literature of their own.[31] They had their own "Fathers of the Church." But far from being placed on a pedestal, the late antique Christian past was treated as a body of living truth, to be applied to every situation of their own times. In that sense, there was no past, any more than the directions of a modern technical manual linger on the "past" of the scientific discoveries which enable a car-engine to be repaired or an electric current to be switched on. What mattered was that the past still "worked" in the present. Thus, for example, when, in 688, archbishop Julian of Toledo wished to console a gout-ridden colleague by composing a meditation on the joys of the life hereafter, he did not choose his own words. Instead, he made a series of extracts from the works of long-dead Fathers of the Church. In the form of extracts which could be easily read and reread, their message was focused on the reader with all the condensed energy of a laser beam. By these means, a doctrine, which all Christians had long taken for granted, would "touch the mind so much more vehemently and pierce the heart."[32]

The problem was not to create a new message nor to contest old ones, but to make sure that a message whose alloy had already been tried and found true in the days of the Fathers of the Church, should sink ever deeper into the hearts of individuals and of the Christian people of entire Churches. Even in its most settled areas, early medieval religion had the aspects of a "missionary religion." Its "ego-ideals" were the preacher, the spiritual guide, and the teacher. Hence, it was not surprising that when two vehicles for the communication of a religious message – the written and the visual: texts and icons – were thought to be in competition with each other, Christian leaders should have clashed so vehemently over which of the two had precedence in the task of "applying" Christianity. In the eighth and ninth centuries, disputes on this topic raged throughout the Christian world, from Iona and Aachen to Jerusalem and Constantinople, at the time of the "Iconoclast Controversy." The dispute was so fierce because both sides felt that they had a duty to discipline not only the minds but even, now, the eyes of the "Christian people committed to their charge."

I trust that in my chapters (notably in chapters 8, 10, 17, and 19) I have done justice to at least a few of the more central moments in this long-term mutation of Christian culture. It is a mutation which is easier to describe than to explain. Let me say, briefly, that the conventional explanation does not satisfy me. Early medieval Christian intellectuals are usually presented as men in a hurry. It is believed that their principal concern was to rescue what they could of a battered inheritance from Roman times in an age of violence and economic collapse. To take one well-known example: the work of Cassiodorus, the sixth-century bureaucrat turned monk, has been seen as no more than a salvage operation. It was believed that this work was carried out, with tragic urgency, on the very edge of the abyss of ignorance and disorder into which Italy and all Europe was about to slide. But (as we will see in chapter 8) the work associated with Cassiodorus' library at Vivarium communicates an entirely different impression. Cassiodorus and his monks did not see themselves in this way. Rather, they set to work inspired by a robust sense of the continuing existence, in East and West alike, of a rich and living tradition. This tradition was not in need of being salvaged. Rather, it needed to be fine-tuned. It needed to be turned into an "applied culture," adjusted to the needs of "modern times." What this "applied culture" may have lost in richness, it more than gained in the manner in which it communicated that here was a living wisdom which had settled down, from the first, frenetic moments of its creation, into the sure and confident stride of a long-distance runner.

In this respect, as I point out in chapter 10, early medieval Europe may not have been very different, in the long-term rhythms of its culture, from the Hellenistic and Roman worlds from which it came. Of the traditions of Biblical exegesis between 430 and 800, it has been said that "the primary desire appears to have been to mop up in the aftermath of genius."[33] But the need to "mop up in the aftermath of genius" is not a characteristic of this period alone. The same could be said of the entire half-millennium between Alexander's conquest of the Middle East and the end of the Roman empire. The blinding release of energy, associated with the Golden Age of Athens, was led, at a lesser voltage, through a teaching tradition which once reached as far as Aï Qanum, in northeast Afghanistan, and which eventually passed through the language barrier between Greek and Latin to dominate the Roman world. Endlessly reproduced, codified, interpreted, and elaborated by schoolmasters and by public intellectuals, it was still active in the days when the young Augustine himself suffered the pains of education in distant North Africa. As Cassiodorus knew very well, an "applied" culture, a Great Tradition carried from generation to generation on the back of its schoolmasters, was nothing new in the history of Europe. What was new was his intention that Christianity, and not a secular culture, should take over from the ancients the well-tried mechanisms of self-perpetuation.

Indeed, it is where it continued to move imperceptibly to the rhythms of a very ancient world that early medieval Christianity often seems most "backward" to us. Like the Greco-Roman world, it was, indeed, a world of schoolmasters – and proud of it. It was also an age whose leaders established a relationship to culture marked by deep existential seriousness. As we will see in chapters 8 and 10, Gregory the Great did not turn away from the classical past either because it was pagan or because he found it to be in an irreparably damaged state. He simply found it a distraction from the main business of life, which was to prepare the soul for judgment.

This reason for the narrowing of Gregory's vision places him against a very ancient background. His choice (though expressed now in Christian terms) was the same as that of any "philosopher" of the Hellenistic and Roman periods. He shared with these philosophers the austere assumption that there was only one permanent and all-important object on which the human mind could always work, slowly but with effect, to bring about irrevocable change: and that was the raw stuff of human nature itself. It was possible to transform the self. Much of the comfort and richness of a culture could and should be sacrificed to that one overriding aim.

What should be stressed is that the drastic focusing of attention which this austere vision of culture implied did not necessarily lead to impoverishment. There is a translucency in the thought of Gregory which is absent in the thunderous abundance of Augustine. Many of the features of Augustine which most appeal to modern persons in works such as his *Confessions* – his intense subjectivity, his fascination with the disjuncture between the inner and the outer person, the haunting sense of a hiatus between the material and the spiritual world – have been thought through by Gregory to more tranquil conclusions. The grinding tensions which gave energy to Augustine have been resolved through long centuries of spiritual guidance. The itinerary of the soul is more carefully plotted and the baffling diversity of human characters is catalogued with the loving precision of a doctor's handbook. The search of the troubled soul for transparency to God led Gregory to use a language where the outer and the inner lead more gently into each other, and where physical signs point without wavering to spiritual realities.[34]

We have entered an altogether more "sacramental" world, different from that of Augustine. It is not a cruder world. But it is a world with different hopes, oriented toward different forms of achievement. The world made sense. It showed the way securely to a beauty which lay beyond itself. Material objects, lovingly constructed and contemplated, could bridge the gulf between human beings and a distant God. It is a world similar to that which had emerged, at much the same time, in the Greek East under the influence of Pseudo-Dionysius the Areopagite. It is a world which has come to rest. Much as a giant star can collapse into fiery clusters under its own unimaginable mass, so, by the time of Gregory and his eastern peers, the exuberant Christianity of the late antique world has pressed itself down, under its own weight. The result, at times, was not depletion, but rather, "precipitates" of rare clarity.

In order to appreciate what this can mean, I would advise the reader to visit the ecclesiastical complex of Sant'Agnese and Santa Costanza on the Via Nomentana in Rome. The fourth-century mausoleum-church of Santa Costanza (originally the tomb of Constantine's daughter) still belongs to an ancient Christianity, revelling unthinkingly in the abundance provided by a wealthy and still classical empire. It is a delightfully confusing world of wicked pinks and bright greens, where pudgy cherubs romp among the garlands of God's paradise. To descend into the stillness of the adjoining early seventh-century church of Sant'Agnese is to enter the world in which Gregory felt at home. St. Agnes hovers silently and alone, set against a bottomless sea of gold, above an apse made as exquisite and translucent as a honeycomb by marble columns. The columns draw the eye, in a moment of uncluttered certainty, from the floating figure above, to the altar, which, itself, is placed directly above the relics below. Heaven and earth are back in place; and, in such a church, they can be seen to join.

"Portions of Paradise": Art, the Sacred, and Gift-Giving in Early Medieval Europe

To stand in a church such as Sant'Agnese is to come close to the principal intellectual and religious agenda of early medieval Christianity. This was a form of Christianity which, in its art and in much of its literature, strove "to remove the dividing line between Earth and Heaven."[35] In Christian worship of the age, "visual art was liberally employed to open doors between this world and the next."[36] Whether this was in a great pilgrimage shrine, blazing with light and heavy with perfume, in an intimate chapel where jewel-studded relic-cases lay on an altar laden with silver and golden plate, sheathed in multicolored silks and screened by intricate surfaces of translucent marble, in the heavy pages of a great, illuminated Bible of the Celtic North, or in the quiet gaze of a Byzantine icon, the Christianity of the period between 400 and 1000 littered Europe and the Middle East with its own equivalents of "arguments in stone." Here were little islands of the holy, where the sa-

cred was concentrated at its greatest intensity and marked out from the profane by all the skills available to a Dark Age society. Each in its own way was
a "portion of Paradise."[37]

It takes a considerable effort to gather together in our minds the sheer
magnificence of early medieval Christianity. The large basilicas of late antiquity survive around the Mediterranean – in Italy, Greece, and Turkey. Their
ground-plans and their floor mosaics, at least, astonish archaeologists by
their frequency all over the present-day Islamic Middle East and in North
Africa. But the majesty of northern Christianity in the early medieval period
is strangely muted. Its buildings paid the price of being, indeed, "directly
ancestral." Unlike the haunting early Christian ruins of the Middle East,
they were built on sites where building has been continuous from the early
Middle Ages onwards. Many were replaced by the Gothic cathedrals which
stand right over them. Many have been devoured by the modern cities of
Britain, France, Belgium, and the Rhineland. Anyone who has driven through
industrial Newcastle looking for the churches associated with the Venerable
Bede knows what I mean. When not swamped in this way by modern developments, the sites around which vibrant microcosms of a Christian order
had once clustered in northern Britain and in Ireland are characterized by an
unearthly emptiness. There is little in the ethereal beauty of present-day Iona
to hint at the solid wealth and artistic skill which had once been massed
around it. Compared with Roman or with Gothic Europe, the achievements
of that age – such as the works of the Venerable Bede and the Book of Kells
– remain strangely "placeless" in our imagination. Because of this, it is only
too easy to slip into the romantic error, which makes the achievements of
northern Christianity in the early Middle Ages appear as brilliant but as
fragile as a streak of winter sunlight over the Atlantic. It is hard to conjure
up the very real solidity of their original grandeur.

Part of the reason, of course, is that not all the visual "arguments" of early
medieval Christianity were "arguments in stone." Many involved the assembly in one place of astonishing examples of portable wealth – jewel-work,
textiles, perfumes, and written pages. These were all too easily scattered to
the winds in future ages, through sale or plunder, in a manner in which the
heavy, locked stones of a Roman city could never be scattered.

But this consideration, in itself, brings us back, for the last time, to a consideration of the economy and the society in which Christian art and architecture were developed at this time. The truth is that the elites of early medieval
Europe were considerably poorer than those of Roman times. Furthermore,
their deployment of wealth was dominated by concerns which did not lead
to the piling up of large architectural monuments. From the Gallo-Roman
bishops of the fifth century through to the Frankish aristocrats and the Saxon

and Irish kings of the seventh century, to the emperors and great popes of the Carolingian age, there is a shabby gentility about the aristocracies of Dark Age Europe which makes the visual and artistic achievements of the time all the more impressive.

For kings and aristocrats had been, in many ways, the principal victims of the general "abatement" of the age. The ending of the relentless system of taxation which had characterized the later Roman empire considerably weakened their ability to extract wealth on a regular basis from their inferiors. No longer policed and bullied every year to pay taxes, the peasantry slipped quietly out of the control of their landlords. Rents fell as taxes vanished. It has been cogently argued, indeed, that in many regions of Europe the Dark Ages were a golden age for the peasantry. Less of their agrarian surplus was taken from them than at any other time in the history of Europe from the foundation of the Roman empire to the end of the *ancien régime*. It was only with the ever more secure establishment of the landed basis of the Frankish aristocracy in the eighth and ninth centuries, under strong and wealthy kings, that the aristocracies could gather in enough wealth to support more ambitious ventures. In that sense, the "Carolingian Renaissance" was a portent for what would later happen in Europe in the Romanesque and Gothic periods. It marked "the beginning of the return to the normal life of grinding extortion from the peasant classes."[38]

In between, the aristocracies had to cut their clothes according to the shape of their cloth. Hence, the enormous importance, in the period between A.D. 400 and 800, of the gift-giving relationship. Though practiced with exceptional intensity in Ireland and Britain, gift-giving was by no means a purely "barbarian" institution: the popes of Rome and the Byzantine emperors were also spectacular givers at this time. What matters is the role which gift giving played in the transfer of wealth in a distinctly sluggish economy. It was based on a "science of the possible." It provided a scenario for magnificence which was most appropriate to the economic capacities of the givers and to the social profile of those whom they wished to impress. This meant, in effect, that spasmodic accumulations of wealth (often made from "windfalls" of plunder and the spoils of war) were disbursed to impress relatively small groups of important people – one's peers and, above all, one's military followers.[39] It goes without saying that holy places received long-term landed endowments. But it was the glory of the gift which lingered in the memory and before the eyes of believers.

As a result of this new rhythm of giving, the urban magnificence which we associate with the Roman period became irrelevant. Right up to the end of the fourth century, in much of western Europe, Roman landowners were assured by the workings of the imperial system of regular and large incomes.

They lavished this wealth on "arguments in stone" – on circuses, theaters, baths, public buildings, and on the boisterous ceremonies which took place in these. In doing this, they aimed to impress thousands of civilians, their "fellow-citizens." And the "ever-chattering stones" of tens of thousands of Roman inscriptions, scattered all over the empire, survive to tell us what they had done.

A few centuries later, in the same areas and often, indeed, within sight of deserted Roman buildings, kings and aristocrats, surrounded by small but indispensable retinues of warriors, would pile gold, silks, and precious objects of all kinds (from Byzantine ivories to the opulent and exotic fur of polar bears) on the altars of small but exquisitely built and ornamented churches and at the gates of the great "holy cities" of the monasteries.[40] Thereby they built up their own "arguments in stone," at lesser overall expense, but in a manner which ensured that local memory would be encrusted with memories of their stunning if spasmodic moments of generosity.

What made such gift-giving meaningful was precisely the sharp structuring of the Christian imagination of the time. Here were places where profane wealth was transformed by contact with the sacred. For, as students of modern Buddhist countries tell us, a system of gift-giving fits very well a certain "shape" of the relations between the local population and those (such as the monks) who both control and "symbolize" in their own persons the presence of the sacred. Gift-giving bridges the sacred and the profane in a manner which enhances the symbolic glory of the sacred while, at the same time, preventing the absorption of the profane. It is "a segregative-connective arrangement" which heightens the boundaries between the two. The kings and the warlords give to the monks. But they do not have to become monks. In the age of Columbanus, of Bede, and of the great abbots of Iona, gift-giving to churches and monasteries did not only bring blessing on the laity. It preserved their identity. For gifts to the sacred, "contribute to mediating between two otherwise polarized and even antagonistic sectors."[41] Gifts created "a sort of buffer zone"[42] between the seemingly irreconcilable values and lifestyles of a Christian clergy and the warrior elites on whose support the Church now depended.

It was in this way that the upper-class laity of Europe came to press in around the Church. Their frequent gifts "served to create familiarity with supernatural powers."[43] We should not think of such gift-giving as an invariably distant, still less as a cynical relationship. Many pressed in around the Church of their own accord. The more pious among them entered with fervor into the spiritualized gift relationship involved in the exchange of confession and absolution. For the exceptionally pious or the exceptionally grateful, children might even be added to the gold, the silks, and the stone. The

Venerable Bede was given to a monastery at the age of seven, as were many leading Christians of the time, all over Europe.

Inevitably, the predominance of the gift-giving relationship defined Christianity as an aristocratic preoccupation. Early medieval Europe was a period of sharply differentiated access to the sacred and to the bodies of knowledge which clustered around it. We must always remember that the most significant division in the Christian Church in this time was not the division between monks and clergy on the one side and the laity on the other. It was between those who could give and reciprocate gifts and those who could not. Abbots, kings and noblemen, priests, lay men and lay women of the upper classes clustered around the churches as equals. They all found themselves, as it were, on the same shelf. They were drawn together in a web slowly woven by the exchange of gifts, of spiritual guidance, and of teaching.[44]

Those who could not give are less easy to see. Compared with the vivid evidence for the piety of the kings and the aristocrats, the faces of the peasantry are largely lost to us in these centuries. I have attempted, in chapters 6, 16, 18, and 19, to find a place for them, and would urge others to do the same. My suspicion is that there is more to discover on this theme. The peasantry were considerably less passive and less isolated from Christianity than we had thought.[45] But their access to it was different, and was frequently judged, by their betters, to be dangerously unconventional.

The final incorporation of the peasantry in the flow of wealth which supported the Church marks, perhaps, the true end of our period. As we will see in chapter 18, by the time of Charlemagne the system of rents and taxes which had been dislocated to the advantage of the peasantry by the unravelling of the Roman empire, had come to be re-established in new forms. Tithes became compulsory on all baptized Christians – peasants among them. And, with the regular extraction of tithes, the Christianization of Europe enters a new rhythm. In many areas, the later ninth century has been called "the age of the parish."[46] The coming together of church and village (often through the intervention of local landlords – lay or ecclesiastical) occurs at this time in many regions.[47] The presence of a church and of a Christian cemetery as a "holy place" for the dead of the village was matched by a quickening of the pace of "admonition" from the pulpit, even at the level of the country clergy. These were the church's counter-gifts for the universal and compulsory gift of tithes.

With these developments, the outlines of a truly "medieval" order began to come into place. From that time onwards, we look back with a certain puzzlement, and yet with a certain poignancy, from the great imaginative distance placed between us and it by the Middle Ages and by the Reformation, at that older Christianity. Yet there had been a time in the first millennium of our era when this older Christianity had covered western Europe with a more diverse and fragile net, and in so doing had dotted the landscape with little "portions of paradise." It is to make this distant Christianity more present to us that this book has been written.

Part I

Empire and Aftermath

A.D. 200–500

CHAPTER 1

"The Laws of Countries": Prologue and Overview

One World, Two Empires

To ensure that we see the history of western Europe in its true perspective, we should begin our account in a city far away from modern Europe. Edessa (modern Urfa) now lies in the southeastern corner of Turkey, near the Syrian border. In the year A.D. 200, also, it was a frontier town, positioned between the Roman and the Persian empires. It lay at the center of a very ancient world, to which western Europe seemed peripheral and very distant.

Edessa was situated at the top of the Fertile Crescent, the band of settled land which stretched, in a great arch, to join Mesopotamia to the Mediterranean coast. It lay in a landscape already settled for millennia. *Tels* – the hill-like ruins of ancient cities dating back to the third millennium B.C. – dot the plain around it. Abraham was believed to have resided in Harran, a city a little to the south of Edessa, and to have passed through Edessa, as he made his way westward from Ur of the Chaldees in Mesopotamia, to seek his Promised Land on the Mediterranean side of the Fertile Crescent.

To the west of Edessa, an easy journey of 15 days led to Antioch and to the eastern Mediterranean, the sea which formed the heart of the Roman empire. To the southeast, another journey of 15 days led to the heart of Mesopotamia, where the Tigris and the Euphrates came closest. This was a zone of intensive cultivation which had supported the capitals of many empires. Here Ctesiphon was founded, in around A.D. 240. Its ruins now lie a little to the south of modern Baghdad. Ctesiphon was the Mesopotamian capital of the Sasanian dynasty, a family from southwest Iran, who took over control of the Persian empire in A.D. 224. The Sasanian empire joined the rich lands around Ctesiphon to the Iranian plateau. Beyond the Iranian plateau lay the trading cities of Central Asia and, yet further to the east, the

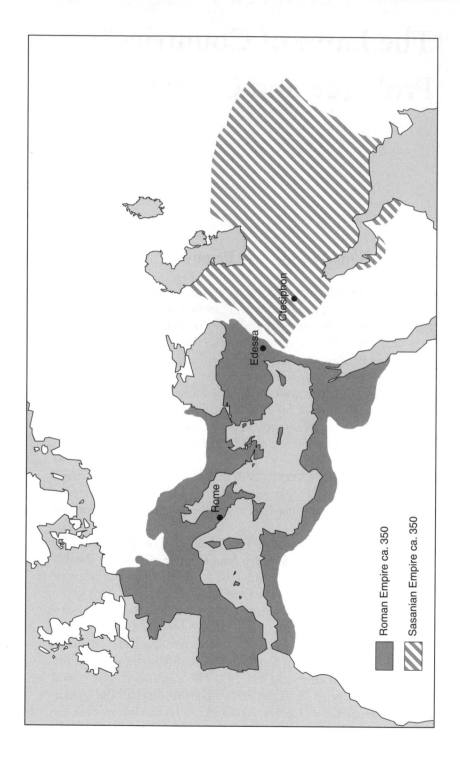

Map 1 The world ca.350: the Roman and Sasanian empires

Roman Empire ca. 350

Sasanian Empire ca. 350

CHRISTIANITY AND EMPIRE ca. 200–ca. 450

	Bardaisan 154–ca.224
	224 Rise of Sasanian Empire
	Mani 216–277
257 Edict against Christians	
	Cyprian, bishop of Carthage 248–258
284–305 Diocletian	
303 Great Persecution	
306–337 Constantine	
312 Battle of Milvian Bridge	
324 Foundation of Constantinople	
325 Council of Nicaea	
	Anthony 250–356
	Arius 250–336
	Athanasius of Alexandria 296–373
337–361 Constantius II	
	Martin of Tours 335–397
	Ambrose of Milan 339–397
	Melania the Elder 342–411
	Paulinus of Nola 355–431
378 Battle of Adrianople	
379–395 Theodosius I	
390 Massacre of Thessalonica	
	Augustine of Hippo 354–430
	writes *Confessions* 397/400
406 Barbarian invasion of Gaul	
410 Sack of Rome	
	writes *City of God* 413+
	Pelagian Controversy 413+
408–450 Theodosius II as Eastern	
emperor	
438 issues *Theodosian Code*	
434–453 Empire of Attila the Hun	

chain of oases that led the traveller, over the perilous distances of the Silk Route, to the legendary empire of China.

In the early third century, Edessa was the capital of the independent kingdom of Osrhoene. Bardaisan (154–fl. 222) was a nobleman and learned figure at the royal court. He represented the complex strands of a culture which drew on both the East and the West. Greek visitors admired his skills as a Parthian (Persian) archer. But, as a philosopher, he was entirely Greek. When a faithful disciple wrote a treatise summarizing Bardaisan's views on the relation between determinism and free will, he began it with a Platonic dialogue between two Edessene friends, Shemashgram and Awida. Yet the dialogue was not written in Greek but in Syriac, a language which was soon to become a major literary language in the Christian churches of the Middle East.

Bardaisan, furthermore, was a Christian, at a time when Christianity was still a forbidden religion within the Roman empire. He interpreted his faith in broad, geographical terms. The point that he wished to make was that, wherever they lived, human beings were free to choose their own way of life. They were not determined by the influence of the stars. Each region had its own customs, and Christians showed the extent of the freedom of the will by ignoring even these customs, and by seeking, rather, to live under "the laws of the Messiah" – of Christ. "In whatever place they find themselves, the local laws cannot force them to give up the law of the Messiah."

Bardaisan's treatise was appropriately named *The Book of the Laws of Countries*. It scanned the entire Eurasian landmass from China to the north Atlantic. It described the local customs of each society – the caste-dominated society of northern India, the splendidly caparisoned horses and fluttering silk robes of the Kushan lords of Bokhara and Samarkand, the Zoroastrians of the Iranian plateau, the Arabs of Petra and of the deserts of Mesopotamia. It even turned to the remote west, to observe the impenitent polyandry of the Britons. Naturally, it included the Romans, whom no power of the stars had ever been able to stop "from always conquering new territories."[1]

Any book on the role of Christianity in the formation of Western Europe must begin with the sweep of Bardaisan's vision. This book studies the emergence of one form of Christendom only among the many divergent Christianities which came to stretch along the immense arc delineated in Bardaisan's treatise. We should always remember that the "Making of Europe" involved a set of events which took place on the far, northwestern tip of that arc. Throughout the entire period covered by this book, as we shall see, Christians were active over the entire stretch of "places and climates" which made up the ancient world of the Mediterranean and western Asia. Christianity was far from being a "Western" religion. It had originated in Palestine and, in the period between A.D. 200 and 600, it became a major religion of Asia. By the year 700 Christian communities were scattered throughout the known world, from Ireland to Central Asia. Archaeologists have discovered fragments of Christian texts which speak of basic Christian activities pursued in the same manner from the Atlantic to the edge of China. Both in County Antrim, in Northern Ireland, and in Panjikent, east of Samarkand, fragmentary copy-books from around A.D. 700 – wax on wood for Ireland, broken potsherds for Central Asia – contain lines copied from the Psalms of David. In both milieux, something very similar was happening. Schoolboys, whose native languages were Irish in Antrim and Soghdian in Panjikent, tried to make their own, by this laborious method, the Latin and the Syriac versions, respectively, of what had become a truly international, sacred text – the "Holy Scriptures" of the Christians.[2]

Less innocent actions also betray the workings of a common Christian mentality. As we shall see, the combination of missionary zeal with a sense of cultural superiority, backed by the use of force, became a striking feature of early medieval Christian Europe. But it was not unique to that region. In around 723, Saint Boniface felled the sacred oak at Geismar and wrote back to England for yet more splendid copies of the Bible to display to his potential converts. They should be "written in letters of gold . . . that a reverence for the Holy Scriptures may be impressed on the carnal minds of the heathen."[3]

At much the same time, Christian Nestorian missionaries from Mesopotamia were waging their own war on the great sacred trees of the mountain slopes that rose above the Caspian. They laid low with their axes "the chief of the forest," the great sacred tree which had been worshipped by pagans. Like Boniface, the Nestorian bishop, Mar Shubhhal-Isho', knew how to impress the heathen: he

> made his entrance there with exceeding splendor, for barbarian nations need to see a little worldly pomp and show to attract them to make them draw nigh willingly to Christianity.[4]

Even further to the east, in an inscription set up in around A.D. 820 at Karabalghasun, on the High Orkhon river, the Uighur ruler of an empire formed between China and Inner Mongolia, recorded how his predecessor, Bogu Qaghan, had introduced new teachers into his kingdom in A.D. 762. These were Manichaeans. As bearers of a missionary faith of Christian origin, the Manichaean missionaries in Inner Asia shared with the Nestorians a similar brusque attitude toward the conversion of the heathen. The message of the inscription is as clear and as sharp as that which Charlemagne had adopted, between 772 and 785, when he burned the great temple of the gods at Irminsul and outlawed paganism in Saxony. Bogu Qaghan said:

> We regret that you were without knowledge, and that you called the evil
> spirits "gods." The former carved and painted images of the gods you
> should burn, and you should cast far from you all prayers to spirits and
> to demons.[5]

It goes without saying that these events had no direct or immediate repercussions upon each other. Yet they do bear a distinct family resemblance.
They show traces of a common Christian idiom, based upon shared traditions. They remind us of the sheer scale of the backdrop against which the
emergence of a specifically western Christendom took place.

The principal concern of this book, however, will be to characterize what,
eventually, would make the Christendom of western Europe different from
that of its many, contemporary variants. In order to do this, let us look
briefly at another aspect of Bardaisan's geographical panorama. The vivid
gallery of cultures known to him appeared to stretch from China to Britain
along a very narrow band. Bardaisan was oppressed by the immensity of the
unruly, underdeveloped world of the "barbarians," which stretched to the
north and south of the civilized world. Grim stretches of sparsely populated
land flanked the vivid societies he described.

> In the whole regions of the Saracens, in Upper Libya, among the
> Mauritanians . . . in Outer Germany, in Upper Sarmatia . . . in all the
> countries North of Pontus [the Black Sea], the Caucasus . . . and in the
> lands across the Oxus . . . no one sees sculptors or painters or perfumers
> or money changers or poets.

The all-important amenities of settled, urban living were not to be found
"along the outskirts of the whole world."[6]

It was a sobering vision, shared by most of Bardaisan's Greek and Roman contemporaries. It was eminently appropriate in a man bounded by
two great empires – the Roman and the Persian. These two great states
controlled, between them, most of the settled land of Europe and western
Asia. Both were committed to sustaining the belief, among their subjects,
that their costly military endeavors were directed toward defending the
civilized world against barbarism. In the words of a late sixth-century diplomatic manifesto, sent by the Persian King of Kings to the Byzantine emperor:

> God effected that the whole world should be illuminated from the begin-
> ning by two eyes [the Romans and the Persians]. For by these greatest
> powers the disobedient and bellicose tribes are trampled down and man's
> course is continually regulated and guided.[7]

It is against the backdrop of a vast world patrolled by two great empires, which stretched with little break from Afghanistan to Britain, that we begin our story of the rise and establishment of Christianity in western Europe.

Who are the Barbarians? Nomads and Farmers

The empires which controlled the settled lands invariably presented themselves as defending "civilization" against the "barbarians." Yet what each empire meant by "barbarian," and the relations which each established with the "barbarians" on its own frontiers, varied markedly from region to region. Western Europe became what it now is because the relations which the Roman empire established with the "barbarians" along its northern frontiers proved to be quite unusual. Compared with the relations between the ancient empires of the Middle East and the nomads of the Arabian desert and of the steppes of Central Asia, the "barbarians" of the Roman West were hardly "barbarians" at all. For they were farmers, not nomads.

We must always remember that "barbarian" meant many things to Bardaisan and his contemporaries. It could mean nothing more than a "foreigner," a vaguely troubling, even fascinating, person from a different culture and language-group. By this criterion, Persians were "barbarians." To Greeks and to an easterner such as Bardaisan, even Romans were "barbarians." But, for Bardaisan as for most Greeks and Romans, "barbarian" in the strong sense of the word meant, in effect, "nomad." Nomads were seen as human groups placed at the very bottom of the scale of civilized life. The desert and the sown were held to stand in a state of immemorial and unresolved antipathy, with the desert always threatening, whenever possible, to dominate and destroy the sown.[8]

In North Africa and the Middle East, of course, there was little truth in this melodramatic stereotype. For millennia, pastoralists and peasants had collaborated, in a humdrum and profitable symbiosis. Nomads were treated as a despised but useful underclass. It was assumed that these wanderers, though often irritating, could never constitute a permanent threat to the great empires of the settled world, much less that they could replace them. Because of a contempt for the desert nomad which reached back, in the Middle East, to Sumerian times, the Arab conquests of the seventh century (the stunning work of former nomads) and the consequent foundation of the Islamic empire took contemporaries largely by surprise. Wholesale invasion and conquest from the hot desert of Arabia had not been expected.

The nomads who had always been feared (and with reason) were, rather, those of the cold north, from the steppelands which stretched from the *puszta* of Hungary, across the southern Ukraine, to Central and Inner Asia. Here conditions favored the intermittent rise of aggressive and well-organized nomadic empires.[9] Herds of fast, sturdy horses bred rapidly and with little cost on the thin grass of the northern steppes. These overabundant creatures, when mounted for war, gave to the nomads the terrifying appearance of a nation in arms, endowed with uncanny mobility. One such confederacy of Huns from Central Asia penetrated the Caucasus into the valleys of Armenia, in the middle of the fourth century:

> no one could number the vastness of the cavalry contingents [so] every man was ordered to carry a stone so as to throw it down . . . so as to form a mound . . . a fearful sign [left] for the morrow to understand past events. And wherever they passed, they left such markers at every crossroad along their way.[10]

The sight of such cairns was likely to stick in the memory. Unimpressed by the desert nomads of Arabia and the Sahara, the rulers of the civilized world scanned the nomadic world of the northern steppes with anxious attention.

Yet, terrifying though the nomadic empires of the steppes might be, they were an intermittent phenomenon. Effective nomadism, in its normal state, depended on the maximum dispersal of families, each maintaining the initiative in maneuvering its flocks toward advantageous pasture, with a minimum of interference from a central authority. To change from herding scattered flocks to herding human beings, through conquest and raiding, under the leadership of a single ruler, was an abnormal and, usually, a shortlived development in the long history of the nomadic world. Even a mighty warlord such as Attila (434–453), despite the fact that he has left an indelible mark on the European imagination, found that his ambitions were subject to insurmountable limits. His ability to terrorize the inhabitants of the settled land was subject to an automatic "cut off." The further from their native steppes the Huns found themselves, the less access they had to those pastures that provided the vast surplus of horses on which their military superiority depended. For a few chilling decades, Attila had extorted tribute from the Roman world. But, within a year of his death in 453, his famous Hunnish empire disintegrated and vanished as if it had never existed.[11]

As a result, the nomadic confederacies played a peripheral role in the history of Europe. The Huns, in the fifth century A.D., were succeeded by the Avars, in the seventh and eighth centuries A.D. But the Avars also settled down, after a few decades of spectacular sabre-rattling. What the Huns and the Avars brought, in the long run, was not the end of the world, as many had feared at the time, but a hint of the immense spaces which lay behind them. The nomad confederacies of eastern Europe and the Ukraine were the westernmost representatives of an international Eurasian world whose vast horizons the settled societies of Europe could barely rival. The movement of precious objects and the borrowing of customs showed this. Garnets from northern Afghanistan, set in intricate gold work that echoed the flying beasts and coiled dragons of Central Asia and China, flowed into the Danubian court of Attila. By the mid-fifth century, such jewelry formed an international "barbarian chic," a sign of high status sported alike by Roman generals and by local kings. Hunting with hawks entered western Europe from Central Asia at this time; and, in the eighth century, the crucial development of stirrups spread to western horsemen as a result of Lombard-Avar contacts in the region between the Danube and Friuli. Up to almost the end of our period, the Avar governor commanding the regions bordering on Vienna still bore a name that was a distant echo of the official title of a Chinese provincial governor.[12]

In eastern Europe, the nomads remained a constant presence throughout this period and beyond. In western Europe, however, the true nomad world, which produced Attila and, later, the Avars, remained remote if imposing. It is important to emphasize this fact. True nomads were rare in Western Europe, yet Romans tended to assimilate all "barbarians" to the rootless and violent image of the nomads which was so current in the ancient world.

Our own image of the barbarians has been colored by Roman attitudes. With us, also, the "barbarian" stands for all that was most mobile and dangerous beyond the frontiers of Rome. In reality, relations between Romans and "barbarians" in western Europe evolved in a significantly different manner. The opposition between "settled" and "barbarian" regions had been charged with great weight for a man of the Near East such as Bardaisan because it was thought to coincide with the ancient opposition between farmers and nomads. But such an opposition was not appropriate when applied to the Roman frontiers of Britain, the Rhine, and the Danube. The ideology of the settled world made it appear as if a chasm separated the populations contained within the frontiers of the Roman empire from the barbarians gathered outside. Their life was portrayed as incommensurable with that of civilized persons, as if it was, indeed, the same as the life of the nomads of the steppes and the deserts.

But the populations of northwestern Europe were not nomads. There was no place along the European frontiers of the Roman empire for the stark ecological contrast between the desert and the sown which made the settled populations of North Africa and the Middle East feel so different from their "barbarian" neighbors. Rather, Roman and non-Roman landscapes merged gently into each other, within a single temperate zone.

If we were to follow only the texts written by Roman authors, we would have little idea of the extent to which life in the world beyond the Roman frontier of the Rhine and the Danube resembled the life of many rural areas within the Roman empire itself. Nor could we guess the extent to which the "barbarian" world came to be molded by the presence of Rome. It is only in the last decades, indeed, that spectacular finds in Germany and Denmark and the new interpretative skills applied to these finds by archaeologists have enabled us to allow the "barbarian" half of Europe to "speak" in its own voice.[13] And what we hear is a world slowly penetrated, on every level, by Roman goods, by Roman styles of living and, eventually, by Roman ideas.

When we enter "free" Germany (as the Romans called it) we do not find creatures from another world. Rather, we have entered a "peripheral economy" attached, in innumerable ways, to the new world created by the Roman empire along the frontiers of the Rhine and the Danube: warriors are buried with Roman swords; chieftains sport Roman dining sets; a kiln for pottery identical with those used in Roman Gaul is set up in Thuringia, over 100 miles east of the Roman frontier. It is the closeness of Rome to central Europe that is surprising, not the notional chasm between "Romans" and "barbarians."

Certain contrasts of terrain between the Roman territories and "free" Germany struck Roman observers. They described the heathlands of the north German plain with their herds of half-wild cattle and the somber, primeval forests which covered the hills of central and southern Germany. But, despite these contrasts, the lands outside the Roman frontiers were inhabited by peoples who shared with the provincial subjects of the Roman empire, in Britain, Gaul, and Spain, the same basic building-blocks of an agrarian society. They too were peasants. They, too, struggled to wrest their food from the heavy, treacherous earth, "the mother of men."

Their overall population was low. It was more dispersed than was the case in many Roman provinces. Farming communities lived in isolated groups of homesteads and in small hamlets, cut off from each other by stretches of forbidding forest and moorland. The villages excavated by archaeologists rarely seem to have contained more than 300 inhabitants. Yet, as is shown in the case of the village excavated at Feddersen Wierde, near Bremerhaven on the north German coast, these could be stable settlements, laid out with care; large barns and buildings hint at increasing social differentiation over the centuries. Along the North Sea coast of Frisia, beyond the last Roman garrisons, the inhabitants defended the arable land against the saltwater tides with the same skill and tenacity as did their neighbors across the sea, the nominally "Roman," British peasants of the Fenland.

Crucial skills of metalworking were practiced; but such skills were virtually invisible to Roman eyes, taking place as they did in the smithies of tiny villages, unconnected by the overarching political and commercial structures which enabled the Romans to bring so much metalwork together, with such deadly effect, in the armaments of their legions. When the German tribes fought each other, the armies they raised were minute and ill-equipped by Roman standards. A German "army" reconstructed from finds at Illerup (in Denmark) seems to have had 300 soldiers armed only with spears, 40 heavily armed warriors, and five leaders. The swords of the elite in this small force were all of them Roman swords.[14]

Livestock played a prominent role among the "barbarian" peoples of the north European plain and elsewhere. Livestock promoted more dispersed patterns of settlement. They were the focus of intense, upper-class competition for mobile wealth, as in the great cattle raids of Irish epic and in the solemn cattle-tributes which expressed the power of chieftains in Germany. Pastoralism on this scale seemed rootless to Romans, who were used to a well-disciplined peasantry, tied to the land and engaged in a labor-intensive agriculture based on cereal crops. But abundant cattle gave greater access to protein, in the form of meat and dairy products, than was common among the undernourished peasants of the Mediterranean. Hence the pervasive sense, among Romans, of the "barbarian" North as a reservoir of mobile and ominously well-fed young warriors. A Roman military expert wrote that "the peoples of the North" live far from the Sun. As a result, they have more blood in their bodies than do the inhabitants of the sun-soaked Mediterranean, whose bodies are "dried up" by heat. No wonder that they make such formidable soldiers![15]

Thus, though viewed by the Romans as "barbarians", the populations of northern and eastern Europe were, first and foremost, farmers. The moment that Germanic villagers and ranchers found themselves confronted by true nomads, such as the Huns, they had no illusion about which world they belonged to. We can see this in the 370s. The first populations encountered by the Huns as they infiltrated the steppelands of southern Russia at this time were the Goths. The Goths were settled to the north of the Danube. Their villages stretched from Transylvania and Moldavia into the southern Ukraine. They were an agrarian people, northern representatives of a peasant economy which had come to cover the landscape, since prehistoric times, in an uninterrupted band that stretched from the Mediterranean to Central Europe and the southern Ukraine.[16]

When the Gothic villagers in Moldavia and the Ukraine began to be subjected to Hunnish raids, in 374, their first reaction was to seek permission to place the Danube between themselves and the Huns by settling in the Roman empire. In return for an offer to provide regular military service, they were allowed to become Roman subjects. They crossed the Danube not so as to "invade" the Roman empire, but as immigrants, who sought to resume their lives as farmers, in a Roman landscape no longer overshadowed (as the Ukraine had come to be) by the truly alien nomads.

Politically, the arrangement turned into a disaster: driven by famine and enraged by the systematic exploitation of their refugee camps, the remnants of the Gothic nobility (soon renamed and known to us ever since as the Visigoths) rallied its warriors to defeat and kill the eastern emperor at Adrianople (Edirne, European Turkey) in 378. Alaric, a Visigothic king, eventually sacked Rome in 410, in the course of a prolonged and inconclusive attempt to gain admission to the Roman high command. But this breakdown of relations happened only after the Visigoths had opted to appeal to Rome against the Huns and the Romans had allowed them in. To call the entry of the Goths into the Roman empire a "barbarian invasion" is profoundly misleading. Despite its unforeseen and damaging consequences, this was a controlled immigration of displaced agriculturalists, anxious to mingle with similar farmers on the Roman side of the frontier. Seen in terms of the long-term history of a shared agrarian civilization which had developed throughout temperate Europe since prehistoric times, the Roman frontier did not mark a chasm between two totally different worlds. It was an artificial divide, destined, within a few centuries, to become irrelevant.

A Middle Ground: The Rise of the Frontier

We must realize, however, that, in the year 200, few Romans appreciated these facts. The ideology expressed by a writer such as Bardaisan was widespread among educated persons in the Latin- and Greek-speaking worlds. "I expect no more to have Germans among my readers," wrote the famous Greek doctor, Galen of Ephesus, an older contemporary of Bardaisan, "than I would expect to be read by bears and wolves."[17]

Such jaundiced views are not altogether surprising. Looking across from their side of the frontier, the Romans saw a society which, by their standards, was totally illiterate. Apart from runes, which developed at this time but were used more for magic than for purposes of communication, the "barbarian" world was a world of entirely oral culture. It was also, palpably, a society dominated by its warriors. Compared with the peasants and slaves who supported them, the warriors of "free Germany" were only a small proportion of the males of each tribe. But they dominated their own societies. Prestige, leisure, access to resources (and especially access to abundant food which would be consumed with gusto in heavy feasting as a sign of the superior status of warriors) and, above all, "freedom" – the crucial freedom of males from dependence on the arbitrary commands of others (as slaves and as serfs) – depended on the ability of young males to participate in battle.

It was the warrior upper crust of "barbarian" society which the Romans watched closely. But they did not do so, inevitably, with anxious attention, in the expectation of imminent invasion. Far from it. What they saw, rather, was a vast and "underdeveloped" landscape whose principal "cash crop," as it were, was an abundant surplus of violent young men. What changed central Europe in the years between A.D. 200 and 400 was not so much an increase of "pressure" on the part of "barbarian" tribes against the Roman frontier. It was the increased "presence" in "free" Germany itself of the Roman empire as a land of opportunity.

The frontier region became a vortex which sucked warrior groups toward it. Faced by a harvest of young men which was so easy to garner, the Roman authorities changed their recruiting grounds from the Roman to the German side of the frontier. Germans rather than provincials filled the ranks of the armies. They served first in "auxiliary" units, but increasingly as fully trained professionals. The emperors always needed troops to fight the bitter civil wars which characterized the third and fourth centuries. This need for soldiers to fight in civil wars sucked Germans across the frontier into wars where, at regular intervals, Romans set about killing Romans, in the deadly clash of fully professional armies, in far greater quantities than they ever expected to kill or to be killed when fighting "barbarians."

As a result of this development, already by the year A.D. 300 a "para-Roman" world, long accustomed to Roman ways and deeply involved in Roman politics, had grown up along the Rhine and the Danube. Far from threatening the Roman order as if from an untamed "barbarian" hinterland, many of the leaders of these warrior societies had already been called upon, in the course of civil wars and even as career soldiers in the Roman high command, to act as the representatives of that Roman order.[18]

Altogether, along the frontier, things were not quite as they appeared. The arrival of the Roman empire in northwestern Europe had set in motion a process which reached its inevitable (but largely unexpected) culmination in our period.

In the first and second centuries A.D., the establishment of large Roman armies on the frontiers and the foundation of Roman-style cities behind them, brought wealth and demands for food and labor which revolutionized the countryside of northern Gaul, Britain, and the Danubian provinces. These regions were suddenly subjected to unparalleled demands. At the mouth of the Rhine, a population of less than 14,000 had to find room for legionary garrisons of over 20,000. The garrisons of northern Britain ate enough food to keep 30,000 acres of land under permanent cultivation. At least 12,000 cattle were needed to supply the Roman army in Britain with leather for its tents and its boots.

On the Roman side of the frontier, hitherto unimaginable coagulations of human population were gathered into newly founded towns. Trier, London, Paris, and Cologne had populations of up to 10,000, even 20,000. They were small-scale yet impressive echoes, in northern Europe, of an urban life associated with the Mediterranean: at this time, Rome had a population which reached a million; the populations of Alexandria, Antioch, and, later, of Constantinople could be counted in hundreds of thousands.

But the towns were only one aspect of a wider process. All over the northern provinces of western Europe the huge fact of empire settled its slow weight on the land. Agrarian society was congealed into more solid structures, designed to aid the permanent extraction of wealth from the tillers of the land. Behind the frontiers, in northern Gaul, great, grain-producing villas (whose owners even experimented with primitive harvesting machines) came to dominate an increasingly subservient peasantry.

It was in this way that the Roman frontier, set in place to separate the Roman world from the squalid lands to its north, became the unwitting axis along which the Roman and barbarian worlds converged. Like a wide depression formed by the weight of a glacial ice-pack, the frontiers of the Roman empire, maintained at the cost of crushing expenditure of wealth and characterized by dense concentrations of settlement, created a novel catchment area. The economic and cultural life of the lands beyond the frontier began to flow into this catchment area. We can see this in small details. Roman garrisons along the estuary of the Rhine came to purchase grain and cattle in the non-Roman territories. The first lines of Latin ever written from beyond the Roman frontiers take the form of a purchase order for a Frisian cow, discovered near Leeuwarden in northern Holland.[19]

The Roman frontiers in Europe were more porous than we think. The spread of Latin loan words in German and Old Irish; the recurrence of Roman motifs in the gold-work of Jutland; the fact that *ogham*, the archaic script cut along the edge of wooden tallies and on standing stones in Ireland, followed a categorization of the consonants propounded by Roman grammarians: these details show a barbarian world slowly changing shape under the distant gravitational pull of the huge adjacent mass of the Roman empire.[20]

As a result of this development, what happened after the year 400 was not what we imagine to have happened when we think of the "fall" of the Roman empire in the West. The Roman frontier was not violently breached by barbarian "invasions." Rather, between 200 and 400, the frontier itself changed. From being a defensive region, which kept Romans and "barbarians" apart, it had become, instead, an extensive "middle ground," in which Roman and barbarian societies were drawn together.[21] And after 400, it was the barbarians and no longer the Romans who became the dominant partners in that middle ground. The Middle Ages begin, not with a dramatic "fall of Rome," but with the barely perceived and irreversible absorption, by the "barbarians," of the "middle ground" created in the Roman frontier zone.

This development, of course, did not happen without suffering and bloodshed. To take one example from northern Britain in the middle of the fifth century A.D.: Saint Patrick (ca.420–490) did not first visit Ireland of his own free will. Patricius (to use his true Roman name) was brutally swept away from his home by Irish slave raiders. A young man who might have gone on to polish his Latin in the Roman schools of Britain found himself set to herding pigs on the rain-lashed coast of County Mayo.

But Patricius' subsequent return to Ireland and the slow implantation of Christianity in what had been an entirely non-Roman island reveals a world that was not entirely dominated by violence. What happened in Patricius' lifetime was the emergence of the Irish Sea as a Celtic "Mediterranean of the North." Around the Irish Sea, the Romanized coasts of Wales and northern Britain were joined to Ireland and the western isles of Scotland to form a single zone which ignored the former Roman frontiers. In exactly the same period, the Frankish kingdom created by Clovis (481–511) represented a return to the days before Julius Caesar, when successful warrior kings had straddled the Rhine, to join Germany with the "Belgic" regions of northern Gaul.

This development coincided with religious changes. The development which we tend to call "the coming of Christianity to the barbarians" has always been acclaimed as the beginning of the western Middle Ages. But seen in a longer perspective, it was no more than the last, most clearly documented and best-remembered phase in the long process by which Roman and "barbarian" regions of northwestern Europe came together along the "middle ground" to form a new zone of high culture.

Western Europe itself looked very different when viewed from the former frontier zones of the empire and no longer exclusively (as Romans had done) from the perspective of Rome and the Mediterranean. To a person of around the year A.D. 700, there was nothing strange in the fact that some of the most polished Latin scholarship of the age should have been produced in monasteries founded by Saxon kings and aristocrats of the kingdom of Northumbria, in what had once been the frontier zone between York, Hadrian's Wall, and southern Scotland. The monasteries of Jarrow and Monkwearmouth, with their well-stocked Latin libraries, which produced a scholar of the caliber of the Venerable Bede (672–735), and the spectacular "Roman-style" buildings set up in northern Britain by bishop Wilfrid (634–709), should not be seen as miraculous oases of "Roman" culture perched, somewhat improbably, at the furthest ends of the earth. They may have been far from Rome; but they lay at the center of a whole new world of their own. From Iona, on the southwestern coast of Scotland, across Anglo-Saxon Britain, to northern Gaul, Bavaria, and, ultimately, to central and northern Germany, a new world had come into being around the former Roman frontiers. The northern Britain associated with the "Golden Age" of Bede (which is well known to British readers) was only one region of the former "middle ground" which blossomed at this time. From Ireland all the way to the Danube, centers of Christian learning came to flourish in what had once been the "barbarian" side of the Roman frontier. Early medieval Christianity was at its most vigorous in regions which, half a millennium previously, had been regarded by cultivated Romans as lands beyond the pale of civilization.

But this, of course, is to anticipate. In the next two chapters, we must turn to the nature of Christianity itself as it developed within the territories of a changed Roman empire in the period between A.D. 200 and 400.

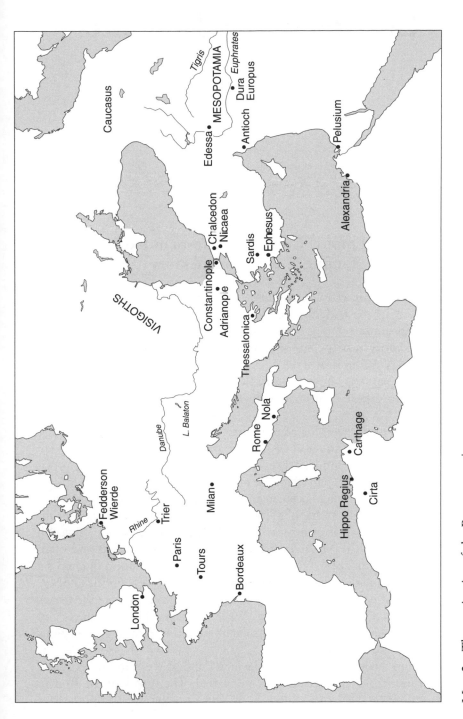

Map 2 The territories of the Roman empire

CHAPTER 2

Christianity and Empire

The New Empire: Crisis and Reform in the Roman Empire in the Third Century

Bardaisan died in around A.D. 222. In the generations that followed his death, the world which he had surveyed in the *Book of the Laws of Countries* underwent profound changes. For both the Persian and the Roman empires, the third century was a time of dramatic reorganization. After 224, the Sasanian kings of Iran turned the loose-knit Parthian kingdom, whose rulers they had supplanted, into a formidable empire. The Roman empire, also, emerged from a period of crisis with the power of the emperors greatly strengthened.[1]

The Roman empire was forced to become a new empire. Renewed warfare along all its frontiers and the emergence, in the Middle East, of the Sasanian empire as a persistent military threat, revealed the inadequacy of the previous structures of the Roman state. We must remember what a fragile institution the Roman empire had been, even at the height of its power, in the first and second centuries A.D. Its inhabitants thought of themselves less as subjects of an empire than as members of a uniquely privileged "commonwealth of cities." Around the Mediterranean, these cities were ancient and often gigantic by the standards of their time: Rome had a population of almost a million, Antioch and Alexandria of around 300,000, and many cities of the Greek East had populations of up to 100,000. These cities were the nerve-centers of Greco-Roman civilization. What happened in their streets and what was written by their inhabitants determined the cultural and religious tone of the Roman world.

Away from the Mediterranean, in the hinterland of Western Europe, cities were less numerous and less densely populated. The towns of the Roman frontier provinces, such as London, Paris, and Cologne, were impressive in contrast to the underpopulated, rural landscapes in which they stood. They had populations of up to 20,000. They were small when compared with the large cities of the Mediterranean. Most towns in the Roman West had populations of around 5,000. They were mere "agrotowns" by modern standards. Yet these towns were seen as privileged oases of Roman civilization. The ruins of even the smallest of them (such as those discovered in Roman Britain) remain impressive. For each town had been consciously built up, by the elites of the region, to serve as an enduring "argument in stone." The towns were showcases. They made visible the power and beneficial effects of the Roman empire. Their monuments were set up by local grandees. They bore the names of those who had paid for them. Statues, baths, circuses, and forums, built by local notables, underscored the privileged position of those who collaborated with Roman rule.[2]

When it came to matters of government, however, the empire was still surprisingly distant in the first and second centuries. Apart from his formidable soldiers, the emperor had few servants. Compared with a modern state, the Roman empire remained profoundly undergoverned. Even in a fiercely controlled province such as Egypt, the proportion of imperial officials to the overall population was one in 10,000.

The empire was kept going not through intervention from on high by officials but, rather, as it were, "horizontally" – through collaboration with an empire-wide upper class, drawn from the elites of the cities. Each city had an *ordo*, a legally-constituted town council. The town council was recruited from 30 to 100 or so of the richest families in the region. As members of the town council, representatives of these leading families were held responsible for running the city and for collecting the taxes of the territory assigned to it. In peaceful (or less provident) times, they exercised virtually unimpeded control over their locality, in exchange for maintaining peace in the cities and a regular supply of taxes for the armies.

Taxation, therefore, was not simply a recurrent event imposed from above: it was delegated in such a manner as to make the distribution of the burden of taxes and their collection a way of life for the leading members of every locality. In Egypt, in the fourth century A.D., one out of every three inhabitants of the large villages were involved, in some way or other, in the administration of taxes and the maintenance of law and order. Even at its most oppressive, Roman government was not strong by modern standards. But, again by modern standards, it was remarkably pervasive. Throughout the Roman world, the upper classes of each city found themselves co-opted into the day-to-day business of running the empire.[3]

From the point of view of the emperors, who had to defend the empire in times of emergency, the disadvantage of this system of indirect rule was that it depended for its smooth functioning on a "cozy" relationship with the city-based elites of every region. The powers of local government were delegated to them, in return for the prompt delivery of taxes which touched little more than 5 percent of the agrarian surplus. These urban oligarchies formed a small and highly privileged group in every locality. The upper classes of the Roman empire never amounted to more than 3 percent of the overall population. Yet they owned a quarter of all the land of the empire and 40 percent of its liquid wealth.[4]

Modern readers have tended to follow the well-satisfied opinion of the urban aristocracies when they described the empire in which they lived, in the first and second centuries A.D. It is customary to speak of this period as "the Golden Age" of the Roman empire. The achievements of the age were, indeed, impressive. But they were fair-weather achievements, which presupposed prolonged peace and unchallenged military superiority on all frontiers. An easygoing system, based on a large measure of indirect rule, was not designed to sustain the strain of continuous hostile invasion and of murderous civil wars. In the course of the third century, all classes in the Roman world had to face up to the unpleasant, day-to-day realities of life in a beleaguered superpower. Between 238 and 270, bankruptcy, political fragmentation, and the recurrent defeats of large Roman armies laid bare the weaknesses of the old system of government.[5]

What was remarkable, however, was not so much this period of collapse, as the speed and determination with which a new system was put in place, after a generation of humiliating uncertainty. The Roman empire over which the emperor Diocletian reigned, from 284 to 305, was an empire in the true sense of the word. The Roman state was considerably more present to all its subjects than had been the case a century earlier.

Most important of all, Diocletian defeated the first and most deadly enemy of all empires – distance. He considered that the Roman empire was far too large a unit to be governed effectively by one ruler. So Diocletian ensured closer control over each major region of the Roman world by delegating his powers to a coalition of co-emperors, known as the "Tetrarchy." The Tetrarchy did not survive for long. But the device was a recognition of the realities of power. In the two centuries from the reign of Diocletian to the end of the western empire in 476, the entire Roman world was ruled by a single ruler only for a period of 23 years in all. For most of the time, the Roman world was divided in two, with an emperor in the Latin West and another in the Greek East. They treated each other as colleagues. They collaborated in ruling the same vast state. By controlling only half of the empire, each was able, in the more manageable region which he controlled, to take over responsibilities which had been delegated, in previous centuries, to local interest groups.[6]

The restored Roman empire was a badly shaken society, anxious for the return of law and order. *Reparatio* and *renovatio* were the slogans of the day. It was not, however, an irreparably impoverished society. Despite an expansion of the army and of the imperial bureaucracy, the overall tax load was usually no more than 10 percent of the agrarian surplus. Such taxes were within the capacities of most peasant communities. In Anatolia, for instance, tax levels reached under Diocletian continued, largely unchanged, until the last days of the Ottoman empire.

What had changed was the presence of empire itself. The empire was no longer a "commonwealth of cities." The elites lost their unique advantages of wealth and local status. They now looked increasingly outside the horizons of their city to the imperial court. The court became the direct and ever-present source of honor. The cities did not collapse in this period (as many scholars once thought). But they now throve only if they remained closely connected with the central government. Constantinople, founded in 324 by the emperor Constantine, was nothing less than a "new Rome." It was spoken of as the "ruling city." For it made the power of Rome directly present to the entire eastern part of the empire. Because it was a center of government, Constantinople became a boom city: by the year 500, its population was almost half a million.

The same process of centralization took place in each province. A *metropolis*, a "mother city," emerged as the permanent capital of each region, leaving other cities in the shade. The provinces themselves became smaller, so that the power of the central government would be brought to bear more directly on less extensive units. All over the empire, the cities survived; but they were now incorporated into a far more exacting and uniform system of government. The cities lost their sense of being unique centers of local tradition. They were no longer thought of as part of an empire made up of a mosaic of vivid communities, each one different from the other. Now what was stressed was what all cities had in common with all others – loyalty to the emperor and his servants.[7]

Outside the cities, also, the extension of the Roman state brought the rulers and their demands closer to those whom they ruled. To take one example, known to us from the papyri discovered in his house: Aurelius Isidore was a canny farmer of the Fayum, in Egypt. Between 297 and 318, he was constantly involved in the annual spasm of activity connected with the collection and distribution of the imperial taxes. Isidore was illiterate, yet he kept his tax documents carefully – lists of assessments, constant petitions to "Your Magnificence" (the local representative of the central government). Isidore even kept a copy of the edict of the emperor Diocletian, which spelled out, with high-flown rhetoric, the advantages of the new tax system. For he needed a copy of this edict to be sure of his rights and duties. Such documents survive only in the dry sands of Egypt. But they must have been everywhere, in the homes of relatively humble provincials throughout the empire. They show a political system forced to bypass the upper classes in order to mobilize the interest and the loyalty of all its subjects.[8]

Religiones: The Ancient Religion

Societies under strain are usually reassured if one aspect, at least, of their accustomed life remains unchanged. For all the dramatic reforms associated with the restoration of imperial power which took place at the end of the third century, most inhabitants of the Roman empire felt that they looked out on a long-familiar religious landscape. Diocletian's empire was still an overwhelmingly polytheist society.[9] It was assumed, as a matter of commonsense, that there were many gods, and that these gods demanded worship through concrete, publicly visible gestures of reverence and gratitude. The gods were there. They were invisible and ageless neighbors of the human race. Knowledge of the gods and of what pleased and displeased them tended to be a matter of local social memory, kept alive by inherited rites and gestures.

Hence the cities were crucial to the notion of the worship of the gods. In the Greek world, in particular, the worship of specific divinities was intimately linked to the history of each city: Athena had always protected Athens; Artemis had always protected Ephesus. Coins issued by cities all over Asia Minor in the second and early third centuries showed with loving precision the exact forms of the temples and statues of their local gods. Polytheism and the notion of the empire as a happy "commonwealth of cities" went hand in hand.[10]

Great emphasis was placed, in traditional Roman circles, on *religio*, the apposite worship of each god. The notion of *religio* stressed (and even idealized) social cohesion. It assumed that correct traditions of worship would be passed on through families, through local communities, and through the memories of proud cities and nations bathed in centuries of history. Each god had his or her own *religio*, just as each city and each locality had its own traditions. Hence *religiones*, very much in the plural – clearly differentiated ways of worship, each one appropriate to a specific god and a specific place – were the hallmark of polytheism in the Roman world. To be a polytheist was to glory in the fact that the gods did not want unity. Rather, they expressed themselves through the infinite diversity of human customs, inherited from the distant past. The words of one of the last great polytheists,

Symmachus, Prefect of Rome in A.D. 384 (responding, by that time, to Christian claims) spelled out attitudes which had been taken for granted by polytheists in earlier centuries.

> Everyone has his own customs, his own religious practices; the Divine Mind has assigned to different cities different religions to be their guardians. . . . To this line of thought must be added the argument from "benefits conferred", for herein rests the most emphatic proof of the existence of the gods. Man's reason moves entirely in the dark; his knowledge of divine presences can be drawn from no better source than from the recollection and the evidence of good fortune already received from them. If the long passage of time lends validity to religious observances, we ought to keep faith with so many centuries, we ought to follow our forefathers who followed their forefathers and were blessed in so doing.[11]

The gods were not airy abstractions. They were vibrant beings, who hovered rank after rank above and around the human race. The lower orders of the gods shared the same physical space as human beings. They touched all aspects of the natural world and of human settlement. Not all gods were equal. Some gods were considerably higher and more distant from human beings than were others. The *religio* that these high gods received depended, to a large extent, on the self-image of their worshippers. Mystical philosophers yearned for the higher gods and, beyond them, for union with the One, the metaphysically necessary, intoxicating source of all being. Such high love for a distant god lifted the soul out of the body, in a manner which made all earthly cares fall silent. Philosophers yearned for union with the One High God.[12]

But, even for philosophers, the other gods were not abolished. They were demoted. They were not denied. Philosophers were superior souls, who did not share the coarse concerns of the multitude. They deserved superior gods. But average gods existed in abundance for average persons. Most gods hovered close to earth. They "stood close by" their worshippers. They were ready to maximize and to maintain, in return for due observance, the good things of life.

It was considered crucial to maintain these diverse *religiones*. For all the gods, high and low, local and imperial, played a role in maintaining civilized life. They protected the Roman empire. A papyrus from the small Egyptian town of Sinkepha shows how widespread this feeling was. The town council commanded a priestess to remember her duties: she must go down to the local temple

> to perform the usual sacrifices on behalf of our lords the emperors and their victories, and the rising of the Nile, and the increase of the crops, and the healthy balance of the climate.[13]

As a devout polytheist, the emperor Diocletian felt just the same. He celebrated the crowning mercy of twenty years of stable rule on a monument set
up in the Roman Forum in A.D. 303. He showed himself at a smoking altar,
flanked by the ever-present gods and surrounded by the animals deemed,
from time immemorial, to be appropriate for a major sacrifice. Diocletian
was a man who took *religio* seriously. The previous year he had declared:

> The ancient religion ought not to be censured by a new one. For it is the
> height of criminality to reverse that which the ancestors had defined,
> once and for all, things which hold and preserve their recognized place
> and course.[14]

New Religion in a New Empire: Christianity before Constantine

Yet, only nine years after Diocletian had erected his monument, the emperor
Constantine entered Rome on October 29, 312, having defeated his rival,
Maxentius, on the previous day, at a battle near the Milvian Bridge, outside
the city. The altars of the gods stood ready, on the Capitol, to receive the
sacrifice appropriate to the celebration of his victorious entry into the city.
But Constantine, apparently, went straight to the imperial palace without
performing any sacrifice. At the time, Constantine's oversight might not have
been interpreted as a breach with the old religion. A ruthless politician, his
first step was to eclipse the memory of Maxentius. He did this by filling the
traditional center of the city with monuments which were totally intelligible
to old-fashioned Romans (such as the triumphal arch, the Arch of Constantine,
which still stands opposite the Colosseum on the road that led to the Forum). These monuments contained no reference to Christianity.[15]

At the same time, however, Constantine let it be known to Christians that
he considered that he had owed his victory outside Rome to a specific and
unique sign from the One God which they worshipped. Writing to Christians, he made plain, in subsequent years, that he owed his successes to the
protection of that High God alone. Over a decade later (at some time after
324) he wrote to the young king of Persia, Shapur II: "Him I call upon with
bended knee, shunning all abominable blood and hateful odors [of pagan
sacrifice]."[16]

Constantine's "conversion" was a very "Roman" conversion. It consisted
in the fact that he had come to regard the High God of the Christians, rather
than the traditional gods, as the proper recipient of *religio*. Worship of the
Christian God had brought prosperity upon himself and would bring pros-

perity upon the empire. He had risen to power in a series of murderous civil wars which destroyed the system of divided empire developed by Diocletian. He occupied Rome in 312. But this did not give him the total power he wanted. Only 12 years later, in 324, did he take over the eastern half of the empire in a series of bloody battles. And he did all this without attributing his success in any way to correct *religio* toward the ancient gods. It was in this pointed absence of piety toward the gods, as the traditional guardians of the empire, that his subjects came to realize that their emperor was a Christian.

Constantine was not a young convert. He was over 40 and an experienced politician when he finally declared himself a Christian. He had had time to take the measure of the new religion and the difficulties which emperors had experienced in suppressing it. He decided that Christianity was a religion fit for a new empire. And so, in A.D. 325, a year after he became sole ruler of the Roman world, Constantine gathered together the Christian bishops of his empire at Nicaea (modern Iznik, Turkey). Nicaea was a city set on a quiet lake equally close to the Sea of Marmara (on whose European shore Constantine founded the city of Constantinople) and to the imperial roads which led up from the East. The Council of Nicaea was supposed to be an "ecumenical" – that is, a "worldwide" – council. It included even a token party of bishops from distant Persia. And what Constantine wished from it was uniformity. Even the date of Easter was agreed upon, so that all Christian churches in all regions should celebrate the principal festival of the Church at exactly the same time. This concern for universal uniformity, devoted to the worship of one God only, was the opposite of the colorful variety of *religiones*, of religious festivals each happening in its own place at its own time, which had characterized the empire when it had been a polytheist "commonwealth of cities."[17]

Constantine died in 337. He had reigned a decade longer than Diocletian, and only nine years less than the emperor Augustus. His choice of a new god as protector of his empire, much less the impenitent success of his reign, could not have been predicted in A.D. 300. We must now look at the Christian churches of the Roman empire to understand the meaning of Constantine's decision to worship their God.

In 312, Christianity had been in existence for over 250 years. The world of Jesus of Nazareth and of Saint Paul was as far distant from contemporaries of Constantine as is the age of Louis XIV from ourselves. Christians presented their Church as having been locked in unchanging and continual conflict with the pagan Roman empire. But this was a myth. In reality, the period after A.D. 250 represented a new situation. Both empire and Church had changed.

The empire had become more intrusive and more committed to an ideological stance. The emperors came to see Christianity, for the first time, as an empire-wide phenomenon. An empire in crisis needed the protection of the gods. It was the duty of the emperors to foster the old religion and to halt "impiety" on an empire-wide scale. The suppression of Christianity was no longer a matter for the "local government" of the cities. Sporadic local violence against Christians and condemnations by local governors, city by city, gave way to empire-wide edicts against the Church as a whole. The first of these was issued in 250, and again in 257. A final set of measures, known to Christians as the Great Persecution, was instituted by the emperor Diocletian in 303. The Great Persecution continued in parts of Asia Minor, Syria, and Egypt for 11 years. It marked the coming of age both of the new empire and of the Christian Church.[18]

The Great Persecution showed that the Christian Church had changed as much as had the empire. It was no longer a low-profile constellation of tiny groups. It had become a universal Church, claiming the loyalty of all believers, at just the same time as the Roman empire had become a true empire, with ideological claims on all its subjects. In the course of the third century, the Church developed a recognizable hierarchy with prominent leaders. The emperors responded to this development. In 303, as in 250 and 257, the imperial authorities singled out these leaders for attack. Bishops and clergy – and not the Christian rank and file – were arrested and forced to sacrifice. Cyprian of Carthage, for instance, was executed in 258. He was declared to be "the standard-bearer of the Christian faction" in the city. Bishops of the caliber of Cyprian were a new phenomenon. He was a well-known local figure. His letters covered every aspect of the life of a large Christian community. They show how the Church had begun to function as a fiercely independent body – a veritable "city within the city."[19]

At a time when the laws of the emperors were regarded as the source of all order (and were carefully collected and preserved even by humble persons) the Church claimed to possess, in the Christian Scriptures, its own, universal code of law. This new "divine law" was attacked. Diocletian ordered that the Christian Scriptures should be taken out of the churches and burned. Even the format of the Christian Scriptures spoke of the urgency of a new age. They were no longer the unwieldy scroll of the classical era. They were *codices*, books as we now know them. The *codex* (from which our word "code" is derived) had developed rapidly in this period of brisk organization. The *codex* was compact and easy to carry. It was bound in such a way as to make its contents final and easy to refer to. Bureaucrats and men in a hurry tended to use the *codex*. So did the Christians. The bound book, rather than the old-fashioned scroll, was an entirely appropriate vehicle for a new

"Law." This law was as unambiguous and as universal in its application as was any law issued by a Roman emperor. And it came from a source higher than any emperor. It was the law of God. The Christian Scriptures could be consulted anywhere, and what they said was applicable everywhere. While the *religiones* of the gods were subject to the vagaries of local custom, and were seldom written down, it was only necessary to open a *codex* of the Scriptures and to read in them the law of God as to which *religio* was correct and which was not. The message was unambiguous: *He that sacrificeth to other gods shall be utterly destroyed.*[20]

Last, but not least, the officials of Diocletian destroyed Christian churches. Christian churches of the third century were relatively humble affairs, assembly rooms created within the existing structures of houses. The church at Dura Europos, on the Euphrates, had been constructed in this manner in the 230s, to house a congregation of barely more than 70. A hundred yards down the street, the Jewish synagogue of Dura was a large building, resplendent with frescoes which showed the deeds of Moses and of other heroes of Israel, and with seats for at least 120 worshippers. The later Christian basilica at Aquileia was 37.4 by 20.4 meters, and could house a congregation of 750. By contrast, the contemporary Jewish synagogue of Sardis was a magnificent building of 80 by 20 meters, with room, that is, for at least 1,500. What mattered, however, is that, in the Christian image of themselves, the Christian churches were "growth points." They welcomed converts, and expected them to remain loyal. To level these walls, therefore, was to halt an institution that was widely perceived to be capable of "runaway" growth.[21]

It is impossible to know how many Christians there were in the empire at this time: up to 10 percent of the population has been suggested, grouped more heavily in Syria, Asia Minor, and the major cities of the Roman Mediterranean than in any other region. But this is a guess. What mattered more is that, in the course of the third century, the Christian communities had expanded rapidly and unexpectedly.[22]

There is little room for the myth that Christians were a perpetually hounded minority, literally driven underground by unremitting persecution. Nor is there any truth in the more modern myth which presents the advance of Christianity as due to the spread of a religion of mercy and equality among the underprivileged. Christianity was by no means the religion only of slaves and of simple folk. Rather, the third century was an age of surprising Christians, of whom the emperor Constantine was only the last. Marcia, the influential concubine of the emperor Commodus, had been a Christian and a protector of the bishops of Rome. Bardaisan was both a courtier and a Christian. His king, Abgar VIII of Osrhoene, was believed to have been a "pious man," even a "believer." Julius Africanus, a Greek polymath from Palestine, was a Christian. He visited Bardaisan, wrote to the great Christian theologian, Origen of Alexandria, and then went to Rome to help the emperor to set up a library in the Pantheon. Newly discovered inscriptions show a more lasting phenomenon: a Christian gentry already established in Asia Minor. In the Upper Tembris valley (southwest of Ankara, Turkey) gentleman farmers, complete with plough-teams, and wives bearing the conventional woman's distaff, speak of themselves, on large gravestones, as "Christians for Christians." One city of the area even boasted a Christian wrestler, known as "the Creeper," who returned to an honorific seat on the town council, having won prizes from as far afield as Brindisi.[23] In around A.D. 300, in southern Spain, a council of bishops at Elvira made rulings on Christian town councillors whose honorific role as "priests" of the imperial cult caused them to be present at sacrifices offered out of loyalty to the emperors; on their wives, who donated robes for the local processions of the gods; on landowners who received consecrated first fruits from their peasants as part of the rent; and on women who had beaten servants to death.[24] It could not be said that Christians were totally innocent of wealth, of slave-owning or, even, of power.

What would have struck a contemporary was that the Christian Church was unlike the many trade associations and cultic brotherhoods which proliferated in the Roman cities. These tended to be class- or gender-specific. Fellow-craftsmen would gather with their equals to dine and worship. Women alone would form societies for the worship of their goddess. The Christian church, by contrast, was a variegated group.[25] In that respect, it was not unlike a miniature version of the new empire. High and low, men and women met as equals because equally subject, now, to the overruling law of one God. Those who entered such churches were encouraged to find in them an orderly assembly. Grown men, married women and children, widows and unattached women: each group was carefully separated, and seated in their appropriate place. Deacons watched the doors to scrutinize incoming strangers: "and let the deacon also see that no one whispers, or falls asleep, or laughs, or makes signs." Social differences were not expunged in such gatherings. They were, rather, handled with an elaborate and pointed courtesy. If a "man of worldly honor" entered a crowded church, the bishop must on no account rise to receive him, lest he be thought to be a "respecter of persons." But the deacon should tell one of the young men to move over: "that they also may be trained and learn to give place to those more honorable than themselves." If a poor man or a destitute stranger should come in, however, it was an entirely different matter: "do thou, o bishop, with all thy heart provide a place for them, even if thou hadst to sit upon the ground."[26]

"All malice will be wiped out": Salvation, Martyrdom, and Penance in the Christian Church

The Christian churches of the third century A.D. were not, in any way, places where the world was turned upside down. What was striking about the Christian groups, rather, was their intense sense of order and of belonging to a network of similar communities which stretched from one end of the Roman world to the other. The message which was preached in these communities was severe: it was about salvation and about sin. It was through this preaching that Christianity emerged as an unusually democratic and potentially wide-reaching movement. It takes some leap of the modern imagination (which has come to be saturated for centuries by Christian language) to understand the novelty of seeing every human being as subject to the same universal law of God and as equally capable of salvation through the conquest of sin, brought about through baptism followed by permanent and exclusive membership of a unique religious group.[27]

Salvation meant, first and foremost, salvation from idolatry and from the power of the demons. "The unity of God and the refutation of the idols" were themes which any Christian lay man or woman was free to expound to outsiders.[28] All past tradition was reinterpreted by such teaching. In polytheist belief, the lower ranks of gods had been treated as ambivalent, moody creatures, capable of being spiteful and manipulable on some occasions and generous and powerful on others. Christians developed this division of the gods in a more radical direction. They ascribed to all gods without exception the unreliable qualities of the lowest gods.

These lower gods had usually been spoken of by polytheists as *daimones*, as invisible, intermediary beings.[29] To Christians, all gods were "demons," in the sense with which we still use the word "demon." They were not just touchy. They were evil. Christians never denied the existence of the gods. Rather, they treated all gods, even the highest, as malevolent and unreliable. The demons were faceless invisible powers, past masters of the art of illusion. They merely used the traditional rites, myths, and images of polytheism as so many masks, so as to draw the human race ever further away from the worship of the One true God. Seen with Christian eyes in the age of Constantine, the immemorial worship of the gods throughout the Roman world was a grand illusion: the ancient rites to which the emperor Diocletian paid such heavy reverence were no more than a tawdry stage-set, set up by the demons so as to stand between mankind and its rightful God.[30]

Nor was this God a distant reality. Christian communities encountered the polytheist world along a front which crackled with demonstrations of divine power. Exorcism, for instance, was a well-known form of religious drama. Cures were effected by driving disruptive spirits from the human body, which they had entered and possessed. Christians used this common practice to teach nothing less than a condensed lesson in the direction of world history. Christ, they believed, had already broken the power of the demons in the invisible world. Now his servants could be seen to drive them from their last hiding places on earth. Exorcism rendered palpable the preordained retreat of the gods, as the demons, screaming the names of traditional divinities, withdrew violently from the bodies of the possessed, when challenged by the name of Christ.[31]

Exorcism was a common practice in the ancient world. Martyrdom, however, was not. In order to enter into the full shock of the phenomenon in the cities of the Roman empire, we have to think away later Christian teaching, which has made us take for granted the idea that men and women should die for their beliefs. At the time, the Christian idea of martyrdom was a dangerous novelty. It turned the religious life of the cities into a religious battlefield. For martyrdom came to be seen (by both sides) as a fully public clash of gods. Christian accounts of the martyrs never emphasized (as we might do) their purely human courage. Rather, the martyrs were presented as men and women possessed by the power of Christ. They had a mighty God in them, and, by their heroic deaths, they trumped the power of the ancient gods of the city.[32]

Even at the height of the Great Persecution, martyrdom was not an everyday occurrence for Christians. But martyrdom did not have to be frequent for its message to inspire horror and awe. Those few who died for Christ made the power of their God seem overwhelmingly present to the many. Even when in prison, the potential martyr was the special joy of the Christian community:

> Let him be esteemed by you a holy martyr, an angel of God or God upon earth . . . For through him you see the Lord our Savior.[33]

In a world where execution was a form of public spectacle, witnessed by the entire urban community, martyrdom was perceived by Christians as an unmistakable sign of the power of Christ. Through the heroism of the martyr, the power of God was displayed for all to see in the very center of every city.

> You could see a youth not twenty years of age, standing unbound and stretching out his hands in the form of a Cross . . . while bears and leopards almost touched his flesh. And yet their mouths were restrained, I know not how, by a divine and incomprehensible power.[34]

The ancient story of Daniel, who had been delivered by God in the lions' den, merged with the figure of Christ and with the victorious power of his Cross, in a setting vibrant with popular associations of contest and victory. The scene just described took place in 308, only four years, that is, before the armies of Constantine, a man already accustomed to looking to heaven for help from "a divine and incomprehensible power," converged on the Milvian Bridge. What Constantine picked up from Christianity was a grass-roots certainty that the Christian God "stood close by" to grant "victory" to his worshippers in every emergency. It was a small step for him to apply this belief to the success of his own armies and to the security of his own empire.

Most Christians were denied the "triumph" of martyrdom. The one triumph that was always possible, however, was the triumph over sin and, eventually, the triumph over death. The Christian funeral was a victory parade. The carrying of the body to the grave took the form of a triumphal progress. The bier was escorted by believers in white robes, carrying radiant lamps. The grave was a place of rest, a *koimétérion* (the Greek word for "lying at rest" is the source of our word "cemetery"), where the dead, and those gathered around the tomb, enjoyed a foretaste of the *refrigerium*, of the joyous refreshment of God's paradise. The living would share in this "refreshment," as they gathered, at regular intervals, to eat and drink at the tomb of their loved ones.[35]

For the community of the living, however, triumph over sin was the principal concern. It was an urgent and difficult matter. We must remember that, in the Early Church, sin (despite the associations that have accumulated around the notion in later centuries) was a largely novel and helpful concept. Like the notion of universal "suffering," which had characterized Buddhism, the notion of "sin" which was current in Christian circles made sense of the world in terms of a single, universal human condition. All human beings sinned, and all could seek to make reparation for their sins. The idea was taken from Judaism. But it was developed in the Christian communities in such a way as to give contemporaries a new language with which to talk about change within themselves and about the relations between their new religious community and the world outside it.

Elements of the new language of sin and conversion already lay to hand even in non-Jewish circles. Christians did no more than sharpen the assertion of ancient philosophers that philosophy was a skill of self-transformation. Philosophers had always attempted to change the minds and the habits of their disciples. Serious persons were expected to file away at themselves, removing their failings so as to produce, like the carvers of Greek statues, a self in which the excrescences of raw human nature were honed down to produce an exquisite, harmonious whole. It was a demanding ideal.[36]

Christians merely claimed to do this better. Their "philosophy" was a God-given "philosophy." The Church was a "school of virtue" open to all. They claimed to be able to transform the human person entirely, through conversion and baptism, in a manner which shocked traditional pagans, as wildly optimistic and, even, as irresponsible – for it seemed to offer easy, "instant" forgiveness of crimes. But, in an age of heady change in all areas of society, Christians held out the prospect of total transformation of the person through conversion and baptism:

> The few commands of God so change the whole man and render him new when the old has been put off, that you do not recognize him to be the same . . . For with one washing, all malice will be wiped out . . . Here is that which all philosophers sought in their whole life . . . He who wishes to be wise and happy, let him hear the voice of God.[37]

Unlike the ferociously individual self-grooming of the philosopher, the handling of "sin" was a communal concern in Christian circles. Sin could be changed into righteousness through reparation to God. And reparation was not a purely personal matter. The small Christian community, gathered frequently within the narrow walls of its churches, was the arbiter of sin. Fellow-believers interceded, before God, for each individual with their prayers. A Christian gathering of around the year A.D. 200 was expected to include gripping scenes of moral "exorcism," through the penance of notable sinners. An adulterer might be

> led in to the midst of the brethren and prostrated all in sackcloth and ashes, a compound of disgrace and horror . . . suing for everyone's tears, licking their footprints, clasping their knees.[38]

Rare though such spectacles might be, they showed that, in the matter of sin, the Christian community meant business.

In the course of the third century, the handling of sin came to be taken over by the bishop. The bishop was presented as the searching mercy of God personified: "first of all judge strictly and, afterwards, receive . . . command the sinner to come in . . . examine him . . . and appoint him days of fasting." Judged by the bishop and supported by the prayers of fellow-believers, individual Christians were able to pace themselves in making due reparation to God for the many frailties that still tied them to "the world" – that is, to that potent presence, outside the Church, of a society which lay in the dark shadow of the demons. *Thy repentance shall be with thee and thou shalt have power over it.*[39]

The Church and Society: Almsgiving

Repentance invited concrete and fully visible reparatory actions. Christians had inherited from Judaism the practice of giving alms "for the remission of sins." This was a crucial inheritance. The notion of almsgiving fused with the notion of repentance in a manner which harnessed the use of wealth in Christian circles to a new system of religious explanation. Money and goods given "for the remission of sins" ensured that wealth gained in "the world" (through craftsmanship, trade, and landowning) flowed, without inhibition, into the Church. The "goods of this world" were "redeemed" by being spent on the religious community.

Even the most humble members of the Christian community were involved in this perpetual mobilization of wealth. The average adherents of Judaism and Christianity were industrious townsfolk. Their hard-won coins "gathered sweat in the palm of the hand," before they were given to deserving causes.[40] But every believer was obliged to give. As a rabbi said, the "breastplate of righteousness," associated with almsgiving, was made up, like the scale-mail armor of third-century cavalry, of innumerable small coins, given frequently by ordinary believers.[41] In the polytheist world of the cities, the proud temples depended on wealthy donors, who might, at any moment, go bankrupt – as happened to many pagan shrines in the course of the crisis of the third century. In a period of financial recession, the Christian communities, with their habits of regular giving by small persons, were better equipped to weather the storm of political insecurity and inflation than were the grandees who supported polytheist worship.[42]

Far from being a cold, cash transaction, almsgiving triggered, at the time, deep-laid imaginative structures that made it seem an entirely appropriate penitential gesture. By giving to the destitute, at the furthest edge of the community, the act of almsgiving made present on earth a touch of the boundless care of God for all mankind. The utter pointlessness of giving to those who, as beggars, could offer nothing in return highlighted the magnificent transcendence of God: "They who are useless to men are useful to God."[43] The gesture of reaching out the hand in mercy to the poor was held to echo (and so to provoke) the gesture that the sinner hoped, above all, from God himself – that his hand, also, would stretch out to offer the supreme gift of forgiveness.

Altogether, the act of giving was a central part of the day-to-day practice of the Christian community. As a result, the churches of the late third century emerged as remarkably cohesive and solvent bodies. Christians were known to look after their own. The churches had created systems for the care of unprotected and afflicted fellow-believers that grew like thick layers of bark around every Christian community. In A.D. 251, the Christian Church in Rome supported – from the gifts of the faithful – 154 members of the clergy (of whom 52 were exorcists) and took care of 1,500 widows, orphans, and destitute persons. The destitute alone were more numerous than the entire membership of all but the largest professional association in the city; and the clergy formed a body as large, and as self-conscious, as the *ordo*, the city council, of any small town.[44] When, at the time of the Great Persecution, commissioners entered the relatively small Christian church at Cirta (Constantine, Algeria), so as to confiscate its treasures, they found a storeroom with 16 shirts for men, 38 veils, 82 dresses, and 47 pairs of slippers for women, as well as 11 containers of oil and wine.[45]

From *religiones* to Religion

The subsequent success of the Christian Church makes it particularly difficult for the historian to assess the position of the Church around A.D. 300. We forget how new to the ancient world and how tentative, even in Christian circles, were some of the notions which we now take for granted. The most novel of all, at this time, was the notion of "religion" as we are now accustomed to think of it. Polytheists knew exactly what *religiones* were: they were precise ways of worshipping the gods, which one neglected at one's peril. But other activities which we, nowadays, instinctively associate with religion were little touched by the gods. Not all of these activities were considered suitable for everybody. Self-grooming and the search for truth tended to be what gentlemen did, under the guidance of well-educated philosophers. Philosophical speculation and moral self-improvement were regarded as upper-class pursuits, not open to the average person. Many philosophers and moralists were pious persons. But philosophy and morality owed little to *religio* – to the cult of the gods. They were thought of as human activities, developed over the ages by human beings. They were learned from and enforced by human beings: by one's father, by one's teachers, and by the frankly man-made laws and customs of one's city. They had not been laid down once and for all in a holy book as the Law of God, as was the case in Judaism and Christianity.

What was surprising to contemporaries about the Christian Church was the extent to which activities, which had tended to be kept separate under the old system of *religio*, were fused into one. Morality, philosophy, and ritual were treated as intimately connected. All were part of "religion" in the wide sense of the term to which we have become accustomed. All were based on the Law of God. They were to be found in their true form only in the Church. In the Christian churches, philosophy was dependent upon revelation and morality was absorbed into *religio*. Furthermore, commitment to truth and moral improvement were held to be binding on all believers, irrespective of their class and level of culture. Hence the remarkable combination of stern moralizing and urgent theological speculation which absorbed the energy of serious Christians, from a wide variety of social backgrounds, in the third century as in all later ages.

In much the same manner, the circulation of wealth was harnessed to a carefully thought out system which linked sin with reparation through almsgiving. All classes within the Church were involved in a dogged mobilization of wealth to build up a single religious community. This wealth was distributed along the margins of the Church in such a way as to suggest that the Christian community had the will and the financial "muscle" to take care of the lowest reaches of Roman society.

Thus, when a continuous spate of laws and personal letters in favor of Christians issued from the palace of Constantine in the decades after A.D. 312, they were received and exploited to the full by a religious group which knew how to make the best of its good fortune. If, in the words of the English proverb, "God helps those who help themselves," the Christian Church, as it had developed in the course of the third century, more than deserved the apparent "miracle" of Constantine's conversion at the battle of the Milvian Bridge.

CHAPTER 3

Tempora Christiana:
Christian Times

"The religion of the Greeks . . . has vanished from the earth": The End of Paganism, Official Version

The religion of the (pagan) Greeks, made dominant for so many years, by such pains, by the expenditure of so much wealth, and by such feats of arms, has vanished from the earth.[1]

Thus wrote a Christian priest, Isidore of Pelusium (a seaport close to modern Port Said, Egypt) in around A.D. 420. All over the Roman empire, articulate Christians, such as Isidore, claimed to enjoy the inestimable advantage, in a time of rapid change, of belonging to a group convinced that history was on their side. They looked back on the century which followed the conversion of Constantine as an age of triumph. They saw the changes of that time against a majestic, supernatural backdrop. Long ago, Christ had broken the power of the gods. When Christ was raised on the Cross at Golgotha, the invisible empire of the demons had crumbled. What happened on earth in the fourth century merely made plain the previous, supernatural victory of Christ over his enemies. It was a "mopping up" operation. The dislodging of the demons from their accustomed haunts – the removal of their sacrificial altars, the sacking of their temples, the breaking of their statues – was presented as the grandiose, and satisfactorily swift, equivalent, on the public level, of the well-known drama of exorcism. In exorcism, the gods were driven from the body of the possessed by the victorious power of the Cross. Now they would be driven, equally brusquely, from the temples, and the sign of the Cross would be carved on the doorposts to mark the triumphant "repossession" of the temple by Christ.[2]

A sense of history moving swiftly to its preordained conclusion runs through much Christian preaching and most Christian narratives of the period. In

404, a group of pagan notables in the small North African town of Boseth (in the Mejerda valley of Algeria) entered the Christian basilica to listen to a sermon by a famous visiting bishop, Augustine of Hippo. What they heard was an exhortation to wake up, to listen to the *strepitus mundi*, the roar of the Roman world, like the unanimous chanting of a great crowd in the circus, as it acclaimed the victory of Christianity.[3]

We should not underestimate the fierce mood of Christians in the fourth century A.D. For centuries, the churches had consisted of small, compact groups, tensed against the outside world. These groups had recently emerged from widespread persecution. It was not a situation likely to breed tolerance of others. Furthermore, as we have seen in the case of the martyrs, Christians made sense of their world in terms of a clash of gods. The power of Christ was pitted remorselessly against the malevolent power of the demons who lurked behind the façade of traditional polytheist worship. The unexpected conversion of Constantine in 312, and his subsequent support of the Church, seemed to be a triumphant vindication of this militant view of the world. By patronizing the Church, Constantine had wished to gain the support of the God of the Christians. Whether he wanted to foster renewed religious violence (this time, by Christians against pagans) is another matter. But the Christian bishops thought otherwise. For them it was now or never. They considered that they had won the right to finish off the struggle with the gods.

For the leaders of the Christian communities now found themselves in a position where they could not afford to lose momentum. Once the Great Persecution had ended, the Christian churches ceased to be small, alienated groups, able to control the behavior of all their members. Large congregations came to contain many wavering believers. For such persons, polytheism was dangerous simply because it was still there: it was still so well established and so seductive. Hence the larger the Church became, the more vital it was for the bishops to "take out" (to use military language) the enemy's positions by pre-emptive strikes. Oracles had remained popular: many were shut down. Great temples were deliberately violated: their doors were broken and their sanctuaries defiled, if only to prove that the gods associated with them were unable to protect their shrines against such sacrilege. Statues of the gods were broken up with deliberate care: their heads, arms, and legs were broken off, so as to deprive them of the divine "life" which their worshippers (and many half-hearted Christians also) had seen in them.[4] These pre-emptive, "first strike" measures were not necessarily expected to convert pagans. They took place, rather, so as to hold in newly converted Christians by removing from them the temptation offered by old places of pagan worship.

The Christian empire was fully implicated in these actions. Emperors had always been expected to have a firm religious policy in order to be sure of the support of the gods. From 250 onwards, and especially during the Great Persecution initiated by Diocletian, the authorities had shown no hesitation in fostering the traditional *religiones* of the empire by "taking out" the Christian Church – by forbidding its meetings and destroying its property and sacred books. Constantine and his Christian successors did the same in reverse. They put very little direct pressure on individual pagans: there were no pagan martyrs. Rather, from time to time, the emperors took measures to render pagan worship incapable of being performed in public. After 312, first Constantine, then his devout son, Constantius II (337–361), and, finally, Theodosius I (379–395) progressively forbade public sacrifices, closed temples, and colluded in frequent acts of local violence by Christians against major cult sites – of which the destruction of the gigantic Serapeum of Alexandria, in around 392, was only the most spectacular.[5]

These governmental actions were sporadic. It was Christian opinion which invested them with an aura of inevitability. Contemporary Christians never treated polytheism as a living religion. It was deemed to have been, from the start, an obsolescent faith, a *superstitio*. In the sharp words of an early edict of Constantine, polytheists might, if they wished, "celebrate the rites of an outmoded illusion," provided that they did not force Christians to join in them.[6] Even in regions of the Roman world where polytheism was not subjected to direct attack, it was allowed to exist only on condition that it was seen to be an empty shell, drained of supernatural power. All over the Roman world, the urban landscape changed. The temples became dead spaces. Their increasingly dilapidated state proclaimed the rise of a new religious group, whose *religio* (the worship of Christ) was officially declared to be responsible for the safety of the Roman empire.

In the late fourth century, polytheism received its modern name. The word "pagan," *paganus*, began to circulate among Christians. This word emphasized the marginal status of polytheism. Usually, *paganus* had meant "second-class participant" – civilian as opposed to regular soldier, lower as opposed to high official. The Spanish priest, Orosius, who wrote his *History against the Pagans* at the behest of Augustine, in 416, added a further touch to this language of exclusion. Cultivated polytheists, urban notables, and even members of the Roman Senate, were told by Orosius that theirs was a religion of countryfolk, of *pagani*, of men of the *pagus*, of *paysans*, *paesanos* – that is, a religion worthy only of illiterate peasants.[7]

Nor was this simply a matter of clerical preaching. The most effective sermonizer of all, in the fourth and fifth centuries, was the newly organized Roman state. The laws of the emperors showed that they took their religious duties with deadly seriousness and that they were open to the petitions of those who did the same. We are dealing here less with direct Christian influence on the legislative program of the emperors from Constantine onward than with the demand of an entire, upper-class society for firm guidelines, from above, on issues which had previously been left to local law and to local public opinion.[8] The position of women came to be more closely defined.[9] Magic, previously treated as an occasional nuisance and a cause of crime, was now outlawed, in universal terms, as a noxious belief.[10]

This ambitious governmental mood left an appropriate monument. In 436, the lawyers of Theodosius II (408–450), the grandson of Theodosius I, met in Constantinople to bring together the edicts of his Christian predecessors in a single bound book, a *codex*. The subsequent *Theodosian Code* appeared in 438.[11] It was the most compact and the most long-lasting monument of this great age of organization. When early medieval Christians looked back to Rome, what they saw, first and foremost, was not the "Golden Age" of classical Rome (as we would tend to do). The pagan empire did not impress them. It was the *Theodosian Code* which held their attention and esteem. It was the official voice of the Roman empire at its greatest, that is, when it was the Roman empire as God had always intended it to be – a Christian empire.

The *Code* ended with a book *On Religion*. This book, in itself, signalled the arrival of a new attitude to religion. Religious belief as such was now treated as a subject for legislation. As we have seen, Romans had always been concerned with the correct performance of *religiones*, with the maintenance of traditional rites. But this attitude had been replaced by the new definition of "religion" which, as we saw, had emerged in the course of the third century A.D. Now it was "thought-crime" itself – wrong views on religion in general, and not simply failure to practice traditional rites in the traditional manner – which was disciplined. In the *Theodosian Code*, extracts from the laws issued from the reign of Constantine to that of Theodosius II were arranged in chronological order. They communicated a rising sense of governmental certainty. There was to be little place, in the new Roman order, for heresy, schism, or Judaism, and no place at all for "the error of stupid paganism."[12]

This hurried mood played an essential role in maintaining the morale of the Christian churches and of their imperial protectors. It was not necessarily shared by the majority of the inhabitants of the Roman world. For all its reforms, the Roman empire remained a mercifully slow-moving place. The absolutism of the emperors was tempered by vast distances and by the continued need (even in a more centralized system) to secure the collaboration of the local elites. It was always more important to ensure that taxes were paid than to smash temples. And if the destruction of a temple alienated the local town councils to such an extent that they were unwilling to help with the collection of taxes, then the temple was likely to remain.[13]

Distant Britain was one such slow-moving society. Sometime in the fourth century, Annianus, son of Matutina, an aggrieved Romano-Briton, from whom an unknown person had stolen a purse with six silver coins, visited the temple of the goddess Minerva Sulis at Bath, so as to place a curse-tablet in the sacred spring of the goddess. The curse contained a conventional list of potential suspects: "whether male or female, boy or girl, slave or free." But it opened with a novel antithesis: "Whether a Christian or a gentile, whomsoever." In late Roman Bath, Christians existed; but they were no more than one category of persons among many; and they were held to be equally subject to the avenging power of an ancient, and still powerful, deity.[14]

Even around the Mediterranean, where Christianity was well known, similar views prevailed. Those who attended the sermons of Augustine, in Carthage and Hippo, considered themselves to be good Christians. But they still carried in the backs of their minds a model of the supernatural world which was not polarized in the dramatic manner proposed by their bishops. Their monotheism was that much less clear-cut. Their belief in the Highest God of the Christians was sincere. But this belief in a new high God did not apply to all aspects of their lives.

> There are those who say, "God is good, He is great, supreme, eternal and inviolable. It is He who will give us eternal life and the incorruptibility which He has promised at the resurrection of the dead. But these things of the physical world and of our present time belong to the *daemones* and to the Invisible (lower) Powers."[15]

To Augustine's hearers, the lower powers, the *daemones*, were by no means impotent beings. Distinguished parishioners reminded their bishop that the gods had, after all, foretold their own withdrawal from their temples, in widely circulated oracles. They argued that Roman religion would not have been allowed by God to last so long, if there had not been some good in it. Faced by a temple, their motto was, "Do not worship there, but do not speak ill of it."[16] For such persons, the venerable religious past of Rome could not be thought of, in its entirety, as a demonically manipulated illusion. They still lived in a multilayered universe. The *daemones* were lower powers, to be invoked for lower needs. They were the protectors of the humble activities of life – of childbirth, of careers, of trade, and of the good things of the earth. They were still there. Nobody thought that they did not exist. And they had not been pushed aside entirely by the austere and exclusive presence of the One God of the Christians. Many of Augustine's parishioners simply expected Christ to coexist, as a High God, ringed with a host of long-familiar "Invisible Powers," to whose oracles they still listened in times of crisis and whose names they still invoked on their amulets and in their healing rituals.[17]

It takes a considerable effort of the modern imagination to realize that, in the fourth and fifth centuries, a large number of Christians, in all regions and of all levels of culture, still thought very much as Augustine's congregation thought. Despite the official version of the Christian Church, which had stressed the dramatic "End of Paganism", the conversion of Constantine only marked, at best, the beginning of the end of polytheism. The Church itself would have to become much stronger, in each locality, before Christianity could claim to have truly triumphed in the Roman world. The Church, in effect, had to conquer the cities.

The Conquest of the Cities

For all their propaganda, Constantine and his successors did not bring about the end of paganism. But what they did bring to the Christian churches was peace, wealth, and, above all, the ability to build up, at a surprising rate, a strong local position. Constantine faced an institution which had already shown itself able to mobilize and redistribute wealth for religious causes. Following the Roman tradition of lavish endowments of the cults deemed most useful to the empire, Constantine became a Christian donor of overpowering generosity. He set up great basilica churches (true "royal halls," as the name *basilica*, from *basileus*, "king," implies) in Rome – Saint Peter's and San Giovanni in Laterano. At Antioch he built a large, golden-domed octagon opposite the newly-built imperial palace. Above all, he built the Church of the Holy Sepulcher at Jerusalem. These churches were sermons in stone. They spoke far more loudly and more continuously of the providential alliance of Church and empire than did any imperial edict or the theorizing of any bishop. They left visitors amazed.

> The decorations really are too marvelous for words [wrote Egeria, a Spanish pilgrim, on Constantine's church of the Holy Sepulcher.] All you can see is gold and jewels and silk . . . You simply cannot imagine the number and the sheer weight of the candles, tapers, lamps and everything else they use for the services . . . They are beyond description, and so is the magnificent building itself. It was built by Constantine and . . . was decorated with gold, mosaic and precious marble, as much as his empire could provide.[18]

We must remember that these churches did not stand alone. What we call a "church" was not an isolated building. It usually stood in a complex of buildings. These buildings included a *secretarium* (an audience hall in which the bishop presided as judge), an extensive bishop's palace, warehouses for supplies for the poor, and, above all, an impressive courtyard, of the sort which stood in front of a nobleman's town house – for charitable banquets, distributions of alms, or, simply, for the faithful to meet and catch up with the news of the town. Augustine's basilica at Hippo, for instance, had room for a congregation of a little over 300. It was not a large church. But it stood in a "Christian quarter" 5,460 square meters in area, with 120 separate rooms.[19]

Such building complexes made palpable the emergence of a new style of urban leadership. Bishops and clergy received immunities from taxes and from compulsory public services. In each city, the Christian clergy became the only group which expanded rapidly, at a time when the strain of empire had brought other civic associations to a standstill. Bound by oath to "their" bishop, a whole hierarchy of priests, deacons, and minor clergy formed an *ordo* in miniature, as subtly graded as any town council, and as tenaciously attached to its privileges.

Furthermore, Constantine expected that the bishop would act as exclusive judge and arbiter in cases between Christians, and even between Christians and non-Christians. Normal civil litigation had become prohibitively expensive. As a result, the bishop, already regarded as the God-like judge of sin among believers, rapidly became the *ombudsman* of an entire local community. Besides this, imperial supplies of food and clothing, granted to the clergy to distribute to the poor, turned the ferociously inward-looking care of fellow-believers for each other, which had characterized the Christian churches of an earlier age, into something like a public welfare system, designed to alleviate, and to control, the urban poor as a whole.[20]

We must remember what this expansion of the Church at the local level meant for the structure of the Roman empire as a whole. The cities had always been the nerve-centers of the Roman world. Roman government worked through them. Even the more forceful Roman state of the fourth century depended on the goodwill of the leaders of urban society for taxation and for the maintenance of law and order. As the fourth century progressed, it became increasingly plain that the Christian bishops, by conquering the cities from the bottom up, were in a position to determine the policies of the emperor. They and their clergy were the local group with whom it was most advisable to remain on good terms. The tail began to wag the dog.[21]

For Christianity remained a grassroots movement. Stunning though the few vast basilicas founded by the emperors at Rome – and, a little later, at Trier and Milan – might be, they were dwarfed by the sheer number of churches, of more moderate size, that reflected the ability of the local clergy to mobilize local loyalties and to appeal to local pride. As far apart as northern Italy and Syria, the mosaic floors of new churches were covered with carefully itemized squares, each bearing the name of the local family which had donated it. Christian villages pooled their resources to cover the Algerian plateau (to name one region only) with solid little "houses of the righteous."[22] In Roman Britain, the church at Water Newton ministered to a tiny community. Nonetheless it had a solid silver chalice, given by a Publianus – "Dependent on thee, I honor thy holy altar" – and a collection of silver ex-voto plaques, marked with the Cross, which did not differ from those offered in the non-Christian shrines of Britain.[23] These were churches built, from the ground up, as it were, by local initiatives. They were not invariably amenable to control by a distant emperor.

Nor were Christian bishops the sort of decorous grandees to whom the emperors had once been content to delegate control of the cities in the first and second centuries A.D. The career of the great patriarch of Alexandria, Athanasius (296–373) showed this only too clearly.[24] In the eventual opinion of Constantine's son, Constantius II, Athanasius was an upstart and a menace to public order:

> A man who came from the lowest depths of society and obtained authority . . . His flatterers . . . applauded, and most of the simple folk took their cue from them . . . The man who led the crowd was no different from a common artisan.[25]

Athanasius was a portent of a new age. He combined an ability to provoke the unrelieved suspicion that his local power, as bishop, was based on peculation and violence, with a gift (a sincere gift, but one that he put to use with great political acumen) for presenting himself as the representative of a timeless and universal Christian orthodoxy, declared forever, in 325, at the Council of Nicaea. He persistently denied legitimacy to his accusers by labelling their views as "Arian" – as those of the followers of Arius (250–336), a learned Alexandrian priest. In this way, Athanasius defended his own growing local power in Alexandria by appealing to all that was most majestically nonlocal and fiercely metaphysical in the Christianity of his times.

Athanasius' career included five periods of exile and many adventures when on the run from his enemies. On one occasion, Athanasius escaped at midnight from Tyre, perched on a raft so as to avoid detection by the harbor-guards. He did so in order to escape the bishops who had assembled at Tyre to condemn him for violence and peculation. Sailing straight to Constantinople, he turned the tables on his enemies by appearing in person, totally unannounced, before an astounded Constantine. Such bravado baffled most of his contemporaries and alienated many. It was only later agreed, by the victorious "Nicene" party, that Athanasius had been the hero of a Christian orthodoxy laid down once and for all at Nicaea. But the story of Athanasius and of his defense of the "Nicene Creed" gained in the telling. It did so especially in the Latin West. By the end of the fourth century, the "Arian Controversy" was narrated in studiously confrontational terms: it was asserted that "orthodox" bishops had defeated "heretics"; and, in so doing, they had offered heroic resistance to the cajolery and, at times, to the threats, of "heretical" emperors.

This view of the "Arian Controversy" was constructed after the event. It contains little truth. But it inspired the career of one of the founders of western Catholicism, Ambrose, bishop of Milan (ca.339–397). Ambrose was not a parvenu, as Athanasius had been. He came from a Roman senatorial family. He built up an originally weak position in Milan by studied acts of intransigence. He stood up to emperors when their religious policies conflicted with his own, and he rebuked them memorably when he considered that they had sinned. To "sin," for Ambrose, meant many things. The emperor Theodosius I was rebuked for "sin" first (in 388) because he had dared to punish rioters who had destroyed a Jewish synagogue, and, once again, only a few years later, for having punished a riot among the inhabitants of Thessalonica by means of a massacre.[26]

The story of Theodosius' penance before Ambrose for the massacre of Thessalonica, in 391, was repeated throughout the Western Middle Ages (and still is repeated today) as the classic example of the beginning of the problem of the conflict of Church and State. At the time, however, this conflict is better seen as a series of trials of strength, by which determined local leaders, the Christian bishops, found out how far they could go in testing the basic structural weakness of the Roman empire – the continued reliance of distant emperors on local interest groups. The expanding power of the Christian churches had placed in the hands of the bishops the levers of power.

The Call of the Wild: Monasticism

Fortunately for the emperors, not every city was as turbulent as Alexandria, nor was every bishop an Athanasius or an Ambrose. The cities did not slip out of the control of the imperial government. The cities remained the spoiled children of the Mediterranean Roman world. The largest cities depended on the favor of the emperor for much of their food supply and amenities. A civic-minded, secular aristocracy still resided in them. The cities could be controlled. It was, if anything, the countryside which proved more intractable. Newly Christianized by more radical forms of Christianity, the countryside always threatened to slip from the orderly embrace of the Christian empire. It was an ebullient countryside. In northern Syria and in many areas in North Africa, population had risen and new forms of village life throve. It was in the countryside that many of the most radical forms of Christianity took root.

This happened in the most spectacular manner in Egypt and in Syria. In 270, in the year that Constantine was born, Anthony (250–356), a comfortable farmer of the Egyptian Fayum, made his way out into the desert, to reemerge, around 310, as a famous *eremités*, a "man of the desert," the model Christian "hermit" of all future ages. In Syria, also, the roads had long been travelled by bands of charismatic preachers who owed nothing to the "world." Pointedly celibate, and filled with the power of the Holy Spirit, their travelling bands were a sight to be seen. They had to be advised not to burst into chanted psalms when passing through non-Christian villages – lest they be mistaken for travelling musicians! They were the "unique ones," the "lonely ones." In Egypt, the Greek word *monachos*, "lonely one," from which our word "monk" derives, soon became attached to such eccentric persons. Unmarried, detached from society either by living in the desert or by their restless movement, the "wanderers" of Syria and the "men of desert" of Egypt represented a new form of radical Christianity, henceforth associated with a new term, "monasticism" – the life of monks.[27]

Nor was this ferment limited to the Roman empire. Further east, in Persian Mesopotamia, Christian radical ideas had led to the foundation, by a visionary, of the first new religion to emerge out of Christianity. Mani (216–277) had grown up in a village south of Ctesiphon. His religion was known as Manichaeism. It made plain, in an exotic form deeply hated by other Christians, the immense potential of an ascetic, "apostolic" missionary movement, based upon monk-like "wanderers." Mani claimed to outdo the previous founders of the great religions of Asia:

> The Lord Zoroaster came to Persia . . . The Lord Buddha, the wise, the blessed one, came to the land of India and of the Kushans (to Central Asia) . . . Jesus the Christ, in the Western lands of the Romans, came to the West.[28]

The "Church of Mani," by contrast, would spread to all these regions. And it did. In the course of time, Manichaeism spread throughout the entire length of the sweep of settled life, from the Mediterranean to China, which had once been surveyed, from Edessa, by Bardaisan.[29]

Manichaeism was a religion carried by ascetic missionaries. The Manichaean "Elect" depended entirely on the laity, the "Hearers," for their food and lodging. Thus supported wherever they went, they travelled far and wide. Manichaeism, like Christianity, was very much a religion of the book. Manichaean manuscripts from as far apart as Middle Egypt and the Turfan Oasis of western Sinkiang show the unmistakable power of the *codex* as the bearer of a universal religious law. A Manichaean Psalm book from Egypt even has a five-page index of contents at the back; and a recent, astonishing discovery, a *Life of Mani*, was exquisitely produced in a miniature format, so as to fit, discreetly, into the robes of a traveller.[30] It was through Manichaean missionaries who joined Asia to Europe that ordinary inhabitants of the Roman empire might glimpse the immensity of Asia, through references, in Manichaean texts, to "the blessed one," the "Lord Buddha."

Checked by savage persecution within the Christian empire, the public appeal of Manichaeism soon waned in the West. This could not be said of the monks of Egypt, Palestine, and Syria. Their fame and example spread rapidly. But the Roman empire was a big place. The Christians of each region made something significantly different of what they heard about the monks. In the fourth-century West, in particular, monasticism existed largely in the eye of the beholder: and these were upper-class beholders. Only persons who could read, who could travel to Egypt and the Holy Places, and who could receive, in their spacious town-houses, visitors from the exotic Christian East were in a position to appropriate, adapt, and simplify the new radical message.

In Syria and Egypt, by contrast, monasticism was infinitely complex. In many ways, it settled down as a humdrum movement. Seen from the Latin West, however, it spoke, in a melodramatic manner, to the disquiets of an entire Christian upper class. The *saeculum*, "the world"— seen very much in terms of their own upper-class culture and their own vast wealth – stood condemned by the lives of these distant, miraculously authentic, Christians. Upper-class Christians, women quite as much as men, became avid readers of monastic literature produced, in the first place, in Egypt. Seldom had *codices* containing the history of obscure foreigners provoked such moral landslides in the lives of influential Romans. The *Life of Anthony* appeared immediately after the great hermit's death in 356. It was ascribed to none other than Athanasius of Alexandria. It was soon available in a Latin translation. In 386, an imperial official from Gaul met Augustine (the future bishop of Hippo) who was, at that time, a teacher of classical rhetoric in Milan.

> He told how . . . on one occasion [two well-placed friends had gone for
> a stroll in the countryside] – it was at Trier, when the emperor was at the
> chariot races in the circus . . . They came to a certain house, the dwelling
> of some "servants of God" [that is, monks] . . . There they found a book
> in which was written the life of Anthony. One of them began to read it,
> marvelled at it, was set on fire by it.

Augustine reacted instantly:

> What is wrong with us? What is this we have heard? The unlearned rise
> up and take heaven by force, while we, with all our culture, remain stuck
> fast in flesh and blood.[31]

Augustine was only one of many successful persons in the West who had
been stopped short, in mid-career, by tales of the desert. A decade previously, Martin (335–397), a retired member of the Imperial General Staff and
future bishop of Tours, had created a monastery on the cliffs overlooking
the Loire outside his episcopal city. His monks were men of good family.
They were careful to wear, not the local wool, but camel's hair imported
directly from Egypt! Martin combined, significantly, the role of an exorcist
with that of a destroyer of country temples. As Bishop of Tours from 371 to
397, Martin re-enacted, in the countryside of Gaul, the victorious rout of the
demons, which, as we have seen, formed the basic Christian narrative for the
spread of the faith. He did so with the collusion of a circle of landed aristocrats. They welcomed the appearance, in their own province, of a *vir
apostolicus*, of a "truly Apostle-like man," endowed with miraculous powers. A disaffected man of culture, Sulpicius Severus (363–425), produced a
Life of Martin in 396. The *Life of Martin* soon became a classic of Latin
hagiography. Here was a saint for new, less quiet times: a prophet raised up
by God in the West, to warn a generation of tepid Christians of the swift
approach of the Last Days.[32]

In 399, the senatorial lady, Melania the Elder (342–411), returned to
Campania from Jerusalem, where she had lived among monks for over 20
years, in a convent established on the Mount of Olives at Jerusalem. When
she had left for Egypt and the Holy Land over 20 years previously, her departure had caused no great stir. Now she returned to a world which had
come to appreciate her presence. Her upper-class relatives flocked to her.
"They thought that they were cleansed from the pollution of their riches if
they succeeded in gathering some of the dirt from her feet."[33]

These dramatic scenes were orchestrated and relayed to each other by a
relatively small group of influential and highly articulate persons. They reflected a growing dissatisfaction in the Christianity of the Latin West. Many

Latin Christians had come to feel that, despite the conversion of the emperors, their world had not yet become Christian enough. It was up to them to change it.

The Power of the *Saeculum*: The New Aristocracy and its Values

The vivid religious history of the fourth century has tended to divert attention from the fact that the religious revolution associated with the reign of Constantine went hand in hand with a social revolution – the creation and stabilization of a new, and self-confident, upper class. The splendid late Roman villas, which dominated the countryside in every province of the western empire, spoke of a world restored. Their occupants – part landowners and part government servants – embraced the new order with enthusiasm. For them, conversion to Christianity was a conversion, above all, to the almost numinous majesty of a Roman empire, now restored and protected by the One God of the Christians.[34]

As a result of this self-confident mood, the Christogram – the Greek letters Chi/Ro (our Ch/r) joined together as a sign of the name of Christ – came to be associated with Constantine's victory at the battle of the Milvian Bridge, and so was placed on every kind of object associated with the affluent way of life of the new aristocracy. To take one recently discovered example: in Pannonia, near Lake Balaton (western Hungary), a hoard of magnificent silverware shows Sevso, a provincial aristocrat – possibly a military man of non-Roman background – at ease in his world. With his favorite horse – carefully marked, "Innocentius" – and his fortified villa, Sevso was there to stay. The main serving dish was made of two and a half kilograms of solid silver, and bore the inscription:

> *May these, O Sevso, for many ages be,*
> *Small vessels, fit to serve your offspring worthily.*

And in Sevso's world, Christianity also had come to stay. The Christogram appears at the beginning of the inscription, directly above Sevso's head, as he presided at his ease over the huntsmen's banquet.[35]

Such persons were prominent also in the cities of the empire. They were Christians, but they had not ceased to be aristocrats. They still needed to celebrate their power. To do this they drew upon ceremonies, art-forms, and literary styles which reached back into the non-Christian past. Large areas of the public life of the upper classes of the Roman empire remained magnificently opaque to the confessional definitions of identity, which claimed, with increasing harshness, to divide the world neatly between Christians and pagans. In this public culture, Christians and non-Christians were free to meet on neutral ground. Men of different *religiones* could collaborate to maintain a Roman world restored to order.

But the creation of a neutral public culture at a time of religious strife depended on maintaining a studied ambiguity. Constantine's new city, Constantinople, was a classic example of this effort. Constantinople was hailed by Christians as a city without temples. Certainly, traditional blood-sacrifice was never performed in the city. But Constantinople was not a city without gods. Constantine had deliberately drained the eastern provinces of their pagan art-works so as to turn his new city into an astonishing open-air museum of the art of the classical world. A "post-pagan" world was not, by any means, necessarily a Christian world.[36]

In this period, also, the Feast of the Kalends of January positively blossomed throughout the empire. The Feast of the Kalends was a New Year's feast. It owed nothing whatsoever to Christianity. It was a feast which celebrated with ancient, religious fervor (although without blood-sacrifice) the unflagging vigor of a Roman order, as this was mysteriously renewed at the start of every year. The consuls who gave their names to the year were nominated on the Kalends of January. All over the empire, the feast of the Kalends of January involved lavish exchanges of gifts between patrons and their dependents, and competitive banqueting, which displayed – and was even thought to guarantee for the coming year – the affluence of individual households.[37]

All over the empire, also, Christian bishops preached with unusual fervor against this particular festival. On one occasion at Carthage (as we now know from a newly discovered sermon) Augustine preached for over two and a half hours on end on the occasion of the Kalends of January.[38] He did so in order to divert the attention of the congregation, by a stunning display of rhetoric, from the murmurous jubilation which surrounded them. He preached in vain. His congregation, though good Christians, were also loyal members of their city: they would not forgo that great moment of euphoria, in which the fortune of the city, and of all within it, was renewed. As long as urban life survived in the West, the feast of the Kalends continued. It was, indeed, so closely identified with the urban life of the Roman Mediterranean that, when, centuries later, Muslim Arabs came took over the great cities of North Africa and the Levant, they found that the Kalends were still celebrated by Christian townsfolk: it was, they said, "a great feast of the Christians." Augustine would not have been pleased![39]

These examples point to the existence of a strong, religiously neutral public culture in the later Roman empire. But the continuance of such a culture depended on the continued stability of West Roman society. Constantine had exploited brilliantly the prosperity which had followed the establishment of a stable empire under Diocletian. But this stability did not last. In 363, the pagan emperor Julian lost a large part of the Roman armies in Mesopotamia. In 378, further legions were annihilated by the Visigoths at Adrianople (Edirne, Turkey-in-Europe). Sevso's Pannonia, to name only one region, became a far from secure place. The late fourth century was an age of renewed civil wars, which involved the stripping of frontier garrisons. In 406, Gaul experienced a major barbarian raid. In 410, Rome was sacked by Alaric the Visigoth. Neither of these was a definitive disaster; but public morale was badly shaken. Pagans began to speak of *tempora Christiana*, "Christian times"; and by "Christian times" they meant, not the stability of the Constantinian order, but a new age, overshadowed by a crisis of authority which led to renewed barbarian raids throughout the Roman provinces of the West. After almost a century of stability in a "restored" empire, the upper classes of the Roman West had to face, once again, the essential fragility of the empire in which they lived.[40]

A Generation of Converts

This sense of growing fragility was heightened by inner landslides. Public disasters often did no more than provide a convenient alibi for restless souls. They enabled such persons to embark on drastic courses that they might not have contemplated in more peaceful times. The career of Pontius Meropius Paulinus (355–431), later bishop of Nola, in Campania (where he had once served as a provincial governor) is revealing in this respect. It showed that, for some Christians, at least, the age of consensus could be publicly declared to be at an end. Paulinus was an Aquitanian senator. He had always been a pious Christian. As a young man, Saint Martin had cured him of an inflamed eye. But he wanted from his religion more than the average, well-to-do Christian had wanted. A politic withdrawal to his estates in northern Spain, caused by a civil war in 389, rapidly hardened into an uncompromising ascetic conversion. Paulinus vanished, for a moment, from upper-class society. He was challenged by his friend and former tutor, the poet Ausonius of Bordeaux, to explain his eccentric behavior. In answering his friend, Paulinus presented himself, in powerful verse, as the classic Christian convert:

> And absolutely, with a master's right,
> Christ claims our hearts, our lips, our time.[41]

It was as Ausonius had feared. "The golden tissue" woven by shared office and by friendships based on a shared upper-class culture had become unravelled. Ausonius was unable to summon Paulinus back to take up his duties as a public figure in Aquitaine.

What disquieted Ausonius was the fact that Paulinus had redefined *pietas*, the essential Roman virtue of loyalty to friends and to one's homeland, in starkly Christian terms. Piety to Christ was all that mattered for him. His loyalties lay with a new group of like-minded friends: "slaves of God, insurgents against the world." These included Sulpicius Severus, the biographer of their shared hero, Martin, the formidable Melania, and, last but not least, a man the same age as himself, a recent fellow-convert, who had become bishop of Hippo in 395 – Augustine. Augustine's *Confessions* appeared in around 397. It was the story of the beginning of a new life, now made fully public, and presented with as exquisite a literary sense as that shown, a decade previously, by Paulinus in his poems to Ausonius.[42]

Augustine's *Confessions* looked back on the youth and vivid adulthood of a successful provincial. But they did so in the light of a new resolve. Augustine now served God as Catholic bishop of Hippo. His past – the flowering of his talents under a traditional, non-Christian system of schooling, his contact with strange doctrines (first, with the Manichees and, later, with the writings of the pagan Platonists), his mother, Monica, his friends, his concubine, the strains of a career driven by "the hope of the world": all this had come to an end, in the summer of 386, with a decision to adopt a life of continence, as a preliminary to seeking baptism at the hands of Ambrose, bishop of Milan.

Augustine wrote the *Confessions* ten years after these events, when he had become a bishop like Ambrose. As bishop of Hippo (Annaba/Bône, Algeria) he was a leading figure in his own province. Conversion from "the world" had not meant a retreat into obscurity. In one way or another, all the great Latin converts to the ascetic life, though they wished to imitate the distant monks of Egypt by dropping off the edge of the world, ended up in positions of prominence in the Catholic Church. Their behavior was watched. Their books were read. Their ideas were hotly discussed. Whether they wished it or not, they had moved from one style of public life to another. What is significant about them all is that not one of them was a convert directly from paganism. They had all come from Christian families. For them "conversion" did not mean a change of belief. It meant, rather, a dramatic hardening of the will to follow a more uncompromising form of Christianity than that followed by the average believer.

Augustine wrote his *Confessions* in such a way as to invest surprising new departures, such as that which he and his friends had experienced, with an overpowering sense of God-given agency. For him the convert emerged as a person sheathed in the will of God. "For *He hath made us and not we ourselves* . . . indeed, we had destroyed ourselves, but He who made us made us anew."[43]

Augustine never doubted this about himself or others. The grace of God worked on the heart, "as if it were a speck of gold in the hands of a master craftsman," hammering the fragile, discontinuous will into an ever firmer, finally victorious resolve. This was no abstract doctrine for Augustine. The life of the Catholic Church, as he saw it, was made up of countless, small victories of grace. To those who had learned to pray with a humble heart, God would always give the grace which fired the will to follow His commands.[44]

Grace, Free Will, and the Church: The Pelagian Controversy

Not every ascetic Christian in this age of great converts was comfortable with such a view. When the *Confessions* were read out, in the company of Paulinus, Pelagius, a devout layman from Britain, walked out of the room. For Pelagius, and his many supporters, the "grace" of God did not work in this manner. God's "grace" consisted rather in God's decision to create human nature in such a way that human beings could follow his commands through the exercise of their own free will. This was grace enough. Human beings had never lost their original, good nature. Everyone was free to choose the good. Once the accretion of evil habits, contracted through contact with the "world," had been washed away through the transformative rite of baptism, every Christian believer was both able and obliged to reach out for perfection. For Pelagius, the Christian was the master craftsman of his or her own soul.[45]

This was not how Augustine saw the matter. From 413 to his death, in 430, the various phases of his great debate with the ideas of Pelagius and his followers (known to us as the Pelagian Controversy) revealed to an attentive audience of educated Latin Christians – not all of whom agreed with Augustine – layer after layer of the message first condensed, with such persuasive power, in the *Confessions*. The controversy placed human agency at the center of attention. The subsequent qualified acceptance of the views of Augustine by the Latin Church, in preference to those of Pelagius, placed God at the center of that agency. Human beings could not simply make themselves good, when they pleased, by their own free will. They depended intimately on God's grace for constant inspiration and support.

The decision to accept Augustine's view of grace rather than that of Pelagius was by no means a foregone conclusion. But by rallying to Augustine, Latin Christians of the fifth century made plain that they needed heroes, not self-improvers. Heroes, as many late Roman persons knew, were made by God. One such hero had been the emperor Constantine. His sense of imperial mission had been fuelled, according to his admirers, "by countless personal manifestations of your Savior and His countless personal visits during sleep."[46] The notion of direct and constant divine inspiration for great deeds was normal at this time. It is this notion which Augustine's views on grace seemed to protect. The words of a fervent supporter of Augustine, a poet and lay theologian, Prosper of Aquitaine, make this plain. The Church could not be built upon mere free will: "the fickle will, that is not ruled by the changeless will of God." What Christianity needed was the certainty that the Church contained members of the elect. The Church would always produce men and women who were the stuff of heroes because filled with the grace of God. For "the elect receive grace, not to allow them to remain idle . . . but to enable them to work well."[47]

In Augustine's world, the "elect" and the "predestinate" were reassuringly visible. In the first case, they were the martyrs. These were universally acknowledged heroes of the faith. Their memory was celebrated in every city of the Mediterranean in massed festivals, which were shot through with a sense of collective triumph and delight. For Augustine, the martyrs were the primary examples of what grace could do.[48] For grace had conferred true freedom on them – the freedom of the militant to act and to endure.

> [Grace gave] a liberty . . . protected and made firm by the gift of perseverance, that this world should be overcome, this world in all its deep loves, in all its terrors, in all its countless ways of going wrong.[49]

But not only the martyrs had received grace in this fully public manner. They were joined, in Augustine's mind and in the growing practice of the Church, by those who had not died for the faith, but had, rather, struggled to uphold and to extend it. These included great bishops, spectacular converts, whose love of God, as Truth, had caused them (like Augustine) to bring a whole pre-Christian culture out of their stormy past into the service of the Catholic Church.

Modern persons do not always share the enthusiasm of those who rallied, at the time, to the views of Augustine. What made his doctrines acceptable, at this time, was his view of the Catholic Church. In this respect, he emerged as far more consequentially egalitarian than was Pelagius. Augustine's theology of grace embraced more believers. It had room both for acknowledged heroes and for the average Christian. Pelagius, by contrast, had little to say to the average Christian. He insisted that all Christians were capable of be-ing perfect and that they should become perfect. He wished to blur the dis-tinction between lay person and monk by making every Christian equally a "convert" and a devout ascetic. He seemed to leave no place for the slow and hesitant progress of the rank and file, whose "conversions" were far from dramatic and far from complete.[50]

Augustine, by contrast, accepted that the Christian Church had come to contain a large number of distinctly mediocre persons. He did not expect every Christian to be perfect. Yet each Christian was equal to every other, because all Christians were equally dependent on the grace of God. Augus-tine's doctrine of election puzzled and shocked many even of his admirers. But he held to it because, in his view, the doctrine was a source of comfort to the humble and a warning to the proud. There was no room in his view of the Church for self-created distinctions, based on the belief that some Chris-tians could make themselves more "perfect" than others. He wrote, for in-stance, with lyrical fervor in support of the virgins of the Church. Communities of dedicated women had sprung up in every Christian community. Virgins mattered vastly to contemporaries. In many churches, they stood behind a chancel screen of glistening white marble, which seemed to condense their rock-like purity. But he also reminded these virgins that some of the greatest martyrs in the North African Church had not been virgins. They had been married women and the mothers of children. The festivals which celebrated the martyrdoms of such married women marked them out, unambiguously, as members of the "elect." Nuns, he wrote, should constantly bear this fact in mind. It was not their self-made virginity that would bring them to heaven, but only their love of Christ. This love of Christ was inspired by the same grace which had led *matronae*, married housewives, such as Perpetua and Crispina, to triumph over death. That same grace was still at work, if in a more humble, less clearly visible manner, in each married member of his congregation. They were equal to the nuns because equally led through life by the grace of God.[51]

Augustine saw the Catholic Church as a united community precisely be-cause it was a community of sinners as well as a community of heroes and of heroines. In Augustine's writings against the Pelagians, we can glimpse the Catholic laity of his own, and of many subsequent centuries. There was room in the church for those

> who indulge their sexual appetites, although within the decorous bonds
> of marriage, and not only for the sake of offspring, but, even, because
> they enjoy it. Who put up with injuries with less than complete patience
> . . . Who may even burn, at times, for revenge . . . Who hold to what
> they possess. Who give alms, but not very lavishly. Who do not take

other people's property, but defend their own: but do it in the bishop's court, rather than before a worldly judge. . . But who, through all this, see themselves as small and God as glorious.[52]

The "Glorious City": Augustine's *City of God*

Human beings could not glory. But an institution could do so. What was truly glorious on earth, for all the imperfections of its individual members, was the Catholic Church. For without Catholic baptism, Augustine was convinced, it seemed impossible (to human minds, at least) that God would grant forgiveness of the original sin which had made all human beings equal because equally estranged from God. For this reason, the Church had to be truly universal. It was the only resting place, on earth, in which a sorely wounded humanity could hope to recover its lost health.

Augustine was at his most disagreeably impatient when faced by groups whom he saw as self-regarding enclaves, deaf to the universal message of the Catholic Church. He insensibly presented the Church not only as the true Church, but as potentially the Church of the majority of the inhabitants of the Roman world. He was the first Christian that we know of to think consistently and in a practical manner in terms of making everyone a Christian. This was very different from claiming, as previous Christians had done, that Christianity was a universal religion in the sense that anyone in any place *could*, in theory at least, become a Christian. Augustine spoke of Christianity in more concrete, social terms: there was no reason why everybody in a given society (the Jews excepted) should not be a Christian. In his old age, he took for granted that the city of Hippo was, in effect, a Christian city. He saw no reason why the normal pressures by which any late Roman local community enforced conformity on its members should not be brought to bear against schismatics and heretics. He justified imperial laws which decreed the closing of temples and the exile and disendowment of rival churches. Pagans were told simply to "wake up" to the fact that they were a minority. They should lose no time in joining the Great Majority of the Catholic Church. The entire world had been declared, more than a millennium before by the prophets of Israel, to belong only to Christ and to his Church. *"Ask of Me, and I shall give you the uttermost parts of the earth for Thine inheritance."*[53]

Hence the supreme importance, for Augustine, of the *City of God*, a book which he began to write in 413, as an answer to pagan criticisms and to Christian disillusionment, provoked by Alaric's sack of Rome in 410. The disaster of the sack of Rome provided Augustine with an excuse to expatiate on a theme dear to his heart. It was summed up in the title of the book, *On the City of God.* For, as in Psalm 86 (87), Jerusalem was the "City of our God," of which "glorious things are spoken." Like the Jerusalem of the Psalms (as Augustine read them) the Heavenly Jerusalem claimed those born in all other nations as potential citizens. A common sin had made all men and all women, quite irrespective of race, of class, and of level of culture, equally aliens from that Heavenly Jerusalem. All were summoned, with stark impartiality, to become Christians and so to begin the long, slow return to heaven, their true homeland. Displaying his command of pagan literature and philosophy to its fullest extent, Augustine deliberately created common ground with his readers, precisely so that, all obstacles removed and all arguments vanquished, they might have no excuse not to slip across that shared ground in order to become potential citizens of heaven by joining the Catholic Church.[54]

Of course, not everybody did this. We have a recently discovered letter which Augustine wrote, at the end of his life, to Firmus, a notable of Carthage. Firmus had attended afternoon readings of the *City of God.* He had even read as far as book 10. He knew his Christian literature better than did his wife. Yet his wife was baptized, and Firmus was not. Augustine informed him that, compared with her, Firmus, for all his culture, even his sympathy for Christianity, stood on dangerous ground as long as he remained unbaptized.

> For what was the purpose of this book? Not so that people might delight in its style, nor learn from it things they had not known before, but that they may be convinced about the City of God – that they should enter into this city without further delay and persevere within it to the end: beginning first with rebirth (in baptism) and continuing within it with rightly-ordered love.[55]

One thing was certain, Augustine's "Glorious City," and its entrance-point on earth, the Catholic Church, was not a small place. It was a "city" for all ages and for every region:

> in a wide world, which has always been inhabited by many differing peoples, that have had, in their time, so many different customs, religions, languages, forms of military organization, and clothing, there have, however, only arisen two groups of human beings [those destined for the "City of God" and those who were not] – groups we call "cities," according to the special usage of the Scriptures.[56]

It was a notion whose unaccustomed sweep and clarity took on new weight and intensity as the churches of the West settled down, as best they could, to face the increasing possibility of a world without the Roman empire.

Virtutes sanctorum . . . strages gentium: "Deeds of Saints . . . Slaughter of Nations"

A World without Empire

In A.D. 418, Augustine received a letter from Hesychius, bishop of Salona (Solun, on the Dalmatian coast of Croatia). Hesychius had written to ask Augustine, in faraway Africa, if the end of the world was at hand. Augustine reassured him. He pointed out that, despite the troubles of the present day, the Roman empire had experienced worse disasters in the course of the third century A.D. At that time, many Christians had thought that the end of the world had come. "For, to cut a long story short, under the emperor Gallienus (253–268) . . . barbarians from all over the world were overrunning the Roman provinces." The anxious Christians of the third century had been proved wrong. The end of the world had not come. In any case, Augustine added, the end of the world and the return of Christ would not come until the Gospel had been preached to all pagan nations. He himself knew of many pagan tribes, untouched by Christianity, far beyond the Roman frontiers of North Africa. A wide non-Christian world still stretched beyond the Roman empire. "The Lord did not promise [to the Catholic Church] the Romans only, but all the nations of the world."[1]

Augustine's calm detachment from the present troubles of the empire may not have comforted the bishop of Salona. Like many Christians who had grown up in the post-Constantinian age, for Hesychius a world without the Roman empire was no world at all.

Yet at the time that Augustine and Hesychius corresponded across the Mediterranean, the prospect of a world without Rome became ever more real in non-Mediterranean provinces such as Britain, Gaul, and western Spain. After the civil wars of the late fourth century and the barbarian raids which began in 406, as a result of the stripping down of frontier defenses caused by the civil wars, the age of peace was over. By the time

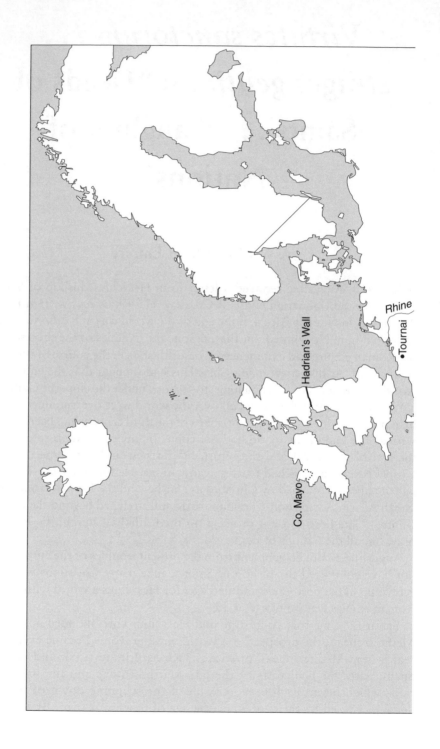

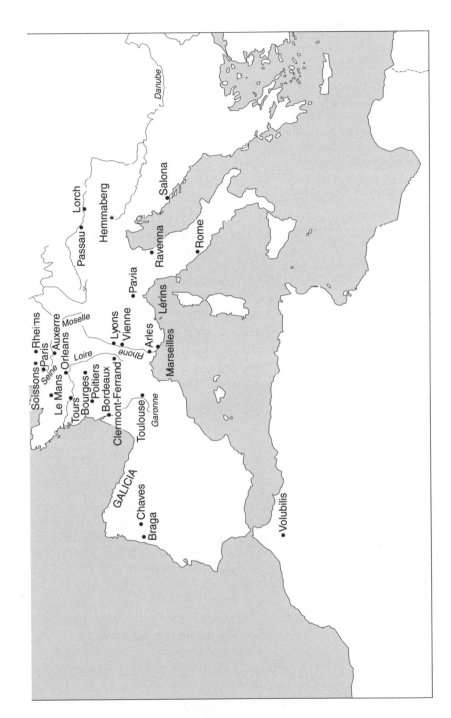

Map 3   Western Europe

WESTERN EUROPE AND THE EASTERN EMPIRE ca. 400–ca. 600

Eusebius of Caesarea 236–340

Vandal Invasion of Gaul 406
Settlement of the Visigoths 418
Beginning of "Barbarian Settlements"

John Cassian 360–435
Hydatius of Chaves 397–470
Germanus of Auxerre 407–447

Vandal Conquest of North Africa
   429–439

Cyril of Alexandria,   patriarch
   412–444

Council of Ephesus 431

Palladius' mission to Irish ca.431

Shenoute of Atripe 385–466

Leo I, pope 440–461

Council of Chalcedon 451

Severinus of Noricum, died 482
Patricius of Ireland, died ca.490
Sidonius Apollinaris 431–489

Resignation of Romulus Augustulus:
End of Western empire 476
Odoacer rules in Italy 476–493

Caesarius of Arles 470–543

Theodoric the Ostrogoth
   rules in Italy 493–526

Clovis king of the Franks 481–511
   wins battle of Vouillé/Voulon 507
   baptized ca.507

Ella Asbeha, king of Axum
   ca.519–ca.531

Gildas writes *On the Ruin of Britain*
  ca.520   Justinian, Eastern emperor 527–565

Gregory of Tours 538–594
  writes *Histories* 576–590

Venantius Fortunatus ca.540–ca.600

Augustine died, in 430, it was already obvious that, unlike the age of Diocletian and Constantine, the present period of dislocation would not be followed by a triumphant restoration of order by the Roman state, as had happened after 300. The military and fiscal apparatus associated with the reformed empire of the fourth century failed, ingloriously, to protect the frontiers.

The West fell apart. It became a patchwork of separate regions. Southern Gaul, especially the region around Marseilles and Arles, along with Italy and North Africa (up to the unexpected and catastrophic conquest of Africa by the Vandals in 429–439) remained "imperial" provinces. For three quarters of a century, until the undramatic resignation of the last emperor, Romulus Augustulus, in 476, Italy and Provence represented a survival, in the western Mediterranean, of the old order of things. Unlike the West, the Roman empire in the East survived intact. If anything, it grew in importance. East Rome was now the senior partner in a world where Roman society in the West was rapidly returning to political conditions which resembled the state of the western Mediterranean before the conquests of Julius Caesar. The Roman order seemed secure along the coastline of the Mediterranean. But, as in the time of Julius Caesar, it now faced the menacing hinterland of a new "free" Gaul – a Gaul without empire.

In the eastern Mediterranean, by contrast, Constantinople rose to the fore as "New Rome." The emperors of Constantinople still stood for Roman law and order as it should be. It was the emperor of the East, Theodosius II, and not his impotent colleagues, the Roman emperors of the West, who drew up and issued the great *Theodosian Code*. Framed in Constantinople, the *Theodosian Code* was promulgated in Rome, in 438, as a potent symbol of the reach of a technically undivided empire. Long after the empire had withdrawn, the *Theodosian Code* formed the basis of all Roman law in the Western provinces. Ravenna, the north Italian residence of the Western emperors, was very much a "little Constantinople."[2]

Elsewhere in the West, in Britain, Gaul, and in the vast hinterland of Spain, the empire was conspicuous by its absence. In these regions, all roads no longer

led to Rome. We should not, perhaps, be unduly surprised by this development. It was not a situation which had been brought about by overwhelming
violence and destruction. Rather, the disintegration of the Roman empire in
the West represented a return to normal in the long-term history of western
Europe. In the first and second centuries A.D., the Roman conquest of the West
had involved the absorption of many regions, each of which differed greatly
from all the others and even more so from the Mediterranean heartlands of the
empire. Intense provincialism had always characterized the western provinces.
For centuries, the local elites had profited by identifying themselves with an
overarching imperial system. But their local position had been made all the
more secure by centuries of Roman peace. And, in the end, local loyalties were
what counted for most. If the empire failed them, they would find their own
ways of looking after themselves and their region.

Yet to do this involved the elites of the western provinces in a painful and
dangerous adjustment. They were *Romani*, "Romans." As we saw in the last
chapter, they were great landowners whose wealth and power had been built
up, in the course of the fourth century, through close collaboration with the
Roman state. They looked back with pride to the strong position which they
had come to enjoy under the restored empire of Constantine and his successors. They were in no mood to sacrifice their highly privileged position as
great landowners and as the guardians of a unique, Latin culture. But, with
the empire no longer available to protect their privileges, they would have to
learn to live in a world in which a hitherto despised group of outsiders,
known to them as "barbarians," were both their partners and, in many ways,
their masters.

In every region of the West, these *Romani* formed a small but determined
group, perched at the top of their local society. What is truly remarkable
about the history of the fifth-century West is the tenacity with which the
Roman local elites renegotiated their own position in a world without empire. The end of the world may not have come, as bishop Hesychius of Salona
had feared. But *a* "world" – a specific religious and social order which many
articulate Christians had come to take for granted for an entire century,
from the reign of Constantine onward until the 430s – was undoubtedly
coming to an end. What emerged, instead, all over western Europe was a
world of "Romans" without a Roman empire. These were the local aristocracies, who now struggled to maintain their power through collaboration,
for the first time, with non-Roman warlords.

What went first, in this period of unrest, were the wide horizons associated with the post-Constantinian Christian empire. We know of one poignant example of this closing in of the old sense of belonging to a universal
empire. Hydatius (ca.397–470) came from Galicia, on the far Atlantic coast

of Spain.[3] Hydatius could not have belonged to a more remote province. Yet even his province had benefited from being part of a world empire. At the age of ten he had visited Jerusalem with his mother. The little boy had been presented to Saint Jerome. But that had been in A.D. 407. When he began to write his *Chronicle*, in 455, Hydatius had been Catholic bishop of Chaves, near the coast of northern Spain, for almost 20 years. He had seen the end of an age. He wrote of himself as caught now

> within Gallaecia, at the edge of the entire world . . . not untouched by all the calamities of this wretched age . . . [faced with] the domination of heretics, compounded by the disruption brought by hostile tribes.[4]

Only a few travellers from the Holy Land passed his way. They could not even tell him when Jerome had died. For all his attempt to keep up with "world events" – that is, with events in regions where the empire still survived – Hydatius grew old in a world whose horizons had come to be bounded by the frontiers of his own province.

Incidents of random local violence formed the main theme of his *Chronicle*. In 456, for example, Hydatius noted that the neighboring city of Braga had been sacked by a Visigothic army in search of quick plunder. The sacking of a city had become a normal event. It was not even a particularly bloodthirsty event. It was the cynical "shakedown" of a Roman city by a small wandering army: "although accomplished without bloodshed, it was lamentable enough." Hydatius' opinion of it was that of a Christian bishop: it was a "partial reliving," in his own sad land, of the tragic plundering of ancient Jerusalem.[5] This, Hydatius implied, was now only to be expected in the world in which he lived.

The end of Roman peace and the loss of the wide horizons associated with the Christian empire were troubling enough to a man such as Hydatius. But what was more painful still was the increasing recognition that regional societies, cut loose from the empire, could maintain a level of order, even of prosperity, but only if they could reach a *modus vivendi* with the "barbarians." But this in turn meant that the *barbari*, the stereotypical "outsiders" of the Roman imperial imagination, had to be allowed to become, in some way or other, "insiders."

This was difficult for many Romans to accept. Romans preferred to speak of barbarians in terms familiar to readers of classical literature. These stereotypes of the "barbarian" had not changed since we first described them in the first chapter of this book. In the fifth century, they were still being deployed in the vivid letters of Sidonius Apollinaris (431–489). Sidonius was a highly cultivated Gallic landowner turned politician. Eventually he found a safe niche for himself as the Catholic bishop of Clermont-Ferrand, in the Auvergne.[6] He wrote at length to his Roman friends about his Visigothic and Burgundian neighbors. They were large men "in unkempt clothes, with furs piled high upon their shoulders" – men dressed, that is, not like Romans, in woven silks that were the fruit of civilization, but in raw products of the wild. He described one such procession of barbarians, as they rode with their leader through the streets of Lyons. They were

> terrifying even in peacetime. Their feet were laced in heavy shoes. They wore green mantles with crimson borders. Their swords suspended from the shoulders . . . pressed against sides girded with studded deer-skins.

Right down to the intricate cloisonné gold-work on their shield-bosses, the ostentatious armaments of such a band "showed, at one and the same time, their wealth and their ruling passion – war."[7] Altogether, they were a rough bunch.

Sidonius wrote many such memorable descriptions of "barbarians" in the 450s and 460s. They implied that "barbarians" should be regarded as if they were exotic men of violence who had arrived from nowhere. In Sidonius' opinion, they could never have a role in the traditional fabric of Roman life. Or, if they did, it would only be as subordinate "allies" of Rome, not as partners and potential masters.

For an influential and vocal group of Roman landowners, it was more comfortable to see the barbarians in these old-fashioned terms. For what Sidonius' letters deliberately suppressed, through conjuring up vivid, classical images of "barbarian" life, was an ugly fact. The barbarians were not at all unlike the Romans. They were *potentes*, "men of power," whose claim to land and taxes rested on their military ability. Far from being wild men of the woods, they were "alternative Romans." Many had been in imperial service for generations. They were products of the middle ground, in which Roman and barbarian customs had come to merge along the frontiers of the empire. They were hard men, but they had already become more than half Roman by the rough standards of their age. They wanted a share in the wealth of former imperial provinces in return for offering what soldiers had always offered – protection and the maintenance of law and order. The writings of Sidonius do not disguise the fact that the majority of "Romans," even among the landowning aristocracy, did not necessarily agree with him. In the course of the fifth century, all over Western Europe, the local aristocracies "voted with their feet" against Rome. Provided that their own local position was not imperilled, they were more than prepared to meet the "barbarians" halfway, so as to set up, in the absence of empire, viable regional power blocs which came to be known as the "barbarian kingdoms" of the West.

Guests of the State: The Barbarian Settlements

The barbarians with whom the local aristocracies dealt had already had many years, even many generations, of experience in collaborating with Roman civilians. Their leaders were as much a product of the achievements of the new empire of Constantine and his successors as were the local aristocracies themselves. The fourth-century Roman empire needed loyal soldiers. It often preferred those soldiers who did not share the values and inhibitions of the traditional landowning aristocracy. Soldiers, indeed, were positively encouraged to be a class apart – to remain alien and abrasive. In any case, for over a century, imperial armies had been filled with foreigners or near-foreigners. They were recruited from frontier areas, where "Romans" and "barbarians" were largely indistinguishable, and even from across the frontier, by drawing directly on German tribes.

What mattered for these *viri militares*, these men of war, was loyalty. As long as the Roman army survived, Romans and barbarians within the army were held together by a common loyalty to the Roman state. This loyalty was summed up in the solemn soldier's oath to the emperor, "to whom faithful devotion should be given . . . as if to a present and corporeal deity."[8] "Romans" and "barbarians" met as equals in the Roman armies because they were equally servants of the emperor and of no one else. They were equally distinctive and equally privileged because connected with a powerful state.

Both Romans and barbarians within the army derived their entitlement to wealth and status from the *cingulum militiae*, from the heavy, golden belt which distinguished them from all civilians. This belt, and other items of their decorations and armaments, were often produced in the imperial workshops of Constantinople, in a style that captured the barbaric splendor of the art of Central Asia and the Danube. Even what now seems most "barbarian" in the jewelry of this time was, in fact, produced by the Roman emperors for the senior officers of Roman armies![9]

In the fourth century, the privileged position enjoyed by the Roman army as a separate group, which stood a little to one side of Roman civilian society, had enabled barbarian warriors within the Roman army to rise to power. The success of such barbarians within the Roman armies provided the model by which more recently arrived groups of barbarian warriors – Visigoths, Burgundians, Vandals, and Saxons – took over Gaul, Spain, Britain, and North Africa in the fifth century. But they now came as substitutes for a

Roman army which had vanished. Inevitably, the takeover itself was not without incidents of violence. But this violence was not continuous, nor was it decisive. For the Roman local elites themselves knew, from long experience of dealing with Roman military men, what to expect of such persons and how best to harness their military skills to their own needs.

It is profoundly misleading to speak of the history of Western Europe in the fifth century as "the Age of the Barbarian Invasions." Such a melodramatic view assumes, in the barbarians, a level of autonomy and of destructive potential which they did not possess. It was, rather, an age of brutal "downsizing." This was caused by the sudden and unexpected relaxation of the power of the Roman state. The situation of the Roman West was more like that of modern Russia and Central Asia, after the devolution of the Soviet empire in 1989, than that of Europe during the horrors of World War II. What frightened contemporaries was not the prospect of endless "barbarian invasions." It was the prospect of a power vacuum in their own region. Hence the speed with which "Romans" found themselves collaborating with "barbarians" – that is, with hard men of military background – to salvage what they could of the old order by creating local centers of strong rule. Local barbarian militias offered defense against further invasion. They maintained law and order. They patrolled the ever-restless peasantry, who were often as alien and as potentially hostile to their own landlords as were any "barbarians." These were the services which the new "barbarian kingdoms" of the West had to offer to the "Romans" who supported them.[10]

In the first generations, at least, the "barbarians" offered their services in the traditional manner. They came as "guests" of the local populations. They were settled among them by agreement with the imperial authorities. Even groups who had shown their military "muscle," as had the Visigoths when they defeated and killed the emperor Valens in 378 and sacked Rome in 410, seem to have been content to agree to such terms. The Visigoths were settled in the valley of the Garonne around Bordeaux in 418. The Burgundians were given garrisons in the middle Rhône and Saône in 430. Detachments of Alan cavalry were stationed along the Loire, within striking distance of the restless coasts of Brittany. As far as we can see, even the Saxon pirates may have first arrived in Britain as the result of an agreement to defend the local aristocracy.

Thus, the barbarian settlers who set up kingdoms around the western Mediterranean were not invaders from "outer space." They were not considered to hold their lands through outright conquest. Rather, in regions such as Spain, southern Gaul, and Italy, the barbarian settlements were the last legacy of a policy of divide and rule – which had kept soldiers separate from civilians, as foreign "guests" in the midst of unarmed populations – which was bequeathed by a failing empire to its provincials.

As a result, the "barbarian settlements" did not involve great social upheaval. The Visigoths of the Garonne valley, for instance, were never more than one sixtieth of the overall population of the region. They were no more prominent than military personnel had been, when they had been stationed on the frontiers. They were settled in such a way as to make them look, as much as possible, like Roman soldiers. Their families received lands, as if they were veterans. They had access to the produce of estates, as if they were regular soldiers billeted on the civilian population. Elsewhere, local garrisons collected a share of the region's taxes for their own use. The heated and inconclusive debates between modern scholars as to how, exactly, the settlement of the barbarians was carried out (whether warriors received land or only a proportion of the taxes of each region) may simply reflect the uncertainty of the time: many devices were used and many deals were struck in a situation which was constantly changing in the course of the fifth century.[11]

But there was one crucial feature of these settlements. They brought to the most fertile heartlands of the Mediterranean, to regions where the Roman landowning aristocracy had always been most firmly entrenched, conditions which had been normal only in the militarized provinces of the extreme north. Over large areas of Gaul, Spain, and, eventually, after 476, even in Italy, military men of non-Roman origin became prominent members of local society.

This situation soon led them to compete with the *Romani* on their own terms. They quickly turned their military privileges into solid, Roman gains – land, gold, clients, and slaves. They displayed their wealth through a Roman style of life. Far from remaining the fur-clad leaders of roving warrior bands (as Sidonius presented them), Visigothic and Burgundian noble men and women rapidly became indistinguishable from their upper-class Roman neighbors. Their Roman neighbors, in turn, rapidly adopted "barbarian" fashions of dress and self-display. Barbarians and Romans owned villas with identical mosaic floors. They were buried in identical marble sarcophagi. They rode to the hunt like any other villa owners – with flowing cloaks and trousers and with the Christogram branded, for safety and success, on their horses' rumps. Theodoric (493–526), king of the Ostrogoths in Italy, summed up this process of symbiosis between two ruling classes in a memorable phrase: "An effective Goth wants to be like a Roman; only a poor Roman would want to be a Goth."[12]

Yet something was new. These "barbarian" soldiers were no longer defined in Roman society by loyalty to a distant emperor. A Visigoth or a Burgundian drew his privileges from serving in the army of his king. Each king had his own royal seat. Visigothic Toulouse was acclaimed as "a new

Rome." Vienne served the same purpose for the Burgundians. Each city acted as the power base of a local militia, which claimed to be the army of a separate *gens*, of a separate tribe, loyal to its own king. The emergence in Continental Western Europe of separate "barbarian kingdoms," each defined as the kingdom of a specific *gens*, of a particular group – the kingdoms of the Visigoths, of the Burgundians, of the Vandals, and, later, of the Franks and the Ostrogoths – marked a new departure.

The emergence of "ethnicity" as the basis of a new ruling class in the post-imperial West was the exact reverse of the process which had led to the formation of a Roman imperial civilization in the West in the first centuries of the empire. At that time, members of very different groups had competed to adopt a shared identity They all claimed (with varying degrees of opportunism) to have become "Romans." Now, the emphasis was placed on the opposite – on ethnic diversity. Different barbarian groups insisted on their separate identities, as Goths, Franks, and Vandals. The Romans with whom they collaborated did likewise. There was a considerable element of artificiality, even of cynicism, in this insistence on ethnic specificity. By the sixth century it would have been difficult to tell at sight who was an upper-class "barbarian" and who a "Roman," and, among the barbarians themselves, who was a Goth, a Vandal, or a Frank. But, in the conditions of the fifth and sixth centuries, separateness, stridently asserted, rather than assimilation, seemed to open up the shortest route to power and wealth.[13]

One factor encouraged this emphasis on an "ethnic" core. The kings ruled through their armies, and armies need manpower. Leading Goths might resemble Romans. But they could not afford to be a closed aristocracy. They depended on the support of large numbers of armed followers who continued to think of themselves as "fellow-tribesmen." With their wives and families, such persons were barely distinguishable, in their economic condition, from the unfriendly Roman populations in which they found themselves. Their Gothic-ness and their right, as free men, to bear arms, was their only claim to privileged treatment. Without it they would have rapidly sunk to the level of Roman serfs. Their muted presence, in the armies of their kings, gave ballast to the "ethnic" definition of each kingdom. It was among such persons that distinctive folk-ways were encouraged to survive. In Burgundian law, for instance, the man who stole a dog in a Burgundian hamlet had to make amends by kissing its backside in public.[14]

But the identification of each army with a specific ethnic group was never complete. Life would have been easier, in the post-imperial West, if this had been so. Modern scholars have long treated these *gentes* – these so-called "tribes" – as if they were compact and clearly defined groups. They were hailed, by nationalist historians of the nineteenth and twentieth centuries, as nothing less than the ancestors of the modern European nations. In reality, active membership in a specific army and the privileges attached to military service – and not ethnic origin in and of itself – defined membership in a specific *gens*. Even though they could count on the support of armed free men of their own tribe, the kings (like the Roman emperors before them) always needed more soldiers. They were not fastidious as to who served in their armies. While each barbarian group may have predominated in the army to which it gave its name, the forces mobilized on many occasions by barbarian rulers were not like "national" armies. They were more like the "Free Companies" of the Hundred Years War – diverse bands, brought together by ambitious impresarios of violence.

In the fifth century, this was a troubling prospect for those who wished to hold on to their "Roman" identity. The barbarian armies were places where a Roman might lose his identity entirely, through serving a "barbarian" king. Like the Ottoman armies, or the Cossacks of southern Russia, the militias of the fifth century were a haven for renegades of every sort – from escaped slaves to Roman country gentlemen whose taste for violence was not satisfied by the excitements of the hunt. Disloyalty to the traditional civilian values of the Roman elites was in the air, fed by countless stories of *Romani* who found that the "barbarians" were not a problem, but an opportunity.[15]

It was, indeed, when barbarians were at their least alien that they posed the greatest threat to influential segments of the Roman population. For barbarians, also, were sincere Christians. As befitted military men, the Visigoths, in particular, had received the faith in the glory days of the empire, in the reigns of Constantius II and Valens. They were committed to what had been the current orthodoxy of the Danubian provinces at that time. It is only in retrospect that we call it "Arianism." But times had changed. Arianism went out of fashion. The Visigoths arrived in Gaul already labelled as "Arian" heretics, unacceptable to "Nicene," Catholic Christians. "Nicene" Catholics looked back to Athanasius as a hero of the faith. They treated intransigent anti-Arian bishops such as Ambrose of Milan as role models for their own, "Roman" religion. The result was a stand-off, where "Romans" and "barbarians" went about their separate ways. Among the Ostrogoths of Italy, Arianism was described, simply, as the *Lex Gothorum*, the "religious law of the Goths." Although it was practiced in churches which would have been identical with those of the "Roman" Catholics, Arianism was treated as a distinct, "heretical" cult. It was not for Romans.[16]

Although they were often pious Arian Christians, most barbarian rulers tended to keep their beliefs to themselves. The only exception was the Vandals in Africa. They felt less secure. Their capital, at Carthage, seemed more vulnerable to naval attack by the orthodox emperors of Constantinople. They also ruled a province accustomed to religious persecution. They simply applied to Catholic bishops the same Roman laws exiling "heretical" bishops which Augustine had justified, at great length, in the interests of the Catholic Church!

Elsewhere, Arian rulers rarely victimized Catholics. Indeed, they shared with them the same religious language. Far from being simple sons of the wild, the Visigothic, Burgundian, and Vandal kings were certain that they knew "correct" doctrine when they saw it. Articulate, Latin-speaking Arian clergymen frequented their courts. The Visigoths proudly ascribed the victories of their armies to their own, "Arian" orthodoxy.[17]

The constant irritant presented by such alternatives ensured that the Catholic Christianity of the western Mediterranean came to see itself, in exceptionally stark terms, as a religion on the defensive. Looking back, from the end of the sixth century, a Catholic bishop, the descendant of a Roman senatorial family from the Auvergne and the valley of the Rhône, Gregory of Tours (538–594), saw the fifth century as a time of dramatic confrontations. As in the days of ancient Israel, the *virtutes sanctorum*, "the deeds of the saints," took place against a background characterized by *strages gentium*, by "the slaughter of warring nations."[18] This was a somewhat stylized vision of what had happened in fifth-century Gaul. What we should remember, however, is that we know so much about Gaul at this time precisely because this was a region which was passing through an acute "crisis of identity." Nobody knew what would happen next and nobody could be certain whether the old ways of being a Catholic, a Roman, or a barbarian would remain valid. Hence, articulate and thoughtful Latin Christians wrote more vividly than ever before about their own times, and espoused with memorable enthusiasm different ways of coping with their situation. Let us look briefly at the role of Christianity in this rapidly changing world.

Defending the Cities: Bishops and Patron Saints

Compared with other provinces, Christianity had not been long established in Gaul. But it had already obtained a foothold in the towns, in the manner which we described in the last chapter. In the fifth century, the towns emerged in Gaul as the nodal points of contested regions. For towns were fortified. Solid walls, many of them built in the insecure days of the third century A.D., surrounded the compact nucleus of what had once been sprawling classical cities. The walls of Clermont, for instance, enclosed only three hectares of what had been an open town of 200 hectares.[19] Apart from the occasional reuse of pre-Roman hill forts, the rural villas which formed the power base of the aristocracy remained undefended.[20] Walled cities stood out, in contrast to an exposed countryside, as enduring symbols of Roman security and authority.

Walls and bishops went together. The *virtutes*, the miraculous deeds, most appreciated in holy bishops in Gaul were those in which their prayers ensured that the walls of their city would hold firm. In 451, Attila's Huns headed for the Loire. The inhabitants of Orléans turned to their bishop, Annianus.

> He advised them to prostrate themselves in prayer and with tears to implore the help of the Lord . . . "Keep a watch on the city walls [he said] to see if God, in his pity, will send us help." . . . When their prayers were finished, they were ordered by the old man to look for a third time. Far away they saw what looked like a cloud of dust [the Roman cavalry of Aetius, along with a Visigothic army, were on their way to relieve the city] . . . "It is the help sent by God." The walls were already rocking under the shock of the battering rams.[21]

But it was essential that not only the walls should hold. The fate of each region depended on the morale of its urban centers. Apart from the occasional, chilling grand raid (such as those associated with Attila) most warfare, in fifth-century Gaul, was a small-scale affair. The control of whole regions was decided by a war of nerves, not by massive engagements. Small bands of marauders would march through the countryside, "destroying the fields, spoiling the meadows, cutting up the vineyards and ruining the olive groves."[22] Their aim was to inflict just enough damage to persuade the local leaders to think twice about offering further resistance: they would pay tribute or open their gates to a new overlord.

The townsfolk were particularly vulnerable to such scare tactics. They needed leaders on whom they could rely, to maintain their spirits and to mitigate the disruptive effects of small, vindictive raids. They found these in the Christian bishops. The intensely communal quality of the Christian churches, which we have seen developing in the cities of the fourth century, now stood out in pointed contrast to a divided and easily dispersed secular aristocracy. The local church became the "fixative" which held whole populations in place. The church's charitable activities palliated the effects of famine and siege. The bishops even helped to keep peasants in their place, through the ransoming and return to their owners of captured serfs. Many such serfs would have profited from the disorders of the time to run away from their masters. Ransoms brought them back home. As bishop of Arles, Caesarius (470–543) ransomed and relocated thousands of uprooted peasants. The silver decorations of his cathedral were melted down to pay for his charities: "Even today, the marks of the axes can be seen on the pillars and screens of the sanctuary where the silver ornaments of the columns were stripped off."[23]

More important still, the buildings of the church spoke of the day-to-day determination of cities to survive and to be seen to survive. The bishops of Gaul vied with each other in placing splendid basilicas in the fortified enclaves of their cities, and outside the city, above the graves of martyrs, in places where the Roman roads passed through extensive ancient cemeteries. Five churches were built in Lyons in this period. The bishops of Tours and Clermont competed to construct cathedrals with room for over a thousand worshippers. At a time when secular building had come to a standstill, these churches represented an impressive coagulation of wealth and collaborative energy. They were the "arguments in stone" appropriate to a new Christian age. They showed that Gaul had by no means become a wasteland. Given energetic bishops and a minimum of security, now gained through collaboration with barbarian local kings, it was plain that the cities could still be filled with new structures, as opulent as giant jewel-cases.

In these churches, daylight was trapped in the unearthly shimmer of gold mosaic and multicolored marbles. To all who entered them, they brought to earth a glimpse of Paradise. As Gregory of Tours wrote of the basilica of his native Clermont:

> In it one is conscious of the fear of God and of a great brightness, and those who pray are often aware of a most sweet and aromatic odor wafted towards them. Round the sanctuary it has walls which are decorated with mosaic work and many varieties of marble.[24]

An age of great basilicas fostered a piety of great assemblies. The mechanisms of reparation for sin, which had long been familiar to all Christian communities, took on a distinctively communal meaning in Gaul and Italy. Group penance, linked to penitential forms of intercessory prayer, was a discipline which curbed the widespread mood of *sauve qui peut*. Solemn moments of communal prayer reduced the temptation, on the part of the rich, to migrate to more secure regions. Great religious ceremonies assembled the local population as a whole in one place, and kept them there for hours on end. The Rogation processions instituted by bishop Mamertus of Vienne, in the 470s, were swiftly adopted by his colleagues. They gathered an entire urban population, and flattened the differences between rich and poor – thereby, it was hoped, inhibiting the reflex of the rich to emigrate to safer locations. They made of small cities "a single fellowship of sighing supplicants."[25]

Collective ventures were not invariably successful. In Paris, Saint Genovefa (Sainte Geneviève) was almost drowned in the Seine as a "false prophet," as a witch and diviner, for urging the citizens to stay where they were as the Hunnish army swept across the plains of Champagne. She and the married ladies of the city kept a lonely vigil in the city's principal baptistery.[26] It was more usual to rally round a bishop who could claim to speak in the name of the ancient Christian heroes of the city. The saintly dead represented collective loyalty at its most familiar and most intense. We have seen how important the festivals of the martyrs had been in Augustine's North Africa. It was the same in Gaul. The graves of local martyrs and of holy persons were visited on a regular basis. Their death-days were celebrated with regular festivals. They were treated as heroic "fellow-citizens." For the saints of old had once stood in the local church praying for the Christian people of "their" city. It was assumed that they still did so. Their spirits remained present at their tombs.

This image of solidarity, based on the loving concern of holy persons for the "family of God," came to be enhanced by the use of terms which carried weighty, public overtones. The saints, also, were leaders. They were *patroni*, "patron saints." They were spoken of as "the boss" – *le patron*, *il padrone*. They were thought of as persons with power and influence. Their *suffragia*, their "suffrages" – the prayers which they offered to God on behalf of their clients – were held to count for much in the distant courts of Heaven. Members of a "celestial Senate house," the saints were invisible aristocrats. In return for protection obtained through their prayers, the saints demanded *reverentia*, fully public tokens of respect, from their pious clients.[27]

We can see this happening in the city of Tours. In the 460s, imperial rule was perceived to have no further chance of asserting itself north of the river Loire. Yet it was precisely at that time that the somewhat unprepossessing tomb of Saint Martin at Tours was given increasing prominence by Perpetuus, the bishop of Tours. Tours stood in a no man's land. It lay in a political vacuum between the Visigothic kingdom to the south and the rudderless frontier provinces of northern Gaul. It now received a gigantic pilgrimage basilica. The mosaics of the shrine showed the miracles of Martin. The inscriptions written beneath them told visitors from all over Gaul what Martin had once done, and so, what his *potentia*, his ever-active power to heal and to punish, might yet do. The inscription on his tomb promised that, at Tours, he would always be present for his worshippers: "Here lies Martin the bishop, of holy memory, whose soul is in the hand of God; but he is fully here, present and made plain by miracles of every kind."

It was a reassuring message. In the courtyard outside the tomb, the possessed roared, their voices rising at times to a howl of alien tongues. They shouted to the saint in garbled Greek, and even in Hunnish. Such foreigners at the shrine were a reminder of a perilously wide world, where the *virtutes*, the effective power of "patron" saints, linked to recognizably "Roman" cities, coexisted with the unquiet movements of alien races.[28]

Bishops as Aristocrats

In the fifth century, the landed aristocracy of Gaul (many of whose grandfathers had been pagans) took over the government of the Church. Of all the experiments in leadership which characterized this fluid century, the "aristocratization" of the Church in Gaul was the most enduring. It placed the cities in the hands of men used to exercising power in a Roman manner. Compared with the tenacious episcopal dynasties of *Romani*, who regarded the major sees of southern Gaul and Spain as their unchallenged appanage for another two centuries, the barbarian kingdoms were an evanescent phenomenon. Barbarian kings, even barbarian kingdoms, came and went. Bishops drawn from the "Roman" aristocracy remained. The real map of post-imperial Gaul and Spain was drawn by its network of episcopal cities.[29]

As a result of this process of the aristocratization of the Church, Gaul became very different from Italy, North Africa, and the eastern empire, whose clergy tended to represent, rather, the middling classes of the cities. Gallic bishops tended to come into their city "from on top." They did not rise through the ranks of the clergy. They were not always popular. But the townsfolk knew at least that their church was in the hands of men who knew what they wanted and what others wanted of them. To take one well-known example: Sidonius Apollinaris (431–489) became bishop of Clermont in 470, after a long career as a politician and a writer. When called upon to justify the choice of an aristocratic bishop for the vacant see of Bourges, he did so with gusto. He made a speech on the occasion, which he later circulated to his cultivated "Roman" colleagues. A bishop drawn from the clergy, he said, would only lead to jealousy. A monk, of course, would be an admirable candidate; but a monk was accustomed to praying to God for the salvation of souls, "not to earthly judges for the safety of our bodies." Simplicius, the son and son-in-law of former bishops, was the ideal choice. He had built a church for the city. He had stood up to the Visigoths. "Time and again . . . he has acted as spokesman of the city, before skin-clad kings and purple-robed emperors." Bourges needed such a man. "A few priests twittered in holes and corners," Sidonius added; but that was only to be expected.[30]

Sidonius was a particularly flamboyant representative of this class of persons. He stood at the end of a generation. What made Gaul unique was not so much that it had an aristocratic episcopate. Other unruly provinces had opted for the same solution: the *Katholikos*, the head of the Armenian Church, was taken from one noble family alone, and would even appear at the altar, celebrating the Eucharist in the fox-fur robes of an Armenian magnate![31] It was, rather, that this development coincided with a religious revolution. Many of these aristocratic bishops had also become monks. A group of persons who had been placed in high office largely so as to reassure their flock that nothing had changed in Roman Gaul, acted as bishops by claiming that, in themselves, everything had changed.

Bishops as Monks

Hence the decisive role of the monastic communities established at Marseilles and Lérins. In the fifth century A.D., Marseilles became again what it had been at the time of its first foundation in the fifth century B.C. It was a bridgehead of Mediterranean-wide culture, perched on the edge of the uncertain hinterland of Gaul.[32] It offered shelter to a remarkable person. John Cassian (360–435) was a Latin-speaking monk from the Dobrudja (modern Romania). He had lived for decades in Egypt. He arrived in Marseilles in 415. Rather than being a practicing monk, he was a gifted theorist of monasticism. His writings placed an entire world in the hands of Gallic readers.[33]

Cassian's *Institutions of the Monastic Life* were written in 420. They provided reports of the monastic life in Egypt, with which to correct over-enthusiastic local experiments. His *Conferences*, of 426, disseminated spiritual guidance in the form of interviews granted to him while in Egypt by the great old men of the desert. In the hands of a skilled writer, the *codex*, once again, helped to bring the traditions of the eastern Christian world close to the West. As Cassian himself wrote, with pride, it was possible, with a *codex* of his works in one's hands, to live in a cell in any part of the world, and still to live as if one were in Egypt.[34]

Cassian, the theorist and the reporter of the lives and opinions of the monks of Egypt, helped to form western monasticism. In an age of increasing fragmentation, Cassian showed that the information networks of the Christian Church could still bridge the great distances between East and West and between "Roman" and "barbarian" Europe.

Equally important, at the time, was the island monastery of Lérins, opposite Antibes, founded in 400 by Saint Honoratus. Lérins was an outpost of the wilderness of Egypt placed within sight of the sun-beaten slopes of the Alpes-Maritimes. It was spoken of as a Circe's Isle from which young men of noble family emerged transformed. Many of those who came to the island did not stay there for long. They re-emerged, after a spell of searching ascetic discipline, to become bishops all over Provence. Arles, in particular, was a crucial see. It was the administrative center of what survived of imperial rule in southern Gaul. A succession of bishops of Arles, most notably Hilary (430–449) and, later, Caesarius (502–543), made Arles a colony of Lérins. By 434, eight sees in southern Gaul were already in the hands of men from Lérins. Spiritual "capital" acquired on the island was "lent out at interest" to an ever-increasing number of churches.[35]

The monastic discipline of Lérins was designed to break forever, in young men of noble family, the springs of worldly pride. Like the drastic Jesuit novitiate of later times, Lérins sent out into the world zealous 30-year-olds from old families, fully capable of deploying the old skills of rhetoric and government, but in a new manner, for a new, high cause. The transformation of the old order began with the body. A harsh ascetic regime changed the body out of recognition. It lost all of its previous aristocratic ease. Luxuriant hair was cut short. The flush of high living was drained from the face by penitential fasting. The proud eye and haughty step of the "natural-born" leader of Gallic society were curbed by a monastic discipline of humility. This deliberately "humbled" body was now ready for new, fully public action.[36]

Not all Gallic bishops of this time passed through Lérins. But they shared a common relation to the ascetic discipline as a way of sloughing off their "worldly" past. Germanus, bishop of Auxerre from 407 to 437, had been an imperial servant. On becoming bishop, "he instantly changed in every manner." He showed this change through his body. He separated from his wife. He wore a hair shirt. He slept on a bed made of piled cinders. He wore a leather bag of relics of the saints tied across his chest. Germanus' body was touched, at every point, by suffering and was now sheathed in the sacred. His biographer described these mortifications with great care. For they cut him off from his past. Yet, once he had shown in this drastic manner that he had abandoned his past as a pampered nobleman, Germanus was free to apply the skills of his aristocratic background to his life as a bishop. His past flowed, in a preordained manner, into his episcopal present:

> The study of eloquence prepared him for preaching, legal doctrine for works of righteousness, marriage to a wife set off his [future] chastity.[37]

The life of Germanus was presented in terms of meteoric energy. His biographer showed him moving from one end of the Roman West to another, always bringing relief and order. In Britain, he baptized a Romano-British

army, before it sallied forth to rout the barbarians to the chant of "Alleluia."
On the Loire, he grabbed the bridle of king Goar of the Alans, bringing to a
dramatic halt the column of mailed cavalry despatched, by the Roman authorities, to crush a tax revolt. When he bore a petition of the provincials to
the distant court of Ravenna, he became the cynosure of the imperial palace.[38]

The *Life of Germanus* was written after his death by a friend of Sidonius
Apollinaris. It was written at an anxious time, when Sidonius knew that his
native Clermont might have to stand a siege. Germanus was a bishop suited
to a dangerous age. His biography was a stirring assertion of the faith that,
once chastened by spectacular ascetic effort, the old skills of public life, exercised by a former aristocrat and public servant, might come again, in higher
form, to serve the Catholic Church.

Bishops even looked their part. We see them in the mosaics of the time,
which represented saints and former bishops. With their quiet eyes, solemn
stance, and sweeping, silken robes, they are recognizably "last Romans."
But they now hovered, in shimmering mosaics on the walls of churches,
above the heads of the Catholic congregation. Their earthly representatives
were supposed to look like them. One had only to look at Epiphanius of
Pavia to know that he would be a bishop:

> His cheeks smiled . . . Well-formed lips made doubly precious the sweet-
> ness of his words . . . His brow was like white, translucent wax . . . well-
> rounded hands with tapering fingers made it a delight to receive a gift
> from him . . . His voice was sonorous, not harsh or rustic . . . nor was it
> lacking in manly vigor.[39]

A View from Rome: Leo the Great and Church Order

Such images of the bishop proved decisive in later ages. In many provinces of
the West, they placed the aristocratic bishop at the center of the Christian
imagination. But, at the time, not everybody regarded the Gallic bishops as
paragons. The bishop of Rome, pope Leo (440–461) viewed with deep dis-
trust the high-handed dealings of a man such as the austere Hilary of Arles.
As befitted an aristocrat, backed by aristocrats, Hilary was an empire-builder.
He had carved out a wide metropolitan diocese for himself through the influence of powerful secular friends. Such actions struck Leo, at Rome, as
nothing less than a "balkanization" of the Christian Church. He professed
to be appalled by such behavior: "inflated by his own pride, he buries himself in Hell."[40]

Viewed from Rome, the world looked very different from the way it looked in Gaul. Even after the Gothic sack of 410, Rome had remained a city with a population of some 200,000. The Western emperors still treated it as the true capital of their empire.[41] It was ten times larger than Paris. Each of its major basilicas was four times larger than any Gallic cathedral. Carefully nurtured memories of the Roman martyrs reached back for all of four centuries. The Roman clergy were a faceless group of men, buoyed up by immense corporate confidence in the absolute rightness of all things Roman. Their bishop, drawn from their ranks, was the last person to appreciate the experimental forms of leadership which had emerged in the rough and tumble of post-imperial Gaul.

The bishop of Rome was called a *papa.* The word meant "grand old man." The word "pope" comes from this courtesy title. But a *papa* of the fifth century was in no way a "pope" as modern persons know him, as the undisputed head of a worldwide Roman Catholic Church. The title *papa,* "pope," was used of any senior bishop.[42] But, as *papa,* the bishop of Rome was expected to play the elder statesman to less experienced regions. Throughout the fifth century, the *papa,* the pope of Rome, could be relied upon to provide authoritative, reassuringly old-fashioned advice on how a well-run church should function: "Let novelty cease to afflict antiquity," wrote pope Celestine to bishops in Spain, "let unease cease to upset the peace of the church."[43] The fact that this advice was frequently inapplicable to local conditions and was usually quietly ignored did not make it any less impressive. This was the voice of Rome. It still carried with it reassuring overtones of stability and correct order.

Individual bishops and clergymen travelled frequently to Rome to seek rulings. In their petitions, they went out of their way to address the bishop of Rome very much as "pope." But these expressions of respect did not necessarily impress their local colleagues. Many of these petitioners were tenacious malcontents. For a Gallic bishop, to appeal to Rome was usually a face-saving alternative to exile. It was a sign that he had lost the support of his local community.

The Churches of Africa, just across the water from Rome, produced a stream of enterprising rascals who appealed to the popes against the judgments of local councils. One was a country bishop, deposed by Augustine and his colleagues for having, among other things, built his episcopal palace from the ruins of houses that he had seized and looted.[44] Such visitors from the provinces did little to increase the respect of the pope and of the Roman clergy for the way in which other Churches managed their affairs. At a time of disintegration and headlong adjustment to new circumstances, Rome stood for a sense of order and for a width of horizons, stretching even beyond the frontiers of the Roman empire, which seemed to make the bishops of Rome, as the successors of Peter and Paul, the true heirs of a Roman world order.

It would, however, be a serious anachronism to see the bishops of Rome as being, at this time, central to the Latin Churches of the West. The bishops of Rome had, indeed, inherited a sense of their city as the center of what had once been a worldwide empire. They even presented Christianity, as Augustine of Hippo had done, as a spiritual empire that could reach beyond even the frontiers of the Roman world. But, on a day-to-day basis, they looked eastward, and not towards the north. What happened at Constantinople meant more for them than what was happening in Gaul.

The imaginative geography of a man such as Leo was determined by the vast fact of the undiminished power of the Roman empire in the East. The empire was technically undivided. An Italian such as Leo, who lived under a western emperor, still felt himself to be directly affected by what eastern emperors decided. As bishop of Rome, Leo was the bishop of the westernmost Christian *metropolis* of a Roman empire whose power had weakened only in distant provinces, across the Alps. In Italy, it seemed as if the empire would last forever.

Furthermore, Leo's position as the bishop of the only major non-Greek city in the empire gave him considerable advantages. The participation of the bishop of Rome, as the major representative of Latin Christianity, was essential to maintaining the balance of power among the Greek-speaking Churches of the eastern Mediterranean. The very fact that, as a Latin, Leo appeared slightly as an outsider to the Greek world gave him, in fact, a considerable advantage. His authority could be appealed to as a "tie-breaker."

"New Rome": The View from Constantinople

For the Churches of the East, the single most dramatic and destabilizing event of the entire century had not been the emergence of local pockets of disorder in the West. Such events were distant to them. What truly mattered was the meteoric rise in their very midst of Constantinople. By the early fifth century, Constantinople had become a world capital. The emperors resided there on a permanent basis. The population of the city was almost half a million. It boasted over 4,000 upper-class town-houses. A mile and a half of wharves were needed to dock the grain ships that fed its inhabitants. With such a city behind him, nobody could know where the ambitions of the bishop of "New Rome," the patriarch of Constantinople, might not lead.[45]

Antioch and Alexandria were ancient Christian cities. They were now as large as Rome itself. The patriarchs of these two cities vied with each other to secure the election of their own candidates to the bishopric of Constantinople. Each sought to discredit the bishop set up by the other. Each attempted, at different times, to bring the bishop of Rome into the struggle on their side. Last but not least, the emperors thought of themselves as "Romans" in a very real sense. They governed through standing for a wider world than that of their Greek subjects alone. In an overwhelmingly Greek-speaking world, Latin nonetheless remained the language of the law and was even spoken at court (much as Spanish continued to be used at the Habsburg court of Vienna). The emperors of "New Rome" had not forgotten the West. Indeed, they were positively anxious to invoke the safely distant prestige of the Latin bishop of Rome, as the imagined guardian of the faith of Saint Peter, as a counterweight to the all too present, ever-insistent claims of the Greek bishops of Antioch and Alexandria.[46]

If, in Leo's eyes, *ambitio*, hard-driving politics, was the besetting sin of the Gallic bishops, the *ambitio* of his eastern colleagues (and especially of the bishops of Alexandria) took place at the very highest level and on a scale which made the activities of a Hilary of Arles seem trivial. The patriarchs of Alexandria were very much the heirs of the unruly Athanasius. And they were a whole century richer. On one diplomatic mission to Constantinople alone, Cyril of Alexandria (412–444) was believed to have distributed to the officials of the imperial court bribes to the value of 2,500 pounds of gold – enough, that is, to feed 45,000 poor persons for one year, and 25 times as much money as a bishop such as Caesarius of Arles had ever been able to raise for the ransom of captives in Gaul.[47]

The councils of the Eastern Church, also, struck Leo as thoroughly "balkanized." The pope's representative to a Church council presided over by Cyril's successor, the heavy-handed Dioscorus of Alexandria, in 449, arrived back in Rome shocked by the violence he had witnessed. He had been forced to flee for safety to the sanctuary of the church in which the council took place, shouting in Latin, to no effect, *Contradicitur*, "I object," as a mob of riotous oriental monks closed in upon him. He later set up in the Lateran baptistery an *ex-voto* plaque to celebrate his deliverance from the violence of eastern bishops![48]

Emmanuel: "God with Us": Christological Controversy in the Eastern Empire

The grand maneuvers set in hand by men such as Cyril and Dioscorus exacerbated and exploited what had become a burning theological problem. The Council of Ephesus (431) and the Council of Chalcedon (451) were successors to Constantine's grandiose experiment at Nicaea. In them, the emperors hoped to obtain the consent of the entire Christian Church to a formula which would resolve a hotly contested issue: how close to man had God drawn near, in the person of Jesus Christ?

On this issue, fifth-century Christians felt that they had entered exciting new territory. The ancient imaginative model of the universe (to which we referred in the last chapter) no longer helped them. This model had stressed the chasm between the higher and the lower reaches of the universe. It gave the human soul a steep upward glimpse, very much from the bottom up, of the hierarchy which it must ascend in order to reach a distant God. The Incarnation of God in Jesus Christ, by contrast, brought the top of this universe down to the very bottom. It placed the ancient model of the universe on its head. As pope Leo said: "It is far less amazing that human beings should progress upwards towards God than that God should have come down to the human level."[49] What mattered less, now, was not how to get from the lowest to the highest, from man to God. The issue was how to understand the unique manner in which God had come down to man – how the highest had been joined to the lowest in the person of Christ. Faced by the person of Jesus, a human figure whose actions and utterances were known in detail from the narratives of the Gospels, the believer had to decide in what way God had been present in Jesus the man and how Jesus the man had been linked to God.

This was far from being a merely theoretical issue, debated only by expert theologians. Large Christian congregations needed to know the answer. They needed to feel that God was with them on ground level, as it were. It was not enough that God should make his will known to a distant human race through a series of special representatives. This was a weakness in previous Christian theology which Athanasius had already spotted and exploited with unrelenting, narrow clarity, in his conflict with the supporters of Arius. Christ was not simply a privileged messenger of God, as Arius seemed to suggest. He was not to be seen only as "a kind of Prefect of the Supreme Sovereign," governing the material universe on behalf of a still distant High God.[50] Rather, Athanasius had insisted, God in person had come down to earth in human form.

Views which thought of Christ as no more than a privileged "representative" of God, and not God himself, had seemed natural to thinkers of the age of Constantine, such as the learned Eusebius, bishop of Caesarea (263–340), the historian of the Church and the biographer and panegyrist of Constantine.[51] To a man such as Eusebius, it seemed as if the victory of monotheism had, indeed, been the victory of a High God, who had reached down to earth, to make his commands plain through a series of privileged representatives of his will, of which Christ had been the greatest and Constantine, on a lesser plane, the most recent.

Eusebius' view had remained dominant for much of the fourth century. But those who supported it made a fatal mistake. It made of God a remote monarch, who acted through agents who were, by definition, different from himself. Emperors were like that. But God did not have to be so distant. In attacking Arius and views associated with men such as Eusebius, Athanasius realized that the Christian people needed to be able to say *Emmanuel*, "God is with us." Christ's life on earth, he had insisted, had not been like "an official governmental visit from on high": it had been the "blazing forth on earth of God Himself."[52]

Throughout the fourth and fifth centuries, the patriarchs of Alexandria, the master-politician Cyril (412–444) and the fatefully over-confident Dioscorus (444–451), rode the tide whose strength, in Christian piety, Athanasius had already sensed.[53] Because Christ had come down to earth among men, it was that much more easy to turn directly to him. The intermediate powers of the *mundus* did not have to be invoked for help in earthly matters. In regions such as Egypt, monotheism became real, not through denying the reality of the lower powers – not through stripping the universe of its shimmering layers of angelic and demonic beings – but through pushing them to one side. All powers were subject to Christ; and Christ, because he had become a human being, was present to his worshippers on all levels of experience.

The unspoken barrier was lifted which had separated spiritual salvation and the afterlife – those high, unearthly things with which Christ, as God, had always been associated – from the humdrum, earthbound concerns of the average Christian. It was possible to call on the name of Jesus in all situations, knowing that, through his incarnation, he had come to know every danger and every temptation, that he had overcome them all, and that his power was still immediately available to help the believer to do the same. In the words of Shenoute of Atripe (385–466), the great abbot of the White Monastery at Sohag in Middle Egypt:

> Try to attain to the full measure of this Name, and you will find it on your mouth and on the mouth of your children. When you make high festival and when you rejoice, cry Jesus. When anxious and in pain, cry Jesus. When little boys and girls are laughing, let them cry Jesus. And those who flee before barbarians, cry Jesus. And those who go down to the Nile, cry Jesus. ... And those whose trial has been corrupted and who receive injustice, let them cry the Name of Jesus.[54]

Backed by such passions, it is not surprising that the great patriarchs of Alexandria acted with such high-handed confidence. Neither is it surprising that each side feared the worst in its opponents. For this worst was nothing less than the fear that God and man would drift apart again, separated by the unbridgeable gulf between heaven and earth implied in the ancient model of the universe.

For Nestorius, who was patriarch of Constantinople from 428 to 431, the Alexandrian solution was repugnant. It seemed to bring God so close to humanity as to implicate an all-powerful and deathless being in the dishonor of suffering. Christ, rather, must be thought of as a man who was uniquely linked to God by a bond of the same quality, though of infinitely greater intensity and permanence, as that which had linked God to any other of his prophets. God's power and majesty were not affected by the Crucifixion of Christ: for it was his chosen human Son and servant, not God himself, who had suffered on the Cross.

When his views were condemned at the Council of Ephesus, Nestorius observed bitterly that the ignorant populace of Constantinople danced around bonfires, chanting, "God has been crucified. God is dead." To join God to human suffering in this manner was a blasphemy which God would not forgive. It came as no surprise to the supporters of Nestorius that, a few years after the condemnation of his views at Ephesus, the Huns flooded into Thrace, looting up to the walls of Constantinople.[55]

The Alexandrians saw the matter very differently. It was vital for them that the Incarnation had made of God and man a single, indissoluble whole – a single "nature." For this reason, the intransigent followers of the theology of Cyril came to be known as Monophysites (from *monos*, single, and *physis*, nature), on account of the manner in which they presented Christ as a unique being, in which humanity and divinity had come together to form a distinctive and undivided whole. "Monophysite" was not a title which they chose for themselves. But it sums up the intensity with which they defended the idea that Christ was a unique being, in which divine and human were joined without so much as the hint of a fissure between them.[56]

Ultimately, no single formula was able to do justice to the very real issue which was at stake. For what counted for those who supported the theology of Cyril against that of Nestorius was an urgent matter. They wished to guarantee the solidarity of God with humankind. This was a real and intimate link, not a mere touching of two eternally distinct spheres – the human and the divine. In Christ, God had, indeed, shared in human suffering. To speak of God as having been, indeed, crucified, in the person of Jesus, was to remind him of the shared suffering which bound him indissolubly, almost organically, to the human race. He could not forget those with whom he had once shared the universal taste of death.

Thus, in the 470s, the "Monophysite" patriarch of Antioch deliberately added to the current form of the litany, "Holy Powerful One, Holy Deathless One," the *risqué* phrase, "Who was crucified for us." He did so at a time of crisis. It was an addition which summed up an entire view of the world. In the main courtyard of the Great Church of Antioch, sympathetic crowds gathered round a street-artist who had trained his parrot to squawk the litany, with the all-important "Crucified for us" at its end. In a time of affliction, no matter how cruelly distant God might seem to be, Monophysites believed that God could be summoned by these words, that spoke to him of his own sufferings as a human being.[57]

The cult of the Virgin Mary as *Theotokos*, as "she who gave birth to God," was pushed to the fore in an atmosphere that demanded one thing of God: that his relations with mankind should rest not on a mere partnership with mankind but on the tender, wordless kinship of shared flesh. The formula adopted by the Council of Ephesus was chosen so as to exclude the views of Nestorius. "The bond of the womb" was the strongest tie of all between human beings. Pleas for mercy to the powerful, at this time, stressed the fact that even the most miserable and undeserving East Roman was a fellow human being, some mother's son, cradled in a human womb and suckled at human breasts. As a result, Mary came to be shown, in the art of the late fifth and sixth centuries, as holding Christ enthroned on her lap, as if he were still tied to her womb. Christ was spoken of, in hymns sung by whole congregations, as drawing his human flesh from sucking the breasts of Mary. For a mother's milk, to ancient persons, was interchangeable with her blood: it was liquid flesh, transferred to the child by suckling. Christ must listen to those who prayed to his mother; for it was she who had rendered him fully human. Only she could remind him, with the authority of a mother, of what he shared with the afflicted human flesh of those who turned to him.[58]

These issues came to divide the Christians of the East in a manner that no emperor could hope to solve. But it was not for lack of trying. The Council of Chalcedon was summoned by the emperor Marcian in 451, immediately after the death of Theodosius II. It was the greatest council ever assembled. Over 600 bishops met at Chalcedon, modern Kadiköy, just across the water from Constantinople. The assembly took place under the watchful eyes of members of the Senate. The emperor was taking no chances. But, unlike his predecessor, Theodosius II, Marcian was a newly installed, military man. Like most monarchs who find themselves in a weak position, as a newcomer to power, Marcian needed to show, as soon as possible, that he could do something decisive and spectacular.

Marcian did not wait for a consensus to emerge among the eastern bishops. Instead, he opted heavily for a theological statement drawn up by pope Leo. Leo's famous *Tome* was presented to the council by the pope's representatives and was accepted by the bishops at Marcian's urging. It was a careful document. Later legend (circulated in Constantinople by none other than pope Gregory the Great) liked to believe that Leo had placed his *Tome* upon the tomb of Saint Peter himself, to have it proofread by the saint.[59] To Latin theologians, it was a perfect statement of the faith. It gave due weight both to the divine and to the human elements in the person and life of Christ. But this was precisely what was wrong with it. To the Egyptian followers of Cyril of Alexandria, Leo's careful balancing of the divine and the human in the person of Christ seemed to suggest that, in Christ, the divine and the human could be separated in the first place. It seemed to lead straight back to Nestorius. It threatened to open, once again, a crevasse between the divine and the human. The opponents of Leo insisted that divine and human had been joined in Christ in such a way that the human person of Christ was totally transfused with divine power. Even the touch of Christ's fingers had been sufficient to bring healing to the sick.[60] In Egypt, in much of Syria, and for many thinking persons elsewhere, the Council of Chalcedon, summoned so as to be the council to end all councils, came to be known as "the Great Prevarication." In their opinion, the council had divided the human and the divine in Christ and had thereby destroyed the solidarity between God and human beings.[61]

Much as modern European Christianity has taken centuries to transcend the issues raised, 300 years ago, at the Reformation, so late antique Christianity remained locked in the issues brought together and, fatefully, left unresolved at the Council of Chalcedon. For the controversy was not caused only by the fine-spun zeal of theologians. The entire quality of a post-polytheist civilization was at stake. The Christians had ousted the gods who had once joined heaven and earth with such ease. They had exalted one God at the cost of making him seem very distant indeed from humankind. They were left to struggle with the manner in which this High God had joined humanity in the person of Jesus Christ. Only by resolving this conundrum could they bring heaven and earth back together again.

These issues spilled out across the frontiers of the eastern empire, to trouble Christians everywhere. Up to as late as the end of the seventh century, the Christological debates which took place in the eastern Churches were constantly discussed in Rome. But they were also known in northern Gaul and even in Britain. In this respect, western Europe had by no means become a separate zone, soundproof to the troubles of the East. As we shall see in chapter 16, verses written in an Anglo-Saxon poem in northern Britain, in around A.D. 700, refer to such controversies – as did a petition of eastern Christian monks addressed to the emperor of China in A.D. 635 (as we shall see in chapter 12).

In the West, however, there would no longer be a Roman empire within which such debates would echo loudly, as they continued to do in the eastern Mediterranean. In 476, the last western Roman emperor, Romulus

Augustulus, was pushed aside. Barbarian kings became the rulers of Italy. It was not until 536, in very different circumstances, that the troops of the East Roman emperor Justinian entered Rome, making it once again an "imperial" city. By that time, however, the Roman empire had become little more than a memory along the frontiers of the West. And these frontiers themselves would soon become the centers of new forms of power, linked to new forms of Christianity. It is to the rapid changes in that crucial frontier zone, which lay at many weeks' journey to the north of Marseilles and Rome, that we must now turn.

CHAPTER 5

On the Frontiers: Noricum, Ireland, and Francia

A Saint of the Open Frontier: Severinus of Noricum

Throughout Western Europe, in the fifth century, the military frontier of the Roman empire came to an end. The life of a holy man, Severinus, who arrived in the province of Noricum (largely in modern Austria) in 454 and died in 482, provides a series of vivid close-ups of how this process happened in one area, along the banks of the Danube.

> At the time when the Roman empire was still in existence, the soldiers of many towns were supported by public money to guard the frontier. When this arrangement ceased, the military formations were dissolved and the frontier vanished. The garrison of Passau, however, still held out. Some of the men had gone to Italy to fetch for their comrades their last payment. But nobody knew that they were killed by barbarians on the way. One day, when saint Severinus was reading in his cell, he suddenly closed the book and began to sigh . . . The river [he said] was now red with human blood. And at that moment, the news arrived that the bodies of the soldiers had been washed ashore by the current.[1]

Severinus was a saint of the open frontier. A mysterious stranger, he came to Noricum as a hermit in around A.D. 454. Some thought he was a fugitive slave; but he spoke the good Latin of an upper-class *Romanus*. Until his death, in 482, he moved along the Danube, from one small walled town to another, preaching collective penance, organizing tithes for the relief of the poor, denouncing grain-hoarders in times of shortage.[2]

Along the Danube, the *Romani* sheltered behind their city walls. These were small towns, with small Christian congregations. The church at Lorch, for instance, held some 200 worshippers – it was only a fifth of the size of a Gallic cathedral.[3] For the townspeople, the Roman empire had already become a distant affair. The empire whose fall in 453 had truly altered their lives was the empire of Attila. The disintegration of Hunnish domination north of the Danube left small barbarian tribes, no longer subject to Hunnish control, free to infiltrate as they wished into the "Roman" territories on its southern banks.[4]

The relations of the *Romani* to the new groups from across the Danube were ambivalent. Much as the mountain chieftains of nineteenth-century eastern Anatolia were said (in an unceremonious but apposite phrase) to "eat" the villages of the plain, to treat the villagers, that is, as a source from which to extract income, so barbarian tribes from across the Danube – such as the Rugi, in the region around Lorch – pressed in to "eat" the Roman cities. They had no wish to destroy them. Instead, they offered the inhabitants high-handed and unpredictable protection in exchange for tribute and occasional levies of skilled manpower. The city-dwellers were "their" Romans. At least no other, rival tribe would "eat" them.

Severinus was remembered for the manner in which he ensured that this rough compact was observed. He moved with authority among competing kings. Gibuldus of the Alemanni quailed before him:

> the king declared to his armed men that never before, either in battle or in any peril, had he been shaken with such violent trembling.[5]

The uncanny hermit was held to control their fortunes. He predicted the rise to power of one local warrior, Odoacer, who would eventually, as a general, oust the last emperor, Romulus Augustulus, and who ruled Italy from 476 to 493:

> at the time [Odoacer] was a young man, tall and clad in poor clothes. He stooped for fear of hitting the roof of [Severinus'] cell . . . "Go to Italy [the saint said]. Go, now covered with mean hides; soon you will make rich gifts to many."[6]

On the frontier, religious boundaries which meant so much for the civilian populations of the Mediterranean counted for little. Severinus extended his blessing to all tribal leaders, Catholic, Arian, or pagan. What mattered more was security. Always short of manpower, and particularly of skilled craftsmen, the barbarians across the frontier absorbed *Romani* at an alarming rate. Slave-raiding was a grim feature of life on the frontiers. To use *Romani* whom one "ate," by selling them as slaves or relocating them among the wood villages of Moravia, was the most heinous breach of all in the tacit compact between the Danubian townsfolk and their protectors. Queen Giso of the Rugians did just that. She was swiftly punished. Her son, Friderichus, wandered by mistake into the blockhouse in which skilled foreign slaves were kept, set to work producing royal jewelry. They seized him and held him as hostage for their own release.[7] It is a grim glimpse of the human cost, for many, of the emergence of brittle new societies, which came into being once the "Roman" and the "barbarian" sides of a frontier region imploded, as it were, to form new cultural and social units.

In the case of the *Life of Severinus*, the glimpse of the last days of a Roman frontier took place from a safe distance. Severinus' biography was written in 511 by Eugippius. Though a refugee from Noricum, Eugippius had become the abbot of a monastery which overlooked the Bay of Naples. A distinguished neighbor and patron of the monastery was none other than the former emperor, Romulus Augustulus, who was now living on a comfortable pension in a villa which still bore the name of its former owner, Lucullus, the famous Roman gourmet of the time of Augustus! Eugippius was at the center of a circle of learned Roman aristocrats, men and women. He even made for them an anthology of the works of Saint Augustine. Noricum was a long way away from such persons. Eugippius' story of the end of Roman urban life on the distant Danube merely served to heighten the sense of security which still reigned around the Bay of Naples in Italy.[8]

In fact, only the upper classes of the cities of Noricum had emigrated to Italy. The Christian graves of humble *Romani* continued, for centuries, to cluster around Severinus' church at Lorch. Their Christianity, largely deprived of clerical leadership, became a folk religion – to such an extent that memories of distinctive Early Christian, late Roman practices, such as public penance, survived into modern times in the folk songs of Slovenia.[9]

It was largely the frontier districts that were exposed to violence and disruption. Away from the dangerous banks of the Danube, in the Alpine hinterland of Noricum, large basilicas, modelled on the churches of northern Italy, flanked by hospices and pilgrimage shrines containing exotic relics, continued to be built long after the death of Severinus. On the Hemmaberg, which rose above the river Sava (in Kärnten or Carinthia), the narrow plateau was covered with no less than four large churches. It was a thriving pilgrimage shrine similar to the many others which stretched across the Christian world of the late fifth century, from Saint Alban's in Britain, through Saint Martin's at Tours, to the new sanctuaries of Symeon Stylites, in northern Syria, and that of Saint Menas in Egypt. Romans and barbarians, even, one suspects, Catholics and Arians, came together at such a center, to visit relics placed above ancient healing springs.[10]

An Age of Tyrants: The End of Roman Britain

What happened in Noricum happened also in Britain. The withdrawal of the Roman armies, after 406, left a power vacuum on the island. An entire governmental elite vanished. The buried treasures which lie in such numbers beneath the soil of East Anglia, speak of the sudden loss of an imperial order. In one such hoard, recently discovered at Hoxne, 14,600 gold and silver coins had been stowed away in wooden chests. The tableware alone included 78 silver spoons. A woman's golden body-necklace weighed 250 grams. A collection of heavy armbands, of the cosmopolitan "barbarian" workmanship sported by Roman officers all over the empire, indicates the hasty departure of a *vir militaris* of the old style.[11]

Yet, despite the withdrawal of the Roman government, the surviving elites of Britain felt that they could look after themselves, without an empire to protect them. But things did not work out in Britain as they had done in Gaul. The settlement of Saxon pirates in around 440 as billeted "guests" in the traditional late Roman manner proved a failure. Small Saxon bands, free from governmental control of any kind, came to settle permanently in Britain where the English Channel met the North Sea. They made their way up the Thames valley, effectively severing southern Britain from the Midlands. Along with other soldiers of fortune (such as the Irish chieftain, Cunorix MacCullen, who was buried, with an Ogham commemorative stone, at Wroxeter, near the Severn) Saxons participated in the civil wars in which local leaders of Roman background fought each other for control of the island. Thus, to speak of a single Saxon "invasion" and "conquest" of Britain is misleading. Small groups of Saxons were only one factor among others in a society which had collapsed in upon itself once the artificial supports provided by the Roman imperial system were removed.

We should never forget how primitive the Roman economy was, and especially in the frontier areas. In Britain, as in many other areas of western Europe, towns, trade, currency, and extensive building (those "arguments in stone" which so impress the Roman archaeologist) were not sustained naturally by overall prosperity and by commercial activity. They depended on the forced mobilization and circulation of wealth through relentless taxation for the support of the Roman armies. Once that great machine had been brought to a halt, in a "post-imperial" world, the economy of the entire island of Britain (and, one suspects, of other areas of western Europe) rapidly lost its sophisticated Roman face. Britain slipped back into conditions more brutally simplified even than the Iron Age societies which had preceded the coming of the Romans.

What archaeologists of post-imperial Britain have discovered is a flattened landscape. The towns stood largely empty, without coins and without extensive trade even in objects as simple to produce and to move around as pottery. Former luxury villas were turned into farmhouses. Wooden buildings replaced the stone halls of Romans. Embattled hill-forts overlooked a countryside now defended by extensive earthworks erected as much against fellow-Britons as against invading barbarians. Far from destroying Roman Britain, the Saxons slowly fought their way into a world which had already ceased to be "Roman" once its elites ceased to have a part in the massive tax structures set up by the late Roman state.[12]

It was not until the 570s that Saxon kings entered as conquerors the walled cities of western Britain. As they entered Bath, where the great shrine of Minerva Sulis had once stood, they were vastly impressed by what they saw:

> Wondrously ornate is the stone of this wall, now shattered by fate. The precincts of the city have crumbled. The work of giants has rotted away ... There were bright city buildings, many bathhouses, a wealth of lofty gables.[13]

Only at that time (in the sixth century, that is, and not in the 440s) did the Saxons weave for themselves a more flattering narrative to justify their unexpected rise to dominance. They now claimed to be the lineal descendants of heroic shiploads of warriors whose leaders, Hengist and Horsa, had sailed direct from the North Sea coast of Jutland to seek, in Britain, their Promised Land. The idea of the "Coming of the Saxons" was a myth. It throws no light whatsoever on what happened to Roman Britain in the century that immediately followed the withdrawal of the empire.[14]

We lack an account of a holy man, such as Severinus of Noricum, to describe the process by which the Saxons settled down to "eat" the Romano-Britons and the Romano-Britons to "eat" themselves. We know very little about the Christianity of Roman Britain. The Church may have been less securely established in Britain than elsewhere. The grip of the Church on large walled cities was central to the history of Gaul. But the cities of fifth-century Britain may have been "ghost towns." Large Celtic hill-shrines, dating from prehistoric times, dwarfed the small churches set up in the cities and on the estates of rich "Roman" landowners.

But there may have been other reasons for this lack of high profile on the part of the Christian clergy. They seem not to have played the "representative" role which they took on so successfully in Gaul. Here Britain may have suffered from the distant backwash of theological controversies which had raged around the Mediterranean. We have seen how important the conflict between Augustine and Pelagius had been in the formation of the Catholic Church in Africa, Italy, and Gaul. Pelagius had come from Britain. Many British bishops were suspected of being loyal to the views of their fellow-countryman. This loyalty may not have been purely personal. The atmosphere of a declining province may have favored Pelagianism. The Pelagians of Britain may have thought of themselves as "Old Christians," as an embattled minority in a superficially Christianized province. In this they would have resembled the first supporters of Pelagius at Rome. They were a self-chosen group of "saints," a heroic few, proud to remain a morally superior minority in a land of violence and bad faith. The passionate moralism of a later British writer such as Gildas (who wrote around 520) may well have reflected the mood of earlier, Pelagian Christians. In the sixth century, this heavy emphasis on the moral purity of the few may well have led to the rise in western Britain and in Ireland of notoriously uncompromising forms of monasticism. Altogether, in post-imperial Britain, the monks and bishops were critics of their society. They did not claim, as in Gaul, to be its leaders.[15]

We can only glimpse this story at a distance in our fragmentary sources. But it is fascinating for what it tells us about the role of Christianity in general in the post-imperial West. This was an age of drastic economic simplification, which accompanied political "downsizing" in many regions. In Britain, it seems as if old Roman centers had vanished and even the simplest forms of goods had ceased to circulate. Yet networks of information survived. At a high level, groups of committed religious experts, literate clergymen in Britain as elsewhere, maintained a quite surprising degree of inter-communication with each other. Continental controversies were debated and Continental styles of Christian piety still spread widely, linking Gaul, Britain, and, eventually, Ireland. In a world where the infrastructure provided by the Roman state had sunk to a pre-Roman level, Christian writers and, one suspects, humbler Christian pilgrims and patrons of local churches seem to have stood out like crests of higher land. The intervisibility of one crest to the other, over extensive distances, gave a sense of scale and unity to members of a Christian elite (such as those who read the vigorous Latin of Gildas) at a time when the local societies around them had sunk in upon themselves.[16]

Whatever the Christian religious experts might do, real power, in Britain, fell, by default, into the hands of men of war. Unlike Gaul, "tyrants," successful local chieftains, and not "Roman" bishops dominate the history of fifth-century Britain. Many of these "tyrants" came from the under-Romanized, highland zone of northwest Wales and northern Britain. Their ancestors might have borne Roman names such as Tacitus; but they now spoke of themselves in Welsh. In the Y *Gododdin* of Aneirin, the sub-Roman princes of the north appear, by A.D. 600, as epic heroes, in a Celtic tradition. It is the chieftain's mead, "yellow, sweet, ensnaring," and not the solemn oath of the professional soldier to his emperor, which now sent young men to their deaths, among "the war horses and the blood-stained armor."[17]

Yet the British princes still held court, if now in timber halls, within the framework of the stone forts on Hadrian's Wall. They celebrated their power by lavish gift-giving on the *Ddyw Calan Ionawr*, the high, imperial day of the Kalends of January, denounced, throughout the Roman world, by Christian bishops. They thought of themselves as Christians. They gave "gold to the altar" before each campaign, as well as "gifts to the bard." If they perjured themselves, they did it on Christian altars; just as, when they murdered their kinsmen, they did so in the sanctuary of Christian monasteries.[18]

Further south, in western Britain, hard men defended a drastically simplified, but still "Roman" provincial landscape. The "tribal" cities founded by the Romans still formed the basic territorial units into which the land was divided. Estates were organized around former Roman villas. Documents continued to be drawn up in Roman form. The new hill-forts may have maintained at least some echo of "imperial" splendor, in the habits of feasting which took place there and in the bestowal of Roman titles on members of the courts of warrior kings. Certainly, a sense of "Roman" pride survived, linked to the idea of being "fellow-citizens" tensed against despised barbarians from outside. The Romano-British notion of being "citizens" together was the root of the word *Cwmry*, the Celtic word for Wales, which originally meant "the fellow-citizens."[19]

Not surprisingly, these beleaguered Britons were not greatly concerned that the Saxons should have remained pagans. A man such as Augustine of Hippo might believe that the Catholic Church had indeed been promised *all the nations of the world*. But most Roman Christians did not share Augustine's breadth of vision. Their world tended to stop at the Roman frontier. The Britons were old-fashioned *Romani* in this respect. They felt that Christianity was too precious a thing to waste on mere barbarians. Saxons could be expected to continue their unsavory pagan ways – much as the Christian Visigoths of Gaul were not expected to be other than Arian heretics. Only when the nature of the frontier itself changed would a common Christianity emerge, of a sort that would embrace Romans and barbarians alike.

"From the ends of the earth": Patricius in Ireland

Hence the most significant development of all took place to the west of Britain. Hadrian's Wall ceased to be an effective boundary. Once the barrier of Roman control was removed, the northern and western parts of Britain and the hitherto utterly non-Roman eastern coast of Ireland came together to form a single "Celtic Mediterranean" of the north. The settlements of the Dalriada Irish (the *Scotti*, the "freebooters", of our texts) linked Ulster with Galloway and the coast of Scotland as far north as the Isle of Skye, in an Irish hegemony maintained by fleets of seven-benched rowboats. Wales and the estuary of the Boyne faced each other: Irish kings took British wives, and new coins of the most Christian emperor, Theodosius I, appear as votive offerings in the Irish temple of New Grange. On the western tip of Cornwall, Tintagel became a fortress city, sporadically supplied with prestige goods – wine, oil, and lamps from Africa, even from Egypt. Ogham stones, signs of extensive Irish settlement, appeared throughout southwestern Wales. Latin terms of trade and military status, borrowed from the sub-Roman society of western Britain, now seeped into Old Irish.[20]

Not all aspects of this discreet flow of persons and ideas had been peaceful. By 430, substantial colonies of British Christian slaves must have existed along the east coast of Ireland, along with the "Roman" British merchants who collaborated with the Irish warlords to stock the fields of Leinster with new labor and the households of the chieftains with new women. What mattered is that the existence of these miserable persons was noted by a leading intellectual from southern Gaul. Prosper of Aquitaine, as we have seen, was a defender of the extreme views of Augustine. He later became an adviser to none other than pope Leo. In a treatise against the Pelagians and in his Chronicle, he noted with pride that a bishop, Palladius, had been sent to "the Irish who believe in Christ." Palladius' mission was seen by him as the logical consequence of a campaign to halt the spread of Pelagianism in Britain (in which we saw Germanus of Auxerre to have been involved). For Prosper this meant that, at one and the same time, a "Roman" island was made "Catholic," and a "barbarian" island Christian.

Prosper's record of the "mission of Palladius" tells us more about how a Mediterranean Christian gentleman viewed the edges of the world than it does about what actually happened. Palladius' mission may have had some impact on the region of Leinster, which looked out across the sea to the still partly "Roman" estuary of the Severn and southern Wales. But, seen from Rome, the Irish mission was something of a "moon shot." It showed, to the great satisfaction of Prosper and of his patron, pope Leo, that the Catholic Church was truly universal, and that, as the bishop of Rome, Leo had a particular responsibility for Christians beyond the frontiers of the empire. The patriarch of Constantinople claimed a similar right to supervise Christians "in barbarian lands." His care extended from the imperial capital to the Christian communities scattered around the Black Sea, in the Caucasus, in the Crimea, and across the Danube. Leo was not the sort of man to be outdone by an eastern colleague. To "land a man on the moon" – that is, to place a Christian bishop in a totally non-Roman Ireland – showed the majestic reach of the Catholic Church, as Augustine had defined it, as a City for all nations.[21]

We are fortunate, in the works of Patricius (later known as Saint Patrick), to possess a set of remarkable documents which tell the inner story of another such mission to the Irish. Like the *Life of Severinus*, Patricius' story of his life suddenly takes us to a frontier region at the furthest end of the Roman world. Sometime in the 440s, Irish raiders fell on an unknown city of Britain. A well-to-do 16-year-old, Patricius, the son of a deacon, from a family of town councillors, was among the captives. He served as a slave on the Atlantic coast of County Mayo. Yet Patricius emerged from this experience as very much the Severinus of the north. In his exile, he turned to an ascetic brand of Christianity to which he had given no thought when he was a young man from a clerical family in Britain.

> My faith grew and my spirit was stirred, and as a result I would say up to one hundred prayers in one day and almost as many by night . . . and I would wake to pray before dawn in all weathers, snow, frost and rain; and I felt no harm . . . as I now realize, it was because the Spirit was fervent within me.[22]

Patricius escaped from slavery, returned to Britain, and, once ordained, decided to go back to Ireland. It was a hotly contested step for a British bishop to take. Patricius' subsequent career in Ireland was dominated by the same concerns as preoccupied the bishops in Gaul, such as Caesarius of Arles. He intervened, as a bishop, to control the terrible movement of persons connected with the slave trade. When Coroticus, a British warlord, raided a Christian community in Ireland, the letters sent by Patricius, asking for the return of all baptized Christians, were rejected: Coroticus and his warriors "roared with laughter at them." To Coroticus, Irish "barbarians," whether baptized or not, could never hope to count as "fellow-citizens of Romans."[23] Patricius was disowned by his British colleagues as a charismatic maverick. He was accused of having made a profit from his mission – collecting, for his own purposes, the splendid jewelry which high-born Irish women piled, as votive offerings, on his altar.[24]

Patricius' *Letter to Coroticus* and his subsequent *Confession* are so well known, as coming from the pen of a man later famous as Saint Patrick, the patron saint of all Ireland, that we forget what remarkable documents they were. They are the first pieces of extensive Latin prose to be written from beyond the frontiers of the Roman world. Their tone is startlingly universalist. Patricius took on the full *persona* of Saint Paul. He was a Spirit-filled man; "a stone, lying deep in the mud." God had set him on high for one purpose only: "Look, we are witnesses that the Gospel has been preached to the point beyond which there is no one." Though summoned by his colleagues to return to Britain, he declared that he would stay among the Irish, "to serve a people just now coming to the faith and which the Lord has chosen from the ends of the earth."[25]

Patricius was an exact contemporary of Severinus, in faraway Noricum. He also was a saint of the open frontier. But his letters show him on the defensive. When he died, perhaps in around 490, it was far from certain that his mission would survive.

What ensured the permanent success of the Christian communities in Ireland was the quickening pace of exchanges around the "Celtic Mediterranean." These exchanges led to the establishment of Christian communities along the eastern coast of Ireland in the course of the late fifth and early sixth centuries. But the Christian churches of eastern Ireland remained unusual. For the first time in centuries, Christians found themselves in a position where they were members of a minority religion in a pagan land. The Irish churches had few of the grandiose ambitions and collective intolerance which had characterized the post-Constantinian Christian empire and the confidently Christian urban centers of Gaul and Italy. Christianity tended to spread family by family and *túath* by *túath* – small tribe by small tribe. These tribes were tiny units. Over 150 of them existed at the same time in Ireland. Christian groups, therefore, had to fit into a society made up of tightly interlocking, but separate, fragments.[26]

The religion of some families, but not of others, the Christian churches enjoyed an almost total absence of persecution. Christians were considerably less concerned with how they might Christianize their neighbors than with how to preserve their own identity. An early synod, the so-called *First Synod of Saint Patrick*, forbade Christian clergymen to act as guarantors for pagans. Christians were not to swear oaths before a druid. The kilt, also, and the heroic, flowing hair of a chieftain were deemed unsuitable in a bishop:

> Any cleric . . . who is seen without a long tunic and does not cover his private parts [was condemned, as were those] whose hair is not cut short as a "Roman" should.[27]

As a result, the great narratives which had recounted the expansion of Christianity around the Roman Mediterranean meant little in this northern land. We meet no violent persecution by the heathen, no dramatic exorcisms, no conversions of great rulers, no spectacular destructions of pagan temples. Instead, with a few exceptions, later Irish legends of Saint Patrick lingered by preference on problems that were dear to the heart of a resolutely non-Roman society.

The narratives of Patricius' mission were designed to explain problems which an Irish, not a Mediterranean, Christian needed to explain. This was a land were visiting strangers were entirely dependent on the goodwill of those who decided to receive them. How had Patricius, a non-Irishman and a Christian, been received into a pagan land? Irish writers dwelt on the reserve of "natural goodness" in Patricius' first hosts which must have led them, although pagans, to offer hospitality to him, although, as a total stranger from across the sea, he had no previous claim upon them.[28]

Ireland, also, was a land in which social relations were established through the exchange of gifts. The Irish insisted on a correct balance of gift and counter-gift. In that case, Christian writers asked, how was it possible that, in exchange for no more than a few Latin words of blessing written on pages of white parchment, this Christian stranger could have charmed from so many hard-fisted chieftains so much solid wealth? For Patricius and his successors had been able to receive from the laity of Ireland land, gold, cattle, even their own daughters, as nuns given to Christ.[29] To get something for nothing was the ultimate feat of the trickster. Hardly surprisingly, the legends which recounted Patrick's first imagined progress through Ireland came to form a cycle which merged with the pagan annual festival of the *Lughnasa*. For at the *Lughnasa*, Lugh, the archetypal trickster god of Celtic mythology, had, like Patrick, tricked out of grim winter, in return for mere words, the solid riches of the next year's harvest.[30] To present a missionary as a trickster-god, rather than as a triumphant exorcist and destroyer of temples, was an unusual way of remembering the coming of Christianity to a northern land.

Northern Gaul: Clovis (481–511) and the Rise of the Franks

We know of Patricius' mission only from his own writings. No one mentioned Patricius at the time. This was not the case with the formation, in northern Gaul and along the Rhine, of a new-style kingdom of the Franks – soon known by the all-embracing term of *Francia* – in the reign of king Clovis (481–511).[31]

After the 460s, northern Gaul resembled Britain. It was a land without empire. Its leading inhabitants had begun to accept this fact. This is shown by a significant change in local burial customs. *Romani* and barbarians alike, whether Christian or pagan, came to be buried bearing arms. For weapons, fine brooches, and heavy belts, the former insignia of the *viri militares*, were what now distinguished any leader of local society.[32]

In this increasingly militarized world, the Franks were by no means newcomers. Many had served in the high command of the imperial armies in the fourth century. To take one example: Bauto, a Frankish chieftain in imperial service became consul in 385 and received a panegyric on that occasion, in Milan, from none other than the young Augustine. He took care to have his daughter brought up at Constantinople, in the palace of a Roman fellow-general. She married the emperor Arcadius: thus the son of Arcadius, Theodosius II, the originator of that most Roman of Roman documents, the *Theodosian Code*, was at least one quarter Frankish! Franks such as Bauto were already honorary Romans. They claimed to be descended, like the Romans, from the Trojans. Priam had been their first king. They had only recently – so Franks close to the Rhine frontier chose to believe – come to Germany from ancient Troy![33]

Not every Frank was like Bauto. The Franks who were led by king Childeric, in the 470s, were wilder men. Childeric was a Merovingian. Later legends made the Merovingians the descendants of a Frankish queen who had coupled with a sea monster when swimming in the North Sea, the legendary home of heroes.[34]

We cannot be certain what contemporaries made of this story. What we do know is that, when Childeric died in 481, the burial which he received at Tournai left a studiously composite image of his power. Discovered in 1653, Childeric's grave is the most splendid barbarian burial yet known in Europe. But it was also, in part, a Roman burial of a man who claimed to be a Roman official. It lay near a Christian basilica, outside a Roman city. Childeric carried a Roman official signet ring, with which to seal his documents. It bore his portrait. The magical long hair of a Merovingian "long-haired king" fell over the folds of the robe of a Roman official. Only in 1983 did further excavations reveal large pits filled with horse skeletons. Lavish horse-sacrifice, in the pagan manner, had taken place at the funeral of Childeric the "Roman" Frank – and possibly within sight of the Christian basilica.[35]

Childeric's son, Clovis – Hlodovech, "glorious warrior" – inherited the many strands of his father's authority in Gaul. He was a pagan; yet he received a letter from Remigius, the Catholic bishop of Rheims: "May justice proceed from your mouth."[36] From the very beginning, Clovis wished to be king of the Franks in a new, more forceful style. When Soissons fell, in 486, and the Franks divided the booty, Clovis, though still a pagan, was careful to please the Catholic bishop. He ordered the Franks to set aside the sacred vessels plundered from Christian churches. One such item was a precious ewer, probably used to pour wine into the Eucharistic chalice. The manner in which booty was usually divided can be seen in the many exhibits, in modern museums, of what is now known as "hack-silver." Exquisite late Roman silverware was summarily chopped into equal squares, so that the war-band should draw equal amounts of silver, in small pieces, as dividends at the end of a raid. Such careful hacking implied a strictly egalitarian code, appropriate to violent young men. Not surprisingly, a warrior objected to Clovis' high-handed suggestion that he reduce the pool of precious metals available to his companions, by setting aside Christian plate:

> [he] raised his battle-axe and struck the ewer: "You shall have none of the booty," he said, "except your fair share."

A little later, Clovis made the man stoop, on parade, to pick up his axe.

> King Clovis raised his own battle-axe in the air and split his skull with it. "This is what you did to my ewer at Soissons."

It was a sharp lesson in the new prerogatives of royalty.[37]

At the same time, Clovis may have issued, in Latin, a law code for his Franks. The *Lex Salica*, the *Laws of the Salian Franks*, took the paganism of the Frankish inhabitants of the Rhine estuary for granted. It protected with special penalties the great gelded boars who had been set apart for sacrificial banquets: for boars were the bristling, magical guarantors of the waving growth of the cornfields. The law was particularly concerned to regulate the legal status of humble Frankish farmers over against the neighboring *Romani*. As *Franci* (perhaps from *Frekkr*, "the fierce ones"), weapon-bearing Franks, even the poorest, could stand high in Gaul. But they were told all this in a Latin text, issued by a king who used Latin advisers. Clovis intended to rule Romans and Franks alike as firmly as had any *Romanus*.[38]

By the end of his life, in 511, Clovis had altered the entire nature of Frankish kingship. He eliminated a confederation of Frankish "royal" chieftains, and ensured that the kingship was held by his own Merovingian family alone. Later generations of Franks relished the violence and cunning that went with every move of Clovis' rise to dominance. To take one example: Clovis bought out the war-band of Ragnachar of Cambrai with arm-bands of fake gold:

> This is the sort of gold [he replied, when they discovered the trick] which a man can expect when he has lured his lord to his death.[39]

In old age, he wished to finish the job:

> he is said to have made the following remark about the relatives he had destroyed. "How sad a thing it is that I live as a stranger like some solitary pilgrim, and that I have none of my own relatives left to help me when disaster threatens." He said this, not because he grieved for their deaths, but because in his cunning way he hoped to find some relatives still alive whom he could kill.[40]

Forceful kingship on such a scale required some change, or, at least, some novel elaboration of traditional worship to do justice to the ambitious aims of the king. Old gods might be promoted or new gods introduced. The Christian god could be one such newcomer. The tradition initiated by Constantine's conversion to the Christian god would have been totally intelligible to any Germanic warrior. Decisive battles, preferably with hereditary enemies, were expected to be associated with a show of divine power. Yet Clovis moved slowly. He took a Christian wife from the Arian Burgundians, in around 490 – queen Chlothild. Yet he did not take the obvious further step of adopting Arian Christianity. He showed that he did not wish to join the "family of princes" formed by the barbarian rulers of the western Mediterranean. For most barbarians in western Europe, Arian Christianity was a truly cosmopolitan religion. A shared Arian faith, which was pointedly different from that of their Roman subjects, linked the Visigoths of Toulouse with the Vandals of Carthage and the Ostrogoths, now firmly established under their king Theodoric, at Ravenna.

Clovis may have sensed that he could hold out for yet more undivided loyalty on the part of his *Romani*. Elsewhere, to the south of the territories of the Franks, the continued, tacit segregation of "barbarians" from the Catholic civilian population, as *ex officio* Arians and military men, echoed the highly compartmented structures of the late Roman state. These structures had survived in more settled provinces; but they were out of date in a northern Gaul where the distinction between soldier and civilian had been eroded. There was no reason why all the inhabitants of a region should not share the same religion, and, even less, why a ruler should be excluded, as a heretic, from the faith of his subjects.

Troubled by the rise of the new power of the Franks in northern Gaul, the Arian Visigoths of southern Gaul were prepared to do everything, barring an official conversion to Catholicism, to enlist the whole-hearted loyalty of their own Catholic subjects. In 506, the Visigothic king, Alaric II, issued an abbreviation of the *Theodosian Code* – the *Breviarium Alaricianum*. It bore his own name. It was ratified by Roman provincial aristocrats and by Catholic bishops. In the same year, although an Arian, he summoned the Catholic bishops to Agde, for the first kingdom-wide council of the Catholic Church ever to be held in Gaul. The bishops were delighted:

> and then, with our knees bent to the ground, we prayed for the kingdom [of Alaric] . . . so that the Lord might expand the realm of him who had permitted us the opportunity to meet.[41]

For Clovis, it was now or never. Such loyalty shown to an Arian ruler by grateful Catholic bishops, if once consolidated within the Visigothic king-

dom, would have blocked forever the road to the south. Now was the time
to turn south against Alaric II. In 507, he deliberately sought an oracle from
the Catholic shrine of Saint Martin at Tours:

> He loaded [his messengers] with gifts to offer to the church . . . "Lord
> God," said he,"if you are on my side . . . deign to show me a propitious
> sign as these men enter the church, so that I may know that you will
> support your servant Clovis." . . . As they entered the church, it hap-
> pened that the chanter was just beginning to intone the antiphon: *For
> thou hast girded me with strength unto battle; thou hast subdued under
> me those who rose up against me* [Psalm 18:39].[42]

The warlike verse was blessing enough for the coming campaign. Clovis'
invasion of the Visigothic south came to be seen only in retrospect as an anti
Arian crusade by a Catholic king. At the time it may not have had a strong
religious tone. It was a show of force, ostensibly intended to collect arrears
in tribute. Its real purpose may have been to test the loyalty to the Visigoths
of the southern *Romani*. In that case, Clovis was mistaken. Far from welcoming the Franks, the Catholic nobility of the Auvergne, including the sons
of Sidonius Apollinaris, turned out in force to support the Arian Visigoths
against these fierce interlopers from the north. But Clovis beat them all the
same. A entire southern society, Catholics and Arians alike – along with
their king, Alaric II – died together, at the fateful battle at Vouillé (or, possibly, at Voulon), south of Poitiers, in the early summer of 507.[43]

Clovis knew how to celebrate his triumph in a suitably Roman and Catholic style. On Christmas Day 508, he was baptized with his entire army by
Remigius, Catholic bishop of Rheims.[44] A force of up to 3,000 men, these
soldiers were the effective "people of the Franks." Many of them may have
been renegade Romans. They had fought in the south. They had wider horizons than did the boar-sacrificing peasants of their northern homeland. They
were easily persuaded to follow their king. It was a memorable occasion.

> The public squares were draped with colored cloths, the church was
> adorned with white hangings, the baptistery was prepared, incense gave
> off clouds of perfume, sweet-smelling candelabra gleamed bright, and
> the holy place was filled with divine fragrances . . . [all those present]
> imagined themselves transported to some perfumed paradise.[45]

On the return from his defeat of the Visigoths, Clovis had brought part of
the spoils of war to the altar of Saint Martin at Tours. There he was met by
ambassadors from the eastern emperor, Anastasius, who saw in this northern upstart a counterweight to the Ostrogothic, Arian rulers of Italy. He sent

to Clovis scrolls of appointment as an honorary consul. Like the great imperial generals of an earlier age, Clovis rode on horseback from the basilica
into the city, scattering gold coins. Some even remembered that he had been
acclaimed as an "Augustus."[46]

Kingdoms without Rome: North Africa and Axum

Although the Frankish kingdom is the best-known to modern Europeans, it
was not the only Christian state to emerge along the edges of the Roman
world in this period. Far to the south, in what is now Morocco and western
Algeria, Moorish chieftains of the High Atlas absorbed the Roman cities of
the plains. They emerged as common "kings of the Moorish and Roman
peoples." The symbiosis of Berber warrior highlanders with Latin-speaking
townsfolk ended only with the arrival of Islam. A Roman-style town council, recorded in Latin inscriptions, survived at Volubilis, near the Atlantic
coast of Morocco, up to the 650s. Moorish kings adopted Latin names. The
Berber ruler who held the Arab armies at bay in the late seventh century bore
the name Caecilius, a common Latin name in Africa, once borne by none
other than Saint Cyprian! Through their influence, knowledge of Christianity penetrated the oases of the deep Sahara, so that, in the Touareg language,
the word for any sacrifice, *tafaske*, was derived from the Christian high festival of Pascha/Easter.[47]

A similar development also occurred at the southern end of the Red Sea,
where the trade of the entire Indian Ocean came within easy reach of Alexandria. The warrior kingdom of Axum straddled the straits of Bab el Mandeb.
This kingdom joined the highlands of northern Ethiopia (a formidable reservoir of warlike tribes) to the Yemen. The Yemen was a wealthy region at the
southwestern tip of Arabia. It was famous for its buildings and its lush, green
terraces, maintained by sophisticated irrigation works.

The kingdom of Axum was the forerunner of the later Christian kingdom
of Ethiopia. It was a remarkable echo, at the far end of the Red Sea and on
the edge of Africa, of Constantine's Christian empire. Due to their contacts
with the Roman empire, through Alexandria, the rulers of Axum had long
identified Christianity with strong kingship. Since the reigns of Constantine
and Constantius II, the solid coins of Axum, minted from local gold, had
borne the sign of the Cross. Whatever the religion of the majority of the
population, Christianity was very much the religion of the court. It was espoused by conquering overlords, whose campaigns, ranging as they did from
Aden to the Blue Nile, were as vigorous as any undertaken by Clovis. They
celebrated their conquests in inscriptions placed upon stupendous granite

stelae, higher than any Egyptian obelisks, and with memorial thrones, set up in the mountain redoubt of Axum, at a distance from the Red Sea coast.[48] Ella Atsbeha (ca.519–ca.531) was a younger contemporary of Clovis. His inscriptions, and those of his successors, echo the same warlike verses of the Psalms as were heard by the messengers of Clovis when they first entered the basilica of Saint Martin at Tours.

> The Lord strong and brave, the Lord mighty in battle . . . in Whom I believe, who has given me a strong kingdom . . . I trust myself to Christ so that all my enterprises may succeed.[49]

"This latter-day Israel": A New History for New Kingdoms

What is remarkable about the Christian kingdoms which emerged along the periphery of the former Roman empire is that, despite extensive borrowings from local Roman practice and occasional diplomatic relations with the court of Constantinople, they did not wish to see themselves exclusively as miniature Romes. Because they were Christian, they could also claim to belong to a history without Rome. They could look past the Roman empire to the Old Testament. The *Kebra Nagast, The Glory of the Kings* (the foundation legend of the medieval empire of Ethiopia, whose nucleus may go back to the age of Ella Atsbeha) treated the East Roman emperors as no more than accommodating northern partners of an Ethiopian imperial dynasty, which claimed to be descended from Menelik, the son of Solomon and the Queen of Sheba.[50]

We know of the rise of Clovis principally from the account of Gregory, the Catholic bishop of Tours. Gregory's account of Clovis advanced no such ambitious claims for the Franks as we find for the kings of Ethiopia in the *Kebra Nagast*. But when he wrote his *Book of History*, in the 580s – a full 70 years, that is, after the events he described – it is surprising how little attention he paid to Clovis' relations with the East Roman emperors. Instead, Gregory placed great emphasis on Clovis' supposed hatred of Arian heretics. He also recorded, without a hint of moral condemnation, the king's unsavory rise to power among the Franks. For Gregory, the Catholic bishop, the career of Clovis was a career worthy of an Old Testament hero. For Clovis resembled, not a Roman emperor, but, rather, the morally flawed but energetic and warlike king David. It was better to be remembered as resembling a king of the long-past ancient Israel than as having once been courted as an ally by the existing East Roman empire.[51]

When, in 520 or later, the British cleric, Gildas, wrote the only surviving description of his war-torn island, his *On the Ruin of Britain*, he also saw the Romans as strangers to his story. For him, what mattered were his "fellow-citizens," the Britons. And he wrote of the Britons as "a latter-day Israel." Like Israel, they were an erring people, and Gildas was their Jeremiah, threatening divine punishment for their sins at the hands of foreign nations, especially the Saxons.[52]

As a sinning Israel, Britain now had a history of its own. The Romans, for Gildas, were no more than the "worthy allies" of the ever-fickle Britons. They were admirable and orderly, but essentially foreigners. Gildas identified the Romans almost exclusively with their army. They were now gone forever, leaving mighty walls across the island as a testimony to their military genius.[53]

Gildas is so fascinating an author for us because he wrote a highly intricate Latin and may have lived in a part of Britain where Roman traditions still lingered tenaciously, despite the collapse of many recognizably "Roman" economic and social structures. His scathing pamphlet *On the Ruin of Britain* represented the victory of a "textual community" of readers of Latin over the cramped circumstances in which actual "Romans" now lived in early sixth-century Britain. He wrote a vigorous Latin intended to be read by small enclaves of learned Christians scattered all over Britain. As a Christian writer, Gildas evidently felt that the Old Testament did better justice to his stormy times than did fading memories of a Roman empire.

His older compatriot, Patricius, showed the same decisive change of perspective. Patricius' Latin was not simply "failed" Latin. It was a different Latin – a Latin modelled deliberately and with great skill on the alien, Hebrew cadences of current Latin translations of the Old Testament.[54]

Altogether, we are dealing with a subtle but decisive change. From Hadrian's Wall to the Atlantic coast of Morocco and the Horn of Africa, the idea of Rome had shrunk to ever smaller dimensions. Rome and its history were no longer central to the imagination of the inhabitants of the former periphery of the empire. A sense of the Roman past was replaced by a different past – the past of the Old Testament. This past was brought close through the Holy Scriptures. It described, vividly and appositely, the turbulent warrior kingdom of ancient Israel. It was a past better suited to the stormy present than were memories of imperial Rome.

With the emergence of such distinctive authors and religious leaders as Gildas and Patricius in the far north, and with the emergence of the kingdom of the Franks in northern Gaul and along the Rhine, we have entered a new age. As we shall see in the next three chapters, the Christian regions of the Mediterranean world – Spain, southern Gaul, Italy, and the Eastern empire –

maintained and transformed legacies which they had inherited directly from Roman times. Further to the north, however, a significant break had occurred. A new world, with a new sense of the past, had come into being along the middle ground which had developed through the joining of Roman and barbarian regions along what had once been the northwest frontier of the Roman world.

Part II
Divergent Legacies
A.D. 500–600

Map 4 Western Europe, excluding the British Isles

CHAPTER 6

Reverentia, rusticitas: Caesarius of Arles to Gregory of Tours

The Battle for the *Mundus*: The Natural World between Paganism and Christianity

On February 15, 495, despite previous warning from the pope, a group of Roman senators made sure that the annual purifying ceremony of the *Lupercalia* was performed at Rome. Once again, naked youths dashed through Rome, as they had done since archaic times. What shocked the pope was that the senators concerned were not pagans. They were good "sons of the Church." But they were public figures. They knew what Rome needed after an anxious year of epidemics and bad harvests: in their rowdy runaround, the "Young Wolves" – the *Luperci* – would cleanse the city in preparation for another year. In the city with the longest Christian tradition in the Latin West, collective memory still looked back to the world of Romulus and Remus.[1]

Even if the gods and their ceremonies were banished from the city, they still hung above it in the heavens. We must remember that late antique persons, Christian as well as pagan, did not look up into an empty sky. The *mundus*, the physical universe as a whole, remained filled with numinous powers. To look up at the stars was to see "heavenly bodies" in the true sense. The stars were the radiant "bodies" of the gods. And the Sun was the most radiant of all. Sheathed in glory, the Sun demanded respect. In 440, pope Leo was shocked to learn that, when they reached the top of the flight of steps that led up to the shrine of Saint Peter, many good Catholic Christians would turn their backs to the saint's basilica, to bow, with a reverential gesture, toward the rising sun.[2]

In many ways, Rome was exceptional. Even after they had become Christian, the senators of Rome remained fiercely loyal to the memories of their city. They continued to treat Rome as a gigantic "theme park" of the pre-

Christian, Roman past.[3] But the problems faced by the bishops of Rome were not unique. All over the Mediterranean world, the cities and the rural landscapes were thought of as nestling in the embrace of a natural world that was heavy with religious meaning. The natural world, the *mundus*, was shot through with unseen powers who had yet to take on Christian faces.

This then was the situation which confronted Christian preachers in the fifth and sixth centuries. The Christian Church had emerged, by A.D. 500, as the sole public religion of the Roman world. Paganism had been officially abolished. But the real battle with paganism in western Europe had only begun. For this battle was not fought out with the old gods of Rome in their clearly recognizable, classical form – with statues, temples, and ceremonies. It was, rather, a battle for the imaginative control of the *mundus*. The natural world, from the highest heavens to the humble earth in the fields, had to be "demystified," because only when "demystified" in this way could the natural world be filled up again, but now with Christian figures, most especially with the figures of the Christian saints.

In Italy, Gaul, and Spain, Christianity had established itself only on the fringes of what remained a dauntingly wide world. Christianity had risen to prominence as a religion of the Roman towns.[4] In the course of the fifth and sixth centuries, it came to penetrate the countryside. But what we call "the winning of the countryside" was a piecemeal matter. It was due to a variety of potentially conflicting initiatives. It should not be seen exclusively as a spreading outward of Christian belief and Christian organization, from the cities into the countryside, conducted under the aegis of urban bishops and clergy.

The bishops, certainly, played their part in the Christianization of the countryside. By 573, for example, the bishops of Tours, in Gaul, had placed some 24 churches in villages in the Touraine.[5] But the bishops were not the only persons responsible for bringing churches to the peasantry. All over Europe, from southern Italy to Portugal, great landowners began to set up chapels, monasteries, even substantial basilicas on their estates. Modern archaeology has revealed remarkable examples of a transplantation of Christianity from the cities into the countryside by this means.[6] The history of the rural church is often the last act in the long history of the Roman *villa*. As with the Roman *villa*, the implantation of a church had economic and social effects. Local markets had always taken place at pagan country shrines on the estates of landowners. Now these shrines were replaced by a church. This was a time when local markets had become more important. The breakdown of wider trading networks made each region more dependent on its own, short-distance exchanges, which took place at rural markets marked by these new churches. The spread of Christianity in the countryside of western Europe is linked to processes of which we still know little – to the redistribution of trade and of patterns of settlement in a post-imperial age.[7] In wilder areas of forest and mountain, Christianity had come first, not from the cities, but from local monasteries and hermits.[8]

By the year A.D. 550, therefore, Christianity was present all over the countryside. But what was far from certain was what kind of Christianity this would be. The bishops of the city were seldom faced with stubborn rural paganism. Rather, they were faced with varieties of "home-grown" Christianity, which constantly threatened to slip beyond their control. The principal concern of articulate bishops in the sixth century was not how to suppress paganism. It was how to impose a "correct" interpretation on a bewildering range of religious practices, most of which claimed to be "Christian." This was a major task, for western Europe was a profoundly rural society. It lived from the land. The natural world absorbed the energies of over 90 percent of the inhabitants of every region, as farmers and as pastoralists. They depended every year on the erratic fortunes of the weather and on the harvest. For such persons, the natural world was far from being a neutral space, as it is to us today. The stars and the planets still spoke of the ancient gods. The lower reaches of the universe were filled with angels and with demons. The clouds, in particular, were thought of as a perpetual zone of combat between demonic and angelic powers. In an agrarian world, human existence depended on the outcome of unseen struggles in the upper air. The power of the demons might be revealed, at any time, in the crash of thunder and in the violent hailstorms which scythed the vines and battered the crops.[9]

It was not enough to have placed a single, exclusive God at the head of the *mundus*. Nor was it enough, even, to have brought that God down to the lowest level of the universe, to move as a human being among other human beings in the person of Jesus Christ, in a manner which Christian theologians of the fourth, fifth, and sixth centuries struggled so hard and for so long to express (as we saw in chapter 4). Christianity had to make sense to populations who had always thought of themselves as embedded in the natural world, and who had always expected to be able to impinge upon that world, so as to elicit its generosity and to ward off its perils, by means of rites which reached back, in most parts of Europe, to prehistoric times.

Triumph or Bad Habits: Narratives of Christianization in East and West

We should not underestimate the sheer range and complexity of the preexistent sacred landscape against which the Christian churches came to perch in western Europe. Remains of Roman paganism littered the countryside from Britain to southern Italy.

Deserted temples with their time-worn idols still stood out as foreboding, uncanny presences: "stark as ever . . . outlines still ugly, faces still grim."[10] Pagan worship had been officially forbidden since the end of the fourth century. Nonetheless, shrines remained active in many remote regions all over the West. As late as the 690s, in parts of Spain, votive offerings were still being made to idols. Springs, crossroads and hill-tops continued to receive little piles of ex-votos. Trees continued to be draped with votive pieces of cloth.[11]

Each region had its own sacred landscape. Physical features, trees, and animals were bathed in imaginative associations which still owed nothing to Christianity. In Gaul, for instance, holiness still oozed from the earth. Even today, the region has some 6,000 holy springs.[12] At the other end of the Mediterranean, in Egypt, we find a similar situation. The spectacular rise of the Christian Church at the expense of the pagan temples merely distracted attention from the humble day-to-day relation between humans and the sacred along the valley of the Nile.[13] In that area, little had changed. In Egypt, the animal world retained its numinous association with the gods. Once a raven alighted on a wall beside a group of Christian laymen, who had come to consult the great Christian abbot, Shenoute of Atripe (385–466). They instinctively turned to greet the bird: "Have you good news in your beak, raven?" For the raven was a prophetic bird. To lay Christians in fifth-century Egypt, the raven, with its prophetic cawing, meant as much as did the exhortations of a great Christian abbot.[14] To Shenoute, the prospect seemed endless:

> Even if I take away all your household idols, am I able to cover up the sun? Should I build walls all along the West [the Egyptian *Amente*, the land of the gods and the dead], so that you do not pray towards the sunset? Shall I stand watch on the banks of the Nile, and in every lagoon, lest you make libations on its waters?[15]

Different Christian regions faced the situation in very different ways. The Christians of the Greek East tended to see their world in terms of the triumphant narrative which had emerged in the age of Constantine. As we saw in chapter 3, they tended to treat the present as a bright new age. They were "Christian times." The power of Christ on earth had brought about a mighty transformation. Christian writers pointed out that Christian holy men now perched on mountains once sacred to the gods; that Christian churches rose triumphantly from the foundations of levelled temples; and that the names of the gods were forgotten, while those of the saints and martyrs were on everyone's lips.[16] Even when churches were not built directly on top of temples, they were still spoken of, in self-confident inscriptions, as if they had been.

> The dwelling place of demons has become a house of God.
> The saving light has come to shine, where shadows covered all.
> Where sacrifices once took place and idols stood, angelic choirs now dance.
> Where God was angered once, now God is made content.[17]

The sense of a pagan past which had been irrevocably defeated led to a certain tolerance of legacies from the classical world. Pagan monuments had lost their power to disturb Christians. To take a small example: the statues of Augustus and Livia continued to stand in the civic center of Ephesus, but they now had the sign of the Cross discreetly carved on their foreheads. Thus "baptized" in retrospect, they looked down serenely on the Christian bishops assembled by Theodosius II – a most orthodox ruler, but also the direct successor of Augustus – at the momentous Council of Ephesus of 431.[18]

This did not mean, in fact, that many regions of the Eastern empire were Christianized any more rapidly than were those of the West. The Greek intelligentsia continued to include distinguished pagans: Christians called them "Hellenes." They were the proud upholders of the culture and the gods of the Greeks. Athens remained a university city, in which known "Hellenes" taught Christians with full public support until A.D. 529.[19] Nor was the countryside entirely Christianized. Perched at a safe distance from major cities, in the prosperous mountain valleys of Anatolia, Lebanon, and northern Mesopotamia, pagan villages looked down, largely untroubled, on the disciplined plains, where the new religion had been declared to have triumphed – at least, officially.[20] Yet Eastern Christians were undisturbed by the existence in their midst of considerable pockets of paganism. The fact that they lived in a successful and stridently Christian empire was enough to persuade them that theirs was a basically Christian world.

In Western Europe, by contrast, different attitudes prevailed. The collapse of the Roman empire in the West seriously weakened the Constantinian myth of a Christian empire, whose manifest destiny had been to banish all paganism from the face of the earth. The rulers of the barbarian kingdoms were sincere Christians. They maintained and reissued the laws of the Christian emperors against paganism in every form.[21] But they ruled an increasingly localized society, in which the power of the state was weak. As a result, the burden of making the world appear Christian fell on the shoulders of the local bishops and their clergy. City by city, region by region, it was conscientious bishops who set the pace in grappling with the pagan past. It was up to them to declare which practices were "pagan" and which were not, which should be abolished and which could be treated as innocent survivals, devoid of religious meaning.

We must remember that we are dealing with the history of a singularly silent process. All over Europe, local bishops and individual households made up their own minds about what to do with the pagan past. The Latin bishops whose views have come down to us (largely because their writings were copied out and circulated) are interesting because they had one thing in common. They tended to take their cue from the more inward-looking and pessimistic streak in the thought of Augustine of Hippo.

As we saw in chapter 3, Augustine's victory over the views of Pelagius ensured that the Catholic Church in the West would not think of itself as a body of "saints" – a Church made up of heroic converts who had totally abandoned their pagan past. Human beings were too weak for that ever to happen. Rather, each believer had to continue, even after conversion and baptism, to battle with the tenacity of evil customs within himself or herself. And these "evil customs" inevitably included parts of the pagan past. Telltale traces of habits picked up in a society which had only recently become Christian marked the behavior of many Christians. It was worse for educated persons. The gods continued to linger in their minds, for the Roman history and the Latin literature that they learned at school were saturated with mentions of a glorious pagan past.

In such a view, paganism could never be treated simply as a *superstitio*, as a bankrupt religious system which lay safely outside the Church. It had not been definitively overcome by the establishment of a Christian empire, as many Christians had believed in the triumphant mood of the fourth century. Rather, paganism was now seen to lie close to the heart of all baptized Christians. It was always ready to re-emerge in the form of "pagan survivals." Such "survivals" attracted attention. For they were treated as evidence of the force of evil habits at work within the Church itself. As a result of this somber view of the Church, the master narrative of Christianization, as it came to be propounded from henceforth in the Latin West, was not one of definitive triumph. It was, rather, one in which an untranscended pagan past perpetually shadowed the advancing footsteps of the Christian present.

"The unceasing voice": Caesarius, Bishop of Arles (502–542)

The Christian preacher who provided future generations with a classic statement of this distinctive mood was Caesarius, bishop of Arles from 502 to

542.[22] Caesarius was devoted to Augustine. He even died, reassuringly, on the same day of the year as had the great bishop of Hippo.[23] Caesarius adapted Augustine's own sermons, preached a century before at Carthage and Hippo, to the townsfolk of Arles and the peasants of Provence.

A conscientious bishop of the early sixth century, Caesarius set little store by originality. To copy the sermons of a great predecessor was simply to equip oneself with timeless skills against a timeless enemy. When it came to the Devil's long, sly siege of Christian souls, time stood still and distance did not matter. Sin and temptation did not change. What every preacher must learn were, as it were, the right chess-moves with which to check the eternal chess Grand Master, the Devil. These chess-moves did not vary from place to place or from time to time. They were always available in the form of standard admonitions to withstand particular temptations and to avoid particular practices. Hence there is nothing surprising in the fact that the sermons which Caesarius first copied from Augustine in Arles came to be copied out again, with equal zeal, three centuries later, to be applied in newly converted regions of central Germany (as we shall see in Chapter 18). The paganism of Germany might be different from that of Provence. But the Grand Master who stood behind it, the Devil, had remained the same.[24]

What Caesarius accomplished by his sermons was a pastoral *tour de force*. He domesticated the daunting immensity of the pre-Christian spiritual landscape of Provence. Paganism, for him, was not a set of independent practices, endowed still with the allure of a physical world shot through with mysterious, non-Christian powers. Rather, he presented paganism as no more than a fragmented collection of "survivals." It consisted of a set of "sacrilegious habits" and inert "evil customs."[25] In the words of a slightly later council of Gallic bishops, paganism was only so much "dirt from the gentiles" inadvertently tracked into the Church on the feet of heedless believers.[26] It was not a religious system in its own right. For Caesarius, the only paganism that mattered was the paganism which lingered within the Christian congregations.

Caesarius did not mince words on those who indulged in such practices. In Arles, he was remembered for his "unceasing voice" as a preacher. On one occasion, he even closed the doors of his basilica, lest members of his congregation walk out before the sermon. He told them that when they stood before God at the Last Judgment, they would not be free to leave the room![27] Beneath the deliberate simplicity of his preaching style, Caesarius was very much a Gallo-Roman noble and a product of the austere monastic discipline instilled at Lérins. He had a strong sense of belonging to an elite. Paganism was not only repugnant to him. He thought of it as culturally inferior to his own well-groomed version of Christianity. To fall back into pagan ways was, quite frankly, to show lack of grooming. It was to behave like *rustici*, like boorish peasants, who, being devoid of reason and unamenable to culture, were driven by brute passion alone.[28]

In Caesarius' opinion, one did not even have to be a pagan or a peasant to be a *rusticus*. Sophisticated urbanites were warned by him that failure to abide by the strict sexual codes upheld by their bishop betrayed *rusticitas*, lack of decorum. In bed anyone could behave like a *rusticus*. To make love on Sundays, or when one's wife was menstruating, was to act no better than a peasant; and the results, he pointed out, appealing to a grim medical tradition, were children such as would befit indecorous tumblings – deformed children, lepers, epileptics.[29] The pruning of *rusticitas* of every kind among baptized Christians, and not the eradication of paganism itself outside the Church, was the principal object of a bishop's pastoral care.

To prune *rusticitas* in this way meant that Caesarius had to challenge an entire mentality. He had to dethrone the ancient image of the world. In his preaching, the *mundus*, the physical universe, was drained of its autonomy. It had no life of its own apart from that given to it by the will of God.

Caesarius approached this problem from many directions. Time, for instance, was detached from nature. Time no longer registered the organic throb of the natural world, as this was shown in the changing of the seasons. Instead, Christian time registered the great acts of God in history. Christian festivals celebrated the moments when God had brushed aside the *mundus* to deal directly with mankind. Hence his particular aversion to the feast of the Kalends of January. It was not simply the folkloristic junketing which upset him. The feast of the Kalends set a pagan notion of the swaggering birth of the year (a notion deeply rooted in ideas of the seasonal renewal of nature) against the divine humility of Christ's birth at Christmas.[30] He fastened with the same precise awareness of their "pagan," cosmic message, on the names of the days of the week. Since imperial times, the days of the week had carried the names of the gods. They reminded humans of the gods who ruled the earth from their thrones on the ominous, unblinking orbs of the planets. Following Augustine, Caesarius urged Christians to count the days of the week from the Lord's Day, as *prima feria*, *secunda feria*. (This manner of naming the days has been adopted only in Portugal. Elsewhere, as we know, the names of the days of the week still echo the names of the gods. By Caesarius' high standards, Portugal must count as the only fully Christianized country in Europe!)[31]

Above all, human beings were denied the possibility of impinging on the workings of the *mundus* through their accustomed rituals. To think that human wills could intervene to change the course of nature in a material world where all events depended on the will of God, was, in the opinion of

Caesarius, the height of stupidity. During an eclipse of the moon, the citizens of Arles would join in, with loud hurrahs, to "help the moon in her distress." Shouts of *Vince luna*, "Up with the Moon," encouraged the bright neighbor of the human race to shake off the engulfing powers of darkness. To Caesarius, this was nonsense. The moon hung above Provence, untouched by such "sacrilegious sounds." It was as distant, as opaque to human hopes and as unaffected by human rituals, as it is to us today. Only its darkened face, at times of eclipse, might be read by Christians as a "sign," given by God to warn mankind. The sudden darkness that fell across the moon was the frown of his anger.[32]

It would be a long time (perhaps not until the death of peasant Europe itself in the course of the nineteenth century) before the mentalities denounced by Caesarius changed irrevocably. The mysterious intimacy of man and nature, established since prehistoric times, could not be broken by a few sermons. What we find, rather, are scattered hints that a slow process of compromise was at work in Arles as elsewhere. Many Christians attempted to find some "fit" between their present religious practices and the patterns of an earlier time.

In this slow process of adjustment, Christianity often held the initiative. The attention which Caesarius gave to paganism as, essentially, a set of inert "habits" which survived within his congregation, gives us a seriously incomplete image of the religious life of the time. We tend to think only in terms of "pagan survivals" within the Church. We do not often give attention to the adaptation, by non-Christians, of Christian rituals.[33] Yet non-Christians and Christians alike had remained intensely interested in exploring new ways of making contact with the *mundus* and the invisible powers within it. They needed these powers as much as they had before, and they were quite prepared, despite the disapproval of their bishop, to experiment with new combinations of rituals.

A lively process of the borrowing of rituals between pagans and Christians appears to have taken place in both directions. Pagan communities borrowed Christian signs and rites. The sign of the Cross would be made at sacrificial banquets. The names of Christian angels and saints would be shouted at the solemn toasts around the table.[34] Above all, monks and clergymen came to offer services which non-Christian ritual specialists had previously provided. Caesarius disapproved; but there was nothing strange in their behavior. Many members of the clergy must have come from former pagan priestly families. They had always enjoyed a reputation for possessing special knowledge of the supernatural. Now it was they who used special blessings, special oils, and special passages from the Christian Scriptures so as to make amulets and remedies for the faithful.[35]

Around Arles, Christianity even lent its own distinctive flavor to fundamental agrarian rites. For instance, the ceremony of the splashing of the
fields with sacred water, associated with seasonal lustration ceremonies, which
had fortified the harvest in the drought-prone climates of North Africa and
Provence, was postponed slightly, at this time, to coincide with the day of
the baptism of Christ in the Jordan. By this small change, the ancient powers
of water were reinforced by the vast new potency ascribed by Christians to
the rite of baptism.[36] Nor were all members of the clergy as inflexible in their
stance toward seasonal festivals as was Caesarius. In late sixth-century Spain,
an exuberant urban clergy were tempted to bless the fun: they were condemned by their bishops for chanting the Christian chant of *Alleluia* (the
quintessential cry of joy associated with the Easter liturgy of the Resurrection) at the feast of the Kalends of January, thereby adding a Christian note
to the euphoria of the birth of the new year.[37]

Reverentia: the Gaul of Gregory, Bishop of Tours (573–594)

It would require a measure of poetry, such as the plain-spoken Caesarius did
not possess, to bring about the imaginative Christianization of the *mundus*.
The spread of the Christian cult of the saints in the course of the sixth century did more to place a Christian face upon the natural world than did the
preaching of a man such as Caesarius. For the cult did not depend on the
"ceaseless voice" of a sermonizer. It aimed, rather, at creating tenacious religious habits that could be observed by all members of the population.

These religious habits focused on the notion of *reverentia*. By *reverentia*
sixth-century Latin Christians meant a reverential attention to the saints.
This attention was directed primarily to major urban shrines, which had
already become pilgrimage sites (as was the shrine of Saint Martin at Tours,
whose origins we saw in chapter 4). But it was also brought to bear at any
number of places and in all kinds of situation. *Reverentia* created "habits of
the heart." It assumed that the saints were still active and present on earth,
and that good and bad fortune depended on the manner in which they were
treated by their worshippers. Reverence of that kind – a readiness to see the
hand of the saints in day-to-day affairs – was the one sure answer to *rusticitas*.
The Christian saints dwelt in heaven, in the presence of God. But, when
approached with *reverentia* by those who prayed to them on earth, the saints
were expected to prevail on God to touch the *mundus* at every level. Their
interventions met the daily needs of believers. A sense of their presence in-
fused a natural world, in which people had always sought the sacred, with a

new quality. The saints brought to their shrines and to the landscape a touch of Paradise.

The man whose vivid and abundant writings were devoted to maintaining this view was Gregory, bishop of Tours from 573 to 594.[38] Born in 538 (a few years before the death of Caesarius), Georgius Florentius Gregorius came from a different region and from a very different generation from that of the bishop of Arles. Caesarius had been an old-world southerner. Roman emperors still ruled Provence when he was a child. Gregory's family, by contrast, came from further north, from Langres, Lyons, and the Auvergne. He had known no other rulers than the Frankish kings of the Merovingian dynasty. His elevation to the bishopric of Tours took him yet closer to the northern heartland of the Merovingian kingdom, to *Francia* proper.

Much had happened in western Europe between the days of Caesarius and the time when Gregory became bishop of Tours. As we shall see in chapter 7, the emperor Justinian (527–565) had attempted to put the clock back in the western Mediterranean. He reconquered all North Africa for the Roman empire and nearly conquered all of Italy. He eventually ruined the Roman social order in Italy by his failure. Worse yet, between 542 and 570, bubonic plague burned out the heart of the once formidable eastern Roman empire and emptied the coastline of the western Mediterranean. Further inland, in Gaul, the plague struck the southern provinces with which Gregory was most familiar. By the end of Gregory's life, power and, with it, cultural confidence had begun to tilt insensibly away from the Mediterranean and toward northwestern Europe.

Gregory was a loyal, if occasionally critical, subject of the Merovingian Frankish kings.[39] He expected them to be powerful defenders of the Catholic Church. He urged them not to waste their energies on unnecessary family feuds.[40] The Merovingian kingdom was not the Roman empire as the Roman empire had wished itself to be seen – a formidable, centralized, and bureaucratic state. But neither was it a society that had slipped into aimless barbarism. Rather, Gaul under Frankish rule was not all that different from what a provincial society had been like, in reality, in the last centuries of the Roman empire, once we take away the grandiose self-image with which the empire had invested its rule in the provinces. It was a confederation of regions. Each region was ruled, in a rough and ready manner, by its local aristocracies in the name of a distant court.[41]

What had changed was the texture of these aristocracies. They were no longer made up of civilians. Among the Franks, military men predominated. And the local "Romans" were quick to imitate their Frankish peers. The carrying of arms and the presence of armed retinues were features of everyday life, even within the walls of Christian churches. Violence was in the air.

But, as in any other "medieval" society dominated by a weapon-bearing nobility, violence was carefully rationed. It was controlled by calculations of political advantage[42] and by complex codes of honor.[43] The Gaul which Gregory surveyed was an untidy society. But it was by no means a society ruled by the law of the jungle.

For the Frankish kings had brought order to Gaul. The rise of Clovis and the establishment of a strong monarchy in the former territories of the Roman *limes* in northern Gaul and along the Rhine (which we described in chapter 5) brought stability to the entire province after the desperate uncertainties of the fifth century. Gaul had not gone the way of post-imperial Britain. A strong enough state emerged, around which the local aristocracies could rally. Gaul was safe. Its frontiers were protected. An *ancien régime* which had barely weathered the storms of the previous century settled back to regroup itself, within a "low-pressure" but stable political system.

Foreigners were quick to notice the stability of Gaul. In 566/7, the Italian poet Venantius Fortunatus came to *Francia* from Treviso (in the Veneto, just south of the Alps).[44] Educated in Ravenna, this ingenious Italian immediately presented himself as an Orpheus fallen among northern barbarians. He made much of his own self-image as a refined representative of southern grace among the harp-twanging *leudes,* the "strong men," of the Frankish court. This, of course, was a literary pose. In reality, Venantius was happy to become the client of persons who were as secure in their own, Roman culture as he was. As he sailed along the Moselle and visited great bishops in their country estates, travelling across Gaul all the way from Trier to Bordeaux, he could observe that a larger measure of old-world solidity existed in Gaul than in his native Italy.[45]

For within the lifetime of Gregory of Tours, the accustomed map of Europe had turned upside down. It was Fortunatus' Italy, and not Merovingian Gaul, that was "the sick man of Europe." Italy had been ravaged by incessant wars. It was in the grip of an economic depression which threatened, in many areas, to bring urban life to an end in what had once been the most heavily urbanized region of western Europe. Except for a thin strip along the coastline, Mediterranean commerce had withdrawn from the peninsula. By contrast, the under-urbanized, agrarian world of northern Gaul had not been subject to such violent dislocation.[46] In the regions which lay on the edge of Gregory's diocese, around Paris in the Seine valley and further to the north and east, toward the old *limes,* a new, non-Mediterranean economy had begun to enable the Frankish aristocracy and their Roman collaborators to accumulate wealth in a manner that would prove decisive for the future position of *Francia* in western Europe. Venantius Fortunatus had come to the right place at the right time. He soon became a friend of Gregory of

Tours. He was happy to end his life as bishop of Poitiers, dying a little after his friend, some time around A.D. 600.

Old "Roman" families had survived all over Gaul, from the Rhine to Aquitaine. In the course of the sixth century, they merged with the Franks to form a new class of *potentes*, of "men of power" of mixed Frankish and Roman descent. The lay members of this new aristocracy were united by a shared Catholicism and by a shared avarice. They were firmly in the saddle in every region. Those *potentes* who survived the occasional feuding frenzies of the great, as they circled around the courts of rival Merovingian brothers, could expect to thrive.

And in this new mixed nobility, made up of Frankish and Roman "men of power," none throve more than did the Gallic bishops. The 110 bishops of Gaul had changed over the years. From being the upholders of the morale of beleaguered Roman populations, in the dangerous fifth century, they had settled down to become crucial figures within the new Frankish kingdom. The local aristocracies needed them. They were constantly appealed to as arbiters, as peacemakers, and as diplomats. Each, in his own city, was law and order personified. This was not simply because many bishops had been aristocrats. They were sincerely looked up to as the "high priests" of their region. When consecrated, the bishop would be carried into his city on a high sedan chair, in a ceremony once reserved for Roman consuls. His actions as judge and peacemaker were thought to make real on earth the justice of God and of the saints. He was responsible for orchestrating the solemn ceremonies which brought down the blessing of God on the community as a whole.[47]

Whether they came from old "Roman" families (as Gregory did) or had risen to the top as royal servants, many of these bishops were fabulously rich. To take one example: Bishop Bertram of Le Mans was the bearer of a Frankish warrior name, "Glorious Raven," from the great bird which pecked at the bodies of the dead on the battlefield. Bertram's will shows that by the time he died he had amassed a private fortune of 300,000 hectares, scattered all over western Gaul.[48]

The bishops presided over the distributive system connected with almsgiving and with pious donations. In this capacity, they "redeemed" the wealth of the laity by turning it into spectacular shrines and buildings. In a society where personal display was of the greatest importance for Romans and Franks alike, the bishops were expected to demonstrate the importance of their Church by stunning displays of wealth.[49] In so doing, they performed nothing less than a kind of supernatural alchemy. In their hands, gold and precious objects were transformed. Flickering, flame-red gold, which stood in the imagination of Christian contemporaries for all that was most cruel, most labile, and, ultimately, most rigid and "dead" in this world, was "re-deemed" and brought alive by being offered to the sacred.[50]

The altar vessels and the great gold-encased and jewel-studded shrines which covered the bodies of the saints in Gaul spoke of a magical transfer effected by the bishop. By lavishing wealth on the saints, the bishop had sent "treasure" on to heaven to benefit the souls of the donors. And this "treasure in heaven" was reflected back to earth in shrines which shone like frozen drops of supernatural splendor. The shimmer of the tomb was a guarantee of the further "blaze" of miraculous power which a saint, especially if he had been a famous bishop, was expected to show from beyond the grave. The tomb of Saint Eligius (Saint Éloi), bishop of Noyon from 641 to 660, throbbed with such splendor that it had to be covered with a linen cloth during Lent, throughout which time it sweated with veiled miraculous power![51]

Merovingian Gaul was an intensely localized society. The bishop was identified with his city. Each city had its own galaxy of local saints. In the course of the sixth century, these cities changed. Many lost their Roman shape. They became, instead, ceremonial centers. Large areas in each city were kept by their bishops as carefully maintained oases of the holy in the midst of a profane and violent world. Bertram's Le Mans had 18 churches, Paris as many as 35. Cities were no longer enclosed, organized spaces, as Roman towns had been. Some cities, such as Paris, had "evaporated." Its principal residents had spilled out into the surrounding countryside. Paris was surrounded by a galaxy of shrines. Beyond the shrines lay the administrative villas and hunting lodges of a largely rural aristocracy. Yet even those towns which had lost their Roman shape remained "Roman" in that they acted as the center of their region. They were still dominated by the castle-like Roman walls of what had become the bishop's "inner city."[52]

Ever since early Christian times, the bishop was supposed to act as the "lover of the poor." But, in sixth-century Gaul, the bishop did not merely support the indigent. He poured wealth and energy into maintaining an entire urban community.[53] The image of the good Catholic bishop as a "father" of his city was formed in this period. It became what was, perhaps, the most long-lasting institutional ideal in Western Europe. It changed little until the very end of the *ancien régime*.

> With all his social grace and his appearance of worldliness, [he] fulfilled his duties as a bishop as though he had no other cares to distract him. He visited hospitals, gave alms generously but judiciously, attended to his clergy and religious houses. He found time for everything yet never seemed busy. His open house and generous table gave the impression of the residence of a governor. Yet in everything it was becoming to the Church.[54]

This could be the description of any Merovingian saint-bishop. It is, in fact, the great spiritual writer, Fénelon, acting as bishop of Cambrai, in 1711, as he is described in the *Memoirs* of Saint-Simon! The criteria for a good bishop had changed so little in a thousand years.

Gregory's World: *Reverentia*, Justice, and Peace

Gregory came from a group of families who had helped to build up such a world in Gaul. He was the great-grandson, the grandnephew, and the nephew of bishops. He grew up a grave child, surrounded by grave relatives. *Reverentia* for the saints was a family tradition. His father always carried a gold medallion full of relics round his neck: they protected him from "the violence of bandits, the dangers of floods, the threats of turbulent men, and attacks from swords."[55] Gregory himself made his first religious "remedy" as soon as he could read. A good Catholic boy, he alleviated his father's gout with a supernatural recipe described in the Book of Tobit. The *codex* of the Holy Scriptures, not the whispered, oral lore of *rustici*, was to be his guide. Not for him the fluid, homespun world of the magical healer, who "whispered chants, cast lots, tied amulets around the neck."[56]

Gregory made plain that he was no *rusticus*. When struck by frequent illnesses, he knew how to approach Saint Martin as a friend and as a great *patronus*, a stern protector. His hopes and fears had been molded over the years by the vast ceremoniousness which characterized the relation of late Roman clients to their patrons. In every eventuality, Saint Martin was his "patron" – his lord and protector: "I approached the tomb, I knelt on the pavement, I wept."[57]

Bishop of Tours by the age of 34, Gregory expected all Catholic Christians to show the same deep reverence for the saints as he did. It was, indeed, essential for his position as bishop that they should do so. Tours had all the disadvantages of being an "open city." It was a pilgrimage center which lay at a crucial crossing of the Loire, linking Frankish northern Gaul to "Roman" Aquitaine. Tours also lay at the joining point of rival kingdoms. In the 20 years of Gregory's episcopate, Tours wavered in and out of various kingdoms, ruled by conflicting members of the Merovingian dynasty. Gregory found himself being governed, in turn, from Metz, from Soissons, and from Burgundy. His diocese was ravaged by frequent punitive raids. At regular intervals, the basilica of Saint Martin was filled with high-placed persons, who had sought sanctuary at his tomb. As bishop of Tours and guardian of the shrine of Saint Martin, Gregory had the duty to protect and to intercede for many an unsavory character. He had a unique opportunity to watch the *potentes* of Gaul at their worst and at their most vulnerable. Dealing on a day-to-day basis with such persons was not calculated to increase his faith in human nature.

We must remember that it is from this viewpoint that Gregory wrote his *History.* He looked out on Gaul from the sanctuary of "his lord" Saint Martin. Though a friend and admirer of the elegant Venantius, he wrote in "rustic" Latin. But this was not so as to address peasants, nor because no one in Gaul was capable of doing anything better. Gregory deliberately chose to write a rough Latin for rough men. He wrote to warn the *potentes* of future ages, Frankish and Roman alike. For them, an unpolished Latin, well on the way to becoming French, was the language which they would have shared with Gregory and his clergy. It was in this language that they needed to be warned.

To call Gregory's book a *History of the Franks* is seriously misleading. Sin and retribution for sin, not ethnicity, was Gregory's all-consuming interest. In writing the history of his own times, Gregory ensured that the misfortunes of well-to-do sinners, Frankish and Roman alike, would be long remembered. He did not lack material: he describes, often in memorable detail, the violent deaths of some 30 politicians. He wrote of them because he was convinced, and needed to convince others, that those who came to a bad end did so because they had offended God and his saints. The Frankish general, Guntram Boso, for instance, died so stuck through with spears that he could not even keel over. Gregory knew why. Spasmodically pious, Guntram had also consulted a pagan prophetess. It had done him no good. Gregory made sure that contemporaries would remember Guntram for what he was:

> an unprincipled sort of man, greedy and avaricious, coveting beyond measure the goods of others, giving his word to all, keeping it to none.[58]

But Celsus, the Roman, was no better:

> a tall man, broad of shoulder, strong of arm, haughty in speech, quick in his reactions, and learned in law. He would often seize the possessions of the Church . . . One day in church he heard a passage being read from the prophet . . . *Woe unto them that join house to house, that lay field to field.* He is said to have replied: "This is a poor look out! Woe then to me and my children!"

He was right. His son died childless, "bequeathing the greater part of his possessions to the Church from which his father had stolen them."[59]

"A Touch of Paradise": Gregory and the Spiritual Landscape of Gaul

As the guardians of a moral order represented on earth by the bishops, the saints drew themselves up to their full height in the cities of Gaul. The world of Gregory's *History* is a largely urban world, which cried out for justice and peace. It was his duty as a bishop to provide this, and he was convinced that, in so doing, he was merely making plain, on earth, the intense sense of justice of his patron, Saint Martin. Yet Gregory also wrote further books of *Wonders* (of miracles). In them he described wonders at the tomb of Saint Martin and at the tomb of Saint Julian at Brioude. Further wonders made up the *Glory of the Confessors*, the *Glory of the Martyrs*, and a *Life of the Fathers*. He even wrote a treatise on the stars, which included a catalogue of the wonders of nature. These books of *Wonders* are as extensive as his *History*. Their sheer size and loving circumstantiality mark a new departure. It is as if Gregory had reached out with his pen to catch the infinitely varied spiritual landscape of his region in a fine web of Christian words.[60]

Gregory had good reason to write as he did. He was little concerned with the survival of paganism in Gaul.[61] But he was deeply worried by the ease with which alternative versions of Christianity sprang up whenever he and his Catholic colleagues relaxed their vigilance. Wandering preachers, bearing relics and claiming to represent none other than Saint Peter himself, had even had the impudence to visit Tours when he was absent![62] Prophetesses emerged in country districts. They attracted large crowds and gathered much wealth by claiming to be able to seek out thieves and to divine the hidden sins of others.[63] When bubonic plague struck Berry, in 571, the hermit Patroclus found himself faced by a formidable rival. A woman called Leubella claimed to have been visited "by the devil, falsely appearing to her as Saint Martin . . . He gave her objects which, so he said, would save the people."[64] Leubella's imagination was as filled with the figure of Saint Martin as was that of Gregory.

What Gregory confronted, in the countryside of Gaul, was not tenacious paganism, surviving unchanged in a peasant world which was untouched by the Catholicism of the cities. What he found, rather, was a world characterized, in city and country alike, by fertile religious experimentation. Christian rituals and Christian holy figures were adapted by local religious experts to serve the needs of persons who would have considered themselves to be good Christians. It was important, therefore, for Gregory, that reverence for the saints, in its correct Catholic forms, should be seen to touch every aspect of the countryside of Gaul. The saints, as Gregory understood them (and not as persons such as Leubella claimed to know them) must be seen to have been able to meet every local emergency, to account for every local legend, and to be associated with every beneficent manifestation of the sacred.[65]

To ensure this, Gregory worked and wrote ceaselessly. As a result, the natural world regained some of its magic. Nature, of course, was not presented by Gregory as throbbing with a numinous life of its own, independent of God. But the natural world was seen by him as if it were a heavy, silken veil. Its rustling surface betrayed the presence, hidden close behind it, of the saints of Gaul. For Gregory, a "relic" was a physical fragment, an enduring "trace" that had been, as it were, left behind in the material world by a fully redeemed person, a saint, who now dwelt in God's Paradise. A pious friend of Gregory's once told him how the water brought from the spring of a martyr's shrine changed into sweet-smelling balsam. Gregory was not surprised. "These are authentic relics, which the power of the martyr has picked out with a touch of Paradise."[66]

Paradise stood very close to a sixth-century Christian such as Gregory. It was no abstract heaven, but rather a place of superabundant vegetation, jewel-like in its radiance and bright color. Gregory reported how a nun had once had a vision of this Paradise:

> they came to a great spring. Its water shone like gold and the grass around
> it glowed as if with the sparkling light of myriad gems . . . "This is the
> well of living water, for which you have thirsted for so long."[67]

Relics brought Paradise into the present. The churches of sixth-century Gaul made this plain. It is a sadness, for the historian, that so many of the great Early Christian basilicas of the cities of modern France have long been replaced by Gothic cathedrals. As a result, Merovingian Gaul seems a more depleted place than it was in reality. At the time, however, one only had to enter any shrine which housed a relic of the saints to find oneself in "a fragment of Paradise."[68] Incessantly lit, at great expense, with oil lamps made fragrant with aromatic substances, the basilicas of the saints in Gaul stood out in a dark, violent, and malodorous world as places where Paradise could be found on earth.[69]

If we go to Italy, we can still see mosaics of the sixth century similar to those which could have been seen in the basilicas of Gaul. They showed the saints standing in Paradise, on a bright green earth, dotted with scarlet flowers. But at times, so Gregory thought, the very flowers of that Paradise might drop to earth. The priest of the shrine of Saint Julian at Brioude (a sanctuary greatly favored by Gregory and his family) once entered the sanctuary in the depths of November, to find the tomb of Julian and the floor around it strewn with gigantic red roses:

their fragrance was overpowering. These roses were so fresh that you might think that they had been cut at that very moment from living stems.[70]

To come to the tomb of a major saint, such as Saint Martin at Tours, was to breathe in a little of the healing air of Paradise. The fragrance of incense and of scented oil filled the sanctuary around Martin's tomb. But that fragrance was only a symbol of the real, healing breezes of Paradise which wafted from the tomb. To be healed at such a place was to experience a sudden flowering of the body. When he described cures performed at the tomb of Saint Martin, Gregory lingered, in gripping detail, as much on the physical rhythm of each cure as on its outcome. For the rhythm of the cure itself showed dried and ruined human flesh regaining the first, exuberant good health associated with Paradise and with the Garden of Eden. A withered hand changed: "like a sponge intensely soaking up liquid . . . the skin became red as a rose." "You might see his pale countenance become rose red." A child crippled by malnutrition "blossomed again."[71] He had been touched for a moment by the all-healing abundance of Paradise, from which Adam had been cast out and in which Saint Martin now lived.

It was important for Gregory that these experiences were not limited only to his own city and to the tomb of Saint Martin. His faith in the multitude of the saints and in the closeness of Paradise led him to embrace, in a single, untroubled vision, the countryside of Gaul. As we have seen, his experience as a bishop, responsible for the sanctuary of Saint Martin at Tours, had not led him to expect many saints among his average contemporaries, the well-to-do and the powerful of Merovingian Gaul. Our impression of the violence and instability of political life in Merovingian Gaul is due largely to the gusto with which Gregory recounted, in his *History*, the misfortunes of such people, as fitting punishments for their neglect of the saints.

By concentrating on such scenes of violence, as if they summed up all that we needed to know about Merovingian Gaul, we forget the other side of the story as Gregory tells it to us. Notorious sinners were not the only people whom Gregory chose to describe. Looking back on the long history of Christian Gaul, Gregory allowed optimism to prevail. Over the centuries, the Christian churches of Gaul had produced, and still produced, in his opinion, a number of persons, of both sexes and of every class, race, and region, who now lived in Paradise. Their relics were everywhere, scattered throughout the entire Christian world. In every region, there were specks of dust unlike all other specks of dust, fragments of bone unlike other fragments, tombs unlike other tombs. Some were already clearly visible: among the late Roman sarcophagi piled up in a ruined hill-top villa, one might be covered by a silk-embroidered veil, with a lamp burning before it – it was a tomb whose miraculous powers proved that it housed a holy person.[72] Other hints of the continued presence of the saints were more discreet. A fragment bound in a silken ribbon emerged unscathed from a bonfire.[73] Sweet voices could be heard singing among the dark lanes of tombs outside Autun.[74] An intermittent glow and a whiff of heavenly fragrance among the brambles of a deserted hilltop in Touraine betrayed the presence of a "place of Christians," long deserted and taken over by secondary forest after the raids of A.D. 406.[75] These unearthly events were intimations that innumerable holy men and women, dwellers of Paradise, stood ready, in all places, and even in the most out-of-the-way areas, to help Catholic worshipers in their everyday needs. They peopled a landscape that had once seemed opaque to Christianity.

Through these many saints, Paradise itself came to ooze into the world. Nature itself was redeemed. Because of his faith in the proximity of Paradise, Gregory allowed sacrality to seep back into the landscape of Gaul. The countryside found its voice again, to speak, in an ancient spiritual vernacular, of the presence of the saints. Water became holy again. The hoof-print of his donkey could be seen beside a healing spring, which Saint Martin had caused to gush from the earth at Nieul-les-Saintes.[76] Trees also regained some of their majesty. The tree that Martin had blessed beside the road at Neuillé-le-Lierre, in Touraine, was still standing, though now dead; for its bark had been entirely stripped away for medicinal remedies.[77] All over Gaul, great trees bloomed profusely over the graves of saints. Gregory looked on such trees with happy eyes. They no longer spoke to him of pagan rites - of bright rags fluttering from branches which drew their strength from the dark and questionable powers of the earth. Rather, they brought down from heaven to earth a touch of the unshackled, vegetable energy of God's own paradise. They showed that the soul of the holy person buried nearby "now flourishes like a palm-tree in God's paradise."[78]

Gregory's unflagging pace as a raconteur tends to lull us into believing that he has told us everything that we ever need to know about Frankish Gaul. This is not so. He was fiercely regional in his interests. He looked back, by preference, into the past of the small Roman towns of southern Gaul. He tells us very little about the spreading northern territories of the Frankish kingdom and nothing whatsoever about Britain and Ireland. He took for granted that he belonged to a wider, older Christendom, defined by Roman cities and their saints. He saw Tours as one Christian city among many, placed at the northwestern corner of a wider Christian world, which stretched southward as far as Volubilis, on the Atlantic coast of modern Morocco, and eastward, across Italy and North Africa, to the territories of the eastern empire, and, beyond the eastern empire, to Persian Mesopotamia and the Zagros mountains. Gregory still felt part of the international Christian culture of the Mediterranean and the Middle East with which we began this book, in the time of Bardaisan. What happened in distant Edessa, and even in Persia, was quite as important to him as what was happening in northern Gaul and in the Frankish Rhineland. By the time that Gregory died, in 594, however, the eastern Mediterranean and the Middle East world had undergone decisive changes. Let us, therefore, follow in our next chapter the destinies of the eastern Roman empire in the sixth century – a century dominated by the reign of the great emperor Justinian (from 527 to 565). Then (in chapters 8 and 11) we will return, once again, to the West, to deal with men who, although they were roughly the same age as Gregory of Tours, came from very different worlds from his own and left a very different imprint than he had done upon the Christianity of western Europe – to the Roman pope, Gregory the Great (540–604), and to the Irishman, Columbanus (540–615).

CHAPTER 7

Bishops, City, and Desert: East Rome

"To maintain good order": Bishops and their City in the Eastern Empire

In August 452, only ten months after the fateful Council of Chalcedon, Peter the Iberian, a former Georgian prince, was elected bishop of Maiouma, the harbor city of Gaza on the southern coast of Palestine. He was faced by a fervent congregation, which threatened to burn down the basilica, with himself inside, if he did not celebrate for them at once the Great Liturgy as their bishop. When he reached the solemn prayer of consecration and broke the sanctified bread of the Eucharist, blood gushed from the loaf and covered the entire altar. He turned, to see Christ at his side:

> Break the bread, bishop . . . I have done this for my glory, that everyone may know where the truth is and who are they who hold the orthodox faith.[1]

Peter, in fact, was an uncompromising opponent of the Council of Chalcedon. Not everyone (certainly not pope Leo!) would have considered him "orthodox." But both Chalcedonians and anti-Chalcedonians agreed that it was the duty of a bishop to act as the high priest of his city. The bishop's solemn celebration of the Eucharist at the Great Liturgy was a public rite which ensured God's favor for the entire community. The bishop's relations with his city were expressed by formal ceremonies. The text of the ceremony of a bishop's entry into his city has survived from the sixth century. On entering, the bishop blessed the chapel at the city gate by surrounding it with clouds of incense. Then he led his clergy, chanting supplications, through the city, where he would offer incense at the Tetrapylon – the four-columned monument which marked the center of the city. After celebrating

THE EASTERN EMPIRE ca. 500–ca. 650

	Symeon Stylites 390–459
	Severus of Antioch 465–538
	Barsanuphius of Gaza 470–547
	Justinian 527–565
	issues *Codex Justinianus* 529
	Nika Riot 532
	Building of Hagia Sophia 533
	issues *Digest* and *Institutes* 533
	Reconquers Africa 535
	Rome 535
	Ravenna 540
Plague 543–570	Khusro I Anoshirwan 530–579
	sacks Antioch 540
	Fifth Ecumenical Council:
	Condemnation of the Three
	Chapters 554
	Jacob Baradaeus sets up
	"Jacobite" church 543–578
Lombard invasion of Italy 568	
	Slav and Avar penetration of the
	Balkans 550+
	John of Ephesus 507–588
	John Moschus 560–634
	Leontius of Neapolis 570–650

the Great Liturgy in his cathedral church, he retired to his palace. There he received the town council and the representatives of the imperial government.[2]

The public rituals performed by the bishop and his clergy made the city holy. His presence as honorary chairman of the town council, assisted by the local notables, made it orderly. Quite as much as in the Gaul of Gregory of Tours, bishops of the eastern empire were public figures in their cities. As in Gaul, some were spectacularly rich. In A.D. 610, the patriarch of Alexandria had 8,000 pounds of gold in his church's treasure. He supported 7,500 indigent persons on his poor-roll (when Gallic bishops barely supported more than a hundred.) The trading fleets of the patriarch sailed from Alexandria to as far as Morocco and Cornwall.[3]

But the great patriarchs were an exception. Unlike Gaul and Spain, there were few landed aristocrats among the clergy. The average bishop in the East Roman empire was a careworn and humdrum person. He was a glorified town councillor. He owed his position to the manner in which he stood between his city and an imposing imperial administration. In the eastern empire, the imperial system created by Diocletian and Constantine had remained in place. Reaching from the Adriatic to Mesopotamia, the eastern empire covered an area almost as vast as the later Ottoman empire. Bishops in the eastern empire were cogs in the machine of a fiercely intrusive and centralized governmental system.

By A.D. 500 the Christian bishop and his clergy had been encouraged by the emperors to take over many of the duties which had once been performed, in classical times, by the town councils.[4] To be a clergyman gave one prestige in the city. One bishop complained that local notables wanted to buy their way into the clergy for no other reason than to be seen in public "in the robes of a clergyman."[5] The church had become the new avenue to local status and prestige.

The building of churches provided new opportunities for display. In the fifth and sixth centuries, the clergy were responsible for a wave of new building which changed the urban fabric of the cities of the Middle East. Archaeologists continue to be surprised by the number of large, new churches, paved with mosaic, that have been discovered all over the modern Balkans, Turkey, Syria, Israel, and Jordan. Many of these churches were placed in the center of the cities. Their floors were covered with exuberant mosaics containing inscriptions which praised the generosity, piety, and intelligence of the bishops and clergy who were their founders.[6] Even in relatively small villages in Syria and elsewhere, the clergy dedicated to the altars large pieces of silverware, each of which bore their own names and those of their family.[7] Church building on this scale signalled the definitive triumph of Christianity in the East Roman empire. Christianity no longer presented itself as a militant creed, locked in struggle with the religion and culture of a pagan world. In a Christian empire, Christianity was now thought to hold the high ground of an entire civilization. It was an age of synthesis, marked by great confidence that the ancient skills of classical Greece – rhetoric, poetry, history-writing, philosophy, and art – could be used to express the Christian message.[8]

On a more practical level, the imperial government used the clergy as its local watchdogs. Bishops were commanded to use "sacerdotal freedom" to report to the emperor governors guilty of graft or incompetence. Bishops validated the weights and measures used in the marketplace, and ensured that the city's walls were maintained.[9] It was they who represented the emperor to their cities. Imperial mandates were now read aloud to the local notables in the bishop's audience hall. They were then posted for the entire city to read in the porch outside the local church.[10] The bishop of Bostra "performed a service to his city" by building his own jail to house and feed criminals awaiting trial.[11] At times of crisis, bishops even blessed and discharged the catapults which lined the city's battlements – as did the bishop of Theodosiopolis (Erzerum, eastern Turkey), killing a Hunnish chieftain with a stone thrown from the catapult "of the church," named the "Saint Thomas."[12] Altogether, the bishops of the east were deeply identified with the defence and stability of their cities, and so with the fate of the empire:

> It is the duty of bishops [wrote the patriarch of Antioch to a subordinate] to cut short and restrain the unregulated movements of the mob . . . and to set themselves to maintain good order in the cities and to keep watch over the peaceful manners of those who are fed by their hand.[13]

Thus, the urban life of the largest political unit in the Mediterranean was firmly based on the conscientious mediocrity of its bishops. Contemporaries identified the coalescence of bishop and city as the keel which gave stability to the empire on the local level. But local politics were not everything. The Christian Church claimed to be universal and in possession of universal truths. The issue remained whether bishops, who were quite prepared to maintain law and order on the local level in their cities, could ever be persuaded to adopt a formula of belief which would make the Church as much a unity, from the doctrinal point of view, as the empire which protected it.

As we have seen in chapters 3 and 4, ever since the reign of Constantine, the achievement of doctrinal unity was held to be the *raison d'être* – indeed, the crowning achievement – of a Christian empire. But the passions aroused before and after the Council of Chalcedon had shown that this unity would be extremely difficult to achieve. It was not for lack of trying. Throughout the late fifth and sixth centuries, the imperial government was convinced that, given the right mixture of command and persuasion, a strong imperial line on Christian dogma would create a united, "orthodox" Church. This course of action failed. And it failed most blatantly during the reign of one of the most self-confident rulers ever produced in the Roman empire, the emperor Justinian (527–565). Justinian's defeat showed that the Christian empire was not, perhaps, as harmoniously united as the ideology of the time had led many public-spirited bishops to expect. East Roman society proved to be more complex, and to contain more poles of loyalty in matters of religion, than the emperors and their servants, the bishops, had reckoned with. In the long run, neither the East Roman state nor the cities through which it ruled proved to have sufficient coercive force or moral authority to impose religious unity.[14] It is important to see why this was so.

"The Church of Satan": Secular Traditions in the City

In the first place, the bishops had less moral authority than their official position in the cities might suggest, for the cities themselves were only partly Christian. In heading the cities, the bishops found themselves implicated in all that was most impenitently profane in East Roman society. The triumphal narratives of "instant" Christianization through victory over the gods left much of the past intact in the East Roman cities. All over the empire, the monumental decor of the cities remained standing. Statues of gods and of former pagan emperors could be seen on every street. In Oxyrhynchus, a minor city in Middle Egypt, for instance, a statue of the last pagan emperor, Julian the Apostate, was still standing. It had the reputation of descending from its pedestal at night, to stalk unwary passersby.[15]

Though now dominated by impressive Christian monuments, there was much in every East Roman city that spoke of forms of celebration and of attitudes to power and prosperity which owed nothing to Christianity. Theaters were still standing. One might now enter a theater through a gate on which the Cross had been placed over the traditional invocation of the *Tyché*, the numinous good fortune, of the city. But in the theater itself, little had changed. Clouds of incense still gave an air of mystical solemnity to the spectacular ballets of the pantomime dancers, whose miraculous leaps and sinuous gestures often took place against a backdrop of mythological friezes carved in stone. Such backdrops (like the theaters themselves) dated from classical times. They were already centuries old. Altogether, the theater stood out as a solid fragment of a very ancient past in the middle of the new Christian city.[16]

Those who attended the theater paid little attention to the warnings of their clergy: "I do not go that I may believe, but I go that I may laugh. It is a game; it is not paganism."[17] Even in the long-Christian city of Edessa, the arrival of a troupe of Greek dancers was a major event:

> there came round again the time of that festival at which the heathen tales were sung; and the citizens took even more pains about it than usual. Lamps were lighted [before the dancers], and they were burning incense and holding vigils the whole night, walking about the city and

praising the dancers until morning, with singing and shouting and lewd behavior . . . they neglected also to go to prayer [and] . . . they mocked at the modesty of their fathers, who, quoth they, "did not know how to do things as we do."[18]

The bishop often found himself responsible for the maintenance of such shows. At the end of the sixth century, the patriarch of Antioch returned from Constantinople with a troop of pantomime dancers and with government funds to rebuild the Hippodrome. His enemies accused him of rebuilding "the Church of Satan."[19] But, although he was a bishop, he had acted as a conscientious public figure. He reintroduced the pantomime so as to keep the population of his city happy in times of distress.

For each city still needed its "Church of Satan." The Hippodrome (the place of chariot races) was crucial to the youth culture of the East Roman cities. And in the fifth century, this youth culture changed, with dramatic consequences. Young men – and especially the privileged sons of the civic elites – had always supported competitive activities in their cities. Now this competition became both more clear-cut and more uniform throughout the empire. Each city came to be officially divided between two principal "factions" – the "Blues" and the "Greens." These groups were encouraged to vie with each other in supporting rival performers of all kinds in the theater and in the Hippodrome. The competition was particularly fierce between the rival teams of "Blue" and "Green" charioteers. The frequent bloody clashes between rival gangs of supporters of each faction were tolerated because the shows themselves had taken on an imperial tone. They took place to celebrate the city's loyalty to the emperor. Even the rivalries of the factions contributed to this atmosphere of strident loyalism. For the competition of the factions ensured that, in all cities, all heads remained turned toward the emperor and his representatives. Gathered in their separate benches in the hippodromes and theaters of all great cities, assembled at the center of the city or at the city's gates on state occasions, the young men of the "Blues" and the "Greens" actively competed to show their enthusiasm for the distant emperor. They would strive to outdo each other in chanting loyal acclamations for the emperor and in denouncing his enemies.[20]

These factions were utterly profane and unusually inclusive. As young men of the "Blue" or "Green" factions, religious outsiders, such as Jews, had exactly the same rights as did "orthodox" Christians. All had a place on the benches of their local hippodrome. And what was celebrated, in the chariot races, was, quite frankly, *Tyché*, Lady Luck. The Hippodrome was both a public Wheel of Fortune and a public Victory Parade. It celebrated the heroic skills of the charioteers, who turned blind fortune into victory, as they whirled at headlong speed around the racecourse. The popular imagination linked these triumphs on the racecourse to the eventual triumphs of the empire itself. Everyone was involved, from the emperor downwards. It was from the imperial box at the head of the gigantic Hippodrome of Constantinople that the emperor met "his" people. And he did so by sharing the same passions as themselves. He also was the supporter of a faction. Hence, although the Hippodrome was denounced by Christian writers as the "Church of Satan," it stood for a mystique of empire which reached back deep into the Roman past. In the hard-driving East Roman state of the sixth century, good fortune and victory had remained the stuff of life in a "Roman" empire.[21]

"Sustained by their prayers": Asceticism and Society in the Eastern Empire

Hence a paradox of East Roman society. In the West, the bishops felt increasingly secure in their control of the surviving towns. They tended to look out from these oases of carefully maintained Christian propriety to confront a spreading countryside where Christianity seemed less securely rooted, and certainly less easy to control. In Syria and Egypt, by contrast, it could appear as if the cities, the centers of imperial government and the place of residence of most bishops, were enclaves of profane living in the midst of a population made up of God-fearing farmers. Along the Nile, villages that had once cohered around their pagan temples now found a new cohesion in their Christian clergy and a new identity in their fervent loyalty to the Monophysite patriarchs of Alexandria. It was through the activities of clergymen that Syriac and Coptic became major literary languages. Though both languages had deep roots in the pre-Christian past, they were identified with a triumphant Christian present. Coptic and Syriac still remained the liturgical languages of major local Churches in the Middle East.[22]

The agrarian society of northern Syria, around Antioch and Aleppo, was, indeed, new and thriving. Since the fourth century, expanding population had taken over marginal lands. By A.D. 500 northwestern Syria was a populous landscape, dotted with villages. The remarkable churches which were built by the villagers have survived to this day. Spectacular hoards of silverware have recently emerged from the area. They give an impression of the wealth which local landowners were prepared to lavish on local churches. An entire new Christian world had come into existence to one side of the cities.[23]

Prosperous and ostentatiously pious, the world of the countryside, in northern Syria and elsewhere, expressed its cohesion through great pilgrimages to spectacular holy men and to the monasteries associated with them. Thousands would stream out from the new villages, to gather every year at the shrine of Saint Symeon Stylites. Symeon was the first "column saint." (He derived his name from *stylos*, Greek for "column.") He had stood in prayer for some 30 years, until his death in 459, on top of a 60-foot column, on the edge of the limestone massif which still bears his name, the Jebel Sem'an. This massif lay within view of the main road which led from Antioch to the Euphrates. A new, dramatic form of Christianity had emerged, in a new Christian landscape, in the vital defensive zone between Antioch and the eastern frontier.[24]

It is important to explain the influence of persons such as Symeon Stylites in East Roman society. They drew their power from the fact that the most significant divide of all in the Christian imagination of the East Roman empire was not that between town and countryside. It was between the "desert" and the "world." This was a notional chasm. It separated two closely juxtaposed spaces: the "desert" was associated with the "angel-like" life of the ascetic, the "world" with the more hesitant Christian behavior of the *kosmikos*, of persons "in the world." Unlike the ascetics of "the desert," persons "in the world" were caught in obligations to society. For that reason, they were not free to give all of themselves to Christ. "Worldly" persons could be lay men and lay women. They could also be busy bishops and members of the clergy. Compared with this basic notional division between those of the "the desert" and those of "the world," all other divisions of the East Roman world – between town and country, between the urban bishop and his rural diocese, even between clergy and laity – seemed insignificant. The "world" as a whole was overshadowed by the presence of "angel-like" holy men associated with the "desert."

In this respect Eastern Christianity differed significantly from the West. In the West, a strong current of opinion, which went back to Augustine, expected that the triumphant grace of God would show itself within society, in the form of holy persons who were, more often than not, called to be leaders of the Catholic Church. Grace enabled such persons to "overcome the world." And they usually did this in the service of the Catholic Church, as bishops and clergymen. Holiness and ecclesiastical office tended to converge, to produce the sort of bishops whom we met in the world of Gregory of Tours – rulers of cities and the embodiment of law and order in Gaul and in other western regions.

This was not so in the East. In Syria and Egypt, and elsewhere in the territories of the Eastern empire, the Holy Spirit was thought to have raised up holy men and women in great numbers outside society, in the desert. Their authority came from the fact that they remained in the desert, to one side of the institutional structures of the Church. In Egypt and Syria, this "desert" was no impenetrable wilderness. It often lay within easy walking distance of towns and populous villages. By the sixth century, the country-side of Syria, Egypt, and Palestine – especially the Judaean desert outside Jerusalem – was flanked by impressive monasteries. These monasteries were characterized by solid buildings. They were miniature villages, often lying at the center of a ring of carefully constructed hermits' cells. Most were perched within sight of the settled world. There was nothing wild or make-shift about them, but they stood for "the desert" in sharp contrast to the "world."[25]

For only in the "desert" – that is, in a place to one side of settled life – could a few great ascetics bring back, through long penance and hard labor on their own bodies, a touch of the angelic glory which Adam had enjoyed in the Garden of Eden.[26]

Hence a significant difference between East and West. A western bishop, such as Gregory of Tours, tended to look for traces of Paradise among the holy dead. In the eastern Mediterranean, by contrast, living persons were thought capable of regaining Paradise on earth. In Egypt, farmers would run up to scoop the sand from the footprints of Apa Apollos, as he walked near his cell, on the edge of the desert. They would take this sand back to sprinkle on their fields in the valley below. The holiness of Apollos had turned the dead sand, the antithesis of the green valley of the Nile, into the richest earth of all – the earth of Eden.[27] It was the same in Syria. Clouds of heavenly incense regularly surrounded the column of Symeon the Younger (521–592), the precocious imitator of Symeon Stylites. At the age of seven, Symeon the Younger wandered off from Antioch to settle in the mountains near the city (the modern Samandağ – Symeon's Mountain, to the west of Antioch/Antakya). Symeon was believed to have played with mountain li-ons, calling them "kitty." Settled on a high mountain-top, yet still accessi-ble to pilgrims from Antioch and elsewhere, Symeon was believed to have brought back to earth, in his own lifetime, the sweet smell of Paradise, and a hint of Adam's innocent mastery of the animal kingdom.[28]

"Angelic" holy men did not abandon the world, in the sense of severing all relations with it. Rather, in the imagination of contemporaries, they trans-formed its wild edges. They ringed a careworn society with the shimmering hope of Paradise regained. They effected a symbolic exchange on a deep imaginative level. Having drained from themselves all hint of the dark pas-sions that ruled the world, they validated the world by constantly praying for it:

assistance flows from their bones to all creation.
Civilization, where lawlessness prevails,
is sustained by their prayers.
And the world, burdened by sin,
is preserved by their intercession.
The earth, heaving with controversy,
is upheld by them.
Troubled with speculation,
their vigil fills it with calm.[29]

This mystical symbiosis of "desert" and settled world was central to the spiritual lives of Eastern Christians. For the spectacular lives of a few great saints formed the model for the activities of innumerable, less famous ascetics whose reputation for holiness led them to be sought out by persons "in the world." Holy persons – men, in the desert, and women, more usually in the safer seclusion of the towns and villages – were constantly available to offer spiritual counsel and the support of their prayers. Not all of them were members of the clergy.

Holy men and women were the true democrats of Eastern Christendom. Paradoxically, it was their awesome austerity which enabled them to fulfill this role. For, seen with the eyes of an "angelic" person formed in the "desert," all persons of all ranks and status, of all vocations and levels of culture, were equal, because equally sinners, caught in "the world." Clergy and laity were alike. Equally caught in the "world," each, in their different manner, limped slowly toward the kingdom of Christ. Emperor or peasant, bishop or lay person, monk or prostitute, each needed the advice of holy persons and the constant support of their prayers. Ascetic representatives of the "desert" met the deep longing for solidarity and for spiritual guidance which the official leaders of the Church – bishops and clergy now deeply implicated in a largely urban world of power and status – could not provide.

We possess a precious record of the spiritual guidance offered by two major holy men in this period: the *ostraka* – the inscribed shards of pottery – which record the requests sent to Apa Epiphanius in his cell among the empty temples of Thebes, in the late sixth century, and the remarkable collection of *Questions and Answers* associated with the great old man, Barsanuphius (470–547), an Egyptian recluse settled outside Gaza. Both holy men moved with ease from providing exacting spiritual direction to a small group of disciples to offering firm and humane advice to married persons "in the world."

An elderly priest asked Epiphanius how he should spend the last years of his life:

broken, lying abed, carried in and out . . . A great grief is in my heart,
night and day . . . be so good as to appoint to me prayers and a regime of
fasting convenient to my sickness and old age, and even if it be lying
down, I will fulfill them.[30]

As for Barsanuphius of Gaza, he supplied the notables of the region with
moral counsels which upheld, from the awesome darkness of his permanently closed cell, ancient standards of grace and courtesy. Should a landowner allow a Jewish neighbor to use his wine press?

If, when it rains, God causes the rain to fall on your fields and not those
of the Jew, then you can refuse to press his wine. But He is full of love for
all mankind . . . why should you, then, wish to be inhumane rather than
merciful?[31]

What is abundantly plain in these vivid interchanges is the power of prayer
ascribed to holy persons. Those who consulted Barsanuphius placed their
souls in his hands, and expected to be protected and guided through his
prayers.[32] As a result, the religious life of eastern Christians of all classes and
in all regions was crisscrossed by subtle and unbreakable threads of spiritual
dependence on individual guides, who were often identified with specific
local traditions. It was a form of religious "networking" that was unusually
tenacious and potentially fissiparous. It counted for more in the lives of many
pious persons than did the notional unity to which the emperor and the
bishops were so strenuously committed.

On one thing, however, Barsanuphius was firm. *Kosmikoi* and monks
alike should avoid contact with heretics. They should never be drawn into
debate with them. "Heretics," for Barsanuphius, included Monophysites who
bitterly opposed the Council of Chalcedon. This was the problem. A remarkably unified empire did not possess a unified Church. The forceful reign
of Justinian witnessed the failure of the most energetic attempt yet made to
reassert, from Constantinople, a single imperial faith.

"The fortunate race of the Romans": Justinian (527– 565) and his Empire

It is easy for the historian, with the benefit of hindsight, to foresee Justinian's
failure. Contemporaries, however, face their world generation by generation. The generation which came into its prime in Constantinople in the
520s was characterized by a quite exceptional combination of anxiety and
high purpose. They knew that they lived in a changed world. The Roman

empire of the West had fallen. In Constantinople, this was an ominous event. Pagans ascribed it to the suppression of sacrifice to the gods, Monophysites, predictably, to the Council of Chalcedon.[33] No longer simply a "new" Rome, a replica of Rome offered to the East, Constantinople now stood alone as the capital of the "true" Roman empire. To call this empire "Byzantium," and its subjects "Byzantines" (from Byzantium, the former site of Constantinople), is a modern practice that denies the continuity with the Roman empire to which the men of the sixth century were fiercely attached. They thought of themselves as members of "the fortunate race of the Romans."[34] Learned folklore, treasured in government departments, and recorded by the scholar-bureaucrat, John Lydus, insisted that the Praetorian Prefect's court used the plural form, "we," because it had been used by Romulus and Remus, when they sat in judgment. It was also believed that the uniforms of the guards of the imperial bedchamber had been designed by Romulus, who had received the pattern from Aeneas![35] Latin remained the language of the law. Though mediated by serviceable Greek and Syriac translations, Latin, "the Roman tongue," continued to be used as the sacred language of a "Roman" state – as opaque but as redolent of uncanny continuity with the distant past as the Latin of the pre-Vatican II Catholic Mass used to be.

In Constantinople, the opinion was that if the West fell, it had been because the western emperors had not been "Roman" enough. They had failed to flex the muscles of empire which were still available to those who governed in New Rome. The yearly budget of the East Roman empire was 8,500,000 gold pieces.[36] Eighty thousand tons of grain arrived each year at Constantinople as part of the tax levy of Egypt alone. The emperor Anastasius (491–518) had left 320,000 pounds of gold (23,000,000 gold pieces) as an unspent surplus in the imperial treasures. No state west of China could mobilize such sums on a regular basis.

Petrus Sabbatius Justinianus – the future emperor Justinian – came from the upper Vardar valley, near Skopje (in the former Yugoslav republic of Macedonia), from a Latin-speaking periphery of the empire, halfway, as the crow flies, between Constantinople and Rome. In 527, Justinian succeeded his unprepossessing uncle, Justin, who had reigned from 518. Like that other outsider, the Corsican Buonaparte, who raised France to glory in the name of the Revolution, Justinian threw himself headlong into the new myth of Constantinople as the true Rome, the heir of Rome's manifest destiny. He was convinced that he knew more clearly than did any of his predecessors what a Christian Roman empire should be like.[37]

Justinian had an outsider's intolerance for the compromises and anomalies that had made possible the smooth running of a splendid, but slow-moving, system. Theodosius II, for instance, had been content to declare that pagans no longer existed in his empire. This meant, in fact, that many men of skill and high culture who were loyal to the old religion were allowed to play a public role as long as they kept their beliefs to themselves. Not so Justinian. In 528, all pagans were given three months in which to be baptized. In 529, the pagan professors of philosophy at the Academy in Athens were forbidden to teach in public. All knowledge was Christian knowledge: it could not be taught by "persons diseased with the insanity of the unholy Hellenes."[38]

Justinian also knew what it was to have an up-to-date code of Roman law. The *Codex* of Theodosius II appeared to him to have been a half-hearted effort. Justinian set the lawyer, Tribonian, to work with a team of experts, to compile a *Digest* of the entire corpus of Roman law: 1,528 law-books were read through and condensed into 800,000 words. The *Institutes*, prepared at the same time, provided a streamlined new textbook for the law schools at Beirut. The *Codex Justinianus*, the *Justinianic Code*, brought the *Theodosian Code* up to date. The *Codex* appeared in 529; the *Digest* and the *Institutes* in 533.[39] The Roman law which was later revived in medieval Europe, and which became the basis of all subsequent codes of "civil" law in western Europe and the Americas, as well as the basis of the imperial law of Russia up to 1917, was not a direct legacy of ancient Rome. It all came from Justinian. It drew upon the works produced by a team of lawyers in Constantinople, driven, for five hectic years, by a man determined to test to its limits the possibilities of the empire he had come to rule. Justinian had done

> what no-one else had dared to hope to achieve and to decide on . . . But we stretched out our hands to Him, Who can, by His mighty power, grant ultimate success to quite impossible enterprises.[40]

The reform of Roman law set the brisk tempo for a further decade. For a time, it seemed as if Justinian could do anything. Then, on January 13, 532, Constantinople exploded. For the first time ever, the Blue and the Green factions united, under the common rallying-cry of *Nika*, "Conquer." They wished to replace Justinian's advisers, and eventually to overthrow Justinian himself. Thirty thousand citizens died in a massacre inflicted by Justinian's troops on a panic-stricken crowd trapped in the Hippodrome. Four days later, the huge roar of the firestorm that consumed the entire center of Constantinople still drowned every other noise.[41] Yet recovery came quickly. Characteristically, Justinian used the destruction to go beyond his predecessors. The city's main basilica was replaced by the stupendous new church of the Hagia Sophia, now known as the Aya Sofya of Istanbul, the Church of the Holy Wisdom.

Hagia Sophia was dedicated only five years after the *Nika* riot. For all future ages, it became the enduring symbol of Justinian's piety and of Constantinople's position as the center of the orthodox Christian world. The Hagia Sophia was also a symbol of empire. It was, indeed, so powerful a symbol that the great Ottoman architect of the sixteenth century, Mimar Sinan, strove to rival it in a series of stupendous domed mosques. As a result, Justinian's great church lives on, as the standard mosque of the Ottomon empire, in areas as far apart as Mostar in Bosnia and Damascus in Syria.[42]

At the time, however, the new church was a prodigious gamble. A structural engineer's nightmare, the piers which supported one main arch began to sway outward under the weight of masonry piled ever higher upon it, and the columns beneath others began to flake from the strain. Justinian was said to have urged the builders to continue. Sure enough, the completed arches settled under their own unimaginable weight. As he first entered the completed building, Justinian was believed to have exclaimed: "Solomon, I have outdone you!"[43]

In the years in which the Hagia Sophia was being built at Constantinople, Justinian set out to reconquer Italy and Africa. Between the summer of 533 and 540, Carthage, Sicily, Rome, and eventually, Ravenna, fell to Justinian's armies. It was a seemingly effortless demonstration of imperial power. A large navy landed small, highly professional contingents, supplemented by deadly Hunnish horse-archers. Divided among themselves, the armies of the Vandals and the Ostrogoths crumbled. Once again, it seemed as if Justinian had brought off the impossible.

> We have good hope . . . that God will grant us to rule over the rest of what, subject to the ancient Romans to the limits of both seas, they later lost through their easy-going ways.[44]

A large part of the coastline of the western Mediterranean, from Carthage to Volubilis and from Sicily to Istria (including, for a time, a line of ports along the southern coast of Spain, centered on Cartagena) fell back into the imperial order after no more than a century of barbarian rule. And this was not a passing moment in the history of the western Mediterranean. In Italy and North Africa, it brought the empire back for centuries. Carthage remained an imperial city until 698, Ravenna until 751. The present-day name of the hinterland of Ravenna, the Romagna, marks it as former "Roman" land – a little *Romania*, overlooking the Adriatic Sea, down which ships sailed frequently to Constantinople. Throughout the early Middle Ages, the popes were subjects of the East Roman emperors. Up to A.D. 800, every papal document sent to western bishops and to western rulers was dated by the regnal year of the emperor in Constantinople, the pope's true lord and master.[45]

Our knowledge of the reign of Justinian has been overshadowed by the account of his wars. This was in part because of the writings of a gifted contemporary. Procopius of Caesarea had served as secretary to Justinian's victorious general, Belisarius. He set to work as a historian in the classical Greek tradition of Herodotus and Thucydides. In the classical tradition, war was expected to furnish the principal theme for any writer of history. It is this aspect of the reign of Justinian, along with the intrigues of the emperor's court, which have become best known to most modern readers.

Procopius' image of Justinian was seriously lopsided, yet it still dominates our overall picture of East Roman society at the time.[46] In one respect, however, Procopius understood very well one aspect of the mentality of a Roman emperor. Justinian shared with his predecessors a healthy zest for conquest. It was how he wished to be remembered. Procopius describes the mosaic which Justinian set up in the entrance hall of the imperial palace. It showed the sort of triumph which any ruler of "the fortunate race of the Romans" would have dreamed of.

> On either side are war and battle, and numerous cities are being cap-
> tured, some in Italy, others in Libya [the classical term for North Africa
> as a whole]. The Emperor is victorious through his lieutenant, the gen-
> eral Belisarius, who returns to the Emperor with his whole army intact,
> and offers him booty, namely kings and kingdoms and all things that are
> prized by men. In the center, stand the Emperor and the Empress Theodora
> . . . They are surrounded by the Roman Senate, one and all in a festive
> mood . . . They smile proudly as they offer the Emperor divine honors
> because of his achievements.[47]

The Plague of 543 and its Consequences

The bubonic plague, however, was nature's rare, but deadly, comment on an expanded empire and on the creation of an Asia-wide economy which went with this expansion. East Rome was a revived empire, anxious for goods. It lay at the northwestern end of the trade routes of the Indian Ocean. Justinian's gold pieces, the imperial *solidi*, were admired in distant Ceylon as those of the greatest empire in the world.[48] Justinian's navies reunited the western to the eastern basin of the Mediterranean. Ceramics of unusual uniformity circulated throughout the eastern Mediterranean. Compared with the frag-mented patterns of distribution which prevailed in large areas of the hinter-land of western Europe, the continued movement of North African pottery along the coastline of the southern and eastern Mediterranean points to a consumer economy, linked to the prosperity provided by a unified state.[49]

We do not know for certain from where the bubonic plague came, when it escaped its deadly pocket – perhaps from the Middle Ganges but, more likely, from the Great Lakes of Central Africa. But once released, it moved swiftly. By the summer of 542, it was in Pelusium, the port at which the Indian Ocean trade of the Red Sea entered the Mediterranean. It emptied the coastal cities. Along the principal highroads of Syria and Asia Minor it left a swathe of deserted villages, of roadside inns filled with corpses, and an uncanny silence over the land, as the harvest lay ungathered on either side of the road.[50]

The plague soon reached Constantinople, rapidly killing a third of its population. It almost killed Justinian himself, leaving him with appreciably less energy. His old age lacked the driving vigor of the early years of his reign. His laws shrank to a trickle. Theological negotiations occupied an increasing amount of his time. By the year 563, Justinian was 81. That year, he left the capital for the first time in over 50 years. He crossed the highlands of Anatolia as winter approached, in a pilgrimage to the shrine of the Archangel Michael at Germia (Yürme, near Ankara). It was a most unusual journey for him to take. But the shrine was noted for its immemorial fishpond, a source of miraculous healing. Justinian may have sought healing. He had been chronically ill for years. He needed yet more life to complete his ambitious plans. But he died only two years later, in November 565. The empire which he had taken over with such high hopes was no longer the same.

Relatively small-scale societies can regain momentum after the first dislocating impact of the plague, as happened in Europe after the Black Death of 1348. But a vast empire, already stretched to its limits, had less chance of recovery. Plague remained endemic in the Middle East until the middle of the eighth century. Periodic outbursts of plague eroded the human resources of the great empires which struggled to control the region. Plague, in particular, burned out the heart of the maritime world on which the military exploits of Justinian had depended and crippled the provisioning of the cities of his empire. Away from the sea, the countryside was less exposed to massive infection. It recovered more quickly. Both within the empire and outside its borders, a world less identified with cities, and especially with the cities of the coastline, became that much stronger.[51]

The sheer size of the empire had placed vast fiscal resources at Justinian's disposal. After 542, this size became Justinian's most unrelenting enemy. Each distant frontier had to compete with every other for the allocation of diminished resources. Italy and the Danube lost out to the most formidable emergency of all. The fear of Persia had always been central to the strategic thinking of the emperors of Constantinople. Now this fear was realized. Under Khusro I Anoshirwan (530–579) the Persian bid to join Mesopotamia to the Mediterranean coast was on again. The head of a vast empire which stretched from Mesopotamia across the Iranian plateau into Central Asia, the Persian King of Kings enjoyed a perpetual military advantage. From 540 to 628, the "running ulcer" of war with Persia dominated the politics of the East Roman empire. The clash of superpowers throughout the Middle East, in a series of military and diplomatic encounters which ranged from the Caucasus to Yemen, made the other frontiers of the eastern empire seem of secondary importance.[52]

Italy was instantly neglected. Reduced to a military sideshow, imperial rule could not be securely established throughout the peninsula. An entire, old-world provincial society died in Italy, as the Po valley and the Apennines became an uncertain frontier region defended by a handful of imperial troops, first against the remaining armies of the Ostrogoths and, a decade later, against the war-bands of the Lombards, who arrived in northern Italy in 568.

The Lombard invasion proved decisive for Italian society. It coincided with nothing less than a social revolution. The final frontier established after 568, between the "Roman" enclaves along the coast of Italy and territories controlled by Lombard dukes and kings, was not only a military frontier. It exposed a deeper social and geographical fissure in Italian society itself. The line of the frontier between the territories controlled by the East Roman empire and those controlled by the Lombards coincided with the division between coastline and hinterland, which had developed as a result of the recession of Mediterranean trade after the impact of the plague of 542. Lombard rule represented a victory of a more rural world over a weakened, imperial Mediterranean.[53]

Along the Danube, also, and as far south as the Aegean, great gashes began to appear in the imperial structure. After 550, Slavic tribes penetrated the mountainous hinterland of the Balkans. They reached as far as Greece and the Dalmatian coast. Small groups of farmers and pastoralists, stolidly indifferent to imperial pretensions, the Slavs welcomed Roman runaways and captives. They incorporated them with ease into their own tribal system. For that reason, they grew at a rapid rate. The *Sklaviniai* – the areas of Greece and the Balkans controlled by the Slavs – were an ominous sign. As with the Lombards in Italy, so with the Slavs; their settlements were not the result only of military conquest. They showed that an entire landscape had come to reject the imperial order. Established in the hinterland, away from the coast, the *Sklaviniai*, in effect, were stateless zones. Their inhabitants, Slav and "Roman" alike, were happy no longer to pay taxes or to provide soldiers for the emperor. If they identified with an imperial system at all, it was with the new nomad confederacy of the Avars, an avatar of the empire of Attila, which formed along the Danube in the 580s.[54]

The Quest for Unity

Despite so many violent dislocations, following the plague of 542 and the revival of war with Persia, Justinian maintained the momentum of his quest for religious unity. Authoritarian as only a Roman emperor could be, he was not a violent man. He simply expected those around him to be swept into sharing his own, terrifying certainty on matters of belief. As emperor, he had considered it to be his duty to reform the inherited body of Roman law. In theory at least, the entire legal system of the empire came from his head alone. He approached Christian doctrine in the same way. He was confident that he could reinterpret the entire tradition of the Greek Fathers of the Church (a tradition which both sides held in common) so as to make the decisions of the Council of Chalcedon acceptable to Monophysite dissidents.[55]

Justinian was not unrealistic in these negotiations. He went for the "swing vote." His main concern was to convince theologians in Syria and Asia Minor. He did not concentrate on Egypt, which he knew to be a monolithically Monophysite province. Syria, however, was more equally divided between Monophysites and Chalcedonians. In any case, Syria and the highlands to its north were the frontier provinces which now had to face continuous attack from the revived Persian empire. Justinian's theological politics were directed toward that crucial area.

When Justinian thought it necessary, he could be a good listener.

> He sits unguarded in some lobby of the Palace to a late hour of the night, and enjoys unrolling the Christian Scriptures in the company of aged priests.[56]

He knew when to compromise. He shared with the Monophysite opposition a deep reverence for the theology of Cyril of Alexandria. One of the principal reasons for Monophysite opposition to the Council of Chalcedon was that it seemed that Cyril (though dead by that time) had not been sufficiently respected by the council. He was denied a total posthumous victory. The bishops at Chalcedon had praised the theology of Cyril, but they made a fatal mistake in Monophysite eyes. They had accepted as "orthodox" a group of Syrian bishops – most notably Theodore of Mopsuestia, near Antioch, and Theodoret, bishop of Cyrrhus, also near Antioch (modern Nabi Khoury on the Syrian–Turkish frontier). These bishops were known to have attacked Cyril vehemently. It seemed to Justinian that the part of the proceedings of Chalcedon which accepted these bishops as orthodox could be disowned in order to appease the Monophysite supporters of Cyril. Cyril's critics would be declared, retrospectively, to have been "heretics." The Council of Chalcedon had been wrong to accept them back into the Church.

It took a decade of tortuous negotiations before a fifth "worldwide" council (in fact, a mere 156 bishops, drawn from the core of Justinian's empire) decided, in 553, to disown the three, long-dead theologians, who were the *bêtes noires* of the Monophysites. This meant the formal condemnation of what became known as the *Three Chapters* – a tripartite dossier of the works of Theodore of Mopsuestia, Theodoret of Cyrrhus, and Ibas of Edessa.

Justinian's enterprise in condemning the *Three Chapters* had lasting and disastrous effects upon his relation with the Churches of western Europe. Because of the decisive role played in it by the *Tome* of pope Leo, Chalcedon had been regarded by Latin clergymen as "their" council. Every part of it was held to be above criticism. Justinian paid little attention to western opinion. The pope, Vigilius, was browbeaten into accepting Justinian's drastic reinterpretation of the meaning of Chalcedon. He was bundled on to an imperial ship which had sailed up the Tiber to fetch him to court. On one occasion he was dragged from sanctuary in the church of the papal delegation in Constantinople with such violence that the heavy marble altar, whose column he had grasped, almost collapsed upon him.

This was not the way that bishops were accustomed to being treated in the West. Altogether, it was an ugly incident. It made the "universal" empire of Justinian appear small and shabby in Latin eyes. Latin opponents of Justinian's decision on the *Three Chapters* treated East Rome as an alien world, truly "Greek" in its devious and tyrannical ways. A further, doctrinal fissure opened up in Italy. The newly established kingdom of the Lombards sheltered a vocal group of conservative Latin clergymen in northern Italy. They asserted that they would not accept directives on dogma handed down by the emperor to cities in the "Roman," imperial parts of Italy – to Rome and Ravenna.[57]

Justinian, however, was quite prepared to sacrifice the good opinion of the Latins to make sure of Syria. What is remarkable is that the Monophysites, who stood so close to Justinian in their basic assumptions, remained unimpressed even by his attempt to make the Council of Chalcedon inoffensive to them. Driven too fast for too long, the complex mechanisms of imperial persuasion no longer worked.

An emperor who wished to command clergymen also had to know how to cajole. In the first decades of his reign, Justinian had done this with considerable success through his remarkable consort, Theodora. Theodora was known even to her Monophysite admirers, quite candidly, as "Theodora, formerly of the brothel."[58] The empress had been a circus performer and, later, the kept woman of a provincial governor. We are told of her sexual escapades in great detail by Procopius who, as a disillusioned politician, wrote a memorable *Secret History*. In the *Secret History* Procopius savagely caricatured the emperor whom he had once praised. He portrayed the misspent youth of Theodora with memorable obscenity.[59]

But Procopius gave only half the story. Theodora was a good example of how East Romans expected sudden conversions, even of the most unlikely persons. She settled down, her professional life behind her, as a devout Monophysite. She became close to the great theologian, Severus of Antioch (465–538), whose works she read in editions specially prepared for her in large, formal script.[60] One suspects that Justinian was more fascinated by Theodora's intense converted state than by the intricate sexual *savoir faire* ascribed to her by Procopius: she was yet further proof that, in Justinian's empire, reform was always possible.

Theodora's patronage had kept the Monophysite leaders in play. Bishops and abbots dispossessed by Justinian were settled by Theodora in respectable retirement in Constantinople, temptingly close to the court. By this means they were also kept at a safe distance from their restive flocks. In the early part of his reign, Theodora represented a principle of unofficial tolerance which the forceful Justinian could not allow himself to show in his public pronouncements. When Theodora died, in 548, Justinian was disconsolate. His subsequent handling of religious opposition did not show the same certainty of touch.[61]

New Solidarities: From Imperial Church to Dissident Communities

By the 550s, the provinces themselves had changed. Less could be done through the cities. Though backed by force and substantial bribes, Chalcedonian bishops nominated by the emperor lacked authority. They were frequently discomforted by reminders of the desert, in the form of intransigent Monophysite holy men who came in from the country. In the middle of one imperial campaign to impose a Chalcedonian bishop on the city of Amida (Diyarbekir, eastern Turkey), Symeon the hermit, who usually lived in the neighboring mountains, suddenly appeared in the main basilica: "a strange and outlandish sight . . . clad in a patchwork of rags made of sackcloth and carrying the Cross on his shoulder."[62] Symeon urged the congregation not to submit to the "impious" Council of Chalcedon. He was a reminder that the precious essence of sanctity was not to be found upon a bishop's throne, but out in the hills.

In Syria, the plague had accelerated a long-term development by which town and country came to level up with each other. For Monophysite clergy to lose control of the cities was no longer to be rendered marginal. It was to "relocate," much as a modern business might relocate from a deteriorating down-town. Bishops took up residence in great monasteries connected with large villages. In these villages, the local aristocracy had built substantial houses and had endowed churches as impressive as any that could be found in a city. In Egypt, Syria, and elsewhere, informal networks based on great villages had become as important as were the urban structures of the imperial administration and the imperial Church.[63]

The Monophysites were quick to take advantage of this weakening of imperial control. Between 542 and 578 Jacob Baradaeus (Burdona, the "rag man"), the Monophysite bishop of Edessa, took the fateful step of ordaining an entire Monophysite counter-hierarchy. The Monophysites would no longer compete, as one theological party among others, to control the single Church of the empire. They would have a Church of their own. Jacob always wore the wild rags of a Syrian holy man. He travelled incessantly all over the eastern provinces, "causing the priesthood to flow like great rivers." He set up 27 metropolitans and was said to have ordained 100,000 clergymen. Not surprisingly, the Monophysites came to be known as "Jacobites," from the numerous ecclesiastical progeny of Jacob Baradaeus.[64]

The Monophysite Church which Jacob created was not like the old Church of the empire. It was not a vertical structure, where separate urban communities were piled one on top of the other, in a pyramid which culminated at Constantinople. It consisted, rather, of a set of region-wide networks. Town and country were equal, because equally covered by the long tentacles of a shared religious identity. Monophysite clergymen travelled along these tentacular systems of loyalty – visiting a monastery here, a holy man there, ministering to a village community on the edge of the Syrian desert or encouraging a confraternity of pious lay persons established in Constantinople. This is the world revealed to us by the *Ecclesiastical History* and *Lives of the Eastern Saints* written by the remarkable Monophysite, John, the titular bishop of Ephesus (507–588). John's heroes and heroines were all part of a fluid but tenacious group of "orthodox" (that is, Monophysite) believers. Religious ideas flowed rapidly along such Monophysite networks, bypassing the accustomed structures of the city-based state Church.[65]

Even the frontiers of the empire were ignored by the Monophysite community of believers. In the course of the sixth century, Monophysite missionaries created what has aptly been called a "Commonwealth" of Christian kingdoms along the periphery of the empire. The Armenian aristocracy rejected Chalcedon in 551. Far to the south, Axum and Nubia became independent kingdoms, loyal to the Monophysite beliefs of Egypt rather than to the faith of the emperors of Constantinople. Arab sheiks on the borders of Syria emerged as major patrons of Monophysite monasteries. Monophysite clergymen travelled with ease among their co-religionists from Constantinople to Persian Mesopotamia. The heavy collective sense of a single urban community joined around the celebration of the Eucharist, with which we began this chapter, gave way to a world of juxtaposed, extended networks which stretched through town and village alike. Chalcedonians and Monophysites lived side by side, without mingling, throughout the Middle East. Each felt that they had more in common with distant co-religionists than with their "heretical" neighbors in the same city.[66]

The generations after Justinian were marked by disastrous wars with Persia, by increased violence between "Blues" and "Greens," and by the strengthening of the dissident, Monophysite Churches. But they also coincided with a flowering of hagiography. The stories of the saints written in the eastern empire are the equivalent of the writings of their contemporary, Gregory of Tours. Their authors shared with Gregory an urge to map out all aspects of the sacred as it impinged on day-to-day life. But the form these stories took was subtly different from the form taken by the hagiography of Gregory of Tours. Gregory wrote to record the moments and the places where Paradise had come close to earth. In the eastern empire, by contrast, Monophysites and Chalcedonians wrote so as to uphold the solidarity of their respective Christian communities. Each did so by exploring the manner in which God's grace penetrated, through miracles and holy persons, into every nook and cranny of society.

The works of East Roman hagiography of this time represent the autumn fullness of a distinctive Christian culture. They followed a century of experiment in rendering Christianity universal throughout the empire. The great basilica churches of the eastern world had become places of newly elaborated liturgical drama. They offered a form of "sacred theater" which strove to rival the ever-present "Church of Satan" – the ancient theater and the Hippodrome. The hymns of Romanos Melodes, a Syrian immigrant to Constantinople who wrote in the days of Justinian, filled the churches with a new, high form of religious poetry. Borrowed from Syria, the chanted hymn, the *kontakion*, was a religious form as novel and as stunning, in its own way, as the Baroque *oratorio*.[67] Monophysites and Chalcedonians would not have disagreed with each other so passionately, if they had not shared a spiritual world in which the great themes of Christ's incarnation and suffering on the Cross had reached new peaks of drama in the liturgy, preaching, and hymn-writing of the age.[68]

As we saw at the end of chapter 4, the issue of the joining of divine and human in Christ raised, in its most intense form, the issue of the solidarity between God and human beings, and so, also, of the solidarity between fellow-Christians. It was a concern which the staunchly Monophysite writer John of Ephesus shared with two convinced Chalcedonian writers of the early seventh century, John Moschus (ca.560–634) and Leontius of Neapolis in Cyprus (ca.570–650). While the bishop of Tours had looked mainly to the ancient dead and to the world of nature to find there all-redeeming traces of God's Paradise, writers such as John of Ephesus looked, rather, into the great cities and villages, to scan the heaving, faceless mass of the poor. If Christ could be found there, then he could be found everywhere. He had not abandoned a fragmented and disillusioned Christian world.[69]

John's Monophysite theology may have made him particularly prone to look to the poor in this way. For if Christ had taken on human flesh with such absorptive power as to render it divine, the humblest human body, because it bore the same flesh as Christ, was as charged with sanctity as was the Eucharist itself. To flout a beggar was to trample on flesh mysteriously linked to Christ and so to trample on God himself. John wrote of how two ladies, Susanna and Euphemia, emerged as the leaders of the Monophysite opposition in Amida at the time of Justinian's persecutions in the 540s. In a region of cruel winters, they put relentless pressure on the rich to support the poor who lay shivering in the streets of the city. Townsmen quaked when they saw Euphemia bearing down upon them, with "her quick and rapid walk . . . with her toes bruised and her nails torn." She would rebuke them for neglecting their fellow-believers. "While God is knocked down in the streets and swarms with lice and faints from hunger, do you not fear Him?"[70]

It was in this manner, with an emphasis on the Christ-like nature of the common man, that sanctity was thought to have flowed back from the desert into the settled land. A sense of the intrinsic holiness of one's fellow-Christians provided a new way with which to express the solidarity of the Christian community, in a world where solidarity was all too easily lost in a cruel and abrasive age, in which the fellow-feeling which had once supported the citizens of classical cities had evaporated. The following anecdote circulated among the *Sayings of the Fathers* that formed part of the great reservoir of spiritual guidance that was available to average Christians in the eastern empire:

An important person took great pleasure in watching wild-beast shows, and hoped for one thing only, to see the fighters wounded by the animals. One day he fell into danger and cried to God: "Lord, come to my help in this misfortune." Then the Lord came to him, His body covered with wounds, and said: "This is how you wish to see me; how then have I the strength to help you?"[71]

Poignant anecdotes such as this mark the end of an age. Large Christian groups, Chalcedonians quite as much as Monophysites, were prepared to forget ancient loyalties to their cities. Religion provided them with a more certain, more deeply felt basis of communal identity. Even when they lived in villages and cities where their own Church predominated, they had come to see themselves, first and foremost, as members of a religious community. They were fellow-believers. They were no longer fellow-citizens. Although, at the time, the thought remained unthinkable even for extreme Monophysites, within a century after the death of Justinian, the populations of Syria and Egypt, having fallen under Muslim rule, would even forget that they had once lived under a Christian empire.

CHAPTER 8

Regimen animarum:
Gregory the Great

"The Holy Commonwealth": Italy and the East Roman Empire

At the end of the sixth century, Rome and significant parts of Italy had been ruled from Constantinople for over half a century. They were provinces of the Eastern Roman empire. Ever since the arrival of the armies of Justinian in Rome, in 536, the city had become the "window on the West" of the emperors of Constantinople. This was an empire of awesome dimensions. Mosaic inscriptions were placed in the great churches of Rome so as to make clear the notion of "worldwide" imperial rule which governed the policies of Justinian and his successors:

> May the enemies of the Roman name be vanquished throughout the entire world by the prayers of Saint Peter.[1]

Yet, of all the major cities of the empire, Rome was by far the most desolate and the most exposed to danger. After the decades of inconclusive warfare which followed Justinian's invasion of Italy, Rome was a ghost of its former self. Its population had dropped to around 50,000.[2] It was a city perched on the far edge of an empire whose fate was being decided, over 1,600 miles to the east, in a relentless, losing war with the King of Kings of Persia. The sheer size of the eastern empire rendered its Italian provinces peripheral.

As we saw in our last chapter, the inhabitants of Italy found themselves triumphantly incorporated in the "Roman" empire of Justinian; and then, within a decade – after the plague of 543 and the resumption of war with Persia – they were left to their own devices. They had to defend themselves as best they could in a region worn down by decades of intermittent, vindictive warfare.

WESTERN EUROPE ca. 500–ca. 650

ITALY

Boethius 480–524
  writes *Consolation of Philosophy* 524

Benedict of Nursia 480–547
  founds Monte Cassino 529
  writes *Rule* ca.546

Cassiodorus 490–583
  founds monastery at Vivarium
    (Squillace) ca.550
  writes *Institutes of Divine and Human
    Learning* 562

Gregory the Great 540–604
  papal representative in Constantinople
    579
  delivers *Moralia in Job*

  pope 590–604
  writes *Regula Pastoralis* 591
  writes *Dialogues* 594
  mission to Saxons in Kent 597

Vision of Fursey ca.630

Vision of Barontus 679

GAUL AND SPAIN

Convent of Caesaria at Arles 508

Radegund 520–587
  founds convent of the Holy Cross
    at Poitiers 561

Conversion of Visigoths to
  Catholicism 589

Isidore of Seville ca.560–636

Columbanus 543–615
  arrives in Gaul 590
  founds Luxeuil
  founds Bobbio 612

Jonas of Bobbio, *Life of
  Columbanus* ca.640

Gertrude of Nivelles dies 659

Not for the last time in its history, Italy became a "geographical expression." It fell apart into a patchwork of intensely particular regions, each of which made its own terms with foreign invaders – East Romans or "barbarian" Lombards. The Lombards came to Italy in 568, allegedly summoned from the Danube by East Roman generals. They took over the Po valley and, by occupying Spoleto and Benevento, they gained control of the Apennines, the mountain spine of Italy. What was left to the empire were the coastal plains. On the east coast of Italy, the empire controlled Ravenna and the coastline of the Adriatic. Across the Apennines, Rome, the coastal plains of southern Italy, and Sicily were imperial territory. They looked to Constantinople.

The social and ecological divide between a coastline washed by the Mediterranean and the more rough and self-sufficient hinterland, which, as we have seen, had already begun to emerge in mid-sixth-century Italy, now coincided with a political frontier. After 580, much of the hinterland of Italy was controlled by Lombard "armies" – by local militias consisting, largely but never exclusively, of Lombard warriors. The coastal plains were held by equally localized, armed groups of self-styled "Romans," who claimed to be loyal subjects of the distant emperor of Constantinople.

To the "Romans" who inhabited imperial territory, the Lombards were the "enemies of the Roman name" *par excellence*. They were regarded as "the most unspeakable nation."[3] Tales of atrocities committed by Lombard war-bands were recounted with horror by refugees from central Italy as they arrived in Rome.[4] The Lombards were treated, by the occupants of the imperial territories, as savage intruders, who had terrorized the populations of Italy. In reality, each region of Italy, in embracing or rejecting the Lombards, voted with its feet for or against Justinian's view of what a "Roman" empire should be. The areas which accepted Lombard rule were like the *Sklaviniai* of the Balkans. They were regions which had grown tired of empire. A strong state was not for them. Lombard garrisons were the lesser of two evils. The worse, by far, was the return of East Roman tax collectors and the imposition, on conservative provincial churches, of the doctrinaire rulings, in religious matters, of authoritarian East Roman emperors. As a result, the ideological frontier between "Roman" and "barbarian" in Italy was drawn with particular sharpness. For beneath the labels of "Roman" and "Lombard" different groups of Italians, in different regions, opted tacitly for different styles of rule, the one "imperial" and linked to the fate of a distant, eastern Mediterranean state, and the other more intensely local, rooted in the hinterland and drawing on the wealth of the Italian countryside.[5]

Of the two sides, the representatives of the empire were always the more explicit. They stressed the contrast between themselves and the "barbarians." Confronting the Lombards along the estuary of the Po, an imperial viceroy, the exarch, took up residence at Ravenna. In the exquisite palace church of San Vitale, the altar was ringed by mosaics placed on the lower walls of the apse. They showed Justinian and Theodora in their full imperial majesty. They had been put up, at great expense, as soon as Ravenna fell to the imperial armies in 540. The mosaic portraits of the imperial couple and their entourage ensured that they would remain ever-present to the Catholic clergy of Ravenna who gathered at their feet, in the sanctuary around the altar. Nothing could have made more plain Justinian's overpowering, personal commitment to maintaining the "orthodox" Catholic faith in every city of his empire.[6] And the "orthodoxy" of Justinian was the basis of his claim, as Roman emperor, to universal rule. The state represented by the exarch of Ravenna was not just any state. It was spoken of by its representatives as the "Christian Commonwealth," even as the *sancta respublica*, the "Holy Commonwealth."[7]

For generations to come, not only the Lombards, but also the other kingdoms of the West – the Frankish kingdoms and Visigothic Spain – maintained a healthy respect for the ability of the East Roman empire to reach out to destabilize distant "barbarian" kingdoms. As late as the 660s, a clergyman sent by the pope from Rome to Britain was detained, in Francia, as an East Roman agent. He was accused of having been sent to stir up the Saxon kings against the Franks.[8]

Each kingdom took its own precautions to cordon off Justinian's "Roman" empire. This was particularly the case with the Visigothic kingdom of Spain. Under Justinian, the eastern empire had established outposts in southern Spain. Greek pirates harried the Spanish coast and "Roman" troops were involved in Spanish civil wars. The effect of interventions by such "Romans" was to alienate Visigothic Arians and local Catholics alike. This happened especially among the wealthy and cultivated Catholic bishops of southern Spain (led by the bishops of Seville) where the East Roman presence had proved most troublesome. Ways were sought to deprive the "Roman" empire of its principal ideological advantage – the claim that, as a Catholic empire, it had a monopoly of orthodoxy over against "outer barbarians" such as the non-Catholic, Visigothic kings. Not surprisingly, therefore, in 589, the Visigoths accepted Catholicism under their king, Reccared. They did so on their own terms and from their own Catholic bishops. It is significant that the pope at Rome was held at arm's length throughout the entire process of conversion. Only later was the pope informed of Reccared's decision, for the pope was known to be a loyal "Roman" subject of the eastern emperor. Even he could be suspected of being an imperial agent.[9]

The conversion of the Visigoths, and the strident royal propaganda which announced the foundation of a Catholic monarchy, common to Goths and Romans, showed a new self-consciousness on the part of the western "barbarian" kingdoms. Goths and Franks now claimed to be both Catholic and "barbarian," and proud of it. In this way, Justinian's reconquest had acted as a catalyst far beyond Italy. The Frankish and Visigothic kings were forced to offer to their own subjects an answer to the ideological challenge presented by the mystique of a "Holy Commonwealth" – by Justinian's East Roman ideal of an orthodox empire called by God to conquer barbarians.

Roma invicta, "Unconquered Rome": The Senatorial Aristocracy of Italy

Italy at the end of the sixth century was a very different place from the Italy of former times. The wars which followed Justinian's reconquest and the subsequent infiltration of the Lombards had brought to an end a very ancient world. In the first half of the sixth century, the culture and society of Italy had been dominated by the senatorial aristocracy of Rome. This aristocracy included families whose pedigrees reached back for centuries, beyond the reign of Constantine. They still met in the ancient Senate house, at the end of the Roman Forum. As we saw in chapter 6, members of these families maintained archaic pagan ceremonies as part of the folklore of their city, without any sense that such actions were inappropriate in a Christian age. They even minted their own bronze coins. These showed Romulus and Remus suckled by the wolf and bore the legend *Roma Invicta,* "Unconquered Rome."

For such persons, the abdication of Romulus Augustulus and the end of the Roman empire of the West, in 476, was a non-event. They still owned large parts of Italy. They collaborated with new, "barbarian" rulers, first with Odoacer (476–493) and then with Theodoric, the king of the Ostrogoths (493–526). As bureaucrats and ambassadors, they placed their traditional *savoir faire* and their vast prestige at the service of their new masters. This small group kept Italy recognizably "Roman" on their own terms.[10]

It was the return to Italy of the new "Roman" empire of Justinian which spelled their ruin. As politicians, landowners, and residents of large and vulnerable cities, they bore the brunt of a prolonged and peculiarly destructive war between the East Romans and tenacious Ostrogothic armies. But they were not only the victims of war. They suffered most from the empire which had claimed to deliver them. In the early sixth century, the dominance of the Roman senatorial aristocracy in Italy had been based on collaboration with an easygoing "barbarian" government which was anxious for their support.

They paid few taxes. Now they found themselves subjects of a formidably well-organized state which taxed even its richest citizens as relentlessly as anyone else.

Worse than that, the old aristocracy was no longer necessary. The new "Roman" empire brought with it a new social order. The Rome-based magnates had been absentee landlords on a prodigious scale. There was little love lost between them and the petty gentry in the provinces of Italy, who envied their power and managed their scattered estates on their behalf. With the reconquest of Justinian, the aristocrats were pushed aside. They were replaced by an alliance between "emperor's men" – East Roman officials and army officers – and the petty gentry of the provinces who had grown up in the shadow of the great senatorial families. This new class of provincial gentlemen formed the backbone of the "Roman," that is, the imperial, order in Italy. They were military men, with little traditional culture. In this respect, they differed little from their opposite numbers, the "barbarian" Lombards and their Italian collaborators in the hinterland of Italy. After generations of unquestioned dominance by cultivated aristocrats, late sixth-century Italy, for good or ill, was a world which offered most to the small man.[11]

What was threatened, in this social revolution, was the very existence of a leisured class, and of the styles of culture and religion that went with such a class. Up to A.D. 550, money had been available, especially in Rome, to maintain the huge expense of aristocratic libraries. These libraries would house, copy, and circulate an ever-growing body of Christian literature. At the beginning of the century, the philosopher and theologian, Boethius (480–524) was able to work, undisturbed for years on end, in his Roman library. Light filtered through alabaster windows on to cupboards stocked with Greek and Latin books. Boethius came from one of the oldest families of Rome. A skilled translator, he made technical works of Greek philosophy available in Latin. He knew that his Italian contemporaries lacked the cosmopolitan culture which he still enjoyed. They could not read anything that was not in Latin.

When Boethius was imprisoned and faced execution for treason, in 524, he wrote a *Consolation of Philosophy* which would dominate the sensibility of the Christian Middle Ages precisely because it bore no sign of Christianity. Its exploration of the relationship between divine providence and human misfortune and its exaltation of the courage of the lonely sage cut deeper into what was truly universal in the human condition than could words taken from any one religious group. Although he was a devout Christian, Boethius was also a Roman. He chose an ancient wisdom, shared by all, with which to reflect on a life about to end in torture and death.[12]

Antiquarius Domini: "Book-producer of the Lord" – Cassiodorus and the Vivarium

It is a tribute to the undiminished ambitions of learned Italian Christians that, despite the increasing disruption brought about by Justinian's wars, they attempted to take advantage of the wider horizons opened up through their incorporation into the eastern empire. The pious senator, Cassiodorus (490–583), was a striking example of the determination and flexibility of a cultivated representative of the old régime.[13] As a young man, Cassiodorus had served as spokesman for the Ostrogothic kings at Ravenna, remaining at his post as late as 537, when their kingdom was already doomed. He was proud of what he had done. He made a collection of the edicts and letters of his Ostrogothic masters, called the *Variae*. They give a unique view of a Roman conducting "business as usual" under barbarian masters.[14]

Cassiodorus then spent frustrating years, as a middle-aged man, in Constantinople. He saw Italian interests progressively pushed to one side at court. Yet he still returned with high hopes to Italy. A man of increasing piety, he had assembled an impressive library of Greek and Latin Christian books, and had conceived an ambitious cultural program so as to put them to good use.

Earlier, as a Christian landowner with an eye to his own retirement, he had founded a monastery on his estate, called Vivarium (from the neighboring fish-pond), outside Squillace, at the toe of Italy, near modern Catanzaro. Vivarium lay among orchards beside a happy stream. It was the center of a large estate, supported by the rents of a well-disciplined peasantry. Cassiodorus intended these local farmers to regard the monastery as a little "city of God," radiating Christianity in a land where the countryfolk were tempted still to turn to ancient holy groves.[15]

Backed by the high ridges of the mountains of Calabria, Vivarium looked out over the Ionian Sea. It seemed to have its back turned on Rome and Ravenna. But the isolation of Vivarium was only apparent. The sea itself had become an imperial, "Roman" sea. The sea-routes from Rome, Sicily, and Carthage to Ravenna and Constantinople passed by the toe of Italy, close to Vivarium. Cassiodorus' endeavors affected a wide circle of persons. He provided texts, commentaries, and judicious "updates" on issues of theology shared by Greek and Latin Christians as far apart as Constantinople and Spain.[16]

Cassiodorus moved his library to Vivarium in around 550. As he outlined his hopes, in the *Institutes of Christian Culture* (a text finalized in 562), Cassiodorus presented his monastery as a place where the classics of Latin

Christian literature would be copied and circulated, where translations of Greek works would be undertaken, and where the basic skills of Latin grammar and rhetorical analysis were maintained, as a *sine qua non* for the understanding and the accurate copying of the Scriptures. Small textbooks were carefully prepared as "teach-yourself" volumes, designed to meet the needs of the average reader. These books made the culture of a very ancient world available to a less privileged generation, which could no longer count on having teachers available, in their locality, to explain difficult texts to them by word of mouth.

We, who live from printed texts and read silently, must remember what a change this must have involved for many of Cassiodorus' contemporaries. Classical education had been a noisy business. It involved the training of the voice to speak in public. Even in its preliminary stages, Latin culture was passed on by largely oral methods. Reading aloud and memorizing texts through recitation had played as much of a role in Roman education as it still does in Islamic schools in Africa and Asia. The bustling life of the cities had included the raucous voices of schoolteachers, shouting out the intricacies of Latin grammar to their pupils, in little cubicles curtained off to one side of the forum. Now those voices had fallen silent in much of Italy. Cities could no longer pay for public teachers, nor aristocrats for private tutors. For the first time, books were that much more free to take on a life of their own. Books, and not the human voice, explained other books. We last hear of Cassiodorus at the age of 81. He had returned "to my old friends, the orthographers": a basic textbook on Latin spelling was what his monks now needed. They came from a post-war generation, for whom the leisured erudition of the *ancien régime* in Italy was a thing of the past. Such persons needed the help of skilled scribes and readers, such as had gathered at Vivarium. Cassiodorus' ideal, in his later years, was to act as the *Antiquarius Domini*, a "Book-Producer of the Lord."[17]

With the advantage of hindsight, it is easy to think of Cassiodorus' activities as no more than a salvage operation. We all too readily imagine him gathering in what little remained of the aristocratic culture of Christian Italy, and making it available, in a brutally simplified form, to an age that was fast slipping into barbarism. To see Cassiodorus in this manner is to overlook his sincere and serene pride. He did not think of himself as standing at the end of an age. Rather, he was confident that he could draw on a rich tradition that only needed to be adapted intelligently to "modern times."[18]

In his opinion, the Latin Church had possessed, for centuries, its own, complete "Library of the Fathers." The works of the great Christian Latin authors of the fourth century – Ambrose, Jerome, and Augustine – now lay in his book-cupboards, resting sideways on their shelves. Elsewhere, in more luxuri-

ous libraries than that of Vivarium (such as Rome and Seville), author portraits of these great figures looked down on the reader from above the cupboards in which their works lay. Cassiodorus intended to remind the Christians
of his own day that, as Latins, they had a culture of their own of which they
had every reason to be proud. As the westernmost province of the eastern
empire, western Christians were encouraged, by Cassiodorus, to draw on the
richness of the Greek world. He assembled a team of Greek translators to
make many of the basic texts of Greek Christianity available for Latin readers.
But he also insisted that the Latins had their own rich tradition. His pride in
Latin Christian literature was a discreet answer to Justinian's high-handed
treatment of the pope and his neglect of the opinions of the Latin Churches.[19]

The activities of Cassiodorus as late as 580 show that, in the quiet world
of texts, the social revolution associated with the imperial reconquest had
not brought about the end of the world. A rich legacy of Latin texts had
survived the dislocation of war. The issue would be how these texts would
be used, by whom, and to what purpose. In this matter, the personality and
peculiar spiritual trajectory of a young man who had grown up as a "Roman
of Rome" in the late 550s and 560s, while Cassiodorus was setting his library to work far away in southern Italy, would prove decisive. This very
Roman young man was Gregory, the future pope Gregory the Great.[20]

The Young Gregory: From the Clivus Scauri to Constantinople

Gregory grew up in a family palace on the Caelian Hill, beside the Clivus
Scauri. The house itself and the view from its terraces summed up the world
in which he found himself. The house was over two centuries old.[21] It abutted the reception hall of a further magnificent palace of the age of
Constantine.[22] The house looked out directly, across the Via Appia (the
modern Via San Gregorio), to the Circus Maximus, the Palatine, and (further to the right) the Arch of Constantine and the Colosseum. This was a
view of the heart of classical Rome. And it was dead. In the fourth century,
over 1,500 chariot races had taken place every year in the Circus Maximus.
Now the great racetrack lay deserted. It had not been used for almost half a
century. The gigantic palace complex on the Palatine Hill was deserted, except for the small office and chapel of an East Roman governor, nestled at its
foot, beneath gigantic cliffs of ancient brickwork. In and around the Forum,
the occasional crash of falling masonry showed that Rome, the Rome of the
pagan past, had not been levelled by invading barbarians. It had simply been
allowed to fall down through neglect.[23]

The view to either side, along the Aventine and the Caelian hills, told a different story. The mansions on these hills had witnessed the birth and triumph of an idea of Rome linked to the Christian aristocracy. To the left, on the Aventine Hill, two centuries previously, in the 380s, Saint Jerome had been patronized by noble ladies, before he left for the Holy Land, so as to produce what any sixth-century person, such as Cassiodorus, would have acclaimed as his *chef d'oeuvre* – a definitive Latin translation of the Bible, known as the Vulgate. Across the Clivus Scauri, near the church of Santi Giovanni e Paolo, a relative of Gregory's, pope Agapetus, had continued this tradition of learning. Agapetus installed a library containing the Fathers of the Church. In 536, he had planned, in collaboration with none other than Cassiodorus, to set up in Rome teachers of Christian literature, supported through public subscriptions. The subscriptions would doubtless have been collected from pious aristocratic families, living, like Gregory's own family, in their ancient mansions.[24] Behind the Caelian Hill, on the way to the Lateran Palace of the popes, the remarkable rotunda-church of Saint Stephen, San Stefano Rotondo (founded by a pope of the late fifth century), showed what ecclesiastical building could still do to place a Christian mark on the skyline of the ancient city.[25] Beside it was a hostel of the poor, connected with the former palace of the Valerii, another Christian clan known to Saint Jerome.[26] Set back a little from the deserted center of ancient Rome, this Christian Rome, patronized for over two centuries by Christian aristocrats, was far from moribund.

Later ages liked to believe that Gregory's family came from one of the oldest senatorial houses of Rome, the Anician family to which Boethius had belonged. This may not be so. He came, in fact, from a more interesting segment of the local nobility. His family had derived their status from being members of the Roman clergy. They were defined, therefore, not simply by their pedigree but by their active piety and by their experience of clerical authority. Gregory's grandfather had been pope Felix III (483–492). Felix had built the first church – now Santi Cosma e Damiano – to be set up in the Roman forum. The large inscription in the apse made plain that the church was Felix's own, fully public largesse to the Roman *plebs*.[27]

But sheltered piety of an ascetic sort (which looked back to the example of Saint Jerome) was equally important in such a family. This was a style of piety which still left room for devout and well-read lay persons. In this respect, Gregory took for granted a Mediterranean-wide ascetic sensibility, which was common to both the Latin and the Greek worlds. He shared the basic assumption of all East Romans: lay persons had the same vocation to sanctity as did monks. What held lay persons back from full perfection were *curae*, the manifold "cares" of "the world," associated with a life constrained by obligations to society. But the "desert" was still within reach for such persons, provided that their hearts had been touched by compunction and by a sharp yearning for God. They could flee from their cares, if only for a moment. They could set time aside so as to create new "habits of the heart." They could learn to pray. They could seek advice and comfort from holy persons (and we saw how important such contact with holy men was for lay persons throughout the eastern empire). Above all, they should read the Scriptures on their own, as carefully (Gregory later wrote to a courtier in the palace of Constantinople) as they would read an imperial edict, "so as to learn from God's own words to know God's heart."[28] For Gregory, as for his East Roman contemporaries, the ascetic call to experience the presence of God was open to everyone. Lay persons were challenged to pursue such piety to the best of their ability, quite as much as were the more sheltered monks.

This was a style of piety which assumed literacy and leisure. It was also a style in which women were not only the equal of men. They were, if anything, the unspoken models of male behavior. The secluded position of upper-class women had provided a centuries-old pattern for a tranquil and devoted style of life. Men could practice such a pious style of life, while remaining "in the world," only with the greatest difficulty. For men were that much more firmly tied to their public roles. They had to act as judges, administrators, soldiers, and landowners. Many of these roles were cruel; all were time-consuming. It was harder for men than it was for women to endure a life robbed of public profile, so as to live a semi-reclusive existence, "in" the world, as it were, but not "of" the world.

In Gregory's own family, the alternation of public eminence in the men and reclusiveness in the women was taken for granted. Gregory's aunts lived a life of sheltered piety in the family palace. It was a life with fluid boundaries. A sense of *noblesse oblige*, and not convent walls, kept the young girls apart from the "world." They were not nuns. They were pious, leisured ladies, living in their mansions like the many other "Christ-loving" ladies described in the Greek and Syriac hagiography of the sixth century. Only the youngest aunt rebelled. She married (of all persons!) a steward of the family estates – an aspiring member of just that class of petty gentry which had been held at a distance for so long by the great families of Rome.[29]

As befitted a young aristocrat, Gregory became Prefect of Rome in 573. At that time, he thought that the life of a devout layman, living a pious life in "the world," was within his powers to achieve. This was the sort of life which Boethius the philosopher had lived. It was only a little later that Gregory decided that he should renounce "the world" and become a monk. It was a decision based upon acute disquiet. He felt that he lacked the moral strength to combine a life of public "cares" with a religious vocation. He had to seek the shelter of a monastery.[30]

In around 575, he turned his father's house on the Clivus Scauri on the Caelian hill into a small monastery placed under the protection of Saint Andrew. The monastery was still very much a Roman gentleman's abode. It included a courtyard, with a *nympheum* (a row of niches in which fountains played) at one end, above which he placed honorific portraits of his mother and father. It was later said that his mother, Silvia, would bring the daily ration of cooked vegetables, served on the sole remaining piece of family silver, for Gregory and his monastic companions.[31]

Gregory knew of the *Rule* of Saint Benedict, the great abbot of Monte Cassino. But his monastery on the Clivus Scauri was not a rural settlement, as Benedict's monastery had been. It was still recognizably a Roman palace. It was a center of fierce asceticism and, above all, of heavy learning. Gregory ruined his health by austerities: from then onwards his energies were sapped by constant illness. In the manner of a late Roman man of learning, he breathed in the wisdom of the past, especially through prodigious bursts of reading in the works of Saint Augustine. This was the life for which he considered himself best suited – not the life of a pious lay person "in the world," but a secluded life, undertaken for his own good, lived without "worldly" cares, as a monk devoted to the contemplation of God.

Gregory would always present himself to others against the background of this short idyll. What had begun, for him, with a recognition of his own inability to live the life of a normal, pious nobleman had brought him (like the monks of the desert) to the edge of Paradise. But the idyll did not last. Gregory had fled to a monastery to avoid the pious layman's exposure to worldly cares. Within a few years, he had fallen back, once again, and, this time heavily and forever, into just such a life of "care." To join the Roman clergy was to re-enter public life at its most exacting. Given the clerical traditions of his family, Gregory could not escape this call to duty. He was made a deacon of the Roman Church and sent to Constantinople as papal representative in 579.

At Constantinople, Gregory lived in the palace set apart for papal visitors, close to the seashore (near the church of Saints Sergius and Bacchus - the present day Küçük Aya Sofia), at the foot of the hill that carried the awesome mass of the Hippodrome, the Imperial Palace, and the Hagia Sophia. This was not Old Rome, whose secular heart was empty. At New Rome, Gregory had reached the exuberant center of all earthly power.

Given the frosty climate of the court, and its lack of interest in Italian affairs, Gregory found time to continue his monastic existence. He later claimed to know no Greek. But he did so when denying authorship of works which circulated in Greek under his name. Though a Latin, Gregory, as the representative of the bishop of Rome, was expected to have a say in the theological life of the capital. In the Greek world, great churchmen were praised for possessing "elegant fingers, apt for writing on matters divine."[32] Eutychius, who was patriarch of Constantinople when Gregory arrived, had introduced himself, at once, by distributing complimentary copies of his theological treatises to leading members of Constantinopolitan society. He sent them

> among the houses of the leading senators, both to men and to women
> . . . and with his book, he sent the message, "Read and learn."[33]

These writings, as Eutychius' biographer pointed out, showed that the patriarch had

> lived on such familiar terms with the Great Fathers [of the Greek Church]
> that he breathed in the words of Basil [of Caesarea], Gregory [Nazianzen],
> and Dionysius [the Areopagite] no less than he breathed in the very air.[34]

Only an ignoramus, the biographer added, could disagree with Eutychius' conclusions. Gregory was one such ignoramus. He rebuked the patriarch for his views on the resurrection.[35] Plainly, the 30-year-old Latin had been breathing in somewhat different Fathers than had Eutychius the Greek.

   It was to a small circle of like-minded Latin friends, brought together at Constantinople by the "cares" of their respective Churches, that Gregory began to make plain what he himself had "breathed in," during his readings on the Clivus Scauri. It was a strikingly distinctive vision of the Christian life.

"Thundering forth . . . hidden meanings": Gregory's *Moralia in Job*

From the works of Augustine Gregory had taken Augustine's fierce longing to return to God.[36] For Gregory, all of human life was an exile. Human beings had been cast out of Paradise, and yet the desire for Paradise – to stand in rapt contemplation in the presence of God – still pulled at them. It was a desire as tantalizing as the gathering of saliva in the mouth for a meal that never came,[37] and as subtle as the smell of a ripe apple into which one would never bite: Gregory spoke to his hearers about the smell of ripe apples carried on beds of straw in a cargo ship as it crossed the sea, the sweet scent rising, still, above the stench of salt and bilgewater.[38] Earthly cares and the heaviness of the body dragged even the most perfect away from the vision of God. Heaven, Hell, and a heaving ocean swept by the winds of temptation and earthly distraction existed in every soul.[39]

Yet God was always close. He was far closer, indeed, for Gregory than he had been for Augustine.[40] Gregory was sure that he could see God's hand in every detail of the material world. God's mighty whisper filled the universe, seeking a way into every soul.[41] Every temptation was intelligible, every illness and every disaster was a personal touch of his hand, even the aching sense of the absence of God was a merciful trial, a concession to human frailty which would be all the more gloriously rewarded in heaven.[42]

Those who first listened to Gregory at Constantinople, and who later read his works, would always feel that they had been taken across a mighty ocean.[43] Every desire of the soul had been evoked, every subtle temptation and every obstacle to spiritual progress had been serenely delineated. Gregory even sketched out the ultimate temptation which Christians would experience at the end of time. He spoke to his hearers, in calm but chilling words, of the approach of Antichrist and of the utter impotence which would fall in the Last Days upon the established Church, leaving it naked and exposed, without a public role. To listen to those words in the capital of the most powerful Christian empire of the time, beneath the shadow of the Hagia Sophia, that fully public monument of Justinian's piety, was truly, for late sixth-century persons, an exercise in thinking about the unthinkable. Yet, in the end, the desire for God would bring the souls of the elect back to Paradise, even out of that terrible world of the future – a world where the Christian religion was stripped of public support, as if the conversion of Constantine had never happened.[44]

It was precisely in his immense precision that Gregory revealed that two centuries had elapsed between himself and Augustine. For, when speaking of temptation, compunction, and the desires of the soul, Gregory spoke with the compassion and liberating precision of an abbot in the tradition of the Desert Fathers. At those moments, John Cassian, who had brought the expertise of the monks of Egypt to southern Gaul (as we saw in chapter 4), was closer to Gregory than was Augustine. Centuries of spiritual guidance, of *colloquia*, of leisurely "talk-ins" on the virtues and the vices, of innumerable conversations of monks with their spiritual guides and of anxious lay persons with their local holy men (such as we saw occurring all over the eastern Mediterranean around figures such as Barsanuphius of Gaza and Epiphanius of Thebes) gave to Gregory's exposition a texture which was unmistakably that of its own time. Gregory reached beyond Augustine, even beyond the Latin West, to draw upon a tradition of spiritual guidance which had come to belong to the Mediterranean world as a whole. Whether expressed in

Latin, this tradition had become almost a learned folklore, a wisdom of the soul common to all spiritual guides.[45]

he feature, however, made Gregory starkly different. His spiritual guidance did not take the form of anecdotes or of letters of advice. Rather, he deliberately derived his insights from an extended, allegorical exegesis of an entire book of the Bible – the Book of Job. In doing this, Gregory was the heir of a long tradition of allegorical reading, in which every line, indeed every word of the Bible, if read with prayer and with "spiritual" understanding, would reveal a secret for the present day – some balm, some consolation, some warning made available here and now, thousands of years after the days of Job. This was what Gregory was convinced that his hearers needed – to see themselves by reliving, word by word, the Book of Job.

It is his choice of this particular form of allegorical exposition which has rendered Gregory distant from us. Augustine's exploration of the journey of his own soul, in the *Confessions*, still speaks to modern readers. But by pouring his spiritual experience into the alien form of allegory, Gregory seems to us, by contrast, to have drained all life from it. His insistence that every movement of the heart had its exact equivalent in the involuted Latin echo of a Hebrew text appears to us not only arbitrary but fussy, fine-spun, and (most unforgivable of all for modern readers) endlessly repetitive.

Yet this is not how a sixth-century listener would have heard Gregory. To enter any book of the Bible was to listen to the voice of God which still spoke, in its insistent whisper, to every soul. There was no reason why God, who spoke in so many ways to humankind, should not also have spoken in code. In that case, every line and every word of a book known to have come from the Spirit of God must be treated as heavy with meaning. It bore a message. And the same Spirit which had written the books of the Bible lingered now, waiting to be awakened, in the heart of every pious reader.[46] Devout Christians could be trusted to get the message, much as servants long familiar with their master could divine, from barely perceptible changes in his expression, what new command, what new advice he had in store for them.[47] To make an allegorical exegesis of a book such as the Book of Job was to follow a guiding thread, valid for all times, all places, and all persons, placed cunningly by God in the text of a holy book, so as to help the soul in its long, winding journey back to Paradise.

Hence, for Gregory, spiritual wisdom and the exegesis of the Bible went together. In that, he belonged to the same tradition as Cassiodorus. A holy text stood at the center of his world. There is a fresco of Saint Augustine from Gregory's time, placed in the Lateran library of the popes. It stood above the collection of Augustine's works. It showed Augustine, Gregory's hero, as Gregory himself wished to be seen – sitting at a reading desk, he

stares into the text of an open Bible. Here was Gregory's ideal:
book only, called by God, like Gregory, "to thunder forth in F
the hidden meanings [of God's Word]."[48]

Gregory entitled his commentary the *Moralia on Job*. By this he meant a
guide for the moral life derived from contemplation of the Book of Job. In
doing this, Gregory made clear that he had no wish to be known as a theologian. He was to be a moral guide. It was the stuff of the soul which concerned him, in every situation and in every turn and twist of its daily struggle
with itself. In his insistence on moral issues, Gregory was a throwback. He
brought into the late sixth century an ancient strand in Roman thought – the
austere tradition of ethical guidance earlier associated with the Stoic sages.
Gregory's emphasis on the examination of one's motives, on the need for
consideration of one's response to every situation, the perpetual awareness
of the inner self laid out before the quiet eyes of God are themes which hark
back to the letters of Seneca and to the *Meditations* of Marcus Aurelius.[49]

Gregory took this choice to act as a moral guide with good reason. Seneca
had spoken to the rulers of the Roman world, urging them to rule themselves, with unflinching integrity, before they ruled others. Those gathered
around Gregory in Constantinople were in a similar position. They lived, by
preference, like monks; but they knew that they would soon return to positions of power in their respective Churches. The friend whom Gregory met
at this time and to whom he would dedicate the written version of the *Moralia
in Job* was one such person. Leander, Catholic bishop of Seville, had come to
Constantinople as a diplomat. He was the only intimate contact which
Gregory had with that proud, closed kingdom far to the west.[50] Both he and
Gregory needed to harden their souls, through contemplation and scrupu-
lous self-examination, before they stepped back into the cares of rule associated with episcopal office.

"The giants groan beneath the waters": Pope Gregory (590–604)

In 590, Gregory's fate was sealed: he was made pope. "Under the pretext of
becoming a bishop, I have been led back into the world."[51] Until his death,
in 604, Gregory saw his life as pope in terms of a single phrase from the
Book of Job: *Behold, the giants groan beneath the waters.*[52] A man who had
passed, for a few years, into the contemplative stillness of monastic seclusion, Gregory found himself crushed beneath the oceanic pressures that
weighed on every Catholic bishop in the sixth century. Few bishops had
more cares than those who supported the massive structures of the East

Roman state; and none had more care than did the bishop of Rome, perched, as he was, on the frontier between the empire, the Lombards, and the far from welcoming "barbarian" kingdoms of the west.

In the first place, the pope was the city of Rome. The pope fed the city from "the patrimony of Saint Peter." This patrimony consisted of over 400 estates, located, for the most part, in Sicily (where they covered over one nineteenth of the entire surface of the island). Furthermore, the pope and his colleague, the bishop of Ravenna, were the bankers of the East Roman state in Italy. Only the Church possessed the treasure and the ready money with which to pay the East Roman garrisons and to advance sums of cash to a penniless administration.[53] It was Gregory who had to write, ceaselessly, to remind the emperor of Constantinople and those around him that Italy existed.

It was Gregory, also, who had to deal with the Lombards. He negotiated constantly with neighboring Lombard warlords and attempted to contain their aggression by corresponding regularly with the newly created Lombard court at Pavia. With grim humor, he described himself, on one occasion, as

> bishop not of the Romans, but of Lombards, [a flock] whose flag of truce is the sword and whose good will gestures take the form of atrocities.[54]

Though he found himself on a particularly dangerous frontier, Gregory knew that what he did in Rome was not unusual. It was only what was expected of him as the bishop of a major city of the empire. At much the same time, the patriarch of Antioch had fed the entire East Roman army as it passed through his city on its way to the Persian front. Speaking in Greek, the patriarch had reminded the assembled officers, a motley body of professionals gathered from as far apart as the Danube and the Caucasus, that they were "Romans," and that they should behave in a manner worthy of descendants of Manlius Torquatus![55]

What was harder for Gregory to deal with was sullen resentment within the city of Rome itself. His election had not been universally popular. The Roman clergy was a tight oligarchy, largely drawn from the local nobility. At a time when, as we have seen, the social structures of Italy were crumbling around them, they at least formed a traditional elite, linked to predictable careers, the reward of predictable, gentlemanly accomplishments. They had tended to admire monks, but from a safe distance. They did not wish to be ruled by one. Least of all did they wish to be ruled by a man such as Gregory, who exhibited a sharp contempt for "earthly" status and for "earthly" culture, such as only a renegade aristocrat was capable of showing.[56]

Microsoft Internet Explorer

Outlook Express, ...

927.9019
check VA
Adam Lane

been the practice
ld at the Lateran
s as members of
long-haired dar-
Many of the most
Rome. Even when
mmon ties of as-
al elite of kindred
onasteries and to
monks.[59]
ast. There monk-
irch, whose bish-
s, the occasional
as a high-minded
bishop of Tella/

he was used [every day] to raise his understanding upwards by the study of spiritual things for the space three hours . . . and for three hours more, from the sixth to the ninth hour (this is, in the early afternoon), he continued in joy and peace with every man, and in interviews with those who came to him for necessary business.[60]

Recently returned from the East, Gregory had every reason to wish that his own life was so crisply divided, and with so little apparent tension, between the ideal of contemplation and the cares of office. He had to reassure an Italian audience, and especially the Roman clergy, who were not used to monk-bishops, that to be a monk, drawn to contemplation, did not mean that he would relax in any way his urgent concern for the souls of his congregation.

"The art to end all arts": The *Regula Pastoralis*

The book which Gregory wrote on this occasion proved decisive for the entire future of western Europe. For Gregory alone, of all his contemporaries, had found himself forced to write, with a rare combination of scholastic finesse and deeply personal disquiet, about the exercise of spiritual power: "*Ars artium regimen animarum*: The art to end all arts is the governing of souls."[61] The phrase was taken from a Greek Father, Gregory Nazianzen. It set the tone for the short treatise which Gregory published in 591, the *Regula*

Pastoralis, the "Rule for Pastors." Gregory took care to circulate copies of the *Regula Pastoralis*. It was soon known in Francia. It even appeared in Greek. It was Gregory's tract for his times and the justification for his own peculiar, quasi-monastic style of rule.

One thing was certain in Gregory's world – power was there to stay. Gregory lived in a world where Christianity now touched every level of life. Power, in such a world, meant attention both to the most exalted and to the most humble aspects of existence. We have seen what powers in secular life came to be exercised by bishops such as Gregory of Tours in Gaul and by Gregory's colleagues throughout the eastern Roman empire. Bishops were expected to do anything. On the plateau of Spain, they were responsible for the rounding up of stray horses.[62] In Sicily, at a slightly later time, the bishop of Palermo could even be nominated, by the local governor, as an inspector of brothels![63]

The issue was how this surreal accumulation of duties could possibly be combined with the care of souls. How could the active life of a bishop remain linked to an ideal of spiritual wisdom nourished, as Gregory had nourished his friends on the Clivus Scauri and at Constantinople, on the contemplation of God and on rapt attention to his Word? Gregory thought that he had found the answer in the figure of the Apostle Paul. Paul was the ideal pastor. Here was a man, Gregory pointed out, whose activities had moved in an unbroken flow from the heights of mystical contemplation to laying down rules on the conduct of married persons, even on the correct times when they should or should not have marital intercourse. Paul the contemplative had entered the "third heaven," "and yet, with heartfelt empathy, he surveys with care the average person's marriage bed."[64]

Condescensio, a compassionate stepping down to the level of every person in the Christian Church, was the key to Gregory's notion of spiritual power. It was "condescension" in the best meaning of the word. It echoed the vertiginous act by which God himself, in the person of Jesus Christ, had bent to earth, to touch every aspect of the human condition. Christ also had both prayed on the mountain-top and gone down into the cities to heal the sick and to comfort the down-hearted.[65] Based on the models of Saint Paul and of Christ, the ideal pastor of Gregory must learn to be "intimately close to each person through compassion, and yet to hover above all through contemplation."[66] It was an ideal of spiritual guidance as intimate and as all-inclusive as that of any East Roman holy man.

It was the intimacy of the care of souls which concerned Gregory. He paid little attention in his treatise to public preaching. He gave no guidance on how to give a sermon. What interested him, above all, was face-to-face spiritual guidance. With characteristic exhaustiveness, he enumerated 39 different types of spiritual condition – and their opposites! – and recommended how each of them should be addressed.[67] Sometimes the spiritual governor must besiege proud souls. He must "penetrate the souls of his subjects," to "open a door into the heart" by "the shrewdest questioning."[68] But at other times, Gregory adds (with the magnificent inconsequentiality of a true guide of souls) a "kind word" at the right time can work miracles![69]

Once again, in writing the *Regula Pastoralis*, Gregory drew deeply on the thought of Augustine. But he was no epigone. On the issue of spiritual power, he had thought more urgently and more consequentially than ever Augustine had done. The *Regula Pastoralis* had the clarity and cutting edge of an industrial diamond. Its reflections on the difficulties and the opportunities of a bishop's life were compressed into crystalline hardness by Gregory's reflection on his own experience.[70] Gregory knew that he and his colleagues had to wield real power. He insisted that this should not dismay them: *God does not reject the powerful, for He Himself is powerful* (Job 36:5).[71] What mattered, rather, was that this power should be wielded, with humility and unflinching self-awareness, for the good of others.

The *Regula Pastoralis* was Gregory's meditation on the nature of spiritual power. Profoundly abstract, it could be read in many ways. It could be viewed as a handbook, a guide to conduct for the ideal bishop, abbot, or clergyman. As such, it placed the souls of entire congregations in the hands of a spiritual elite. They were to be the "subjects" of a new generation of "doctors of the soul." But the *Regula* was written, also, as a critique of the existing episcopate. For, judged by the standards on which Gregory insisted, many a bishop was no better than a lay person. A bishop without skill in the rule of souls was not a bishop.

> *They have come to reign, but not through Me; princes have arisen, and I know nothing of them.* (Hosea 8:4)[72]

The rule of souls was not a job for amateurs. Amateurs – magnates turned bishops, in Gaul; emperor's men, in the sees of Italy and the Roman East – were what Gregory feared most. His *Regula Pastoralis* warned them to think twice before undertaking the unique "weight of the pastoral office." Those who ruled in the Church must know how to rule and why they ruled – for rule they must.

Gregory was helped in his fierce precision by the fact that the Christian Church, in Italy as elsewhere, harbored a number of small but highly significant communities in which power over souls had long been exercised at its most absolute and its most searching – that is, in the monasteries. Gregory himself had lived for a time in a small monastic community – in the monastery that he had set up in his house on the Clivus Scauri. There he had exercised the powers of an abbot. He had found that it was a terrifying power. On one occasion, for instance, he had allowed a man to die alone, without the comfort of his fellows, for a single sin of avarice.[73]

Gregory knew the *Regula*, the *Rule*, of Benedict and wrote the only account that we have of Benedict's life. Yet Benedict was not close to him. He was a figure of the now-distant past. He had died in around 547. Benedict's monastery at Monte Cassino no longer existed. It had been sacked by the Lombard war-band of duke Zotto. The story of Benedict's life came to Gregory, like the ghostly bells of a sunken city, from a world before the furious impact of the Lombards. But this did not matter. In Gregory's opinion, to read Benedict's *Regula* was to seize the essence of the man.[74]

The *Rule* of Benedict was not the only monastic "Rule" available in Rome. Many such "Rules" circulated at the time. Each was treasured as the condensed life's wisdom of recognized masters of the art of souls. What plainly struck Gregory about Benedict, as he read Benedict's *Rule*, was his rare *discretio* – Benedict's unfailing sense of measure and his spiritual insight. Here was an abbot of inspired certainty of touch, who knew how to lead his tiny flock of monks through every spiritual and material emergency. And he had done this by exacting absolute obedience. Each monk was bound to his abbot and to his fellows by an awesome code that was summed up in a single phrase: *obedientia sine mora*, "obedience without a moment's hesitation."[75] In the *Rule* of Benedict, absolute power over souls demanded absolute integrity of purpose and absolute clarity as to its final aim.

The sort of monastery which Benedict had ruled and which Gregory knew from his own experience was a small community. Italian monasteries seldom housed more than 30 monks.[76] They were not large, impersonal institutions. The monks lived as close to each other as inmates in a modern prison cell. They knew each other intimately and, alas, at times they could hate each other with the same crazed intensity. They were never out of each other's sight. At Compludo, in northwestern Spain, the prior would linger for a moment at nightfall in the cottage-like dormitory of the monastery, surveying the beds, "that, by observing each monk more closely, he may learn how to treat the character and merits of each."[77]

One could have no illusion as to the skill required to govern such small, cramped groups as a true *abbas*, a "father." As *abbas*, the abbot was truly the "father" of his monks. He was the representative among them of God the Father. His words must work their way, like God's own leaven, into the soul of each and every monk. To do this required constant vigilance, insight and adaptability.

he must vary from one occasion to another, mixing soft words with threats, the sternness of a schoolmaster with the tenderness of a father ... And let him be aware how difficult, how arduous a thing it is to govern souls and to put himself out to serve so many different temperaments.[78]

The *Regula Pastoralis* was to be Gregory's equivalent of Benedict's *Rule*. It was a *Rule for Bishops*. This was a daring solution. As we have seen, Christians, in both the West and in the eastern Roman empire, had come to see their bishop as a distant and majestic figure. He was the exalted representative of law and order in their city. He was a judge, an administrator, a high priest. Now Gregory placed the most intimate and penetrating model of power available to the Christian experience of his time – the abbot's exercise of his authority over monks – at the heart of the bishop's role. He gave episcopal power a sharply pastoral stamp.

It was the rare consequentiality of Gregory's treatise which ensured its success in the ensuing centuries. For the *Regula Pastoralis* proved to be a book for all occasions. Gregory had been deliberately vague when he spoke of the person of the *rector*, the "ruler" of souls. He often assumed that the *rector* would be a bishop. But the spiritual authority of which he spoke in studiously general terms could also be exercised by an abbot, a clergymen, even by a king or a pious layman in a position of authority. Each in their own way could be seen as responsible for the care of souls.

What Gregory had unwittingly created was a Europe-wide language of power. For, by the year 600, western Europe had become a mosaic of contrasting political systems. Much as a single official language tends to become dominant more rapidly in a region characterized by a great diversity of local languages, so Gregory's studiously undifferentiated notion of the Christian *rector* spread with ease throughout these different systems, as far apart as Spain and Ireland. Above all, Gregory's pastoral language spilled over easily into thought about the responsibilities of Christian lay rulers. His heavy emphasis on the responsibilities of the ruler for the souls of his subjects was immediately adopted, by the Spanish clergy, to lend an added note of solemnity and urgency to the moralizing legislation of the Visigothic kings of Spain. It bolstered their attempt to set up a "Holy Commonwealth" of their own, in answer to the ideology of the East Roman empire.[79] A little later, in a very different world, Gregory's emphasis on the finesse and consensus-building qualities required of a Christian ruler and guide of souls seemed to do justice to the more tentative powers of Celtic chieftains in the far, non-Roman north.[80]

In all his writings, Gregory was assured of a lasting literary future. For he wrote with a lapidary, almost gnomic certainty. His phrases seemed like great, smooth stones, polished by constant, deeply meditated use. He was eminently repeatable.[81] And in what he wrote on the duties of the Christian *rector*, he created the language of an entire governing elite. With the *Regula Pastoralis* to guide them, the kings and clergy of Latin Europe no longer needed to look to the surviving "Christian empire" of East Rome to guide them. Gregory had given them a mission to rule and code of conduct as clear and as all-embracing as any that had once inspired the governing classes of the Roman empire. "Gregory's intervention permanently raised the ceiling of expectation for those in public office, in the medieval West and beyond."[82]

But this is to anticipate. In the ancient world, rulers set the tone, not by books of political theory, but through the manner in which they themselves interacted with their subjects in highly visible situations. Here Gregory played his part to perfection. A Greek writer (John Moschus, whom we met in the last chapter) describes how John the Persian had come all the way from northern Iraq to visit Rome. There he met Gregory. When he bowed to make the customary reverential prostration, Gregory checked him: the pope was no "lord." Then Gregory bent forward and, with his own fingers, he placed three gold coins in the monk's hand. This was Gregory's *condescensio* in action.[83]

Gregory's correspondence tells the same tale. They document a distinctive style of rule. The 866 surviving letters collected in his *Regestum*, his *Register of Correspondence*, were no more than the tip of the iceberg. Quite apart from his correspondence with the court at Constantinople and with other western rulers, Gregory, as pope, was the center of a network of patronage and administration which stretched from Marseilles and Sardinia to Sicily and Carthage. It has been calculated that as many as 20,000 letters may have been written from Rome in the years of Gregory's pontificate. This may be too much.[84] But Gregory certainly found himself constantly called upon to rule. Sixty-three percent of his letters were rescripts: they were answers to requests for a ruling on administrative and ecclesiastical matters. And not all these rescripts were form-letters. Many would have involved delegations to Rome, in which it was possible to meet Gregory and to see him in action, in the sort of solemn interviews that we know of from the story of John the Persian.

Copies of the letters that were sent out were selected, each year, by Gregory himself. They were transcribed each year into a large papyrus volume. The letters, as we have them in the *Regestum*, were, in many ways, Gregory's own memoirs of his years as pope. They document a master of souls in action. The word "subtle" recurs frequently, in innumerable contexts. Precision, finesse, studied courtesy, mediated in the localities by chosen representatives of exclusively clerical or monastic background close to Gregory's own views, were the signs of a new broom in the Lateran Palace. So, also, was the occasional letter of rebuke for those who failed to live up to the code laid down in the *Regula Pastoralis*. The bishop of Salona (Solun, near Split) was the proud ruler of a "Roman" imperial enclave on the Dalmatian coast. He was a bishop of the old style. He justified his lavish banquets by an appeal to the hospitality of Abraham. Gregory was not amused.

> In no way do you give attention to reading the Scriptures, in no way are you vigilant to offer exhortation, rather, you ignore even the common norms of an ecclesiastical way of life.[85]

On his epitaph, Gregory was acclaimed as *consul Dei*, "God's consul." But such reminders of continuity with the Roman past were largely wished upon him. For all his links with Rome, Gregory did not think of himself as a "last Roman." He saw himself, rather, as a *praedicator*, a man called to give warning at the end of time. The ruins of Rome play such a poignant role in his writings because they were a statement of the obvious. They spoke plainly, and to everyone, of the swift and hidden race of history toward its end. More prosperous societies might delude themselves that God's time stood still for their benefit. The crash of falling masonry in Rome, and, indeed, the entire state of post-Lombard Italy, formed "an open book" for all to read. "Once the world held us by its delights. Now it is so full of disasters that the world itself seems to be summoning us to God."[86] What mattered now was *praedicatio*, the gathering into the Christian Church of what remained of the human race, so as to face the dread Judgment Seat of Christ.

It was a thought calculated to greatly concentrate the mind. For Gregory, the age of *praedicatio* was not an age of panic. It was, rather, an age of unexpected excitements. Like soft dawn light creeping beneath a door, Gregory saw, in his own age, a subdued recrudescence of the miraculous powers which had once accompanied the first advance of the Apostles. In 594, his *Dialogues* – a collection of miracles discussed in a series of conversations between himself and his friend, Peter – announced to the Christian world that, in recent times, Gregory's native Italy had been filled with vibrant holy men and women. They had been sent by God, in the last days of the world, to warn mankind.[87]

The *Dialogues* make plain that, for Gregory, a *praedicator* did not have to be a bishop, or even a "preacher" in the strict sense. Often holiness spoke for itself. Preaching to the Roman people, Gregory would begin with his usual allegorical flights of exegesis. These were what one expected of a learned bishop in a great see. Often read aloud by Gregory's secretary when he himself was too tired to preach, they were as opaque, but as elevating in their own way, as an organ recital. But then Gregory would suddenly descend from the heights. He would end with a simple tale of a miracle. This showed his listeners how close to heaven they already stood without knowing it. Servulus, a poor man known to them all, had died in the courtyard of the church of San Clemente. Did they know that he had heard the angels singing around him as he died?[88] The pious count Theophanius died at Civitavecchia. Did they know that, on being opened, his sarcophagus had wafted "a fragrant odor, as if his decaying flesh were swarming with spices rather than worms"?[89] A hurricane had blown down some buildings. If God could so move "a gentle breath of air" to such violence, what do they think the wind of his anger would be like, when he came to judge sinners on the Last Day?[90]

In the *Dialogues*, Gregory looked out all over Italy for signs, for flashes from the other world, as it were, that would wake up sluggish Christians before it was too late. Fortunately, bishops were not the only ones who could give warning. Old abbot Florentius, perched in the woods above Subiaco with a pet bear who always knew the correct hours for prayer, had, in his time, drawn a whole countryside to Christ as effectively as did any sermonizer.[91] Driven by his ideal of the preacher as moral guide and warner of the last days, Gregory's Christianity, as it appears in his *Dialogues* and in his *Homilies on the Gospels*, "was a missionary religion, in its flexibility, adaptability and understanding of fundamental human problems."[92]

Miracles of *praedicatio* had, indeed, begun to happen on a truly "missionary" scale around him. In 589 (just after Gregory returned to Rome from Constantinople) the entire political elite of the last, non-Catholic, Arian kingdom of the West, the Visigoths of Spain, adopted Catholicism. An entire "nation" joined the Church. As we saw, Gregory was studiously excluded from this development. But it confirmed his best suspicions of his age:

> This is the change which the right hand of the Most High hath wrought.
> It was [he wrote, to the Visigothic king, Reccared, who had sent a belated, somewhat parsimonious gift of shirts for the poor at St. Peter's] a new miracle in our time. My feelings are roused against myself, because I have been so sluggish . . . while, to gain the heavenly fatherland, kings are working for the gathering-in of souls.[93]

Gregory had not long to wait. It is a grim comment on the conditions of early medieval Europe that slave-traders were among the most effective, if unwitting, missionaries of the age. They brought about the forcible transfer of whole populations. In 593, Gregory had watched the peasants of the Roman Campagna, "tied by the neck like dogs," driven in herds to the north by Lombard raiders, to sell to Frankish dealers from across the Alps.[94] In 595, similar dealers brought to the markets of Gaul parties of *Angli*, tribesmen from the Saxon kingdoms of Britain.[95] They were a timely reminder, for Gregory, of pagan nations to whom the Gospel had yet to be preached, before the end of the world could come.

The appearance of these sad figures may have coincided with a delegation from the king of Kent, Ethelbert, who had already married a Frankish Christian wife. Here was a "nation" that might be "gathered in." Gregory was not a man to be outdone by a Visigothic king. He himself would provide the *praedicatio* for this strange kingdom. In 597, an exceptionally large party, headed by a monk from Gregory's own monastery (named, significantly, Augustine) received permission from Ethelbert to settle in the royal center of his kingdom, in the ruins of a Roman town that was later called Canterbury.

The fate of Gregory's mission, when it arrived in Kent, will be described in chapter 15. But there is no doubt as to the high drama of the mission as viewed by Gregory himself from Rome and as presented by him to his colleagues. In July 598, he wrote to the patriarch of Alexandria:

> While the people of the English, placed in a corner of the world, remained until now in the false worship of stocks and stones, I resolved . . . to send . . . a monk of my monastery to preach to that people . . . And even now letters have reached us . . . that both he and those who were sent with him shine with such miracles that the miracles of the Apostles seem to live again in the signs that they exhibit.[96]

Ten thousand *Angli*, he added, had been baptized at Christmas. It was, altogether, an amazing happening, worthy of the end of time.

Gregory died in 604. He had come to expect the unexpected. But even he could hardly have foreseen how unusual the future might yet be. Within a century, a new Christianity had emerged in northern Europe. The first attempt to write a *Life* of Gregory was made in a monastery perched on the edge of the North Sea, close to Hadrian's Wall.[97] Streanaeshalch (modern Whitby, in Yorkshire) may have been a former pagan grove. Now it was a monastery in which an abbess ruled male monks. It had been founded for a lady of royal Anglian blood, who bore the name of a Valkyrie, abbess Hild. We have come a long way, within a century, from the Caelian Hill in Rome. In the next chapters we will trace the profound changes which made possible the emergence of a new Christianity of the north in the generations after the death of Gregory I.

Part III

The End of
Ancient
Christianity

A.D. 600–750

CHAPTER 9

Powerhouses of Prayer: Monasticism in Western Europe

The End of Ancient Christianity

Gregory the Great has been called, with some justice, "the last ancient man." In the century which followed his death – the seventh century – the Christian world changed dramatically. In the Middle East, a new world religion was born only a few decades after the death of Gregory – Islam. The consequent Arab conquests marked the end of the ancient world order in the Middle East and in North Africa. Equally important, for western Europe, was the emergence of a new cultural zone in northwestern Europe, in the Frankish kingdom of northern Gaul, in Ireland, and in Saxon Britain. Gregory could not have been aware that, while he was pope in Rome, a distant Arab – the prophet Muhammad, already a man of 30 – would begin to seek God in the mountains of the Hijâz. Nor could he have foreseen the long-term consequences of two events of which he was aware: one was the arrival in northern Gaul of the vivid Irishman, Columbanus, which took place in 590, the year in which he himself became pope, and the other was the mission which he himself sent, in 597, to the pagan Saxons of Kent. We will deal with these two sets of events – the rise of Islam in the Middle East and the creation of a new religious culture in northwestern Europe – in subsequent chapters (in chapters 12 and 13 for the Middle East, and in chapters 14 and 15 for the British Isles). Taken together, these two very different and unrelated sets of changes, which took place at the two furthest ends of the existing Christian world, in Ireland and in Arabia, changed forever the face of Christendom. The seventh century, and not the inconclusive political crisis that we call the "Barbarian Invasions" of the fifth century, witnessed the true break between the ancient world and what followed.

But a religious culture does not change only under the impact of dramatic crises. It also changes slowly and surely over the centuries within itself and under its own momentum. These changes had already begun in western Europe in the sixth century, before the days of Gregory the Great. The most important of these changes was that monasticism began to take on a different profile. It became notably more prominent within the Christian Church. In significant parts of Europe, it changed its function in a manner that came to look straight forward to the great monasteries of the Middle Ages. Secular Latin culture also changed greatly, in the course of the sixth century, in the former Roman territories of Continental Europe. In the non-Roman areas of Ireland and western Britain, it took on an entirely new form. Finally, the intervention of Columbanus and his Irish monks (who were very much the products of the new form of Christian Latin culture developed in Ireland) acted as a catalyst for changes which had already been under way for a century. Northern Gaul was transformed as a result. These three changes will be the subject of this and the next two chapters. In this chapter, I will describe the changing role of monasticism, then (in chapter 10) I will deal with the changing meaning of secular culture in Continental Europe and in the British Isles, and last of all (in chapter 11) with the impact of Columbanus on the northern Frankish kingdom, and with the consequent emergence of a new style of Christian piety.

It is important to linger on these three developments. The seventh century appears to us to be something of a trough in the overall development of European civilization. It is awkwardly placed between the last centuries of the ancient world and the creation of a new world, which we associate with the age of Charlemagne and with what we tend to call (whether rightly or wrongly, we shall see) "the Carolingian Renaissance." We tend to hurry through the intervening centuries, which stretch between the fall of Rome and the Carolingian empire.

By doing this, we overlook the fact that the late sixth and seventh centuries were truly seminal. Between A.D. 550 and 650, Western Christianity finally took on the face which it would wear throughout the Middle Ages and into modern times. "Our" Christianity was created in the seventh century and not before. Not only did Christian institutions change, with the rise of impressive monasteries. Issues which had not greatly concerned Christians of former centuries (or which had concerned them in an entirely different manner) came to take on new prominence.

This mutation did not involve a change in doctrine. It was based, rather, on a profound change in the imagination. The result was nothing less than a new view of sin, of atonement, and of the other world, which, in turn, laid the basis for a distinctive notion of the individual person and of his or her fate after death. These remained central concerns of western Christianity up to the Reformation and beyond. On these issues, western Christians of around the year 700 had begun to think and to feel in a manner that made them closer to us than they were to western Christians of an earlier time. For this to happen, the imaginative patterns of a very ancient, Mediterranean Christianity had to lose their grip. The process which we will follow in these chapters, therefore, amounted to nothing less than what has been described as "The End of Ancient Christianity."[1]

Monasticism in Mediterranean Western Europe

By the year 600, at least 220 monasteries and convents existed in Gaul.[2] In Italy, we have records of around 100.[3] With few exceptions, monasteries still clung to the contours of a very ancient world. In Gaul and Spain, they clustered close to the Mediterranean, in the former, highly Romanized areas of the south. They were associated with the former Roman cities. Convents of nuns gathered (in part for protection) within the city walls. Monasteries of monks tended to be suburban. Monasteries were often associated with the great shrines which had grown up in the cemetery areas outside the city walls. Both convents and monasteries lived under the shadow of the urban bishops. It was the bishop who protected and supervised them. Bishops were often the most zealous founders of monasteries.[4]

Altogether, monasteries and convents were thought of as adjuncts to the religious life of the cities. Compared with the impressive basilica churches and shrines that had been built in and around the cities in the past two centuries, monasteries and convents were inconspicuous. Many were converted town-houses (as was the monastery of Gregory the Great on the Caelian Hill) or re-adapted farmsteads.

This was true even in Italy, where the abrupt distinction between the rich plains of Rome and Naples and the wild hills that jutted out from the central mountain spine of the Apennines made many monasteries seem as remote and unearthly as if they were perched in the middle of the Egyptian desert. But this was not the case. The city was always close to hand. Benedict's first monastery at Subiaco was hidden in a cliff-face, in the midst of steep, heavily wooded ridges. But it was only 50 miles from Rome. The name, Subiaco, from *Sub Lacum*, "below the lake," was derived from the artificial lake of a large, nearby villa, which had been built by none other than the emperor Nero as a summer retreat from the heat of Rome. Benedict's final and more famous monastery, Monte Cassino, was on a wild hilltop; but it looked down over the main road that linked Rome to the Bay of Naples.

What an early sixth-century visitor to Monte Cassino would have encountered was not the "city set upon a hill" that it later became. A chapel of 7.60

by 15.25 meters (the size of a village church) would have stood on the site of a ruined temple, surrounded by what would have looked like a complex of small farmhouses. By the eleventh century, this church had become a major basilica (of 46.2 by 19 meters) and the hilltop was covered, like a fortress, with large stone buildings.[5] Cassiodorus' Vivarium, founded on a major estate close to his native city of Squillace, was exceptionally grand. It was not the average monastery, either in its economic security or in its scholarly activities. We often glimpse tiny establishments. At Luni (on the Ligurian coast, near the marble quarries of Carrara) we know, from a letter of Gregory I, that a monastery – to which he gave his approval – consisted of no more than a house with ten beds and two oxen together with two slaves to do the ploughing.[6] Most monasteries were poor. Benedict insisted that his monasteries should attempt to be self-supporting.[7] But this ideal was seldom realized. Monks usually shared in the general poverty of their region. They were as vulnerable to shortages as were any other small farmers. Frequently, they had to be bailed out by pious lay persons. By the time of Benedict, alms "for the poor" often meant, not alms for the local beggars, but contributions to the "poor" monks of the local monastery.[8]

We should not think of early sixth-century monks as great landowners. Many monasteries were established on marginal lands. Only in such a way could the monks be given land without cutting into the neighborhood's limited pool of good arable land. We see this happening in Spain. Monks in monasteries in Galicia, on the edge of the Pyrenees, found that they had to abandon the life of a gentleman farmer. It was not enough to grow grain in the valley. Like it or not, they must take to the wild hills as shepherds. The abbot explained that

> most monasteries would scarcely have enough food for three months if there was only the daily bread of the region to eat, which requires more work on the soil than in any other part of the country.

He added that they should console themselves by remembering that the Patriarchs Abraham and Jacob had also herded sheep![9] Altogether, monasteries in western Europe had not yet become places whose occupants enjoyed the same degree of prestige as did their colleagues in Egypt and Syria.

It is important to stress the relatively low-profile quality of early western monasticism. Monks did not yet enjoy the high status of a holy caste, totally separate from the laity, which they enjoyed in later centuries. Rather, monks, nuns, and lay persons found that they had much in common with each other compared to the bishop and his clergy. For monks and nuns were an awkward, "amphibious" group. They were neither lay persons nor clerics. They were plainly different from the laity. On entering the monastery, they had solemnly abandoned all claims on their private property. They could not marry and rear families. They wore ostentatiously nondescript, "religious" dress. But few monks were ordained, and, as women, no nuns were. They were a singularly colorless group. They stood between a laity, where differences of status (particularly in the upper classes) were asserted vehemently – through dress, gesture, and tone of voice – and often defended with violence, and a clergy which was also arranged in a clear hierarchy, due to the right of the bishop to ordain priests and other, lesser members of the clergy, and whose public role in the cities was undisputed.

Yet the laity plainly needed monks and nuns and wanted them to stand out as special in a way that they did not expect the clergy to be. The pressure on monks to be special is shown by small but significant changes. By the middle of the sixth century, the monastic tonsure came to be introduced in many regions. "Tonsure" (from the Latin *tondere*, to cut short or shave) became a clear statement of the separation of the monk from the lay world. It involved cutting the hair on the top of the head. This was an almost folk-loristic ritual, chosen from a pool of lay practices that had always treated hair as significant. How hair was grown and how it was cut carried an instant social message. Romans expected teenage boys to dedicate their first beard at a temple. Christian Romans continued the practice at martyrs' shrines. "Barbarians" regarded the forcible cutting of hair as an assault on their honor. So the tonsure emerged, quietly and without theorizing, as a sign that, on admission to the monastery, the monk was both consecrated to God and humbled, by the loss of his hair, beneath the rule of the abbot. It was a ritual worked out between the monks themselves and a laity who wished them to look different in a way that everyone would understand.[10]

For the laity had also begun, at this time, to offer their children at an early age to monasteries and convents. Child nuns could be offered as early as six, little monks at the age of ten. These children had been "offered" to God and to the monastery – hence the term "oblate" from the Latin *oblatus*, "offered." They had some freedom to choose whether they would remain in the monastery when they grew older. But it was not a freedom that many dared to exercise against the wishes of their family. Most oblates remained in the monastery to which they had been given.

The growth of the practice of "oblation," along with the emergence of the tonsure, shows the extent to which the laity treated monasteries as an adjunct to their own piety. Based on appeals to the Old Testament story of how Hannah (previously childless) had dedicated her first-born, Samuel, to the temple, the vowing of children was a regular practice for those afflicted by infertility or illness. Like any other product of nature, children were the gift of God quite as much as was any good harvest. Why, then, should children not be offered to God much as the "fruits of the earth" were offered? Children were offered as a counter-gift to God for the fertility which he had bestowed on human bodies in the same way as he had bestowed fertility on the fields.[11] More cynically, of course, parents frequently used monasteries and convents as depositaries for unwanted children – and especially for girls, who required dowries if they were to be married.[12]

Tonsure made the monk look distinctive. The practice of "oblation" ensured that children often grew up in monasteries, totally sheathed in a distinctive, monastic culture. Both practices seemed to make the monks more separate from the lay world. Yet this is only half of the story. Both practices showed that monasteries depended on a tacit symbiosis with the laity. They adopted lay rituals and they accepted recruits in a way that fed into the reproductive and marital strategies of their lay neighbors.

This means that monasteries and convents should not be seen as totally enclosed communities. Rather, they followed with unusual sensitivity the shifts of Christian piety in the world around them. It was lay persons who wished to join monasteries and convents or to offer their children to them in fulfillment of vows. It was lay persons who wished to stay close to them so as to benefit from the example, the prayers, and the spiritual advice of their inmates. It was, above all, lay persons who came increasingly to wish to endow and protect them, even if they did not themselves become monks or nuns. What was demanded of monasteries and convents throughout this period did not change only as a result of the work of bishops and of monastic organizers. The demands changed as a result of the constant, mute pressure of lay expectations.

"A school of the Lord's service": The *Rule* of Benedict (ca.480–ca.547)

First and foremost, lay persons agreed that monasteries were there to deal with sin. This is shown very clearly in a letter which Gregory I wrote to the emperor Maurice in 593. Drained by his wars with Persia, the emperor desperately needed manpower for his armies. As a result he issued an edict which forbade persons liable to military service to become monks. Gregory protested immediately. Surely the emperor must realize, he wrote, that such a law was intolerable: "for there are many persons who, unless they abandon all [and enter a monastery] cannot gain salvation in the sight of God."[13] Lay persons were, of course, capable of salvation. But monasteries existed for the exceptional cases. They gave freedom to those called to a sharper, more exacting style of Christian life. They sheltered sensitive souls in love with God, as Gregory himself had been. But they also existed for the amelioration of sinners. Many sinners needed "conversion." For sixth-century Christians, indeed, "conversion" had come to mean not a change of belief but a change of life. It meant joining a monastery so as to "purge" one's sins.

The *Rule* composed by Benedict for his monks at Monte Cassino owed its later influence to the manner in which he assumed that, as converted sinners, monks needed to begin with the basics. Monte Cassino was not expected to be a "Paradise regained" in an unearthly desert, as in the heroic days of the monks of Egypt. In Benedict's opinion, these days were long past.[14] What Italian monks of the early sixth century needed was a *Rule* "for beginners." His monastery was to be a "school of the Lord's service."[15] It was an elementary school. Upper-class persons, who had attended such schools, knew what this meant. As boys, they had struggled to internalize the crystalline precision of "correct" Latin under the cane of a schoolmaster. Now, in a monastery, as grown men, they were expected to go back to a school of morals which was as exacting, in its own way, as any Roman school. They were to subject their behavior to meticulous supervision, accompanied, when necessary, by instant punishment – blows from the strap included.

In an intensely status-conscious society, the most heroic self-mortification of all for a monk was to submit himself, in this manner, to the rule of an abbot. Gregory I tells the story of the son of a local notable who found himself, as a monk, standing behind Benedict, his abbot, holding the lamp while Benedict sat dining:

> "Who is this," he thought to himself, "that I should have to stand here holding the lamp for him while he is eating? Who am I to be acting as his slave?"[16]

Hence, the extreme sensitivity which Benedict showed to the issue of blotting out social differences. This was achieved, in the first place, by an utterly uniform code of dress. These were to be cheap reach-me-downs, bought in the local market. Thus, the cowl and robe of medieval monks, which plays so large a part in modern romantic visions of the Middle Ages, began as the sixth-century equivalent of a farmer's blue jeans.[17]

Seen from the outside, monasteries were like the slave households to which Romans would long have been accustomed. All monks were equal because all were placed under the fatherly but absolute control of their abbot. Monasteries were small places of intense discipline, carved out against the grain of normal social relations in a late Roman society. They were maintained by innumerable, hard-won victories over the self on the part of former free men.

"The cool refuge of chastity": The Convent of Caesaria at Arles (508)

Throughout the Christian world pious monks and nuns had always enjoyed a reputation for possessing the power of prayer. It was believed that such persons could pray to God on behalf of their fellow-Christians. As we saw in chapter 7, the importance of holy men and holy women in East Roman society depended on the belief that they possessed an unusual capacity to move God by their prayers. They were constantly asked to intercede on behalf of their lay clients.

What changed in the West, in the course of the sixth century, was the emergence of the belief that entire convents and monasteries possessed a collective power of prayer that was somehow stronger than the prayers offered by any one holy person. It is a subtle but decisive shift. Convents and monasteries came to be seen as more than sheltered places where individuals sought holiness. They were treated as holy places in themselves. A well-organized monastery could function as a powerhouse of prayer on behalf of the community as a whole. Hence the growing importance placed, in monastic rules all over Europe, on those qualities which rendered the community gathered in a monastery or convent capable of collective holiness and, hence, of effective collective prayer.[18]

We can see this development most clearly in Gaul. It first affected women. Nuns rather than monks led the way.[19] This in itself is significant, for the need for a powerhouse of prayer made up of women placed the greatest weight of expectations on those who, in many ways, were closest to the lay world. Women could never be priests. Given the prevalence of rape and violence in a countryside frequently ravaged by warfare, women could not seek out a "desert" for themselves in the hills and woodlands of Italy and Gaul. They had to stay close to town. All over the Christian world, women's monasticism had begun very much as a branch of family piety. A pious household would be proud to have "its" virgin. She would be secluded in the back of the house. She would be visible only as she proceeded (with due modesty) to the local church and back, to join her "sisters in religion" in the local virgins' choir. But it is precisely this enclosed and faceless quality which caused the virgin to be valued so highly, for it placed sanctity in the very heart of the profane world. The pious virgin was a human relic, encased in the midst of the city. Virginity brought a particularly charged form of the sacred and placed it alongside the profane world in a way that the more distant heroism of desert monks, the models of male monastic piety, could not hope to do.[20]

For virgin women carried their sanctity with them in an utterly tangible form. Their bodies were intact. They had not suffered the penetration of intercourse or the disruption of childbirth. While men had to work hard, through ascetic discipline, to present to the lay world reassuring physical signs of their holiness, a woman, as a virgin, was believed to carry an intact soul fully revealed through an intact body. The fact that this body had been left untouched seemed to show awesome self-control on the part of the woman (given late antique Mediterranean notions of the vulnerability of women to sexual temptation). In reality, it frequently did show very real heroism and determination on the part of the young girl: her wish not to marry was only too easily overridden by her parents. And, once the girl's dedication as a nun took place, it showed something even weightier. It made visible the sheer will of an entire family and of the convent which the family patronized to say "hands off" to the world at large. A woman of their family, in "their" convent, had been made sacred and was not available to others.[21]

In reality, of course, a woman's holiness was achieved through a Christian ascetic piety that did not differ greatly from that of monks. Pious women faced the same austerities. They engaged in the same struggle to overcome their own self-will. If they were girls from cultured families, they engaged in the same bouts of intense meditative reading as did any monk. Augustine's monastic rule circulated at this time in two forms, with only the Latin gender switched, from masculine to feminine, according to whether it was intended for a monastery or for a convent.[22] But the holiness of a woman nonetheless gave a different message to the lay world. It spoke with mute certainty, in a language that was understood since pagan times, through a miraculously intact body. It was from bodies charged with such associations that sixth-century persons thought that they could create the most effective power-houses of prayer.

In 508, Caesarius of Arles (of whom we have already heard in chapter 6) set up a convent under his sister, Caesaria. The *Rule* which he composed for her in 512 became a classic.[23] He brought together an unusually large group of women (200 in all) in a single convent of St. John. He deliberately placed this group in buildings that abutted the walls of the city itself. By their position beside the city walls, they were marked out as the spiritual protectors of Arles, at a time when the city was under constant danger of siege.[24]

Caesarius imposed total seclusion on the nuns. Once they entered the convent, they would never leave it. They had sought out, in the convent, "the cool refuge of chastity."[25] He then subjected every detail of their life to meticulous control. He even went so far as to sketch, in the manuscript of his *Rule*, the precise shape of the haircuts which the nuns should have.[26] Such a community was well worth the care which Caesarius put into it. For what

Caesarius had created, out of a pool of pious women gathered together by his sister, was nothing less than a "holy place" as effective as the shrine of any local saint. This was an environment where the "world" (and, it was hoped, even sin itself) stopped at the convent door.[27]

Caesaria's nuns were recruited with care from the daughters of the elite. Like the virgin priestesses of Roman times, their purity was held to protect the city as a whole. Their unearthly seclusion and carefully paced life of prayer and reading made of them the Vestal Virgins of the new Christian city. The convent of Saint John had something of the ancient holiness of a temple precinct about it. It was a precinct that must never be breached. When a fire broke out in the convent buildings, the nuns were remembered as having huddled together in the empty cistern that lay in the center of its courtyard until the flames died down, rather than abandon their seclusion by passing back through the door which led out into the city of Arles.[28]

"To pray for the peace of the kingdom": Radegund of Poitiers (520–587)

Precisely because it stressed a stunning juxtaposition of the utterly sacred and the profane, a woman's piety could act as a bridge between the new barbarian, military elites of northern Gaul and what had previously been a largely "Roman" form of religion, cultivated by the leisured and still largely civilian elites of the south. Impressive royal women had begun to do this early in the century. Queen Caratene, the estranged wife of king Chilperic II of the Burgundians, was praised both for her generosity to the poor and for a form of secret piety that was greatly valued at the time. She always wore a hair shirt beneath her royal robes.[29] No practice signalled so effectively the intimate bringing together of the sacred and the profane. Beneath the embroidered robes of a public figure, the queen carried real flesh, mortified by ascetic discipline. Caratene brought a sliver of intense holiness into the midst of a hard-driving, largely military court.

The Burgundian kingdom had lain in the Rhône valley, close to Caesaria's Arles The woman who brought this style of piety to the Frankish society of northern Gaul came as an outsider from across the Rhine. Radegund (520–587) was a woman of royal stock from Thuringia.[30] She had grown up as a Christian in a region far removed from the heavily Romanized Provence of Caratene, Caesarius and Caesaria. She was brought to Francia in 532 as a young captive, after the destruction of her country, in order to become the unwilling wife of king Chlothar of Neustria. At that time, Chlothar controlled much of northwestern Gaul, around Soissons. In a new and hostile environment, the young teenager sheathed herself with an intense sense of the sacred. Isolated in a royal villa at Athies, near Soissons, Radegund would lovingly clean the chapel of the villa. She gathered up the dust from the altar "and reverently placed it outside the door, rather than sweep it away." She would lead her companions in solemn processions, carrying a home-made wooden cross.[31] During Lent, like queen Caratene, she wore a hair shirt (given to her by a holy nun) beneath her royal robes.[32]

Finally, Radegund shook herself free from her husband. In any case, she had only been, at best, the "chief wife" of Chlothar, who was exuberantly polygamous, as Merovingian kings were supposed to be. She forced the bishop of Noyon to accept her as a nun, by the simple expedient of dressing herself in the robes of a nun and advancing to the altar, demanding to be consecrated.[33] In her new inviolate status, as a "dedicated" person, Radegund emerged as a gift-giver in truly royal style. For a Merovingian queen, robes, jewels, and great gold-studded belts were far more than mere ornaments. They were the physical condensation on her person of the magical aura of royalty. Radegund piled these on the altars of churches or chopped them up to be sent to local hermits, thereby transmuting them into "sacred" wealth offered by a "sacred" queen.[34]

Her austerities made her admirers shudder. Hers was a piety grounded on her own body. She was even said to have branded her arm with the sign of the Cross: "to cool her fervent soul, she sought to burn her body."[35] She brought her body into contact with all that was most loathsome to an upper-class person. She regularly bathed the poor, massaging with her own hands the scabby, worm-eaten heads of beggar-women.[36] By such extremes of highly physical piety, she brought a touch of fierce holiness to the highest levels of society in Frankish Gaul.

When Radegund moved to Poitiers, in 561, to found a convent of her own, she placed it, like the convent of St. John at Arles, in a section of the city's walls. She adopted for her nuns the *Rule* of Caesarius for Caesaria. Her convent was to be a similar holy place. She then did something which Caesaria had not done. She used her status as a member of the Christian "family of princes" to obtain nothing less than a relic of the Holy Cross itself, direct from the emperor of Constantinople. It was an altogether appropriate relic for such a woman to obtain. It linked Radegund to the memory of Constantine and of his mother, Helena, who was believed to have uncovered the true Cross at Jerusalem. In doing this, Radegund shrank time and distance: "What Helena had done in the East, Radegund did for Gaul."[37] The arrival of the True Cross at Poitiers brought a touch of international, East Roman piety into a Gaul which, up to then, had been largely devoted to the cult of local saints.

But the relic of the True Cross had a deeper and more personal significance for Radegund. Radegund was a queen, "a noble sprout from royal
stock."[38] Had she remained "in the world," she might have proved to be a
"blossoming bough" whose fruit, in the form of children, upheld the
Merovingian Frankish dynasty. Instead, she had allowed her potentially fertile body to become as dead and dry as was the dry, hard wood of the relic of
the Cross. To a Christian poet who meditated on such things – none other
than Venantius Fortunatus, summoned by Radegund to Poitiers to do justice
to the occasion – the dry fragment of the Cross was the most fertile object in
the world. For the Cross was the true Tree of Life, always blossoming and
heavy with the fruit whose taste healed humankind.[39] Radegund, the infertile queen, whose body had been rendered dry and hard by arduous austerities, was its most appropriate guardian. She and her nuns were the truly
fertile ones, for they "carried Christ in the womb."[40]

In many ways, Radegund's convent of the Holy Cross looks forward to a
new style of piety.[41] The relic of the Cross was kept in a special chapel. This
chapel lay at the heart of the monastery. In it were stored "those precious
gems which Paradise holds and which Heaven hoards."[42] It was a treasure-
house of holy things. And only Radegund, her nuns, and a few, chosen visitors were allowed to have access to it.

In the deliberate seclusion of the relic of the Holy Cross, we are dealing
with an intensely focused sense of the holy, shielded from the world by
virgin women. This was different from the old-fashioned holiness associated with the great urban shrines of Gaul. That had been a holiness where
a touch of Paradise had been open to all. In Tours, and elsewhere, as we
learn from Gregory of Tours, heaving crowds of men and women alike
would stream in and out of the basilicas. They gathered in glorious disorder around the holy tombs, "like bees in full swarm."[43] This was not the
case in the convent of the Holy Cross. Access to the holy was restricted.
Because of this, the holiness associated with the convent seemed to be that
much more vibrant and more awesome, as befitted a convent thought to be
a powerhouse of prayer.

The delicate scent of a royal court lingered at Radegund's Convent of the
Holy Cross. She received courtly personal poems, accompanied by baskets
of strawberries, from Venantius Fortunatus.[44] A potted laurel stood in her
cell. One of her nuns was delighted to recognize the sounds of a love song
that she had composed in her youth, drifting through a window from a festival below.[45]

But the monastery had a serious purpose. At a time when a highly localized devotion to urban patron saints was the most usual form of Christian
piety in Gaul, Radegund thought in "imperial" terms. Her prayers embraced

the Frankish kingdom as a whole. She and her nuns were the spiritual guardians of that state and of the kings who struggled to control it.

> She taught us all to pray incessantly for their stability . . . She imposed assiduous vigils on her flock, imploring them to pray incessantly for the kings.[46]

By the time that Radegund died, in 587, she had shown how intense, melodramatic piety practiced by the secluded few might act as a powerhouse of prayer to support the entire Frankish kingdom. In the largest and, in many ways, the wealthiest, political unit in western Europe, monasticism had become a fully public institution, identified with stability and political success.

The Making of a *Sapiens*: Religion and Culture in Continental Europe and in Ireland

The "Rustic Roman Tongue"

The decisive development of monasticism in the course of the sixth century took place in a Continental Europe which was still recognizably Roman. The populations of the entire western Mediterranean continued to speak Latin. The coastline of North Africa, also, was Latin-speaking up to and beyond the Arab conquest. As late as the eleventh century, the inhabitants of Gafsa, an isolated oasis in southern Tunisia close to the Sahara, still spoke what they called "Latin."[1] We are dealing with a paradoxical development. Latin won its final triumph as the spoken language of most of the former territories of the Roman empire in the very last, more desperate centuries of Roman rule. Had the empire fallen when the "Roman peace" was at its height, in the second century A.D., Latin would have vanished along with the empire in much of western Europe. Celtic would have re-emerged as the dominant language in Gaul and much of Spain. France and Spain might well have become Celtic-speaking countries, as Brittany and Wales are today. It was only in the last century of the empire that the slow pressure of bureaucrats, landowners, and the Christian clergy ensured that Latin replaced languages which had existed since prehistoric times.

By the year 600, the victory of Latin was assured around the Mediterranean and throughout much of Gaul. A simple Latin, shared by all classes, replaced the previous local languages, with the exception of Celtic in Brittany and Basque in the Pyrenees. As we will see in chapter 19, this Latin later came to be known as the "rustic Roman tongue." It was from this workaday "rustic" Latin that the "Romance" languages of Italy, France, Spain, and Portugal developed.[2] As far north as the valley of the Moselle, in France, and deep into the northern valleys of the Alps, as far as Bavaria, the population spoke some form or other of the "rustic Roman tongue."

The Decline of the Schools

The consolidation of Latin on the ground took place at a time notorious for the recession of Latin studies at the top of society. In chapter 8, we followed the erosion of the Latin culture of the leisured upper class in the course of the sixth century in Italy. We saw the reaction to this decline of men such as Cassiodorus and Gregory the Great. Similar developments took place in Gaul and Spain.[3]

They are easily summarized. Education had always been a preserve of the upper classes of the Roman world. But these upper classes had been fluid. Gifted boys from small towns (such as Augustine, later famous as bishop of Hippo and author of the *Confessions*, whom we met in chapter 3) could mingle with the great on the strength of their command of a Latin punctiliously modelled on great, classical authors. Their speech and writing betrayed deep immersion in the works of Cicero and Vergil. This education was provided in the cities, and specially in the major cities. Those in search of a classical education found themselves travelling around an "archipelago of cities" where education was to be found. These cities stood out in high relief in a world where "rustic" Latin was spoken everywhere, but where refined Latin and the civilization could only be found in a few privileged places. We should never underestimate how "rustic," indeed, how "barbarous," large tracts of the Roman world remained, from the cultural point of view, long before the "Barbarian Invasions" occurred. In the fourth century, for instance, Augustine had moved from one small town, Thagaste (Souk Ahras in modern Algeria), to a provincial center, Madaura (Mdaourouch, Algeria) and then, at considerable cost to his father, he finished his studies in the great city of Carthage. Later he went on to teach in Carthage, Rome, and Milan. His was a success story; and it was a success story that clung to the contours of the Roman cities.[4]

In the fifth and sixth centuries, the cities of the West could no longer support the expense of maintaining their schools. This happened in part because the old alliance between classical culture and the exercise of power was weakened. In the later empire, highly educated civilians had acted, as it were, as a Mandarin class, spread all over the empire. They owed their homogeneity to a remarkably uniform education. It was they who kept government going, both at court and on the local level. They passed on the commands of rough men – of military emperors and, later, of "barbarian" kings – in acceptable, old-fashioned form. The career of the young Cassiodorus as spokesman of the Ostrogothic kings of Italy (which we saw in chapter 8) showed that it was still possible, in early sixth-century Italy, for a classically educated Roman to remain a valued figure in a "barbarian" court. In doing so he appealed to the old division between civilians and the military. Romans, he said, were glorious for their eloquence, Ostrogoths for their feats of arms.[5]

But in many kingdoms, most notably in Francia and in Visigothic Spain, the old distinction of military and civilian had broken down. A mixed aristocracy had emerged. These men knew that they served their king better, and received more generous rewards, if they opted at an early age for military careers rather than spend their time, at the feet of a schoolmaster, learning the Latin classics. Thus it was not only financial difficulties which led to the drying up of the urban schools. It was the competition of possible career paths among the aristocracy of major kingdoms, such as the Franks and the Visigoths, which led young men of "Roman" background, quite as much as "barbarians," to neglect their Vergil in favor of the more profitable and (as we would say) the more "relevant" arts of war.[6]

"Worldly wisdom": The Classics and the Christian Church

Thus, in Roman times, a shared classical education had been the marker of an empire-wide upper class. By the year 600, this class had splintered. Its members faced a variety of career choices, many of which did not require the sort of uniform education which we associate with the "classical" Latin world. Throughout western Europe, from southern Italy to Spain and Gaul, the militarization of the upper classes was the most decisive change of all. But it was the most silent. We know far more about the vocal split, within the upper classes themselves, between those who still upheld an ideal of "worldly wisdom" (based on what remained of a traditional education in the classics) and those who considered such "worldly wisdom" to be at best a distraction and at worst a legacy of paganism.[7]

We should not underestimate the strength of this current in the sixth-century Church. Nowadays we speak somewhat nostalgically of "the classical tradition," and are concerned by its decline over much of western Europe in this time. Many serious contemporaries, however, thought that they faced sterner choices. A well-educated and intellectually sophisticated man such as Gregory the Great was quite capable of thinking that "the classical tradition" was not for him. It was no more than "worldly wisdom." Since Roman times, "worldly wisdom" had been a badge of status for the upper classes. It bolstered the status of men "in the world". It often rendered them confidently oblivious to the call to amendment of life delivered by ascetic

Christians. Gregory observed that "worldly wisdom" encouraged pride in noblemen and intellectual competitiveness, leading even to heresy, in clerics. It had no message for the serious Christian. It was all froth and no content. Altogether, Gregory dismissed "worldly wisdom" not so much because it was tainted by its undoubted pagan past. Rather, he treated it as an unwelcome distraction. It hindered the mind from concentrating on the main business of life, which was to steel the soul for the Last Judgment.[8]

We are dealing with the insensible but irrevocable narrowing down of an entire tradition.[9] This narrowing down was as important for the fate of classical Latin studies as was economic recession and the opening up of alternative careers for the upper classes. Those who propounded this austere view of culture were by no means persons deprived of education. Many were high aristocrats, whose families had been better able than were lesser persons to escape the effects of the general recession of education. If Augustine had lived in the sixth century, he would not have been able to receive the education which brought him to the top. As a member of the Roman nobility, however, Augustine's great admirer, Gregory the Great, had succeeded in maintaining a high standard of Latinity. At Rome, he lived in a world of tutors and great libraries such as could not be found in the provinces.

Men such as Gregory still existed, scattered all over Mediterranean Europe, in Italy, southern Gaul, and southern Spain. Many had received what we might call a "private" education. They had been taught at home by learned members of their family or by a learned local bishop. They could still draw on the resources of family libraries or of libraries collected by churchmen. Their culture and *savoir faire* still led them into leading positions in the Church. But, whether they had become monks or not, their minds had passed through the monastery. They consciously opted to devote their talents to the study of the Bible and to the grimly practical task of amending their own lives.

This new seriousness amounted, in many ways, to the most drastic inner mutation of Latin culture to occur in the centuries which followed the end of the empire. But it had been long prepared in Christian circles. The great generation of converts of the late fourth century – Jerome, Augustine, Paulinus of Nola – had argued vociferously for and against the relevance of "worldly wisdom" to the Christian. They often took up extreme poses against the pagan classics. These extreme statements were belied by their practice, which often showed them to be men steeped in the ancient tradition. But the invectives of Jerome and others still echoed loudly in the sixth and seventh centuries.[10]

Nor was such a narrowing down of culture (drastic though it was) an altogether unique event in the long history of the ancient world. It did not necessarily betray a moment of irreparable breakdown. Rather, the history of Greek and Roman civilization had always been marked by a characteristic pendulum swing. Moments of exuberant creativity were repeatedly followed by long periods of retrenchment. And this pendulum swing was marked by constant alternation between periods of creativity in literature and in speculative philosophy followed by long periods of single-minded preoccupation with ethical problems. How educated persons should groom themselves; how they should conquer their weaknesses; how they should overcome pain and console themselves in moments of grief; how they should stand in relation to their fellows and in relation to the gods: these were issues pursued by ancient philosophers, for centuries on end, with remarkable singlemindedness.[11] They meant more to a vocal (if somewhat eccentric) segment of the Greco-Roman elites than did the enjoyment of literature and the thrill of speculation. For, as the proponents of the ethical tradition pointed out, these issues were about real life. They involved giving serious thought to the real sufferings and choices faced by real men and women. To have a grasp on these ethical issues and to develop a carefully thought-out scheme for moral self-improvement was to do something that was regarded as truly serious. It was to understand, not through speculation, but, existentially, through life itself, what life was about. In a very real sense, it was to achieve "wisdom."[12]

The ecclesiastical culture of the late sixth- and seventh-century West was dominated by a "culture of wisdom" overwhelmingly directed to moral issues, which was analogous, in many ways, to the strenuous concern for moral improvement which had dominated philosophical thought in the Hellenistic and Roman periods. In chapter 8, we saw what the adoption of a "culture of wisdom" meant for Gregory the Great. His writings were intended to mark a decisive shift towards what he called *moralitas*. By this he meant far more than "morality." It was nothing less than the transformation of the self, through the amendment of sinful habits and the development of "compunction" – a sharp stirring of the heart which fostered the love of God. When Gregory expounded the Book of Job to an inner circle, it was the "moral" message of the book which concerned him – hence its famous title, the *Moralia*.[13]

Gregory was acutely aware that he wrote for a new elite which needed "wisdom." His readers were powerful figures in their respective regions. They were bishops and great abbots. His *Regula Pastoralis*, his "Rule for Pastors," was addressed to persons like himself. They had been pushed to the top of society all over Europe by the rise of the Church. They were *rectores*, rulers of souls in a spiritual empire, whose actions had an immediate effect also in the secular world. Gregory wrote to tame and to direct ecclesiastical power. He did not wish the new bishops and abbots to be theologians or rhetors. He paid hardly any attention to preaching skills. Rather, he wanted bishops, clergymen, and monks to be men endowed with "wisdom." For only those possessed of "wisdom," developed through long meditation on the Bible and through fear of the Last Judgment, could rule their "subjects" as true "doctors of the soul." As in the Roman empire of the days of Seneca, the reform of conduct was considered essential. Rhetoric, philosophy, even theology, could be dispensed with. What mattered was the formation of a new elite of bishops and abbots, who were urged (as the Romans addressed by Seneca had once been urged) to rule themselves before they ruled others.

"Subtlety of words": Secular Culture in the "Barbarian" West

We must remember, however, that this severely purposive view, though it was strenuously upheld by a new elite of monks and clergymen, never stood alone in Continental Europe. Secular culture of a kind was maintained by other members of the upper classes. This culture lacked the impressive uniformity of earlier times, which had been based on relentless insistence on "correct" Latin grammar and syntax. But vivid little oases of self-conscious Latinity were maintained. Power did not reside only in arms. There was still some room left for eloquence. Both the Visigothic kingdom and the Frankish kingdoms centered on courts where displays of old-fashioned Latin rhetoric and poetry were still appreciated.[14]

When Venantius Fortunatus came to northern Gaul, in 567, he did not meet a Frankish elite that consisted only of illiterate warriors. He met a man such as Gogo the *referendarius*, the lord chancellor and tutor of the young kings. Gogo's letters were written in a style that was acclaimed as "succulent and florid." Through these letters, he maintained literary friendships with fellow-members of the ruling class in a manner that had changed little since the fourth century, when the letters of Ausonius and Paulinus of Nola had crisscrossed Spain, Gaul, and Italy.[15] As late as the middle of the seventh century, young men were sent to the court of the Frankish kings so as to learn "the subtlety of words."[16] This steady trickle of young men, eager to gain "subtlety of words," ensured that, in western Europe, power still bore, at times, an old-fashioned Latin face.

The chanceries of the Frankish kings of Gaul and of the Visigothic kings of Spain still needed a high-flown Latin with which to impress their neighbors. In the seventh century, the Visigothic kings emerged as formidable legislators in a tradition continuous with the *Theodosian Code*. Laws collected by the emperor of Constantinople in 438 were still being reissued and added to in Toledo, at the court of the Visigothic kings, as late as the end of the seventh century.[17]

The Frankish kings of the north were less given to formal legislation of this kind. But in southern Gaul, at least, as in Spain and Italy, the law remained a Roman law. The practice of Roman law demanded an ability to write and to read. Hence, practical Latinity reached down, through royal officials, through the Church and through the great landowners, to touch local societies all over the West. For legal documents, written in the workaday cursive script of local notaries, remained essential for members of the elite. Their titles to property, their wills, their pious foundations, their marriage settlements, and even their political trials demanded long sheets of papyrus, carefully written up with legal formulae that had developed, without any significant break, from Roman times.[18]

Pathetically few examples of these papyrus documents survive compared with the large number that must have been produced all over early medieval Europe. Hence the excitement of the few documents written on more durable material, which have recently been discovered by archaeologists. They give a glimpse of a Latin legal culture which reached right down the social scale to touch the lives of local landowners and their peasants. Wooden estate documents have been recovered from North Africa. Written in 493–96 (20 years, that is, after the formal end of the western empire), they show that the laws determining the distribution of the olive crop between landlord and tenants had not changed since the days of Hadrian in the early second century.[19] Similar legal instruments have been found, scratched on tiles for the use of villagers in seventh-century Castile.[20]

We should remember the persistent "background noise", throughout the West, of a low-level but tenacious Latin secular culture. When bishops such as Caesarius, Gregory of Tours, and Gregory I stressed the fact that they themselves had chosen to use a simple, "rustic" style, they did not do so because they or their audience could read and write nothing else. Far from it. What they offered was a literary equivalent of *nouvelle cuisine*. Their "rustic" style was designed for those in search of spiritual health. The bishops knew very well that, in the wider world, there were some lay persons and even many clerical colleagues who still preferred a hearty "banquet of words" of the old kind. Fragments of "worldly" literature continued to be produced throughout the sixth and seventh centuries because they carried resonances of old-world solidity and grace, as did the late Roman marble sarcophagi which members of the elite would reuse for their own burials, the classical gems and the late antique silverware which ornamented the altars of the churches, and the carefully chosen columns of Roman marble with which they decorated their shrines and palaces. They were reminders that a long and opulent Roman past still had a place in the present.[21]

The Making of a *Sapiens*: Sixth-century Ireland and West Britain

What the inhabitants of Continental Europe appear not to have known is that, further to the west, on islands embraced by an Atlantic Ocean which was believed to guard the very end of the world, a significantly different form of Latin Christian culture had come into being. This had been created, in the course of the sixth century, where the coasts of western Britain and eastern Ireland faced each other across the Irish Sea.

In our fifth chapter, we saw how this new cultural zone had been created, in the course of the fifth century, as a result of the quickening of contact between eastern Ireland and Britain, which formed the background to the mission of Patricius (later Saint Patrick). We will deal, in chapter 14, with the further spread of Christianity in Ireland.

For the moment, what needs to be stressed is that, in this new cultural zone, Latin was a totally foreign language, to be found only in a few, infinitely precious books. The mother tongues of those who read these Latin books were two distinct branches of Celtic – British (the ancestor of Welsh) and Old Irish. These two dialects of Celtic were not mutually intelligible, and, at this time, neither of them was a written language. Hence, those who wished to share a common Christian culture found themselves forced to use a Latin based on Christian books as their only vehicle of written communication. Only in a Latin patiently learned from books could British and Irish Christians with any pretensions to learning write to each other, teach each other, argue with each other and enjoy the pleasure of denouncing each other.[22]

What is remarkable is the manner in which, despite the collapse of so much that was "Roman" in Britain, and the absence of Roman culture in any form in Ireland, embattled enclaves of Latin learning sprang up in both countries. They maintained a lively "inter-visibility," through constant contact one with the other throughout the late fifth and sixth centuries. The Irish Sea, which had previously marked the westernmost frontier of the Roman empire, was now open. It was frequently crisscrossed by travelling religious experts. Irish sources long remembered how a British sage Vinniau (Saint Findbarr in Irish) had come west to Ireland "over the swelling sea, bearing [scriptural] law."[23]

By the end of the sixth century, a network of Latin-using monks, clergymen, and scholars stretched from southern Wales and along the coast of

Ireland from Leinster to Antrim. This network stood out in high relief in a world which was still only partly Christianized, and which owed little or nothing to Rome.

There were certain dilemmas which Welsh and Irish men of Latin learning did not share with their Continental colleagues. "Secular" or "worldly" Latin did not exist for them any more than did spoken Latin. What they had to hand was the Bible and a selection of vivid texts of Latin Christian literature of the late fourth and early fifth centuries – the cultural debris of a ravaged Roman province, that had been preserved in western Britain and Wales after the collapse of Roman society in large areas of the island. At a time when Cassiodorus, at Vivarium, boasted a library stocked with carefully prepared volumes, Irish and Welsh scholars made do with a limited number of texts, copied into unprepossessing, functional *codices*. The great illuminated Gospels that we associate with the Celtic world were not created until two centuries later. In the sixth century, the Irish made do with mere scraps compared with what was still available in Mediterranean Europe.[24]

It is important not to exaggerate the cultural riches of sixth-century Ireland. An enthusiastic nationalist tradition has claimed that an entire range of classical Latin books were transported to the island at the time of the "Barbarian Invasions." They were saved by the Irish from the barbarism into which, so these enthusiasts assert, Continental Europe had irrevocably sunk. Books are still written entitled "How the Irish Saved Civilization."[25] This is a myth which has no scholarly support. It is also a myth which overlooks the true originality and creativity of Irish Christian culture at that time. For what Irishmen and West Britons lacked in books, they more than made up for through the intensity and originality with which they read what books they had, and the zest with which they applied their reading to substantially new situations. The Irish did a lot more than "save" the relics of classical civilization. They created something new.

First of all, from these scarce materials, they created an entire new Latin. This was not the self-consciously "simple" Latin upheld by Continental monks and bishops. For it was not tensed against existing, upper-class rivals in the secular world, who still used a florid Latin for purely "worldly" purposes. It was, in many ways, an older Latin than that of sixth-century Europe. It was closer to the dramatic style of the great monk-aristocrats of fifth-century Gaul. It was a deeply premeditated language, often sprinkled with rare words found only in Latin handbooks, endowed with a complex syntax, which spaced the sonorous Latin phrases in such a way as to endow their message with the tension and the sense of pace of poetry. We saw, in chapter 5, how Gildas had used such a Latin to denounce the sins of his fellow-Britons. Altogether, it was the Latin of a small, self-chosen caste of *sancti*, of unflinching Christians perched on the edge of the world. Through Latin, they spoke intensely to each other; and they assumed that all other Christians, all over Europe, through the very fact that they also possessed Latin books, must also be speaking the same way as they did.[26]

The cultural ideal of these circles was the *sapiens*. This was a man who had mastered Latin from books, who had made his own the wisdom of the Bible and of a Christian inheritance made available in a few, stubbornly valued texts, and who knew how to deploy this hard-won knowledge in a Latin rhetoric calculated to communicate the awe and the urgency of such wisdom.[27] Seldom, in the history of Christianity in western Europe, do we meet men creating, so zealously and in so short a time, a "Christianity of the mind", a Christianity, that is, conjured up from texts alone, that carried the reader back, almost 200 years, to the world of Saint Jerome, to John Cassian, and to the first, raw impact on Western Christians of news of the monks of Egypt.

These texts were read as if time and distance had collapsed. The monks of Egypt, and the advice which John Cassian had drawn from them, was held to belong fully to the present of the monks of Britain and Ireland. They did not in any way share the gentle pessimism of their Italian contemporary, Benedict. As we saw in chapter 9, Benedict thought that such feats were not for the monks of his own day. The renowned austerity of what we call "Celtic" monasticism derived, in part, from a distinctive style of reading Christian texts. What had been brought to Ireland and Britain, through books, was the heroic Egypt of the fourth century. The Irish wanted to experience to the full the rigors of the Egyptian desert. They were prepared to perch on offshore rocks in the Atlantic in order to do so.[28]

"Medicine for sin": The World of the *Penitentials*

Hence, what developed in the British Isles was a radical local variant of the "culture of wisdom" which held such an appeal to men like Gregory the Great in Continental Europe. The difference between the two areas was that, in Continental Europe, a monastic "culture of wisdom" had emerged slowly and needed always to defend itself against powerful alternatives within the same Latin culture. In Ireland and Britain, the overwhelmingly non-Roman structure of society ensured that, within the Latin tradition of local Christianity, no such competitors existed. The *sapientes*, the "men of wisdom," dominated the world of Latin texts.

As Christianity progressed in the British Isles, these "men of wisdom" were called upon to regulate large Christian communities. This was a challenge of the first order, such as Gregory the Great, who lived within the boundaries of a massively Christian state, could barely have imagined. Up to the middle of the sixth century, Christianity may well have been a minority religion in Ireland. Western Britain had been officially Christian since the days of the Roman empire. The British kingdoms extended over a far wider area than modern Wales (which has remained the core of Celtic speech in Britain). But, in the sixth century, they were shaken by the advance of Saxons from the eastern seaboard. The Saxon advance often involved acculturation. Conquered Britons abandoned their Christianity to join a new, self-confident elite of pagan Saxons. The urgent writings of Gildas showed that a sense of menace hung over the British Church.[29]

Thus, both in Ireland and in western Britain, the identity and the stability of the Christian community was a matter of real urgency. In potentially fissile and threatened congregations, the problem of how to deal with sin had to be faced with unaccustomed rigor. The answer of the *sapientes* consisted in the elaboration of an unusual system of penance and atonement for sin, called by scholars by the somewhat clumsy name of the system of "tariffed penance."[30] Each particular sin had to be confessed to a spiritual guide, who was usually a bishop, a priest, or a monastic director. A precisely calibrated penance, in the form of a fixed period of prayer, fasting, and similar self-mortification, was assigned to each sin. Once this penance had been performed, the sinner could be considered absolved in the eyes of God.

The fierce asceticism associated with monasteries in west Britain and Ireland was made possible by the belief that all sins – even the most horrendous – could be atoned for by penance. Writings about the monks of Egypt had taken this for granted. Spiritual guides in the British Isles shared in an attitude which, as we saw in chapter 9, was widespread also in Continental Europe: the monastic life was there, in large part, to enable repentant Christian to "purge" their sins. But they treated the actual process by which sins were purged with a new, liberating precision.

They followed the accounts of Egyptian monasticism which had been made available to the Latin world by John Cassian, as we saw in chapter 4. Cassian had described how the wise men of Egypt delineated the eight principal vices and the antithetical virtues by which these vices were cured. Each sin was spoken of as an illness. The duty of a spiritual guide was to draw on his wisdom to search out and to apply the correct "medicine for sin," appropriate to each failing. Now, in the middle of the sixth century, and some 4,000 miles away from Egypt, the wise men of Britain and Ireland claimed to extend this basic categorization of the vices and their antidotes to cover every possible sin. There was no human sin that could not be itemized and healed.[31]

But "tariffed penance" not been developed, in Ireland and western Britain, only for monks and nuns. It was meant to meet the needs of the Christian community as a whole. The basic assumption of the system was that while sin was serious, it was manageable. Sin embraced all aspects of human life. There was no sin too trivial to be confessed and atoned for. But then, no sin was so horrendous that it could not be forgiven, provided the sinner confessed it and showed his or her sincere repentance by taking on a clearly defined period of penitential self-mortification. Troubled average Christians (and not only ascetics) were offered an opportunity to gain, and constantly to regain, the favor of God. This was a society where Christians constantly looked for the hand of God in every notable fortune and misfortune. Those whose had "purged" their sins through confession and penance could be that much more certain to enjoy divine protection and good fortune.

As in Continental Europe, notorious sins had always cried out for some dramatic form of "closure." Spectacular sinners had to be excluded from the church and then let in again after due atonement had been offered. There was nothing unusual in this element in the *Penitentials*. What was unusual was the insistence that the system of "tariffed penance" was not reserved for emergencies only. Ordinary lay persons with sins on their conscience could approach a priest or some other spiritual guide and "purge" their consciences through confession and through accepting a measured penance.

As we will see in later chapters, confession and penance were not imposed on all believers, as they came to be imposed in the Catholic Church from the year 1215 onwards. Penance was a "medicine," and only the very desperate or the spiritually sensitive went out of their way, at this time, to seek it. But, precisely because it had a strong "elective" element in it, the system contributed decisively to the creation of an inner ring of Christian lay persons, who felt particularly bound by ties of confession, penance, and atonement to their local church or monastery.[32]

We know of this system from the many little manuals of penance, known as *Penitentials*, which were necessary for its functioning.[33] The *Penitentials* consist of lists of sins and of their appropriate penances. They are blunt texts. In their description of sins they are nothing if not precise. A single *Penitential* can range from explosive cases of perjury and bloodshed to the most intimate details of sexual behavior. Fornication by a bishop is mentioned alongside intercourse with animals, masturbation, intercourse with one's wife "from behind, in the manner of dogs," and sexual play by small children.[34] Entire scenarios of temptation are described, and the appropriate penance for each act is laid down:

He who [as a monk] loves any woman, but is unaware of evil beyond a few conversations, shall do penance for forty days. But if he has kissed and embraced her, one year . . . He who loves her in mind only, seven days. But if he has spoken [his love] but has not been accepted by her, forty days.[35]

Not surprisingly, modern readers of the *Penitentials* are alternately appalled and fascinated by so much circumstantiality.[36] Their sixth-century authors were less easily shocked than we are. Such things happened. They could be confessed. If they were confessed, they would be forgiven.

But the example of the monks of Egypt, with their emphasis on the availability of "medicine" for every sin, was not the only strand that went into the making of the *Penitentials*. They also represent an attempt to mold society according ideals found in the Old Testament. In the "holiness code" of the Book of Leviticus the wise men of the British Isles found an all-embracing code of behavior, based on the avoidance of various forms of "pollution." This code had guaranteed the order, the identity, and the sovereign dignity of the people of Israel. It made of Israel a "people of God."

The Old Testament was now invoked to do the same for the Christian communities of Britain and Ireland. Like the Book of Leviticus, the message of the *Penitentials* was that the Christian life was a high art, a matter of conscious craftsmanship, undertaken by a people brought close to God. Trivial sins with light penances – such as sexual peccadilloes and lack of decorum in the presence of the Eucharist – were still to be treated, as it were, as so many false notes. They had to be pointed out and corrected, lest they spoil the solemn melody of a "holy people" set apart by God (as Israel had been set apart) for his service. A Christian community where confession and penance for precise sins were taken seriously (and we can imagine many communities in Ireland and Britain where they were not!) was a community which, like the ancient people of Israel, had a proper sense of the order of things. It could be sure of the blessing of God. And a convent or a monastery in which the laws of penance were observed with heroic diligence was a place of guaranteed "holiness," an island of divinely ordained order in the midst of a rough world.[37]

Behind the crabbed Latin of these texts, we can also sense the living texture of the Celtic societies in which they were first elaborated. These were societies without empire. Roman styles of rule had collapsed in western Britain in the course of the sixth century, and they had never existed in Ireland. No strong state existed to enforce law and order from on top. Instead, the peace of society was maintained, as it were, "horizontally," by a balance of power, established through constant negotiations between roughly equal kin-groups. Any injury to one group, or to any member of the group, would be met by violence on the part of the other. But violence could be bought off. It could be atoned for by compensation.[38]

The exchange of threat and compensation, through which members of a "stateless" society maintained the peace and upheld among themselves a rough equality of status, was carried out in the name of honor. Honor – *enech*, "face," in Old Irish – was the mercurial essence of all social relations in the Celtic world. To insult or injure a person and his kin-group, or to fail to meet agreed obligations to them, was to "leave shit on the face." To avenge oneself of such an insult was to "wash clean the face." To offer compensation to offended neighbors was to "wash their face" – to acknowledge and restore their damaged honor.

The "law of the face" covered all eventualities. To walk through the fence set up by a farmer around his house without his permission was to breach his honor. Compensation had to be offered.[39] To "spoil the face" of a king was a serious matter: "Bringing shame on the countenance by raising a conspicuous lump . . . Let a heavy penalty accompany that disgrace."[40] We are dealing with a society knit together by an endless balancing and testing of honor. It was characterized by conflicts which tested the honor of rivals and by endless negotiations which restored this honor, through intricate forms of compensation and mutual surety.[41]

The *Penitentials* frequently incorporated local law directly in their own rulings. Nothing if not practical, their authors knew that in no other way would peace be established in a community made up of Irish or British Christians. A clergyman guilty of killing, for instance, had to make two kinds of compensation. He had to fast for ten years in exile under the guidance of a spiritual director. But then he had to return home, pay the blood-money to the victim's kin, and offer to work for the parents of the dead man, as a substitute son, so as to "warm" their old age as their son would have done, by laboring for them on their farm.[42]

But the *Penitentials* did more than this. They assumed, in many ways, that an analogous relation existed between God and the sinner as between an offender and the person of higher status whose "face," whose honor, he had damaged. To do penance was to restore the honor of God. Hence, as in the Irish law of damages, no sin was too trivial or too drastic not to be compensated for by penance. The face of an injured God demanded to be "washed clean" by the self-abasement and penitential self-mortification of the sinner, much as the "face" of a superior or of an angered kin-group would be "washed clean" by compensation.

Yet this was not all. In an evenly balanced society, such as that of Ireland, compensation did not mean only the restoration of honor to the offended party through the humiliation of those who had infringed that honor. For compensation, duly offered, removed, from those threatened with revenge, the potential dishonor of suffering violence or mocking. Both parties were expected to emerge from such negotiations with their honor equal. The faces of each had been "washed clean" by a correctly conducted process of atonement. In the same way, in the *Penitentials*, atonement to God meant more than an appeasement of his anger. It also meant that the sinner had been "washed clean."

Last, but not least, as in daily life in Ireland and western Britain, "washing clean" through the compensation of penance was expected to occur frequently, and to be offered promptly. Altogether, the *Penitentials* assume an almost neighborly closeness to God, which encouraged persistence in calling for his forgiveness and, above all, a very real confidence that, once atonement had been offered, forgiveness would come. As we saw in our last chapter, the religion of Gregory the Great had a "missionary" quality about it. It was marked by an endless capacity to take pains for the "care of souls." Though they sprang from very different roots, the Celtic *Penitentials* shared the same "missionary" zeal. They were the product of men confident that they could set up, in their own land, an echo of the holiness associated with the monks of Egypt and with the ancient people of Israel. They were also confident that this holiness would be achieved by bringing to all who wished it, well-tried and effective "medicine" for their every sin.

Prelude to Exile: Columbanus at Bangor (570–590)

The Irishman Columbanus was an outstanding product of this distinctive culture.[43] He was a *sapiens* learned in Latin texts and a fierce guide of souls, well-acquainted with the Irish and West British circles which had produced the first *Penitentials*.[44] Born in Leinster in around 550, Columbanus (the Latin for "little dove") became a monk at the ascetic settlement of Bangor (Bennchor), some 20 miles along the southern shore of the Lough of Belfast. It was a settlement ruled by abbot Comgall. Comgall was notorious for his strict rule, designed to break the proud will of young scholars such as Columbanus. Only five miles away, at the head of Strangford Lough, the Briton Vinniau (Saint Findbarr) had settled at Movilla (Mag mBili), bringing with him, from western Britain, memories of his master, the formidable Gildas.[45]

Bangor was a monastery where, under the hands of scholars, a scant resource of old Latin texts had been made to blossom. To take one example: intense meditation on one phrase alone, found in the few letters of Saint

Jerome which were available in Ireland, had enabled the monks of Bangor to write verses on the birth of Christ whose exultant solemnity echoed similar verses, inspired by the same passage in Jerome, written, in distant Poitiers, by the Italian Venantius Fortunatus. Both creations were independent of each other. Bangor seems to have had no direct contact with the Continent.[46] Yet its monks shared in the same stock of precious Latin books, and knew how to set them to work with as much skill as the refined Venantius. As a *sapiens* of Bangor, and the master of many Latin books, Columbanus had good reason to expect that wherever he moved in Europe he would find himself beneath the same Latin sky.

In 590, Columbanus asked Comgall for permission to undertake the terrible mortification (for an Irishman) of leaving the island, so as to live as a stranger among total strangers. Of all the penances which an Irish monk might face, self-exile "for the love of God" was the most drastic. It meant a total loss of social identity. An exile was supposed to roam the world, cut loose from his native community, as lonely as a wolf.[47] Yet exile was also a course of action which offered to a middle-aged ascetic and scholar, such as Columbanus, something more than a loss of self. It gave him a free hand to create his own version of a proper monastery – that is, an Irish monastery – on the alien soil of northern Gaul. He arrived in Gaul, in 590, at the age of 40, with a retinue of fellow-Irishmen as his disciples, never to return to Ireland. The year 590 was the same one in which Gregory the Great, a man almost the same age as Columbanus, became pope in Rome. Let us see, in the next chapter, what this remarkable man would do in Europe, and what would be the long-term consequences of his activities.

CHAPTER 11

Medicamenta paenitentiae: Columbanus

"Coming from the world's end": Columbanus in Europe

When he arrived in Continental Europe, Columbanus remained very much the *sapiens*. He never lacked for books. He soon received a copy of Gregory's *Regula Pastoralis*, perhaps as a gift from the pope himself. He wrote to Gregory that it was a book "sweeter than honey to the needy."[1] But, despite his reverence, Rome remained a distant city to him. The frontier between the territories of the East Roman empire in Italy and the "barbarian" world to their north was, perhaps, the most clearly drawn line on his map of Europe. He kept to the "barbarian" side of this line, seeking out marginal zones in which to settle his colony of "strangers." From 590 to 610, he was at Luxeuil, in the Vosges, in eastern France. Later, he passed along the Rhine and across the Alps to Bobbio. The site of Bobbio was offered to him by Agilulf, the king of the Lombards, close to the river Trebbia, on the edge of the Apennines. He died at Bobbio in 615. But his work was continued, with the greatest zeal, by his non-Irish disciples – by Franks from northern Gaul, Burgundians from the more "Roman" valley of the Rhône, and by Italians.[2]

As befitted a *sapiens* from Ireland, Columbanus had brought with him to Francia something of an enclave mentality. He was fiercely loyal to his teachers and to the precious stock of books that he had already mastered. Columbanus and his Irish monks persistently shocked the local Gallic bishops by celebrating Easter on a different date from everyone else. But, for Columbanus, his Easter was the "true" Easter, celebrated on the date that he had learned in Ireland. In Ireland, he had followed a dating system which had been approved of by Saint Jerome. His masters at Bangor had taught him that any other system for determining the date of Easter was "laughable." The Easter calculations used in Gaul struck him as "trendy" and unreliable. Columbanus instantly wrote to Gregory as one *sapiens* to an other to take up the matter with him. He addressed the pope, in his best Irish Latin, as "fairest Ornament and most honored Flower, as it were, of worn-down Europe." He wrote to tell the pope that it was he who was out of step. Had Gregory not read his Saint Jerome? "How then, with all your learning . . . do you favor a dark Easter? An Easter proved to be no Easter?"[3] No reply from Gregory has survived.

At the end of his life, Columbanus wrote once again to a pope. This time he did it at the request of king Agilulf. He rebuked pope Boniface, a successor of Gregory, for having given way to the emperor Justinian's disastrous decision to bypass the Council of Chalcedon by condemning the Three Chapters (of which we heard in chapter 7). He assumed that the pope would accept his rebuke. Columbanus spoke of himself with rococo humility as "that little dove, that sport of nature, that rare bird." Who was he, he added, "a bumptious babbler" and "a slow-witted Irish pilgrim," to tell the pope what to do? And then, of course, he did so – and in no uncertain words. Boniface was not to sit on the fence. He was "to remove the cloud of suspicion from Saint Peter's chair." Columbanus professed to be shocked by "so much mortal sloth" in Rome, "I, coming from the world's end, where I have seen spiritual leaders truly fighting the Lord's battles . . . am quite astounded . . ."[4]

Disciplina disciplinarum: The Training of All Trainings: Columbanus' Monasticism

If we turn from the *Letters* of Columbanus to his *Monastic Instructions* and his *Rule* we see how Columbanus, though he alienated many, could emerge, in Francia, as a figure to be treated with awe and followed by many with ardent loyalty. It was his monks who heard him at his most urgent. His *Instructions* were preached in Latin to a monastic group made up of many "nations" – Irishmen, Franks, Burgundians, and Romans of the south. They were the equivalent of the more pensive *Moralia* of Gregory I. Their message had a starkness which makes even Gregory, for all the urgency of his belief in the approach of the Day of Judgment, seem to belong to a sunnier world. Like Gregory, the God of Columbanus was deeply present to him:

> This is no God which dwells far from us that we seek . . . For He resides in us like the soul in our body . . . Ever must we cling to God, to the deep, vast, hidden, lofty and almighty God.

And God had promised to those who served him: *I shall dwell in them and will walk in their very midst.*[5]

But this would happen only when the will and the body had lost their pride and their fierce lust. The body itself was a sight of horror. But this was because the body, with its labile flesh and slimy fluids, was no more than the horrifying externalization of something infinitely more slippery and corrupt – the "insatiable, rabid leech" of the unbroken will.[6]

Because of their untamed wills, human beings lived in impenetrable darkness. There is no sense in Columbanus, as there is in Gregory, of that ancient, Platonic mysticism, in which Paradise, though lost, might yet still linger in the mind, tantalizing the soul like the subtle whiff of the scent of fresh, ripe apples in a malodorous world. For Columbanus the corrupted will had brought humanity up against a blank wall.

> How miserable is our state! The things we ought to have loved are so remote and undiscovered and unknown to us . . . O wretched man that you are! What you see you ought to hate, and what you should love you do not know.[7]

This is the reason why they had come to his monastery:

> This in fact is the training of all trainings – the *disciplina disciplinarum* – and at the price of present sorrow it prepares the pleasure of unending time.[8]

There was no doubt as to the amount of "present sorrow" which Columbanus laid down for his monks. In the early days in the Vosges, his monks lived off the land, gnawing bark in times of famine.[9] Even in the more stable settlement at Luxeuil they lived a life where they could hardly claim a moment as their own. Theirs was the heroic rhythm of the ancient monks of Egypt, not of contemporary Italy (where the wise Benedict – whose *Rule* Columbanus knew – had left room, in the day's schedule, for a summertime siesta!). In the middle of winter, the pre-dawn service involved the chanting of Psalms for two and a half hours, followed by a short nap only before the next service began.[10]

> Let him come weary to his bed and sleep walking, let him be forced to rise when his sleep is not yet finished. Let him keep silence when he has suffered wrong. Let him fear the superior of his community as a master, love him as a father, and believe that whatever he commands is healthful to himself . . . For though this training may seem hard to hard men, that a man should always hang from the mouth of another, yet by those who are fixed in their fear of God it will be found pleasant and safe.[11]

Medicamenta paenitentiae: The Medicines of Penance

"Pleasant and safe" would hardly be the way that a modern person might characterize life under the *Rule* of Columbanus. But the secret of the success of Columbanus lay in his transparent confidence that the "training of all trainings" would work. Ground down by mortification, the will and the body would finally surrender to the presence of God: pain would be turned into desire.

> Thus do Thou enrich my lantern with Thy light, I pray Thee, Jesus mine
> . . . that constantly I may see, observe, desire Thee only . . . and that Thy
> love may own us all, and Thine affection fill all our senses . . . and that
> such affection may be in us impossible of quenching by the many waters
> of this air and land and sea.[12]

The darkness would end, and they would find themselves in light.

The best commentary on the expectations which the preaching of Columbanus aroused in those who heard him is in the second book of the *Life of Columbanus*, which was written in 639–43 by his disciple, Jonas. In this he narrated a series of deathbed scenes. This was entirely appropriate, for they showed that the way to heaven lay through the convents and monasteries founded under the influence of Columbanus.

The great convent of Burgundofara (later known as Faremoutiers, in the valley of the Marne) was founded by a disciple of Columbanus. Jonas describes in gripping detail the deaths of many of its nuns. Ercantrudis, for instance, lay dying at sunset in her darkening cell.

> After that, as black night rushed in and the last glimmer of light faded on
> earth, Ercantrudis [the nun] asked them to extinguish the lamp that burned
> in the cell where she lay.

Ercantrudis no longer needed the lamp. For her, the darkness had ended.

> "Do you not see," she said, "what splendor comes? Do you not hear the
> choirs [of angels] singing? . . . *Oh give thanks to the Lord for He is
> good; for His mercy endures forever.*"[13]

Faremoutiers was a convent in which it was believed that every sin could be forgiven. The nuns confessed their sins three times a day.

> For it was the monastery's custom to observe the rule that each woman
> should purge her mind by confession . . . erasing the least hint of spir-
> itual weakness by pious disclosure.[14]

The psalm which Ercantrudis heard the angels sing at her death was the same psalm which the nuns had sung as they processed out of the church every day, having received forgiveness for their sins.[15]

Jonas, the biographer of Columbanus, claimed that his hero had introduced the *medicamenta paentitentiae*, the "medicines of penance," to Gaul at a time when they had come to be neglected.[16] By this he meant that Columbanus had brought a fierce asceticism, directed at every stage by forms of confession and penance which, as we saw in the last chapter, had been developed by spiritual guides in sixth-century western Britain and Ireland. It was the Irish system of "tariffed penance" which gave those who followed Columbanus the confidence that, by following his "training of all trainings," they would go straight to heaven, "purged" of their sins. The convents and monasteries which sprang up all over northern Gaul after his death were treated as mighty powerhouses of prayer precisely because they were known, also, to be powerhouses of atonement.

Frankish Society and the New Monasticism

The life of Columbanus and the subsequent arrival of other Irishmen (from other areas, which did not necessarily share the same traditions as Bangor) closed the gap between the Frankish society of northern Gaul and the hitherto unknown world that had grown up across the water. A new cultural zone, characterized by distinctive forms of religious life, was created in northwestern Europe in the course of the seventh century. The Channel, even the Irish Sea, ceased to exist. Ireland, Britain, and the lands north of the Seine came closer together than they had ever been in Roman times.

In describing this process, it is important to maintain a sense of perspective. Columbanus and the *sapientes* of the Irish Sea represented a highly distinctive form of Christianity. But nobody thought of them (and least of all did they think of themselves) as out-and-out "exotics." Columbanus presented himself as "Irish" only when it suited him. Equipped with bristling Latin, he acted with an almost total disregard of his Irish origins. He inspired and admonished Frankish bishops and Roman popes alike as one *sapiens* to another, as one learned man moving among his equals. He felt himself to be part of a network of religious experts which stretched without a significant break across Latin Europe from the Irish Sea to Rome.

Nor did the introduction of a new ascetic fervor combined with the newly developed system of "tariffed penance" constitute an entirely new departure in the history of western Christianity. In the Frankish world, Columbanus came not as a revolutionary but as a catalyst.

This does not mean, however, that the changes which he and his Frankish disciples helped to bring about were not significant. His intervention marked the beginning of a dramatic shift in the geographical location of monasticism and the culmination of the long process, which we described in chapter 9, by which monasteries came to take on a leading role in society. In the rich valley of the Seine, and its northeastern tributaries, the Oise, the Aisne, and the Marne, Columbanus found the most secure and prosperous region in western Europe. Known as Neustria, the "New Western Lands" of the Franks, or simply as *Francia* (from which we derive the modern word for France), this was a region of royal courts and of impressive royal and aristocratic villas. These were true palaces, towns in miniature. They controlled a wealthy countryside where Roman cities had never been prominent.

In northern Gaul and, further to the northeast toward the Moselle and the Rhine (in what was called Austrasia) a new Frankish aristocracy had come into being. They were no longer adventurers and henchmen living off spasmodic royal bounty. They were heavily intermarried with Gallo-Romans. They were acutely aware of the fact that they had become great landowners on a truly "Roman" scale. They felt the need to leave a permanent mark on estates which they now controlled in perpetuity. Such persons were newly arrived to power. Honor and gift-giving, the essence of social relations in Columbanus' Ireland, were matters of great importance to them also. Given the economic resources which they controlled, what they had to give was spectacular by Irish standards.[17]

For all his desire to live as a stranger among total strangers, Columbanus rapidly found himself implicated with powerful lay persons, Frankish kings and aristocrats, who wanted to tap into the vibrant holiness which he offered. Those who approached Columbanus thought instinctively in terms of the gift exchange. They would endow and protect monasteries and convents in return for having a powerhouse of prayer and atonement in their midst. They sought the surge of honor and prestige which came from close association with a holy place. Thus, Columbanus' first major settlement at Luxeuil may well have been the gift of a king, Theuderic II (596–612). Though elk and aurochs roamed the Vosges and Columbanus himself would walk the woods, whistling down from the trees a squirrel which would perch on his neck and run in and out of his cloak, the monastery was placed in a dilapidated Roman spa, surrounded by classical statues. It was an ancient, royal place.[18]

In 610, Columbanus failed to meet this royal gift with the correct counter-gift of his blessing. He refused to bless the sons of Theuderic II by his concubines. Columbanus and his Irish monks (but not the Franks) were told to leave. By giving nothing in return for royal gifts, they had forfeited the hospitality which the king had offered them. In the course of this stormy exchange between Columbanus and Theuderic, cups of wine sent by the king to Columbanus exploded on the holy man's table. The miraculous incident made plain that Columbanus would have no part in such gifts. Memory of the incident was treasured among persons who valued the gift-exchange, Franks and Irish alike. The exploding cups were a sign of the electric charge that ran through any gift relationship which bound these new monks to their lay patrons.[19]

Despite Columbanus' exile, Luxeuil came to thrive. Ruled by Frankish disciples of Columbanus, it became a large community of 200 monks. It was recruited from and was frequently visited by the top aristocracy of Frankish Gaul. Its manuscripts betray the bureaucratic skills that were practiced at the Frankish court. This skill in letters was now applied to the copying of holy texts. With former bureaucrats from a royal court among its inmates, Luxeuil soon became something of a Vivarium of the north.[20]

But kings were not the only patrons of monasteries and convents. For the first time, we find large numbers of Frankish landowners of the north anxious to found monasteries and convents so as to place islands of untouchable holiness in the midst of their estates. These monasteries and convents were not discreet country cottages, as earlier monasteries had been in the Roman south. They functioned much as the great Roman villas had done in northern Gaul. They were economic centers which gathered an entire countryside around them. They often consisted of a group of churches and buildings which were deemed so holy that no lay person might enter them. Many were surrounded (as in Ireland) by extensive earthworks, which marked them off as "holy cities" in miniature.[21] They were set in a countryside of waving wheatfields, served by the most advanced technology of watermills. They were the "honor" of the Frankish families who founded them made concrete and untouchable.[22]

To take only one example, this had happened to the family of Burgundofara. The visit of Columbanus to the residence of her father, Chagneric, was long remembered. It had "ennobled their home."[23] Faremoutiers, the convent founded by Chagneric and ruled by his daughter, Burgundofara, was a convent whose reputation for holiness was based on the utter purity of all its members. Each nun strove, as we have seen, to end her life totally "purged" of sin. The stories of the dramatic deaths of nuns of Faremoutiers made plain that here was a place where heaven touched earth. The holiness of the convent irradiated an entire agricultural region, much as the enclosed convent of Caesaria, within the walls of Arles, had protected the city.

These convents and monasteries were outstandingly rich. They had endowments of up to 20,000 hectares of land. They were protected by royal "immunities." Royal agents and the local bishops alike suspended their rights to visit them, thereby making them appear all the more untouchable and holy. Far from weakening their prestige by doing so, the Merovingian kings positively basked in the glow of a holiness which they themselves had a hand in creating, through declaring them to be special, "immune" zones.[24]

What the kings gained from their grants of immunity was what Radegund had once provided, at the convent of the Holy Cross at Poitiers: power-houses of prayer for the kingdom. The monastery of Corbie was founded in around 661, by king Chlothar III and by his impressive queen, Balthild (a former Saxon slave from across the Channel). The charter of immunity made plain what the royal couple expected:

> that on account of this benefit the holy congregation may love even more to pray for the mercy of the Lord for the stability of our kingdom.[25]

Corbie later received, in the form of gifts from the royal warehouse at the Mediterranean port of Marseilles, regular supplies of olive oil (for the perpetual lamps of its church), Cordova leather (to bind its books and to provide soft shoes for its monks), quires of papyrus imported direct from Egypt, even dates and pistachios. Every year, some 3,650 kilograms of precious goods were carried north, across Gaul, in 15 wagons.[26] Relics from the Holy Places, carefully labelled and wrapped in precious silks woven in Constantinople and Iran, were placed in the shrines of the monasteries and convents of Neustria. They represented a worldwide Christian order, now brought together with appropriate grandeur in the new lands of northern Francia.[27]

Districtio: "a strict accounting": Sin and Penance in the Western Church

The new monasticism associated with the "medicines of penance" brought to Gaul by Columbanus was so popular because it had given an up-to-date, crisp answer to an ancient question. For centuries, East Roman Christians had approached the holy men of Egypt, Syria, and elsewhere, with one blunt inquiry: "Give me a word, Father. How can a lay person – a person 'in the world' – be saved?"[28] Western Christians had done the same, if in a less explicit manner. The answers varied greatly from region to region, even from bishop to bishop and from mentor to mentor. No uniform system existed in Latin Christianity for the imposition of penance and the forgiveness of sin. What could be done with sin, indeed, remained an open question.

Many bishops looked back to what they imagined to have been the heroic days of the Early Church. There, it was believed, sin, penance, and forgiveness had been weighty matters, accompanied by a group drama of exemplary intensity, such as was described in chapter 2. As we saw in chapter 3, the emperor Theodosius I had sought penance of this kind from Ambrose, bishop of Milan, in 391, after the massacre of Thessalonica. He was remembered to have stood in church, startlingly divested of his crown and imperial robes, until he was re-admitted by Ambrose to the Eucharist in a splendid ceremony of reconciliation. Such high events were good to remember. Penance of this kind continued, but it was largely concerned with the very public sins of very public persons. Theodosius needed to undergo dramatic penance so as to restore his own credit in the Christian community. But what we call "public" penance of this kind was not the only form of penance that was available.[29]

For the average believer, the tradition established by Augustine in his controversy with Pelagius proved more significant. As we saw in chapter 3, Augustine denied that any Christian could ever be without sin, even after baptism. Penance, for him, was not to be directed only toward major sins (what Augustine called "capital" sins: that is, mortal sins). Penance must also touch those failings of everyday life which reminded all believers, all the time, of their fallen human nature. Such "light" sins were significant, but their penance was slight. In Augustine's opinion, it was sufficient to recite every day with sincere regret the phrase from the Lord's Prayer, *Forgive us our sins, as we forgive those who sin against us*, and to show that one meant what one said by giving alms generously to the beggars crowded around the church porch. Penance, for Augustine, was not a spectacular remedy for occasional great sins. It was, rather, a frame of mind. It was a lifelong process, because sin, also, was the lifelong companion of the Christian.[30]

It was Gregory the Great who added a final, distinctive tone to the Augustinian tradition of perpetual penance. His contribution derived, in many ways, from a very ancient Roman past. The aristocratic tradition of moral guidance, represented by Seneca and others, had always urged its practitioners to adopt a never-ceasing attitude of "displeasure with the self." Adepts must subject themselves to relentless inner cross-examination, so as to lay bare their failings and to correct them.

To this venerable, almost instinctive tradition, maintained among the Roman elites, Gregory added the entire world of the Desert Fathers, with their unflinching emphasis on the constant inner struggle of the monk and on the need for candor in revealing all sins to a spiritual guide. Both Columbanus and Gregory had read their John Cassian. They drew the same conclusions from him: all sins mattered; and all must be examined with medical precision if they were to be "healed."

Hence the austerity of Gregory's message. The more Christians strove for perfection, he believed, the more clearly they would see their own imperfection. For this vision of the self Gregory uses the word *horror*. By this, he did not mean the fear of Hell. Rather, he referred to a nightmare sense of vertigo experienced by pious persons at the sight of the sheer tenacity, the insidiousness, and the minute particularity of their sins.[31] The righteous were encouraged to make their own the *districtio*, the "strict accounting", of God himself.[32] They must look at themselves as God saw them – that is, with the clarity and the divine impatience of an utterly just being, for whom a shoddy, unfinished soul was not enough.

These long-term developments reached back to the early fifth century. As a result, confession and penance became part of a religious quest in itself. The East Roman question, already posed in Egypt and Syria in the fourth century – how can the lay person be saved? – had become, by the sixth century, the principal form of piety throughout all Christian regions, in East and West alike. To seek forgiveness of sins, by whatever means of atonement was made available by local custom, was a concern that united monks, nuns, clergy, and lay persons of both sexes all over Latin Europe. All serious Christians wished for this. But, of course, not all Christians were serious Christians. Those who sought penance – be they lay or clerical – were the spiritually alert. They were often the well-to-do, who had time for spiritual matters and wealth to support spiritual guides. To use a phrase coined to describe the working of penance in seventh-century Ireland, they were an "elective elite."[33] They were not the average, unthinking Christian. No obligation to confess existed in the Church at this time. Rather, confession and the "medicines of penance" were actively sought out by pious persons.

For such persons, the Celtic system of "tariffed penance" did not come as a totally exotic novelty. It aroused no opposition. Its lists of sins and penances were easily adopted. They lent a final note of somewhat brittle precision to a religious culture already dominated by a penitential mentality. Columbanus, as we saw, appreciated the *Regula Pastoralis* of Gregory I. Though separated by hundreds of miles and each the product of a highly distinctive culture, the two men met as equals. Both belonged to a "culture of wisdom" whose highest ideal was the "doctor" who brought "medicine" to the soul.

Journeys of the Soul

The widespread "penitential" mentality also led to greater preoccupation with death and the afterlife. In the literature of the time, the moment of death stepped into the foreground. Seldom had the deathbeds of the saints been presented in such gripping close-up. For death was the test of penance. It was on their deathbeds that the souls of the saints were shown to have been "purged" of sin. As we have seen, Gregory's *Homilies on the Gospels* and his *Dialogues* lingered on the deaths of saintly persons: globes of light rose to heaven, angels were heard chanting, and the air became heavy with unearthly fragrance.[34]

The atmosphere of Gregory's *Dialogues* also suffused Jonas' *Life of Columbanus*. The message was the same. It was unatoned sin, and not the heavy, physical body, which stood between the self and God. Once sin was gone, the soul could move, with triumphant ease, into the other world. Sisetrudis, a nun at Faremoutiers, had been warned in a revelation that she had 40 days in which to finish off her penance. After 37 days, two angels took her soul to heaven, for a *districtio* – a strict accounting – of her remaining sins. On the fortieth day, the angels reappeared. Her account was cleared. Sisetrudis' soul was ready:

> "I would go now, my lords, I would go now and delay no longer in this life of cares . . . I am now better prepared for the road" . . . And all who attended her departure heard an angelic chorus singing in full harmony.[35]

The emphasis on a glorious, light-filled death was not, in itself, a novelty. The martyrs and the great monks of Egypt were believed to have passed to heaven in such a way. What was new was concern for those who, very obviously, did not stand such a chance of doing so. For if entry into heaven depended on complete atonement of one's sins, through penance, it was very hard to see how the average believer would ever get to heaven. It is for this reason that seventh-century Christians, in the West, turned, with novel precision and with a heightened sense of drama, to the issue of the passing of the soul.

Gregory devoted the entire fourth and last book of his *Dialogues* to exploring this topic. He knew that he was touching on a recent concern, which had not played an important role in previous Christian tradition. In his opinion, God was warning Christians, in the last days before his coming, by sending visions which revealed, more fully than ever before, the outlines of the fate of the soul immediately beyond the grave. It was like a landscape whose basic outlines were becoming visible, for the first time, in the half-light that precedes the dawn.[36] The landscape of the other world included, of course, a well-known Heaven and a Hell whose horror was only hinted at. But it also included a new, intermediate region characterized by agonizing delay. "Unpurged" souls seemed blocked there. A learned, seemingly pious

but pig-headed deacon, known to Gregory's family, once made an appearance, after his own death, in the thick steam of a Roman thermal spa. He
begged a startled bishop for his prayers. The prayers worked. He was not
there next week. Plainly his soul had resided for a time in an intermediate
zone, as painful for him as the scalding, suffocating steam of a thermal
spring.[37]

Stories such as this marked, in retrospect, the beginning of a new age.
Medieval persons looked straight back to the fourth book of Gregory's *Dia-*
logues as the foundation charter of their own distinctive belief in Purgatory
– that is, in an intermediate region of "purging" fire, where souls waited for
a given period before they could enter heaven.[38] But yet more dramatic and
explicit visions would soon follow. The seventh century saw the flourishing
of a new Christian genre – tales of the "Voyage of the Soul."[39]

In around 630, the Irish abbot Fursa, from County Louth (a little south of
Bangor, on the east coast of Ireland), passed through a "near death" experience.[40] It was not pleasant. Though protected by angels, he was pursued by
demons, raising the blood-curdling battle-yell of Irish warriors. But they were
not merely hostile. They knew their *Penitentials*. They claimed him for their
own. They said that he had not atoned for every one of his sins.

> He has often uttered thoughtless words. It is not fitting that he should
> enjoy the blessed life unscathed ... For every transgression that is not
> purged on earth must be avenged in heaven.[41]

On the way back, Fursa was engulfed in a billowing fire, which threatened
to burn him:

> for it searches out each one according to their merits ... For just as the
> body burns through unlawful desire, so the soul will burn, as the lawful,
> due penalty for every sin.[42]

He emerged at last with the side of his face scarred. For, at the very last
moment, a sinner to whom he had granted easy penance in return for the gift
of a cloak was hurled against him, from out of the fire.[43] Very much a product of the new cultural zone of northwest Europe, Fursa soon left Ireland for
East Anglia. As he relived the terror of that vision, he was seen to sweat with
fear in the icy winter chill of the North Sea.[44] He died in Francia, and his
story was circulated in northern Gaul.

It was not a tale calculated to reassure lay persons and those who had only
recently left the lay life to seek atonement in a monastery. One such person
was Barontus, a nobleman who, in later life, had joined the monastery of
Logoretum (now Saint-Cyran-en-Brenne) near Bourges. A retired royal offi-

cial and not a notable sinner – just a middle-aged man with three marriages and many concubines on his conscience – his experience was as frightening as was that of abbot Fursa.[45]

In 679, Barontus fell dangerously ill. It seemed to him that he was taken on a journey to Heaven and Hell. The issue was whether Barontus, the late convert, belonged to the angels who guided him toward a distant heaven or to the clawed, toothed demons who jostled his poor soul as it floated through the air above the countryside of Bourges. In Barontus' struggle on the edge of death, it was his entire identity, conscious and unconscious, that was at stake:

> Blessed Peter, addressing the demons, asked politely: "What crime do you have against this monk?" The demons answered, "Major sins! . . . He had three wives . . . He has also committed other adulteries and many other sins . . ." And they went over all the sins that I had committed from infancy onwards, including those which I had totally forgotten.[46]

He returned to earth, greatly shaken, to tell his tale. The story ends with a citation from the *Homilies on the Gospels* of Gregory the Great. "Let us consider how severe a Judge is coming, who will judge not only our evil deeds but even our every thought."[47]

The Rise of the Other World

What is remarkable about such visions is the attempt to piece together a story of the soul after death. Stories which delineated the soul of each individual in terms of its precise individual sins and merits had not been widespread at an earlier time. Nor had so starkly "otherworldly" a perspective on human life been common. Up to this time, Christians had tended to be more interested in how the other world entered – and entered deeply – into this world. Paradise was thought to lie close to hand. So did the icy, mischievous shades of the demons. They were both to be sensed in this world.

When a Christian of an old-fashioned cast of mind, such as Gregory of Tours, surveyed the landscape of Gaul, it had kept for him much of its ancient magic. As we saw in chapter 6, he wrote of a Gaul that contained islands of Paradise, fully palpable, in the here and now, as was shown by miracles of healing and exuberant fertility that occurred in their vicinity. Limbs were restored. Trees blossomed. Mysterious roses were scattered over the floor of a saint's shrine. In the same way, Gregory of Tours detected chilling touches of Hell, characterized by the smoking fevers, by the screams of the possessed, and by the vengeful fire which showed that the wrath of the saints was at work on earth. Touches of Heaven and Hell impinged on the day-to-day life of Tours. They showed that Saint Martin was still "fully present" at his shrine. The blaze of such a shrine in the present eclipsed speculations, in those who guarded it and visited it, about their own fate in another world. Compared with glimpses of paradise on earth, associated with the great shrines of Gaul, the outlines of the other world (and particularly of its intermediate zones) remained indistinct.[48]

For Gregory the Great, by contrast, and for those who came to share his views in the course of the seventh century, it is as if the Christian imagination had taken on a significantly different tilt. It looked away from this world, so as to peer into the world of the dead. Manifestations of the other world in this world certainly occurred. Demons remained active. Saints performed miracles. Paradise opened, visibly, to receive holy persons. But these intrusions of the other world into this world seemed somehow less important. The color drained from them, in comparison with gripping evocations of the dread last journey of the soul. This was the drama on which seventh-century authors lingered by preference as far apart as Ireland, Spain, Rome, and Gaul. For what truly mattered for those who wrote was now the dread occasion when, at the moment of death, the individual soul confronted the massed ranks of angels, saints, and greedy demons who guarded the thresholds of Heaven and Hell.[49]

Heightened interest in the fate of the souls of average Christians after death caused western Christianity to become, for the first time, an "otherworldly" religion in the true sense. Religious imagination and religious practice came to concentrate more intently on death and the fate of the dead. This happened because leading exponents of the new "culture of wisdom," such as Gregory and Columbanus, had caught the entirety of human experience in the strands of a single net. All aspects of human life could be explained in the light of two universal principles – sin and repentance.[50] Sin explained everything. Secular rulers exercised their power (so Gregory had said) so as to suppress sin and to encourage repentance. History happened according to the same rhythm. Disasters struck and kingdoms fell because the sins of the people had provoked the anger of God. Prosperity came when the people repented of their sins and regained the favor of God. Even the early medieval economy worked to the rhythm of sin. Massive transfers of wealth to monasteries and great shrines occurred for the "remission" of the sins of their donors. Above all, the human person was seen, with unprecedented sharpness, as made up of sin and merit – and nothing else. And death and the afterlife were where sin and merit would be definitively revealed by the judgment of God.

Thus, it was the emphasis on sin which gave to the average Christian an interest in the hitherto dim world of the dead. Previously, Christian believers had been, perhaps, happier and more confident of their salvation. But the other world to which they hoped to come had been more faceless. Apart from great, well-known saints, the identities of individual believers tended to be swallowed up in the golden haze of paradise. By contrast, for good or ill, the timorous Barontus had a face. It was a face sharply etched in terms of his "purged" and "unpurged" sins. These sins made him distinctive. He saw himself as built up, like a coral reef, by his individual sins and his individual virtues. They gave his personality a continuity which reached back even deeper than his present memory of himself. Barontus' otherworldly experiences may seem bizarre to us. But they addressed with new precision the problem of how much of the present self survives, as a unique individual, still subject to the laws of sin and repentance, even beyond the grave. For this reason, the journey of Barontus has rightly been described as "a first sketch of the awareness of the self on the part of the individual in Western Europe."[51]

The Christianization of Death

These writings circulated among a spiritual elite and reflect their concerns. But they were not sheltered concerns. Barontus had recently been a lay man, and his vision shows us very plainly what was on the mind of lay men and women in the circles in which Barontus had moved. Death itself had become a problem for Christians. It takes some effort of the imagination to realize the extent to which this had not been the case in earlier centuries. What we call "the Christianization of death" was a centuries-long process, which entered a crucial phase at this time.[52]

It is important to stress the slowness of this process. We cannot know for certain whether Christians of the ancient Mediterranean world had been more confident than were pious persons in the seventh century that they would go to heaven. What we do know is that they retained complete confidence in the ancient Roman traditions of the care and burial of the dead. In the Christian communities, as among non-Christians, death, burial, and the subsequent "care" of the dead were matters for the family. The clergy had a singularly little role in such matters. In cities, the dead were taken outside the walls and placed in private, family graves. Christians frequently lay among pagans. In the fourth and fifth centuries, there was no such thing as a clearly delineated "Christian" cemetery. A feature of Christianity which we now take for granted was simply not there.[53]

What really mattered for Christians of the fourth and fifth centuries was not the fact of common burial alongside other Christians (though, plainly, as Christianity progressed, most family graves in a given area would be the graves of Christians) but common membership of the Church. In many regions, the graves emphasized the fact that the dead were *fideles*, baptized Christians. Their families offered food, wine, and money at the Christian Eucharist so that their dead should still be "remembered" as part of the Church. But the relationship between the "remembrance" of the dead and their fate in the other world provoked little speculation. The gravestones themselves were singularly mute: most were content to announce that the dead persons were "in peace." This may have meant no more than that their spirits were "at rest" because they had been properly buried and cared for by their kin. There was no such thing as a notion of distinctive "Christian" burial. A proper Christian burial was the proper "Roman" burial of someone who happened to be a Christian.[54]

In the course of the fifth and sixth centuries, these very ancient burial practices changed significantly in only one respect as a result of the cult of the saints. To be buried near a holy grave was to gain the hope of standing beside the saint, one's patron and protector, on the day of the resurrection. Like iron filings suddenly regrouped around a magnet, the ancient cities of the dead changed, as Christian graves pressed in around the shrines of holy persons. Even the immemorial boundary between the city of the living and the city of the dead, outside its walls, was broken down. In many towns, the dead came to be buried inside the city, so that they could rest near the altars of urban churches. This change, however, affected only the privileged few. Members of the clergy, kings, aristocrats, and notably pious lay persons sought out the shelter of the saints.[55]

Burials beside the saints occurred largely in the Roman cities. For the vast majority of the population, "Christian burial" in a "Christian" cemetery was a matter of little importance. We only expect that it should have been important because of the later rise of Christian cemeteries and of the notion of burial in Christian "holy" ground. But this decisive development – the rise of the Christian cemetery – does not truly belong to our period. It was a later development. It showed the coming of a truly "medieval" order, which was not yet conceivable in the seventh century.[56]

What did matter, however, was what the Christian family could do for the dead. Here the seventh century was a decisive period. For it is in this century that the family's "care" of the dead, which had been largely independent of the clergy, came to strike up a closer alliance with the clergy. The clergy defined more clearly the rituals which they had to offer; the laity, for their part, incorporated these rituals more intimately into their own care of the dead.

In upper-class circles, the penitential mood of the seventh century strengthened this alliance of laity and clergy. We can see the crucial change occurring in small ways. For the first time, in Christian grave inscriptions, the soul is made to speak to the living, not about its past (as was normal in Roman times) but about its present, anxious state. Gravestones presented the dead person as possessing the soul of a "sinner." They begged for the prayers of others. The gravestone of a certain Trasemir, in the south of France, is covered with three great protective crosses. Along the top, the inscription reads: "Pray, all men, for the soul of Trasemir."[57]

The issue, then, was who prayed best. For the powerful the great new monasteries were powerhouses of prayer for the dead. But, even when they were scattered throughout the countryside, as they now were in northern Gaul, monasteries and convents were special places. Average believers needed some other, more generally available form of help for the souls of their loved ones.

The tradition validated by the *Dialogues* of Gregory the Great emphasized the Mass as the only ceremony which could truly help the soul in the other world. Previously the fate of the soul of the dead person had been considered to be as much a part of the "care" of the family as was the burial of the body. Despite frequent expressions of disapproval by leading clergymen, Christian families had continued for centuries to "feed" the dead by eating around their tombs. Even their "offerings" on behalf of the dead at the ceremony of the Eucharist were thought of as an ethereal form of "feeding" their lost ones. Gregory of Tours tells of a lady in Lyons who would regularly offer Gaza wine of the highest quality for the Eucharist in memory of her husband. A deacon drank the wine himself and put *vin ordinaire* in the Eucharistic chalice. The husband appeared to his wife in a dream, and complained that he did not appreciate being "fed" with vinegar![58]

Only in the seventh century did the Eucharist – the Mass – lose this quality of a "meal" relayed from the family to the dead. The Mass came to be spoken of, rather, as a "sacrifice" which only a priest could offer. The laity could contribute nothing to this "sacrifice." And the Mass was offered at a time of danger. The soul was now thought of as being placed in a position of peril in the other world. Its sins might outweigh its merits and so expose it to being waylaid by the demons, as abbot Fursa had been waylaid. The ancient rituals performed by the family, such as bringing food and drink to "nourish" the soul, could not allay so sharp a peril. Only the Mass could do that.[59]

This was a more anxious view. But it was, in many ways, a more "democratic" one. Not all people could hope to allay their anxieties by being buried beside a saint, as the well-to-do and the exceptionally pious had been buried, or to be remembered in the prayers of a great monastery. By contrast, emphasis on the celebration of the Mass as the only ritual which was truly necessary for the care of the dead enabled a "grassroots" Christianity to spread all over northern Europe. By A.D. 700, even the smallest tribe in Ireland had its own Mass priest. They took care to maintain him. They held him to strict accountancy. They watched his chastity carefully. For they needed to have a man among them who could celebrate a valid Mass on behalf of their dead kin. He performed for them the one ritual which was now deemed basic to a Christian group, by "singing for the absent ones" (the dead).[60]

"All the Inhabitants of Europe"

By the year A.D. 700, Western Christianity had taken on features which would continue from that time until the present day: a highly individualized notion of the soul and a lively concern for its fate in the afterlife; a linking of the Mass to a notion of the "deliverance" of the soul, which opened the way to the medieval doctrine of Purgatory; a widespread emphasis on confession as a remedy for sin; a landscape dotted with prestigious and well-endowed monasteries. Little of this had been there in around the year 500.

Between the days of Saint Benedict, in the early sixth century, and the establishment of the monastic system of northern Gaul, in the course of the seventh, a very ancient Christianity, common to the eastern and the western shores of the Mediterranean, slowly lost its grip on the minds and habits of Christians in many regions of the West. In that ancient Christianity many of the features of the medieval Latin world which we now take for granted as, simply, what Christianity is and always has been, had not existed or, if they had existed, they did not enjoy such prominence in the Christian imagination. Many of the new features which came to prominence in Western Christianity in the course of the seventh century do not exist in the Orthodox Christianities of the East. In Eastern Christianity, very different views of the afterlife led to very different attitudes to death and to the commemoration of the dead. The notion of Purgatory, in particular, remained ill-defined.[61] It was the changes of the seventh century which, for good or ill, have caused Western Christianity to stand alone among its Christian neighbors.

Many of these developments happened at the greatest speed, and in their most articulate form, in a world that had begun to tilt away from the Mediterranean. In the course of the seventh century, northwestern Europe found its own voice. Small details show this. When Gertrude, abbess of Nivelles (south of modern Brussels) died in 658, it now mattered to her biographer that it was on Saint Patrick's Day. Her spiritual adviser had been an Irishman. He may even have been the brother of abbot Fursa. Gertrude's Irish adviser was loyal to the memory of Patrick, the favored patron saint of his region. Gertrude feared the approach of death and the dread journey of her soul. He assured her that Patricius would come to her at the moment of death, to lead her soul safely to heaven. This is our very first reference, in a Continental source, to Patricius. After two centuries, the eccentric Romano-British bishop had finally come to Europe as one of the great saints of the north.[62]

Furthermore, Gertrude's family (from which, eventually, Charlemagne would be descended) was spoken of as famous "to all the inhabitants of Europe."[63] It was a self-conscious use, by a Frankish writer, of an old geographical term to speak about a new reality. This was not Europe as distinct from Asia. It was "the West," a distinctive definition of Europe, as seen from Ireland, Britain, and Francia.

As "Europe," the northwestern frontier regions of the former Roman empire had come to be aware that they possessed an identity of their own, different from the less familiar lands to their south and east. Just how different the ancient, eastern heartlands of Christianity would become, in the decades when Gertrude ruled at Nivelles, and for what reasons, will be the subject of the next two chapters.

CHAPTER 12

Christianity in Asia and the Rise of Islam

"A kingdom which shall never be destroyed": East Rome in Asia

In 591, a party of Turks from eastern central Asia arrived at Constantinople. They bore the sign of the Cross on their foreheads.

> They declared that they had been assigned this by their mothers; for when a fierce plague was endemic among them, some Christians advised them that the foreheads of their young be tattooed with that sign.[1]

These Turks had come from what is now Kirgizstan, some 2,300 miles east of Constantinople, close to the borders of modern China. They had learned about the sign of the Cross from the Christian communities which were established along the entire length of the Silk Route, which led from Antioch, through Persia, to China.

Christians of the East Roman empire of the sixth century knew that they lived in a wide world. Thirteen days of travel to the east of Antioch took them to the frontier of the Persian empire, to Nisibis (Nusaybin, eastern Turkey), the first city in Persian territory. Then the distances seemed to stretch endlessly, into furthest Asia. Eighty days of travel east of Nisibis took the traveller beyond Persia into Central Asia, to the great oasis cities of Merv and Samarkand. A further 150 days were required to reach Hsian-fu, the western capital of China.

We know these distances from the writings of a pious merchant from Antioch (known to us by the colorful but misleading name of Cosmas "Indicopleustes" – Cosmas the India-Sailor).[2] Cosmas had traded down the Red Sea to Axum and Socotra. He knew, through the accounts of fellow-merchants, of communities of Christians from Persia settled along the

Map 5 The Middle East, from Constantinople to Iran

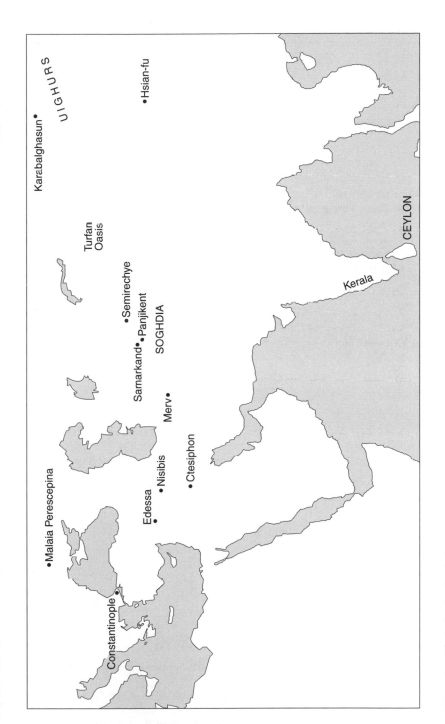

Map 6   Christianity in Asia

THE MIDDLE EAST ca. 450–ca. 800

	Yazdkart II, King of Kings 439–457
Battle of Avarayr 451	
P'awstos Buzanderan writes *Epic Histories* 470	

	Barsauma, bishop of Nisibis
	  470–496
	Khusro I Anoshirwan, King of Kings
	  530–579

Cosmas Indicopleustes writes *Christian Topography* ca.550	
	Khusro II, King of Kings 590–628
Heraclius, emperor 610–641 defeats Khusro II 627	

	Muhammad 570–632
	  begins to receive *Qur'ân* 610
	  flight from Mecca to Medina 622

Battle of Yarmuk 636	
	Battle of Qâdisiyya 637
	Eastern Christians at Hsian-fu 638
	Calif Mu'awiya 661–680
	Ummayad Califate 661–750

	Calif 'Abd al-Malik 685–705
	  builds Dome of the Rock
	  in Jerusalem 691/2

Conquest of Spain 711	
Defeat of Muslims at Constantinople 717	
Battle of Poitiers 733	
	Calif Hisham 724–743
	Abbasids replace Ummayad Califate 750
	Foundation of Baghdad 762
	Calif Harûn al-Rashid 786–809

Coromandel Coast and in Ceylon. These colonies of Christian merchants from the Persian Gulf were the originators of the modern "Saint Thomas' Christians" of Kerala.

Cosmas' *Christian Topography* (written in around 550) was an optimistic tract. For him, the earth was reassuringly flat. Heaven stretched above it like a vast dome. There were no Antipodes, as pagan philsophers vainly imagined. No unknown races lurked at the other side of a round earth. Cosmas felt that he could survey the entire world. And in the immense territories of Asia, Christianity appeared to be the dominant religion. It was already the religion of one world empire, the empire of the Romans, and it was widespread in the Persian empire also.

Cosmas was fortified in these views by a sense of divine providence. Because it was the empire in which Christ had been born, the Roman empire was destined to last forever. He applied to it the prophecy of the Book of Daniel: *The God of Heaven shall set up a kingdom which shall never be destroyed* (Daniel 7:14).

> The empire of the Romans thus participates in the dignity of the kingdom of Christ, seeing that it transcends as far as can be . . . any other power and will remain unconquered until the end of time.[3]

Cosmas found room for the Persian empire, also, in the divine scheme of things. This was a frankly pagan empire, associated in Christian minds with the Persian *Magi*, the grave pagan priests from whom our word "magic" is derived. Zoroastrianism was the religion of the "Magi." It was the state religion of the Persian empire. The second greatest power in the world, and the neighbor of the Christian empire, had remained as staunchly pagan as the Roman empire had been in the days of the emperor Diocletian. But this did not worry Cosmas. For the Magi had come to Bethlehem to pay homage to Christ when he was born. The Three Wise Men of the Gospel account were regarded, by eastern Christians of this time, as Persian ambassadors. By coming all the way to Bethlehem, they had come to recognize the supreme lordship of Christ, as the King of Kings. In Christian mosaics of the time such as that in Sant'Apollinare Nuovo in Ravenna – the Wise Men are shown approaching Christ, as he is carried on the lap of the Virgin Mary, who is seated on an imperial throne. They wear the exotic trousers and Phrygian caps with which Persian ambassadors were shown, on imperial monuments, when they brought tribute to the Roman emperor.

> As regards the empire of the Magi . . . it ranks next to that of the Romans, because the Magi, in virtue of their having come to offer homage and adoration to the Lord Christ, obtained a certain distinction.[4]

In the generations which followed the death of Justinian, it did, indeed, seem as if Asia had become a smaller place. The terrible incursion of the plague, in 542–3, had been a reminder that the East Roman empire lay at the western end of a commercial system which included all of Asia and the Indian Ocean. The Silk Route also became more active, as the Chinese empire expanded westward, making its presence felt deep into Inner Asia, as far as the Tarim Depression and the great oasis of Turfan. After 550, embassies from Po-tzu, from Persia, were a regular occurrence at the court of the Chinese emperor at Hsian-fu. Even Antioch and Syria were described, for the first time, in Chinese gazetteers of the "Western Lands."[5] Small Christian communities, adapting differently to different environments along the way, were part of a steady trickle of information, merchandise, and displaced persons which took place along the entire length of the Silk Route, from Antioch to China. We should not underestimate the "conductivity" of such a route. News travelled quickly along it. A monk writing in the monastery of Qenneshre, on the banks of the Euphrates, mentioned a total eclipse (in the year 627), which could have been observed only in western China![6]

"Two powerful kingdoms who roared like lions": East Rome and Persia: 540–630

The "shrinking" of Asia at this time was in part the result of renewed conflict in the Near East. In Mesopotamia, Syria, and Palestine, the Christian populations were divided between two world empires. Those in the west (in what is now modern eastern Turkey, Syria, Jordan, Palestine, and Israel) were subjects of the Christian empire of East Rome and those to the east (in an area which coincides roughly with modern Iraq) belonged to the pagan, Zoroastrian empire of Sasanian Persia. These two empires were spoken of as "the two eyes of the world."[7] For almost 70 out of the 90 years between 540 to 630, they were at war. From the Caucasus to Yemen in the south of Arabia, and from the steppelands of the Euphrates to eastern Central Asia the two superpowers maneuvered incessantly to outflank each other. As a result, the inhabitants of the Near East found themselves caught between "two powerful kingdoms who roared like lions, and the sound of their roaring filled the whole world with thunder."[8]

The warfare between East Rome and Persia was highly professional and murderous in its impact. Nothing like it occurred in Western Europe. At a time when Justinian's armies in Italy were seldom larger than 5,000, armies of up to 50,000 men clashed in the plains and foothills of northern Mesopotamia. Brigades of heavily armored Persian cavalry rode in tens of thousands across the plains and steppelands of Syria. Ancient cities endured sieges, cap-ture, and the deportation of their entire populations: this happened to Antioch in 540 and to Apamea in 573. In terms of cost, bloodshed, and human suf-fering, the "Barbarian Invasions" of Western Europe were no more than minor dislocations compared with such campaigns. This was the real face of war.[9]

Yet, just because it was highly professional warfare, waged by strong states, its impact, although atrocious, was limited. The 70 years of warfare between East Rome and Persia eventually led to the exhaustion of the two states who conducted it. But it did not lead to a total destabilization of society and to a breakdown of law and order. Paradoxically, indeed, the societies over which the armies of Rome and Persia fought remained wealthy and self-confident in a manner which contrasted, in an increasingly ominous manner, with the bankruptcy of the states who were supposed to defend them.

From Antioch eastward to Edessa and south to Gaza, the cities of the Christian empire remained the centers of government. But they no longer bore an entirely classical face. Their temples were closed. The traditional *agora* which marked the center of public space was replaced by the court-yards of great Christian cathedrals. In many cities, the ancient, grid-like streets of the Hellenistic age were cluttered with artisan shops and bazaars. Open spaces gave way to more enclosed and inward-looking forms of housing. The cities of the age of Justinian and his successors were alive; but they were alive now with a different spirit. They were less dedicated to a self-consciously "classical" ideals of public space and of the comfort and entertainment of their citizens. Theaters and public baths gave way to markets and to untidy agglomerations of inward-looking, deeply private houses.[10]

And, in any case (as we saw in chapter 7) the countryside had levelled up with the cities. The sixth century was the heyday of the Christian village. In modern Syria, Jordan, Palestine, and Israel, the boom of village life contin-ued past the years of the plague. If anything, after the plague, districts in the hinterland throve at the expense of the Mediterranean cities. In Jordan, for instance, village life reached ever further into the hinterland, up to the very edge of the Arabian desert. The Beduin of the steppes, and not the Mediter-ranean, provided the villagers with a new market.

Many of these were large villages, as populous as any city. In the village of Rihab (modern Jordan) nine churches were built between 533 and 635. Made up of houses consisting of closely linked, enclosed courtyards, these villages presented a closed face to the outside world. The only public buildings in them were the churches. Villages such as these often supported monasteries, many of which were centers of teaching and learning in their own right, as creative as any urban school. It was in this distinctive environment of great villages and their adjacent monasteries that the Monophysite "dissidence" throve and defied the efforts of Justinian and his successors to bring them back to the state Church.[11]

At the Crossroads of Asia

Most paradoxical of all, the generals and the troops who fought across these Near Eastern landscapes were usually foreigners to the region. The armies of the "Romans" were largely recruited in Asia Minor and the Balkans; those of the Persians came from the closed world of the Iranian plateau and from the steppes of Central Asia. To enter Syria from Constantinople was to descend from the Anatolian plateau into a different world. To descend from Iran into Mesopotamia was also to find oneself among foreigners. Both empires fought to control a Syriac-speaking "heartland" whose language they did not understand. As for the inhabitants of the region – the political and military frontier between the two empires meant little to them. Syriac-speaking Christian villages stretched on both sides of the frontier, without a break, from the Mediterranean to the foothills of the Zagros. It was possible to travel from Ctesiphon, the Persian capital in southern Mesopotamia, to Antioch, speaking Syriac all the way.

Despite the ravages of war, the sixth-century Near East was crisscrossed by travelling clergymen and intellectuals for whom the political frontier between Rome and Persia was irrelevant. Culturally and religiously, Syria and northern Mesopotamia were a vortex. It was a region where ideas and forms of piety and culture met, were transformed, and spread westward to the entire Mediterranean and eastward as far as western China. In Italy, Cassiodorus (whom we met in chapter 8) modelled his cultural program, in part, on what he had heard of the great Christian Academy founded by Syriac-speakers at Nisibis, on the Persian side of the frontier. He was amazed to hear of such a large school, in which Christian Biblical exegesis was taught in public, much as the classics had been taught in Rome. On the Roman side of the frontier, at Resh'aina (near Tel Halaf in modern Syria), Sergius, a priest and physician, made a Syriac commentary on the *Organon* of Aristotle in the 530s. Sergius had no doubts as to the importance of his enterprise:

> Without these [without Aristotle's logical works] neither can the meaning of medical writings be attained, nor can the opinions of philosophers be understood, nor, indeed, can the true sense of the divine Scriptures be uncovered . . . For education and advancement in the direction of the sciences . . . cannot take place without the exercise of logic.[12]

He had made the work of Aristotle available for his fellow-Syrians in Syriac. Working in Rome, as we saw in chapter 8, Boethius had done the same, by translating Greek texts into Latin. But the work of Sergius was soon carried across distances of which Boethius, in Rome, could not have dreamed. Within a few years, the Syriac guide to Aristotle was in the hands of Sergius' colleague, a Syriac-speaking bishop of Merv, a great oasis city on the northeastern frontier of Persia, some 1,200 miles to the east of Syria, in what is now Uzbekistan.

Syrians felt that they stood at the crossroads of Asia. They knew that they saw more widely than did the proud Greeks who formed the core of the eastern "Roman" empire. To take one example: a later translator, Severus of Sebokht (d.666/7), refers to the system of "Indian" numbers. This system was quickly adopted by the Arabs. Hence, the numerals we use today are called "Arabic numerals." They are considerably easier to use than are the clumsy numbering systems of the Romans and the Greeks. Severus instantly appreciated the importance of this Indian invention:

> Had they been aware of these, the Greeks, who imagine that they alone have reached the summit of wisdom just because they speak Greek, would perhaps have been persuaded . . . that there are other people who have some knowledge![13]

Culturally and socially, the political frontier between East Rome and Persia meant little. The true frontiers of the sixth- and seventh-century Near East were ecological. The plains of Palestine, Syria, and Mesopotamia formed a "heartland" of Syriac-speaking populations, most of whom were Christians. But these plains were surrounded, as in a mighty arena, by foothills leading up to high mountains. To the west lay the Taurus mountains and the high plateau of Anatolia; to the north, the Hakkari mountains and, behind them, the Caucasus; to the east, the Zagros mountains stretched southward from the Caucasus to the Persian Gulf, cutting off the high, dry plateau of modern Iran from the rich, alluvial plains of Mesopotamia.[14]

Everything in this world depended on the presence of rain. In northern Mesopotamia, the foothills of the high mountain systems received ample snow and rain. They were rich in fruit trees, grain, olives, and wine. They were dotted with great monasteries. A mountain range between Edessa and Nisibis, still known as the Tur 'Abdin, "the Mountain of the Servants of God," had over 80 monasteries. Many of these have survived as Christian monasteries up to this day. They are masterpieces of stonework, and notable for their immense water-cisterns.[15]

Only in northern Mesopotamia, at the foot of the mountains, was rain-

based, "dry" agriculture possible. Southern Mesopotamia, in Persian territory, depended entirely on a carefully maintained system of irrigation, leading from the Tigris, the Diyala, and the Euphrates. What is known as the
Fertile Crescent linked Mesopotamia to the Mediterranean. This belt of settled land was largely made up of Christian villages. To its north lay mountains and rain; but to the south lay a gigantic wedge of arid steppeland,
which was the northernmost reach of the great Arabian desert. Here under
200 millimeters of rain fell every year. One had to travel south over 1,500
miles of wasteland, among tribesmen who spoke only Arabic, before reaching green again on the edge of the Indian Ocean. In the southwest corner of
the Arabian peninsula, the mountain settlements of the Yemen (watered by
the same rains from Africa as caused the yearly flooding of the Nile) were
covered with miraculous green. Here a sophisticated, Arabian society throve,
supported by systems of water catchment and by irrigation from great dams.[16]
Five hundred miles to the west, across the southern end of the Red Sea, the
well-watered mountains of the Christian kingdom of Axum (the future empire of Ethiopia) completed the great oval of watered and unwatered lands
which made up the sixth-century Near East.

"The patrimonial faith": Armenia between Persia and Rome

Each of these regions was affected, and each differently, by the confrontation between Persia and East Rome. Let us begin in the mountains of the
north. The ambivalence of a frontier area was made particularly plain in the
case of Armenia. The high mountain valleys which stretched between Mesopotamia and the Caucasus were a reservoir of military manpower. Like the
Swiss *Landesknechten* or the Scottish Highlanders of later times, Armenians
were prominent in the armies of both empires. They came from a culture
which relished heroes. A seventh-century arithmetic exercise for Armenian
schoolboys went as follows:

> I heard from my father that, in the times when Armenians were fighting
> the Persians, Zarwen Kamsarakan performed memorable feats of prow-
> ess. Attacking the Persian army, he killed half on the first attack . . . a
> quarter on the second . . . and an eleventh on the third. Only 280 Per-
> sians survived. How large was the Persian force before he laid them low?[17]

Armenia looked both east and west. In its social structure and lay culture
it was a westward extension of the feudal society of Persia. Yet it was not a
Zoroastrian country. Christianity had entered the mountains of Armenia

from the Syriac-speaking plains around Edessa and from the river valleys which led up from Greek-speaking Caesarea in Cappadocia to Karin/ Theodosiopolis, which is now Erzerum in eastern Turkey. Under king Trdat III (298–330) and his adviser Grigor, "Gregory the Illuminator," Armenia became a nominally Christian kingdom. This happened in around 314, at the same time, that is, as the fateful conversion of Constantine in the Roman empire. Armenia did not survive for long as an independent kingdom. In 387, it was divided between Rome and Persia.[18]

But what did survive, across the new political frontier, was a common Christianity. Armenians on both sides of the frontier belonged to the same Armenian Church, under a single Armenian *Katholikos*. The unity was sealed by the flowering of a newly created Christian culture. The Armenian alphabet was created around 400 by Mesrop Mashtots (who died in 439). While Coptic and Syriac had been the final adaptation, to Christian purposes, of millennial literate cultures, the clerical elites of Armenia moved, within 50 years, from an oral culture into literacy. As a result, Armenian historiography echoed directly the preliterate world of the epic minstrels. Accounts of Christian saints and kings were structured around notions of power and heroism which belonged to the feudal world of the Iranian plateau. This was a literature with a strong substratum of Iranian oral epic. Nothing like it existed in the Christian Near East, or, indeed, anywhere in Europe, until the flowering of Old Irish, at the other end of the Christian world, in the seventh and eighth centuries.[19]

Not all Armenian clergymen approved of the social milieu which produced such heroic tales. Despite triumphal narratives which looked back to the formation, in Armenia, of the first non-Roman Christian kingdom, in the heroic age of Trdat and Saint Grigor, the conversion of the warrior aristocracy of Armenia had been a slow process. In the disabused words of P'awstos Buzand (Faustus the Bard, who wrote around 470):

> [The Armenians] did not receive Christianity with understanding . . . but as some purely human fashion, and under duress . . . Only those who were to some degree acquainted with [book] learning were able to obtain some partial inkling of it. As for the rest . . . they cherished their songs, their legends and epics, believed deeply in them and persevered in their old ways, in their blood-feuds and enmities.[20]

If these proud warriors related to the Church at all, it was in the manner of the warrior elites of the barbarian west. They approached the Church much as the aristocrats of northern Francia approached the monasteries of Columbanus. They came as princely donors. They were careful to make offerings "for the forgiveness of their sins." But they had little intention of

amending their own pre-Christian ways. One *Katholikos* (described disap-
provingly by P'awstos) saw this only too clearly:

> [The *Katholikos* Yohan would] go down on all fours, braying with the
> voice of a camel . . . "I am a camel, I am a camel, I bear the sins of the
> king; put the sins of the king upon me" . . . And the kings wrote and
> sealed deeds for villages and estates and put them on Yohan's back in
> exchange for their sins.[21]

P'awstos' realistic estimate of his fellow-countrymen was not popular with
his ecclesiastical colleagues. Armenian Christianity required heroic foundation myths if it was to survive at all. This was provided by an epic encounter
between the Christian aristocracy of eastern Armenia and their overlord, the
Persian King of Kings. At the famous battle of Avarayr, in 451, a faction of
the nobility, led by Vardan Mamikonian, died fighting against the Persian
army of the King of Kings, Yazdkart II (439–457).

Yazdkart had attempted to impose Zoroastrianism on their country. But the
Christian nobles did not fight the representatives of Yazdkart so as to become
independent of the Persian empire. They fought so as to remain faithful vassals
of the King of Kings, even though they were Christians. They regarded it as
unjust that they should be expected to become Zoroastrians. They wanted to
retain their honor and their standard of living as the marcher-lords of the Persian empire, whose secular *mores* (religion apart) were so like their own.[22]

The brilliant narratives of Lazar of Pharp, in around 500, and of Elishe
Vardapet, Elishe the Teacher, ensured that the 1,036 Armenian warriors
who fell at Avarayr would be remembered forever after as Christian martyrs. Vardan and his companions were presented as the heirs of the Jewish
Maccabees. Like the Maccabees, they were faced by a formidable empire.
Their ranks were thinned by the apostasy of many of their fellow-noblemen
to Zoroastrianism. Yet Vardan and his army died to preserve the "traditions
of their fathers." Their loyalty to Christianity took the form of a solemn
"Covenant," sworn upon a copy of the Gospels. It was a Covenant which
embraced nobleman and peasant alike. On both sides of the frontier between Roman lands and Persia, all Armenians were henceforth expected to
be loyal to a single "patrimonial faith."[23]

Furthermore, the "patrimonial faith" of Armenia took on a form of Christianity which made them different from the despised Syrians of the lowlands
of Persian Mesopotamia. The Armenians opted for Monophysitism. By so
doing, they made the Armenian Church independent of the staunchly anti-
Monophysite "Church of the East," the Church of the Syrian Christians of
Mesopotamia, which was the principal representative of Christianity in the
Persian empire.[24]

In all of this, Armenian writers presented their heroes as avatars of a militant Israel. In Armenia, the Old Testament and the warlike history of the People of Israel were put to use in the present in a manner which was similar to the appeal to Old Testament models made by clerical writers in the warrior kingdoms of the west.[25]

"The Church of the East": Persian Christians and the School of Nisibis

To the south of the warlike highlands of Armenia, in the Syriac-speaking lowlands, it was not a heroic battle but an ecclesiastical event which determined the future identity of the various Christian communities of the region. The Council of Chalcedon also happened in 451. We have already followed (in chapters 4 and 7) the repercussions in the Eastern empire of the failure of the greatest imperial council of all times. By the middle of the sixth century, a Monophysite "dissident" Church had become established throughout the eastern provinces of the Roman empire. A tentacular network of counter-bishoprics, monasteries, and village priests and holy men of anti-Chalcedonian views stretched from Egypt, Nubia, and Axum across the Fertile Crescent, entering the territories of the Persian empire as if no frontier stood in its way. Based on an unusual combination of theological sophistication and intense, Christ-centered piety, Monophysitism, in its various forms, was the dominant, and certainly the most vocal, faith of the western Syriac world.

The "Church of the East," however, rose to the challenge. This was the Church of the Christian communities in Persia, the "Empire of the East." This Church is often called "the Nestorian Church" and the Christians of Persia, "Nestorian Christians." Like many ecclesiastical labels forged in a time of controversy, it is a "lamentable misnomer."[26] The leaders of the Church in Persia were conservatives. They deeply disapproved of the radical Christology of the Monophysites. They believed that God had graciously revealed himself fully to the human race through a chosen human being, Jesus Christ. But God had not blurred his identity with that of Christ. He had not suffered with Christ on the Cross, as the Monophysites appeared to say. In the opinion of the Church of the East, this was a terrible doctrine. It ascribed suffering and loss to God himself. They thought that the Council of Chalcedon had not gone nearly far enough in opposing the blasphemous absurdity – that God could suffer like a human being – which seemed to be sweeping the Syrian world of the west. The bishops assembled at Chalcedon had failed to do their job:

> Owing to their feeble phraseology, wrapped in an obscure meaning . . .
> they found themselves standing at a cross-roads and they wavered.[27]

In taking such a view, the "Church of the East" was loyal to its roots. Until the very end of the fifth century, the Christian communities in the Persian empire had been an eastward extension of the religious culture of the church of Antioch. The great Antiochene exegete, Theodore of Mopsuestia (350–428), had created the intellectual climate which produced Nestorius. He was revered by his admirers throughout Syria and Persia as "the Universal (that is, the World-class) Exegete." No Persian Christian wished to disown the seemingly bottomless wisdom of Theodore, a past master of Scriptural exegesis.

We saw in chapter 4 how the extreme views of Nestorius had led to the crisis which provoked the Council of Ephesus of 431 and the Council of Chalcedon in 451. But, compared with Theodore, Nestorius was little known in the "Church of the East" before Syriac translations of his works appeared in the middle of the sixth century. Rather, it was the hard-line Monophysites, bitter enemies of Nestorius, who used the term "Nestorian" as a slogan of abuse.

After Chalcedon, Monophysites came to predominate in Edessa. Edessa was the sister city of Nisibis. It was the first major city on the route from Nisibis, on the Persian side of the frontier, toward the west. As a result of the "takeover" by Monophysite radicals at Edessa, boundaries hardened. For the first time in the history of Syriac-speaking Christianity, it became increasingly difficult to come to study at Edessa from Nisibis, only a few days' travel across what up to then had been a largely dormant frontier. In 489, the school for students from Persia in Edessa was closed. At the same time, the churches in Persia rallied, explicitly, to anti-Monophysite doctrines, thereby founding what has been known, ever since, to Western scholars (largely on the strength of Monophysite polemics), as the "Nestorian" Church.[28]

From 470 to 496, Barsauma was the bishop of Nisibis. A high-handed man, Barsauma was accused by later Monophysite writers of having deliberately pushed the "Church of the East" into accepting the heresy of Nestorius in order to seal the frontier between Rome and Persia. Each empire would now have a different, and mutually hostile, form of Christianity within its frontiers. But the split between the "Church of the East" and its western neighbors was the result of a far longer development. The Christians within the Persian empire had begun to feel at home. They no longer looked westward, toward the Roman empire.[29]

In the fourth century, most Christians in Persia had been "Roman" foreigners. They were descended from the thousands of Syrians who had been brought back from Syria to Mesopotamia as captives by Shapur I in the 260s. But times had changed. Christians now came from the Iranian population itself, either through intermarriage or, occasionally, through conversion. Pehlevi (middle Persian) joined Syriac as the other language of the Church of the East. It was Persian Christians, and not only Syriac-speakers from northern Mesopotamia, who penetrated the markets of Asia. A sixth-century eastern Christian cross – a distinctive, quasi-cosmic symbol, half a Cross and half an ancient Mesopotamian Tree of Life – has been discovered as far east as Travancore, with a Pehlevi inscription.[30] Pehlevi, also, would have been the language of the successful Christian entrepreneurs who controlled the pearl fisheries of the Persian Gulf. Their bishops needed to warn them to allow their divers to rest on Sundays. Christian Rogation ceremonies took place, along the shore, to clear the waters of giant sharks. Such persons did not think of themselves as "Romans" *manqués*, but as Persians who happened to be Christians.[31]

The emergence of a silent majority of Persian Christians in the hinterland coincided with a dramatic transfer of Syriac high culture to the Persian side of the frontier in Mesopotamia itself. Nisibis became one of the great university centers of the Near East.[32] Students from all over Mesopotamia flocked to Nisibis, the new "Mother of Wisdom." In its methods of teaching, the school of Nisibis may have resembled the schools established in the large Jewish villages of southern Mesopotamia. Unmarried young men, distinguished by a semi-monastic style of life and dress, settled in the cell-like rooms of a former caravansary. They would memorize the Psalms, the New Testament, and passages from the Old Testament, along with the works of Theodore of Mopsuestia. The intensive work of memorization formed the basis, also, of the intricate chants and specially composed hymns which were the glory of the eastern Christian, as of every other Syriac, liturgy. Headed by a teacher such as Narsai (around 480–90), who wrote over 300 religious *Odes*, the school of Nisibis was to be a training-ground for religious poets as well as for exegetes.

In the culture of the Syriac-speaking world, holy books were supposed to saturate the heart. They did so by being translated into melodious sound, carried by the magical sweetness of the human voice. Unlike the Vivarium of Cassiodorus, this was no hushed world, in which the written text alone spoke to the reader, as a solitary, silent instructor. By contrast, the Syriac world, in east and west alike, was filled with sound. Hence the importance of the *qeryana*, the "reading aloud" of the Scriptures. Through the *qeryana*, the Syriac language was raised to a new pitch. It became a tongue rendered sacred through the repeated, exquisite recitation of the Word of God. Exegesis itself was not a purely intellectual probing of the text of the Scriptures. It was a reliving of the Scriptures through recitation combined with a reverential "robing" of the Word of God, in the form of explanations and amplifications of the Biblical text, in a manner which closely resembled the Midrashic techniques of the rabbis. In a Syrian church, the "reading" held the center of attention:

> Now there was present . . . a great learned priest who had gone out to the porch of the church to meditate upon the outline of his sermon, which he wished to deliver in a learned manner . . . But when the deacon, Mar Jacob, had begun to recite the Psalm, the sweetness of his voice so greatly attracted the attention and mind of everyone . . . that the learned priest cried out with a loud voice: "Fie on you, young man, for the sweetness of your voice has . . . driven out of my mind the thoughts which I had wished to gather together!"[33]

Carried in this way, on the voices of young men, a culture based upon reading aloud the message of God in the church was particularly well suited to the task of "internal mission" which maintained a remarkable degree of cultural and religious unity among the Christians of the East, whose churches stretched from Mesopotamia to China. A large Christian cemetery discovered at Semirechye, in eastern Kazakhstan, shows that Christian communities survived up to the time of the Mongol empire in the thirteenth century. The gravestones show how this could be so. Eight hundred years after the founding of the school of Nisibis, and over three months of travel from Mesopotamia, the "Church of the East" had maintained a quite distinctive style of transmission for their religious culture. The tombs were inscribed in a bold Syriac script which had changed little over the centuries:

> The year 1627 [that is, from the foundation of Antioch by king Seleucus! – A.D. 1316] . . . in the Year of the Dragon, according to the Turks. This is the grave of Sliha, the famous Exegete and Preacher . . . son of the Exegete Petros. Praised for his wisdom, his voice was raised like a trumpet.[34]

From Mesopotamia to China: The "Church of the East" in Asia

The expansion of the "Church of the East" was due to the sheer size and strategic position of the Persian empire. The Persian territories of Mesopotamia were no more than the western fringe of a political system which reached as far as the middle of Asia. The rulers of this empire were aggressively Zoroastrian. Yet their strong rule indirectly fostered the spread of Christianity throughout an officially pagan empire. The Sasanians (to call the rulers of the Persian empire by their local name, from the dynasty to which they belonged) tamed the fragile flood-plains of the Tigris and the Euphrates. In some regions, they almost doubled the area of settlement and maintained levels of irrigation unequalled before modern times. As a result, their empire was hungry for manpower. Khusro I Anoshirwan, "of the Immortal Soul" (530–579), and Khusro II Aparwez, "the Victorious" (591–628), renewed the policy of Shapur I. Their wars against East Rome were slave-raids on a colossal scale. Thousands of Christian captives were settled in new towns and villages both in Mesopotamia and along the fertile but precarious oases which edged Central Asia. From Mesopotamia, Christians gained a foothold on the plateau of Iran, the traditional heartland of Persia, and from Central Asia the roads lay open as far as China.[35]

For the Christian communities within his empire, the King of Kings was a formidable but studiously distant presence. The pressures toward religious conformity which were so strong in East Rome and in the Christian kingdoms of the West did not weigh as heavily upon the subjects of the Sasanian empire. The occasional aristocrat who converted to Christianity was subjected to gruesome public execution, as a renegade from Zoroastrianism. Zoroastrianism was known as the *beh den*, "the Good Religion." It was considered to be too good a religion to be wasted on non-Persians. It was, indeed, a compliment to the Armenians on the part of Yazdkart II that he thought them capable of sharing the "Good Religion" of true Iranians. Syrians were not expected to join this very exclusive club. Usually, as long as subject religious groups were loyal and paid their tribute, they were not greatly troubled. Unlike the Christians of East Rome, who shared in the euphoric myth of an eternal Roman empire, blessed by Christ and inhabited (apart from the Jews) by Christians only, the Christians of the East learned to live among non-Christians, under a non-Christian state. It was a lesson which would prove invaluable to them in succeeding centuries.[36]

Christians emerged at the court of Khusro II as privileged royal servants, somewhat like the "King's Jews" of medieval Europe. Shirin, his principal wife, was a devout Christian. Yazdin of Kerkuk (in northern Iraq) was Khusro's all-powerful financial minister. Yazdin was acclaimed as "the Constantine and the Theodosius" of the Church of the East.

When the armies of Khusro II broke the defenses of Syria, after 610, these high-ranking Christians joined with gusto in the spoliation of their "heretical" East Roman neighbors. When Jerusalem fell to the Persians, in 618, the relic of the True Cross made its way to Mesopotamia. It was intended for the royal palace at Dastkart. Dastkart was set, appropriately enough, within sight of the ruins of ancient Nineveh, from which the Assyrians had struck at Jerusalem 12 centuries previously. But the True Cross ended up as the treasured property, not of the pagan King of Kings, but of the eastern Christian community of Yazdin's Kerkuk.[37]

Moving with little difficulty in a pluralistic society, groups of eastern Christians fitted with ease into the vast horizons which opened up from Persian Central Asia. They joined other groups in the cosmopolitan oasis city of Merv, and soon settled, also, among the Turkish nomadic tribes who acted as the overlords of the trading cities of eastern Central Asia.

From there they established themselves east of the Oxus, along the foothills of the Hindu Kush and the Tien Shan mountains, in the autonomous cities of Soghdia. The Syriac copy of a Psalm, made by a Christian schoolboy, with which we opened our account of the spread of Christianity in the first chapter, was made at Panjikent, a major commercial center in Soghdia, near Samarkand in modern Uzbekistan.

The Soghdians were wide-ranging merchants. Known to the Chinese as men "with mouths full of honey, and gum [to catch every penny] on their fingers," their journeys knit Asia together. Many became Christian. An eastern Christian cross with a Soghdian inscription has been found as far away as Ladakh, on the route to Tibet. Through the Soghdians, Christianity became a religion of the nomads who gravitated around the western frontiers of the Chinese empire.[38] Syriac formed the basis of the script of the Uighur kingdom of southern Mongolia. Most surprising of all, the Mongolian word for "religious law," used of Buddhism – *nom* – may be a distant echo, through Soghdian, of the Greek *nomos*, "law." A central Greek concept was carried as a loan word in Syriac – *namûsa* – to the heart of Asia.[39] In the course of four centuries, Bardaisan's "Law of the Messiah", with which we began our first chapter, had travelled a long way!

In the Turfan oasis of western Chinese Sinkiang, invaluable manuscripts of Manichaean scriptures were found. As we saw in chapter 3, Manichaeism was the perpetual *Doppelgänger* of Syrian Christianity. It also reached Inner Asia at this time, and would survive in China until the fourteenth century.[40] In the nearby village of Bulayiq, a Christian church was found. Its library included a Soghdian translation of the *Antirrheticus* of Evagrius of Pontos (346–399). This was a work on the spiritual struggle of the monk, written in Egypt by a man who had been the friend and adviser of none other than Melania the Elder, the heroine of Paulinus of Nola, whose dramatic return to Italy from the Holy Land we described in chapter 3. Translated into Syriac,

Evagrius had become the master of the art of contemplation in the Syrian world. Now an ascetic text of Evagrius was being read in Soghdian, in an unimaginably distant setting, close to Buddhist monasteries which housed its exact equivalent, a guide to ascetic living entitled *The Sutra of the Causes and Effects of Actions*, also in Soghdian translation.[41]

In 635, eastern Christians submitted a "Defense of Monotheism" to the Chinese emperor at Hsian-fu. Three years later (in the same year, indeed, as Jerusalem was lost to Muslim invaders), a Christian monastery was established in Hsian-fu and works of Syriac theology, derived ultimately from the fourth-century Antiochene culture of Theodore, the "Universal Exegete," were formally placed, in Chinese translation, in the imperial library, among the many *exotica* of the distant western lands.[42]

"Trapped on a rock between two lions": The Arabs between Two Empires

As we have seen, the development of Christianity in both the Persian and the Roman regions of the Near East took place against the background of an escalating conflict between East Rome and Persia. Each of the two super-powers of western Asia had reached out, far into Inner Asia, to seek allies and commercial advantages in an effort to tip the balance in a struggle for total control of the Middle East. After 603, it was as if the keystone of an ancient arch had collapsed. The days of Xerxes or, alternately, the days of Alexander the Great had come again. First, the Roman empire seemed to collapse. Between 610 and 620, Antioch, Jerusalem, and Alexandria fell to Persian armies. Then, in 627, the emperor Heraclius (610–641) struck back into the heart of the overextended empire of Khusro II. In a brilliantly un-conventional strategic move, he fell on Mesopotamia from the north, straight from the Caucasus. He led an army reinforced by nomadic cavalry drawn from the steppes around the Caspian Sea. He burned the palace of Khusro at Dastkart. He celebrated Christmas Day 627 in the great church at Kerkuk. Khusro II was murdered. The True Cross was returned in triumph to Jerusalem, accompanied by Heraclius himself – the first and last East Roman Christian emperor ever to set foot in the Holy Places.

Heraclius' triumph took place against the background of a war-weary Middle East. The cities of the Fertile Crescent had been emptied by massive deportations. The olive groves around Antioch had been hacked to the ground in vindictive raids. Large areas of Mesopotamia were awash again, through neglect of the royal dams. More dangerous still, for the continued existence of the two existing empires, local leaders throughout Syria and Mesopotamia had learned, again and again, for over a generation, the necessary art of surrendering, with good grace, to foreign conquerors.[43]

In this long war, one area of the Near East had attracted little attention. It was taken for granted that the Arabs of the steppelands and the deep desert of Arabia were insignificant. Local Christians wrote of them with contempt:

> There were many people between the Tigris and the Euphrates who lived in tents and were barbarous and murderous. They had many superstitions and were the most ignorant people on earth.[44]

It was assumed that such ignorant starvelings were easy to control. One wily Arab sheik advised another to play the part of the "desert Arab" when he visited the Persians.

> Put on your travelling clothes, gird yourself with your sword, and when you sit down to eat, take big mouthfuls . . . eat much and appear hungry . . . for this pleases the king of Persia . . . For he thinks that there is no good in an Arab unless he is a hungry eater, especially when he sees something which is not his accustomed food. If he then asks, "Will you master your Arabs for me?", say, "Yes."[45]

And yet, in the course of the sixth century, the Arabian peninsula had been drawn into the religious and political confrontations which had swept the settled land. The Arabian peninsula became a gigantic echo-chamber, in which the conflicting political and religious options of the Near East were closely observed, and the weaknesses of the competing empires were sharply assessed. By ignoring the Arabs, the inhabitants of the settled land had been lulled by immemorial stereotypes into a false sense of security.

The total separation of the desert from the sown had been a myth purveyed for millennia by the governing classes of the empires of the Near East. Though frequently repeated up to this day, there was little truth in this myth. All along the steppelands which ringed the villages of Roman Syria and Persian Mesopotamia, Arabic-speaking tribesmen were partners in the economic life of the region. Food could not move without their camels. Marginal land would not remain fertile without the dung of their herds. The goods produced by the large villages would find no market if they did not pass, southward, into the lands of the Arabs. Like the Roman *limes* in Europe, the ecological frontier between the settled land, blessed with the gift of moisture, and the arid desert was not an absolute boundary. It was a middle ground. Along the western hinterland of Mesopotamia and the eastern edges of Syria and Palestine, in a wide belt which stretched from the outskirts of Antioch to the Gulf of Aqaba, settled populations and nomads found themselves drawn together, despite the differences in their languages and social structures, despite much mutual suspicion, and despite the veritable "cascade of contempt" which poured from high places upon the heads of the Arabs.[46]

In the first place, the increasing demands of war between the two empires rendered the Arabs indispensable. Arab sheiks controlled the vital routes across the steppelands which joined Roman Syria to Persian Mesopotamia. It was an Arab ally who led the army of Khusro I Anoshirwan straight to Antioch, across the steppe, in 540. The Arab tribes found themselves drawn into the confrontation between the two great powers. A wide defensive zone, in which the Arabs played a crucial role, developed along the borders of Syria and Persian Mesopotamia. It was if they were "trapped on a rock between two lions, Persia and East Rome."[47]

Faced by this situation, the Arab leaders could always merge back into the desert. The arid steppeland was a place of refuge and a reservoir of tribal fighting men, feared for their swift raiding. But (like any other barbarian leaders along the Roman frontiers) they preferred to exploit their position so as to control the entire middle ground on both sides of the ecological divide between the desert and the sown. Sheiks of the Jafnid family of the Banu Ghassân were major landowners in Syria and patrons of the local Monophysite church. They left their mark on the landscape (much as the Frankish aristocracy left their mark on the fields of northern Gaul) by founding monasteries at permanent watering places where settled land and desert met. There they would set up their encampments and would set their herds of war-horses to graze on the rich grass. These monasteries were long remembered by Arab writers.

> They built monasteries in pleasant places, abounding in trees, gardens and water-cisterns. Their [liturgical] plate was in gold and silver. The curtains in the churches of brocaded silk. They placed mosaics on the walls, and gold and images upon the ceilings.[48]

At Resafa (Rusâfa in modern Syria, west of the Euphrates, some 20 miles south of Raqqa) the Banu Ghassân controlled the greatest religious shrine in the Arab world.[49] Resafa was also called Sergiopolis. It was the "city of Saint Sergius." Sergius had been a Roman soldier who was executed as a Christian in the Great Persecution. At that time, Resafa was no more than a frontier fort, perched in an apparent wilderness. East Romans called it "the Barbarian Plain." But the "Barbarian Plain" was no longer empty. Or, rather, those who lived in it were visible, for the first time, because they were Christians and they were useful. As Christians, the Arab tribes of the steppes met Syrian, Greek, and Persian Christians of the settled world in a common devotion to Saint Sergius. They would seek baptism there. Sergius, Sarjûn, or Sargis in Arabic, became a favored "Christian name" among the Arabs. Arab leaders availed themselves of the sacrality of the site. The leading sheik of the Banu-Ghassân, al-Mundhîr, may even have held the meetings where he presided as a tribal judge in a domed building where the relics of Sergius himself were kept, a short distance outside the walls of the sanctuary city.[50] Christianity and leadership among the tribes went hand in hand along the Syrian frontier.

But this was the case also on the Persian side of the desert. The sheiks of the Banu Lakhm at Hira, on the Persian frontier, were also Christian. The court of the Banu Lakhm at Hira was a gathering place for some of the greatest Arab poets of the age. Hira was a "camp." But, like Resafa, it was also a Christian holy city. It was the burial place of *Katholikoi* of the Church of the East and the scene of heated disputes between Nestorians and Monophysites.[51]

The message of these northern camps was quickly transmitted to the south. Religious confrontation was in the air. On the edge of the green mountains of Yemen, the oasis city of Najrân sheltered an oligarchy of Christian merchants who were as rich as any in Edessa or Alexandria. Najrân thought of itself as the Resafa of the south. In 523, the Arab clans of Najrân were brutally crushed by a Himyarite Arab king in Yemen, Dhû Nuwâs, who had opted for Judaism. By so doing, Dhû Nuwâs hoped to create, in the rich lands of southern Arabia, a "Davidic" kingship which was independent of the Christian powers.[52] As we saw in chapter 5, Dhû Nuwâs was eventually defeated by the Axumite Christian, Ella Atsbeha, a warrior king as enterprising and as convinced that he had God on his side as was his contemporary in the distant northwest, Clovis, the king of the Franks.

But the Christian conquest of Yemen did not take place before the pros and cons of Christianity and Judaism had been hotly debated, in Arabic and in a manner which resounded throughout the Arab world. Far from the inhibitions imposed by dominant orthodoxies, the central issues of both faiths were open to fierce contention: was Christ divine or was he a mere human being? Was he greater than Moses or simply a crucified sorcerer? Altogether, had Christianity and the forms of Christian piety which had developed by the sixth century (monasticism and the cult of saints and relics in particular) been a great mistake? In the words of a former Christian bishop who had converted to Judaism:

> In truth, if you were to meet the prophets of old, they would have spat in your face . . . for you have chosen corrupted ways which are false and aberrant.[53]

"My servants, the righteous, shall inherit the earth": Muhammad and the Preaching of Islam

Such debates would have been unthinkable in the orthodox empire of Justinian. But they were perfectly normal in Arabia. For the historian, there is nothing remarkable about the fact that, around the year 600, Christianity and Judaism were well known throughout the Arabian peninsula. What is remarkable, rather, is that, in the person of Muhammad of Mecca (570–632), the Arabian peninsula produced a prophet who, in the opinion of his followers as of all later Muslims, had received from God authority to transmit, to his fellow-Arabs, God's own, definitive judgment on both Christianity and Judaism.[54]

Muhammad grew up in Mecca, a city in the Hijâz, in the same years as Columbanus settled in Luxeuil and Gregory the Great lamented the ruins of Rome. Some 600 miles north of Najrân and a good 1,000 south of the frontier villages of the Roman empire, Mecca was an unprepossessing place. Untouched by rain, unlike Yemen, it was one of a number of settlements made possible by the existence of a spring of water. It maintained itself as best it could through trade with similar settlements, which were scattered all over the central and northern parts of the Arabian peninsula. Its inhabitants were "townsmen" only in the sense that they controlled a settled area.

The Arabian peninsula was not an empty space, crossed only by nomads. It had many settlements like Mecca. They were tiny ecological cracks in the austere, lava sheath of the Arabian desert. Their population outnumbered the true nomads. But they depended on these nomads for the circulation of goods on which each settlement depended. They shared with the "Arabs of the desert" a common deposit of social values. They were tribesmen. In the absence of a state, safety depended on membership of a clan which was prepared to defend its members, its livestock, and its wells against all comers. It made little difference whether one lived in a settlement or as an Arab of the desert: whichever way, the tribe was everything. The townsmen also shared in the constant shifting of a pan-Arabian pecking order. Some tribes were "strong" and "noble" and others were "weak" and easily pushed to one side. Above all, they shared the only form of stunning wealth which societies bereft of material goods tend to create with exuberant abandon: they spoke the richest language in the entire Near East. Arabic had already acquired a "classical" homogeneity, through the constant interchange of poets and storytellers. An Arabic script had been developed and was used for inscriptions in many parts of Arabia. This was a world where words carried. What was known and thought in distant Resafa, Hira, and Najrân, was clearly heard in the oasis settlements of the Hijâz.[55]

It was once thought that the key to the emergence of Mecca at the time of Muhammad could be found in the fact that the Hijâz lay along great caravan routes, which carried the trade of Yemen and the Indian Ocean northward to the Mediterranean. There is little truth in this view.[56] The "international trade" which mattered more, in the Arabia of Muhammad, was a trade in religious ideas, carried with remarkable "conductivity" from north to south. And this trade in ideas gained immensely in explosive content as it entered a tense world where tribe was always pitted against tribe and oasis against oasis. Some tribes of central Arabia had adopted Judaism. Others, such as the Banu Ghassân, were known for their Christianity. Religious differences were part of the ceaseless battle for prestige between the tribes. Faced by an open world, already polarized between Jews and Christians, Persians and East Romans, the dominant family of Mecca, the Quryash, were proud to remain frank idolaters. In a world where Jews and Christians, and even the great empires of the Near East, had come uncomfortably close, they thought it best to stand to one side and wait.

Not so Muhammad. In 610, at the age of 40, the visions began to come. They came from the One God (in Arabic: Allah), "the Lord of the Worlds." For the next 20 years, the messages came irregularly, in sudden, shattering moments, up to his death in 632. In them, so Muhammad believed, the same God who had spoken to Moses and to Jesus, and to many thousands of humbler prophets, now spoke again, once and for all, to himself. Vivid sequences of these words from God were carefully memorized by Muhammad's followers. They were passed on by skilled reciters throughout the Arabic-speaking world. For these were nothing less than snatches of the voice of God himself speaking to the Arabs through Muhammad. They were not written down until after 660, in very different circumstances from the time of their first delivery. When written out, they came to form the single book known to us as the Qur'ân.[57]

Qur'ân and the Syriac *qeryana* come from the same root *qr'*, to read, to cry aloud. Both accorded the fullest measure of authority to a religious message when it was carried, directly, by the human voice. A once-skeptical Meccan was believed to have described his experience in listening to such a "reading." Like the learned Syrian preacher who listened to the "reading" of Mar Jacob, he was shaken by what he heard:

> I thought that it would be a good thing if I could listen to Muhammad . . .
> When I heard the Qur'ân [that he was reciting] my heart was softened and Islam entered into me. By God [said another], his speech is sweet.[58]

But for Muhammad's followers, this was no Syriac religious ode, not even a Psalm of David, a human composition offered by man to God. What Muhammad recited was, rather, a direct rendering of the eloquence of God as he spoke to the human race. This God had never ceased, throughout the ages, to "call out" to all nations, through his many prophets. Now this voice repeated itself, in Arabic, in a final and majestically definitive summation.

It was this aspect of the Qur'ân which instantly offended Jews and Christians. For the messages relayed by God through Muhammad claimed to undo the past. His messages declared that neglect and partisan strife had caused Jews and Christians to slip away from, even to distort, the messages which they had once received from their prophets, Moses and Jesus. Christians were told, in no uncertain terms, that they had erred. They were warned by God that the Christological controversies which had absorbed their energies for so many centuries were based on a gigantic misunderstanding. Jesus had not been God and had never claimed to be treated as if he was God:

> And behold [at the Last Judgment] God will say: "O Jesus, son of Mary! Didst thou say unto men: worship me and my mother as gods in derogation of God?" He will say: "Glory to Thee. Never could I have said what I had no right to say." (Qur'ân v:119)

Though they played an essential role in defining the position of Muhammad's later followers in a world of Jews and Christians, the messages directed against Judaism and Christianity were less central than was the message which Muhammad brought to the Arabs themselves. He was acutely conscious of having been sent by God to his fellow-countrymen to warn them, in clear Arabic, to change their pagan ways. They were to return to the original purity of an uncorrupted past. They were to realize that they were the descendants of Abraham, the father of Ishmael. The Ka'ba of Mecca (a local shrine erected around a meteorite) had been the spot where Abraham himself had sacrificed to the one, true God. Now the Quraysh had filled it with idols. In reclaiming the Ka'ba for his worship alone, Muhammad and his followers would regain for Mecca the powerful blessing of God.[59] All who heard this message should surrender themselves to the will of God. For this was what all religious persons had done since the beginning of time.

The name adopted by the new religion, "Islâm," and the word used to describe its adherents, "Muslims," came from the same Arabic root, *slm* – to surrender, to trust in one God. It summed up an entire view of history. It was a history where, in what truly mattered for human beings – that is, their relationship to God – nothing had ever changed. Islam and Muslims had always existed. In all past ages, trust in God and the rejection of all other

worship had invariably distinguished true monotheists from ignorant poly-
theists. God had fostered this monotheism by sending his prophets to the
Jews and to the Christians. Those who accepted sincerely the messages of
Moses and Jesus were Muslims without knowing it.[60]

Now the Arabs were summoned to partake in the same, perennial faith.
And if they did not, they would be lost. The gaunt ruins of so many dead
cities, which lay along the caravan routes of the Arabian peninsula, spoke to
Muhammad quite as clearly of the swift approach of the Last Judgment as
the ruins of Rome spoke to his older contemporary, pope Gregory. Both
men, the Arabian prophet and the Roman pope, thought of themselves as
sent by God to warn a world in its last days:

> Do they not reflect in their own minds? Have they not travelled the land
> and seen what was the end of those before them? They were superior to
> them in strength: they tilled the soil and populated it in greater number
> than these have done. (Qur'ân xxx:19)
>
> But how many countless generations before them have We destroyed?
> Canst thou find a single one of them now, or hear so much as a whisper?
> (Qur'ân xix:98)

If the Arabs listened to God's warning, however, they might face a very
different prospect:

> Before, We wrote in the Psalms: . . . *My servants, the righteous, shall
> inherit the earth.* (Qur'ân xxi:105, citing Psalm 37:22)

A remarkable group of young men, caravan merchants and warriors, had
been the Companions of Muhammad throughout his career. They had defended his cause with arms, in the authentic Arab manner. They had "striven
hard," risking their wealth, even their lives, to maintain his honor and safety:
the word *jihâd*, usually translated as "holy war," originally meant little more
than to "strive" to keep one's end up in a world which took tests of martial
courage for granted. For young tribesmen, raiding the camels of one's rivals
and showing one's prowess by making members of "weak" tribes back down
was fun, and not particularly lethal fun. To fight the new Companions of
Muhammad, however, was not fun. It was lethal, for the Companions fought
in earnest. They did so in order to defend their religion. Very soon they
struck out, to "humble" stubborn opponents. They cited as warrant for their
deadly seriousness as warriors the behavior of the frontier troops of the East
Roman empire. Those soldiers had been stationed on the edge of the desert
by Christian emperors so as to protect churches and monasteries. They also
fought so as to humble unbelievers. For inhabitants of the settled empires,

there was nothing strange in the idea that warfare was blessed by God. But, within Arabia itself, the sheer aggression of the followers of Muhammad changed the rules of the game.[61]

In 622, Muhammad and his Companions emigrated to the more northerly oasis of Medina. This was a *hijra* – an emigration of a leader and his armed band to find a new place to settle. By this move, they had re-created themselves as a new tribe, a small nation in arms, like any other Arab tribe, but more determined. In all later centuries, Muslims would count the years from the date of the *hijra* to Medina. In 630, Muhammad and his Companions returned in triumph to Mecca. They purged the Ka'ba of its idols. Unlike the destruction of temples in the Christian empire, this was not acclaimed by Muslims as a victory over the ever-present demons. The purging of the Ka'ba was more like the restoration of a painting. A veneer of ignorant practices, piled up over the centuries, was scraped away to reveal the original, simple temple, uncluttered by idolatry, where Abraham had once worshipped the true God in Mecca.[62]

The year 630, which marked the return of Muhammad to Mecca, was the same year as the emperor Heraclius had brought the Holy Cross in triumph back to Jerusalem. It was a moment of high emotion. Heraclius was believed to have dismounted and walked the last 200 miles to the Holy City on foot, like a rejoicing pilgrim.[63] Only two years later, 1,200 miles to the south, Muhammad died, in 632. Muhammad's Companions survived the death of their leader. Having gained respect throughout Arabia by forming a confederation of towns joined together by a common acceptance of Islam, they were able to offer their allies conquests of which they had not dared to dream.

This was not surprising. To seventh-century persons, it was not particularly shocking. The Companions of Muhammad were blunt men in a society inured to war. They were as convinced as the emperors Justinian and Heraclius had been that God blessed the armies of those who trusted in him. They intended to use their armies to *inherit the earth*. As an Armenian writer reported it:

> They sent an embassy to [Heraclius] the emperor of the Greeks saying: "God has given this land as an inheritance to our father Abraham and to his posterity after him. We are the children of Abraham. You have held our country long enough. Give it up peacefully, and we will not invade your country. If not, we will retake with interest what you have withheld from us."[64]

The imagined reaction of Heraclius, reported in an eastern Christian source, was equally revealing. A military challenge from the "tents" of the south, at a time when the frontiers of both empires had been fatally weakened by decades of warfare, was only to be expected. But this would be different:

> This people [the emperor said] is like an evening, between daylight and nightfall, neither sunlit nor dark . . . so is this people neither illumined by the light of Christ nor is it plunged into the darkness of idolatry.[65]

Let us see, in our next chapter, how the Christian populations of the Near East adjusted to the gigantic Arab empire which seemed to be founded on a troubling anomaly. In their opinion, Islam was an "in-between religion". It was not pagan. It closely resembled Christianity and Judaism. Yet it was like neither of them. It was something entirely new. It was another monotheistic faith, thrown up by the political and religious turmoil of the Near East. And like Christianity, Islam also was convinced that it alone represented the culmination of God's purposes on earth.

CHAPTER 13

"The Changing of the Kingdoms": Christians under Islam

"The fourth kingdom . . . greater than all other kingdoms": Responses to the Arab Conquests

In around 634 a group of Jews were arguing in Carthage with Jacob, a fellow-Jew who had recently converted to Christianity. As always in debates between Jews and Christians, the issue was whether the Messiah had come or was yet to come. Jacob was convinced that the Messiah had already come, in the person of Jesus Christ. It was obvious to him, from the events of recent times, that the end of the world was at hand. There was no time left for a future Messiah – only for the coming of Antichrist, to be followed swiftly by the Last Judgment. For the last great empire of world history was passing away:

> Up to our times the frontiers of the Roman empire stretched as far as Ireland and Britain . . . to Persia and the East. The statues of the emperors in bronze and marble appeared everywhere. By the command of God, all nations obeyed the Romans. Now we see that the Roman world is brought low.[1]

Jacob and his opponents had heard of Muhammad. Only two years after Muhammad's death, troubling news from Arabia made some Jews think that perhaps he was the "prophet" sent by God to announce the coming of the Messiah. In a letter to Carthage, a Jewish partner reported that the Byzantine general in command of the frontiers of Palestine had been killed in one of the first Arab raids:

> When the general was killed by the Arabs, I was at Caesarea . . . People were saying "the general has been killed," and we Jews were overjoyed. And they were saying that the prophet had appeared, coming with the Arabs, and

that he was proclaiming the arrival of the Anointed One, the Messiah who was to come. I stopped . . . and paid a visit to a certain old man well-versed in the Scriptures, and I said to him: "What can you tell me about the prophet who has appeared among the Arabs?" He replied, groaning deeply: "He is a false prophet, for prophets do not come armed with the sword" . . . So I inquired and heard from those who met him that there was no truth to be found in the so-called prophet, but only the shedding of men's blood."[2]

The Arab victories of the subsequent years left the inhabitants of the Near East, Jewish, Christian, and Zoroastrian alike, stunned. In 636, the East Roman army was crushed on the steep eastern slopes of the Golan, at the battle of the Yarmuk (in modern Syria). A year later, at Qâdisiyya (in modern Iraq), the Persian army suffered a similar fate. Egypt fell in 642. Crossing the Zagros on to the plateau of Iran, the Arabs routed the last Persian king at Nihâwand, in 642, and soon controlled Central Asia as far as Samarkand. Carthage fell in 698, and the Visigothic kingdom of Spain collapsed in 711. At the same time, far to the east, Arab armies were raiding northern India and had made contact with the western outposts of the Chinese empire. Nothing like this had happened since the days of Alexander the Great. It was the greatest political revolution ever to occur in the history of the ancient world. For the first time in human history, the populations of the archipelago of settled regions which stretched from Morocco and Andalusia to Central Asia and the Punjab found themselves part of a single political system.

Christian contemporaries of this revolution could do justice to so immense a change only by invoking the vision of the succession of great empires in the Book of Daniel. In the succession of empires, Rome had, up till then, been treated as the last empire. As we saw, Cosmas Indicopleustes, and with him the majority of East Roman Christians, Greek and Syrian alike, regarded this as a source of pride and confidence. Their empire was the empire of Christ. It would last for as long as time itself would last. But now, only two generations after the writing of the *Christian Topography*, time had lurched forward. The age of Rome was over. Its end was in sight. The new "kingdom of the Arabs" had replaced Rome. It was the final, gigantic flare-up of human grandeur, pride, and violence before the return of Christ to earth and the Last Judgment. Christians who witnessed the events of the seventh century felt that they were participating in the last "changing of the kingdoms," which had been predicted in the Book of Daniel:

> This fourth, arising from the south, is the kingdom of the sons of Ishmael [the Arabs] . . . *The fourth beast, the fourth kingdom, shall arise, which shall be greater than all other kingdoms, and it will consume the whole earth.* (Daniel 7:23)[3]

The military and social reasons for the success of the Arab conquests have rightly fascinated historians.[4] But there is an aspect of these conquests which needs to be remembered. They took place among intensely religious populations who held deeply felt views on the course of human history and on the manner in which God intervened in the world. It was these pre-existing systems of explanation which were mobilized to cope with the shock of sudden conquest. As a result, we can listen in to the voices of the Christian communities of the Near East, whose diversity we examined in the last chapter, as they tried to make sense of their position in a changed world.

A sense of the approaching end of time was in the air. It is a sign of the openness of Muslim Arabs to the religions around them that many Muslims appear to have shared in the anxieties of their Jewish and Christian subjects. Pious Muslims were by no means always as self-confident as the ideology of their empire encouraged them to be. They felt that they were men in a hurry, working in the twilight of the last days. They constantly feared that the entire enterprise of Islam might fail. In around 700, *Hadith*s, "Sayings of Muhammad," were passed around the garrison cities of Syria. They were far from optimistic. The catastrophic defeat of the East Roman armies in Syria had, for the moment, cleared the empire out of the Near East, up to the edge of the Anatolian plateau. But Constantinople and the heartlands of the East Roman empire remained unconquered. They were protected on the sea by a formidable navy and on land by the bleak uplands of Anatolia. The Christian empire of East Rome, the empire of *Rûm*, might yet strike back. *Hadith*s circulated in which Muhammad had warned his followers:

> Persia is [only a matter of] one or two thrusts and no Persia will be after that. But the *Rûm* [the East Romans] . . . are people of sea and rock . . . Alas, they are your enemies to the end of time.

Nothing could be certain:

> Islam has started as a foreigner [to all lands] and may again become a foreigner, folding back [on Mecca and Medina] like a snake folding back into its hole.

To stand watch for one night on the coast of Syria, scanning the horizon for the dread return of the East Roman navy, was deemed a more pious action than to spend all night in prayer in the Ka'ba of Mecca.[5]

"Justice flourished in his time and there was great peace": The Ummayad Empire, 661–750

From the Arab point of view, the most surprising development of the seventh century was the survival of their empire, and its eventual transformation from a momentary "kingdom of the Arabs," whose leaders happened to be Muslim, into a true Islamic empire, built to last. We should not allow hindsight to dull our sense of the extreme unlikelihood, in the 630s, that such an outcome would happen. Nor should we underestimate the doggedness and creativity of the Muslim elites and their collaborators in having created, by the year 700, an unambiguously Arab and Islamic state.

In themselves, the victories of the Arabs along the weakened frontiers of the settled land might have done little more than produce large areas in Mesopotamia and Syria which resembled the *Sklaviniai* of the Balkans. After the first momentum of the conquests was spent, and the unity generated by success had dissipated, these regions could easily have become lawless frontier zones, withdrawn, if only for a short time, from the immemorial grip of empire. The ancient empires would have returned, after a brief interlude of Arab rule.

This possibility was always present in the seventh century. The Arab armies were recruited from tribesmen. Their first loyalty was to their own tribes and not to Islam. The commanders of the Arab armies were Muslims; but they knew very well that it was on the energy of the tribes that the success of their armies depended. At the battle of Qâdisiyya, for instance, the Arab armies had been mauled on the first day by a significantly larger and well-trained Persian army. During that night, the Muslim leader, Sa'd bar Abî Waqqâs, lay on the roof of a house, listening to the troops around the campfires, in an attempt to assess their morale. What he heard reassured him. In every tribal compound, the sound of poets and reciters of genealogies filled the night air, boasting in high Arabic the martial valor of their clan. He knew that they would win next day.[6]

Such raw material might win battles. But it was unlikely, by itself, to create an empire. The Arab leadership was riven by feuds. In 656–61 and again in 683–92 the Arabs of the western, Syrian territories were pitted against the eastern Arabs of Iraq in fierce civil wars. Yet, despite these strains, a permanent Islamic empire emerged. This was partly due to the skill with which the Arab rulers of Syria enlisted the active collaboration of the surviving members of the provincial elites, both Persian and East Roman. Coming after generations of breakdown, where anything could have happened, the vast new state was not only the result of conquest. It was the result of the ability of its rulers and public servants to turn conquest into law and order. And this ability came from a firm vote on the part of the silent majority of the settled populations of the Near East for the stability of empire – of any empire – over potential anarchy.[7]

It is interesting to see how Christians in the Near East regarded this development. Writing in Syriac in northern Mesopotamia in 687, John bar Penkâye remembered the Arab conquests of the 630s with horror:

> God summoned against us a Barbarian Kingdom – a people that is *not open to persuasion* (Isaiah 65:2) . . . whose comfort lies in meaningless bloodshed, whose pleasure is to dominate all nations, whose wish is to take captives and to make deportations.[8]

But those times now lay in the past. John had nothing but praise for the Arab Calif Mu'awiya (661–680). For Mu'awiya had brought an end to civil war.

> He became king, controlling the two kingdoms, the Persians and the Byzantines. Justice flourished in his time and there was great peace in the regions under his control. He allowed everyone to live as they wanted.[9]

We can appreciate the hopes and fears of a man such as John bar Penkâye if we look at the Near East with the eyes of persons who still remembered the days of Heraclius and of Khusro II Aparwez. Then the Fertile Crescent had been a corridor for conflicting armies (as it remained, in times of civil war, between rival Arab armies). But, once the military frontier between Rome and Persia had been expunged by the Arab conquest of Syria, Iraq, and Iran, the Near East became a more natural unit. Its separate parts fell together after centuries of division. Strong rule which maintained this unity was good for everyone.

The new Islamic empire was associated with the rule of the Ummayads of Syria – the family of Ummaya, members of the clan of the Quraysh, from which the Calif Mu'awiya had come. This empire linked the former subjects of East Rome and Persia in a single political and economic system, whose local administrative underpinning was recognizably continuous with all that had gone before.

We need only go to the monuments created by the Ummayads to appreciate what this could mean. They show that the Near East had become a common market of artistic skills. To take one example: The Ummayad palace of Khirbet al-Mafjar, now known as the Hisham Palace from its supposed connection with the Calif Hisham (724–743), stands a little outside Jericho in modern Palestine. It lies near the road across the Jordan into steppelands which had once marked a military frontier. But, after the establishment of the Islamic empire, the steppes beyond Jericho marked no more than the starting point of routes which continued without a break, within the territories of a single state, as far as Central Asia. The cultural frontier between the world of Persia and the Mediterranean world of Rome had been expunged. Looking at the astonishing stone-carving, mosaic, and stucco-work discovered in the Hisham Palace, we realize that two once separate worlds had come together to create something new.

They are strange to look at. The mosaics of the great private bathhouse are recognizably East Roman in design and layout; and yet there is a sense of color and of tight pattern which makes them look more like woven carpets. The stucco-work has the same exuberance as we find in the palaces and hunting lodges of Persian kings on the Iranian plateau; and yet it includes figures gesturing like Roman rhetors in carefully folded togas. Modern stereotypes of what an Arab, Muslim world should look like are undermined by this art. It is neither recognizably Muslim nor particularly Arab as we now imagine "Muslim" and "Arab" to be, when we think of the Islamic world. This art was new. But it did not come from the desert. Nor did it owe anything to Islam. It was created by the joining of the two sides of the Fertile Crescent. What we call Islamic art began with a mutation of old traditions brought about through the creative splicing of elements taken from the hitherto divided cultures of the western (East Roman) and the eastern (Persian) regions of the Near East.[10]

At the same time, a profound transformation also took place in the ideology of the elites of the Arab empire itself. This was, in many ways, a reaction to the troubling richness and wide horizons which had been opened up by the Arab conquests. The pressure of civil war led to a need to assert a common and fully public ideology – a mainstream on which all sides of the Arab, Muslim community could agree. There was a real danger that the Muslim community would disintegrate and that Muslims would lose their identity. They would sink back into the rich world revealed by monuments such as the Hisham Palace. A remedy for this danger could be found only in the assertion of a common Islam and in an increased emphasis on a common Arab heritage. In religious and literary circles, both the Muslim and the Arab aspects of the new empire were stressed with a new urgency.

The Qur'ân was written down in 660. In the Qur'ân, the messages of Muhammad seemed to be removed from time and space. Though delivered in Arabic and to Arabs, they were for all places and all peoples. These messages were now rendered intelligible by commentaries and by supplementary narratives which placed Muhammad and his preaching in a hyper-real, strictly local, and Arabian context. The exact circumstances of Muhammad's utterances and actions in Mecca and Medina were evoked with loving circumstantiality. By this means, the landscape of the Hijâz was fixed forever in the minds of Muslims as far apart as Spain and China. This was where their history began.[11]

And it was a pan-Arabian history. Muhammad had shown dislike for the "Arabs of the desert." He regarded them as boastful, feral men, heedless of religion and capable of destroying their newborn daughters by burying them in the sand.[12] In the later tradition, however, this dislike was muted. The "Arabs of the desert" and the city dwellers were treated as fellow-Arabs. The nomads were accepted. They were spoken of as "the root of the Arabs and the reinforcement of Islam."[13] Barbarian settlers in western Europe had created histories for themselves in the same way. It helped to make them separate from the populations with whom they had mixed. As we saw in chapter 5, the Saxons of Britain came to speak proudly of their "coming" to the island in ships across the sea. In so doing they turned generations of desultory migration and symbiosis with the local populations into a single, heroic moment of invasion. But nothing which happened in barbarian western Europe equalled the energy with which the Muslims of around 700 mobilized a sense of their own Arabian past. The creation of an Arabic historical tradition was one of the great intellectual achievements of the early Middle Ages.

The sense of the past which was achieved through this creation of tradition tacitly excluded all outsiders to Arabia. Jews and Christians, Persians and East Romans were allotted "walk-on parts," but little more. The immensely rich but inward-looking Arabic historical tradition virtually ignored the intimacy and the complexity of the relations between the Arabs and the other cultures of the Near East, which we described in the last chapter. This has to be recovered from other, non-Arabic sources.

An Empire Gains its Public Face: Language, Coinage, and Mosques

As a result of these pressures, the state set in order by the successors of Mu'awiya, notably by the Califs 'Abd al-Malik (685–705) and al-Walid (705–715), was a defiantly Islamic, Arabic state.

On the ground level, administrative practice continued as before. East Roman families continued to collect the taxes in Syria and Egypt, Persians did the same in Mesopotamia and Iran. Seen from below, little had changed. But this was not the case at the top. At the governmental level, the empire took on a firm, public face. After 699, Arabic became the sole official language of the bureaucracy. At the time, the change affected only those involved in the business of administration. But the Califs also used the same, overwhelmingly visual means for making their presence felt in the world at large as had been used by the East Roman emperors. They used coins which everyone saw. After many experiments, a new gold and silver coinage was issued in 693 to replace the coins of East Rome, which had previously circulated as legal tender, or had been copied, with adaptations, in the Calif's mints. Now the coins were cleared of all representations of the human figure. Only passages from the Qur'ân, in a firm Arabic script, could be seen on them.[14] Even the milestones came to bear Arabic inscriptions, including the Muslim confession of faith, the *shahâda*: "I confess that there is no God but the One God, and that Muhammad is his prophet."[15]

By the year 700, the public spaces of Syria, Egypt, and Iraq had begun to look distinctively Muslim and Arabic. Arabic could be seen on coins, inscriptions, and textiles. A little later, under the Calif Yazid II (720–724) the Cross (which had been the sign *par excellence* – almost the "national flag" – of the East Roman Christian empire founded by Constantine) was removed from public places.[16]

Above all, Muslims seized on the traditions of public building which had led, in East Rome, to stupendous monuments such as Constantine's church of the Holy Sepulcher in Jerusalem and Justinian's Hagia Sophia in Constantinople, as we saw in chapters 3 and 7. They were fully conscious of the need to compete with Christians. It was in this spirit that the Calif al-Walid built the Great Mosque in Damascus:

> For he beheld Syria to be a country that had long been occupied by Christians and he noted the beautiful churches still belonging to them, so enchantingly fair and so renowned for their splendor [such as the church of the Holy Sepulcher in Jerusalem] . . . So he sought to build for the Muslims a mosque that should prevent them from looking with admiration at the Christian churches, and that should be unique and a wonder to the world.[17]

The Great Mosque of Damascus, which al-Walid began in 705, revealed very clearly what the Muslim rulers of the empire wished. They followed, in a new idiom, a thoroughly Roman ideal. They created public spaces in which to make stunning visual statements of the prosperity and innate superiority of their empire. Mosques were perfect for this purpose. The word mosque comes from *masjid*. The word has survived virtually unchanged in Spanish as *mezquita* – a testimony to centuries of Arabic-speaking Muslim rule. It meant "place of worship." The mosque was a place for fully public worship. The entire Muslim community was expected to assemble in their mosques at regular times, and especially on Fridays. Unlike the Christian churches, even

the greatest of which still maintained a sense of secluded mystery, the mosque
– in the largely rainless climate of Syria, Egypt, and Iraq – was an open-air
meeting place. Used for prayer, but also for preaching, for announcements
of important news and for discussions, the open courtyard of the mosque
served both as the forum and as the parade-ground of a religious "nation in
arms."

Al-Walid created his mosque by the simple and drastic device of enclosing
the former religious heart of the city. He included in this enclosure both the
gigantic temple of Jupiter and the Christian shrine dedicated to John the
Baptist, later known to Muslims as Yahya. Before 705, the Christian church
had been shared as a place of prayer by Christians and Muslims. This was a
normal practice in the yearly years of Muslim rule.[18]

The mosque was a statement of imperial grandeur and a monument to
victory. It was resplendent with marbles and columns known to have been
taken from conquered royal palaces. It was sheathed with mosaic work which
was said to have been provided, by way of tribute, by humbled East Roman
emperors.

Yet this very ancient message of victory also carried with it a strong
and distinctively Muslim religious charge. As we saw in the case of Gregory
of Tours, in chapter 6, Christians had always believed in Paradise as a
garden of delights. Muslims shared this belief. But, in Christian churches,
this was an otherworldly Paradise, conjured up in the depths of great,
enclosed shrines. In the Great Mosque believers did not enter into a building. Rather, they stood in the open air. Their Paradise was all around
them. The courtyard of the mosque was a vast pleasure-garden, surrounded
by scenes in glittering mosaic of palaces set in vivid greens, among streams
of sparkling water. It was full of light, bright color and water. Such a
mosque was an image on earth of the Paradise promised to true believers
in the Qur'ân.[19]

A little earlier, the Calif 'Abd al-Malik had made an even more aggressive
statement of the superiority of Muslims to all other religions. In 692, he
began to build the Dome of the Rock on top of the deserted site of the former
Jewish Temple at Jerusalem. The new dome towered above the dome of
Constantine's Church of the Holy Sepulcher. Inside, the mosaics around the
base of the dome bore inscriptions from the Qur'ân. These are the first evi-
dences that we have of the Qur'ân as a written document (for no early copies
of the Qur'ân have survived). And they were put there with a purpose. They
showed that the Calif wished to make plain to visiting Muslim pilgrims that,
in God's definitive judgment, the entire past of Christianity had been weighed
and found wanting. The inscriptions were taken from verses of the Qur'ân in
which Christians were rebuked:

> Oh People of the Book [that is, Christians, defined by their possession of Holy Scriptures] do not go beyond the bounds of your religion . . . Jesus, the son of Mary, was [only] God's Messenger . . . It is not for God to take a son . . . The true religion with God is Islam. (Qur'ân iv:171 and iii:19)

There was even a strong belief at that time that, at the Last Judgment, God himself would set up his throne upon the Temple Mount, and would judge the Christians according to these clear messages contained in the Qur'ân.[20]

There was no doubt about it: the founders of the Islamic empire believed, as unthinkingly as did their Christian contemporaries, that there was a direct relationship between the favor of God and the foundation of great empires. The foundation of their own, Islamic empire proved that Christians, Jews, and Zoroastrians had been wrong and that they themselves were right. As one Arab Muslim told a local Christian hermit: "It is a sign of God's love for us and His pleasure with our faith, that He has given us dominion over all peoples and faiths."[21]

Cities, Segregation, and Control: Muslims and their Subjects

Such was the public face of the Islamic empire in around the year 700. But it is important to remember that in the seventh and eighth centuries the Near East was utterly unlike the predominantly Muslim and totally Arabic-speaking world that it is today. Islam was the religion of only a tiny minority of the overall population of the region. Massive conversions to Islam did not begin until the Middle Ages, at a time after the period covered in this book. The Arabs were scattered widely throughout the Near East. They soon became dominant in areas which abutted the steppes, such as Syria. Elsewhere, they were a distant presence. They were dwarfed by the civilian populations among whom they lived, much as the barbarian settlers in the Mediterranean regions of the western empire in the fifth century had been dwarfed by the Roman provincials.

Compared with the barbarian settlements in the West, however, the Muslims lived a strangely segregated existence. Muslims thought of themselves as soldiers on campaign, and not as farmers or landowners. They received handsome rewards in cash and food in exchange for being permanently available for war. They were known to each other and to the outside world as *muhâjirûn*, as persons in a state of unceasing *hijra*. They were permanent emigrants. They followed the example of Muhammad when he had led his

Companions to Medina. They were armed men, settled in temporary residences, always prepared to move on.[22] Islam was the religion of military camps. These camps soon grew into great cities. Basra and Kufa were founded within a few decades of the first conquests along the edge of southern Iraq. They served as great "ports of entry" for the populations of the Arabian desert. The tribes of the desert would be gathered in them and would then be sent out for further campaigns. Garrison cities of this sort sprang up all over the Islamic empire.

Such settlements were called *amsâr* (the plural of *misr*), "cities." They were like the great legionary camps of Roman times. One such city, 'Anjar, was founded in around 714 on the route which joined Damascus to Beirut. It was surrounded by a rectangular wall, 370 by 310 meters, with 40 towers. Inside, the spaces were laid out within a perfect grid pattern, with wide avenues radiating from a central column. Nothing so purely "Roman" had been built in the Near East for centuries. Yet new elements were placed in the ancient framework. One quadrant was devoted to the governor's palace flanked by a large mosque. The residential area was made up of large, walled compounds, each looking in on itself around a central courtyard. There was no forum.[23]

Like the great cities of the New World in the first centuries of the Spanish empire, the new Muslim cities of the Near East were vivid but encapsulated centers where the culture and religion of the conquerors were everywhere. But they were perched against a landscape where little had changed. In the cities, the Muslim community was largely self-perpetuating. Massive influxes of slaves took place on a scale which had not been seen since the Roman conquest of the Greek East. There was room for such slaves in the great houses of the Arab leaders. Through the practice of concubinage and polygamy, the descendants of slave-women came to grow up in a totally Arab and Muslim environment. Many of the greatest Arabic poets, grammarians, lawyers, and theologians of the Muslim world were the descendants of a generation of slaves brought to Iraq from Iran and Central Asia. Supremely confident in their ability to reproduce themselves, physically and culturally, Arab Muslims felt no need to reach out to make converts among the subject religions of their empire.

Protected in this way by a sort of religious and social apartheid, the Christians of the Near East settled down to live with their new masters in a state of perpetual ambivalence. Their position within the Islamic state was far better than the status of non-Christians, Jews and pagans, in the Christian empire. Under the Christian empire of Justinian, as we saw in chapter 7, pagans and other religious minorities were subject to constant pressure to convert. After his triumphal return to Jerusalem, the emperor Heraclius had extended the policies of Justinian to include the forcible baptism of the Jews.[24]

Nothing like this happened in the first centuries of Muslim rule. Jews and Christians were treated as "Peoples of the Book." According to the messages of Muhammad, they had received from God their own prophets and their own valid Scriptures. They may not have lived up to their original saving message. They were, as it were, failed Muslims. But they still deserved respect on the strength of their possession of holy books.

Christians paid a special poll-tax – the *jizya* – in return for the "benefaction" of being allowed to continue to practice their religion undisturbed. The *jizya* tax was intended to make plain their subordination. It was paid by individuals and not (as the land-tax was paid) by communities. Its administration required an elaborate and vexatious system of registration, such as only a strong empire, backed by a professional bureaucracy, could have imposed. Even the moment of payment was supposed to emphasize the subordinate position of "people of the book" over against Muslims. Lawyers insisted that those who offered the *jizya* must be careful to present the money on their upraised palms, in such a way that their hands should never be seen to rise above those of the Muslim recipient! In return for this mark of inferiority, Christians and Jews were left free to carry on their lives under the protection of an Islamic empire. They could continue their religious practices, under their traditional leaders, as long as they supported the Muslim armies with their wealth, through taxes. For Muslims, the massive presence of two superannuated religious dispensations merely highlighted the triumphant novelty of Islam. Individual converts to Islam were, of course, welcome. But forced conversions were not favored. At that time, they would have broken down the carefully constructed compartments into which the populations of the Near East were organized, so as to bear the weight of the last and greatest empire of all times.[25]

As a result of this situation, Islam rested as lightly as a mist along the contours of what had remained a largely Christian landscape. In provinces which were distant from the centers of Muslim power, in upper Egypt and in northern Iraq, local Christian elites remained firmly in control for centuries. They administered the taxes and proudly maintained the churches and great monasteries of their region. A Christian holy man in the foothills of the Zagros gained privileges for his convent through curing the favorite horse of the local Muslim emir.[26]

Indeed, there was always far more contact between Christians and Muslims than the official ideology of both sides would allow us to suspect. Muslims frequently consulted Christian hermits and even joined in Christian ceremonies. It was the Christian clergy and the Muslim lawyers who had to draw firm boundaries: the laity often did not see why they should not mix with fellow-monotheists.[27] As a result of generations of barely noticeable symbiosis Christian and Jewish legends and ideals poured into the traditions of Islam. Within two centuries of the Arab conquests, the image of Jesus, in Islamic legend, had come to be modelled on vivid memories of the great monks of Egypt and Syria. Always spoken of by Muslims with the greatest reverence, Jesus – the Isa' of the Qur'ân – was imagined as a great ascetic, dwelling in desert places, praying and weeping abundantly.[28]

All over the Syriac-speaking territories of northern Mesopotamia, pious Christian notables continued to endow schools and monasteries in which cultural activities which had changed little since the days of Justinian continued up to the days of the Crusades and the Mongol invasions of the thirteenth century. Altogether, Near Eastern Christianity settled down for the long haul. How the different Christian communities would fare in coming centuries depended very much on their geographical position, their relation to Muslim centers of power and, even more decisively, on the traditions and view of their own history of the individual churches.

Christian Attitudes to Islam

Near to the centers of power, in Palestine and Jordan, the Muslim armies had passed swiftly northward, leaving behind them villages where churches were still being built in the very year that Roman rule collapsed in Syria. Jerash, for instance, was a city still dominated by its ancient pagan temple. One small mosque only appeared in Jerash, alongside 15 fully-functioning Christian churches. The local manufacturers of terracotta lamps at Jerash solved the problem of the emergence of yet another world religion by inscribing them, on one side, in Greek, with "The Light of the Christians is the Resurrection," and, on the other, in Arabic, with "In the Name of Allah, the Merciful, the Compassionate."[29]

At the court of Damascus, Christian civil servants continued to play a crucial role. Long before the Arab conquests, Damascus had a large population of settled Arabs. A leading Arab Christian, Mansûr, had been responsible for the taxes of the region under the emperor Heraclius. Mansûr's son, Sarjûn (Sergius: like so many Arabs, he was named from the great saint of Resafa), served the Ummayad Califs. He supervised the taxes of the entire Middle East. Only in A.D. 700 did Sergius' son – Mansûr bar Sarjûn – leave court. A typical member of a pious East Roman family devoted to public service who had turned to religion, Mansûr, like Gregory the Great in Rome, abandoned the "cares" of office to become a learned monk. He is known under his monastic name, John: John of Damascus – John Damascene – a prolific writer in Greek and a founding father of the medieval Orthodox tradition.[30]

The case of John of Damascus showed that it was possible for an Arab to be many things in seventh-century Damascus. A fragment of a book of the Psalms intended for public reading in church shows how complex the situation must have been on the ground. It is written in Greek letters; but the language is Arabic![31] Plainly, a clergy accustomed to using Greek as the language of learning (and unable or unwilling to use the written Arabic associated with the Qur'ân) would conduct the services in Arabic for what had long been a largely Arabic-speaking population. These were settled Arabs. Yet, at the same time, an Arab Christian, al-Akhtal, emerged as one of the greatest poets at the Ummayad court. Proud of wearing the Cross and loyal to *his* saint, Sergius, al-Akhtal was particularly valued by his Muslim patrons. He brought to a court of *nouveaux riches* from the Hijâz memories of the good old days of "pure" Arab poetry, associated with the Lakhmid Christian court of Hira. These two Arab Christians were near contemporaries. But they took two different roads. John, son of Sarjûn, ended his life as the last great Father of the Greek Church. Al-Akhtal, by contrast, though equally a Christian, led his hearers back to the golden days of Arabic verse, as it had been practiced, before Islam, among the Arabs of the Persian frontier.[32]

In a complex city such as Damascus, individuals were free to take many roads. The Christian communities as a whole, however, found themselves burdened by their own distinctive pasts. Each Church reacted very differently to the new situation. They did so in terms of their previous history. The Chalcedonians had been the state Church of the Near East. They came to be known, quite simply, as "Melkites" – as "the Emperor's People." The collapse of the East Roman empire was a cruel blow for them. The extensive toleration of Christians under Muslim rule is rightly appreciated as a sympathetic feature of the first centuries of the Islamic empire. But seventh-century "Melkite" Christians, used to the East Roman empire, were in no mood to be thankful. They did not greatly value tolerance. What they had been used to was an official Church which dominated public space, in the manner which we described in chapter 7. To be stripped of this public persona was an unforgivable humiliation.

Yet all was not lost. Prolonged controversy with Monophysites, and more recently, under Heraclius, with Jews, had taught local Chalcedonians how to look after themselves. A characteristic genre developed at this time. It consisted of *Questions and Answers* which included vigorous imaginary debates with religious enemies. In the under-governed empire of Heraclius (where whole provinces lived for decades under Persian rule) state orthodoxy could no longer be imposed by force from on top. Hostile groups lived cheek by jowl. They argued with each other incessantly. Texts such as the genre of

Questions and Answers enabled the "orthodox" Chalcedonian believer to meet any challenge, delivered anywhere and on any topic, with a brisk return of fire.[33] By treating Jews and all Christian groups with even-handed indifference, the Islamic empire merely declared a permanent open season for religious disputes between Jews and Christians, Chalcedonians and Monophysites. Unlike the days of Justinian, no group could use state power to silence the other.

Anastasius of Sinai was a learned Chalcedonian. He had worked among "Roman" captives from Cyprus, set by their Arab masters to work in the lethal asphalt deposits of the Dead Sea. He wrote an encyclopedic catalogue of answers for every kind of religious doubt. He also recorded a series of *Stories to Strengthen the Faith.* Anastasius knew his Muslims at close hand. He knew that they believed that a man predestined to die fighting in the holy war would bear on his face unmistakable signs of his impending "martyrdom." He also knew that some Christians had become Muslims and that many others treated Islam as no more than an innocuous variant of their own religion. He wrote to warn such people. When 'Abd al-Malik began to construct the Dome of the Rock, Anastasius was told by pious Christians in Jerusalem that they had actually heard at night the cries of the demons, as they helped the Muslims to clear the debris from the Temple Mount. The demons were helping, "their allies, the Saracens [the Arabs]" to make the site ready for the supreme blasphemy of 'Abd al-Malik's shrine. Anastasius also told the story of two Christian sailors who had visited Mecca. At night they saw a hideous form arise from the earth to devour the meat of the camels and goats offered, in sacrifice, around the Ka'ba. This proved, Anastasius insisted, that the sacrifice at the Ka'ba was no "true sacrifice," instituted by Abraham. Muslim sacrifices were ghoulish rites, which would never ascend to Heaven as pleasing to God.[34]

By contrast to Chalcedonian "Melkites," the Syrian and Egyptian Monophysites of the "Jacobite" church were no great lovers of the Arab nomads. But they arrived at less dramatic conclusions than did the humiliated Chalcedonians. God had "nodded his assent" to the Arab conquests. They were a punishment on the East Roman emperors for having persecuted the true – that is, the Monophysite – Church:

> When He saw that the measure of the sins of the Romans was full to overflowing . . . He stirred up the sons of Ishmael and enticed them hither from their southern land . . . Yet it was by striking a bargain with them that we secured our deliverance. This was no small gain, to be delivered from the tyrannical kingdom of the Romans.[35]

The New Hellenism: History and Learning in the Syrian World

In order to justify their claim to be the true Church, the Monophysites became the remembrancers of the Near East. Monophysite historians of the Church constantly turned back to the fateful decisions of the Council of Chalcedon, the "Great Prevarication," and to the persecutions which the upholders of the true Monophysite faith had suffered from successive East Roman emperors in the fifth and sixth centuries. As late as the 760s, Chalcedonians and Monophysites presented the Muslim governor of Alexandria with rival petitions:

> The Chalcedonians sent him a letter [only] a few spans long ... and when he read it he laughed and shook his head.

The Monophysites, however, knew their late Roman history. They recounted in detail, from contemporary sources, the disastrous consequences in Alexandria of the Council of Chalcedon – persecutions, lynchings, punitive massacres.

> When the judge heard that, he clapped his hands together and said to those around him: "Oh, what a tyrannical deed was that!"[36]

For Middle Eastern contemporaries of the young Charlemagne, events which had happened three centuries earlier, in the 450s, and which had taken place in the now-distant East Roman empire, were still contemporary history.

Hence the tenacity of the grip upon the past exercised, especially, by the Syriac-speaking (and largely Monophysite) Christians of northern Mesopotamia. Far from marking the end of an age in northern Mesopotamia, the Arab conquest may even have fostered intellectual developments which had begun in pre-Islamic times. The seventh and eighth centuries saw the creation of an "eastern Hellenism" – the flowering of elite culture in a Syriac which was permeated by Greek forms.

It is revealing to see how this happened. The great monasteries of the region were central to the emergence of this last Syriac transformation of ancient Greek traditions. These monasteries were not the well-disciplined and somewhat monochrome "powerhouses of prayer" which had emerged in western Europe. They were large settlements, ringed by walls. The monks practiced many forms of asceticism, some of them highly individualistic. Most major monasteries boasted their own "stylite" hermits, set on columns near the monastery, and many hermits, settled in the neighboring caves. But there was room also in such places for an educated elite. Like Cassiodorus, monks would often bring with them into the monastery an entire "worldly" culture. As abbots, bishops, and teachers, they would continue high standards of literacy and of intellectual inquiry.

There were many such people in the Near East of the sixth and seventh centuries. The Syrians were not members of a warrior elite, as were the aristocrats of Francia and Visigothic Spain, for whom the "subtlety of words," associated with Latin literature, meant less and less. Rather, they were civilians who were used to careers as highly literate public servants. In the East Roman empire, they had to be bilingual. In the days of Justinian and Heraclius, Greek was as much part of their cultural world as was Syriac. The mother of one future monk and bishop (John of Tella, a city in eastern Turkey) sent him to serve in the office of the local military governor. To qualify for the job, he went to a Greek school "to learn the letters and wisdom of the Greeks." It was only as a result of his religious vocation that John began to read and to memorize the Psalms in his native Syriac. Yet he went on to a monastery which specialized in the study of the greatest and most Greek of theologians, Gregory Nazianzen. John was typical of the biculturalism which was taken for granted in the Syrian churches of the period before the Arab conquests.

Far from breaking this tradition, the Arab conquests merely hastened the absorption into Syriac of the Greek elements in the bilingual culture of Syria. As with the translations of Boethius in Rome, translations of Greek works met the needs of a learned class which had ceased to be bilingual, but which still valued contact with "the letters and wisdom of the Greeks." They still wished to read Greek works, even if only in translation. The *Iliad* of Homer was translated into Syriac by Theophilus of Edessa (695–785) in around 750.[37]

If literature can be defined as "language transfigured by the play of form," then much of later Syriac literature is language transfigured by Greek form.[38] It was a literature based on intensive schooling in Syriac monasteries. This schooling maintained, in Syriac, educational traditions which reached back for a millennium to the schools of the Hellenistic age. Students were taught to analyze grammar and to adhere to strict rules of composition. The hand book produced by Anthony of Tagrit (a monastery on the Tigris in modern Iraq) proclaimed, in Syriac, that ancient rhetoric was alive and well in Mesopotamia. Other nations might use words. But they did so,

> as a peasant uses a table, not knowing how it was put together. An Arab may praise, blame or incite to battle, yet may never have learned the fair art of Demosthenes.[39]

Anthony knew no Greek. But he knew what it was to write well, like a Greek. It is a statement of classical values which we do not expect to hear from an inhabitant of Mesopotamia in the age of Charlemagne.

From Antioch to China, Syriac remained one of the great languages of culture of medieval Asia. And, with Syriac, time stood still. In the West and in Constantinople, drastic changes in book production led to the adoption of a new, more compact script, known as "minuscule." After the ninth century, the flowing script of Greek and Latin manuscripts of classical and late antique times became unreadable to the average clergyman. Books which were not recopied into "minuscule" script at that time were as good as lost to future ages. A crevasse of this nature, between the present and the past, did not open up in the well-stocked monastic libraries of Syria and northern Iraq. Up to this century, any learned Syriac-speaker could take up and read a manuscript written in the age of Justinian.

The *Histories* produced by the Syrians of northern Mesopotamia were world chronicles. Each began with Adam and followed with attention the fate of the Christian Church throughout the Near East. They described the vicissitudes of their own region against a majestic background. The sequence of events was slotted into a chronological system which counted the years all the way back to Adam. What they described were God's eternal dealings with the human race. All the vicissitudes of human life, from the rise of great new empires (such as the kingdom of the Arabs) to the incursions of locusts, brigands, and tax-collectors, were written about as if they happened according to one basic rhythm: sin and repentance. Sin brought affliction, repentance brought peace and prosperity. There was a strong sense of *déjà vu* about such chronicles. The world of the Hebrew prophets, who had foretold the extinction of Israel, was little different from the world of eighth-century northern Mesopotamia as it faced the stresses and strains of Muslim rule:

> Here Jeremiah was of great use to us . . . He should now come and cry
> out not over one nation and city, Jerusalem, but over all nations.[40]

Such chronicles highlighted the afflictions of their own times and region. These were God's response to the sins of its inhabitants. But the very repetitiveness of the story was a subliminal source of comfort. There was nothing new or necessarily irreversible about the Arab conquests. It had happened before. The empires of Rome and Persia had passed away. Throughout these afflictions, God was always present to protect his Church. As in the days of the people of Israel, the times would change again.

The chronicle tradition was one of the most carefully nurtured and long-lasting forms of culture in the Christian Near East. It was the product of a remarkably stable culture, living at peace behind the frontiers of a great empire. In the course of the seventh century, the culture of the East Roman empire almost foundered completely under the hammer-blows of Muslim invasions. Entire tracts of the history of the seventh century were not recorded by Greek chroniclers. In Edessa, many miles from the war zone of eastern Anatolia, Syrians kept the record straight. They plotted the events of the seventh century year by year. When, in the ninth century, Byzantines attempted to revive their own chronicle tradition and to fill in the lacuna in historical memory inflicted by the crisis of the seventh century, it was to Syriac chroniclers that they turned.[41]

And the tradition continued. The great *Histories* of the Monophysite Church, compiled from earlier writers by Michael the Syrian (1166–1199) and by Gregory Abu al-Farâj, known as Barhebraeus (d.1286) look back without a break to the fifth century A.D. To read them is to catch an unmistakable echo of the world of late antiquity in contemporaries of Richard Coeur de Lion, Saint Louis, and Marco Polo. The Mongol Laws of Chingiz Khan, wrote Barhebraeus, have gnomic elements: they reminded him of the *Gnomai* of Gregory Nazianzen. As for their shamanist belief in the journey of the soul, this, of course, says the learned Syrian, with over a thousand years of unbroken culture behind him, can be found in the writings of Aflatûn – of Plato – when he discusses the doctrine of the transmigration of souls![42]

"Walking the Roads to China": The Church of the East under Islam

For the eastern Christians of the former Persian territories, Muslim rulers were, if anything, a marked improvement on the erratic patronage of a pagan King of Kings. It was the Zoroastrian state religion of Persia which was well and truly humbled by the Arab conquests. The loss of the monarchy and the impoverishment of the Iranian aristocracy broke the back of the "Good Religion." Zoroastrians were appalled by the Arab conquest:

> The Good Religion was ruined and the King of Kings was slain like a dog. They eat the bread of the land. They have taken away the sovereignty from the emperors.[43]

But not so the Christians. The Eastern Christians of Iraq positively welcomed the establishment of a strong, frankly monotheist empire.

> Before calling them, [God] had prepared them beforehand to hold Chris-
> tians in honor . . . How otherwise could naked men, riding without armor
> and shield, have . . . brought down the proud spirit of the Persians?[44]

The hierarchy of the Church of the East benefited from an empire whose
horizons were even larger than those of the Sasanians. In the 780s, at a time
when Harûn al-Rashid was launching his last great expeditions into East
Roman Anatolia and when the armies of Charlemagne fought their bitter
campaigns in the woods of pagan Saxony, eastern Christian bishops were at
work on the edge of the world, in regions "destitute even of Arabs and Jews,
who confess One God, the Creator of Heaven and Earth."[45] They hacked
down the holy trees of the pagan mountain tribes of the Caspian highlands.
They revived the Christian mission in Hsian-fu. Timothy I (780–823), the
Katholikos of the "Church of the East," took full advantage of the new
situation. He reminded a bishop, who had asked for a pension with which to
spend a comfortable retirement in Baghdad, that Christian monks who possessed nothing but their staff and satchel, were walking the roads that led to
India and China. He even planned a new bishopric "for the peoples of Tibet."[46]

Taxes and Language: The Beginning of Islamization and the Triumph of Arabic

As we have seen, these very different Christian communities had all been
able to maintain their identity under Muslim rule. To a large extent, they
were even able to carry on with the cultural and religious agendas which
they had inherited from late antiquity. They gave way very slowly to the
pressure of Islam. In northern Mesopotamia, however, we can see, through
the shocked pages of the *Chronicle of Zuqnîn* (a world chronicle that came
to be preserved in the Monophysite monastery of Zuqnîn, near Diyarbekir
in eastern Turkey) how the Islamization of the Near East began.

As with most miseries associated with this zone of great empires, it began
with taxes. The world of the Christian villages, whose resilience we described
in chapter 12, finally gave way when the economy gave way under the pressure of taxes and of the demands of passing armies in times of civil war. For,
as in the Roman empire, it was civil war, and not barbarian invasion, which
caused most disruption to the inhabitants. The collapse of the Ummayads, in
750, and their replacement by Arab armies from eastern Iran turned northern Mesopotamia into a corridor through which conflicting armies passed,
as they had done in the sixth century. An age of prosperity came to an end. It

was bankruptcy and bad government, and not direct pressure to convert brought to bear by an Islamic state, which opened the way for conversion.

The situation also affected the Muslims of the area. They had changed. They were no longer a distant, dominating class. The greater degree of professionalization of the Arab armies rendered the services of many Muslims unnecessary. They left the great garrison towns and settled among the surrounding populations. In so doing, they brought Islam to Christian towns and villages for which the new faith had previously been a distant matter.

An entire underclass of "demobilized" Muslims developed. They suffered as severely from misgovernment and from the effects of civil war as did their Christian neighbors. Often they shared the afflictions of the Christians. They contributed to collections of money made by local Christians for the ransom of captives taken from their neighborhood. But, because they faced impoverishment and loss of status, they competed all the more fiercely with Christians for the one insurance against disaster which a Near Eastern society could offer – land in the villages. The *Chronicle of Zuqnîn* describes how, in around 770, the Muslims took advantage of a period of warfare and crippling taxation "to wriggle among the poor villagers like worms in wood." Only then did mass conversions begin in earnest. Impoverished villagers

> turned to Islam faster than sheep rushing to water . . . They would boast and look down on us, saying . . . "you are godless, and holding as it were on to spiders' webs."

These converts became outcasts among their own people. Even "the color of their face, their body odor, and the look of their eyes" showed that they had abandoned the "sweet smell" of Christian baptism. But they were not particularly welcome to the Muslims. Drawn from Syriac-speaking villages, their Arabic was minimal. The Muslims called them "The 'These-There'": for they only knew enough Arabic to point to things![47]

Ultimately, it was the victory of Arabic which opened the doors to Islamization. The spread of Arabic eroded the elaborate compartmentalization of Near Eastern society on which the earlier centuries of tolerance had been based. Religious and linguistic segregation had protected the Christians. The spread of Arabic removed this protective barrier. Yet the religious effects of the spread of Arabic were delayed. The elites of the different Christian groups soon came to share in the widespread enthusiasm for the new language of the Arabs. The Arabs thought of their language as the tongue of the "clear-spoken ones." It was a Semitic language akin to Syriac. But, as we saw in our last chapter, Arabic had already developed, in the harsh conditions of Arabia, an overwhelming richness and precision. It was as sharp and flexible "as the blade of a rapier." Arabic soon emerged in the Near East as something more than the official language of an empire. It was increasingly seen by Christians and non-Arabs as the one language in which every human thought and every human feeling – from love, war, and the desert hunt to the most elevated of metaphysical abstractions – could be expressed.[48]

By A.D. 800, it was the allure of an entire profane culture, expressed in Arabic, and not Islam itself, which caused the Christians of the Islamic empire to forget their own rich heritage. As a Christian wrote in Cordoba, in 852/4:

> Many of my fellow-Christians read verses and fairy-tales of the Arabs, not in order to refute them, but to express themselves in Arabic ever more correctly and elegantly . . . Alas! All talented Christians know only the language and the literature of the Arabs . . . They express themselves . . . with more beauty and more art than do the Arabs themselves.[49]

If the clergy were to remain in control of their own laity, they had to learn Arabic and to participate in the new Arabic culture. To take one example: the Chalcedonian Christian, Theodore abu Qurrah (ca.740–ca.825), wrote most of his works in Arabic. He kept pace with Muslim theological debates. When he defended the worship of icons, passages from the Qur'ân and sayings ascribed to Muhammad were what engaged his attention. The debates on the same issue which raged at Constantinople at the same time meant nothing to him. An Arabic-speaking Christianity had come to look to Islam for its vocabulary and for its theological agenda, and not to the Greek West.[50]

The transfer of the center of the Islamic empire from Damascus to Baghdad, which was founded in 762, completed the triumph of Arabic among the Christians of the Near East. Baghdad lay close to the imposing ruins of Sasanian Ctesiphon. Eastern Christian administrators and doctors were as much in evidence in the court of Harun al-Rashid (786–809) and his successors as they had been, two centuries before, in the reign of Khusro II Aparwez. The legal restrictions imposed on the "Peoples of the Book" weighed lightly on this extensive class of non-Muslim technocrats. Arab littérateurs complained of this. The large Christian community in Baghdad even forced up the price of fish, through buying so much on the days of their fasts!

> The Christians now have costly mounts and thoroughbred horses. They have packs of hounds and play polo, wrap themselves in costly fabrics and affect [pure Arab] patronymics.[51]

Learned Christians were essential to the new Muslim ruling class as doctors and as astrologers. Altogether, they were human artesian wells. Only learned Christians who had retained knowledge of Syriac, and who enjoyed intermittent contacts with Greek-speaking fellow-Christians, could tap the vast subterranean reservoir of medical, scientific, and philosophical knowledge which had slowly seeped into the Syriac churches which were now subject to the Islamic empire. Men whose culture reached back to the days of the foundation of the School of Nisibis now became transmitters of Greek learning to the Arabic-speaking elites of Baghdad.

To take only one example: the eastern Christian court doctor, Hunayn ibn Ishaq (d.873) worked carefully as a translator. He would compare old Syriac translations (made in the days of Justinian) with Greek texts which had become available in Baghdad through diplomatic missions to Constantinople. As a result of his activities and those of his colleagues, more works of Galen came to circulate in Arabic than were ever available in the Greek-speaking world of East Rome – not to mention translations of Euclid, Ptolemy, and much of the logical and metaphysical tradition of late classical philosophy.[52]

For Christian translators and their Muslim readers alike there was something reassuringly neutral about such subjects. As far back as the fifth century, Syrian Christians had tended to value a philosophical and technological culture which was soundproof to confessional differences. Now, at the Muslim court of Baghdad, a perennial "Greek" wisdom was patiently put together, in Arabic, part by part, like the reconstruction of a great dinosaur – an awesome antediluvian creature, untouched by the bitter religious confrontations of modern times. It was as fellow-philosophers, *falasifa*, bound by the value-free rules of *kalâm*, of logical argument, and not as religious adversaries, that Jews, Christians, and Muslims could meet with courtesy, "to bargain with each other . . . as brothers who share in the goods that they inherit from a single father."[53]

Islam, East Rome, and the West

Events such as these took place at the fulcrum of a very ancient world, at Damascus, Edessa, and Baghdad. They were far away from that northwestern tip of Eurasia which had begun to call itself, a little self-consciously, "Europe." To Muslim observers, East Rome, *Rûm*, was the only Christian region which really mattered. Constantinople was the capital of the last, proud empire to resist the call of the Prophet. It was the "hard-necked" state *par excellence*.[54] The East Romans replied in kind. Their image of Islam became the basis of all later Western images of the Muslim world. It had none of the nuances which we find among the Christians of the Near East. Greek and Latin sources never spoke of "Muslims." They regarded Islam as a purely ethnic religion. Muslims were "Saracens", "Ishmaelites," or "Hagarenes" – that is, descendants of Ishmael, Abraham's bastard son by his servant Hagar. Islam, for them, was no more than "a new, deceptive heresy." It was not even a very interesting heresy. They saw it as an incompetently plagiarized form of Christianity, thought up by Muhammad so as to give a cloak of religious respectability to the ravages of his bloodthirsty nation.[55]

Constantinople, the heart of the East Roman empire, remained the goal which Muslim armies strove to reach. It is a measure of the resilience of the Christian empire of East Rome that it took them 800 years to do so. Constantinople finally fell to the Ottoman Turks in 1453. Had it done so at the height of the Arab invasions, the entire history of western Europe would have been very different. East Rome was the only state which offered prolonged resistance to the Arab armies. Naval expeditions were sent against Constantinople in 672 and 717. The last, elaborately orchestrated campaign to take Constantinople ended in disaster. In 717, the emperor Leo III used "Greek fire" to destroy the Muslim fleet. This was an explosive combination of naphtha and potassium which detonated into a gigantic, burning oil-slick on the water. The secret of "Greek fire" had recently been brought to Constantinople by Syrian refugees from the oil-rich areas of northern Iraq.[56]

> Many other calamities befell [the Muslims] at that time, and made them learn by experience that God and the all-holy Virgin, the Mother of God, protect this City and the Christian Empire, and that those who call upon God are not entirely forsaken, even if we are chastised for a short time on account of our sins.[57]

The empire of *Rûm* was always present to the Muslims. By contrast, the West was a distant place. It was viewed by Muslims much as it had been viewed by previous civilized Near Easterners, Greeks and Syrians. It was a vast, indeterminate land, inhabited by unkempt and warlike peoples. It was marginal to the great "changing of the kingdoms" which had taken place in the ancient heartlands of civilization.[58]

Seen from the West, it was the East Roman empire which had absorbed the shattering impact of the Arab advance. To Christian countries further north, these great events were still distant matters. They apparently caused little anxiety. In around 680, Arculf, a Frankish bishop, made his way to the Holy Land. He travelled without apparent molestation in a land very different from his native Gaul. He observed that no wagons were to be seen: camels, and camels only, carried all loads.[59] The Holy Places were as they had always been. The Arab conquest had made no difference. The great Church of the Ascension on the Mount of Olives still glowed like a beacon above Jerusalem:

> under the terrible and wondrous gleaming of these [lights], pouring out copiously through the glass shutters of the windows, all mount Olivet seems on fire, and the whole city, situated on the lower ground nearby, seems to be lit up.[60]

Arculf did note that "the unbelieving Saracens" had built themselves "a church" in Damascus. But that is all. He returned peacefully to Constantinople to see "the Emperor of the World" – appropriately called Constantine IV – bending to kiss the fragment of the relic of the Holy Cross, which Heraclius had saved from Jerusalem as Syria collapsed before the Arabs.[61]

Even after the Arab conquest of Spain, in 711, no one in the north was certain that the invaders who had reached the western Mediterranean had come to stay. In conquering Spain, the Arabs took over a loosely connected kingdom, where the state had been weak in comparison with Near Eastern empires. Former Visigothic Spain did not provide for the Arabs of the West the same springboard for further conquest as the former, heavily administered East Roman provinces of Syria and Egypt had done for the Ummayads of Damascus. The Ummayads controlled territories which enabled them to launch near-annual attacks on *Rûm*. The Arab conquerors of Visigothic Spain did not inherit such resources. They could never penetrate into the far north. When one Muslim raiding party reached as far as the Loire, in 733, it was easily crushed by Charles Martel, the nephew of Gertrude, abbess of Nivelles, and the grandfather of Charlemagne, at the famous battle of Poitiers. But Poitiers was no Constantinople. The Muslim threat to the rest of western Europe was largely confined to the Mediterranean regions of Gaul. For the kingdoms of the north, the Arab invasions were basically a matter for the "Romans" to worry about. In around 730, a Saxon lady from southern Britain was warned not to travel south to the Mediterranean. She was told that she should wait "until the attacks and threats of the Saracens, which have lately manifested themselves in the lands of the Romans, should have quieted down."[62]

In 724, a party of Saxons from Britain actually reached Syria as Christian pilgrims. Their strange clothes caused a stir. A local Muslim dignitary declared that they meant no harm. He had seen such men: "they wish only to fulfill their religious law." They came from "the Western shores, where the sun sets . . . and we know of no land beyond their islands, but only water."[63]

Their leader, Willibald, returned to Europe – but not before being arrested by the authorities for attempting to smuggle precious balsam out of Palestine in the hollow of his pilgrim's staff! – to become, eventually, an abbot in southern Germany.[64]

Northern Europe had changed greatly since the 630s. The pious Saxon pilgrims came from a region that had barely been touched by Christianity in 630. Between 630 and 730, with the conversion of the British Isles, an entire new, northern dimension was added to the Christianity of the West. Arculf's account of the Holy Places was written down, complete with careful illustrations, not in Gaul, but at Iona, a great Celtic monastery perched off the western coast of Scotland. Unimaginably far away from the "changing of the kingdoms" which would prove decisive for the future history of Asia and of Africa, a northern European world had come into its own. It is to the "western shores" – to the Irish and to the Saxons in Britain – that we must now return.

CHAPTER 14

Christianities of the North: Ireland

The New North

In the same decades of the seventh century as saw the last triumphs of the East Roman empire in the Middle East and then its sudden collapse before Arab invaders, the northern peripheries of the Christian world took on a new and distinctive profile. Far to the north of Continental Europe and the Mediterranean, in the British Isles, in Scandinavia, and even further east, between the Baltic and the Black Sea, we meet societies in which new forms of power were being created, new religions were tested, and exotic goods avidly sought out. We see this most vividly in the great hoards which accompanied the burial of successful rulers. Over a thousand miles east of Rome and 700 miles north of Constantinople, one such grave was discovered at Malaia Pereščepina, in the Ukraine. It may be connected with a Bulgar prince, who, in the 630s, had played a crucial role in the diplomacy of the emperor Heraclius. It contained, in all, 20 kilograms of golden objects, gathered from Constantinople, the Balkans, Iran, and Central Asia.[1] At the other end of Europe, overlooking the North Sea, the spectacular complex of Saxon burial mounds at Sutton Hoo, perched on the coast of Suffolk, is equally impressive in the variety of its objects, and in the mobilization of labor that must have gone into their creation. They were erected at some time after 650. The principal excavated mound contained a ship 26 meters long, weapons, and a selection of ornaments that showed contact with Denmark and southern Sweden, jewelry made from 4,000 garnet chips (such as would have required the full year's labor of 17 skilled craftsmen to create), gold coins from Francia, spoons and a great silver dish from Constantinople, Romano-British enamels, and yellow silk from Syria. So magnificent a setting-aside of wealth to be given over forever to the earth echoed the sumptuous burial of Childeric, the pagan father of Clovis, which (as we saw in chapter 5) had taken place at

Map 7 The British Isles and the North Sea

THE BRITISH ISLES ca. 500–ca. 750

Columba ca.520–597
    founds Iona 565

                                        Ethelbert king of Kent 580–616
                                        Mission of Augustine to Kent 597

                                        Edwin of Northumbria 616–633
                                        Oswald of Northumbria 643–642

                                        Foundation of Lindisfarne
                                            from Iona 634

                                        Oswy of Northumbria 642–670

                                        Synod of Whitby 664

                                        Benedict Biscop 628–690
                                            founds Jarrow and Wearmouth
                                            674 and 685

                                        Wilfrid of York 634–706

                                        Theodore of Tarsus 602–690
                                            Archbishop of Canterbury 668–690

Muirchú, *Life of Saint Patrick* 695
                                        Caedmon ca. 680

Adomnán abbot of Iona 679–704
    writes *Life of Columba* 697
    imposes *Law of Innocents* 700

Compilation of the
    Senchas Már 720

                                        Bede 672–735
                                            writes *Ecclesiastical History
                                            of the English People* 731

Production of the
    Book of Kells ca.750

Tournai a century previously. But there is one disturbing difference – recently discovered human skeletons arranged around another mound at Sutton Hoo imply, perhaps, that not only horses, but also human beings, were sacrificed on the occasion of a great royal burial.[2]

In the recent excavations of Gudme, on the island of Funen in Denmark, we can glimpse the sheer zest which went into the creation of such hoards. Gudme – the Place of the Gods – lay between the North Sea and the Baltic. It was placed where the land met sea, the source of strange goods from over the water. It was dominated by a gigantic wooden hall (of 500 square meters – as large as a sizable Christian church) surrounded by the workshops of craftsmen. In these workshops, an unprecedented range of foreign objects (gathered by plunder, tribute, or gift-exchange) were transformed, by the magic of skilled craftsmen, into prestige goods that were distributed as royal bounty. This was the alchemy by which all that was most foreign was turned into a source of local power and prestige for rulers and their aristocracy.[3]

Gudme was not alone in Scandinavia. Between the fourth and the sixth centuries, Roman gold was transmuted into an astonishing abundance of luck-bearing amulets, known as *bracteates*. Four thousand were discovered at one time in Ostbornholm near Gudme. They may have been returned to the sea as votive offerings. Many of these amulets were based on Roman coins. Constantius II, the conscientiously Christian son of Constantine, lived on for centuries in the distant north, transformed into the image of a war-god! In such a world, successful warrior kingship and a demonstrative relationship with victory-bringing deities went hand in hand.[4]

These societies were not in any way cut off from the rest of the world. Nor were they placid backwaters, whose inhabitants preserved unchanged the traditions of a barbarian, "tribal" society. Few societies of the West in the sixth and seventh centuries were changing as rapidly as they were. New, more forceful styles of rule emerged. New customs and origin myths were invented, often under the guise of "immemorial" tradition. Local religion was subject to constant manipulation to meet new needs, and "exotic" religions were scanned with considerable interest, in the hope that, like the exotic goods which passed though the magical hands of craftsmen, these religions, also, might provide new sources of power, blessing, and healing. In this troubled landscape, which stretched across the North Sea from Denmark to the coasts of Britain and, further to the west, in Wales and Ireland, self-contained "barbarian" tribes, ruled by unchanging "tribal" custom (the ideal alike of a former generation of romantic historians and of many students of Christian missions) were not to be found. When Christian missionaries came to northern regions, they spoke of "barbarians ... as yet unploughed by the ploughshare of preaching." Their largely rhetorical complaints have made us assume that this soil must have been particularly heavy. In fact, it was sandy soil: it was light and already ready to shift into any number of different formations under the impact of exotic goods and of internal social strains.[5]

A New Religion for the Elite: Sixth-Century Ireland

The case of Ireland makes this plain. In the course of the sixth century, Christianity emerged as the dominant religion because it was adopted by the royal and noble families who controlled Irish society. This was due in part to the growing links between Ireland and western Britain. Only a short distance across the water, West Britain would have impressed the Irish. It was characterized by proud, post-Roman Celtic kingdoms and by impressive enclaves of "Roman" Christian scholars. But the emergence of an aristocratic Christianity in Ireland itself was also an answer to a potential crisis of Irish society.

Celtic Ireland was the oldest society in Europe, in that it had not experienced the disruption of the imposition of Roman rule. But this did not mean that it had not changed, and changed greatly, over the centuries. A period of "slump", of aimless violence and recession of cultivation, came to an end in the fourth century A.D. as a result of a "boom" in the provincial economy of Britain in the last century of secure Roman rule. As the Roman defenses of Britain collapsed in the fifth century, trade was followed by extensive slave raiding. Patricius was brought to Ireland with "thousands" of his fellow-Britons.[6]

A society such as Ireland could easily be swamped by so massive an influx of foreign slaves. Like most "barbarian" societies, made up of small, face-to-face communities, Ireland was fiercely stratified. Each *túath* (commonly called, for the sake of convenience, a "tribe") was a tightly interrelated group, which often claimed common ancestry. Each occupied a tiny ecological niche. A *túath* was frequently named from the "plain" that it controlled – a patch of arable land surrounded by mountains and bogland. Such a "plain" could support only a midget community. A small class of persons of royal and noble descent (perhaps no more than 70 families in each *túath*) dominated the local farmers. These aristocrats were known as *errid*, "men of the chariot," from memories of archaic warfare which had long since vanished. They dominated the farmers through their control of the livestock of the region.

The inferiors of the kings and nobility were called "base clients," *aithech*.

The services which "base clients" owed to their lords took many forms, but especially they owed them hospitality – which meant, in effect, that they fed them and their retinues for a substantial part of each year. Service was given in exchange for a formal gift of cattle that was essential for every farm. But the base client kept his farm and he, also, carried weapons. They were not serfs, as they would have been in most areas of Continental, "Roman" Europe. They could be bullied only to a limited degree.[7]

From top to bottom, therefore, Irish society was a society held in balance by an intricate web of mutual obligations created by gifts. In this society, nothing was for nothing. In chapter 10 we have seen how the Celtic system of compensations, which was echoed in the "tariffed penance" of the Celtic *Penitentials*, ensured that every injury and failure to meet obligations had to be atoned for by gifts. In the same way, the structure of Irish society depended on the assumption that every gift incurred the obligation of a return.

But, again like most "barbarian" societies, the nobles and the farmers had in common the precious quality of "freedom." This was highlighted by the fact that they were slave-owners. Unarmed, without rights, the slave was the ever-present, dark alternative that lay beneath the brittle world of free men, in which nobles and farmers endlessly balanced their rights and obligations to each other and "washed the face" of their respective honors by elaborate gestures of compensation. Slaves had no part in that world. To bring too many slaves into such a small society, and especially slaves from one area (Britain) joined by a single faith and ministered to by clergy of the energy of Patricius, was to invite trouble. Later Irish legends would claim that the opponents of Patricius had prophesied that "He will free slaves, he will exalt base kindreds through the grades of the church."[8]

The course of the sixth century showed how this fear (though it was a realistic one at the time) came to be resolved.[9] What we call the "conversion" of Ireland was, in fact, the decision of the nobility of the land to make their own, quickly and very much on their own terms, the religion of their foreign slaves. In so doing, they came to share in the Christian culture of the Celtic, British world which lay so near, across the Irish Sea. The result was a remarkable variant of Christianity, created, in the course of the sixth century, by the collaboration of Irishmen and West Britons.

"In the terrible clashing of battles": Saint Columba (521–597) and the Hegemony of Iona

We have already met, in chapters 10 and 11, a truly remarkable example of the type of learned man and ascetic leader produced by this collaboration –

Columbanus (ca.550–615). Columbanus was the very first Irishman to become famous on the Continent of Europe. But Columbanus belonged to the second generation of established Irish Christianity. Far more important for the history of Ireland and Britain was a man who bore a similar name – Columba, later known as "Colum Cille," Saint Columba, the "dove of the Church."[10] Columba belonged to an earlier generation. He was born in 521. Within his lifetime, Christianity changed from being the religion of an articulate minority to become the exclusive faith of powerful royal clans. It was not until Columba was almost 40 that the *feis Temro*, the solemn sacral act by which the high king of Tara (Temair) slept with the guardian goddess of the land, was celebrated, for the last time, by Dermot mac Cerball, in 558.

Columba was the first leading Christian to come from a royal family. He belonged to the Cenél Conaill – the "kindred of Connell" – of Donegal and Tyrone in northwest Ireland. They were Uí Niall (O'Neill) descendants of the great "Niall of the Nine Hostages", the former high king of Ireland. Unlike the usual "tribal" levies of farmers and their lords, the warrior retinues of these northern O'Neills meant business. In 561, they defeated their southern O'Neill cousins, the rightful kings of Tara, at the unusually bloody battle of Cúl Drebene. A few years later, in 563, Columba decided to leave Ireland as a penitential exile. Whether he was shocked by the slaughter or implicated in it through his family connections we do not know. He sailed northward, across the sea to Scotland. There he settled in Iona, in the territories of a different Irish clan, the Dál Riata. These Irish eventually gave their name to Scotland, for they were known as *scotti*, the name for sea-rovers.

Columba arrived at Iona in around 565. In that year, at the other end of the Christian world, the great emperor Justinian lay dying, in southern Italy Cassiodorus was engaged in quiet scholarship in his monastery at Vivarium, in Gaul Gregory was about to become bishop of Tours. Columba stayed at Iona until his death, in 597 – it was the same year that Gregory the Great's mission to the Saxons landed in Kent.

Columba came to Iona as an act of self-inflicted exile, following the Irish tradition of seeking to live among strangers which would later lead Columbanus to Gaul.[11]

> There is a grey eye that looks back at Ireland: It will never henceforth see the men of Ireland nor their women.[12]

Walking the island, Columba once picked up with tenderness an exhausted crane from Donegal that had landed at his feet: like himself, the noble bird was an exile, far from home.[13]

Iona lay between northern Ireland and Scotland. It was cut off from the mainland of Argyll by a stretch of "glass-green" sea. Here was the classic "desert" of Egypt, the home of the great monks of old, now re-created, in a Celtic idiom, in the remoteness of an offshore island in the wild Atlantic. There was a touch of Paradise Regained about the island. On Iona the hard laws of nature in a warrior society were miraculously held in suspense. A knife blessed by Columba would no longer draw blood.[14]

Yet, in reality, Iona was situated at the center of the political world of the North, on the seaways where Ireland and northern Britain met. Columba eventually returned to Ireland, on a few, ceremonious occasions, to visit "his" monasteries – client monasteries founded by his disciples and his kindred – all over Ireland. But, even in Iona, Ireland was never far away.

> He heard his companions . . . talking on the way about two kings . . . "My dear sons [he said], why do you gossip idly about these kings. For both of those you mention were recently killed by their enemies and their heads cut off . . . Sailors will arrive today from Ireland and will tell you this."[15]

Iona emerged as the center of a spiritual empire which stretched from Ireland along the northwest coast of Scotland as far as the Hebrides, Loch Ness, and to the north of the Great Glen of Scotland. Within half a century of Columba's death, the "family" of Iona had been built up. This was a constellation of client monasteries and bishops, similar to the pyramid of client tribes gathered around him by a strong high king. It was an unusually extensive spiritual empire. It stretched from western Scotland deep to the southwest into the heart of Ireland and, to the southeast, it reached down throughout northern Britain, through the influence of its sister monastery, Lindisfarne. Lindisfarne is still known as "Holy Island." It was an island acting as a "desert," similar to Iona, cut off by tidal waters from the mainland. It looked out on the North Sea, some fifty miles to the north of Hadrian's Wall.

In 635 the Irish monks of Iona converted the leading Saxon warlords of the north – the Northumbrian dynasty of Bernicia. This extensive kingdom straddled Hadrian's wall. It controlled the lowlands of Scotland and cast its shadow (and with it, the shadow of an Irish Christianity, based on Lindisfarne and ultimately loyal to Iona) as far south as the river Thames.[16]

Saint Columba had become the greatest saint of the north. And he had done this because he was the saint of a warrior upper class. It was to him that they turned.

> Some kings were conquered in the terrifying crash of battles and others emerged victorious according to what Columba asked of God through the power of prayer.[17]

Men of war, even "bloodstained sinners," had escaped certain death in battle through chanting Irish hymns in his honor.[18] In a quiet landscape, ringed by the hills of Scotland, the battlefields of Ireland and Britain remained always present to the community of Iona. Through the continued protection of Columba, the monastery of Iona was believed to hold in its hands the fortunes of the competing warrior kingdoms of the north. The subsequent abbots of Iona were chosen from among the kin of Columba, that is, they were of the same high blood as the kings to whom they offered their blessing.

The man who drew up the final version of the *Life of Columba*, a hundred years after the saint's death, was as impressive a representative of the new, aristocratic Christianity of Ireland as was Columba himself. This was Adomnán, a descendant of Columba's kinsmen, who was abbot of Iona from 679 to 704.[19] In his day, Adomnán was the greatest ecclesiastical politician of the northern world. He was one of the few early medieval churchmen who enjoyed sufficient authority to control warfare. In 700, he persuaded 51 kings and 40 churchmen to agree to the *Cáin Adomnáin*, Adomnán's Law, an Ireland-wide *Law of Innocents*. The *Law of Innocents* protected women and clerics from the effects of intertribal violence.[20] The ability to create such a law was a sign of the way in which Columba's spiritual empire had worked its way deep into the fabric of political life in Ireland and beyond.

We met Adomnán at the end of the last chapter. He turned the reports of a Frankish bishop recently returned from Muslim-occupied Palestine and Syria into a booklet *On the Holy Places*. He scanned the entire world with the tranquil eyes of an Irish *sapiens* in his country's great age of Latin learning. Though he lived in a monastery that was unimaginably distant to most Continental Europeans, he received visitors (possibly students) from Francia. He checked the bishop's report against accounts of the eastern Mediterranean in the texts of his own library. His comments on forms of Christian worship encountered in the Holy Land show that he wrote as one *sapiens* to others, wherever they might be. He shared with them up-to-date religious concerns which preoccupied an intellectual elite scattered all over Europe, as far as Rome and Constantinople.[21] A learned Irish abbot and descendant of kings, the last thing that he would have considered himself to be was "out on a limb," out of date, or in any way "peripheral" to Europe.

Competition and the *Lives* of the Saints

Adomnán's *Life of Columba* marked the culmination of an age in which great monasteries and ambitious bishops had carved out for themselves extensive ecclesiastical "empires" in Ireland. In this process of empire-building, the monasteries had a distinct advantage. In a world without Roman towns, whose solid walls and long-established populations guaranteed the status of their bishops, great monasteries, such as Iona, were the few fixed points in an ever-changing landscape. Bishops and clergy existed in abundance in Ireland. Each *túath* was proud to have its own hierarchy.[22] But these local figures lacked glamour. They belonged to the humble world of the small tribes. Their status rose and fell as each tribe passed from one powerful over-king to another. For to be a successful king in Ireland was to have ambitions wider than one's own *túath*. It was to make one's court the focus of a whole pyramid of minor communities, each committed (as base clients were committed to their lord within each *túath*) to providing regular services, food renders, and tokens of honor.

The bid for the ecclesiastical equivalent of over-kingship was taken on by monasteries and sanctuaries such as Iona in the far north, the shrine of Saint Brigit at Kildare in Leinster, and the vocal "metropolitan" see of Saint Patrick at Armagh. Each strove to amass dependent monasteries and bishoprics.[23] As a result of fierce competition, these religious centers emerged as the equivalent of the great high places of pagan times which had once acted as intertribal joining points. In a major Christian monastery or episcopal center, monks, students, and their dependents could be numbered in hundreds. In a land without large conglomerations of population, great monasteries were the nearest things to cities.[24]

Paradoxically, it was Christian poetry written in Irish that celebrated the pagan high places of Ireland. Many of these had ceased to function for centuries before the coming of Christianity. Only the outlines of their earthworks and the great burial mounds containing prehistoric passage graves survived. But the landscape was still charged with their mute presence. The glories of these places were now evoked, as if they had only recently passed away. They provided an epic backdrop for the thriving, pan-tribal sanctuaries of Christian times:

> *Tara's great fort withered with the death of her rulers:*
> *Great Armagh remains with a host of venerable heroes.*
> *It has been quenched – great the downfall – the*
>   *pride of valiant Loegaire:*
> *The name of Patrick, splendid, famous,*
>   *this is the one which grows.*[25]

The bishops and abbots who entered into this competition for the ecclesiastical equivalents of high kingship in Ireland were as intensely aware of their social status as were any of their near contemporaries, the aristocratic bishops of Gaul. A seventh-century bishop of Kildare faced off a rival in this memorable, Old Irish poem of defiance:

> *Are your horns the horns of a buffalo? . . .*
> *Is your land the Curragh of the plain of Liffey?*
> *Are you the descendant of a hundred high-kings?*
> *Is your church the shrine of Kildare?*
> *Do you keep house with Christ Himself?*[26]

Such competition brought about a sudden flowering of Irish hagiography. Each major center strove to bring its long-dead founders into the present. Cogitosus' *Life* of Saint Brigit of Kildare (who died in 520) was written in around 675. It told a story from a very different age. Brigit had been a slave-girl (though of Irish, not foreign descent) in a still largely pagan world. But that world now lay in the distant past. Cogitosus' account culminated on a triumphant note, with a description of the saint's present shrine – a tomb of shimmering gold and jewels, surrounded by chandeliers and royal treasures, worthy of any Merovingian bishop, and housed in an exquisitely carved wooden church on the rich plain of the Curragh. "This site," Cogitosus concluded, "is open to heaven."[27]

Challenged by the claims of Kildare, Muirchú moccu Machtheni soon followed, in around 695, with a *Life* of Patricius, written to defend the prestige of the see of Armagh. In the case of Muirchú's *Life* of Patricius, we can do what is seldom possible for a historian. We can measure the exact extent to which an imaginative chasm had opened, in the course of two centuries, between the hesitant Christianity of the late Roman frontier and the triumphant new Christendom of seventh-century Ireland. For Muirchú had Patricius' *Confession* and *Letter to Coroticus* before him as he wrote. We can see how these texts, now two centuries old, were read by seventh-century eyes. But Muirchú's eyes were not those of a modern scholar. He gave his readers what they wanted. This was not an eccentric British bishop, but a religious leader larger than life, cut to the measure of the modern "heirs" of Patricius, the great bishops of Armagh.

In Muirchú's *Life*, Saint Patrick (as we can now call him, having abandoned the humble Patricius of history) is made to confront Loegaire (Leary), the high king at Tara,

> where was the greatest kingdom of these peoples, the capital of all paganism.

In a triumphant confrontation with the king and his druids, Patrick

> drove an invincible wedge into the head of all idolatry . . . For the faith
> of idols [so Muirchú asserted] was wiped out on Patrick's arrival and the
> Catholic faith filled every corner of the land.[28]

Even the proud Coroticus (readers of chapter 5 of this book will doubtless
be pleased to hear) was duly punished for his contempt for Patrick. He was
turned into a wild fox![29]

"The sewing together of church and people": Christian Communities in Ireland

These literary fireworks took place in vivid Latin against the background of
a tight economy. It was difficult to accumulate wealth in Ireland. A landscape of small farms ringed by large herds of cattle might seem prosperous.
But it was open to the vagaries of north Atlantic winds and rain. A summer
in which "the wind would not disturb the tails of the cattle from the middle
of spring to the middle of autumn" was a dearly wished for ideal; it was not
the reality of Irish farming.[30]

Quite apart from the climatic vulnerability of the land, what wealth existed in Ireland was hard to tap. "Base clients" – small farmers owing dues –
were the foundation on which the intense aristocratic culture of Ireland rested.
But, unlike the serfs of "Roman" Europe, "base clients" carried arms and
owned their own farms. There was a strict limit above which they could not
be exploited. At a time when Visigothic bishops rode around the countryside
of Spain with retinues of up to 60, lawyers in Ireland declared (admittedly
somewhat conservatively) that a retinue of 12 was all that a local king or
bishop should maintain.[31] The local community could not and would not
support any more. There was nothing in Ireland equivalent to the stunning
accumulation of thousands of acres around newly founded monasteries, which
took place at the same time along the valley of the Seine in Frankish Gaul. By
contrast, in Ireland, high kings, major bishops, and abbots of monasteries
engaged in intense competition to extract wealth from a land of strictly limited resources – marks of honor, food-renders, rights of hospitality here, a
proportion of local fines there. These were slim pickings. But they created a
mentality. They stressed the fact that every gift, every offer of wealth or
service implied an obligation to give something in return.

This insistence on the return of gifts affected the implantation of Christianity on the ground in Ireland. What the Christian Church offered was presented, quite frankly, as a "gift" in return for a "gift." The laity supported
the clergy and the monasteries in various ways by offering their wealth and

services. In return, the local church or monastery was expected to offer the counter-gift of Christian blessing – baptism, "the Reading" (of the Psalms and the Gospel: that is, church services on regular occasions), confession, penance and absolution, and, at the end of life, prayers for the dead, and, for the favored few, burial near the church or in the cemetery where the monks awaited their "resurrection" on the last day. This was particularly true for the small churches and monasteries in each local community. It was by a punctilious exchange of gifts between the laity (the people of the *túath*) and the church that "the sewing together of church and people" took place, on the local level, all over Ireland.[32]

It is important to emphasize the distinctive nature of this ideal of reciprocity. The laity were not seen as the "subjects" of the clergy, as tended to be the case in Continental Europe. Rather, they thought of themselves, in a very Irish manner, in terms of entitlement. Their gifts gave them access to the blessing that was to be had in the little wooden and stone churches (often set among groves of what had recently been pagan holy trees)[33] and in the monasteries, with their enclosures marked out by stone crosses, flanked by "holy" graveyards.

But, as was usual in Ireland, entitlement varied from group to group and from class to class. The first obligation of a monastery was to its own clients. In a slippage of language that tells us much about the impact of Christianity on Irish society, these clients were called *manach* (plural *manaig*) from the Latin "monk." Each abbot, in fact, ruled a monastery without walls, through the network of dependent farmers that he controlled. It was along thin but strong lines of personal dependence, perpetually created and re-created by gifts (the gift of blessing being met by the gift of hospitality and labor), and not through anything as uniform as pastoral care of the faithful, parish by parish, as had come to be the case in many parts of Continental Europe, that Christian practice spread into the Irish countryside.[34]

The *manaig* were the privileged clients of the church, even if they were not its only clients. Their position makes clear a crucial feature of the Irish situation. As we have seen in chapters 10 and 11, the penitential practices evolved in Britain and Ireland and brought by Columbanus to the Continent depended, for their application, on a desire on the part of the laity itself to seek forgiveness. Confession and penance were not imposed on the Christian population as a whole (as would be the case in later Catholic practice). Rather, they were the concern of an "elective elite."[35] Monks and clergymen were expected to have a "soul friend," an *anmcharae* – a confessor, without whom they were "like bodies without heads."[36] But members of the laity in Ireland also sought penance according to the extent to which they were enmeshed with their local church and monastery. This depended on the degree of their piety and on the intensity of their sense of entitlement. Within a wider, nominally Christian population, an inner ring formed around the church, made up of pious lay persons, the *áes aithrige*, the "people of penance."[37]

Because of pressure from the laity itself, the *Penitentials* tell us more than most modern persons want to know about the sexual practices of married persons. But this was because, as the clients of monasteries, lay people demanded the same careful attention as was enjoyed by the monks themselves. This included confession, penance, and forgiveness. Not all encounters with a monastic confessor were punitive. Even the austere Columba was consulted by a woman about an ugly husband with whom she could have no sexual pleasure. His prayers rescued the situation:

> For the husband I hated yesterday I love today. For during the night, I know not how, my heart was changed within me from loathing to love.[38]

Others, of course, did not participate with such zest in the new Christian system. The Christian clergy had few illusions about the world in which they lived. It was a world ringed by extensive areas on which Christianity had little or no purchase. They expressed this situation in traditional terms. The Irish had tended to divide their landscape into concentric circles. At the center was the home and around it was grouped the comforting presence of fully domesticated animals, extending from the dog (who might enter the house) to the cow and the domesticated pig. But beyond them, in the world of the boglands, the woods, and the mountains, there lurked the grim antithesis to well-ordered living. When Patrick turned the proud Coroticus into a fox which fled into the woods, he was merely making plain that the warlord's feral heart belonged to the wild world that ringed the placid settlements in the plain.

Monasteries arranged their sacred spaces in a manner that echoed an ancient mapping of the landscape according to moral criteria. Only monks could enter the monastic church itself. That was for "holy persons." But, in the great courtyard outside the monastic church, there was room (as in the farmyard outside the farmer's home!) for the more domesticated species of lay person: "we let enter the crowds of local people who are not given to much villainy."[39]

The monks knew that, in seventh-century Ireland, a further, concentric band of persons lurked in the moral equivalent of the wild. The worst examples of these were bands of landless, unmarried young men – "kings' sons," exiles and outlaws – who lived a wild existence in the woods and boglands. Eating horseflesh, marked by sinister tokens of their vows of vengeance, frequently employed by the powerful as "enforcers," these groups shadowed

Irish society like the grey shapes of the wolves, the *cú glas*, the "grey dogs" – packs of savage creatures who had broken loose from human control.[40] Human wolves, untamed warriors and brigands, occupied the unchurched edges of society. They were a constant presence at the time. The Old Irish word *laech* was applied to them. It was derived from the Latin *laicus*, "layman."[41] These were the ultimate "laymen," men incapable of penance, whose feral life highlighted, by contrast, the little networks of mutual obligation that bound "lawful Christians" to their church.

A resolute profanity characterized much of the life of Ireland, and especially, as one might expect, of the warrior elite. These were hard men, not much given to penance. Many a noble hall in Ireland continued to be filled with "vehement and foul people . . . boasting and bellowing."[42] In the *Lives* of Irish saints, the "holy" sound of the saint's hand-bell was vividly contrasted with the blood-curdling yell of warrior bands, "sons of death" bent on revenge.[43] In Ireland, paganism was not definitively overcome, as Muirchú's legend of Saint Patrick implied that it had been. It was, rather, pushed to one side, away from the brightly lit centers of life, now occupied by Christianity, and out on to the fringes of a landscape which still, one suspects, had plenty of room for the wild and for the non-Christian.

"The blessed white language": Christian Literacy and Pre-Christian Tradition in Ireland

On the ground, the "Christianization" of Ireland was a distinctly piebald process. The truly remarkable achievement of the sixth and seventh centuries was, rather, the Christianization of one section of Irish society – the Irish learned class. This took a quite distinctive turn.

The complexity of Irish society had created a need for experts. "Speakers of the law," *brithemain*, were the guardians of legal memory. Poets, *filid*, "seeing men" endowed with an almost uncanny gift for remembering the past, moved freely all over Ireland. Honor was their business. They laid down "the law of the face." They made reputations by their poems of praise, and ruined them by their satires. Seldom had two such distinct classes of learned persons come to the fore in a "barbarian" society as the guardians of purely oral lore.[44] And never before had such classes fastened, with such alertness, on the most "exotic" of all goods to come into Ireland from the outside world – the skill of letters.

The emergence of writing on stones in *ogham*, in the course of the fourth century A.D., shows that an arcane script was already valued in Irish circles. The arrival of Christian Latin culture, in the next century, gave the learned classes what they needed – the opportunity to write.[45] In Irish memory of the seventh century, Patrick appears, always, as a bearer of books. His clergy advanced through a land without writing, holding their wooden writing tablets "like drawn white swords."[46] In churches that he founded, he would leave (so legend said) Psalters written in his own hand.[47] To join the Church, as a monk or clergyman, was to obtain, at once, an entire new skill.

> When Patrick was on the road, he saw a gentle young warrior herding pigs . . . Patrick preached to him, baptized, tonsured him and gave him a Gospel book.[48]

Furthermore, it was believed that Patrick had established a special relationship with the learned classes of Ireland. Dubtach maccu Lugair, a member of the *filid*, had been the first to show him signs of respect when he arrived at Tara. Dubtach then explained to Patrick the laws of Ireland. It was agreed between them that most of them were consistent with "natural law." They did not need to be corrected greatly to bring them into harmony with "the blessed white language" of the written Scriptures, the "law of the Letter."[49]

> After the men of Ireland believed in Patrick, the two laws were joined, the law of nature [the ancient laws of Ireland] and the Law of the Letter . . . And anything, in the practice of the lawyers, that was not opposed to the word of God in the Law of the Letter and to the consciences of believers was confirmed.[50]

Of the traditional experts of Ireland, only the druids, the purveyors of non-Christian religious knowledge (who may, in any case, have had less interest in the deployment and preservation of words by writing than did lawyers and poets) were banished to the "wild." They sank to the level of common sorcerers. The other learned classes established a symbiotic relationship with the Christian clergy.

However much the lawyers and poets of Ireland might value the inherited culture which preceded the arrival of "the blessed white language" of the Latin Scriptures, they shared with Christian bishops and abbots, who were drawn from the same noble class as themselves, a determination to uphold the social order in Ireland. Far from destroying a traditional culture (as has frequently been the case when literacy impinges on non-literate societies) the introduction of literacy into Ireland unleashed a surge of creativity within the most traditional sectors of Irish upper-class society. Newly endowed with the skills of literacy, the guardians of traditional law and of traditional memory, the lawyers and the poets, entered with gusto into a new age.

But, of course, to carry authority, they had to write in Irish, not in Latin. Hence the emergence of Old Irish as a written language. Honed to a remarkable degree of homogeneity by experts who would frequently travel from one end of the Irish-speaking world to the other, Irish went into letters with surprising rapidity and speed.[51] Nothing like it had happened before in Europe.

The only parallel to what happened in Ireland was a contemporary one, but from the other end of the world. As we saw in chapter 13, the Muslim Arabs of the seventh century set about creating an entire historical tradition for themselves. Due to the influence of the Qur'ân, which was first written down in the 660s, the poetry and narratives of pre-Islamic Arabia were caught in texts. A totally new, "barbarian" language, destined to conquer the Middle East, made the leap into literacy in exactly the same century as did the learned men of Ireland.

Like Arabs, Irishmen did not suffer from false humility as to the beauty and complexity of their native tongue. Irish had "the best of every language and all that was widest and finest in every tongue."[52] But there was a significant difference. The Qur'ân had been written in Arabic for Arabs. The books which Patrick and his successors brought to Ireland were written only in Latin. Hence the traditional learned class in Ireland confronted a double challenge. To put their own traditions into writing in their own language, they must first learn the "blessed white language" of the Latin Scriptures. They went to school as clergymen and monks. We can even catch them at work. Irish appears first in the form of "glosses" – little notes of the Irish meaning of words and phrases in Latin copies of the Gospels and similar ecclesiastical texts. A little later (in monasteries outside Ireland, in Continental Europe) we even meet them reading the classics. "Vergil was a great poet" is written out in Latin; and then there is added in Irish, "and he is not easy, either!"[53]

As far as we know, no learned persons in Ireland gained their literacy in any other setting than in Church schools largely dedicated to the learning of Latin. Nor did they set it to use outside the bounds of the Church. Old Irish literature was not used against the Church, as if it were a residue of "native," pagan values, pitted against the new religion. What was written down in Irish at this time had nothing about it that was defiantly pagan, or even notably exuberant. Rather, written Irish was just one face, among many, of a clerical culture still dominated by Latin.[54] It enabled the clergy and its allies to adopt, in Irish, a tone of command. What was produced were legal texts. Legal texts met a sharp concern for social order in an upper class formed through an alliance of clergymen, poets, and lawyers. Here were men of the same class, all of them used to ruling. Legal texts helped them to define themselves. They laid down the status of bishops, clergymen, and monks in an intensely hierarchical society. They regulated the exchanges between pious lay persons and their local churches. They recorded, in Irish, the rights of major sees. We must remember that legal texts circulated only among the members of the learned classes. In its day-to-day practice, Irish law never went the way of Roman law: written documents were of little or no importance in the process of witnessing and adjudication which took place at the level of the local community.[55]

We will deal, in our very last chapter, with the terms on which memories of pre-Christian Ireland were allowed to linger, through written literature, in the Christian present. A vivid literature of Old Irish tales, whose pre-Christian elements are unmistakable, grew up in Ireland at a later period. This literature has always been regarded, by modern persons, as the peculiar glory of the Celtic world. But the flowering of Irish vernacular literature took place in a later, more relaxed age. In the seventh century, issues of authority and of social order were central. It was not a time for epics and fairytales. Rather, the great collections of Irish law that would be followed, in Ireland, until the sixteenth century, were put together in this period. Forms of legal practice, many of which reached back to at least 1000 B.C., passed into writing at this time, through the pens of Christian scribes, to enjoy a further millennium of use.[56]

Of all the Latin books brought into Ireland, it was the text of the Old Testament which formed the bridge between the two worlds. Its influence was decisive. As we saw in the case of the *Penitentials*, the Old Testament had given Celtic Christian communities, in Ireland and Britain, a vision of an entire society, organized around the principles of sacredness and pollution. But it did more than that. The earthy texture of much of the Old Testament provided Irish Christians with a mirror in which to see their own society more clearly. From the practice of polygamy to the flaunting of the heads of decapitated enemies, there was nothing that happened in "barbarian" Ireland that had not happened in the Old Testament. This meant, in effect, that the blessing of God might rest upon the ways of the Irish as it was known to have rested on the Chosen People of Israel, despite their rough ways. At the very least, the past customs of Ireland could be seen as "their" Old Testament: they were seen as practices suited to a period of preparation for the coming of the Gospels. At best, the existing laws of Ireland could be seen as bringing a touch of the majestic strangeness of ancient Israel into the present day.

The classic statement of this view is contained in the great collection of Irish law, known as the *Senchas Már,* "The Great (collection of) Tradition." The "Great Tradition" was put together around A.D. 720. It marked the end of an epoch of extraordinary creativity. It declared the unity of an entire new Christian region. It was a code written for all lawyers in the entire Irish-speaking world. In size and comprehensiveness no single legal compilation had appeared to equal it in western Europe since the *Theodosian Code* of 438. In it, the ancient laws of Ireland were brought into the Christian present, by being treated as if they were an adjunct to the Old Testament.

Altogether, the use of the Old Testament in the *Senchas Már* and other texts provided Irish lawyers with a firm middle ground in which to stand between the Christian present and traditions inherited from the past of their own land. Polygamy, for instance, was forbidden in the Christian churches, although it continued to be practiced throughout Ireland. Yet polygamy was taken for granted in the Old Testament. Who was to tell which law was the better? Validated by the example of the Old Testament, polygamy might yet have a place in Christian Ireland. In the words of a contemporary law text:

> There is dispute in Irish law as to which is the more proper, whether many sexual unions or a single one. For the Chosen People of God lived in a plurality of unions, so that it is not easier to condemn it than to praise it.[57]

In such ways, a sanguine view of local custom was allowed to develop, under the aegis of appeals to the practice of the Old Testament. The "sewing together" of church and people in Ireland, in the sixth and seventh centuries, had resulted, by the beginning of the eighth century, in a "sewing together" of pagan past and Christian present that was unique in the history of Europe. Let us turn now to the pagan Saxons of eastern Britain to see what very different use they made, in the same period of time, of the "exotic" goods brought to them – also from overseas – by Christian missions.

CHAPTER 15

Christianities of the North: The Saxons of Britain

"A barbarous, fierce and unbelieving nation": Saxons and the Christianity of Britain

In early 596, a mission headed by Augustine, the prior of Gregory's family monastery on the Caelian Hill, set out for Britain at the behest of Gregory the Great. As we saw at the end of chapter 8, they had been invited by Ethelbert, the pagan Saxon king of Kent. Later writers stressed the fact that they went in fear:

> They were paralyzed with terror. They began to contemplate returning home rather than going to a barbarous, fierce and unbelieving nation whose language they did not even understand.[1]

We must be careful, however, not to make too much of this reaction. The British Isles were not a "Darkest Africa," to use a phrase coined by Victorian missionaries. In making contact with the pagan Anglo-Saxons, Christians from Europe did not come to societies which had previously known nothing of Christianity.

Indeed, it was only contemporary Christians (and scholars who are content to follow their opinion) who spoke of the unconverted pagans of the North as if they lived in a world of their own, in enclosed communities, mired in ancestral custom. We have seen that, in the rapidly changing world of the North, this was not at all the case. The pagans with whom Christians came into contact in this period were, by and large, alert entrepreneurs of the supernatural. Religion had always been an important part of their lives. They had as little prejudice against foreign religions as they had against foreign goods. These were "exotic" things, to be scanned carefully and with intelligence to see if they could be "recycled" at home, as additional sources of prestige, power, and knowledge of the other world. Though this process of scanning is usually made to appear self-interested and merely instrumental in Christian sources (and in many modern accounts of the process of Christianization) we should never underestimate the subtlety and the sheer zest for new forms of access to the supernatural that went into contact with Christianity at this time.[2]

We saw, in chapter 5, how the Saxons had established themselves in Britain. It was a piecemeal business. They did not drive the local inhabitants before them. Rather, they rose to the top in a time of political collapse, establishing themselves securely in certain enclaves, while leaving others relatively untouched. By the year 597, pagan groups known as "Saxons" had taken control of about a third of the island of Britain. They had been known by that name to outsiders since Roman times, and would continue to be called "Saxons" by the Welsh and Irish, who maintained a very "Roman" attitude toward them. To the Britons who still controlled the western parts of the island they remained, simply, "the Nation of the Thugs."[3] The Saxons dominated a great triangle which ran along the entire eastern seaboard of Britain, from Hadrian's Wall to Kent. They had conquered much of the southern, Channel coast as far as the Isle of Wight and had penetrated up the Thames deep into the Midlands. By the 570s, they had reached the valley of the Severn. We met them last, in chapter 5, wondering at the Roman ruins of recently conquered Bath.

In all of western Britain, from Cornwall to Ayrshire in southern Scotland, the Saxons faced Christian Celtic kingdoms which were far more extensive than modern Wales, and which had become more consolidated since the first chaotic days that followed the withdrawal of Roman rule. The Christianity of these kingdoms had been strengthened by the monastic renewal which had done so much to establish a remarkable Christian culture on both sides of the Irish Sea.[4] With the foundation of Iona, this Christianity, built by a collaboration of Irishmen and West Britons, reached as far north as the Highlands of Scotland. It was only the Saxons who called these western Britons "Welsh," from *wealh, wealisc,* "foreigner."

Nor had Christianity vanished entirely from the Saxon areas of Britain. The Saxons of eastern Britain were overtly pagan. But this did not exclude considerable "subliminal" awareness of Christianity. They had "Welsh" slaves and, in many areas, pagan Saxon lords controlled a peasantry for whom Christianity had survived, even without an organized clergy, as a "folk religion". Such "folk Christianity," practiced by a conquered people, was largely invisible to outsiders. Irish Christians in Iona wrote of the "whole of the land of the Saxons" as "darkened by the shadow of heathendom and ignorance."[5] The monks sent by Gregory the Great evidently felt the same. Yet, when Augustine finally arrived in Kent, in 597, he soon learned that the shrine of a local Christian martyr, called Sixtus, was visited by the Britons of Kent. The shrine dated from Roman times. The Britons themselves knew little about the martyr; but they had continued to worship at his grave. What Augustine encountered was a humbled, but recognizable, remnant of what had once been a community of Romano-British Christians. Such communities must have existed elsewhere, in other parts of "Saxon" Britain.[6]

Thus, the pagan kings and aristocracies of Saxon Britain with whom Augustine and his monks made contact may have been formidable and unfamiliar. But they themselves were not ill-informed about Christianity. The issue was not whether Christianity would "come" to a world that knew nothing of it. Christianity was already there and the Saxons knew it. What was at stake, rather, was not only "whether" the various Saxon groups would accept Christianity, but also, once they did, "which" Christianity it would be and "how" it would be thought as having come to them.

Christianity and Overlordship: Ethelbert of Kent (580–616)

Augustine arrived at the far south of the Saxon settlements, at a time when Saxon society all over the island was still in a state of flux. Like other northern societies, from Ireland to southern Sweden, aggressive dynasties, with more effective military retinues and greater control of local resources, had begun to turn societies that had known little or no state system into "kingdoms." Though fragile as spiders' webs compared with the post-imperial solidity of the Frankish and Visigothic kingdoms, these new political units represented a decisive change. After 560, the O'Neill dynasty in Ireland came to cast a more grandiose, harsher shadow of "empire" over the land: hard-dealing warrior kings, they fought to create ever larger pyramids of client kings, who would provide them with yet more goods and services. In the areas of Britain controlled by the Saxons, similar hegemonies emerged. As in Ireland, the locus of such power shifted frequently. But the outlines of power had become firmer and more irrevocable over the years.

Prestige and links with the past counted greatly for such rulers. There were still many pasts from which they could choose. Rome survived as a memory. Established within the walls of Roman forts along the North Sea, the kings of East Anglia claimed to be descended both from the war-god, Woden, and from "Caesar." A large bracteate medal discovered in a Saxon grave at Undley, Suffolk, combines the image of a northern war-god with a scene of Romulus and Remus suckled by the wolf![7] In Britain, the Saxons had long held the eastern coastline. This meant that they could draw their traditions from at least two worlds. There was the North Sea world, which reached northward as far as Scandinavia. As we have seen, from the excavations at Gudme in Denmark, this world was marked by a confident, experimental paganism, such as may be echoed in the ship burial at Sutton Hoo. But, to the south, where the North Sea flowed into the English Channel, Christian Europe was close. The estuary of the Rhine, the Channel coast of Neustria and a Seine valley increasingly dominated by great monasteries, were as close to the Saxons of Britain, by ship, as was the hinterland of their own country.

Though Kent might seem infinitely distant to monks who came from Rome, Saxon Britain, in fact, was the close neighbor of the most self-confident Christian region in northern Europe. Saxon kings appreciated, though from a safe distance, the solid success represented, throughout northern Europe, by the Christian Frankish kings. They exchanged slaves gained in their internecine wars for the wealth of the Frankish Rhineland. Frankish sources spoke of the markets of Gaul flooded with Saxon slaves, "more numerous than flocks of sheep."[8]

The Saxon "kingdoms" were made up of agglomerations of dependent chieftaincies, bullied into submission and tribute. To be a successful over-king required both charisma and an ability to make one's presence felt over wide areas. Above all, to be an over-king meant that one must be able to control the "exotic" goods which were entering the land in increasing amounts as a result of contact with the North Sea, with Continental Europe, and with the Celtic West. Along with the spoils of war, it was from their monopoly of exotic goods that strong kings were able to reward their followers. They strove to create around them, in their palaces, a warrior elite dependent on royal generosity alone.

A foreign religion was simply one such exotic good. It was essential that the king should not allow religious novelties brought from overseas to penetrate society in such a way as to strengthen any group other than himself and his followers. Traditional scholarship has tended to stress the privileged religious position of kings in the Germanic world. Unlike the kings of Ireland (who were largely men of violence, watched over by a self confident learned class) the kings of the Saxons have been treated as "sacral" experts. Forms of "sacral kingship" are ascribed to them. They are said to have been held responsible for the well-being of their subjects and for the religious rituals which achieved this well-being. At the time, however, Saxon kings may not have enjoyed a religious role based on immemorial tradition. In a fast-changing world, they acted, in matters of religion as with everything else, so as to pre-empt competition. They, and they alone, would be responsible for missionaries, and for distributing the rare goods of a new religion, which had come to Britain from across the sea.[9]

Thus, in marked contrast with sixth- and seventh-century Ireland, where an entire learned elite was implicated in the adoption of Christianity, in the Saxon kingdoms, the kings and their court went out of their way to hold the center of attention. The spread of Christianity among the Saxons was remembered very much as the "coming" of a new religion from a distant and prestigious source. It took place at royal courts. Its establishment was seen in terms of memorable gift-exchanges between Saxon kings, Christian missionaries, and the outside world which they represented.

This, at least, was the official story. It was a story which deliberately overlooked the nuances of what must have been a complex process of adaptation, not invariably linked to high politics. It was also a story which rendered the Christian Britons invisible. To adopt Christianity from outside (indeed, from Rome itself) was to give the fragile Saxon kingdoms, the "Nation of the Thugs," a triumphal new charter for their occupation of Britain. Yet, in parts of western Britain, Saxon kings and magnates may well have received their Christianity from neighboring British princes, whose courts they often frequented, as exiles and temporary allies.[10] But no glory was attached to remembering gifts received from the "Welsh," the *wealh*, the "foreigners" *par excellence*. Up to the 630s, at least, the Celtic kingdoms of western Britain remained formidable. They were not always in retreat. Any debt incurred to them for the "gift" of Christianity was best left forgotten.

This was the situation which Augustine found when he arrived in Kent. It was a situation which imposed its own, indigenous rules on the actions of his mission. With a party of 40 monks, accompanied by Frankish interpreters, Augustine headed an impressive retinue. He met, in Ethelbert of Kent (580–616), a Saxon king determined to use every asset – including the new religion – to maintain his own distinctive, local style of hegemonial overlordship.[11]

Ethelbert knew how to control foreigners, lest the world they represented should undermine his own prestige. He had been married for 15 years to a Christian Frankish princess, Bertha. Bertha had been free to practice her own religion, with a Frankish chaplain-bishop. They had been allowed to use a Romano-British church that lay a little outside the Roman walls of Canterbury, on the Roman road which led to the coast. But Ethelbert was in no mood to receive baptism from the Franks, nor, apparently, were they eager to insist on it. They did not want a Christian equal, and Ethelbert had no intention of becoming the spiritual "sub-king" of rulers with hegemonial ambitions that were quite as marked as were his own. To receive baptism from Rome was a different matter. By accepting baptism from a representative of pope Gregory, Ethelbert could hope to make contact with the safely distant, imagined center of the Latin Christian world. Beyond Rome, he would gain recognition from the Roman emperor himself, the greatest ruler in the world, whose subject the pope was known to be.

Gregory's letters to Ethelbert were welcome in Kent. They were accompanied "by numerous gifts of every kind." These showed that the pope intended "to glorify the king with temporal honors." Bertha was told that her piety was well spoken of in the imperial palace of Constantinople. Ethelbert was told that he could imitate Constantine, a ruler who had

> converted the Roman State from the false worship of idols . . . together with the nations under his rule [so that he] surpassed his predecessors in fame.[12]

Yet, when they arrived, Augustine and his party found themselves confined to an offshore island. Ethelbert would meet them only in the open air. He would not enter a building, lest, as sorcerers, they swayed his judgment. It was a gesture to his more conservative followers. Ethelbert showed that he would not allow himself to be "bewitched" by the religion of these foreigners, in such a way as to forsake traditional rites without due consultation with his own nobility.[13]

We do not know when Ethelbert was baptized. But even when Augustine found himself free to preach in Kent, his monastic community at Canterbury resembled a cordoned-off residence of privileged foreigners – valuable but potentially disruptive persons, best kept under surveillance close to the royal court. Only in 601, when Ethelbert seemed for a time to be sure of his control of the Thames estuary, through dominating Essex and the large emporium established at the former Roman city of London, did more ambitious ecclesiastical schemes emerge. It was only then (and perhaps as a result of information from Augustine on the successes of Ethelbert) that Gregory set out his plan to revive the entire ecclesiastical structure of the former Roman province of Britain, with a metropolitan bishop at London and York, each with 12 colleagues under his supervision. To be patron of such a structure would have given Ethelbert the Britain-wide "presence" for which he strove.[14]

Even then the missionaries could not move fast. As befitted a Christian ruler, Ethelbert had been urged to "suppress the worship of idols, to overthrow their buildings and shrines."[15] In fact, no dramatic burst of temple-breaking (such as had characterized the heroic days of Saint Martin of Tours and the reign of Theodosius I) accompanied the arrival of the new religion. Gregory wrote that pagan shrines were not to be destroyed. Rather, they were to be reconsecrated with holy water. The solemn sacrificial feasts that had challenged the gods, through the reckless gift of so much food, to grant the counter-gift of fertility to the crops and livestock, were to be replaced by Christian banquets on the feasts of martyrs. These banquets would take place in wooden booths set up outside the new churches; but they would continue to carry the same associations of divine good cheer.[16]

We should not mistake this famous letter as evidence for tolerance of paganism. Gregory wrote it as a good subject of the supremely self-confident eastern empire. From Italy to Upper Egypt, temples had been taken over. Crosses were carved on their doors and lintels. Churches were built in them. As we saw in chapter 6, this gesture made plain that, within the territories of the "Holy Commonwealth," all temples had been superseded by a triumphant Christian dispensation. Yet Gregory did not simply follow East Roman practice. He justified the measure with a characteristic sense of what was best for the "care of souls."

> It is doubtless impossible to cut out everything at once from their stubborn minds: just as the man who is attempting to climb to the highest place rises by steps and slow stages, not by leaps.[17]

It was a ruling which left room for flexibility. The evolution of Christian language in Saxon Britain also betrayed a similar process of enforced adaptation to local conditions. *Pascha*, the Latin version of the Jewish feast of Passover, the *Pesah*, was still the word used in all Romance languages. It was adopted, unchanged, in Old Irish. But in England, as in all other Germanic-speaking lands, *Pascha* became "Easter." The name was frankly derived from *Eostre*, the pagan goddess from whom the month was named. The joy of a pagan spring festival was allowed, by Christian writers, to pass its name on to the principal festivity of the Christian year. It became the joy of "Easter."[18]

Of greater long-range importance even than the fate of temples was the fact that Augustine provided Ethelbert with a skill with which he could shine as a new Clovis to his people. He issued "with the advice of his counsellors a code of law after the Roman manner." Clovis' *Salic Law* had recently been reissued by the Frankish kings It was very much a token of the special status of the Franks in northern Europe. But while the *Salic Law* was written in Latin, Ethelbert's *Laws* were issued in what we now call Anglo-Saxon. It is a remarkable indication of firm purpose and adaptability. Within a decade, unknown Roman or Frankish scribes, working with a Saxon king, had turned a Germanic dialect into a written language.

They did so in order to create documents which would protect their Church. The *Laws* made plain that the new foreigners enjoyed the personal protection of the king. They began by stating that theft of "the property of God and the Church" required twelve-fold compensation. Even the honor of a

Christian priest was proclaimed – and in the vernacular – to be as sensitive as that of the king himself, and to be worth nine-fold compensation.[19]

Screening and Acceptance: From Ethelbert of Kent to Edwin of Northumbria (616–633)

Ethelbert had been a hegemonial ruler in the intensely personal style of his Saxon peers. When the power of Ethelbert waned, and the old king eventually died in 616, the Christianity based on Kent suffered from the change. Ethelbert's son, Eanbald, was determined to maintain his position by marrying Ethelbert's second wife. The clergy disapproved of such a marriage. So Eanbald returned, for a time, to pagan sacrifices. Elsewhere in southern Britain, the Christian hegemony associated with Ethelbert quickly unravelled. In Essex, the pagan sons of a king who had been a client of Ethelbert reminded their bishop that Christianity, also, was subject to Saxon codes of gift-exchange. It was only fair that they, who had given so much to the bishop, should be given his "gift" in return. Though pagans, they demanded the Eucharist.

> When they saw the bishop, who was celebrating solemn mass in church, give the Eucharist to the people, they said to him "Why do you not offer us the white bread which you used to give to our father . . . If you will not oblige us in so trifling a matter as this, you cannot remain in our kingdom."[20]

For Redwald, a king of East Anglia whose power was on the rise, Christ might be a distinguished new guest. But he had to learn to live with other, local gods: "in the same temple he had one altar for the Christian sacrifice and another small altar on which to offer victims to devils." A descendant of Redwald, a good Christian who died in 713, remembered being shown this temple as a little boy.[21]

It is in this atmosphere of competing traditions, perhaps, that the Sutton Hoo burial mounds were constructed. They did not stand for an immemorial heathenism. Rather, they showed that great wealth and power were now available to Saxon kings; and that this wealth and power did not necessarily have to wear a Christian face.[22]

These anecdotes provide a unique glimpse of indigenous value systems at work along the northern frontiers of Europe. Christianity reached the Saxon kingdoms on sufferance and, for well over a generation, its representatives were carefully "screened" by kings and noblemen who knew exactly what they wanted from a foreign religion.

Altogether, the establishment of Christianity among the Saxons followed in the footsteps of a politics of prestige, conducted through the exchange of gifts and of women. In 625, Paulinus, an Italian disciple of Augustine, at last reached York. But he did so in the retinue of Ethelbert's daughter, Ethelburga, who had been given as a wife to the formidable overlord of northern Britain, Edwin. Despite his marriage, Edwin took some years to decide to become a Christian. Like Clovis, he did not convert until he had won a stunning victory over his rivals. The victory put him in control of a windfall of booty and tribute. Booty would enable him to offer substantial rewards to his followers. He could form a new aristocracy, pliable to his wishes. It would be a Christian aristocracy.

When Edwin accepted baptism, in 628, he ensured that it was a thoroughly royal occasion. He summoned his followers for a public debate. Memorable sayings were exchanged. Old retainers waxed wise.

> This is how the present life of man on earth, King, appears to me [said one] in comparison with the time which is unknown to us. You are sitting feasting with your earldormen and thegns in winter time; the fire is burning on the hearth . . . and all inside is warm; while outside the wintry storms of rain and snow are raging; and a sparrow flies swiftly through the hall . . . it flits from your sight, out of the winter storm and back into it again. So this life of man appears but for a moment: what follows, or, indeed, what went before we know not at all. If this new doctrine brings us more certain information, it seems right that we should accept it.[23]

This was how Saxons liked to remember the occasion on which they had changed their minds in matters of religion.

More forcibly still, the pagan high priest Coifi, who had until then been debarred by taboo from joining the king in war, received a warhorse and a spear, with which to desecrate his own shrine. This was the principal sanctuary of the southern branch of the Northumbrian Saxons, at Goodmanham, near Hull.[24] Previous Saxon ideas of the sacred had been based upon sharp ritual distinctions between male and female, war and peace. They involved all classes and all sexes in wooing the earth for her fertility. The priest's gesture showed that these distinctions could be brushed aside. Wealth and prosperity were not to be found at a shrine hedged by taboos. They now lay with the warhorse and the spear. Both were gifts of the king. They were only to be found at the king's hall and among the young men of the king's war-band. Because it was less tied to the land and its cults, many of which concerned women and simple farmers, Christianity emerged as an entirely appropriate religion for the all-male (and frequently unmarried) war-band of a warrior king, which lived a prestigious life a little to one side of settled society.

In northern Britain, Christianity may well have survived from Roman times in large areas, among recently conquered British populations. But Edwin made sure that his new Christianity was to be found only where the king was. Moving north along the spine provided by the surviving Roman road which linked York to Hadrian's Wall (now known as the Devil's Causeway), Edwin was preceded by a royal banner that may well have been borrowed from memories of Roman practice. He also made his presence felt at the northern end of his extensive hegemony. A royal center had been recently created at Yeavering. Yeavering stood on a landscape made solemn by the presence of prehistoric earthworks. Excavations have revealed large wooden halls, built for prolonged feasting and supplied by livestock from the neighboring hills.[25]

It was at Yeavering, in around 630, that mass baptisms and preaching took place. On one occasion they lasted for 36 days on end. Edwin had ensured that the "coming" of Christianity to the Saxons of northern Britain was a royal moment. Such moments were long remembered in the kingdom of Northumbria. An elderly priest told the historian Bede, in around 730, that he had been told by an old man, of how

> he had been baptized at noon by bishop Paulinus in the presence of king Edwin with a great crowd of people . . . [Paulinus, he remembered] was tall, with a slight stoop, black hair, a thin face, a slender and aquiline nose . . . at once impressive and terrifying.[26]

A History for the English: Bede (672–735)

Yet Edwin had only a few more years to live. His death in battle in 633, when fighting a formidable alliance between Celtic Christian kings and a major pagan Saxon warlord from the Midlands – both equally anxious to cut Edwin's "empire" down to size – was followed by the collapse of Christianity in his kingdom. Paulinus and Ethelburga fled by sea back to Kent. They had little to show for their stay in the north other than a great golden cross and chalice, Christianized remnants of the once-famous "treasure" of Edwin.

It was the Irish Christianity of Iona which saved Christianity in the north of Britain. The successor to Edwin, Oswald, had been baptized at Iona when an exile, fleeing from Edwin himself. For what later became known as the kingdom of Northumbria (the kingdom of the Saxons north of the Humber) had consisted of two separate regions, each with its own royal family. Edwin represented the more southerly, York-centered group in the Saxon confederacy (Deira) while Oswald came from the northern group (Bernicia), which had settled both to the south and the north of Hadrian's Wall. Since the days of the Roman legions, this area, which stretched as far north as the Grampian mountains of southern Scotland, had attracted warriors, and may have nursed memories of "imperial" grandeur. Oswald died in 642, but he was succeeded by Oswy, from 642 to 670 (the first Saxon king to have been born a Christian and one of the few to die in his own bed) and Ecgfrith, from 670 to 687.

Oswald's "northern" option proved decisive. For it brought the northern Saxons, through Iona, into the orbit of the Christianity of Scotland and northern Ireland. We have to abandon modern nationalistic prejudices (which tend to draw firm lines of division between the English, Scots, and Irish) in order to appreciate the significance of the new cultural zone that was created by the conversion of Northumbria. For the rest of the seventh century, a Christianity formed in Iona stretched in a great arch joining what is now northern England, Scotland, and Ireland. Iona stood at the northern apex of this arch. One side of it stretched southeastward, from southern Scotland to the Midlands of England; the other reached southwestward from Iona into the Midlands of Ireland. A constant traffic of Christian religious experts linked the various parts of this new zone. Many leading Northumbrians (Oswald among them) were bilingual in Irish and Saxon. Christian Saxons studied in Ireland. Irishmen (including the visionary Fursa, of whom we heard in chapter 11) and the pupils of Irishmen were known all over Saxon Britain as far south as the river Thames.

The great arch based on Iona swept far to the north. It bypassed the former cultural zone created by Irish and western Britons around the Irish Sea in the sixth century. It left the Celtic kingdoms of the "Welsh" to one side. On the frontiers of Northumbria, the Britons were in retreat. They had become more isolated than in the previous century. The Northumbrian Saxons had no wish to look to them to receive the "gift" of Christianity. By contrast, to acknowledge a debt to the immensely prestigious Irish was entirely acceptable.[27]

And, in the gift-exchange between an "exotic" Christianity and its Saxon patrons, the Northumbrian kingdom was the greatest gift-giver of all. The victories of the Northumbrian kings against the British gave them land, booty, and slaves. The efflorescence of Christian culture in seventh-century northern Britain is known as the "Golden Age of Northumbria." It was a "Golden Age" which rested on much real gold.[28]

The fact that we know so much about the fortunes of Christianity in Saxon Britain is due to one remarkable product of the "Golden Age of Northumbria." Bede (Baeda: later known as the Venerable Bede) came from a Northumbrian family. Born in 672/3, he grew up among monks. At the age of seven (that is, at an age when warrior sons, also, were entrusted to a foster-father) he had been given by his parents to the abbot of Wearmouth. Wearmouth and its sister monastery, Jarrow, formed a pair, placed along the estuary of the river Tyne where modern Newcastle now stands, only a few miles away from the North Sea end of Hadrian's Wall. They had been set up and equipped at great cost, between 674 and 685, by a succession of noble and royal patrons. Built in stone, "in the Roman manner," they dominated the estuary and looked out to sea, as did the royal barrows at Sutton Hoo. Like Sutton Hoo, they spoke of the spectacular wealth of the ruler (in this case, king Ecgfrith) who had endowed them. Only a truly successful king could afford to take so much wealth, which might have circulated among his followers, and cast it, beyond recall, into an exotic institution which (like Sutton Hoo, but in a Christian idiom) was intimately connected with the glorious memory of the dead.[29]

It was only as an old man, after a life spent largely in writing commentaries on the Scriptures (the "hard" science of a *sapiens* of the seventh century), did Bede settle down to write his *Ecclesiastical History of the English Nation* in 731. The *Ecclesiastical History* came half a century after the great flowering of Irish hagiography and a decade after the appearance of the *Senchas Már*. But, like these, it was written to declare a definitive triumph of the Church. Saxon Britain, like Ireland, had become a Christian land.[30]

But while the Irish took the unity of their law and language for granted, Bede went out of his way to create a new unity. He viewed Britain as a whole, much as Gildas (whom he had read with care) had done. He endowed the Saxon kingdoms with a providential role in the island. They were not merely the scourge of the sinful Britons, as they had been for Gildas. They were a new people, united, if in nothing else, by their common adherence to Catholic Christianity. Bede was the first author to speak of the disparate groups of settlers no longer simply from the outside, as "Saxons". He talked of them from the inside. He used a name which the tribes of Northumbria and others had used for themselves. He treated them as a single *gens Anglorum*, a single "nation of the English." He did this in part because Gregory the Great, who knew no better, had used the same undifferentiated term. But he also used the term because he wished to present the *gens Anglorum* as a single people, like the People of Israel, newly established in their own Promised Land, the island of Britain. He dates the end of his history by the "285th year after the Coming of the English to Britain."[31]

In Bede's writings we can watch, as seldom elsewhere in Europe, the process by which Christianity came to create notions of "national" unity that would (for good or ill) look straight to the present day. Within one crucial generation, between 700 and 731, two regions of the British Isles received, from the pen of Christian, Latin writers, legends that would prove decisive for their future sense of identity: Muirchú moccu Machtheni gave the Irish a Saint Patrick who claimed to be the patron of the entire island, and Bede gave the nondescript patchwork of military adventurers who had settled in eastern Britain the common name by which they have come to be known in later ages – the "English." Centuries later, but also under the influence of readers of Bede's *Ecclesiastical History*, they would come to speak of their country as "England."[32]

But Bede, of course, was not a modern nationalist. He wished to make sense of the history of his own times in terms of sin and punishment. He treated the "English" – the "Angles" – as a single group so as to hold them responsible before God, as a group, for their sins, exactly as the People of Israel had once been held responsible. And, as in ancient Israel, so among the *Angli*, it was the behavior of the kings which tipped the balance of God's favor toward the people as a whole.

Such a view was favored by Bede in part because it imposed a merciful simplicity on a complex process. When it came to the great sins of recurrent apostasy and frank syncretism, against which the Christian missions had to battle constantly (as Bede well knew from his own pastoral experience), it was simpler to blame it all on bad kings. This had been the case, also, in the Old Testament accounts of the People of Israel. It was easier to do this than to linger over the complex hesitations of an entire population.

By the same token, the flashes of peace and grandeur enjoyed by the *Angli* under major hegemonial rulers, such as the kings of Northumbria, could be ascribed to their willingness to accept the faith and to listen to Christian bishops. Bede presented the missionaries, bishops, and great holy men of his century as worthy heirs of the Hebrew prophets. They were vivid figures, whose interventions were as drastic (and as mercifully intermittent in the day-to-day life of a warrior society) as had been those of a Samuel or an Elijah at the time of the warring kingdoms of Judah and Israel.[33]

Bede dedicated his *Ecclesiastical History* to a king – a literate man, whose piety soon forced him into exile. He made sure that good kings would be remembered even in their most spectacular reverses. Unlike the accepting but disabused account of Clovis by Gregory of Tours, a raw sacrality – the product of fiercely maintained local memories – flickers around a figure such as king Oswald of Northumbria. Oswald was Edwin's successor. He had been baptized at Iona. Even the moss from the wooden cross which Oswald had erected when he fought his first decisive battle in 635 (at Heavenfield, under the shadow of Hadrian's Wall) continued to heal the faithful up to Bede's own days.[34]

Fluent in Irish, Oswald was very much the product of an Ionan Christianity. At Iona and its sister-monastery at Lindisfarne, the great abbots knew how to reverse the values of a warrior society in their own behavior. They would, for instance, make a point of never riding on horseback (the prerogative of a nobleman). They trudged the length and breadth of their extensive diocese on foot – a stunning gesture of humility in men of royal blood.[35]

As a king, Oswald also knew how to invert the codes of the war-band at moments of high Christian festival. He showed that "hack silver" could be used in unexpected ways:

> the story is told that on a certain occasion, one Easter Day, when he sat down to dinner with bishop Aidan, a silver dish was placed on the table before him ... They had just raised their hands to ask a blessing on the bread when there came in an officer of the king ... telling him that a great multitude of poor people from every district were sitting in the precincts and asking alms of the king. He at once ordered ... the dish to be broken up and the pieces divided among them. The bishop, who was sitting by ... grasped him by the right hand, and said, "May this hand never decay."[36]

Sure enough, the blessed hand of Oswald was cut off when he died in battle in 642. It was preserved undecayed in a chapel in the royal fort of Bamburgh, overlooking the North Sea, close to the Iona-like "Holy Island" of Lindisfarne. The earth on which Oswald had fallen, even wood from the stake on which his head had been fixed by his enemies, worked miracles. His last battle-cry, a prayer for the souls of his doomed retinue, became proverbial.[37]

The elaboration of the cult of Saint Oswald took place in the same decade as Muslim armies, staffed by warriors who regarded themselves as potential martyrs, swept into Syria and Iraq. Oswald became the first warrior king in Europe who, simply by the fact of having died a violent death in battle, was believed to have gained the supernatural powers usually associated with a Christian martyr or ascetic.

Oswald, however, belonged to a distant, heroic age, which Bede tended to idealize in order to castigate his more comfortable times. Oswald made a good story. But what had mattered in the period between 640 and 700 was not so easily recounted. In this period, a substantial and irrevocable change set in. Once they had tested the new religion to their satisfaction, the kings of Saxon Britain and their aristocracy (not only in Northumbria, but all over the island) emerged as givers to the Church on a heroic scale. Slowly but surely, in the course of the seventh century, Saxon Britain came to resemble northern Francia, as we have described it in the decades that followed the impact of Columbanus. It was a rich world, where kings and their courtiers sought to atone for their sins and to secure the future fame of their families.

Altogether, Britain, Francia, and parts of Ireland moved to the same rhythm at this time. Each region boasted a generous and wealthy local aristocracy determined, whether as monks or simply as the patrons of monks, to transfer to their own homeland vivid microcosms of a once-distant Christian order. They would rebuild a new cultural world from the "exotic" cultural goods that had come to them originally from across the sea. They would capture, in a way, some of the magic associated with the original source of these goods, in a distant world across the sea. They did this by "mirroring" essential features of that distant world, almost in miniature, in their homeland. It is to this remarkable process of relocation that we must now turn, in order to understand what the new Christianities of the North shared with other regions and how they differed significantly from the very ancient, Mediterranean Christendom on which they drew with such enthusiasm at this time.

CHAPTER 16

Micro-Christendoms

"A boundless store of books": Benedict Biscop (628–690) and the Library of Wearmouth

Looking back over a remarkable century, Bede lingered with particular affection on moments when the presence of books unleashed, in the privileged few who handled them, a sense of breathless hurry. In his *Life of Cuthbert* (the saintly bishop of Lindisfarne, who died in 689), Bede recounted how, when Cuthbert was at the abbey of Melrose, in southern Scotland, in around 664, the old prior Boisil had summoned him.

> "I warn you not to lose the chance of learning from me, for death is upon me. By next week my body and voice will have lost its strength."
> "Then tell me what is the best book to study. One that can be got through in a week."
> "Saint John's Gospel . . . I have a commentary in seven parts. With the help of God we can read one a day and perhaps discuss it if we want."[1]

When Bede himself faced death in 735 in the monastery of Saint Peter at Wearmouth, he was gripped by the same sense of urgency. Some texts still lay unfinished.

> "I cannot have my children learning what is not true [he said] . . . Take your pen and mend it, and then write fast." Then Wilberht [his pupil] said: "There is still one sentence . . ." And he said: "Write it! There now, it is written. Good." And then [in Christ's words]: "It is finished."[2]

Only then did Bede sit back in his chair to await death. He prepared for death by reciting an Anglo-Saxon Christian poem on "that last, forced journey," the passing of the soul.[3] But he had written over 40 books in a flawless Latin. Scholarship had been his life.

> I was born in the territory of this monastery. When I was seven years of age I was, by the care of my kinsmen, put into the charge of the reverend abbot . . . From then on I have spent all my life in this monastery, applying myself to the study of the Scriptures; and, amid the observance of the discipline of the Rule and the daily task of singing in the church, it has always been my delight to learn or to teach or to write.[4]

Behind Bede's achievement lay two generations characterized by the massive transfer of goods from Gaul and Rome to northern Britain. The unusual wealth of the kings and aristocracy of the frontier kingdom of Northumbria had made this possible. Biscop Baducing (628–690) – later known as Benedict Biscop – was a wealthy Northumbrian nobleman turned monk.[5] He founded the monastery of Jarrow in 674 and that of Wearmouth (where Bede lived most of his life) in 682. Wealth meant the ability to move with ease across Europe, not as a penniless pilgrim, as Columbanus and other Irishmen had done, but as a Christian aristocrat, in search of Christian goods. On six occasions, beginning in 653, Biscop travelled to Rome. Even his name, "Benedict," came from abroad. It signalled his enthusiasm for Saint Benedict, the author of the *Rule*. He returned to Northumbria with a "boundless store of books of every kind." An entire library, collected by this northern magnate as he made his Grand Tour of Christian Italy, arrived at Tyneside – along with an Italian expert on the style of chanting practiced at St. Peter's in Rome, relics, icons, embroidered silks (one of which was so valuable that it was sold to the king in exchange for three large estates), experts in glassware from Gaul and "masons who could build a church for him according to the Roman manner which he always loved."[6] The entire church of St. Peter's, Wearmouth (now known as Monkwearmouth) survives to this day. It was unusually high and narrow – 30 feet high, 16.5 feet wide, and 64 feet long. The basilica at Jarrow was larger – 90 feet long and 19 feet wide. At Jarrow, the church was flanked by a substantial dining hall – 91.5 feet long and 26 feet wide. These were some of the largest stone buildings to be set up in northern Britain since the abandonment of Hadrian's Wall.[7]

Benedict Biscop and his successor, Ceolfrith (another aristocrat who became abbot from 688/9 to 716 – that is, when Bede was in his prime) attracted royal gifts.[8] The twin monasteries housed some 600 monks. They were maintained by the services of many thousands of tenants. Bede had access to over 300 books, some of which had once belonged to Cassiodorus' Vivarium. It was the largest library to be assembled north of the Alps at this time.

But the library of Wearmouth, though outstanding, was by no means alone.

A steady drift of books into Britain ensured that fragments of a Mediterranean world, whose history we have followed in previous chapters, now came to rest at the far end of Europe. Each book opened a window down the centuries. For instance, one Gospel produced at Lindisfarne was based on a manuscript that had originally been produced in the early sixth century, at the monastery of Eugippius. The manuscript had come a long way. In chapter 5, we met Eugippius. He was the author of the *Life of Severinus*. He had lived through the end of Roman rule along the Danube; but he had ended his life as the neighbor of Romulus Augustulus, the last emperor of the West, living in retirement. Eugippius' monastery overlooked the Bay of Naples. And Eugippius' Gospel, itself, claimed to be based on a copy of the Gospels once owned by Saint Jerome! We know of all this because this information was solemnly copied out at the end of the newly produced Gospel book by a Saxon or Irish scribe.[9]

We must remember that the arrival of so much book learning involved a reorganization of local resources as dramatic as any that had once accompanied the establishment of Roman legions along Hadrian's Wall. Hundreds of unmarried men had to be supplied and fed. We must remember that monks such as Bede did not labor in the fields. The monasteries needed to be supported. They received as endowments large estates, amounting to thousands of acres in all. Vast flocks of sheep and herds of cattle roamed the uplands of Northumbria, earmarked for the monks. For sheep and cattle were more than food. They provided the hides with which to make parchment (made from sheepskins) and the greatly appreciated vellum (made from the skins of calves). Thousands of sheep and calves were needed. The skins of over 500 sheep were required to make one large Bible. Altogether, by modern standards, book production involved an immense outlay of labor and resources. To write a book was the equivalent of putting up an entire building. To assemble a library was a crushing investment. If one wished to possess the works of Gregory the Great, for instance, one had to create, by patient copying, an 11-volume set made up of 2,100 parchment folios. It would have weighed almost 50 kilograms (while the modern standard edition weighs only 3!). To copy the four Gospels took up to eight months.[10]

And these books were not produced for local scholarship alone. Books were more than aids to learning. They were often treated as gifts. They carried messages of friendship, submission, or dominance across the widely separated Christian regions of Europe. Nothing shows this more clearly than the production and subsequent fate of a manuscript produced between 688 and 716 at Wearmouth – the *Codex Amiatinus*. The *Codex Amiatinus* is now on show in the Biblioteca Laurenziana in Florence, and is named from Monte Amiato, where it came to rest in the Middle Ages. It was only one of three large copies of the entire Bible, called a *pandect* (an "all-inclusive" volume), that were produced at this time in Wearmouth. It was based on an Italian original – the *Codex Grandior*, "The Larger Codex," which had been prepared at Vivarium by Cassiodorus himself. This Grand Codex arrived at Wearmouth when Bede was a boy. It was copied out with its sentences and paragraphs marked out for easier reading, and the text was carefully brought up to date according to the Vulgate translation of Jerome. In 716, Ceolfrith, abbot of Wearmouth, set out to Rome with a retinue of no less than 80 monks. He intended to place one copy of the great new *codex* on the tomb of Saint Peter. Weighing over 35 kilograms, it was intended to be a spectacularly appropriate counter-gift to Saint Peter, the protector of the monastery of Wearmouth, from Peter's loyal client, Ceolfrith, "an Abbot of the Ultimate Land." Ceolfrith died on the way. The *Codex Amiatinus* finally came to rest in Italy. So perfect a copy was it that it was long taken to be, not the product of a late seventh-century Northumbrian monastery, but a Bible produced in Italy at an earlier age. It was spoken of as "the Bible of Gregory the Great"![11]

"First of the English race to introduce the Catholic way of life": Wilfrid of York (634–706)

The transfer of so many cultural goods from Mediterranean Europe to northern Britain was a piecemeal process. We should not overlook the surprising gaps in the flow of texts and the patches of deep ignorance of the Mediterranean past which could occur in northern monasteries at this time. Bede and his colleagues did not survey the culture of Christian Europe with the effortless ease that is made possible, for us moderns, by outline histories of the period. It was only in his old age, for instance, that Bede realized that the majestically "Roman" Grand Codex with which he had, as it were, grown up in Wearmouth, had been prepared by none other than Cassiodorus. He never knew that Cassiodorus had written the *Institutes*. The "Christian senator" remained a distant figure for him. He had little idea when he lived and where he lived.[12]

The seventh century in Britain was an exciting age. But, as was only to be expected in a society suddenly saturated by exotic goods from across the seas, it was a time calculated to breed false certainties and to encourage forms of ecclesiastical "empire-building" based on competing local customs.

From Ireland to Kent, each area in the British Isles had developed, as it were, its own, distinctive "micro-Christendom." These had been built up through the skilled deployment of resources (often slender resources) that usually had come to each region from abroad. Each region was convinced that its own local variant of a common Christian culture was the "true" one.

Each believed that it mirrored, with satisfactory exactitude, the wider macrocosm of worldwide Christian belief and practice. The religious leaders of every region claimed to possess at home a set of customs and doctrines which were ultimately derived from "true" centers of Christian learning and practice in a wider world. Seldom have so many appeals been made, as in the seventh century, to membership of a universal Christian community; and never before had they been made with such insistence, so as to build, from the ground up, as it were, so many vibrant and idiosyncratic versions of "true" Christianity.

The kingdom of Northumbria was one area where the creation of conflicting "micro-Christendoms" led to dramatic moments of conflict. For Northumbria stretched far to the north, into a world dominated, through the monastery of Iona, by the Christianity of Ireland. Yet Northumbrian supremacy also reached as far south as the Thames. It had absorbed areas that were exposed to Continental, "Roman" influence. The kings of Northumbria were givers on a heroic scale. But they (and other Saxon kings) needed to know which were the correct building blocks for setting up their own "micro-Christendom" – a local Christendom, that is, which mirrored the majestic certainty of a "true" Christianity, preserved somewhere in distant lands.

Such a need explains the meteoric career of a man such as Wilfrid (634–709). Wilfrid was the first native Saxon to become archbishop of York. He held that office only from 669 to 678. In 678, he was unceremoniously exiled by the king of Northumbria, who resented the power of an over-mighty bishop. Wilfrid's ecclesiastical empire was dismembered by his episcopal colleagues. But what Wilfrid achieved at that time, as a young man in his late thirties, was sufficient to polarize the Northumbrian churches for the remainder of the century.[13] For Wilfrid and his supporters remained convinced that he and he alone was the first bishop of English race "to introduce the Catholic way of life to the churches of the English."[14]

Like Benedict Biscop, Wilfrid was a Northumbrian nobleman. More a courtier than a warrior, he made his way through service in the retinue of queen Eanfled, the wife of king Oswy (642–670). Wilfrid used his royal contacts to travel to Gaul and Rome. On the first occasion he even accompanied Benedict Biscop. But he sought out more than books in Rome. He found, in the shadow of the great shrine of Saint Peter, a guaranteed source of personal superiority.

> In the oratory dedicated to Saint Andrew, he humbly knelt before the altar over which the four Gospels are placed, and prayed the Apostle . . . to obtain for him keenness of mind to learn and teach the nations.

Then he placed himself in the hands of a Roman archdeacon. The archdeacon

> made him word-perfect in the four Gospels, and taught him the rule [of
> how to calculate the date] of Easter, of which the Irish and Britons, be-
> ing schismatics, were ignorant.[15]

He returned to Northumbria through Gaul, where he added a further touch of "Roman" authenticity. This was the round tonsure on the crown of the head, which was said to have been worn by Saint Peter himself. Such a tonsure would distinguish Wilfrid and his eventual followers from the Irish monks of Iona, who, at that time (as we have seen) dominated the Christianity of Wilfrid's native Northumbria. For the "tonsure of Peter" was a very Mediterranean affair – a "crown" placed on the head by cutting the hair at its top. The "Celtic" tonsure, by contrast, involved the vertical mutilation of one's long-flowing hair – a cutting away of the hair above the forehead, as dramatic as a scalping – which signalled the Irish monk's abandonment of his warrior status.[16]

When Wilfrid arrived back home, in around 660, sheathed in inflexible certainty, he could not have picked more explosive topics for debate than the issue of the correct date of Easter and the correct form of the tonsure. Nor could he have picked a more opportune moment in which to push forward his views. Under king Oswy, the Northumbrian kingdom had to face the consequences of its triumphant expansion. It risked falling apart. Through the island-monastery of Lindisfarne, the northern regions of Northumbria were tenaciously loyal to the memory of Saint Columba. What "his" monks did and had always done was "true" Christianity. But, looking south, Oswy faced a southern Britain closely linked to the Continent of Europe through Kent and increasingly overshadowed, from across the Channel, by the Frankish Church.

Oswy was a shrewd survivor. He had already ruled for over 20 years. He wished to retain his grip on the south, even if it meant weakening the links between the Northumbrian kingdom and Iona. Bishops of his own choosing – and not Irishmen of royal blood, whose claim to rule sprang from their kinship to the O'Neill High Kings of Ireland – would be given the chance to create their own ecclesiastical "empire" under the shadow of his kingdom. At the age of 30, Wilfrid was the sort of man he needed.[17]

The two issues – the Roman against the non-Roman tonsure and the correct annual dating of Easter – were designed to engage the passions of lay persons and clergymen alike. In an almost totally illiterate society, the precise nature of visible gestures and the precise timing of festivals spoke volumes. Conflicts over fully visible practices counted for more than any conflict of ideas. Styles of hair had never been neutral. All over Europe, and not only in the British Isles, each hairstyle made a clear declaration of identity, distinguishing laity from clergy, warrior from farmer, "Roman" from barbarian.[18] As for Easter, differences in the method of calculating on which day Easter would fall in a given year led to situations where, in certain years, the followers of different traditions would celebrate Easter as much as a month apart. In an area where the two customs met, such as Northumbria, uncertainty on the correct date of Easter affected the timing of mass baptisms of the newly converted (which usually took place at the high festival of Easter) and upset the rhythms of the royal court, where (as we saw in the case of king Oswald) a warrior-king was expected to show his most exuberantly Christian face at the Easter feast.[19]

Altogether, the debate took place in a world where externals were everything. Honor was a matter of the "face"; and loyalty, the most precious commodity of all in a warrior society, demanded that one wear one's heart on one's sleeve. To treat external matters, such as the cutting of one's hair and the day of one's principal festival, as if they were matters of indifference was to remove from the entire fabric of profane and ecclesiastical society the vital bond of demonstrative loyalty. Hence, to challenge the customs of the great monastery of Iona was to do nothing less than to pit loyalty to Saint Columba against loyalty to Saint Peter, and to render Oswy, as king of Northumbria, the arbiter between the two.[20]

At a council summoned by Oswy at the royal monastery of Streanaeshalch/ Whitby, in 664, Wilfrid was allowed by the king to tell bishops and abbots, who had been loyal members of the great monastic confederacy of Iona, that their founder, Saint Columba, may have been holy, but he had been out of touch with the rest of Europe. On the date of Easter, he had been misled "by a rustic lack of sophistication." Only the despised Britons and the monks of Iona, now identified by Wilfrid with the rude nations of the distant north, were isolated. "Few as they were, and placed on the extreme boundaries of the world," they should join the larger unity which young Wilfrid represented.[21]

In some ways, Wilfrid had pushed triumphantly against an open door. His claim that the Irish were isolated was a caricature. The Irish churches had kept in touch with Europe. Ever since the days of Columbanus (who had now been dead for half a century), the conflicting systems of Easter dating had been discussed. The southern Irish had already opted for a "Roman" Easter. Iona, the bastion of Christianity in the far north, was already in danger of being pushed to one side by its southern Irish rivals. As early as 630, Cummian (Cumméne the Tall), a formidable *sapiens* from southern Ireland, spent a year in seclusion (so he claimed) studying this urgent and arcane matter. He wrote to warn the great abbot of Iona that he and his community were out of step. They should remember that they were no more than a "pimple on the chin of the earth."[22] Thus, when they listened to Wilfrid's denunciations at Whitby, many Irish and Saxon supporters of the customs of Iona must have thought that they had heard it all before, and from fellow-Irishmen.

As archbishop of York, from 669 to 678, Wilfrid claimed to be an out-and-out "Roman." But his actions made clear that, in reality, he wished to out-Irish the Irish. He was a prince of the Church, and an ecclesiastical empire-builder in a mold to which the British Isles (Irish and Saxon alike) had grown accustomed. Wilfrid was unlike his fellow lover of things Roman, Benedict Biscop, the self-effacing monk. He knew how to be larger than life. He was notorious for "the number of his monastic foundations, the vastness of his buildings, his countless followers arrayed and armed like a king's retinue."[23] He regularly travelled with a retinue of 120 (twice that of a Visigothic, Spanish bishop and ten times that of a minor Irish king!). For all his unpopularity at certain periods in his career, Wilfrid was remembered with zest if not with affection. He brought to the kingdom of Northumbria a touch of "style," such as had long been admired in the episcopal magnates of Gaul and which the great abbots of the north, such as Adomnán of Iona, displayed with little inhibition when they trod the Irish scene.[24]

Saxon society, we should remember, did not have a learned class like the lawyers and poets of Ireland. Wilfrid's learning was that much more of his own making, and, for that reason, that much less inhibited. But he gave the Saxons of Britain the sense of making contact with a font of learned tradition. He radiated knowledge of the correct, "Roman" forms of Christendom. He carried relics of Roman saints with him at all times. Every day he bathed his body in ice-cold holy water.

Wilfrid, indeed, was an awe-inspiring figure. He had a gift for remaining sober at royal banquets. He was "endowed with a wonderful memory for texts." Yet Wilfrid also retained a Saxon aristocrat's gift for establishing intense friendships. As far apart as Britain, Gaul, Frisia, and Italy, Wilfrid moved as a distinguished foreigner from court to court, bearing with him the mystique of a noble exile, his heart filled with arcane lore. Magnetically omniscient, Wilfrid was sought out as a foster-father for their sons by members of the Northumbrian nobility. He forwarded their careers even when they did not become monks. (One suspects that Wilfrid's ability to draw followers from the ranks of the lower aristocracy was one of the reasons for his downfall in 678: he threatened to replace the king as a source of protection and bounty). Beyond Northumbria, he attracted enthusiastic patronage from royal dynasties and local chieftains as far south as the Channel coast.[25]

Above all, Wilfrid knew how to use wealth. His monastery at Ripon was placed between York and the wild mountain spine of northern Yorkshire. It was endowed with the wealth of newly conquered British churches in the area. It stood on a frontier, as a veritable fortress of "Roman"-ness. The church was dedicated to Saint Peter.

> The altar was . . . covered with purple woven with gold . . . Wilfrid stood in front of the altar, facing the people, and in the presence of kings read out in a clear voice the lands which previous monarchs and now they themselves had given him for the salvation of their souls . . . [And] he had written, for his soul's sake, a book of the Gospels, done in letters of purest gold on parchment dyed in purple.[26]

Across a page of imperial purple, unmistakably "Roman" letters were written in gold – in a solemn rounded script known as "uncial." This script, with its majestic layout, brought an unmistakable touch of Roman grandeur to the edge of the Yorkshire Dales.[27]

Later in his career, Wilfrid founded an even larger church at Hexham. To do so, he cannibalized the stones of Hadrian's Wall. This was a basilica church of Continental proportions. It was 100 feet long and 65 feet wide. It had room for a congregation of over 2,000. As his biographer wrote: "We have never heard of its like north of the Alps." At Hexham, "the crypts of beautifully dressed stone [on which it is still possible to read Roman military inscriptions taken from the Wall itself!] . . . and the many winding passages and spiral staircases" were designed to echo exactly, in miniature, the haunting catacombs of Rome and, especially, the galleries which led down beneath the floor of Saint Peter's at Rome to the tomb of the Apostle.[28] Silver squares showing the heads of Apostles (votive plaques whose style reaches back to the pagan temples of Britain) and a hoard of reproductions of the keys of Saint Peter, discovered at Hexham and at other sites associated with Wilfrid, showed that Wilfrid intended his churches to be centers of pilgrimage. The great church at Hexham was to be a "Rome" of its own, placed within reach of the Christian populations of northern Britain.[29]

Bede appears to have looked back to Wilfrid with a certain disquiet. Despite his own, strict views in favor of the "Roman" Easter, he never disguised his respect for the sanctity of the monks of Iona and the bishops whom they had sent to Northumbria after 635. In describing them, "as a truthful historian should," he drew an implied contrast between an ascetic bishop such as Aidan and the lordly Wilfrid. In so doing, Bede may have made the Irish missionaries of the north appear, in retrospect, to be more open to the masses and, generally, more sympathetic (altogether more like Bede himself) than they had been in reality. The Irishmen had been somewhat awesome figures – proud sons of kings, wandering with the somewhat uncanny detachment of royal strangers among the "harsh and uncultivated" Saxons.[30] But, despite their misgivings over his style of churchmanship, Bede and his generation knew that Wilfrid, with his strident, entrepreneurial "Roman"-ness, had been the pace-setter for their own more secure enjoyment of the cultural riches of the Mediterranean.

"To restore the monumental fabric of the Ancients": Encyclopedias and Autonomy in Seventh-Century Europe: Visigothic Spain 589–711

The vividness of figures such as Wilfrid tends to make us forget that Wilfrid and those around him were only playing out (on a stage peculiarly well lit by contemporary sources) a situation which affected the entire extent of Christendom, from Europe to the Middle East. The seventh century was characterized throughout western Europe by a massive "involution" of the economy. Entire regions fell in upon themselves, drawing little from the outside world. The decline of trading networks in the western Mediterranean coincided with the disruption caused by the Arab invasions, and with the consequent hardening of political and confessional boundaries all over the eastern Mediterranean and the Middle East. The movements of a few distinguished travellers, such as Benedict Biscop and Wilfrid, gained their significance precisely from the fact that they had rarity value. Such figures stood out as the bearers of exotic goods and of foreign knowledge to regions locked in the cultural and religious equivalent of a "subsistence economy." Throughout the Christian world, Christian churches had become profoundly regionalized. Christianity was a patchwork of adjacent, but separate, "micro-Christendoms." Each region needed to feel that it possessed, if in diminished form, the essence of an entire Christian culture. Such a need was sharply felt in the British Isles, but it was by no means limited to it.

Hence the emergence, at this time, all over Christendom, of "encyclopedic" works, which organized all previous knowledge in easily accessible form. These were not seen by contemporaries as mere bloodless digests of a once-rich past (as modern scholars tend to view them). Far from it. They were greatly valued. Like high-energy vitamin capsules, they reassured contemporaries that the total nourishment of Christian truth was still available. What had once been scattered with insouciant abundance through so many great, long books, not all of which were now available at any one time in any one region of Europe or the Middle East, could be absorbed in compressed form. Knowledge encapsulated in lists of extracts, in sentences of gnomic brevity, and in neat abridgments would be "activated" and set to work in the urgent and deeply existential task of building up a local Christendom.

The phenomenon can be seen to happen in Christian regions as far apart as Spain, Armenia, and Persia. Already in around 600, the writings of Theodore of Mopsuestia (the great scholar of the school of Antioch who died in 428) were presented, by the Nestorian teachers of Nisibis (Nusaybin, on the south-eastern frontier of Turkey), as if they contained the sum total of human knowledge. Theodore was said to have assembled the "scattered limbs" of wisdom, and to have made of them "a single, perfect statue."[31] The omniscience ascribed to one great teacher guaranteed the cultural integrity of the Christian Church in Persia. It enabled the "Church of the East" to stand out as a cultural region of its own, resistant to penetration by rival Christian theologians.

A little later, in 665, the Armenian savant, Ananias of Shirak, in his *K'nnikon*, claimed to have brought back from his travels in the Greek world a complete summary of cosmology and chronological computation. Significantly, his encyclopedic work included the rules for calculating the date of Easter. It was his gift to "this country, the heritage of Saint Grigor, the land that loves Christ."[32] Equipped, in this way, with a comprehensive guide with which to avoid "false Easters" based on incorrect calculations, Armenia could henceforth do without the Greeks.

The example of this encyclopedic tendency which is best known to western Europeans came from the Visigothic kingdom of Spain. Bishop Isidore of Seville (ca.560–636) was the younger brother of Leander of Seville, the friend of Gregory the Great. Immediately after Isidore's death, his *Etymologies* were published by his disciples. This was a 20-book summation of all knowledge. It took the form of separate entries on the "origin," and hence the meaning, of significant terms used in all the pagan and Christian books that were available to Isidore. The *Etymologies* promised to introduce the reader to the riches of all past generations of Latin wisdom.[33] Isidore's *tour de force* confirmed the hopes of an entire local elite. He gave them all they would ever need to know. He enabled them

> to view, in his own person, the full *tableau* of ancient wisdom . . . After Spain had suffered so many blows, God raised him up to restore the monumental fabric of the Ancients, lest, through senile loss of memory, we slip back into rustic ways.[34]

In the case of Spain, as in the case of other conflicting Christian regions, there was a competitive edge to such collections of knowledge.

The Visigothic kings of Spain and their episcopal advisers, of whom Isidore was among the most enthusiastic, wished to create their own version of a "true" Christian commonwealth in thinly disguised competition with the "kingdom of the Greeks" – the self-styled "Holy Commonwealth" of East Rome.

As we saw in chapter 8, when dealing with the distinctly cool relations between Gregory the Great and the Visigothic kingdom of Spain, the competition between Spain and the East Romans was very real. The Visigoths had reason to be edgy. The Visigothic monarchy was elective and, as a result, was prone to civil war. Justinian had taken advantage of just this weakness to invade southern Spain at the time of a disputed succession. Even after "imperial" garrisons had been dislodged from the southern coast of Spain, in the 620s, the eastern empire remained a threatening presence in Carthage, Sicily, and Rome. East Roman ships might yet return to dabble in Spanish politics.

Having established a firm alliance with the Catholic bishops through their conversion from Arianism in 589, the Visigothic kings of Spain succeeded in holding together for over a century the largest undivided political unit in seventh-century Europe.[35] It was a remarkable achievement, maintained, in part, by intermittent bursts of solemn words. Like the imperial codes of East Rome, the royal laws of the Visigothic kings covered all subjects and claimed to solve all problems. They ranged from occasional, grandiose mandates for the forcible baptism of Jews throughout the kingdom[36] to lists of compensations for injuries caused to villagers by local bulls.[37]

On 17 occasions, between 589 and 694, the entire Catholic episcopate of Spain was summoned to councils which were held at the new royal capital of Toledo. Perched on a defensible spur above a bend of the river Tajo, Toledo lay on the edge of the plateau of Castile in such a way as to command, without being absorbed by, the rich but vulnerable provinces of the Mediterranean south. Toledo was spoken of as a "new Jerusalem." Its hilltop crowned with palaces and shrines, it was a solemn urban theater where bishops and kings together acted out the great hope of a self-sufficient "micro-Christendom."[38]

It is interesting to see, in the light of the prominence which such issues took on also in the British Isles, the importance attached to the uniform observance of "correct" Catholic rituals in Spain. The councils of the Spanish Church laid down that major festivals were not to be celebrated on dates determined solely by local custom. Each must be observed on the same day throughout the kingdom, "as it is celebrated throughout the entire world."[39] The "entire world," in fact, amounted to the territories controlled by the Visigothic kings.

> Let one norm of praying and singing the Psalms be preserved through-
> out all Spain and [the Visigothic parts of] Gaul . . . nor should there be
> any further variation among us in ecclesiastical custom, seeing that we
> are held within the same faith and within a single kingdom.[40]

Like fissures opening in a heavy building, cultic anomalies were treated seriously as the first, troubling symptoms of a wider potential for disorder. The
Spanish bishops condemned incorrect tonsures on monks and clergymen and
the use of incorrect forms of chant in the liturgy.[41] In a vast country, which
took months to traverse, the symbolic unity produced by insistence on a
single set of ecclesiastical practices was crucial. Divergences in such small
but highly charged matters were as much a cause for alarm as was desertion
from the royal army, rebellion, or the constant hemorrhage of the labor
force caused by the escape of slaves and by the movement of vagrants across
the threatening immensity of the plains of Castile. One could never be too
careful, "for it is in such a way that divine wrath has caused many kingdoms
of the earth to pass away."[42]

In 711 the worst happened, and precisely from the direction which the
Visigothic kings had always feared. Predictably, it also happened at a time of
civil war, when the authority of the newly established king Roderich (Rodrigo)
had been eroded by aristocratic dissension. On this occasion, however, it
was not the East Romans who entered Spain from their tiny outposts along
the coast of Africa, but the more determined Arabs and their numerous Berber
allies. The Visigothic kingdom, though "established with ancient solidity,"
was the only western Christian state to fall, with ominous speed, to the armies of the "unspeakable Saracens."[43]

Far away in Northumbria, Bede noted the fact, as he read the story of
Abraham, Ishmael, and Hagar in the Old Testament. The present-day Saracens
fulfilled the prediction first spoken about their ancestor, Ishmael:

> *For he shall be a wild man and his hand will be against every man* (Gen-
> esis 16.12). For now their hand is against all to such an extent that they
> have rendered the entire length of Africa subject to their rule and the
> greatest part of Asia, and even a part of Europe, hostile and opposed as
> they are to all other nations.[44]

Before this disaster, the most characteristic product of the Spanish "micro-
Christendom," the encyclopedic work of Isidore of Seville, had already been
enthusiastically received all over northern Europe. Irish clerical scholars fas-
tened on the *Etymologies*. It was just what they needed. They called it the
Culmen, "the summit of all learning." Such a book gave members of the
Christian clergy, a caste defined by their arcane learning, the means to mas-

ter the entire exotic world which had been opened up to them by their mastery of the Latin tongue. Through the *Culmen* of Isidore, all Latin wisdom might come to their native land. It could be believed, in subsequent centuries, that the learned men of Ulster had given away their knowledge of the epic cycle of their tribe – the *Táin*, the story of the Cattle Raid of Cooley – in exchange for a single copy of the invaluable *Culmen*![45]

"The philosopher . . . the archbishop of far-away Britain": Theodore of Tarsus at Canterbury (668–690)

The Northumbria in which Bede grew up faced the same problem of creating an ordered and self-sufficient Christian culture as did other Christian regions, most notably the Visigothic kingdom of Spain. But Bede's Britain was a more open world. The inhabitants of the island had an almost embarrassing range of traditions from which to choose so as to build up their own "micro-Christendom." Nothing shows this more clearly than the extraordinary figure of Theodore of Tarsus, the great archbishop of Canterbury whose activities, from 668 to 690, coincided with the youth of Bede.[46]

Theodore was born in 602, that is, when Gregory the Great was still alive. He came to Britain in his late sixties, from a world that owed nothing to the Latin West. He had grown up in Tarsus, in Cilicia (on the easternmost end of the Mediterranean coast of modern Turkey) near Antioch. As a boy, he would have seen the Persians sweep past Tarsus into Asia Minor. As a young man (had he not already fled the area) he would have witnessed the fall of Antioch to the Arabs, in 637. He eventually came to Rome as a refugee.

Theodore of Tarsus belonged to a generation of extraordinary Greek scholars on the run. Many sought to flee the advance of the Arabs by settling in the extreme western end of the East Roman empire, at Rome and Carthage. They were men of ascetic vocation, used to being "strangers." They moved all over the East Roman world from one monastery to another. They were the nearest equivalents, in the Mediterranean world, to their contemporaries in the British Isles – the great Irish "pilgrims" and *sapientes*, men of wisdom, such as Columbanus.[47]

They could be as cantankerous as Columbanus had been. From the safety of their western retreats, they instantly engaged in bitter controversy with the emperor of Constantinople and his ecclesiastical advisers. Since 633, the imperial government at Constantinople had attempted, once again (as we saw Justinian to have done, in chapter 7) to find a formula of agreement with the Monophysites of Syria and Egypt. It was part of a desperate attempt to form a united front of all Christians against the Arab invaders. But to the embittered refugees in Rome and Carthage, it seemed as if this compromise went too far to placate their ancient enemies, the Monophysites.

The emperor had wished to proclaim that Christ was truly human and truly divine, but that the core of his being, his will, was unique and utterly undivided. Christ never suffered the normal human agony of indecision. He had a "Single Will" – hence the term Monothelite, from *monos*, "single" and *theléma*, "will." To the opponents of this "Monothelite" formula, it appeared that such a view robbed Christ of his full humanity, and made him that much less accessible to human beings. They thought that the "Monothelite" formula implied that Christ had not truly wept, and that, when faced with the prospect of crucifixion, Christ had not felt, for a moment, the full weight of human indecision and of human horror at the approach of death, before deciding freely to go forward to his fate. Such feelings were possible only in a being which possessed free will, and who could feel the terrible pull of alternatives like any other human being. Christ, for them, was not a divinely serene automaton, his human will engulfed in the will of God.[48]

The full working out of this theological issue need not concern us here. But it did concern those around Theodore at Rome. A few years before Theodore was chosen to go Canterbury, the imperial government had reached out to crush opposition with the extraordinary brutality of a regime reduced, by the Arab invasions, to a state of perpetual emergency. In 655 one pope (Martin I) and in 662 one leading Greek refugee theologian (Maximus the Confessor) were arrested, mutilated, and left die to in exile. The pope who chose to send Theodore as archbishop to a distant land, Vitalian (657–672), wanted to maintain good relations with the emperor by avoiding controversy. Theodore, a learned Greek refugee in his prime, was a potential trouble-maker. He was better out of Rome. He was unexpectedly nominated as archbishop of Canterbury in "Great Britain" – by which East Romans meant "Outer, Faraway" Britain. Theodore set out for the far north, accompanied by an experienced Latin adviser, the abbot Hadrian. Roman sources spoke of him henceforth as "Theodore the philosopher, archbishop of Great Britain."[49]

It was precisely his learning and his long experience, as a refugee, of divergent customs which ensured that Theodore was a spectacular success in Britain. Entering his seventies, he travelled everywhere. Within a few years, this man, a native of what is now southeastern Turkey, who remembered the city of Edessa and the great churches and monuments of Constantinople, found himself at Lindisfarne, blessing a church made of carved oak, thatched with reeds "in the Irish manner."[50] Faced by the saintly bishop Chad, who still insisted, in the manner of a monk of Iona, on touring his diocese on foot, the elderly Greek picked up the saint and set him on top of a horse. He told Chad that it was his duty, as a bishop, to travel in the most efficient way possible, if he was to look after the faithful as he should.[51] Used to the small cities of Asia Minor and Italy, where the bishop was expected to act as a "father" to the faithful in a small region, the vast ecclesiastical "empire" of Wilfrid shocked him. He colluded in Wilfrid's deposition and in the dismemberment of his overblown diocese. Up to his death, at the age of 88, Theodore ruled all the churches of Saxon Britain from the see of Canterbury.[52]

But it was as a "philosophus," a man of diverse and exceedingly exotic learning, that Theodore took the learned classes of the British Isles by storm. The success of his "school" at Canterbury shows that Ireland and Britain were joined in a single "sound-chamber," where every word spoken in one island resonated in the other.

Irish collections of canon law cited the "judgments" of Theodore on matters of ecclesiastical practice. Irish scholars surrounded him at Canterbury, harrying the old Greek with questions, "like a pack of hounds baying at a wild boar run to earth." And Theodore answered them courteously, sharing with them a store of information gathered from distant Christian regions. He discussed their *Penitentials* with them. He approved of most of their rulings, with a few reservations. To eat horseflesh was taboo in Ireland. But among the Greeks and Romans, he pointed out, eating horses was not so charged an issue. It was simply "not the custom" to do so. Questioned on matters of "tariffed penance," Theodore approved. His own experience among eastern Christians led him to applaud the system of meticulous confession and penance developed by "doctors of the soul throughout Britain."[53]

We can now listen to Theodore at work through a recently published manuscript of a commentary on the Bible.[54] This commentary reflects his teaching at Canterbury. It shows that, in Britain, his eccentricity, as a Greek from the region of Antioch, turned out to his advantage. For the school of Antioch had always stressed the "literal" meaning of the Bible. The Bible, for them, was not simply an aid to meditation. In this they differed markedly from the traditions which had stressed an "allegorical" approach to the sacred text.

As we saw in chapter 8, Gregory was an outstanding representative of the allegorical method. For him, the Bible was a great encoded message, sent by God to cast fire into the heart. It echoed with the mighty whisper of God. It was for this "whisper" that the devout Christian should listen, reading the Bible, as it were, "between the lines" – paying less attention to the text itself than to a message from God which lay beyond the text. The school of Antioch, by contrast, saw the Bible first and foremost as a challenging text. Its different books had been written at specific times, by specific authors. One had first to discover exactly what these authors meant before one could go on to draw upon the Bible to nourish higher flights of contemplation. It is a view which modern scholars take for granted to such an extent that we forget that it was Gregory's meditative approach which dominated an early medieval West preoccupied with the building up of souls, and the scholarly Theodore who was the rarity.[55]

For Theodore, therefore, the Bible required explanation at the most basic level. The reader had to be told what a given word actually meant, what the immediate concern of the author of a given book had been, to what precise historical context and to what customs he referred. This was a basically "encyclopedic" approach. And the scholars of Britain loved it. It provided them with just what they needed – an introduction that gave them a purchase on the unimaginably distant, Middle Eastern world in which the Bible was set.

On this subject, Theodore was a fountain of recondite information. He explained the meaning of Greek, Hebrew, and Syriac words. He described the entire ancient Near East – its habits of dress, its food, its forms of social relationships, its festivals – so as to provide a setting for the Old Testament. He described with almost archaeological exactitude the journeys of Saint Paul. Through Theodore's eyes, students from Ireland, Northumbria and southern Britain were able to see the landscapes of the Middle East. It was as near as they could come to the distant world with which we began our account of the rise and spread of Christianity. Theodore even told them about Edessa, the city of Bardaisan, (modern Urfa in eastern Turkey). In Edessa, he said, watermelons grow to so great a size that a camel is required to carry two of them, slung in baskets on either side of its hump.[56] It was the last "close-up" of the Middle East, from the mouth of a native of the region, which western Europeans would enjoy until the time of the Crusades.

"The work of angels": Lindisfarne, the Book of Kells, and Northern Art

What is truly remarkable about the Northumbria in which Bede grew up was the continued diversity of its local ecclesiastical cultures. Although the "Roman" Easter became dominant in the north, so that even the monks of Iona accepted it in 716, no "Roman" uniformity settled over the province. Culturally not all roads ran to Rome. Many roads still ran to Iona, and from Iona to northern Scotland and Ireland. As the production of the *Codex*

Amiatinus for abbot Ceolfrith made plain, Bede's own monastery of Wearmouth was fiercely committed to a "Roman" style, based on Roman manuscripts. But only 50 miles to the north, in Lindisfarne, the challenge of "Roman" grandeur posed by Wilfrid was met by vigorous competition. Hence an extraordinary flowering of manuscript production took place in a "native" style. This flowering was the answer of the north to Wilfrid. It produced some of the greatest artistic achievements ever to come out of the "Celtic" world.[57]

In a Christian region where books of any kind were rare objects, the Christian mystique of copying the Scriptures was yet further tinged with the magical awe that had always surrounded the *áes dana,* the "people of skill," the master-craftsmen whose legendary cunning provided secular rulers with the ornaments and jewelry appropriate to their status. We need only look at Irish jewelry of this time (such as the great Tara Brooch which would have held the cloak of a king around his shoulder) to see how men of skill could work magic with small quantities of raw gold and fragments of semi-precious stones. They turned these raw materials into objects of haunting subtlety. Looking at such a brooch, the eye was pulled inward into a charmed world of interlaced patterns and writhing beasts. Such jewelry made concrete the "face," the honor, of its wearer.

In the same way, the craftsmen of the great monasteries covered the vellum pages of Gospel books with exquisite illuminations. These craftsmen were the *áes dana* of the "High King of Heaven." They caused the honor of God to blaze from the page. They were not simply copying a text. They were turning parts of the holy text into the equivalent of jewelry. We have a description of an Irish craftsman, the monk Ultán, as he set to work somewhere in Northumbria to produce a Gospel book:

> he could ornament books with fair markings, and by this art he made the shape of letters so beautiful, one by one . . . For the Holy Ghost ruled his very fingers.[58]

The most spectacular example of this art may well have been prepared at Iona by a successor of Adomnán. It came to rest in the shrine of Saint Brigit at Kildare, where it was called "the High Relic of the Western World." At some time, perhaps in around 750, this remarkable Gospel had been given by the abbot of Iona as a gift from one mighty Irish shrine to another (much as Ceolfrith had brought his great book from Wearmouth to Saint Peter at Rome). It is now known, from the last place in which it rested, as the Book of Kells.[59] A twelfth-century traveller to Ireland, Gerald of Wales, recorded his impression of its pages:

If you look at them carelessly . . . you may judge them to be mere daubs . . . You would see nothing subtle where everything is subtle. But if you take the trouble to look very closely and to penetrate with your eyes to the secrets of the artistry, you will notice such intricacies, so delicate, so subtle . . . so involved and bound together, so fresh still in their colorings, that you will not hesitate to declare that all those things must have been the work not of men but of angels.[60]

"Now must we praise Heaven-Kingdom's Keeper": Caedmon, *The Dream of the Rood,* and Anglo-Saxon Religious Poetry

The flowering of a "native" style of art in northern Britain went hand in hand with the first emergence of Anglo-Saxon as a language of religious poetry. In order to understand how this could happen, we must concentrate, for a moment, on the process of Christianization in Bede's Northumbria. Christianity had come to northern Britain (as to other parts of the Saxon world) frankly from on top. It was an exotic good, adopted by kings and their aristocracy. Monasteries were the bastions of this upper-class Christianity. A system of bishops and parishes was slowly put in place throughout Saxon Britain; but, as in Ireland, it was the monasteries which held the center of attention. We know more about them because monasteries and convents, and not the humble local clergy, were the principal recipients of lavish gifts and endowments.

As we saw in chapter 11, it was through the foundation of monasteries and convents that the Frankish aristocrats of northern Gaul had sought to leave their mark on the land. The example of Gaul was close to Saxon Britain at this time. There were many such rulers and aristocrats in Saxon Britain who were glad to follow the Frankish example. Many local figures among the Saxons were the descendants of chieftains demoted by the rise of strong kingdoms. They were anxious not to be entirely forgotten. Family foundations, in which upper-class women, as abbesses, played an unusually prominent role by Continental standards, brought Christianity home to their region. Viewing Northumbria from the majesty of Wearmouth, Bede was deeply suspicious of such "family" monasteries. They often failed to endure.[61]

These monasteries were small affairs. The church at Escomb (in County Durham) may have belonged to one such family venture: it was only 24½ feet by 14½ (a third of the size of Wearmouth). But, in a manner similar to what happened in Ireland (as we saw in the last chapter), small centers such as these passed on their Christianity very effectively to an extended "family" of retainers, tenants, and neighbors. They created a "grassroots" Christianity in a way that splendid, royal foundations such as Wearmouth-Jarrow could not do.[62]

We should not be misled by the inward-looking and otherworldly self-image of an early medieval monastery. In reality, the monastery tended to be a microcosm of local society. It owed its success, in large part, to this fact. It shared the values, the limitations, and the skills of its milieu. The monastery was very often a local "noblemen's club" for retired warriors quite as much as it was an island of Latinate book-learning. Even in a monastic settlement as unusual as Wearmouth and Jarrow, studious Latin scholars, such as Bede, were a very small minority among their fellow-monks.[63]

Bede did not expect otherwise. Converted warriors came to monasteries to do something more urgent than master the Latin language. As in northern Gaul, they came to save their souls, through prolonged penance under a strict rule. They saw the monastery as a powerhouse of atonement. In Britain they needed atonement. As we saw in chapter 11, the Frankish courtier, Barontus, in his monastery near Bourges, had only a checkered marital career to answer for when he faced the demons in his vision of the other world. At Much Wenlock (in Shropshire), in the warlike border country between the Welsh and the Saxons, a monk was haunted by far worse sins. He saw "a man upon whom he had inflicted a heavy wound . . . The bloody and open wound and even the blood itself cried out against him."[64]

Sebbi, king of Essex (664–694), was typical of many former warriors who must have retired to monasteries all over Britain. They practiced a penitential asceticism in the hope of a "good death."

> Being of kingly temperament, [Sebbi] feared that, if he felt great pain in the hour of death, he might, by his words and gestures, act in a way unworthy of his character.

An angel granted the old warrior a peaceful passing.[65]

We must remember that, unlike Bede, most monks and members of the clergy had a tenuous grasp of Latin. To write in Anglo-Saxon (as also, to write in Old Irish) was not necessarily to address a lay audience outside the clergy. It was needed so as to educate the clergy itself. Bede urged writing down and memorizing in Anglo-Saxon the basic Christian prayers and formulae. These formulae were to be used by the clergy for their own instruction. He died engaged on an unfinished, projected translation into Anglo-Saxon of the opening chapters of the Gospel of Saint John.[66]

Such uses of the written vernacular, though usually designed for monks and clergymen, inevitably slipped beyond the walls of the monasteries into a purely oral world, without writing but with a lively interest in the new religion. For we must remember the extent to which (in Britain as in Ireland) Christianization often took place, on the ground, through a wide penumbra of half-participants who had gathered around the monastery. Much of this was "self-Christianization," based on a zest for knowledge of arcane matters and on a search for new sources of supernatural power whose force we tend to overlook when we study the relations between the "barbarians" of the north and the new religion.

So strong an appetite for knowledge of the supernatural posed a problem whose outlines we can discern only along the very edges of our evidence. The determination of the upper classes to assert a monopoly over the religious life of their region, through spectacular patronage of Christianity, has inevitably led us to an overwhelmingly "top-down" view of the establishment of the Christian Church in northern Europe. There is no denying the crucial role in this process of kings and aristocrats. But Bede gives us evidence that more was at stake. The upper-class monopoly of Christianity remained fragile. Marginal figures, largely untouched by Latin and even by literacy of any kind, played a crucial role in interpreting the new religion to the majority of their fellows.

Visions came to such persons. Drythelm, a pious married layman in Cunningham, Ayrshire, in southwestern Scotland, had a vision of "awful flaming fire and freezing cold," followed by the view of "a very broad and pleasant plain, full of the fragrance of growing flowers." The angel who accompanied him, however, explained that these were not Hell and Heaven, "as he had often heard of them." They were two intermediate stages of the Christian soul after death, a near-Hell and a near-Heaven, to which believers would go, dependent on the degree to which they had done penance in this life.

On the strength of his vision, Drythelm set up as a hermit near Melrose. He would stand for nights on end in icy water. But Drythelm's vision had not been as terrifying as that which abbot Fursa (whom we met in chapter 11) had experienced. Drythelm did not return scarred by searing flames. On the strength of his vision, he was able to reassure a wide clientele (which included a learned king of Northumbria) that they should believe that the common remedies for sin (penance, almsgiving, and the prayers of friends) could alter the fate of Christians in the other world. This was knowledge worth having: the Christian soul was not caught forever between two seemingly inflexible alternatives – between Heaven and Hell. There was something that ordinary lay persons could do for themselves and for their loved ones. On this all-important issue, Drythelm the lay visionary (and not a scholar such as Bede) was the theologian of his district.[67]

We saw, in chapter 6, that a Gallic bishop, such as Gregory of Tours, was little concerned about resistance from paganism. But he was haunted by the fear that Christianity could, as it were, "take off" as a popular movement led by figures beyond the control of himself and his episcopal colleagues The visions of Muhammad, in Arabia, showed that an entire new religion might arise from such experiences, in a tribal world recently disturbed by the intrusion of Judaism and Christianity. In Northumbria also, a vernacular visionary culture, stirred by Christianity but unamenable to ecclesiastical control, lay dangerously close to the sacred precincts of every great monastery.

Hence the enthusiasm which Bede showed for those visionary experiences which turned out to be amenable to control by the Church. Once such was connected with Caedmon, a dependent of the great royal monastery of Whitby. Caedmon was a client-farmer on the monastery's land. He was in a position similar to that of a *manach* in Ireland. He was a failed poet. His name suggests that he may even have been a Briton. He lacked the Saxon gift for extempore recitation.

> Hence sometimes at a feast, when for the sake of providing entertainment, it had been decided that they should all sing in turn, when he saw the harp approaching him, he would rise up in the middle of the feasting, go out, and return home.

Suddenly, one night, he received the gift. In a dream, he was ordered to sing the story of Creation. Having been tested carefully at the monastery, Caedmon was allowed use his gift. He set to work, turning the stories of the Bible into Saxon heroic verse.[68]

It is significant that this should have happened at Whitby, for the monastery of Whitby (then known as Straenaeshalch) stood for all that was most self-confidently unusual in the Christianity of Northumbria.[69] It was a "double monastery" in northern Frankish style. An abbess of royal blood ruled both nuns and monks. Abbess Hild (614–680) was a living reminder of a heroic, transitional world. She had been the first princess in Northumbria to be baptized, in her teens, by bishop Paulinus. By no means the sheltered product of a cloister, her life fell into two halves. She had lived in the world and been a married woman for 33 years, and she had been a nun and abbess for a further 33.

> So great was her knowledge of affairs that not only ordinary people but kings and princes sought and received her advice. She compelled all those under her to devote much time to the study of the Scriptures [so that five bishops and many clergy emerged from her training at Whitby]. All who knew Hild . . . used to call her "Mother."[70]

As we saw at the end of chapter 8, the first *Life* of Gregory the Great to appear in Europe was written at Whitby. Thus Caedmon claimed to have received the visionary gift to compose religious poetry in Anglo-Saxon verse on the edge of an establishment whose core was royal and highly Latinate.

There was nothing "popular" or "folkloristic," in a modern sense, about such Anglo-Saxon verse. Versification was a noble's skill, an intricate instrument of social memory, usually deployed in warrior epics and in the praise of royal lineages. Just as the illuminators of the Book of Kells turned pages of the Bible into jewelry, to show the status of the High King of Heaven, so Caedmon's poetry began as a praise-poem on the deeds of God.

Now must we praise Heaven-Kingdom's Keeper.[71]

A visionary and royal quality clung to the most powerful example of the Anglo-Saxon religious poetry of the age. The *Dream of the Rood* took the form of a pious Christian's night-time vision of the Holy Cross. It spoke of the Crucifixion of Christ as if it were the blood-soaked death of a warrior king. Death and triumph merged into each other. In a haunting juxtaposition of images, a sheet of blood is seen pouring down behind a triumphal, gold-sheathed Cross – a Cross such as sheathed the relic of the True Cross which Radegund had brought to Poitiers from Constantinople.[72]

Lines from the *Dream of the Rood* were later carved, in runic script, over the edge of a tall stone cross set up in around A.D. 700 at Ruthwell (in Dumfriesshire, Scotland). The cross itself was majestically "Roman" in its monumental carving. It was placed at the heart of a recently conquered British kingdom. It emphasized both the lordship of Christ and, in the heavy gesture of Mary Magdalene as she bent to wipe the feet of Christ with her hair, it evoked the all-important monastic call to penance. It was the product of an ostentatiously non-local style. It echoed the Roman liturgy of the Adoration of the Cross.[73] It brought a wider world into Northumbria. A little further to the west, at Bewcastle, in a former Roman advance post to the north of Hadrian's Wall, a similar cross was decorated with vine-scrolls and a twining border of exquisitely stylized flowers, which reached beyond Rome to Egypt and Iran.[74]

In the same way, the *Dream of the Rood*, though written in Anglo-Saxon and transcribed in runes, was by no means the reflection of a purely local culture. It had been called into existence by a cult of the Cross which stretched from Scotland to Armenia. The *Dream* spoke of the Cross, at times, as a gold-sheathed treasure, hung with jewelled banners. It was in this way that the Holy Cross was set up, in the Hagia Sophia, to be adored by the "emperor of the world" and his court. Bishop Arculf had witnessed the ceremony in 680 and described the scene to abbot Adomnán at Iona.[75] The emphasis which the poem placed on the heroic willingness of Christ to face death echoed issues stirred up by the Monothelite controversy in Rome and Constantinople.[76] As a victory-bringing sign, the Cross was known to warrior aristocracies throughout the Christian world. Only five years after Oswald had set up his own wooden cross to do battle with pagan rivals for the kingdom of Northumbria, an image of the True Cross was placed as a token of their victory, by the warrior aristocracy of Armenia, on the walls of the votive church at Mren, which is now perched in no man's land on the frontier between Turkey and the former Soviet Union, some 2,300 miles away from Ruthwell.[77]

Seen against this wide panorama, the "micro-Christendom" of Bede's Britain was still part of a Christian "global village." It shared with the many "micro-Christendoms" which stretched, like so many beads on a string, from Iona across Europe and the Middle East to Iran and Central Asia, a common pool of images and attitudes inherited from ancient Christianity. Yet the position of the "micro-Christendom" of Britain and of its neighbors, in Gaul, Spain, and Italy, would change dramatically in the course of the eighth century.

In the eighth century, the balance of power in Europe shifted. As missionaries in Frisia and Germany, Anglo-Saxons (as we may now call them, for Bede had effectively given them that name) came to be swept up in the greatest political revolution to occur in western Europe since the passing of the Roman empire. The unprecedented coagulation of military power in the hands of the Frankish aristocracy who supported Charles Martel; the replacement of the Merovingian kings of Francia by a new, "Carolingian" royal dynasty; the absorption by the Franks of large areas of central and northern Europe, from modern Holland to Saxony; the Europe-wide conquests of Charlemagne: within half a century of Bede's death, these developments engulfed the Christian populations of much of continental Europe in a kingdom of truly "imperial" dimensions, known to us as the Carolingian empire. Regional "micro-Christendoms" survived. But at the top of a victorious society, dominated by Franks, their various representatives came together, for the very first time, to create what they considered to be the only true "Christendom" that mattered.

This happened, in part, because few rivals to the Frankish definition of Christendom had survived the political storms of the seventh century. At the western end of the Mediterranean, the magnificently self-sufficient Visigothic kingdom had ceased to exist. The East Roman empire fought for survival against unrelenting Muslim armies. Tied down by warfare on its eastern frontiers, the "empire of the Greeks" ceased to be an effective presence in the

West. As a result of these strains, the East Roman empire passed through a "crisis of identity" as acute as any that had been experienced in the West. It emerged as an empire with a distinctive culture, which we now call "Byzantine." Hence, as a result of the rise of the Frankish empire and the mutation of East Rome, two new and contrasting forms of Christendom emerged in the course of the eighth century. Eastern and Western Christendom began to look very different from each other. It is to the creation of these new Christendoms that we must turn in the four remaining chapters of this book.

Part IV
New Christendoms
A.D. 750–1000

The Crisis of the Image: The Byzantine Iconoclast Controversy

An Empire under Siege: From an East Roman to a "Byzantine" State

> In the days of old [wrote a Muslim geographer] cities were numerous in
> *Rum* [the East Roman empire], but now they have become few. Most of
> the districts are prosperous and pleasant, and have each an exceedingly
> strong fortress, on account of the raids of the [Muslim] fighters of the
> faith. To each village appertains a castle, where they take shelter.[1]

By A.D. 700, the former world empire of East Rome, known to the Muslims
as *Rûm*, had become a sadly diminished state. It had lost its eastern provinces and three quarters of its former revenues. For two centuries on end,
until around 840, it faced near-annual attack from the Islamic empire – a
state ten times larger than itself, with a budget 15 times greater, capable of
mustering armies that outnumbered those of the *Rûmi* by five to one. The
most hotly contested frontier of the Christian world lay, not in western Europe, but a little to the west of modern Ankara, in what had been ancient
Phrygia. A chain of fortified garrison-towns, their walls rapidly piled up
from the spoils of ancient classical monuments, blocked the way which led
from eastern Anatolia, where the Muslim armies would gather, to the valleys
that led down to the Aegean coast and from there to Constantinople. Every
November, a thick blanket of snow gripped the highlands, blocking the passes
and turning the fortresses of Phrygia into "cities of Hell" for the Arab invaders. Winter, and the vast distances of an Anatolian plateau skillfully defended
by East Roman generals, stood between ever-present Muslim armies and the
densely populated villages of the Aegean that were the heart of what remained of the Christian empire.

It was this embattled heartland which survived. Between 717 and 843,

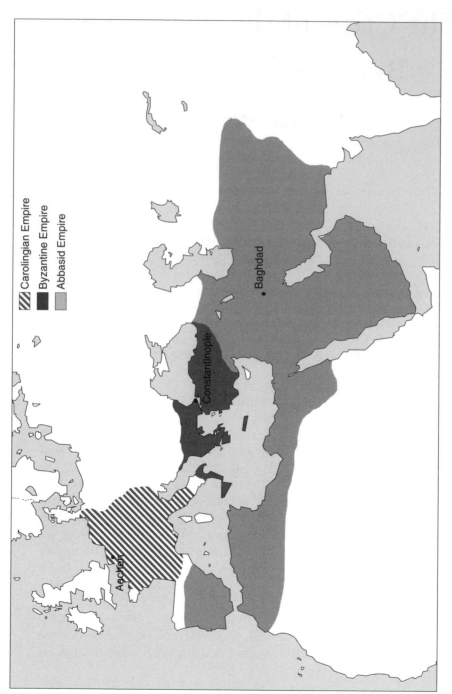

Map 8   A new world, 800: the Carolingian, Byzantine, and Abbasid empires

THE BYZANTINE EMPIRE ca. 700–ca. 843

Pseudo-Dionysius, *The Celestial Hierarchies* ca.500

John of Damascus ca.665–ca.749
  writes *Defense of Holy Images* 726/733

Leo III, emperor 717–741
Constantine V 741–775

Lombards conquer Ravenna 751

Iconoclast Council of Hieria 757

Iconophile Council of Nicaea 787

Charlemagne 768–814
  commissions *Libri Carolini* 793
  summons Council of Frankfurt 794

Emperor Nicephorus killed by
  Khan Krum of the Bulgars 811

Leo IV emperor 813–820
  "Second Iconoclasm" 815+

Nicephorus 750–828
  patriarch of Constantinople
  writes *Antirrhetikos* 818/20

Theodore of Stoudios 759–826

"Triumph of Orthodoxy" 843

western Asia Minor, the coastlines of Greece and the Balkans and, at the furthest edge of the Ionian Sea, Sicily and Calabria were firmly incorporated into a new political system. Ruled from Constantinople, southern Italy was as Greek in the early Middle Ages as *Magna Graecia* had been in ancient times. The modern term "Byzantine" (which we have avoided until now) is apposite for the compact, Greek empire which replaced the old-world grandeur of the "Roman" empire of the East. The emperors continued to call themselves "Roman" and treated the Muslims as no more than temporary occupants of the "Roman" provinces of Egypt and Syria. But they now ruled a more cohesive state, made up of a largely Greek population. Westerners called it, increasingly and with justice, "the empire of the Greeks."

Though reeling from the attacks of outsiders, the new "Byzantine" emperors were very much lords of their own territories. Few barriers stood between them and direct control of their subjects. The old city councils and the civilian provincial elites associated with the cities were swept aside. Four great *Themata* – *Themes*, stationed armies – formed massive regional commands of up to 15,000 troops each. The *Themes* dominated the countryside of Asia Minor. Their generals came from the highlands of the eastern frontier. Many were Armenians. They were often fluent in Arabic. Altogether, the new elites of the empire were hard men, soldiers and ranchers, who did not pretend to possess urban graces. They were a warrior elite, not unlike their contemporaries in western Europe. But they were pious Christians, loyal servants of Christian emperors in a time of constant emergency. The populations they defended were made up, overwhelmingly, of villagers. The ancient cities and the elites associated with them had all but vanished. No urban oligarchies stood between the villages and the central power, as they had done in previous ages. The inhabitants of such a rural society, if they looked outside their village at all, looked up directly to their emperor. They identified themselves through loyalty to a Christian emperor, who shared the same embattled faith as themselves. Their empire was defined by their religion quite as sharply as was the empire of the Muslims. Theirs was the empire of "the baptized people."[2]

At the center of a drastically simplified society, Constantinople stood alone. Other cities had become mere fortresses and market-towns. But even Constantinople was a depleted city. Its population had shrunk to around 60,000. Spacious gardens crept into its center, sheltering monasteries and great pleasure palaces, often built in a new, non-classical Near Eastern style, associated with Persia and with the luxurious life of Arab princes. The inhabitants were largely immigrants from the Balkans. They had lost all sense of the classical past. The ancient public decor of Constantinople spoke to them of a fairytale world, which they understood only dimly. The classical statues which Constantine had lavished on his city now struck them as alien, vaguely threatening presences, out of place in a Christian present.[3]

Yet, in this greatly reduced city, the Imperial Palace, the gigantic Hippodrome with its imperial box, and the Golden Gate, through which victorious armies still occasionally made their entry, remained in place. So did Justinian's Hagia Sophia. In the nearby library of the patriarch of Constantinople, it was still possible to find, and even, with some difficulty, to understand the "orthodox" meaning of the writings of the great Greek Fathers of the Church. The Byzantine Church was increasingly cut off from Latin Christianity and from the Christian communities in the Middle East. It became more compact as its horizons narrowed. It had become no more than one "micro-Christendom" among others. But the emperor and clergy of Byzantium were convinced that in the writings of the "Greek Fathers" and in the traditions of their Church lay the essence of a total "orthodox" system of belief.

Texts of the Fathers were excerpted and arranged in encyclopedic anthologies. The organization of the overwhelming richness of the past into trenchant collections of citations and the resolution of theological problems through manuals of *Questions and Answers* was as necessary a pursuit in Byzantium as it was, at the same time, in the Spain of Isidore of Seville. The Byzantine clergy were as intensely concerned as were the bishops of Spain, that "orthodox" belief should be reflected in uniform traditions of worship observed throughout the empire. Given this situation, the religious life of Byzantium was characterized, not by renewed theological controversy, but by heated debates over concrete Christian religious practices. It is not surprising, therefore, that the custom of venerating painted images of Christ, of his Mother and of the saints became the center of a virulent controversy among the leaders of the Byzantine church.[4]

"If only I see his likeness, I shall be saved": Images and East Roman piety, 550–700

This controversy is known to scholars as the "Iconoclast controversy." To modern persons it has seemed strange that the governing classes of an empire thrown into a period of unparalleled turmoil should have devoted time and energy to deciding how believers should treat religious images. Images that portray religious scenes are now so much part of the imaginative world of western Christians, and "icons" (in the strict sense of individual images of holy persons – Christ, the Virgin, and the saints) are so much part of the religious practice of the Orthodox Church, that it is hard to recapture an age where their presence was hotly contested. But, in around A.D. 730, what was at stake in this issue was by no means trivial. It was about how to find, in a society thrown into a state of perpetual mobilization, fully acceptable symbols around which to rally the religious determination of a much-battered "baptized people." The beleaguered Christians of the Byzantine empire believed that, if they looked to God for help, then they had to be sure that the manner of their worship was acceptable to him. The survival of the empire was at stake.

Those who revered icons called themselves "Iconophiles" – lovers of images – and even "Iconodules" – worshippers of images. They had come to believe that icons brought Christ, his Mother, and the saints down among the Christian people. These holy figures were now in heaven; but they were made accessible on earth through their portraits. The word "icon" comes from the Greek *eikôn*, "image." At the time it meant any representation of a human person. Holy persons could be shown either through their faces alone or in full length. These could be painted on boards (like modern "icons"), but they could also be shown in mosaic or fresco in churches. What mattered is that, since around the middle of the sixth century, these images tended to be set up separately or, if they were part of a larger décor of a church, to receive separate treatment.

A significant change had come about in the visual world of Christians all over the Mediterranean and the Middle East. Ever since the fourth century, Christian churches had been filled with images of holy figures: splendid rows of angels and holy persons could be seen on the walls of every church. But now, some of these images, as it were, "broke ranks." The new images came to be placed, by themselves, in prominent positions: at the doors of shrines, at special places in churches, in public places, outside shops, and in privileged places within Christian homes. Even when they were still part of the overall décor of churches, they were made to look special by being placed in separate panels. This made them "holy" images. They received gestures of veneration: believers bowed deeply before them, kissed them, burnt lights and incense before them, even nailed votive objects to them, as tokens of their power.

Such images made Christ, his Mother, and the distant saints "present" at a precise place, where they could receive the prayers of those who needed them. They met an unchanging need to sense, close to hand, the loving "presence" of invisible protectors. Pagans had made their gods "present" in this way through little pictures and portable statues.[5] As we have seen, living holy men had always played a similar important role in eastern Christianity. By their miracles of healing and their preaching, holy persons "made present" the love and power of a distant God. In the course of the sixth century it came to be believed that portraits of such holy persons could also make them present, even at a distance. These portraits were usually made on small portable tablets, following a long tradition of representing protecting gods, and of memorializing heroes, personal benefactors, and beloved parents. In around 550, a woman who had been healed by a holy man set up a portrait of the saint in the inner quarters of her house. "Being overshadowed by the Holy Spirit which also dwelled in the saint," the image itself began to work miracles. It did so in the privacy of the woman's quarters, many miles away from the mountain-top where the holy man lived. A woman came to the house to be healed of a 15-year-long illness: "For she had said to herself: 'If only I see his likeness, I shall be saved.'"[6]

The incident shows the strength of one current in Christian piety at a time when the empire was about to face its most deadly challenges. If we turn to Rome in the seventh century, we can see the manner in which religious images came to be charged with the hopes of those who regarded them as a special means through which to approach invisible protectors. On one icon of Mary, set up in a special place in the ancient Pantheon (which had been converted into a church in 608) the hand of the Mother of Christ was gilded. It was the hand with which Mary would touch her Son, to remind him of his love for those who prayed before her image. Mary's hand, as it were, was shown in the act of drawing the attention of Christ to the worshipper who stood, praying before the image. In Thessalonica, also, Saint Demetrius was shown with a golden right hand raised in prayer to God, while he laid his left hand on the shoulders of those whom he protected. On such images, what you saw was exactly what you hoped to get: the protection of God made "present" by the prayer of the saint before whom you yourself now prayed.

Nor did these images address purely private needs. Ever since the end of the sixth century, at a time when the empire already felt threatened by invasion from Persia and from the Balkans, images of Christ and the Virgin had been carried in processions to invoke their protection. The solemn movement of an image seemed to make it live, as it swayed above the crowd. To the Iconophiles, images of this kind guaranteed the presence, on earth, of the supernatural protectors whom they represented.[7]

"Inanimate and speechless images . . . which bring no benefit": Images and Their Critics, 600–700

By the year 730, such practices were already well-developed. But they were far from being universal. Even after two centuries, many Byzantines regarded the cult of images as a novel and exaggerated form of devotion. Those who were called (by their enemies) the Iconoclasts, the "icon-smashers," were far from certain that such images were "pleasing to God." Yet, in peaceful times, conflict over the issue might have been indefinitely postponed. This could not happen after the unparalleled series of crises which fell upon the Byzantine empire in the generations before and after the Muslim invasions. The "worship" of images already had its critics. Now such critics would be heard.

In the first place, the worship of images had always been repugnant to the Jews within the Roman empire. When persecuted by Christians (as had happened during the Persian wars of the emperor Heraclius in the 630s) Jews had responded by bitter criticisms of their images. They pointed out that, in his Ten Commandments, God had expressly forbidden the worship of images made by human hands. Now some Christians were inclined to agree with the Jews. God might, indeed, turn his face away from his people because of their idolatry.[8]

A little later, the rise of Islam brought the issue of images into even sharper focus. Islam presented itself as a true and incorrupt religion very much through criticizing contemporary Christian practice. Strict Muslim theologians even claimed that no artist had the right to "endow" an image with "life" by representing a living creature. (Painting was seen as a sort of "cloning" through art, by which the artist reproduced "living" creatures, thereby usurping God's right to infuse them with life.) Muslim art veered away from the representation of the human form. As we saw in the case of the Ummayad Mosque at Damascus and similar monuments, Muslim art and architecture remained magnificent; but it moved rapidly, in the course of the seventh and early eighth centuries, in the direction of abstract, floral imagery, across which moved the steady, Arabic script of citations from the Qur'ân.

Christians under Muslim rule were affected by these developments. In Palestine and Jordan, for instance, Christian churches of this time seem to have acknowledged the validity of Muslim criticisms. The mosaics on the floors of many churches were changed, around 700, so as to replace living creatures with floral designs. It is tantalizing testimony of debates on images which must have taken place all over the Middle East, in Jewish, Muslim, and Christian circles.[9]

Not all of this debate between Muslims, Jews, and Christians touched Byzantium. Their Iconophile enemies accused the Iconoclasts of having been directly influenced by Muslim views. This accusation can be discounted. The Iconoclast emperors, Leo III (717–741) and Constantine V (741–775) considered themselves to be good Christians. And, as good Christians, they believed that the Christian congregations of their empire should not be encouraged to turn, in their time of need, to unreliable objects of devotion. They should not pin their hopes on "inanimate and speechless images, made of material colors, which bring no benefit."[10]

In the opinion of the Iconoclasts, what the Iconophiles presented as "holy" images were no such thing. They were too close for comfort to the little images of the gods which pagans were remembered to have used. The remains of once-vibrant pagan shrines dotted the landscape of Anatolia, over which Byzantine and Islamic armies maneuvered every year. The populations of many areas of Anatolia had only been Christianized for a century or so. The charge that the veneration of "holy" images revived pagan idolatry was easy to believe. It caused particular worry to conscientious bishops placed in the garrison cities of western Anatolia, which lay in the war zone between the Christian empire and its Muslim opponents.

What was never at stake, in this controversy, was whether art itself should continue in Byzantium. The Iconoclast emperors built splendid palaces, filled with animal and human figures. But palaces were not churches. Images might be used in profane contexts. The Iconoclast emperors did not follow the trend toward an entirely abstract art which characterized Islam. But they did believe that images were out of place in Christian churches. To make them special and to "worship" them, as many Christians appeared to have been doing, was an impious action, calculated to provoke the anger of God.

To Purge the Temple: The First Iconoclasm, 730–787

This was an age of emergency, the Byzantine equivalent of the Battle of Britain. What contemporaries remembered in the debate for and against the worship of images were not theological arguments. Rather, what counted for them were incidents in which God appeared to show his displeasure at the "idolatrous" worship of images. One example shows this clearly. When the Muslim armies invested the city of Nicaea, having penetrated down from Anatolia to within easy reach of the Sea of Marmara and of Constantinople itself, a Byzantine officer manning the walls spotted an image of the Virgin. The image had probably been brought out by believers to parade along the walls of Nicaea so as to invoke her protection. He took up a stone and hurled it at the image, knocking it off its stand. He then trampled upon it until the wooden panel broke. Sure enough, the Muslim army withdrew. To the Iconoclasts involved in the defence of Nicaea (but by no means to the Iconophiles!) the officer's gesture had been a pious act. By stopping an "idolatrous" practice, he had pleased God and so caused the withdrawal of the threatening Muslim army.[11]

From 730 to 787, the initiative lay with the Iconoclasts. Iconoclast emperors and their advisers claimed to offer to their subjects something better than icons. They upheld the image of the Cross. The abstract sign of the Cross was a symbol of unquestioned visual power. The Cross was a symbol which every Byzantine Christian shared, and which every Muslim was known to despise. It had the weight of the past behind it. The Cross had been the "victory-bringing sign" under whose auspices Constantine was believed to have won his battles and to have founded the Christian empire. To force the Cross to the foreground, so that it should replace all other images, was the sign of a Christian empire stripped for battle and reunited to its triumphant past. For the Iconoclast emperors, there was no such thing as an "Iconoclast controversy" for the simple reason that their position seemed, at first sight, to be utterly uncontroversial. As so many Roman emperors had done before them, they would save the present by going back to the past. They would revive the days of Constantine. Under the Cross alone, and without the help of icons, true Christian emperors would relive the victories of Constantine the Great, the first Christian emperor.[12]

The emperor who initiated this policy, Leo III (717–741), had the advantage of having begun his reign with a spectacular sign of God's blessing. In 717, he saved Constantinople from a major Arab invasion. As we saw at the end of chapter 13, Leo used the devastating "Greek fire" (a new invention, brought to Constantinople by refugee Syrians who had gained from the petroleum-rich regions of northern Iraq knowledge of the chemistry of substances that would burn on the surface of water) to destroy the Arab fleet which had gathered beneath the walls of the city. Leo's decision to act against images coincided with a terrifying volcanic eruption in the Aegean, in 726. As ashes darkened the sky above Constantinople, a new sign of the Cross, its power acclaimed by an inscription, was set up over the entrance to the Palace. Bishops on the frontier received tacit permission to destroy images in the churches much as they would destroy pagan idols. The Byzantines were the "people of God" like the People of Israel. They now thought of themselves as being as beleaguered as the People of Israel had been. Leo feared that his empire might be altogether deserted by God, as the People of Israel had once been deserted by him, because, by worshipping images, they had lapsed into idolatry.[13]

Thus the first phase of what we call "the Iconoclast controversy" took place in an atmosphere of public emergency. The controversy was not allowed to escalate. Apart from occasional vicious acts of violence by Iconoclast officials (acts which gained in the telling in later, Iconophile histories of the period) a lifeboat mentality prevailed at Constantinople. A small governmental class and an upper clergy, largely recruited from that class, were anxious to maintain what little remained of the Christian empire. They tended to follow a firm, imperial lead.

Leo's son was appropriately named Constantine V (741–775), after Constantine the Great. He knew what he wanted – that his Christian subjects should pin their hopes on trustworthy objects of devotion. As his armies slowly turned the tide of the Muslim advance, he could count on the loyalty of the populations which he had defended so successfully, and on the active enthusiasm of troops who proved increasingly victorious. The soldiers knew that they had won their battles without the help of icons. There was no need for this new Constantine to hurry. Only in 754 did Constantine V assemble a council of the Church, in his suburban palace at Hiereia, to secure a definitive declaration, on theological grounds, of the illegitimacy of image-worship. Only in 765 did he permit the lynching of a leading Iconophile, Saint Stephen the Younger. Next year (after a failed attempt at a conspiracy against him) he singled out for public humiliation lay persons and monks who did not follow the imperial policy.[14]

This policy was clear. Constantine would purge the Church of occasions for "idolatry" just as the pious king Hezekiah of Israel had once "purged" the Temple of Jerusalem of the "idol" of a brazen serpent. By so doing, Hezekiah had turned away the danger of invasion and conquest by the Assyrians. Facing imminent conquest by their "Assyrians," the Muslims, the Byzantine emperors would do the same. They would purge their temples (that is, the churches) of idols (the icons). Sometime in around 750, the large basilica church of Saint Irene was repaired. Saint Irene was a prominent church. It stood between the great church of the Hagia Sophia and the ancient capitol of Byzantium (on the edge of what is now the Top Kapi Palace). Constantine V went out of his way to fill the apse with ethereal green mosaic, in which an entirely abstract sign of the Cross stood out in silver, like a triumphant sign shining from the depths of heaven. Around it, in a stately Greek script, ran an inscription from Psalm 65:

> *Holy is Thy Temple. Thou art wonderful in righteousness.*
> *Hear us, O God our Savior, the hope of all the ends of the earth.*

The combination of an abstract Cross, a renewed church as splendid as the "purged" Temple of Jerusalem, and a triumphal citation from the Psalms was very much the message which the Iconoclast emperors had wished to communicate to their subjects.[15]

"Why is it that the Christians all experience defeat?" The Balkan Crisis and the Second Iconoclasm, 787–842

Not all of Constantine V's subjects, however, had agreed with this particular formula for deliverance. The death of Constantine V in 775 and the weakening of his dynasty led to a drastic swing of policy. When it came to an issue as charged as the safety of the empire, it was a matter of either/or. A council was summoned in 787 by the empress-regent Irene (the widowed daughter-in-law of Constantine V) in the name of her son, Constantine VI, to bring an end to Iconoclasm. This event, known as the Second Council of Nicaea, was a clamorous victory for the Iconophiles. Even the site of the council, at Nicaea, was deliberately chosen so as to make the council appear to be a triumphal re-enactment of Constantine's first "worldwide" council. (The truth was that the bishops did not dare to meet in Constantinople, where opinion was largely in favor of the former Iconoclast emperors.)[16]

Not surprisingly, the restoration of images did not last. By 815, what is known as "the second Iconoclasm" was back in power. For the best part of a century, strong, successful rule had come to be associated with the absence of images. All that was needed was a renewed public emergency for Icono- clasm to be re-instituted as the policy of the emperors. This happened as a result of a major crisis in the Balkans.

The endless warfare between Byzantium and Islam had overshadowed Balkan affairs. Yet, ever since the Great Plague of the age of Justinian (as we have seen in chapter 7) the hinterland of the Balkans slipped out of the con- trol of the Byzantine emperors. The empire retained its grip on the coastline; but in the mountainous hinterland large swathes of territory became "state- less" zones. Slav settlers moved into them. The Slavs kept a low profile. They tended not to produce aggressive military leaders. Rather they looked for leadership to the nomadic confederacies which had formed to the north of the Danube, in the steppelands of Moldavia and the Ukraine. First the Avars and then the Bulgars acted, as it were, as a "counter-empire" to Byzantium. Their presence effectually neutralized imperial attempts to dominate the Slavs and to regain control of the Balkans.

Hence, only a generation after the apparent victory of the Iconodules at the Council of Nicaea, Constantinople found itself overshadowed, once again, by a semi-nomadic Bulgarian Khanate, which had established itself on both sides of the Danube in the course of the eighth century. The Bulgars called themselves "Children of the Huns." They were the most recent example of a nomadic style of overlordship. From their base on the Danube, they threat- ened the rich, disciplined plains of Thrace, on which Constantinople de- pended for its food supply. Though they came to rule large Christian populations, the Bulgar Khans were deliberately opaque to Christianity. In 811, Khan Krum (802–814) defeated and killed the emperor Nicephorus. Nothing like it had happened since the death of the emperor Valens at Adrianople in 378. Krum turned the emperor's skull into a drinking-cup with which to share the wine of triumph with his Slav allies.[17]

Fortunately, Krum died in 814, but not before his armies had reached the walls of Constantinople. Nicephorus' successor, Leo V, knew what he should do. The message was clear. The revived worship of icons had, once again, angered God:

> Why is it that the Christians all experience defeat at the hands of the [pagan] nations? [Leo was said to have asked] I think it is due to the worship of images and nothing else . . . Only those who have not vener- ated them have died natural deaths, and have been escorted with honor to the Imperial Tombs . . .
>
> It is they whom I intend to imitate in rejecting images, so that, having lived a long life, I and my son should keep the empire to the fourth and fifth generations.[18]

With all eyes upon him, at the Epiphany ceremony at the Hagia Sophia, Leo deliberately passed by a representation of Christ and his Mother in the form of a great roundel woven on the cloth that covered the great altar. He made sure that everyone noticed that he did not bow before it. He made clear, by this gesture, that believing Christians should not show an "idolatrous" degree of respect toward religious images. Under Leo's successors, Michael II (820–829) and Theophilus (829–842), images remained out of favor. But, this time, they were ignored rather than attacked.

The "Second Iconoclasm" was the product of cultivated men. It was much less raw and more reflective than were the emergency-driven policies of Leo III and Constantine V. It was less a matter of attacking images as "idols," whose worship angered God, as of questioning the ability of any religious image to capture adequately the unearthly glory of Christ and the saints. As the product of a mere human artist, the icon was doomed to be an unreliable guide to the supernatural realities which it claimed to represent. Consequently, there was no good reason, intellectual or religious, why Christians, who had been provided by God with so many satisfying visible symbols of their religion (the sacraments and the sign of the Cross), should go out of their way to lavish devotion on little painted images.[19]

"Led by visible images": John of Damascus and the Theology of Images

Ironically, Iconoclasm was finally undermined by the success of its imperial sponsors. The pressure of Muslim invasions diminished. The beleaguered Byzantine empire of the 730s clambered back painfully, by the year 840 and afterwards, into the position of a world power. After 840, an unprecedented degree of wealth and leisure returned to the elites of Constantinople. With this came a greater degree of cultural self-confidence. After 840, we find that Greek diplomatic missions to Baghdad made capital out of the superiority of Greek culture. As we have seen, in chapter 13, the Califs greatly prized "Greek" wisdom at their court. Byzantine ambassadors now pointed out that their Greek empire was the fountainhead of all this wisdom. Byzantium, and not the upstart Islamic empire, was the crown of civilization.[20]

Iconophiles of the period after 840 looked back on their own past in a similar mood. After a century of dislocation and hand-to-mouth existence, they had reached a new plateau of culture and sophistication. They dismissed Iconoclasm as a thoroughly un-Byzantine aberration. They claimed that only "half-barbarous" rulers, devoid of Greek culture, could have so mistaken the rich traditions of their Church.

We should not be misled by these assertions. They were made after the event. Throughout the eighth and early ninth centuries, cultivated Greek clergymen had frequently criticized the worship of images. The population, also, had been divided on the issue. In dangerous times, they had no wish to offend God by idolatry. It was a caricature of the past to present it in terms of "barbarous" Iconoclast emperors riding rough-shod over the wishes of a naturally Iconophile population. The equation of the worship of icons with the immemorial traditions of the Greek Church was made only after the victory of the supporters of images.

In fact, a firm Iconophile position emerged for the first time only at the very end of the controversy, in the period between the Iconophile Council of Nicaea in 787 and the official "Triumph of Orthodoxy" in 843. It is important to realize this. The victory of icons did not represent, at the time, the "natural" victory of the immemorial religious ideals of the majority of Greek Christians. Rather, the period of the "Triumph of Orthodoxy" and the measures taken to consolidate the Iconophile position were marked by creative new solutions, which had little to do with the past. What emerged at that time was new and destined to last.

In the eighth century, the Byzantine empire had almost collapsed, only to remake itself into a new state in such a way that it would endure for centuries as a major power in eastern Europe and the Middle East. Without the Iconoclast emperors and their willingness to jettison much of the cumbersome legacy of the later Roman empire, Constantinople would almost certainly have fallen to the Muslims long before 1453. In much the same way, the Iconophiles jettisoned much of the East Roman Christian past. They gained control of the elites of the empire in the course of the ninth century. Having done so, they used their victory to incorporate the worship of images into what was, in effect, a novel religious system. They showed that they were as much "reformers," in their own way, as the Iconoclasts had been. While they claimed to have revived the immemorial traditions of the Church, they were prepared to take control of popular religious practice in a new way and to make it serve their own, new needs. It is their measured synthesis (and not the more dramatic but piecemeal forms of the worship of images associated with previous centuries) which has endured for over a thousand years in all regions of the Orthodox world. Let us look, briefly, at some of the intellectual underpinnings and the consequences of this silent revolution in religious practice.

The consolidation of the Iconophile position was due to three great protagonists. Two were active in Constantinople immediately after the Second Council of Nicaea of 787. The great abbot Theodore of Studios (759–826) showed a hatred of compromise and a fighting spirit on behalf of the worship of icons which fired the lay and religious elites of Constantinople. The theological ideas of the Iconoclast emperor Constantine V were carefully refuted by the patriarch of Constantinople, Nicephorus (750–828), in his *Antirrhetikos* (written in 818–20). Together, Theodore and Nicephorus regained the intellectual high ground for the Iconodules. They promoted the worship of icons from being an intense but largely unreflective practice of many Christians into being a touchstone of orthodoxy. They argued with remarkable intellectual bravura that not only was it permissible to represent central doctrines of the faith (such as the full humanity of Christ) through images, but that, in fact, such doctrines could not be properly expressed *without* images. Icons were not merely useful "illustrations" of the faith. They were a *sine qua non* for its correct expression.[21]

In the long run, however, the most authoritative voice came from a century earlier, and from a long way from Constantinople. The views of a distant and hitherto little-known Syrian, John of Damascus (ca.665–ca.749), only came to be adopted in the generations after the Council of Nicaea. From then on, in Orthodox Christian circles, John Damascene (as he is usually called), was acclaimed as the last great Father of the Church, and his defense of holy images has been held to be the classic statement of the Orthodox position. Yet, although John, like all other Iconophiles, claimed to defend the perennial wisdom of the Church since its earliest days, his writings reveal a comprehensive and thought-through attitude to Christian art that was entirely new. His defense of images was as much a novel departure, in comparison with all that had gone before, as was the radicalism of the Iconoclasts. Let us linger a little, therefore, on the thought of this remarkable man.

John was not in any way a "Byzantine" as this had come to be defined at Constantinople in the war-torn years of the eighth century. He belonged to an older and more open age. As we saw in chapter 13, John was a Christian Arab. He was a pious member of a powerful administrative family of Christian Arabs long settled at Damascus. In the manner of generations of cultivated and pious public servants, John left his father's profession to adopt a life of ascetic retirement, much as Gregory I had done when he retired from the prefecture of Rome to his family monastery. John is said to have become a monk in the great monastery of Saint Sabas, in the Wadi Saba near Jerusalem.

Political frontiers meant little to John. He thought of himself, first and foremost, as an "Orthodox" Christian, a supporter of the Chalcedonian faith with which (as we have seen) the "Byzantine" emperors were still identified. Though probably an Arabic-speaker from his boyhood, as a theologian John wrote and thought in Greek. This was the learned language of his fellow-

Orthodox wherever they might be. When he sat down to write his *Defense of Holy Images* and other treatises in defence of orthodoxy, between 726 and 733, both Muslim and early Iconoclast arguments were already known to him. It was typical of the embattled and authoritarian mood of the Byzantine empire, that only a Christian living under Muslim rule was free to write in defense of images, and that (due to careful Muslim protection of the Christian communities within their domains) he enjoyed complete leisure to do so and had access to unparalleled library resources still maintained in the monasteries of the Judaean Desert. It was also characteristic of the regionalism which had fallen across the entire Christian world, that John's writings only came to be well known in Byzantium after 800. Only then did they come to play an essential role in the formation of a Byzantine theology of images. But it was John's theology of the image which helped to prepare for the definitive victory of Iconophile ideas associated with the "Triumph of Orthodoxy" of 843.[22]

John's most decisive intellectual maneuver was to claim for images the same unambiguous ability to represent the unseen that earlier authors had claimed only for the liturgy and for the sacraments of the Church.

> Images [he wrote] are a source of profit, help and salvation for us since they make hidden things clearly manifest to us, enabling us to perceive realities otherwise hidden to human eyes.[23]

He did this largely under the influence of two remarkable works, the *Celestial* and the *Ecclesiastical Hierarchies* of Dionysius the Areopagite. This crucial author was a Christian Platonist of the sixth century. But John and his contemporaries believed that he was none other than an Athenian philosopher who had become the disciple of Saint Paul. His thought was held to reflect the opinions of the very earliest Christians.

In his treatises, Pseudo-Dionysius endowed the entire material world with a sense of the holy. God lay behind it. He had created the visible universe to act as his own, immense icon. A vast "code" of visible symbols, deliberately placed by God in the world, linked humanity to an invisible God. The physical, visual aspects of Christian worship were part of that great code. God was far above human imagination. But God drew the human race toward him through a proliferation of visible symbols. This was the cornerstone of Pseudo-Dionysius' argument: "we are led to the perception of God by . . . visible images."[24]

Religious images, therefore, were not a mere product of human choice and of human invention. They were essential to God's revelation of himself. They formed a bridge, wished by God himself, with which to cross the vertiginous chasm between the seen and the unseen. The figures which believers saw on icons or on the walls of churches were what God wished them to see. They were clearly recognizable tokens which led the mind to the invisible persons that they represented.

By such arguments John of Damascus answered the acute anxiety which had driven Iconoclast criticism of the worship of images. The Iconoclasts had not trusted the unguided visual imagination. For them, as for many Christians in former centuries, there was no reason why a saint, the Virgin, or Christ as imagined by an artist should be related in any way to the "real" person that it claimed to represent. The contorted, haunting forms of classical statues showed only too plainly how pagans of the distant past had been led by demons to dream up images of their gods. Were Christian "holy" images, painted by mere artists, to be treated as any more reliable? John's symbolic system of the universe, based on Pseudo-Dionysius, answered this criticism with great force. What Christians represented on their "holy" images was, basically, what God, the saints, and the angels wished them to represent, as a merciful concession to the weakness of the human mind.

But there was a price to be paid for absence of anxiety about images. This was the acceptance of guidance from the Church alone. John of Damascus and his successors insisted not only that images had always been venerated, in some form or other. They also asserted that every image that was venerated in their own days had been venerated, in exactly the same form, since the days of Christ and the Apostles. The Gospel written by Saint Luke was said to have included illustrations. These illustrations were the prototype of all future Christian representations of the life of Christ. All images, therefore, reached back ultimately to the days of Christ and the Apostles. It was a breathtaking claim, which made time stand still. But it was made for a good reason – to ensure that not a shadow of doubt could fall between the form taken by images, as they had evolved in ninth-century Byzantium, and the beloved persons whom they were said to represent.[25]

"As she has appeared in visions": The "Triumph of Orthodoxy" (843) and the Training of the Christian Visual Imagination

John's assertion that icons had always been part of Christian worship was further validated, in the ninth century, by appeals to visions. For visions added up-to-date confirmation of the Iconophile belief that the Church had always possessed a complete and totally reliable set of "identikit" represen-

ıly figure. The Christian imagination did not need to fear
tself in vain on arbitrary creations.

ьciate what this meant to Byzantines through one well-known
.. ın 867, a mosaic of the Virgin with Christ on her lap was set up for
..ıe first time in the apse of the Hagia Sophia. The mosaic used all the devices
of a self-consciously revived classical style in a deliberate, even fussy manner, to emphasize the three-dimensional and hence the "real" quality of Christ
and his Mother. Hyper-real by Byzantine standards, the new mosaic was an
awkward presence in that vast and ancient church. Even today it stands out
in marked contrast to the faceless glory of the golden mosaic dome and the
shimmering, multicolored marbles set up, three centuries previously, by the
emperor Justinian. For Justinian was very much a Christian of the early sixth
century. He had made little use of images. Rather, he and his architects had
believed that the sheer blaze of sunlight trapped in the dome and the haunting shimmer of multicolored marbles had done nothing less than bring heaven
down to earth in his great new church.

But, in 867, cultivated Byzantines no longer thought as late Roman persons such as Justinian had done. For them, to look up at the newly installed
mosaic was to look past it. It was to see the apse open on to a scene which
was believed to have always been available to believers, and which had always been exactly as they now saw it. It was to see the Virgin and her child
as they really were, and as they had appeared to believers in all ages. This
was no "imagined" image, the product of the random fantasy of an artist. It
was a real vision, frozen in mosaic.

> Before our eyes stands motionless the Virgin carrying the Creator in her
> arms as an infant, depicted in painting as she is in writings and as she has
> appeared in visions.[26]

After 843, the churches of the Orthodox Byzantine world came to be filled
with such visions, frozen in mosaic and fresco. What Orthodox believers
now saw, on entering a Byzantine church from the ninth century onwards,
was no longer a space throbbing with faceless, shimmering glory, as Justinian's Hagia Sophia had been. But neither would their eye be drawn to a single, heavily charged image, which stood out from all the rest, as an object of
special devotion, as was the case in many seventh-century churches. What
they now saw were rows upon rows of human faces, arranged on the walls
as if they were all staring down upon the worshipper from the great court of
heaven. The saints were brought into the present in orderly ranks. The faces
and figures of saints and Apostles, of the Virgin, and of Christ himself rose
up the walls, from ground level, each one occupying its accustomed, care-

fully allotted space. Every church endowed in this way with imag
Damascus had said, acted as a "spiritual hospital."[27] Sick souls co
any church in the Byzantine world and find in it the same comfortii
of a heaven whose saintly inhabitants pressed in around them on th   ...is
with quiet, clearly recognizable faces.

We must remember that this was not how Christian churches had looked in previous centuries. In the fifth and sixth centuries, the founders and do-nors of new churches, lay persons and clergymen alike, had filled the basili-cas of the eastern empire with every form of visual magnificence. They had striven to bring Paradise down to earth; and it was still a very ancient Para-dise. On the mosaic floors of churches all over the eastern Mediterranean, Paradise lay all around the believer in exuberant floral decorations, in frank hunting scenes, and in classical personifications of the virtues and of the elements. Majestic figures of saints, of the Prophets, of Christ, and of the Virgin were also present on the walls. But they were swamped by a greater, less-focused sense of majesty. In Justinian's church of San Vitale, in Ravenna – to take only one well-known example of a late antique church – many holy figures were represented. But all around them, from the top of the vault to the floors, they were flanked by a bright green jungle of fern-like ornament. The eye of the believer was encouraged to lose itself in this jungle. For it spoke, in a language taken directly from the ancient Near East, of a Garden of Paradise, a place of faceless, vegetable abundance, where the righteous would find their rest. In such a church, the liturgy also made full use of incense, of chanting, and of shimmering lights. It engulfed the senses. In church, worshippers were surrounded with the sights, the smells, and the sounds of Paradise.[28]

After the ninth century, it is as if the heavy atmosphere of Paradise had cleared a little. The liturgy remained as splendid as ever. But what drew the visual imagination of Byzantines was no longer, to such an extent, the idea of Paradise as a place of supra-human joy and abundance, which lay tanta-lizingly close to the material world. As we saw in chapter 6, in the West, Gregory of Tours had looked for such a Paradise. In the East, also, early Muslims sought a similar Paradise in the garden-like mosaics of the Great Mosque of Damascus. By contrast, what was expressed most forcibly in icons was something different. It was the desire to see clearly recognizable human faces of the saints and, through these faces, to enter into a direct relationship with invisible protectors – with Christ, with the Virgin, and with the saints.[29]

The need to establish a relationship with invisible human protectors had driven the early cult of images. Images had made the saints "present" to their worshippers. The need of Byzantine believers to feel that Christ and the saints were close to hand in all their daily emergencies – in sickness, in the swearing of oaths, at the baptism of their children, in childbirth and infertility, at moments of success and of danger – had given to the Iconophiles a "low-profile" tenacity in their defence of images which, ultimately, wore down the high-minded reform of public worship introduced by the Iconoclasts.

From the ninth century onward, however, it was the Church which claimed to control this fierce need for the "presence" of the saints. Rather than attempt to abolish such practices, by effectively excluding them from the regular worship of the Church, as the Iconoclasts had done, the Iconophile clergy, from the ninth century onward, stepped in to take charge of lay devotion. An already existing devotion to icons was "clericalized." It was pulled into the gravitational field of the Church. The clergy now insisted that icons should be concentrated, in an orderly fashion, within the walls of the churches and that their worship should be intimately connected with the regular celebration of the liturgy.

This meant, in fact, a considerable "flattening" of the holiness ascribed to individual icons. In the sixth and seventh centuries, it had been quite normal for a heavy charge of worship to be directed to one particular holy picture in a church, in a city, or in a private setting. That particular painting and that one only seemed to bear the "presence" of an invisible person. It was an "effective," a "miraculous" image, and all others were not. Now all icons claimed equal respect because all of them had been declared equally holy. They were holy because of the holiness of the persons whom they represented and because of their placing in a church where the liturgy was celebrated. Individual icons no longer "broke ranks" as they had done in an earlier time.[30]

Slowly but surely, the visual world of Byzantium had come to be different from its late antique past. Religious images now clustered in churches and (later) in the special "icon corner" of private houses. But they had vanished from places where they had once been scattered with reckless abundance in early centuries. In the fourth, fifth, and sixth centuries there had been no lack of Christian religious images. They were all over the place. Christians had worn images of holy persons embroidered on their robes. Figures of saints and martyrs were stamped on cutlery and on tableware. In Syria, even the doorposts of stables carried images of Symeon the Stylite, so as to protect the livestock within. But these representations were not seen as icons. They were talismans. The holy "presences" portrayed on them acted on their own accord to ward off the demons. They were not meant to engage the eyes of human worshippers. Rather, they were there to beat back the "evil eye" of nonhuman, malevolent powers.

After the ninth century, this function of the religious image was silently abandoned. What came to count, in the view of the clergy at least, was the creation of precise "habits of the heart," through the conscious worship of the tranquil, carefully characterized faces seen on icons. It was on the walls of the churches and in the "icon corner" of the home – and nowhere else – that the saints were "present." It was conscious human prayer addressed to loved and powerful human beings, as believers stood before their icons – and not the mute power of talismans – which saved the faithful from harm in a dangerous world. Those who sought personal protection of a more intimate kind now resorted not to amulets, but to *enkolpia* – to exquisite portable icons, worn around the neck, each of which showed a clearly designated protector-saint.[31]

Altogether, the claim of the Iconodules to have done no more than bring back the ancient traditions of the Church has obscured the extent of their achievement. Never before in the history of Christianity had a determined and highly cultivated elite taken in hand, with such firmness and with such theoretical certainty, the schooling of the visual imagination of an entire "baptized people."

Not surprisingly, of course, icons continued to "break ranks." They still spoke to the heart, and so to fiercely private needs. Meanings clustered around religious images which the theorists of icons could do little to control. Icons did not always function in the manner that their clerical defenders claimed that they should. Miraculous icons, for instance, remained a constant feature of the Orthodox world. They spoke, they wept, they moved. Some even showed the "spirit" which resided in them by spinning around, when carried in processions in Constantinople and elsewhere, as if their bearers were possessed.[32]

Nor did the sharp sense of privacy which grew from standing alone in the silent "presence" of an icon vanish. One could say things to icons which one could never say to one's priest. Up to this day, a part of the marble paving of the narthex of the Hagia Sophia is visibly lower than the rest. A pilgrim to Constantinople in the fourteenth century was told why this was so. It had been worn down by the feet of innumerable believers who came to kiss the icon of the "Confessor Savior," which hung to the left of the doors of the main church: it was the image "before which people confess their sins when they cannot confess them before a father confessor because of the shame."[33]

This late medieval pilgrim, we should note, came from Novgorod, a Russian trading city near the Baltic. By the year 1400, the Orthodox Christianity of Byzantium – and not the Christianity of the Latin West – had become the religion of the Balkans and of much of eastern Europe. Soon Russian Orthodoxy would spread as far as the Arctic Ccircle and, within a few centuries, eastward as far as the Pacific. The greatest and most lasting triumph of post-

Iconoclast Byzantium lay in the diplomatic offensive of the late ninth and tenth centuries which led to the conversion of the Slavs of the Balkans (in around 860), of the kingdom of Kiev in the Ukraine (in 987), and eventually, through Kiev, of the northern Slav lands that came to be associated with Russia.[34]

It is not the concern of this book to recount what was, in itself, a remarkable venture in Christianization. That story belongs to the history of another Christendom, not that of the West. But it is worthwhile remembering, in this chapter, that what the Byzantine state, as a political empire, had lost forever, in surrendering the Middle East to Islam, it more than regained in the form of a spiritual empire which embraced the huge territories of eastern Europe and Russia in Asia in a single Orthodox faith.

For the Orthodox Slavs, Constantinople, and not Rome, was the center of the world and the fountainhead of all culture. In the year 1415, a Russian monk, Epifanij the Wise, wrote to the famous Byzantine icon painter, Feofan (Theophanes) the Greek, who was then working in Russia:

> I ask your Wisdom to paint for me in colors a representation of that great church of Hagia Sophia at Constantinople erected by Justinian . . . Some say that in quality and size it is like the Moscow Kremlin, so large it is to walk around . . . Please represent this . . . so that I can put it at the beginning of a book and imagine myself in Constantinople.[35]

But Byzantium was close not only to the learned. Up to the present, in a vast sweep, from the Balkans to Alaska, it is still possible to step into an Orthodox church and to be confronted with the same vision of a heavenly court, each member of which is clearly defined by a facial expression and by a style of dress that is a recognizable echo of the revived classical art of post-Iconoclast Byzantium. When John of Damascus, a Christian Arab living under Muslim rule, wrote his treatises, in around the year 730, he could not have known that the cult of icons would be the most direct legacy of all of Byzantium to regions and to ages of which he and his contemporaries could not have dreamed.

Byzantium and the West: Charlemagne and the Council of Frankfurt (794)

But this is to anticipate by several centuries. If we return to where we left off, in the West around the year 730, we find a world to which the Byzantine empire had become increasingly distant. The Iconoclast controversy took place in an empire forced to turn in upon itself. Throughout the eighth century, the imperial armies had been pinned down by a seemingly endless defensive war on the eastern frontier. For most Byzantines, the West dropped out of sight. Byzantine control continued in southern Italy. But in order to retain Sicily as the westernmost bulwark of a naval empire based on the Aegean, all Italy to the north of Calabria was neglected. In 751, Ravenna fell to the Lombards. King Aistulf held court in the former palace of the Exarch, and doubtless offered his gifts, as a good western Catholic, on the altar of San Vitale, under the silent gaze of Justinian and Theodora. Rome was next. If the popes in Rome were to maintain their autonomy, they had to look for new protectors.

The popes soon found such protectors. After 751, the northern Franks, and not the emperors of Constantinople, came to be recognized as the arbiters of Italian politics and as the privileged protectors of the popes in Rome. At the Council of Nicaea, in 787, pope Hadrian's envoys from Rome spoke with enthusiasm of the pope's model "spiritual son," Charles, king of the Franks. We know this "Charles," of course, as Charlemagne. Charles had already taken over northern Italy. According to the glowing account of the pope's envoys, he had "conquered all the West" and had even "subjected barbarous tribes to the Christian faith." To the Byzantines at Nicaea, it was unwelcome news. A mere "barbarian" king should not be praised for doing what only "Roman" emperors should do. That part of the pope's letter was not translated into Greek.[36]

When the *Acta* of the Council of Nicaea were sent to Rome and forwarded to the Frankish court in a Latin translation, the clerics around Charles, for their part, were pleasantly disappointed. It struck them as a slipshod and theologically incorrect document. It showed that the Church "of the Greeks" no longer held a reliable form of Christianity. The Latin Church had done better. Latins, they claimed, had realized that images were essentially neutral. Images were not to be "adored," as the Council of Nicaea seemed to suggest that they should be; but neither were they so important that they had to be smashed. In the opinion of the clergy gathered to advise Charles, the Greeks had wasted their energies on a trivial matter. A memorandum on the worship of images was prepared by an expert, Theodulph (the future bishop of Orléans).[37]

The memorandum was read out to Charles and carefully explained to the Frankish monarch. Notes in the margin of the surviving manuscript record Charles' reactions. They provide a precious insight into the outlook of the new master of Europe. Theodulph wrote that the Greek Church should not have acted on its own: "[it] should have sent to the churches of all the regions around it to enquire of them whether images should or should not be adored." *Probe*: "That's it!" was Charles' comment. Theodulph observed that it was the duty of bishops to teach the "people beloved of Christ." *Recte*, "of course!" was what Charles replied.[38]

And when Charles said "of course!" he meant it. When, in 794, he summoned a council of all the bishops of his extensive kingdom to meet in his palace at Frankfurt, he had no doubt as to his role. Like the Byzantine emperors, he also saw it as his duty to reform the Latin Church as a whole. And this Church was exactly like its Byzantine peer, in that it believed that it possessed the fullness of Christian truth. The council declared that the decrees of the "Greek" Council of Nicaea in favor of the worship of images were to be "completely rejected and scorned."[39] Nor were the Byzantines the only victims of this mood of high confidence in the theologians gathered around Charles. Representatives of the great Visigothic Church, now broken by Muslim conquest, were also condemned for heresy. The proud "micro-Christendom" of Spain had derived its theology from long reflection on the works of Augustine and had expressed this theology in a carefully composed, local liturgy. Now this local theology was found wanting. The condemnation of Elipandus, the archbishop of Toledo, for having advocated incorrect views on the human nature of Christ, derived from the local traditions of his Church, was a characteristically high-handed gesture. It was due to the emergence of a new, more academic, standard of orthodoxy, based upon what a group of scholars patronized by Charles considered to be the correct reading of "Roman" texts.[40]

Times had changed. While the eastern empire had been engaged in fighting its way back from the brink of annihilation, a new political order had emerged in the West. It was connected with a new dynasty, with the "Carolingian" descendants of Charles Martel. Both its rulers and its clerical elite were confident that they knew how to absorb and to educate whole new Christian peoples. They made clear, in a decisive half-century, that they would do so in a manner very different from that of the Greeks. By the end of the eighth century, as the Council of Frankfurt of 794 made plain, they were confident that they lived in a uniquely privileged Christendom, and that they were even entitled to an "empire" which could be treated as the equal of the "empire of the Greeks." To find out how this situation came about, we must go back to around the year 700, so as to trace the build-up of Frankish power and the extension of a distinctive form of Frankish Christianity in northern Europe.

Map 9   Continental Europe

CHAPTER 18

The Closing of the Frontier: Frisia and Germany

A New Political Order

The middle of the eighth century saw the emergence, in Europe and in the Middle East, of political systems that had lost contact with their roots in the ancient world. East Rome became "Byzantium." It lost its civilian elites and its worldwide horizons. It became a beleaguered, but more cohesive, state. The Iconoclast controversy showed the extent to which its new rulers were prepared to seek the much-needed favor of God by calling to account customs inherited from a richer, more easygoing past. New men from new territories – in the Byzantine empire, persons of military background from eastern Anatolia – had been forced to build fast, in a world that had lost many of its ancient landmarks.

In northwestern Europe, the Frankish state passed through a similar period of urgent turmoil. The nobility of Austrasia had emerged as a distinct group in the late sixth century. They controlled the frontier territories of northeastern Gaul and the lands east of the Rhine. After 700, they rallied increasingly to a family that came from the Maas/Meuse (in Belgium) and the Ardennes. This family was led by Pippin of Herstal (d.714). Pippin was the nephew of Gertrude of Nivelles (Belgium), whom we have already met (at the end of chapter 11) as an influential abbess. As "mayor of the palace," Pippin of Herstal had acted as the strong "vice-king" to a largely symbolic Merovingian ruler. Pippin's son, Charles, was later named, all too appositely, Charles Martel, Charles "the Hammer." He revived the ancient "terror of the Franks." By the time that he died in 741, Charles the Hammer had shown his supporters what success in war could do, in acquiring new wealth to be distributed among themselves. In 733, he stopped a Muslim army on its way to loot Tours, and, from then onwards, Charles' armies looted the Christian regions of the south and imposed a northern hegemony on them.

WESTERN EUROPE ca. 700–ca. 840

Willibrord 658–739
founds Echternach 698

Pippin of Herstal
mayor of the palace 687–714

Radbod king of the Frisians 685–719

Boniface 675–754
arrives in Francia 716
destroys Oak of Thunor at
Geismar 723/4

Charles Martel
mayor of the palace 715—741
Battle of Poitiers 733

Boniface founds Fulda 744
Condemnation of Aldebert 745

Vergil of Salzburg 745–784

Coronation and anointing of
Pippin II as king of the
Franks 751

Pope Stephen II anoints Pippin II 754

Boniface killed in northern
Frisia 754

Charlemagne 768–814
attacks Saxons 772
conquers Lombards 774
massacres Saxons at Verden 782
Capitulary on Saxony 785

Alcuin of York 735–804
abbot of St. Martin's at
Tours 797–804

Admonitio Generalis 789
Defeat of the Avars 792
Builds palace at Aachen 794
Crowned emperor at Rome 800

Theodulph bishop of Orléans 798–818
writes *Libri Carolini* 793
Ghaerbald bishop of Liège 785–809

Louis the Pious 814–840

Einhard writes *Life of Charlemagne*
824/836

Agobard bishop of Lyons 816–840

Stellinga Revolt in Saxony 841/3

Charles Martel's victory over the Muslims at the battle of Poitiers, in 733, is what is most usually remembered about him. His systematic ravaging of the south of France is passed over in silence. His greatest conquest, however, was less spectacular but more decisive. He took over Frankish Neustria. As we saw in chapter 11, Neustria had been the heartland of Merovingian Gaul. Paris and the rich, well-watered lands around the Seine lay at its center. It was the most stable and prosperous region in Europe. As we have seen, great royal and aristocratic monasteries had sprung up all over northern France in the course of the seventh century. These monasteries were supported by new agrarian wealth. Slowly but surely, the landowners of the region imposed a "seigneurial" system on the peasantry. Greater control of the peasantry enabled the aristocracy to regain, for the first time in four centuries, a level of security and of guaranteed affluence that had once been enjoyed by the villaowners of the Roman empire. In controlling Neustria, Charles controlled the economic and cultural core of northern Europe.[1]

The Frankish aristocracy had rallied grudgingly to the family of Pippin and Charles Martel. For much of his life, Charles Martel found himself faced by bitter enemies in a "winner take all" situation. But once he had emerged as victor, a consensus was formed around him and his family. Given an able leader, the combined aristocracies of Neustria and Austrasia found that they could strike anywhere, from Aquitaine and the Rhône valley to the Rhine estuary, the Black Forest, and the Danube, to extract wealth and to tighten up previous ties of submission. Ranging now far outside their homeland, the Franks became the dominant partners in a confederation of widely differing regions which had always been associated, in a looser fashion, with the hegemonial rule of the Merovingian kings.

The armies which Charles and his fellow-noblemen deployed were far from being exclusively made up of cavalry. Frankish warfare was sophisticated in its combination of horsemen, infantry, and siege-craft. But it was on their horses that the nobles now rode all over Europe, to pillage and browbeat distant regions. And even their horses, apparently, shared their confidence. In the next century, the great theologian Gottschalk, when dealing with the problem of divination, wrote that warhorses possessed a sixth sense: they became more frisky when they knew that their army would win. Accompanying a Frankish campaign, a thousand miles southeast of Francia, along the Dalmatian coast, Gottschalk had asked his godchild to observe the horses. He was proved right. The horses of the Frankish cavalry cavorted merrily, before yet another victorious charge.[2]

What we are witnessing, under Charles Martel, are the first stages of a process which would change the face of Europe in the course of the eighth century. The combined Frankish aristocracy of Neustria and Austrasia were on the way to becoming the first truly international elite since the Roman senatorial order of the fourth century. In Germany, in particular, Frankish noblemen had already penetrated the upper echelons of regions that had always been nominally subject to the Merovingian kings. They would eventually do this, also, as far apart as Italy and northern Spain. Like the Roman aristocracy, they were easygoing on matters of ethnicity and local culture as long as it was they who remained on top. They married into the local aristocracies. They became local landowners. They were quite prepared to judge their inferiors according to local laws. They used the regions in which they had settled as local power bases with which to challenge their colleagues (and especially, at this time, the upstart family of Pippin and Charles Martel). But, like the Romans, they did not lose their sense of belonging to a single, highly privileged group. Frankish noblemen (and their wives – who emerged at this time as tenacious guardians of aristocratic, family memories) watched each other across the length and breadth of Europe. It was "their" kingdom, the "kingdom of the Franks." Eventually, everyone who wished to advance in this new order became Franks (by marrying into the Frankish aristocracy), learned to behave like Franks and sought out the patronage of the Frankish rulers.[3]

Center and Periphery in Christian Europe

At the time of Charles Martel, however, it was far from certain what form the "Frankification" of the elites of northern Europe would take. In this respect, it is important to remember the Janus-like quality of the Frankish kingdom. It had been formed in a Roman frontier zone. In the sixth century, the ancient *limes* had still traced an unmistakable line, which marked the joining of two worlds. The weight of a long Roman and Christian past could be felt along the Moselle, the Rhine, and the Danube. Metz boasted 40 churches, some of which were already 400 years old. At Mainz, solid Roman walls enclosed venerable basilicas. South of the Danube, also, the pattern of a former Roman order was not yet totally expunged. Pockets of Christianity survived as the "folk religion" of "Romans." A Christian slave escaping southward from the woods of Saxony was heartened by the sight of Regensburg, with its ancient Roman walls and stone church.[4]

By the year 700, however, the division along the Rhine had become erased. To the east of the former Roman frontier, a Frankish system of landowning had spilled over from northern Gaul and the Rhine valley, and had begun to penetrate eastward into central Germany along the Main. Southern Germany, also, was affected by the same development. Both in the Black Forest area of the Alemanni and in Bavaria, the Frankish model showed that a local nobility, with strong rulers behind them, could tame a once-evasive peasantry in such a way as to extract an unprecedented surplus of wealth. For the elites of the region, it represented a disturbing and enticing development. Our modern maps of Europe make a clear distinction, along the Rhine, between France and Germany, and, to the north, between France, Belgium, and Holland. They do not do justice to the real frontiers of eighth-century Europe. At that time, the truly important frontier lay between the pagan lands of north and eastern central Europe and a "Frankish" style of society, long identified with Christianity, which stretched from modern northern France across the Rhine and up the Main deep into modern Germany.

The issue, in the early eighth century, was who would benefit from these developments. Greater wealth and authority for the part-Frankish local aristocracies could mean two things. Either these developments placed them in a position to act as poles of resistance to the upstart family of Charles Martel. Or they could be cowed or wooed into joining, with other members of the Frankish aristocracy, in the profitable landslide of his success. Nowhere was the "winner take all" situation which had developed in Francia, as a result of the rise of the family of Pippin and Charles Martel, more plain than in Germany.

It is against this immediate social and political background that we should place the development that has come to be known as the "Conversion of Germany." For the conversion of Germany was part of a larger process, in which the shape of northern Europe itself was at stake. The coming of Christianity to these regions amounted to a closing of the frontier. What had once been an open world, characterized by loose social and political structures and by far greater fluidity in its religious allegiances, found itself drawn into an ever-tighter system of political and religious control.

As a result of this process of consolidation, the lands to the north and east of the old Roman *limes* and its Frankish extension across the Rhine, came to appear truly peripheral. Viewed with Christian eyes, accustomed to the well-established Christianity of Francia, they seemed part of an older world. Frisia and Saxony, from the North Sea coast to the Teutoburger Wald, had remained staunchly pagan. The north German plain had always been a distinctive ecological zone, an extension across northern Europe of the sands of the North Sea. It was a zone of heathlands, abundant cattle, and scattered settlements, populated by independent-minded warrior farmers. The religious frontier between paganism and Christianity had come, for a short period, to coincide with a contrast between two landscapes.

Further to the south, in the region between the upper Rhine and the upper Danube, in what is now northern Switzerland and southwest Germany, in the area in and around the Black Forest, Christianity had long been present. This was the territory of the Alemanni. But the Christianity of the area was not organized on a Frankish model, with bishoprics and large monasteries. Christianity had remained, in effect, a family cult. The archaeology of the region between Strasbourg and Stuttgart shows Christian crosses made out of thin sheets of stamped gold scattered in many graves. At Wittislingen (near Nördlingen), an Alemannic lady was buried with a brooch that bore a perfect Christian epitaph, with classical echoes. But she lay among her family's prestige graves. There were churches. But these were small buildings in stone or wood, built over the grave of their founders, local priests and nobles. Well-organized villages show the presence of these noblemen. But their Christianity is revealed, by archaeology, to have been very much of a "do-it-yourself" nature. Altogether, the territories of the Alemanni provide a fascinating glimpse of a local Christianity establishing itself from the bottom up. This must have happened elsewhere in Europe and in the British Isles. But here we can see it clearly.[5]

Further east along the Danube, Christianity was a folk religion which had survived since Roman times. It had flourished with little clerical control. A pagan sorceress would bring animals to the local church, as a thank-offering for the success of her incantations. The panels around the tomb of Saint Corbinian (d.725), at Freising, included an image of a stallion with a gigantic extended penis. A reminder of an earlier, less discriminating age of ex-votos, it was later removed by Corbinian's more fastidious successors.[6]

In comparison with Francia, with its royal dynasty and aristocratic land-owners, the power of local chieftains in pagan Germany was weak. The Old Saxons functioned without a king. A caste of nobles were content to choose, by lot, a leader whom they would follow in wartime alone. Great holy trees were vital to the Old Saxons. They functioned as the sacral gathering points of their confederacies. Though organized in this apparently loose manner, the Old Saxons proved to be a formidable warrior-society, fully capable of terrorizing and subjugating their neighbors. Yet apart from their unusual social structure and their paganism, they were almost indistinguishable from the Franks, who had frequently made use of Saxon mercenaries. Hence, perhaps, the peculiar bitterness of the rivalry between the two groups. The pagan Old Saxons were what the Christian Franks had once been.

Altogether, the mercurial fluidity of a pagan society such as that of the Old Saxons confirmed the worst suspicions of western Christians. In Francia, Britain, and Ireland, kingship – and an increasingly strong kingship at that – was identified with civilization. An eighth-century Christian author wrote of the outermost edge of the world as ringed by ominously stateless societies, "by brutish peoples, without religion and without kings."[7] The solid structures of the Frankish state and the spectacular flowering of Christianity among the ambitious kings of Britain stood in disquieting contrast to the near-total opacity to the new faith of the kingless Old Saxons. The proper Christian "order" of strong, believing kings was cut down to size by the immense, muted presence, in so much of central and northern Europe, of ancient, less forceful styles of rule, linked to ancient cults.

What is the Frontier? From Roman Limes to Mission Territories

The decision made in the course of the eighth century to convert such peoples to Christianity, by force if needs be, was by no means an inevitable development. Christianity had always thought of itself as a "universal" religion, in that Christians believed that all peoples *could* be Christians, or, at least, that there could be Christians among all peoples. But in Continental Europe, Christians had been slow to draw the conclusion that Christianity *should* be the religion of all peoples, even if this involved having to send "missionaries" to the heathen in distant regions. The idea of the "missionary" seems so normal to us that we have to remember that it was only in this period that anything like a concept of "missions" developed in Western Europe.[8]

Up to then a more old-fashioned, more "Roman" view of the world had prevailed. The Franks assumed, much as the Romans had assumed, that beyond the *limes* a barbarian "back-country" would always exist. It was important that the inhabitants of this "back-country" should be held in check and, if possible, cowed into submission. Those pagans who found themselves on the Frankish side of the old frontier had to be absorbed. In the seventh century, a series of efforts were made by Frankish bishops, many of whom had been disciples of Columbanus, to convert the "un-churched" populations of the Channel coast and the southern side of the estuary of the Rhine (modern Flanders in Belgium). But this was seen as a "firming up" of an untidy frontier. It was not a missionary drive directed to faraway pagans. The populations of the back-country of Frisia and inner Germany were left free to continue their "barbarous" lives. By and large, western Christians on the Continent had not felt the need to reach out to gather in the unruly peoples who lived along the fringes of Christianity.

Things looked different when viewed from the British Isles. In Ireland and Saxon Britain, the imaginative barrier of the *limes* did not exist. What mattered was *peregrinatio*, the act of becoming a stranger to one's country for the sake of God. After that, one could go anywhere. Compared with the elemental wrench of self-imposed exile, by which a man breached the barrier of his own kin and his own small tribe, the ancient frontiers of Europe meant nothing. For a religious exile, everywhere was equally strange. To find oneself among "heathens" was not unusual. Furthermore, if one had become an exile to save one's own soul, the sense of urgency which drove one to that desperate remedy might also lead to a sense of the urgent need to save the souls of others.

As we have seen, the idea of "exile of God" had developed in Ireland. But Ireland was not alone in this. By the year 700, the structures of the newly established Anglo-Saxon churches in Britain were calculated to produce a supply of highly motivated wanderers. The urge to become an exile often coincided with a "middle age crisis." Indeed, the call of exile occurred at the same time of life as the great converts of the late fourth century (such as Augustine and Paulinus of Nola) had experienced the call to a higher life.

But the reasons for their conversion were different. The exiles of the eighth century wanted to get out of ecclesiastical structures in which they felt themselves to be held too tightly. Given to a local monastery at an early age, between five and seven, able men found themselves entering middle age only to confront a dangerous emotional and social situation. Between the ages of 30 and 40, they faced the prospect of becoming abbots or bishops. They would be compelled to settle down as figures of authority among their own kin and region. This meant that they found themselves inextricably implicated in the compromises that had produced, in Britain as in Ireland, an established Christianity that was shot through with deeply profane elements. For a devout person, it was better to leave home, so as to seek elsewhere the clarity of a true Christian order. Among such persons, religious exile and the sharp sense of a Christian order as it should be went hand in hand.

The first of this new generation of strangers, Willibrord (658–739), was a product both of Wilfrid's micro-Christendom in Northumbria and of Ireland. He received his vocation when studying, already as an exile, at Cluain Melsige (Clonmelsh, County Carlow). In 690, he arrived, with a small party of monks, to offer his services to Pippin of Herstal, the father of Charles Martel. Unlike an earlier stranger from Ireland, Columbanus, Willibrord did not offer "medicine" for the souls of Pippin and his entourage. His burning wish was, rather, to save the souls of real pagans. He was encouraged to preach to the Frisians of the Rhine estuary, who had recently fallen under Frankish domination. But he also wished to reach out to pagan peoples as far away as the Danes and the Old Saxons.[9]

We have Willibrord's own Calendar, written in a clear Irish script, with entries in his own hand. It is a glimpse of the new Europe of an exile. It was a wide, northern world held together by the ritual commemoration of saints and dead persons from the distant British Isles: Patrick, Brigid, and Columba, the three great saints of Ireland, appear together with three kings of Northumbria. Furthermore, when writing the date of his seventieth birthday, Willibrord adopted a new dating system: he wrote of it, much as we do, as "A.D. 728" – "in the 728th year from the Lord's Incarnation."

The system of A.D. dating had been elaborated earlier; but it suddenly became important for a small group of men whose sense of time was as majestically universal as was their sense of space. (In this, of course, they had been preceded by the Muslims, who regularly dated the year, throughout their vast empire, from the *hijra*, the fateful journey from Mecca to Medina of the Prophet and his Companions in 622.) Up to then, time in Europe had been regional time. Often, it was time which still looked straight back to Rome. Many regions still used the old Roman "provincial era." This was a time-scale where the years were counted from the year in which the region had been incorporated, as a province, into the Roman empire. Local rulers used their regnal years. And the popes, ever intent on proving that they were good "Romans" and loyal subjects of the Byzantine emperors, placed the regnal years, even the honorary consulships and the tax-cycles (the *Indictions*) of the East Roman emperors on every document that they wrote.

These old-fashioned dating systems were maintained in much of Europe. But in Willibrord's world (as in the dating system used by Bede in his *Ecclesiastical History*) there was only one time because there was only one world-ruler – the Lord Christ, whose reign over all humankind began with the year of his birth. It was a time-frame that all Christians could share. The choice of the "Anno Domini," A.D., dating communicated a sense of time that was as universal, as independent of local traditions, as Willibrord's vision of the world was independent of local frontiers. All time began with the beginning of Christianity and, by implication, all time was about the time it took for Christianity to reach its fulfillment, through the conversion of ever more pagan regions.[10]

Seen across the sea from Willibrord's Northumbria, Frisia was the gateway to Europe. Frisian merchants linked the fast-spending Saxon kings of Britain to the goods of the Rhineland. Precious glasswork, minted silver, even heavy mortars of German stone were exchanged for slaves. Throughout northwestern Europe, Frisian commercial activity brought about the end of a very ancient world. After 670, Merovingian gold coins, greatly reduced but still recognizable echoes of Roman imperial coinage, gave way to silver *sceattas*. These were minted for the use of merchants in a thriving economy now tilted toward the North Sea. Franks and Frisians fought for the control of Dorestad (Duurstede, Holland), an emporium on the Rhine south of Utrecht.

Dorestad became one of the great ports of Europe. In 800, its wooden wharves and merchants' houses covered 250 hectares, while a Roman Rhineland city such as Mainz covered no more than 100. Further north, among the *terpen* – the artificially raised mounds – of modern Groningen and Friesland, a society of free farmers and merchants enjoyed rare affluence. Well fed, they had livestock to spare. They produced large quantities of valuable, tweed-like cloth. Frisia was a standing rebuttal of the growing Christian conviction that paganism was synonymous with underdevelopment.[11]

Pagan Frisia represented a still undecided "might have been" for the entire North Sea. The Frisian chieftain, Radbod (685–719), established a sub-Frankish state on the borders of Francia. He was a strong ruler with the power to command his chieftains and to hurt his enemies. And he was a pagan. Just because he and his aristocracy had, in many ways, come so close to their Frankish neighbors, it was all the more important for him to assert an essential point of difference. Radbod was careful to maintain the pagan rites which gave so much prosperity to his people and which separated them from the Franks.

The Franks, in turn, were prepared to believe the worst of Radbod. It was rumored in Francia that he had upheld the grim practice of the sacrifice of victims, who were chosen by lot and left to drown in the tide as the great North Sea rose to take them to itself. It was later remembered about Radbod that, when once persuaded to accept baptism by a Frankish bishop, he asked whether the majority of the nobles and kings of Frisia were in Heaven or in Hell. The Frankish bishop's answer was unambiguous: all were in Hell. Wherewith the old king stepped back out of the font. He would rather be in Hell with the great men of his lineage than share Heaven with Christians such as the bishop.[12]

Willibrord was not expected to win over men such as Radbod. Rather, Willibrord acted as a consolidator. When the tide turned in favor of the Franks, Willibrord and his monks set to work, in the re-established city of Utrecht, to "weed out" paganism in zones that had fallen under Frankish rule. "Consolidation," however, meant many things on such a frontier. In 698, Willibrord received from Pippin of Herstal a former Roman fort at Echternach, near Trier, in which to found a monastery. Echternach was not a place set in the wilds. It lay near the site of what had once been a magnificent Roman villa. An ancient Roman road, which ran through the lands of Pippin's family, connected Echternach to Utrecht, some 250 miles away.

Echternach throve. It was, in its way, as much a center of Christianization as was Willibrord's frontier bishopric at Utrecht. The local nobility rallied round. They defined themselves through public acts of giving to Willibrord, recorded in charters that were witnessed by their peers. Willibrord was a holy person, a *vir strenuus*, "an active, Apostle-like worshipper of God." He was the favored holy man of Pippin, their own lord. To give to Willibrord was to touch a source of salvation and, at the same time, to join a group of fellow-givers who stood out in their region as loyal to Christianity and to a lordly, Frankish way of life.

The circle revealed by the charters of Echternach is a microcosm of the changes that were affecting the entire region to the north and east of the Frankish heartlands. These men were landowners whose families had, comparatively recently, established themselves in what had once been an inhospitable frontier zone between the Waal and the Maas/Meuse in modern Belgium and Holland. Their ancestors had been quite content to be buried, as chieftains, among their own dependents, in isolated settlements on the land that they themselves had won. They may or may not have been Christians. Those who gave to Willibrord, by contrast, were a new generation. They formed a tight, distinctive group. They were "nobles" in the up-to-date Frankish manner. They were no longer buried with their retainers, but elsewhere, near Christian churches. They had broken with the pre-Christian code that had linked them, as chieftains, to their followers, in death as in life. They were great landowners, and their followers had become mere peasants. They had been greatly enriched by their own lord, Pippin, so they were ostentatiously faithful to Pippin's invisible Lord, the God whom Willibrord served with such Apostolic zeal. It is in these small ways that an open frontier came to be closed, region by region, through the establishment of a new, more tightly organized social system along the edges of the Frankish kingdom.[13]

"So much barbaric lack of order": Boniface in Germany

In 716, Willibrord was joined by an impressive but troubled compatriot from a monastery in southern Britain – a six-foot tall man of 40 called Wynfrith. Wynfrith came to be known as Saint Boniface (675–754), the "Apostle of Germany." He had come to the Continent as a man already gripped by passionate loyalty to principles of order. He was a gifted schoolmaster. He had even written a handbook of Latin grammar. This handbook was utterly up-to-date because totally Christian. In grammar, as in all else, so he declared, "the customs of past ages" must be measured by "the correct taste of modern times." For him, the classical past was irrelevant. All the examples of good style that were cited in his handbook were taken from the writings of the Christian Fathers alone. Wynfrith drew on its opening pages a square enclosing a Cross with the name of Jesus Christ. His own heart remained filled with a similar sense of four-square solidity. He stood for a new form of Christianity, unburdened by the past. He was prepared to shed much of his own past and that of others in favor of a well-organized Christian present. On his first visit to Rome, for instance, in 719, he followed the Saxon custom of taking a Roman name, Boniface. But, unlike Benedict Biscop, he abandoned forever his Saxon name. From henceforth, Wynfrith was Boniface and only Boniface.[14]

Yet, although he saw himself as an exile, the churches of southern Britain remained close to Boniface. His extensive correspondence with his supporters in Britain reveals a particularly poignant aspect of his life. He felt bound to his Christian correspondents "through golden chains of friendship made for heaven."[15] Looked at from Anglo-Saxon Britain, Boniface summed up the hopes of an entire generation, frustrated by the very success of their own, less heroic Christianity. For Anglo-Saxon bishops, monks, and nuns in Britain, it was good to think of Boniface. His letters to noble nuns are moving to read. Less free to follow a man's stern road to exile, they looked to him as a distant, comforting *abbas*, even as a surrogate brother.

Boniface reminded the Saxons of Britain, on one occasion, that the Old Saxons claimed to be kin to them: "we are of the same blood and bone."[16] Indeed, his view of his own mission was deeply influenced by ideas which many Anglo-Saxon clergymen had come to share with the Venerable Bede. As we have seen, as Bede presented it in his memorable *Ecclesiastical History* (which appeared in 731), conversion to Christianity had made the Anglo-Saxons special and had turned Britain into their Promised Land. As an Anglo-Saxon, Boniface intended to re-enact among the Germans the triumphal coming of Christianity to the Anglo-Saxons of Britain. Not everyone agreed with such claims. But, at least, it was agreed in Britain that Boniface lived a heroic, "apostolic" life in a heroic environment. Even a king of Kent wrote to him for a gift of falcons: for he had heard that falcons were "much swifter and more aggressive" in Saxony![17]

Boniface's lifelong friend, bishop Daniel of Winchester, soon plied him with advice as to how to argue with pagans. He must not do so "in an offensive and irritating manner, but calmly and with great moderation."

Among other arguments, he should point out that

> whilst the Christians are allowed to possess the countries that are rich in oil and wine and other commodities [the gods] have left to the heathens only the frozen lands of the North . . . [They were] frequently to be reminded of the supremacy of the Christian world.[18]

Boniface was protected by Charles Martel. Later, in the 740s, he was called upon by Charles' son, Pippin, the future king of the Franks, to act as a "troubleshooter" and reformer in the Frankish church. But he also went out of his way to receive from the popes (between 722 and 739) a series of ever-widening commissions to act as a missionary bishop and supervisor of new churches throughout Germany. In presenting himself as a special servant of the popes, Boniface, once again, was influenced by his own distinctively Anglo-Saxon view of history. He was convinced that the Church in England had been founded through the mission sent from Rome to Canterbury by Gregory the Great. Had this not happened, the English, he believed, might still have been heathen. It was only proper, therefore, that he should turn to the successors of Gregory in order to validate his own mission to the heathen.[19]

In the course of 30 years, Boniface came to leave his mark throughout western Germany, from Bavaria to the watershed of the Lahn and the Weser, beyond which stretched the territories of the unconverted Old Saxons. He always presented himself as having brought light and order to a wild country. But Boniface's letters are so fascinating because they reveal the opposite. They show how little Germany, in fact, resembled the virgin heathen lands which the Anglo-Saxon myth of the missionary had led him to expect. Christianity already had a long and complicated history in central Europe. But that was not how Boniface and those who supported him saw the matter. Thus, when he founded his monastery at Fulda, in 744, he reported to the pope that the monastery lay "in a wooded place, in the midst of a vast wilderness." That was what Romans expected to be told. Fulda, in fact, lay on the main prehistoric trackway that crossed central Germany from east to west. It had been a Merovingian fort. A deserted church was already present on the site. It was far from being lost in the woods in a land untouched by Christianity.[20]

Altogether, nothing in Germany was quite what it seemed. Boniface had been sent, in the words of the pope, "for the enlightenment of the German people who live in the shadow of death, steeped in error."[21] What he found, instead, was much Christianity, and almost all of it the wrong sort. Cultic practitioners exchanged rituals. Pagans baptized Christians. Christian priests sacrificed to Thunor, ate sacrificial meats, and presided at the sacral funerary banquets of their Christian parishioners. Theirs was an oral Christianity, which mangled essential Latin formulae. A Bavarian priest performed his baptisms *In nomine Patria et Filia.* He had confused both case and gender. Boniface doubted that such a baptism was valid.[22] In Hesse and Thuringia, local chieftains were anxious to please the Franks. But they knew the limits of their powers over their followers. They could not bully them to accept Christianity. They had learned to coexist with pagans. It was not to convert a totally pagan population but, rather, to end an age of symbiosis between pagans and Christians that Boniface decided, in 723/4, to cut down the mighty Oak of Thunor at Geismar. This oak had stood at a joining point between half-Christian Hesse and the pagan Saxons. It may well have been visited by Christians as well as by pagans. He was careful to use its holy timbers to build an oratory of Saint Peter, which would serve as a Christian place of pilgrimage on the same spot.[23]

More disturbing yet, for Boniface, were Christian rivals – clerical entre-preneurs who had moved into the new territories from Ireland and Francia. He met these particularly in Bavaria, between 735 and 737 and again in 739–40. Despite Boniface's coldness toward them, many such clergymen were far from being mere adventurers. In Bavaria, they represented a previous missionary establishment, set up largely by Irish "exiles of God," whose methods had proved quite as effective, in southern Germany, as they had been in northern Britain at an earlier time. Vergil, abbot and later bishop of Salzburg (745–784) had once been Ferghil, abbot of Aghaboe (County Laois, Ireland). He was as much a zealous "Roman" stranger as was Boniface. A man of combative esoteric learning, Vergil shocked Boniface by preaching that "there is below the earth another world and other men." The bishop's opinion blended classical speculation on the Antipodes with Irish belief in the world of "the Other Side," a fairy counter-kingdom which flanked the human race. It was a notion calculated to frustrate the efforts of a man such as Boniface. He had striven hard enough to bring Christianity to all the na-tions already known to him. It was dispiriting to be told that there were yet others, as yet unbaptized, on the far side of the earth.[24] Yet bishop Vergil also had the ear of the pope. He was able to intervene successfully with the pope to protect the poor priest who had muddled the Latin of his baptismal formula. The pope told Boniface, sharply, that mere lack of grammatical precision did not invalidate a Christian sacrament.[25]

Far more dangerous than rival bishops were those who, in Francia and Germany, threatened to create their own idiosyncratic version of a Christian mission. They did so from elements long associated with a dramatic style of "frontier" Christianity. In 745, at a Roman synod, Boniface secured the con-demnation as heretics of Clement, an Irishman, and Aldebert, a Frank. Clem-ent and Aldebert stood for very different Christian options from those upheld by Boniface. They offered very different solutions from his own to contem-porary problems.

Take, for example, the views of Clement on the prohibited degrees of marriage. The nature of restrictions on marriage partners was a particularly charged topic at the time among the Franks and in Germany. It was a con-cern driven by a strong sense of the need to avoid incest in a society based on family solidarity and on complicated family alliances. Clement had his own solution. He supported the marriage of the widow to the dead man's brother (a practice abhorrent to Boniface) precisely because it was a practice that was found in the Old Testament. As an Irishman, he did this in the same spirit as that shown by the lawyers of the *Senchas Már.* As we saw in chapter 14, Irish lawyers had appealed to the Old Testament to justify pre-Christian marital practices.

In using the Old Testament in this way, Clement closed the chasm which threatened to open between the non-Christian past and the Christian present of the newly converted populations. He even reassured his flock that Christ had taken out of Hell the souls of all humanity, of all past ages: "believers and unbelievers, those who praised god and those who worshipped idols."[26] This was not at all what king Radbod had been told!

Aldebert was an even greater challenge than was Clement to a man such as Boniface. For Aldebert represented an older strain of Christianity – the Christianity of the charismatic holy men who had brought the faith to so many regions of western Europe and the Mediterranean. Aldebert was born of simple parents. He wrote of himself as a bishop "by the grace of God": so had the eccentric Patricius. His mother had dreamed of a calf emerging from her side: the mother of Columbanus had "seen the sun rise from her bosom."[27] Aldebert, like Boniface, claimed to have received authority direct from Rome. He claimed to know the contents of a letter dropped by Jesus Christ himself from Heaven, that now lay on the tomb of Saint Peter.[28]

Thus authorized by Jesus and by Saint Peter, Aldebert created his own Christian mission. He was said to have considered pilgrimage to Rome unnecessary. He himself was a living relic. Any place where he preached was as much a self-sufficient Christian "microcosm" as was any other. He set up chapels and crosses in the fields and at springs. In the absence of country churches, Anglo-Saxon landowners in Britain had done the same, by setting up just such crosses on their estates.[29] Above all, Aldebert offered instant penance. There was no need to tell him one's sins through confession. He already knew them all. Preaching in the hills around Melrose, Saint Cuthbert had inspired almost the same awe: the villagers confessed to him because they were convinced, by his mere appearance, that he already knew what they had done.[30] Boniface made himself unpopular by securing Aldebert's condemnation. He had taken away from the people of Francia "a most holy Apostle, a patron saint, a man of prayer, a worker of miracles.[31]

We do not know how widespread Aldebert's preaching had been. But the terms of his condemnation, taken together with the manner in which Boniface had set about his own mission and the way in which his example was remembered by successors, hints at a lively debate on how the process of Christianization was to be continued and who could best act as representatives of the new faith.

In many ways, the erratic Aldebert stood for one vivid strand in a very ancient Christianity. As a wandering holy man, he stood closer to Saint Martin of Tours and to Saint Cuthbert than to the new clerical elite gathered around a man such as Boniface. Boniface, by contrast, was not a charismatic figure. Rather, he radiated "correct" ecclesiastical order. His task turned out to be less to convert the heathen than to clear up anomalies and to put an end to long habits of compromise. He had brought from the "micro-Christendom" of Saxon Britain a blueprint of "correct" Christianity which he was quite prepared to impose on the ancient Christianity of Continental Europe.

Boniface soon learned that, judged by his high standards, Gaul and Italy were no less prone to "barbaric lack of order" than were the supposedly wild woods of Germany. In 743, he wrote to pope Zacharias. He had been told by pilgrims who had visited Rome from Germany that the Kalends of January were still celebrated there:

> in the neighborhood of Saint Peter's church by day and by night, they
> have seen bands of singers parade the streets in pagan fashion . . . They
> say that they have also seen there women with amulets and bracelets of
> heathen fashion on their arms and legs, offering these for sale to willing
> purchasers.[32]

If "ignorant common people" from the north saw such unabashed, ancient profanity in the very center of Christendom, they could hardly be expected to pay heed to the strictures of their priests at home. It is a characteristic letter. Over the years, the "depaganization" of Christians had come to interest Boniface as much as did the conversion of pagans.

Boniface wrote this letter when he had become a major figure within the Frankish kingdom itself. After 742, the pope had authorized him to act as the privileged counsellor of Pippin and of other "rulers of the Franks," in summoning councils to effect a reform of the Frankish Church. Boniface's position among the Franks was unprecedented, but his powers were ambiguous. He was not popular. Frankish bishops had their own firm views on how best to set up a Christian order.

In northern Francia and in the Rhineland, Boniface was by no means the hero of his generation. He faced determined opposition from bishops who regarded him as an interloper. He returned their scorn with a vengeance. Many Frankish bishops struck him as standing for all that he had left Britain to escape. They were aristocrats. They believed that a man must hunt; and that a man of honor, even a bishop, must, of course, kill with his own hands the killer of his father (the father being also, of course, a bishop!). It hurt Boniface to mix with such people at court, and to share Frankish good cheer with them at Pippin's great feasts. But he had no option. He wrote to his friend Daniel:

> Without the patronage of the Frankish prince I can neither govern the faithful ... nor protect the priests ... nor can I forbid the practice of heathen rites and the worship of idols in Germany without his orders and the fear he inspires.[33]

Altogether, correct order was hard to find in Francia. Even books were written in a crabbed hand, which strained his failing eyesight. He remembered a copy of the Old Testament prophets which had been used by his teacher in Britain. "I am asking for this particular book because all the letters in it are written out clearly and separately."[34] By now a blind old man, Daniel replied by ordering the transcription of long passages from Saint Augustine on the need for patience when living with evil men. Written in North Africa, almost four centuries before, now copied by an Anglo-Saxon in Winchester for a Anglo-Saxon working in central Germany, these were what a friend could offer, "culled from the works of ancient scholars, things useful to bear in mind in the midst of so much barbaric lack of order."[35]

Altogether, the Franks had been a disappointment to Boniface. Only the new-won lands gave the missionary in Boniface the opportunities for which he craved. Now an old man in his late seventies, Boniface turned back to the far north. He went on a tour of the mission fields in a Frisia barely pacified by Frankish armies. On June 5, 754, his entourage reached Dokkum, on the edge of the North Sea. With its liturgical paraphernalia and great chests of books, Boniface's progress through Frisia was, as he always intended it to be, a splendid sight, designed "to impress the carnal minds of the heathen." Almost by accident, the great man became a martyr. A band of pirates – hard sea-rovers, not indignant pagans – fell on his party. In the great iron-bound treasure chests, which every nobleman carried with him when travelling, they did not find gold, as they had hoped. Rather, they found the heart of Boniface's sense of order. They found texts.

> Disappointed in their hope of gold and silver, they littered the fields with books ... throwing some into the reedy marshes ... By the grace of God, the manuscripts were discovered a long time afterwards, unharmed and intact.

In the Episcopal Seminary at Fulda we can still see one of these books. It is a thoroughly ordinary manual. It contains an anthology of Patristic texts, partly concerned with the Arian controversy – that is, with a theological controversy which had happened four centuries previously, far to the south in the Mediterranean, when there was still a Roman empire in western Europe. It was an unpretentious volume, one of the many strictly functional books from which Boniface hoped to build a Christian order on the shores of the North Sea. It has violent cuts across the margins.It may well be the book which Boniface raised, instinctively, above his head, as the pirate's sword descended.[36]

Paedaogus populi, Educator of the People: The Legacy of Boniface

Boniface had died as a martyr. But he had lived very much as a schoolteacher, bringing order and instruction to untidy lands. It is not that the conversion of Germany was without drama. We can glimpse a small part of the process in a later account of the life of an Anglo-Saxon nun, Leoba. Leoba was a kinswoman of Boniface. She and other nuns had been taken by Boniface from Wimborne in Dorset, and placed in Tauberbischofsheim, southwest of Würzburg. The little community of foreign women did not find themselves among pagans. Instead, they faced a local population which was anxious to have an enclave of "holy" virgins in their midst. They turned hostile only when this reputation for holiness seemed to have been sullied. A crippled girl, who had lived from the food given as alms by the nuns at the convent gate, drowned her illegitimate baby in the nuns' millpond. The villagers were appalled. They claimed that the nuns, these so-called virgin "mothers," had disposed of their love-child in the very water which they used both to baptize the villagers and to drive their mill. By so doing, they had polluted the water of the village. Only days of dramatic penitential processions could reassure the villagers that the nuns were "pure" of guilt. The convent was to be a "sacred" place. Only then could it act as a power-house of prayer and a place of atonement. Far from being indifferent to Christianity, the people of the region had been enraged when it appeared that the holiness which they wanted from a convent had been desecrated by the sins of a nun.[37]

Slowly, after proving that it was indeed a "sacred" place, the convent at Tauberbischofsheim gained support.

> Many nobles and influential men gave their daughters to God to live in the monastery . . . Many widows also forsook their homes . . . and took the veil in the cloister.[38]

Tauberbischofsheim was another link in a Christian network, similar to those formed around the convents and monasteries of Ireland, Britain, and northern Gaul in the days of Columbanus and Bede. It was a smaller version of Willibrord's Echternach. These little nodules of local support for places endowed with an aura of the supernatural, such as Leoba's convent, brought about the "grassroots" conversion of Germany more effectively than did the high ecclesiastical policies associated with the leading missionaries.

Apart from these accounts, however, the supernatural was strangely distant in Boniface's world. What he and his followers considered themselves to have brought, rather, was the miracle of preaching and of "correct" instruction. It is revealing to see the extent to which Boniface and those around him linked up, across two centuries, with the tradition represented by Caesarius of Arles. After a long period of neglect, Caesarius' works came to be copied again in Frankish circles. They were copied in women's monasteries in the Rhineland and instantly put to use in Germany.[39] As we have seen, Caesarius had been a tireless preacher and critic of local semi-pagan customs. He had not been a wonder-worker. Caesarius was a significant model for a missionary to have chosen.

In 743, an *Index of Superstitions and Pagan Practices* was drawn up, in connection with Frankish councils over which Boniface had presided. The list shows practices very different from those of the Mediterranean peasantry, which Caesarius had denounced when he preached at Arles. They mention, for instance, the *nodfyr*, the "fire of need." This was fire created anew by rubbing wood, with all other fires extinguished, so as to fortify the powers of the land against cattle-plague. The *nodfyr* was still lit in Marburg in the seventeenth century. As late as 1767, it was used in the once Scandinavian western Isles of Scotland.[40]

These details hint at a sacred landscape of which Caesarius had never dreamed. But the attitude which brought such a list together was significantly similar to that of Caesarius. The document declared, in effect, that paganism, as such, had ceased to exist. All that the bishops had to deal with, now, were "survivals," "superstitions," *paganiae*, "pagan leftovers." The continued existence of such practices merely showed the ignorance and the stubborn attachment to old habits of an unenlightened Christian people. Such people were "rustic" in the true sense of the word. They were under-educated Christians. They were not pagans. In speaking of popular practices in a tone similar to that once used by Caesarius, the *Index of Superstitions* declared that the ancient gods of Germany were already safely dead. The "superstitious" practices of "rustic" believers were no more than lack of instruction. They did not betray the continued, uncanny presence of the old gods.[41]

It is worthwhile to linger a little on the implications of this attitude. It shows that, in this as in so much else, the eighth century marked a significant change in the mental horizons of the elite of the Christian Church. Christianization was no longer perceived as taking the form of an outright clash of supernatural powers. As we saw in chapters 2 and 3, this had been the principal element in all narratives of the triumph of Christianity. But in the eighth century, victory over the gods could be taken for granted. That victory lay in the past. The real task of the Church, therefore, was a *mission civilisatrice*. Education was as important as miracles.

In this, the revival of the preaching texts of Caesarius of Arles was decisive. It ensured that forms of religious instruction which had once been brought to bear on sophisticated urban populations in the late Roman Mediterranean – in the Hippo and Carthage of Augustine and in the Arles of Caesarius – were now applied in central Europe to the populations of an overwhelmingly rural society, gathered around monasteries and served by parish priests.

From Bavaria to Frisia, the generation of Boniface and of his successors was characterized by a plethora of little books. These are neat books, copied in a business-like manner and meant to be carried and consulted. Books of penance were carefully kept up to date to do justice to the prevalent sins and misdemeanors of the various regions in which they were used. We can even guess which one was used by Willibrord among the Frisians, while others were meant for different regions.[42] Books of rituals were equally important. They provided the correct form of words for the administration of Christian sacraments. Some of these even contain the first, hesitant translations into German of the Lord's Prayer and of the convert's baptismal oath that promised to renounce the gods.[43] Most moving of all, in many ways, were collections of sayings culled from all over Christendom. They were brought together in little volumes, so as to create a new Christian "wisdom literature." An almost folkloristic, gnomic lore, more like riddle collections than the encyclopedic anthologies of the seventh century, circulated in Latin among the clergy of Bavaria and other regions.[44]

These books are all well worn. They had been frequently used. When we see them in modern library collections they are, in their own way, as moving as the compact, slashed volume associated with the death of Boniface. For we are looking at the humble tools which passed the message of Christianity, from the great centers of Ireland, Britain, and the Frankish kingdom to networks of monks and priests working in new lands.

For such people, the missionary was no longer the wonder-working, itinerant holy man. He or she (for the convents played a crucial role in the quiet elaboration and distribution of orderly bodies of information) was increasingly perceived as, first and foremost, a teacher. When Huneberc, an Anglo-

Saxon nun, wished to sum up the life of her kinsman, Willibald, the first bishop of Eichstätt (whom, surprisingly enough, we have already met, at the end of chapter 13, as a pilgrim wandering through the Holy Land in the first century of Muslim rule – such was the range of these religious exiles!), she chose a loaded phrase. Willibald had been the *populi paedagogus*, the Educator of the Christian people.[45] It was a suitable ideal for a world reduced to order. Whether it came in the form of newly founded bishoprics and monasteries, which cast a net of Christian books and Christian teachers over the new territories, or in the form of an agrarian system based upon a greater measure of control over the lives of the peasantry, by the middle of the eighth century Christianity and order had begun to come in earnest, and hand in hand, to Germany.

"To preach with a tongue of iron": Charlemagne and the Conquest of Saxony

In the half-century after the death of Boniface, however, the missionaries were less important in Germany than was the unprecedented power and determination of the Frankish kings. Charles Martel and king Pippin had made the "people of the Franks" frightening, once again, in Europe. From 768 to 814, Charlemagne, the son of king Pippin, made them overpowering.

We need to go back, for a moment, to the last years of Boniface, in order to appreciate the circumstances under which Charlemagne came to enjoy such power. Charles Martel had still to be content to act as "mayor of the palace" to the kings of the Merovingian dynasty. After his death, in 741, the Frankish aristocracy agreed that they needed a "real" king. As also happened in Byzantium, the Franks preferred to move forward, to do something new, by claiming to move backwards. They would leap the centuries and identify themselves with the ancient "people of Israel." The "people of Israel" had chosen their kings so as to be effective, "to lead the people out to war." The "people of the Franks" should do the same by choosing a new king, in fact, Pippin the son of Charles Martel, to replace the ineffective Merovingian dynasty.[46]

In order to validate this unprecedented step, the Frankish bishops and their aristocratic colleagues sought the blessing of the pope in Rome. This approach from the distant north could not have been more welcome. If there was a city of the ancient Mediterranean which had well and truly died and that needed to "re-create" itself, it was the city of Rome in around 750.[47]

As we saw at the end of our last chapter, separation from the Byzantine empire had left Rome exposed to the ambitions of the Lombards. Worse even than the prospect of conquest by the Lombards was the fact that Rome was bankrupt. Byzantine gold no longer circulated in the region. The local coinage consisted of pathetic pieces of gilded copper. Centuries of neglect ensured that Rome had come to look like a bombed-out European city in 1945. The shape of ancient Rome had been lost. The local aristocracy lived in houses that were no different from the simple farmhouses in which they lived in the countryside, built into a landscape where the classical pattern of great forums linked by regular streets had vanished. Huge Christian shrines surrounded by gardens and little monasteries towered above a formless, partly empty landscape, encircled by crumbling walls which marked out the huge extent of the former city. In this atmosphere of decayed gentility (reminiscent of the state of the Venetian nobility, lingering in their decayed *palazzi* in the middle of the nineteenth century), the popes were so poor that one of them could even be suspected of making ends meet by engaging in the slave trade.[48]

Yet the popes and those around them showed amazing tenacity and skill in "re-creating" Rome to meet the needs of its new, northern patrons. By the end of the eighth century, they had brought about a remarkable triumph of urban memory over a truly desolate urban scene. For the beauty of Rome still lay in the eyes of the beholder; and, seen from the north, Rome was still an awe-inspiring city. As we have seen, from the sixth century onwards, former Roman cities in Gaul had also become faceless conglomerations. In the former cities of the north, large, semi-rural spaces were ringed by ancient walls and studded with Christian shrines built around relics of the saints. Such a city (and not a classical city as we might wish to imagine it) was what a northern visitor would expect to see; and, by those standards, Rome was overpowering. It still had a population of around 25,000. Huge churches still dominated the landscape. The papal palace and library at the Lateran were still magnificent. It would have struck visitors as a dream-like temple city as vast as Angkor Wat.

This was not the first time that Rome had re-created itself. In the fourth century, Rome ceased to be the effective capital of the empire. As we saw at the beginning of chapter 6, the local aristocracy successfully maintained the prestige of the city for centuries by presenting Rome (in the words of a modern scholar) as a theme park of the classical past. Now, in the eighth century, a succession of exceptionally gifted popes turned Rome into a theme park of the Christian past.[49]

What they presented was a Rome of the saints and a Rome which was a depository of the order and wisdom of the early Christian past. In Rome the relics of the saints were everywhere. In the words of a graffito scratched at this time by a pilgrim, Rome was "the new Jerusalem, the display case of the martyrs of God."[50] And the visitors who came to worship the saints came also to observe, at Rome, the ceremonies and to find the books which linked them to a Christian past far more ancient than their own.

The visitors now came principally from north of the Alps. By the year 750, Rome had lost its Mediterranean dimension. The Byzantines had withdrawn. The great churches of Spain and Africa lay under Muslim rule. Only the roads to the north lay open. The sort of visitors who came to Rome were men such as Boniface. Such men had a perfect command of Latin, through the careful study of Latin texts. But they could not trust themselves to speak "vulgar Roman". For the Latin of Rome had already come to resemble Italian. Whenever Boniface had something of importance to communicate to the pope, he insisted on writing it down.[51]

The northerners – Irish, Anglo-Saxons, and Franks – found in Rome relics of Christian saints from the earliest days of the Church. They also found texts which claimed to have caught the Christian past in amber. Things had always been like this, so the Romans told them, in Rome. Rome gave the much-needed dimension of antiquity to "micro-Christendoms" which saw themselves, for all their immense creativity, as in need of a past. In Neustria, for instance, liturgical books from Rome, though copied out and adjusted to Frankish custom, were especially esteemed in the Frankish kingdom because they were presented as authentic copies of the Mass-books which had once been used by Gregory the Great. One such "Gregorian" text was known, from its famous patron (the son of Charles Martel), as the "Sacramentary of King Pippin."[52]

Eventually, the blessing and the "authenticity" which only the popes could provide eased the delicate experiment in usurpation by which the family of Charles Martel took over the kingship of the Franks. Duly consulted by the Frankish bishops in 751, Zacharias II declared that Pippin could be made king. The ceremony took place in the most up-to-date manner possible for eighth-century Christians – that is, by a return to the Old Testament. Pippin was anointed as king with oil by the bishops, for the kings of Israel had been anointed with oil.[53]

Not surprisingly, the Lombards reacted to the threat of an alliance between the popes and the new kings of the Franks by occupying Ravenna and by turning south to Rome. Early in January 754, pope Stephen II arrived in Francia, exhausted by a hurried journey across the Alps in the middle of winter, to beg, in the name of Saint Peter, for Frankish help in Italy. It was an unheard-of event. No previous pope had ever made such a journey to the distant north. Arrived in Francia, Stephen repeated the ceremony of anointing in such a way as to designate Pippin's own family as the sole royal stock entitled to rule the Franks. Thus, with papal blessing, king Pippin initiated the "Carolingian" dynasty named from Charles Martel. Stephen got protection for Rome. Pippin invaded Italy so as to check the Lombard advance on Rome. He returned to Francia in 756, after two campaigns across the Alps, with a "heap of treasures and gifts." He had forced the Lombard kings to give him one third of the royal treasure stored behind the high walls of Pavia. There was money for everyone. That was what the Frankish aristocracy expected of a strong and well-blessed king.

When Stephen II came north to Francia, Pippin's eldest son, a solemn seven-year-old, had escorted the battered pontiff to his father's villa. The boy would be known to future generations, in the late, late Latin of Gaul, as Charles *le magne* (from the Latin *magnus*, "great"), as Charlemagne. In 768, Charles became king of the Franks. He had a reign of 46 years ahead of him – a reign longer than that of Augustus and of Constantine.

Charlemagne proved to be a man of truly "Napoleonic" energy and width of vision. He was constantly on the move and constantly planning. In one year alone (in 785) he covered 2,000 miles, pacing the frontiers of his new dominions. Such energy boded ill for the Old Saxons. The fate of the pagan Saxons was crucial to Charles' new concept of Christian empire. Not only were the Saxons pagan, they were a surprisingly aggressive warrior confederacy whose raids affected precisely the areas in central Germany where Frankish settlement and a Frankish style of life had begun to be established.

As had once been the case along the Roman *limes*, so now in the eighth century, part of the danger posed by the Saxon challenge came from the fact that Franks and Saxons had drawn closer to each other. Saxon noblemen had already come to adopt a large measure of Frankish customs. Yet, like king Radbod, they clung all the more tenaciously to paganism so as to differentiate themselves from the Franks. It was all the more essential for the prestige of the Carolingian family that the Saxons, who had come to adopt so much of Frankish ways, should be declared to be outside the pale as pagans, and that, as pagans, they should be well and truly defeated.[54]

In 772, Charlemagne led the Franks into Saxony. They were said to have desecrated the great intertribal sanctuary of the Irminsul, the giant tree which upheld the world. They rode home again, with much plunder, in time for the hunting season in the Ardennes. Next spring the Franks were in northern Italy. In 774, Charles became king, also, of the Lombards. He even made a short visit to Rome. It was the first time that a Frankish king had set foot in Rome. It was also the first time since the fifth century that a western ruler of such power had been greeted in Rome with the sort of elaborate ceremonies which the Romans knew so well how to put on. Charles entered Saint Peter's and, next day, was led through the gigantic basilica churches of the city. In return, Charles proved to be a generous donor. An influx of Frankish silver marked the beginning of a dramatic recovery in the fortunes of the popes, which was made plain by an unprecedented boom in buildings and repairs.[55]

But it was in Germany, and not in Italy, that Charles showed himself to be a ruler as determined to be obeyed in all matters as any Roman emperor had been. The Saxon war was fought along the same routes into northern Germany as had been taken by the legions of Augustus. But this time, unlike Augustus who lost his legions in the Teutoburger Wald, Charlemagne won. It was an unusually vehement war, characterized by the storming, one after another, of well-defended hill-forts. The very flexibility of the kingless society of the Old Saxons prolonged the misery. Total surrender of the Saxons as a whole was impossible. Fifteen treaties were made and broken in 13 years. One Saxon nobleman, Widukind, was able to avoid submission for decades on end. He fled to the Danes and involved even the pagans of Frisia in his resistance.

For a decade, an entire Frankish order was challenged in the north. Charles found himself forced to take over more territory that he had, perhaps, first intended to do. He pressed on from the Weser to the Elbe, entering the northern heathlands, as far as the Danes. The populations of whole areas were forcibly relocated. In 782, he had 4,500 Saxon prisoners beheaded at Verden, southeast of Bremen. Only Romans had been so self-confidently barbaric in their treatment of unreliable neighbors. It is revealing that the victims had been handed over to the Franks by members of the Saxon nobility. For Charles was Roman, also, in the skill with which he played a game of "divide and rule" in "free" Germany. He wooed the pro-Frankish faction in the Saxon aristocracy through lavish gifts and through the promise of incorporation in a new social order that would strengthen their hands against their own peasantry.[56]

In 785, Widukind finally submitted and accepted Christian baptism. In the same year, Charles issued his *Capitulary on the Region of Saxony*. A *Capitulary* was a set of administrative rulings "from the word of mouth of the king," grouped under *capita*, short headings. These were very different in their brusque clarity from the long-winded rhetoric of Roman imperial edicts. They registered, in writing, the invisible, purely oral shock wave of the royal will. The royal will was unambiguous. In theory at least, the frontier was now definitively closed. No other rituals but those of the Christian Church could be practiced in a Frankish province.

> If anyone follows pagan rites and causes the body of a dead man to be consumed by fire ... let him pay with his life.
>
> If there is anyone of the Saxon people lurking among them unbaptized, and if he scorns to come to baptism and wishes to absent himself and stay a pagan, let him die.
>
> If anyone is shown to be unfaithful to our lord the king, let him suffer the penalty of death.[57]

A small body of clergymen (notably Alcuin, a Saxon from Boniface's Britain, who was himself connected with the family of Willibrord) were challenged by such brusqueness to restate, more forcibly than ever before, a view of Christian missions which emphasized preaching and persuasion.[58] But, in fact, when it came to Charlemagne's treatment of the Saxons, most later writers took no notice of Alcuin's reservations. They accepted the fact that, as befitted a strong king, Charlemagne was entitled to preach to the Saxons "with a tongue of iron" – as a later Saxon writer put it without a hint of blame.[59] Force was what was needed on a dangerous frontier. Education began, rather, at home. In the reigns of Charlemagne and his successors, a substantially new Church was allied with a new political system, both of which were committed, to a quite unprecedented degree, to the "correction" and education of their subjects.

CHAPTER 19

"To Rule the Christian People": Charlemagne

Monarchy Making: Aachen and the Court

After 785, Charles controlled the former European core of the Western Roman empire – northern Italy, parts of northern Spain, and all of Gaul – and had absorbed its German and North Sea periphery. He showed what a warrior king could do when backed by unprecedented resources. In 792, he turned against the Avars of western Hungary. In order to ensure supplies for future campaigns, he planned to join the Main to the Danube by digging a canal three kilometers long between the river Regnitz and the Altmühl. He was defeated by the geology of the region. The preparatory diggings for the *Fossa Carolina*, "Charles' Ditch," the Karlsgrab, can still be seen near Eichstätt. They were so impressive that, in 1800, Napoleon's engineers considered resuming the project. In 20 weeks Charles had been able to spend two and a half million man hours, the labor of 8,000 men. Charles was not a warrior-chieftain in a fragile, epic mode. He trod with the heavy tread of a *dominus*, of a lord of Roman determination, capable of deploying resources on an almost Roman scale.[1]

The defeat of the Avars was widely publicized by the supporters of Charlemagne as the destruction of the last great pagan state in Europe. Wagonloads of plunder made their way back to the Ardennes.

> The site of the Khan's palace is now so deserted that no evidence remains that anyone has ever lived there. All the Avar nobility died in the war, all their glory departed. All their wealth and their treasure assembled over so many years were dispersed. The memory of man cannot remember any war of the Franks by which they were so enriched and their material possessions so increased.[2]

Now it was time for Charles to think even bigger than before. In 794, work began on a *palatium*, a palace complex appropriate for an emperor, at a former Roman thermal spa on the edge of the Ardennes, Aachen – Aix-la-Chapelle, "the Waters of the [Imperial] Chapel." Unlike the huge palaces of Constantinople and the Islamic world, from which the ruler dominated large cities, Aachen was set in the countryside. It was a compact affair. The living quarters of the palace were no larger than the residence of a Byzantine provincial governor of the age of Justinian. Aachen it did not need to be large. It was sufficient for it to be a satisfying microcosm. It had all the components necessary for an imperial center: an audience hall, porticoes that led to a large courtyard at the entrance to a round, domed chapel. Only the chapel has survived. It echoed the palace church of San Vitale at Ravenna. A great mosaic of Christ, flanked by the four creatures of the Apocalypse – Christ, that is, as Judge and Ruler of the world who would come at the end of time – filled the dome. Charles sat on his throne on a high gallery, halfway between Christ, his Lord and the model of his own kingship, and the "Christian people" gathered below him. In the eyes of contemporary admirers, he had been raised up by God "to rule and protect the Christian people at this last dangerous period of history."[3]

On Christmas Day, A.D. 800, Charles was in Saint Peter's at Rome, having come south to investigate a conspiracy against the pope, Leo III. Bareheaded and without insignia, as was normal for a royal pilgrim, he prayed at the shrine of Saint Peter. When he arose, Leo – apparently unexpectedly – placed a crown on his head; the Roman congregation acclaimed him as an "Augustus," and Leo "adored" him – that is, the pope threw himself at Charles' feet, as he would have done to his former lord, the East Roman emperor. It was a one-sided attempt, on the part of the pope, to have a say in recognizing, on his own terms, the formidable "imperial" power that had developed, far from his control, at Aachen.[4]

Charles returned north after the ceremony. It was from Aachen that he intended to steer his "Roman empire." For the last years of his life, from 807 to 814, he resided for large periods each year at Aachen, making it a fixed capital – a marked departure from the mobile kingship of earlier times. It was there that he was observed by Einhard, who wrote the classic *Life of Charlemagne* sometime between 824 and 836. A tiny little man from the petty nobility of the Maingau, too small to be a warrior and far too clever to languish as a cloistered monk in distant Fulda, Einhard was educated at Fulda but remained a layman. He supervised the near-perfect copies of Roman bronze-work that can still be seen in Aachen. He knew just how to surprise his contemporaries by carefully chosen references to the ancient world. A jewelled cross that he dedicated to the monastery of Saint Servatius in neighboring Maastricht was set by him on a perfect miniature of a Roman triumphal arch, on which (as a good "Roman" Christian) he placed figures of Christ and the Apostles. His portrait of Charles is equally, unexpectedly Roman. He modelled it on Suetonius' *Life of Augustus*, a rare text, to which this ingenious little man had gained access.[5]

Einhard's Charles was not a sainted king, as Bede had portrayed king Oswald. He portrayed Charles as a man of flesh and blood, a Frank among Franks, just as Suetonius, his model, had gone out of his way to make Augustus, the first emperor, appear, for all his universal power, to be still a Roman among Romans. The realism of Einhard's portrait of Charles was deliberate. By it, Einhard emphasized the links that bound Charles to his principal supporters and to the beneficiaries of his success, the aristocrats who led the victorious "people of the Franks."

> His nose was slightly longer than normal . . . His neck was short and rather thick, and his stomach a trifle too heavy . . . He spoke distinctly, but his voice was thin for a man of his bulk . . . He spent much of his time on horseback and out hunting .. for it is difficult to find another race on earth who could equal the Franks in this activity. He took delight in steam baths and thermal springs . . . [and] would invite not only his sons, but his nobles and friends as well . . . so that sometimes a hundred men or more would be in the water together.

When the great man finally fell ill, the scholars at his court liked to believe that he had spent his last days "correcting books." Einhard knew his Charles better. He wrote that Charles went out, for one last time, to hunt. When he died, on January 28, 814, it was Einhard who recorded the simple epitaph: "Charles the Great, the Christian Emperor, who greatly expanded the kingdom of the Franks."[6]

The consolidation of the "greatly expanded kingdom of the Franks" required a continuous effort at "monarchy-making" such as had not been seen in western Europe since the reformed empire of Diocletian and Constantine. Loyalty could never be taken for granted. In Italy, for instance, Charles' conquest of the Lombard kingdom had broken the Lombard aristocracy. Two hundred of them were taken north as hostages. Frankish noblemen now had the upper hand all the way from the Alps to as far south as Benevento, which remained an independent, Lombard duchy. The monastery of San Vicenzo at Volturno, some 20 miles northeast of Monte Cassino, stood at the tense frontier between Benevento and the "kingdom of the Franks." In 785, the monks of San Vicenzo began to say regular prayers for Charles as their king. No sooner had they reached the Psalm, *O God, in Thy name make me safe*, than abbot Potho, a member of the old Lombard nobility, got up and refused to sing. "If it were not for my monastery," he said, "I would kick the man like a dog."[7]

Charles and those around him were faced by much resentment and by widespread noncooperation, not only in conquered territories but from Frankish families who still resented the rise to power of the Carolingian dynasty. The best that Charles could do, in this situation, was to communicate that, in a shaken world, the new imperial order found at Aachen represented the only effective guarantee of social and religious stability; and that those who joined in would be allowed to thrive at the expense of those who did not.

Charles controlled a spoils system that ramified throughout much of Europe. He manipulated with great skill a reserve of inducements which no ruler had possessed since Roman times. For those who could be persuaded to be loyal, Charles, in his middle age, seemed a reassuringly old-world figure. Lack of loyalty to one's lord, at any level of society, was known to shock him. Associations of equals that seemed to undermine the loyalty of inferiors to their lords – such as local sworn leagues and even the raucous toasting-feasts of Frisian farmers – were savagely punished. They were a "blasphemy" against God and the proper order of society.[8]

Charles summed up in his own style of life a hierarchical social order which insisted on close bonds of loyalty between dependents and their lords. The ceremonial life which developed around Charles at Aachen and in his other palaces did not cut him off from his *fideles*, his loyal dependents. He knew how to combine hierarchy and prompt obedience with studiously relaxed good cheer. The royal court was an image of a lordly, stable society, which any powerful person might hope to re-create, around himself, in his own region, provided that he retained Charles' favor.[9]

It was in this distinctive, very Frankish manner, that ties of loyalty, fostered around Charles at Aachen, reached out, in tentacular fashion, through a "managerial aristocracy" composed of powerful laymen, bishops, and great abbots. Through such persons and their many dependents, Charles was careful to make his will felt in every region of the "greatly extended kingdom of the Franks."

Let us return to the Lord (Isaiah 55:7): Carolingian Correctio

For modern persons, the Carolingian empire – as the empire of Charles and his successors has come to be called by historians (though it was never called this by contemporaries) – is a political and cultural system which is notoriously difficult to hold in focus. It seems, at times, to be improbably grandiose and, at times, to be pathetically weak. This is because we approach it with criteria other than those of its own time.

Most of these criteria come from our modern expectations of what a successful empire should be like. But the self-image projected by Charles and his supporters has made it even more difficult than usual to see his empire in perspective. The Carolingians had no mean opinion of themselves. They rose to power by claiming that they had brought the Franks out of a "dark age." They asserted that the kingdom of their Merovingian predecessors had been characterized by aimless barbarism and by a sad decline in learning. As we saw in chapters 6 and 11, there is no truth in this myth. The Carolingians built on solid foundations, already set in place in Merovingian times, in the Frankish heartlands of northern Gaul.

The effect of the Carolingian myth, however, has been to encourage scholars to judge Charles and those around him according to unrealistically exalted expectations. The Frankish empire claimed to rival the "Roman" empire. As a result, we tend to judge the achievement of Charlemagne's empire by comparing it with the centralized Roman state which had once ruled all of Europe from Scotland to Africa. Not surprisingly, we find it wanting. The scholars around Charlemagne claimed to have "renewed" Latin learning when it had reached a nadir of "rusticity." We take this claim at face value, and so speak of a "Carolingian Renaissance." We are then disappointed to learn that, in comparison with the Humanists of the Italian Renaissance, the scholars around Charlemagne and his successors paid scant attention to what we, nowadays, consider to be the essence of "classical" Greece and Rome. The great scholars of the Carolingian period thought of themselves first and foremost as Christians. They made it abundantly clear that they had little interest in the "classical"world in its own right. That had been a pagan world which had been replaced by Christianity. Altogether, we are left with mixed feelings. The Carolingians do not measure up to our own expectations of what they should have been. We tend to dismiss them. Either they were noble dreamers, who planned to restore all that was best in the ancient world despite the limitations of the "Dark Age" society in which they lived. Or they were pretentious barbarians, who should have known better in the first place than to attempt to imitate the past glories of Rome.

It is, therefore, important to look at what were the "horizons of the possible" for Charles and his contemporaries. They had their own view of where they fitted in to the overall history of Europe. It is revealing that, for the very first time, they spoke of the "barbarian invasions" as if they were a distinct period of history. They believed that this period had come to an end in their own, more fortunate times. Carolingian writers, indeed, were the first to propagate the myth of the "barbarian invasions". They regarded these as an ugly interlude, a dark age placed between the "fall" of the Roman empire (which was caused by such invasions) and the coming of better things, in the form of the Christian kingdom of the Franks.

> Although the whole of Europe was once denuded with fire and sword by Goths and Huns, now, by God's mercy, Europe is as bright with churches as is the sky with stars.[10]

These are the words of Alcuin, an Anglo-Saxon, written in 793. Alcuin had been summoned from distant Northumbria to the court of Charles. After a period of turmoil, Alcuin implied, Charles' empire enjoyed unprecedented prosperity and success because God was pleased with it. It had won the favor of God through having renewed the correct practice of Christianity. This was the "ancient, Roman" world that had been brought back by Charles. It was not the pagan Rome of classical times. Rather, it was the Christian empire of Constantine and Theodosius (with its massive codes of law in favor of the Church) and the Latin, Christian culture that had produced Jerome, Augustine, and preachers of the caliber of Caesarius of Arles.

For Alcuin and his colleagues, the Christian Church, and not the Roman empire, was the most majestic institution ever to have appeared in Europe. The Church reached back without a break for over half a millennium, linking the Frankish kingdom directly to the "ancient" Christian world. The Church embraced all the peoples within Charles' Frankish empire and the neighboring kingdoms of the British Isles. While the past of pagan Rome seemed immeasurably distant to Carolingian clergymen, the same could not be said of the past of the "ancient" Christian Church. It seemed within easy reach. The correct order of the "ancient" Christian Church was alive in the present, as the almost unconscious touchstone of all that was right and proper – much as the American Constitution is more to Americans than a document written by gentlemen of the *ancien régime* a few centuries ago; it remains, also, the touchstone of all arguments on legality in the present-day United States. Christian texts dating from the age of Augustine and even earlier had accumulated in libraries all over Western Europe. These texts were not read as evidence of a long-past period, but as reminders of the timeless presence of God and of his "Law" in all periods. They were still relevant to the present. In that sense, the Early Christian past seemed little removed from the Carolingian present.

Hence our modern word, "Renaissance," fails to describe what the Carolingians intended to do. It was not their aim to conjure up the world of "classical" Rome as if from the grave. Their Christian culture did not need to be "reborn" for the simple reason that they did not think that it had died. It just needed to be reasserted. Their chosen term, therefore, was *correctio* – "correcting, shaping up, getting things in order again." It was a down-to-earth term, suited to the aims of an energetic managerial aristocracy. Their ambition was to make sure that a respected Christian past got on the move again in modern times, much as a large and solid vintage car that had lingered for some time in its garage might soon, with a little effort, be got ready for the road.

But if they failed, then God might again turn his face from them. We should not underestimate the anxiety that was the permanent shadow of the Carolingian program of *correctio*. In this, Charlemagne and his court were very like their near-contemporaries, the Iconoclast emperors of Byzantium. Both believed sincerely that it was possible for the Christian people to err and to incur the wrath of God. Both believed that the imperial power existed so as to correct such errors. But, if the emperors failed in their duty, then God's wrath would be made plain in the decline of the kingdom and in renewed barbarian invasion.

Alcuin wrote as he did because he had received the news of a Viking raid on Britain. It was a warning that the "barbarian invasions" might begin again. The unprecedented, almost indecent prosperity of the Franks had to be paid for by a strenuous effort to "correct," to "shape up" the Christian religion of their new empire. Alcuin ended his remarks with a passage from Isaiah: *Let us return unto the Lord God* (Isaiah 55:7). Thus a rare combination of fear of God's displeasure and confidence that the Christianity of their times could be "corrected" from on top drove the movement that has been confidently misnamed, by modern scholars, "the Carolingian Renaissance."

"And he read in their ears all the words of the book" (2 Chronicles 34:30): Imposing the Christian Law

The movement of "correction" from on top lasted longer than the reigns of Charles and of his son, Louis the Pious (814–840). It mobilized an unprecedented range of persons (lay persons as well as the better-documented monks and bishops). It touched, in very different ways, widely different areas of Europe. The extent of its impact varied greatly from place to place. Indeed, what is truly significant about the Carolingian movement of "correction" was that, although it was vociferously fostered by outstanding figures, it was not masterminded by those figures alone. It drew on a remarkable convergence of aims, which betrayed a hardening of the will to rule, and to rule "correctly," on the part of an entire diffuse governing class. But, provided that we do not allow them to distort our picture of the movement as a whole, a few examples of well-known personalities can serve as test cases.

Let us begin with Charlemagne himself. As emperor, it was Charles' business to uphold the "corrected" Christian order and to make it work. He did this through energetic bursts of consultation with the leading figures of each region. Each group was given its own "law," was urged to live by it, and faced the heavy consequences of imperial disfavor should they fail to do so.

> In this year [A.D. 802] the lord Caesar Charles stayed quietly at the palace at Aachen: for there was no campaign that year . . . In October, he convoked a universal synod [at Aachen] and there had read out to the bishops, priests, and deacons all the canons [the laws of the Church] . . . and he ordered these to be fully expounded before them all. In the same assembly likewise gathered together all the abbots and monks . . . and they formed an assembly of their own; and the *Rule* of the holy father Benedict was read out and learned men expounded it before the abbots and monks . . . And while this synod was being held, the emperor also assembled the dukes, the counts, and the rest of the Christian people . . . and all had the laws of his people read out, each man's law was expounded to each, emended . . . and the emended law was written down . . . And [the *Annals* added, with justifiable pride at the ceremonial recognition of one emperor by another] an elephant [the gift of none other than the Calif Harun al-Rashid of Baghdad] arrived in Francia that year.[11]

Charles was at his most "imperial" on such occasions. This was because he was seen to be acting in a manner that revived, in Christian times, the action of the godly king Josiah, when he had promulgated the rediscovered Law to the people of Israel. Charles was well aware of this precedent. He used it in the prologue of the most extensive statement that he ever issued of the program of "correction" – the *Admonitio Generalis*, the "General Warning" of 789.

> *And the king went up into the house of the Lord . . . and the priests and the prophets, and all the people, both small and great: and he read in their ears all the words of the book.* (2 Chronicles 34:30)[12]

In secular matters, local laws prevailed, each in its own region. The written laws of individual "peoples" were regularly supplemented by oral custom, created by oral forms of pleading and decision-making. Provided that the Franks retained the upper hand, Charlemagne actively encouraged the use of local laws.[13] But this made the "Christian Law" all the more important. In matters of religion the "Christian Law" was the true, universal law of Charles' empire. It was what every baptized Christian had in common with every other subject of Charles' Christian empire.

The "Christian Law" was not intended to supersede local laws. But it did sum up the consensus on which Carolingian society as a whole rested. For the correct observance of Christianity gained the favor of God for the empire. This was a written law. It was contained in texts – in the first instance, in the Bible (the Old and the New Testaments), then in written liturgies, in the rulings (the canons) of the Councils of the Church for the last 500 years, and in the works of the Latin Fathers of the Church.

The insistence that the "Christian Law" should be applied correctly in all regions of the empire pushed to the fore a largely new group of persons. Charlemagne's reforms created an empire-wide "nobility of the pen," drawn from monasteries and from the clergy. This nobility of the pen was recruited largely from the Frankish aristocracy and from those who depended on the aristocracy, as distant relatives and as clients. Thus the learned class of the empire was not unlike its lay relatives. They stood at the top of Frankish society. They were rare birds and they knew it.

When we speak of this group of monks and clergymen, we should be careful not to speak of them as if they alone represented the "Church" and "the clergy." There were many forms of clergymen. The average monk and clergyman was no great master of Latin. He lived in a different world from the highly literate group who ruled the Church. But, like their relatives, the Frankish warrior elite, the upper clergy did not form a class which was cut off from all others. Warrior aristocrats depended on their ability to raise loyal troops through maintaining the enthusiasm of large bodies of men very different from themselves. In the same way, the great bishops and abbots of Charles' empire knew that they also had to use all the skills of command and persuasion which they possessed to bring the "Christian Law" down to every level of their own clergy and to the Christian people.[14]

In controlling the Church, Charles controlled a structure of power which was unusual in its extensive reach and in its ability to penetrate downwards so as to touch many layers of local society. Carolingian Europe was crisscrossed by a network of great cathedral churches and monasteries. The empire of Charles and his successor, Louis the Pious, had 180 episcopal sees and 700 great monasteries (in some 300 of which the emperor had a direct interest). In Germany, in particular, great monasteries such as Fulda, Reichenau, and St. Gall have been appositely likened to Roman legionary camps, settled on the new *limes*. But they were more than that. They inherited a long northern tradition, that had already been operative in Ireland, Britain, and Neustria, by which a monastery, as a locus of the holy, might become the nodal point of the society of an entire region. Carolingian abbots owned estates which made them the landlords of tens of thousands of peasants. They were responsible for mobilizing the local gentry for war. The monasteries received, in return for prayers, thousands of small gifts, often from humble persons.

Since the time of Willibrord and Boniface, indeed, a "social earthquake" had changed the face of Germany. Between half and a third of the land in most villages passed, by donation, into the hands of churches and monasteries. The Church had become an overwhelming presence in every locality. As a result of this new situation, the *correctio* of the Church, in Germany at least, was not imposed from above by a distant circle of idealists. It was a response on the ground level, by local churches, to a new situation of unparalleled power. The Church had to be made orderly and majestic if it was to live up to the expectations of populations for whom the Church had become, for the first time, an ever-present, dominant neighbour.[15]

We should not forget the importance of the highly local nature of the Carolingian churches. The existence of a widespread clerical elite, associated with bishoprics and monasteries scattered all over western Europe, made the Carolingian empire significantly different from the equally reform-minded Byzantine empire of the same time. Byzantium remained a highly centralized empire. The provinces continued to live in the shadow of Constantinople. There were few local centers of cultural life. Culture tended to drain upward to the capital, to gather around the court and the offices of the patriarchate. This was not the case in Charlemagne's empire. Despite the ceremonial importance of Aachen in the last decade of Charlemagne's life, the Carolingian empire never developed a single, all-absorbing center. Instead, the court acted as a "distribution center" both for books and for personnel. Skilled and enthusiastic educators and administrators were drawn to the court and then were sent out to distant bishoprics and monasteries.

Although the court was important as a cultural center in the empire of Charlemagne and his successors, it did not impose a uniformity of culture from on top. Rather, as in the days of the competing cities of the Roman empire, the Carolingian ideal of a "correct" Christianity spread all over western Europe (as Roman city life had done, half a millennium previously) through constant competition between rival local centers, each anxious to outbid the others according to an agreed but flexible standard of excellence. Hence the Crolingian reforms were capable of considerable variation, in different regions and in the hands of different persons.

The first need for such a trans-regional elite (in the age of Charlemagne as under the Roman empire) was for a common code of communication which enabled them to recognize and to feel close to their peers all over Europe. Hence the importance of a particularly well-known figure in the gallery of scholars gathered around Charlemagne – Alcuin of York (735–804). Alcuin was an Anglo-Saxon from Northumbria. He had been lured to Charles' court in 782. He presented himself as standing for the high "Roman" traditions of Bede. He was very much a career scholar. Not a nobleman himself, he shared his compatriot Boniface's dislike for local churches ruled by stylish and unlettered aristocrats. To belong to a great monastery brought its own nobility, and subjected the monk to its own forms of *noblesse oblige.*

> Look at the treasures of your library, the beauty of your churches . . . Think how happy the man is who goes from these fine buildings to the joys of the Kingdom of Heaven . . . Think of what love of learning Bede had as a boy and how honored he is among men . . . Sit with your teacher, open your books, study the text . . .
>
> Look at your fellow-student [he urged a recalcitrant disciple] who has always kept close to God and now holds an eminent bishopric, loved, praised and sought after by all.[16]

Yet Alcuin was not only an Organization Man. He remained an outsider in the tight world of a court dominated by well-born Frankish clergymen and laymen. To this world he brought, from his Anglo-Saxon monastic background, the inestimable gift, for any newly formed elite, of the ability to communicate to his colleagues the sense of belonging to a charmed circle. He did this through intense teacher–student relationships. He fostered a cult of friendship of which his intense penitential piety was the reverse – for the sadness of humankind consisted precisely in having turned away so often from the friendship of Christ.[17]

Alcuin also brought to the court an originally Irish habit, which consisted of bestowing flamboyant nicknames on his friends. Charles, predictably, was "David." This playful streak was a welcome sign. It showed that intellectuals lived, once again, in a world so secure that they could joke with each other and be drawn to each other by elective affinities. But, characteristically for Alcuin, it also carried a didactic message. To be members of the circle of Alcuin, nicknames and all, was to become living avatars of the golden age of ancient Christianity.[18]

Alcuin came to a Francia that had begun to develop the *sine qua non* for a collaborative venture of *literati* – a new, uniform script. What later became known as "Caroline minuscule" was a smaller script, more regular and altogether more legible than its predecessors. Italian Humanists of the fifteenth century, when they discovered Carolingian manuscripts, were so struck by the elegance and solidity of "Caroline minuscule" that they were convinced that they were reading manuscripts written by Romans of the classical period!

In fact, "Caroline minuscule" was the end product of one of those silent continuities that are usually ignored in historical narratives of the early Middle Ages. It was the end product of centuries of experiment by unassuming "technicians of the written word" who had maintained the routines of writing legal documents at the local level and in the courts of barbarian kings, as we saw in chapter 10. Generations of barely noticed pen-pushers had continued at work, in a manner which linked the last centuries of the Roman empire, without a break, to the age of Charlemagne. Now this no-nonsense style of writing emerged as the *sine qua non* for the extensive copying and the public exposition of the "Christian Law."[19]

The "Christian Law" had to speak for itself, to readers of varied levels of competence. But it also had to speak aloud to others. Texts, at this time, were not meant only for solitary readers. They were meant to be read aloud. The Bible, the books of the liturgy, the sermons of the Fathers (especially the homilies of Caesarius of Arles) had to be read out clearly and in an authoritative manner to a wide audience, gathered in large monasteries or in churches. This emphasis on instant intelligibility marked a significant difference between the aims of Carolingian intellectuals and their Roman predecessors. It was not expected that ancient books should speak for themselves. Roman literary manuscripts had lacked punctuation. Words were not separated. Entire sentences and paragraphs merged into each other.

This was not the sort of book that Alcuin intended to produce. He lived in a world that had come to want texts that were "user-friendly." These texts were written out in such a way as to guide the voice of the reader. Capital letters marked the beginning of new trains of thought or of narrative sequences. Punctuation warned the reader instantly when a sentence ended and how the sentence itself fell into separate parts. Even the cadence of the voice between doubt and certainty could be indicated: the question mark is a direct legacy from the age of Charlemagne. When Charles made him abbot of the monastery of Saint Martin at Tours in 797, Alcuin placed the following inscription over the door of the monastery's writing-hall, the *scriptorium*:

> May those who copy the pronouncements of the holy law and the hallowed sayings of the fathers sit here. Here let them take care not to insert vain words . . . May they punctuate the proper meaning by colons and commas [by which Alcuin meant the pacing of the voice according to units marked by punctuation] . . . so that the reader reads nothing false or suddenly falls silent [because faced by an unfamiliar text] when reading aloud to the brethren at Church.[20]

The development of "Caroline minuscule," and the new standards of legibility that went with it, mark a significant breach with the past. Books in Europe were no longer what they had been in the ancient world: they became considerably more like books as we know them. More important at the time, they gradually became the same all over Europe. The diffusion of the "Caroline minuscule" brought to an end the colorful diversity of local scripts that had developed in the sixth and seventh centuries.[21]

Alcuin played an important role in this development. But he stood at the center of a wider convergence of aims. The development of musical notation, which appears from the first time in Europe in Frankish monasteries, reflected a similar desire. Faced with the importation of unfamiliar but prestigeful "Roman" Mass-books, the monks had to establish a standard way of indicating how these should be chanted. Whether through the aid of correctly written texts or through musical notation, contemporaries were determined that the churches and monasteries of Charlemagne's kingdom should be filled with well-organized, authoritative Latin words.[22]

We can see this also at the furthest end of the Carolingian empire, at the monastery of San Vicenzo in Volturno. After abbot Potho's protest, the Carolingians competed with the Lombard dukes of Benevento to kill the monastery with kindness. Standing between the empire and Lombard southern Italy, the monastery was to be a showcase of "correct" religion. The magnificence of its buildings took archaeologists by surprise when they excavated them in the 1980s. The surfaces of the buildings were covered with writing of all kinds – exquisitely carved stone epitaphs, names on tiles, messages painted on frescoed walls. In a large assembly hall, the Prophets of the Old Testament were shown, standing in formidable order, each with an open book which bore a citation from the prophet's message. The magnificent scripts derived from Benevento rather than from the Frankish north. But they conveyed the same message as did the *scriptoria* presided over by Alcuin. Words of command and admonition, uttered by holy persons and caught for all ages in the Holy Scriptures, were what Carolingians thought of when they upheld the "Christian Law." For the "Christian Law" was no abstract code. Nor was it a mere collection of texts meant for private reading. It was a sound. It was a rolling "thunder" of authoritative voices, demanding obedience and demanding it in Latin.[23]

Admonitio generalis: "A general Warning" and the Problem of Communication

This clear Latin, however, was unintelligible to the vast majority of the population of Charlemagne's empire. This should come as no surprise. In Roman times, also, the overwhelming majority of the population would have been illiterate. In Roman times quite as much as in the days of Alcuin and his leisured friends, those who had mastered a correct, classical Latin based on texts were instantly marked out as a privileged group. There was nothing new in that. But Charles' empire was different in that it was divided between populations for whom some form of Latin had remained their spoken "mother tongue," and regions where no one had ever spoken Latin at any time or had not done so for centuries. As an Anglo-Saxon, Alcuin himself had come from such a region. For centuries, in Ireland and Britain (as now in Frisia and Germany), Latin had been a language learned from books. It was a perfect language because it was a perfectly dead language. It was spoken with a fixed pronunciation (which stressed each syllable and altered the sound of many diphthongs) which even learned Continental persons from former Latin-speaking areas would have found hard to follow.

When persons such as Alcuin came to areas of "Roman" speech on the Continent, the Latin he encountered struck him as "barbarous." But this was not because it was written by "barbarians." The exact opposite was the case. This was Latin written by persons who thought of themselves as, in some way, still "Romans." They thought that they were writing Latin when, in fact, they were already writing proto-French. They had not noticed the hiatus between their own, sub-Latin "Roman" language and the "correct" Latin which was to be found in ancient texts.

By creating an elite based upon shared high standards of Latin, based on common texts written in a common script, the Carolingian program of "correction" laid bare for the first time a hitherto largely unobserved barrier: the extent to which Latin, as a learned language, had come to diverge from the sub-Latin languages of southern Europe – what contemporaries called "the vulgar Roman tongue," and what we now call the "Romance" languages: French, Italian, and Spanish. A sudden sense of strangeness fell across a linguistic situation which more easygoing generations had simply taken for granted. What Alcuin and those around him had gained, by creating a Latin culture of remarkable homogeneity and "horizontal" reach, they stood to lose, by cutting off the channels of "vertical" communication, which had made "good enough" Latin still intelligible to persons who spoke Latin-based dialects. "Correct" Latin, if spoken in the manner that scholars such as Alcuin advocated, could not be understood in the "Roman" areas of Merovingian Gaul, Italy, and Spain.[24]

We should not, however, over-dramatize the dilemma that this presented. Highly stratified societies do not necessarily expect their elites to be instantly intelligible to their inferiors. Inferiors can be assumed to "get the message" somehow. It was more important that the elites should understand each other. They still did so in the empire of Charlemagne. It is only with hindsight that the linguistic boundaries of Europe seem to have become fixed at this time. In fact, the Frankish elites were probably bilingual. Aristocrats switched easily from Germanic Frankish to a "vulgar Roman" proto-French. Constantly on the move from one part of the empire to another (with large retinues which would, in any case, have included Latin scribes and interpreters), they crossed without difficulty linguistic frontiers that would become clear only in later ages.

Nor had a chasm yet developed between Latin as the exclusive language of the clergy and an "unlettered" laity which was locked, by default, into local vernaculars. Once again, the real division was between the powerful and the rank and file. "Active" literacy implied the ability to read and write in Latin. This had always been the preserve of the privileged few. As in Roman times, "passive" rather than "active" literacy was the more widespread form of literacy. Many persons in Carolingian Europe could read familiar Latin texts and could decipher the contents of important documents. The average clergyman fitted into this category. He was no Alcuin, and no one expected him to be. By contrast, many lay *potentes* of the Frankish kingdom had maintained the late Roman equivalence of power with the possession of high culture. Just because they were lay persons, this did not mean that they were illiterate barbarians. Despite their studiously maintained self-image as a warrior upper class, defined on all occasions by the wearing of great swords, Frankish gentlemen could be as serious on matters of religion and high thought as any clergyman.

Einhard, the biographer of Charlemagne, is a remarkable example of this class of persons. In the midst of his activities as a Frankish aristocrat, he found time to write abundantly. He wrote a vivid account of how he had brought the relics of Saints Peter and Marcellinus all the way from Rome in order to set up (in the best Frankish manner) a "correct," authentically "Roman" cult site – a Rome away from Rome – on his estate at Seligenstadt. His letters to learned clergymen allow us to glimpse the extent of his grief at the death of his beloved wife, Emma.[25]

The lady Dhuoda is another example of the literate aristocrat. In 841–3, during the reign of Charles the Bald, Dhuoda wrote instructions to her young son at court. It is a fascinating Latin text. Dhuoda addressed issues of daily religious practice and propounded a code of behavior suited to a Christian gentleman. Dhuoda did not write copybook platitudes. She used Latin to express her own ideas. Much of what she wrote was based upon her own personal experience and on the memories of her family. For Dhuoda, God was still "to be found in books," and these books were Latin books.[26]

The problem which faced Charlemagne and his advisers was not that an unbridgeable "communication gap" had opened up, as the speakers of vernacular drifted away from the "high" Latin of the Church. It was the other way round. Those who upheld "correct" Latin felt themselves to be on the defensive. "Rustic" Latin pressed in all around them. The results of such insouciance could be serious. The message of the "Christian Law" might be blurred by the slipshod Latin of those who copied texts and repeated them aloud to the Christian people, "for often, while people want to pray to God in the proper fashion, they yet pray incorrectly because of uncorrected books."[27]

The attempt of Charlemagne to maintain "correct" Latin throughout his kingdom can strike modern persons as fussy and misplaced. Yet Latin was to the Carolingian clergy what icons were to the Byzantines. Serious issues were at stake behind an apparently trivial issue of religious practice. For the new elite, "correct" Latin stood for an entire view of a world restored to order. Its erosion, through *rusticitas*, through slipshodness, hinted at dangers that went beyond issues of language. It opened up a truly daunting vista. Throughout Charlemagne's empire, entire populations had, for centuries, been loyal to a largely oral version of Christianity. Christianity was their traditional religion, and Christianity for them was, in effect, the practice of their region. They often derived their instruction from local priests and from monasteries with few books to their name. The highlights of their Christian life consisted in the excitement of pilgrimages to great shrines, where, in "Roman" areas, the hearers would still be bathed in a Latin liturgy and in sermons read out in a "high tongue," in a Latin that was all the more intimate and uplifting for being a familiar but awesome rendering of their own more blurred and "rustic" speech. (Orthodox Greeks and Russians still have the same experience with the "high" language of their liturgies, as do Arabic-speakers with the "divine," classical Arabic of the Qur'ân.) These forms of easygoing, "vernacular" Christianity were by no means confined only to the lower classes. Entire regions, from the aristocracy and the upper clergy downwards, were committed to what we might call "dialects" of Christianity that were as distinctive and as "rustic," by the standards of the new elite, as was their Latin.

Those around Charlemagne, by contrast, were very much the heirs of Boniface. Like Boniface, they were sincerely concerned to save souls. It was their duty, Charles reminded them, "to lead the people of God to the pastures of eternal life."[28] But like Boniface, also, they were far from certain that the people would reach those pastures if they were not warned often that much of what they thought was Christianity was not Christian at all – that the Latin formulae that their priests used might be invalid (as Boniface had thought, of the priests of Bavaria with their execrable Latin) and, in general, that their religious practices were ill-informed, "illiterate," and superstitious. "Correct" Latin texts were to be the basis of a more wide-reaching reform of piety.

Hence the importance of the major shake-up of the Frankish Church which

Charles expected to carry out in 789 through sending his representatives to all regions. We have the agenda for this shake-up in the form of the *Admonitio Generalis*, the "General Warning," addressed to the clergy and laity of his kingdom. The *General Warning* was meant to be read as the foundation document of a new style of "corrected" Christianity. It appeared in the same year of Charles's reign as the year of the reign of king Josiah on which the king (like Charlemagne!) had rediscovered and read aloud to the people the correct, original text of God's Law to Moses. Like Josiah, Charles strove "by visitation, correction and admonition to recall the kingdom which God had given him to the worship of God."[29]

What is significant is the extent to which the *General Warning* reveals a vigorous, "vernacular" Christianity which, just because it was largely oral, expressed a Christian piety which experts such as Alcuin found difficult to control. Far from being untouched by Christianity, much of Carolingian Europe was characterized by intense religious curiosity and by luxuriant forms of Christian practice. The experts considered these to be in need of constant pruning. It is characteristic that, once again, the *General Warning* condemned the notorious *Letter from Heaven*, which was said to have been written by Jesus and placed by him on the altar of Saint Peter at Rome. As we saw in the last chapter, Aldebert had appealed to such a document. Now, only 40 years after Boniface's condemnation of Aldebert, the *Letter from Heaven* was still making its rounds in Francia:

> that most evil and most false letter which some . . . last year declared to have fallen from the sky [is] not to be believed or read but [is] to be burned lest the people be cast into error by such writings. Only . . . the words of holy authors are to be read and expounded.[30]

In Charlemagne's empire, as previously, there was one communication gap which truly worried the upper clergy. This was not that the "vulgar" might not hear the Christian message. It was that they might hear it from the wrong people. As in the days of Gregory of Tours, the greatest danger did not lie in an unabsorbed paganism. The danger was a Christianity of non-literate and half-literate believers who were convinced of their own essential orthodoxy. When, for instance, in 847, a prophetess called Thiota appeared in Mainz, she was instantly brought before the bishops:

> For she said that she knew a definite date for the ending of the world, and other things known only to God, as if they had been divinely re-vealed to her. As a result, many of the common people . . . came to her with gifts and commended themselves to her prayers. Still worse, men in holy orders, ignoring the teaching of the Church followed her . . . After

she had been carefully questioned about her claims, she admitted that a certain priest had coached her in them ... For this she was publicly flogged by the judgment of the synod.[31]

The case of Thiota reveals an extensive category of persons, from literate clergymen to an unlettered woman, who looked to guidance from Christian visionaries and not from the exponents of "correct" Latin texts.

It was to save souls and to meet the challenge posed by unauthorized preachers of a vernacular Christianity that a council of bishops in Tours in 813 declared for the first time ever that homilies – the selected sermons of former preachers such as Caesarius of Arles – were to be read out in Latin, but that they should also be translated, by the preacher *in rusticam Romanam linguam aut Thiotiscam*: "into the language of rustic Romans or into German (Deutsch)."[32]

The decision taken at Tours has been described as "the birth certificate of French."[33] This is to see it with hindsight. At the time, the decision fits well into a movement of control from on top, which was combined with an ever-greater insistence that the commands of the authorities be fully understood by those who received them.

Throughout his reign, Charles had reached out to impose oaths of loyalty on ever-widening sections of the population. It was an aggressive policy. It rendered all those who took such oaths fully liable, in case of default, to the harsh penalties of "infidelity." The oaths were administered in the vernacular of each region. Those who took them could never claim that they had not understood what was spoken on that occasion. Each person was henceforth engaged by his oath to serve Charlemagne "with all my will and with what understanding God has given me." Like the oaths exacted by Charlemagne, the "Christian people" also must know in their own hearts, through having heard it in their own tongue, the "Christian Law" to which they had given their assent.[34]

We can see the Carolingian system of instruction and control working hardest in the newly incorporated territories of Germany. In a region such as Saxony, there was a very real need for loyalty. Here the danger did not come from charismatic leaders of a non-literate Christianity. It came directly from the pagan past. In Saxony, the gods had remained ever-present. They were alternative lords. Baptismal vows copied out in variants of Old High German included a specific list of renunciations: "and I forsake all the Devil's works and words: Thunor, Woden and Saxnote and all the uncanny beings who are their companions."[35]

One of the most remarkable examples of this drive to communicate Christianity to the newly converted Old Saxons was produced a little after the death of Charlemagne. The *Heliand, The Savior,* retold the story of the Gospels in Old German epic verse. In the poem, Christ was presented very much as "the Lord," in a heavy, Carolingian style (and not in the old, looser manner of an Old Saxon chieftain). His Apostles were his war-band. At first reading, the *Heliand* seems to have sprung, unmistakably, straight from the woods of Germany. Yet the condensation of the Gospel narratives on which it was based was taken from a book originally written in northern Syria in the time of Bardaisan – the *Gospel Harmony* of Tatian. By the vagaries of the circulation of ideas within a worldwide Christendom, this product of the third-century eastern Church had ended up in central Europe. Some of the only fragments that have survived of this much-travelled and mysterious text of the Gospels are in Old Dutch.[36]

The *Heliand* was written for monks and for the local Saxon gentry who supported the monks. It was necessary that lay aristocrats should know the message communicated by Christian books in their own tongue. Christianity in Saxony still depended on a fragile alliance between the Franks and the Saxon aristocracy. In 841, this alliance broke down in a time of civil war. Local artistocrats, involved in the fighting, had to turn for support to their own peasants. It was a dangerous move. The peasants insisted on the revival of the *Stellinga,* the assembly of the warrior peasants associated with the pagan days of Old Saxony. It was an ugly moment. The *Stellinga* was suppressed with exemplary savagery. Carolingian sources described it as having been nothing less than a peasants' revolt and an apostasy from Christianity. Whether this was true or not, the revival of the *Stellinga* was a warning sign. The establishment of a Christian order in large parts of Germany could not be taken for granted, It required constant vigilance.[37]

Toward Medieval Christianity: Tithes and Godparents at Liège

Saxony was a "frontier" province, where the problem of communication took on a notably aggressive tone. But the Frankish empire included many peaceful landscapes with long traditions of Christianity. They stand out as "model regions" much as do the "model regions" (given over to restrained capitalistic free enterprise) in the vast territories of the modern Chinese People's Republic. Ghaerbald, bishop of Liege (785–809), and his successor, Walcaud (809–831), lived in one such region. Liège was close to Aachen. The documents connected with the episcopate of Ghaerbald show that he presided over a Christian landscape that had already become recognizably "medieval." They make us realize how long we have had to wait (almost half a millennium) before features which medieval persons (and we moderns) would take for granted as central to the landscape of Christian Europe made their first appearance.

The most important of these new features was the payment of tithes. Ever since the days of Boniface and king Pippin, royal law had made the payment of tithes compulsory. All members of the population were supposed to deliver a tenth of their agrarian produce to their local church. Some form of gift-giving between the local church and the laity had always existed. We saw this in the case of Ireland, in chapter 14. But this was different. In the Carolingian empire, the imposition of tithes was only one aspect, among many others, of a reinvigorated system for extracting rent and services from the peasantry, to which we referred in the last chapter. It marked the beginning of a new dispensation: "no tax in the history of Europe can compare with tithes in length of duration, extent of application and weight of economic burden."[38]

But the imposition of tithes brought the Church closer to the average Christian community than it had been before. For those who paid it needed to be persuaded in no uncertain terms that the Church was worth it. Not surprisingly, Ghaerbald of Liège urged his clergy both to keep careful lists of tithe-payers and to instruct their congregations on a regular basis. It was important that they should do both. The "Christian people" must understand their faith more fully. They had to be encouraged to embrace with the well-schooled loyalty of good subjects a faith that offered services for which they were now expected to pay on a regular basis.[39]

It was important that each Christian must be made fully aware of the exact nature of their baptismal vows, and so of the extent to which these vows bound them to God and his Church. Ever since the victory of Augustine over Pelagius, the baptism of babies was normal in western Christianity. Instant baptism of the child meant instant incorporation in the protection afforded against the Devil by the Christian Church. In effect, infant baptism meant that the godparents of each child vouched for their godchild. It was they who memorized and repeated the Creed and the Lord's Prayer on the child's behalf. The godparents would stand around the priest or bishop, each carrying a godchild on their right arm or, in the case of older children, with each child standing on the right foot of his or her godparent. It was an ideal occasion on which to remind all present of the basic tenets of the Christian faith and of the binding nature of their oath to the Christian God.[40]

To enforce the baptism of adults without so much as a minimal degree of indoctrination – as had happened in the case of the newly conquered Old Saxons and Avars – shocked a man such as Alcuin. Avars, he wrote, were not like those early converts described in the Acts of the Apostles, such as the centurion Cornelius. A Roman centurion, Alcuin the scholar pointed out, had received a liberal education. As a result, he would have understood the preaching of the Apostle Peter and could be instantly baptized. This was not to be expected of the Avars around Vienna, who – writes Alcuin the scholar! – were "a brutish and unreasonable race, and certainly not given to literacy." The illiterate Avars should be allowed at least a token 40 days of Christian preparation.[41]

In the better-favored regions of Francia, however, Charlemagne took preparation for baptism on the part of the godparents very seriously. In 802/806, Ghaerbald received a letter from Aachen.

> At Epiphany, there were many persons with us who wished [as sponsors] to lift up infants from the holy font at baptism. We commanded that each of these be carefully examined and asked if they knew and had memorized the Lord's Prayer and the Creed. There were many who had neither of the formulae memorized. We commanded them to hold back ... They were quite mortified.[42]

It is a revealing incident. With characteristic resourcefulness, Charles and his advisers had fastened on an informal practice, that had been widespread in the lay world, so as to use it as an instrument of religious instruction. For centuries, all over Europe and also in Byzantium, a sponsor had been asked by the family to "lift" the baptized child from the font. This had been a largely profane ritual. Families had used it to seek out alternative patrons and allies, through involving them in the baptism of their children as "co-parents." It was an ingenious arrangement. It showed the ability of generations of post-Roman persons to impose their own "vernacular" meaning upon Christian rituals by making them serve new social needs. The Franks took the practice very seriously indeed, as a ritual device for cementing social bonds.

Charles and his clergy captured the old Frankish practice of "lifting" the child from the font by making of such sponsors, for the first time, "godparents" in the sense to which we have become accustomed. Godparents were incorporated in the baptismal liturgy. By memorizing the Lord's Prayer and the Creed they were co-opted as the fully cognizant guarantors of the child's oath of loyalty to God.[43]

It is a development that was characteristic of the Carolingian age. In the turning of sponsors into godparents, we are witnessing the ingenious exploitation, to new ends, of a situation that had already existed for centuries in Frankish lay society. In "correcting" the laity, Charlemagne and his advisers did not simply impose new demands on them. They often chose, by preference, to make use of the bridges between the lay world and the Church which the Frankish upper classes had already created for their own benefit.

For centuries, the laity had asked for Christian blessing and had used Christian rituals for their own purposes. Now the Church would, as it were, "call in its favors." Rituals which the laity had already developed in their own interest were now used to bind the laity more closely to the Church, so as to cement their loyalty as tithe-payers and to instruct them in the faith.

"Persons of low intelligence": Agobard of Lyons and the Thundermakers

Altogether, with the scholar administrators of the Carolingian empire we are dealing with a singularly purposeful body of men. In their writings, many of them appear as the first technocrats of Europe. They claimed to know the Christian Law in its majestic entirety. They knew how to guide the Christian people to fulfill its goals. As landlords and bureaucrats, they kept lists of their congregations, for the purpose of extracting rents and tithes. All over Europe, they were more of a presence in the lives of those whom they intended to "admonish" and "correct" than they had been in previous centuries. Faced by Christian practices different from their own, they tended to dismiss such practices, quite bluntly, as unenlightened. One admittedly extreme example illustrates this tendency. Agobard was born in Spain and trained at Aachen. He became archbishop of Lyons in 816, where he acted, also, as imperial commissioner.

Agobard soon found that Lyons was no Liège. The former kingdom of Burgundy, in the Rhône valley, was a Mediterranean region with long traditions of its own. Agobard showed little patience with the "folk Christianity" that he encountered. For instance, he was told that certain persons in Burgundy were believed by all classes to have the power to bring down hail on the fields of their neighbors, and that they were allied to a race of persons from "Magonia," who sailed through the clouds in boats, to take the harvests back to their distant country. This was, perhaps, an aerial version of the Irish belief in "the Land of the Other Side," which may have survived since Celtic times in Gaul.[44]

Agobard was not impressed. A humane judge, he intervened to save four poor wretches who had been brought before him. They risked being stoned to death as inhabitants of Magonia who had fallen to earth. The terms in which Agobard justified his dismissal of the case deserve our attention. For in his defense of his own action, he betrayed a slight but significant shift in attitudes to the supernatural. Previously, it had been taken for granted that demons did, indeed, have control of the lower air, and that ill-intentioned persons frequently allied themselves with the demons to cause harm. Good Christians, by contrast, refused to make contact with the shadowy counter-empire, whose power in the material world was rendered all too palpable by the crash of thunder and by the hailstorms that fell like a scythe upon the vineyards. Everyone believed that holy men and women had been raised up by God so as to hold an all too real counter-empire at bay. Christian priests, monks, and holy persons challenged the demons in the name of the yet greater power of Christ. But the demons remained, nonetheless, a massive presence. They were far from being "popular illusions."

Agobard, by contrast, drained the demonic world of much of its solidity. Agobard was an uncompromising monotheist. The "Christian Law," as Agobard presented it in a series of citations from the Old Testament, proved that all power in the supernatural world belonged to God alone. No human being could influence the weather. Without God's permission, not even the demons had the power to hurt mankind. Demons, of course, existed. But, for Agobard, they were a distant presence. Reports of their activities in Burgundy could be safely discounted. They were merely believed to have been active, and such belief was, in his opinion, a popular illusion. It proved what, as a court-bred scholar, he had always suspected, which was that the uneducated were no more than "half-believers." For "stupidity [was] an essential element in misbelief." Faced by religious practices of which he disapproved Agobard was content to declare that the Devil found it easy to delude

> those over whom he thinks he has the best chance of prevailing, because they have barely any faith and lack the ballast of reason – such as girls, young boys, and persons of low intelligence.[45]

For Agobard, the application of the universal "Christian Law" in backward Burgundy assumed not only that Christianity was true and endowed with greater supernatural power than its rivals: in its authorized exponents, Christianity and cultural superiority could now be assumed to go hand in hand.

Res sacratae, "Consecrated Things": Sacred and Profane in the Carolingian Empire: Theodulf of Orléans

Agobard was an extremist. He was an unusually consequential exponent of a tendency toward a clerical detachment from all forms of vernacular religion that was latent but never dominant in the Carolingian reforms. But this streak of contempt for "popular" practices was never dominant at the time. Agobard was isolated even in his own times. We get closer to the heart of Charlemagne's endeavor if we go back in time to the late 780s. Here we find a writer who expressed, with rare clarity, the manner in which the "corrected" Latin Christianity of the Carolingian empire had taken a path that diverged significantly from its Christian neighbors in Byzantium.

As we have already seen, at the end of chapter 16, Theodulph, the future bishop of Orléans (798–818), had been commissioned in 793 to prepare a memorandum on the cult of images, in the form of a detailed rebuttal of the *Acta* of the Iconophile Council of Nicaea of 787. The memorandum was read out before Charles. The manuscript still contains a precious record of the emperor's comments. The memorandum came to be known (in modern times) as the *Libri Carolini* – Books for Charles. It was not well known at the time: Charles came to consider it too radical a statement to be circulated widely. Nevertheless, partly because it was a semi-secret memorandum, the *Libri Carolini* summed up with unusual harshness attitudes which Theodulph held in common with his colleagues.[46]

It was important for Theodulph to make plain the differences between himself and "the Greeks." The clergy around Charlemagne had much in common with the Iconoclasts of Byzantium. Like the Iconoclasts, they were concerned to reassess a Christian inheritance which had been shaken in the previous century. Like the Iconoclasts also, they intended to root out abuses in worship which had crept into the Church.

In his memoir, Theodulph spells out with great care the basic religious assumptions which governed his own worldview. It was a worldview very different from that of Orthodox Byzantines. For Theodulph, God was a distant ruler, sharply separated from his creatures. God was to his creation "as a lord to his servants." (*Optime*, "Excellent idea!" was Charles' comment at that point.)[47] It was his will alone that bridged the chasm between himself and human beings. He did not offer to the human race a gentle flow of visual symbols, which linked the invisible to the visible world in a seemingly unbroken continuum, as Greek thinkers such as Dionysius the Areopagite and John of Damascus liked to believe. He preferred to make himself known by his commands. Law was God's greatest gift to mankind. When it came to the visual tokens of his will, God had used a stern economy of means. He had granted to his people a few, utterly dependable visible signs through which he had approached them and through which they could approach him. To the people of Israel he had given the Law and the Ark of the Covenant. "Shimmering with so many awe-inspiring and incomparable mysteries," the Ark was a unique artefact. In creating it, the skilled Besaleel, "filled with the Spirit of God," had not followed his own visual imagination but the command of God alone.[48]

The Ark of the Covenant was a work of art untouched by the arbitrary quality that characterized all other forms of artistic creation. Icons, by contrast, in Theodulph's opinion, were not like the Ark of the Covenant. They partook in the frightening indeterminacy of all profane activity. Without its written label,

Theodulph pointed out, an icon of the Virgin could be mistaken for the portrait of any majestic and beautiful woman – even, perhaps, for an image of Venus.[49] Nothing, in itself, guaranteed the "sanctity" of such an icon; for nothing painted in it by the artist had come directly from the will of God, as had been the case when the inspired Besaleel had constructed the Ark of the Covenant.

The Ark of the Covenant was counted among the *res sacratae*. It was a "consecrated," holy object, because its awesome form had been explicitly laid down by God. Such *res sacratae* reflected on earth the eternal will of God. In Christian times, the consecratory prayers of the Mass and the text of the Scriptures acted for the Christian people as the Ark of the Covenant had once acted for the people of Israel. They were truly holy things. They were ordained by God.[50]

When, as bishop of Orléans, Theodulph built his own exquisite little chapel at Saint Germigny-des-Prés, beside the Loire near Orléans, he placed a mosaic of the Ark of the Covenant in the apse above the altar. In a place reserved for "consecrated things," only visual objects known to have been given by God to his people, by his express command, should meet the eye. As bishop of Orléans, also, Theodulph's regulations to the clergy laid especial emphasis on the holiness of the Church and of the Eucharist. He was not over-demanding in his demands on lay persons. It was enough for a Christian to pray twice a day, in the morning and at evening, "You who have made me, have mercy on me" and "God, be merciful to me, a sinner." But they should know what were "sacred things" and what were not. The space around the altar was sacred: no woman was to enter it. The holy vessels used at the Eucharist should be worthy of it. Even the bread offered at Mass should not be "common" bread. And churches, he insisted, were holy places. They should not be used as temporary barns, in which to store the village's supply of hay.[51]

Holy places could be sumptuous. Frankish ambassadors travelling to Constantinople had reported to Theodulph that they had found there many dilapidated basilicas, their roofs open to the sky and their lights untended. The ambassadors had come from a world of imposing shrines. They professed to be shocked to find that Byzantine society devoted so much energy to painting pictures and paid little attention to the fabric of holy buildings. In contrast to Byzantium, in Theodulph's opinion, the world of Latin Christianity was right to value the shrines of the saints and the splendid cases which surrounded their relics. The unearthly brilliance of the gold and jewelled reliquaries in which the relics of the saints were encased showed that "the lords," the saints, were "in" them. There was no doubt that this was where the saints were "present" on earth. Before such objects, the faithful should, indeed, bow with reverential awe – as Gregory of Tours had done, a full two centuries earlier. In Byzantium, by contrast, the "presence" of the saints seemed to be sought all over the place. The eyes of believers strained toward icons, many of which were not even placed in the church, but in the profane setting of private houses, even in bedrooms. In Theodulph's opinion, it was better not to rely on icons. Rather, one should go to a great basilica (such as the shrine of Saint Martin at Tours or of Saint Peter in Rome) and kneel before the saint, who was "fully present" there, in his ancient tomb.[52]

The artistic traditions associated with the sacred in northern Europe tended to support Theodulph's anti-iconic arguments. Early medieval art had turned away from the human face. Stately human figures could, of course, be seen on the walls of basilicas all over the West, from Rome to Bede's Wearmouth and to the shrine of Saint Brigid in Kildare. But these human figures were not singled out as icons. They served, rather, as "books for the uncultivated." They reminded the bulk of the population of Biblical narratives which only the learned could read for themselves in the original text. Pictures were necessary, but they were not "holy things."[53]

The highest art, in the north, had not been concerned with catching the "living" likeness of a human being, as was the case in a classical tradition of human representation which had survived unbroken in Byzantium. The art of the jeweller, and not that of the portrait painter, was the most prized. For the magical cunning of a craftsman consisted in taking raw wealth – precious stones, precious fragments of gold and silver (often unceremoniously hacked from ancient pieces, or in the form of coins extorted as tribute) – and transforming this mass of shimmering metal into condensed signs of power. Hence the skill devoted to the great brooches, to the belts, to the ornamented armor, and to similar regalia by means of which the kings and nobles of Ireland, Britain, and Francia sheathed their own persons with stunning tokens of their status.

The religious artist took this process of transformation one step further. The scribes who illuminated the Book of Kells and the other great Gospel books of the British Isles (which we saw in chapter 16) and the craftsmen who produced the great votive crowns, the crosses, and the relic-cases of Gaul and Spain were not concerned to catch a "likeness." Their task was to take "dead" matter, associated with the profane wealth and power of great donors – precious pigments, the skins of vast herds, gold and jewels – and make them come alive, by creating from them objects whose refulgent, intricate surfaces declared that they had moved, beyond their human source, into the realm of the sacred.

Most important of all was the fact that Theodulph's religious world was dominated by a written text. Carefully copied and passed down through the centuries, the Holy Scriptures stood out as the unique manifestation of the will of God. It was through books, and not through icons, that God had chosen to lead the human race "by the hand." When Moses had taught the people of Israel, he had done so

not by painting but by the written word . . . nor was it written of him
that "He took paintings," but *Moses took the Book . . . and read in the
ears of the people the words of the Book.*[54]

Theodulph and his colleagues placed the words of the Bible at the heart of
their religious culture. A contemporary Irish poem on the ideal monastery
wrote of one such great Bible, placed open in the middle of the church:

> . . . *bright candles*
> *over the holy white scriptures.*[55]

Careful copying and meditation on the Bible were activities tinged with an
edge of mystic joy. This tradition reached back from the age of Theodulph,
over four centuries, through Bede and Gregory the Great, through the Vivarium of Cassiodorus, to the leisured and literate intellectuals of the age of
Augustine and Jerome.

What had changed, over the centuries, was that the Latin book had, by the
time of Theodulph, become a world of its own. It stood out in majestic
isolation from what was now an alien babble of vernacular tongues. To
understand the Scriptures and to explain their contents to the "people beloved of Christ" became all the more urgent. It shocked Theodulph that his
Christian colleagues in the East seemed unaware of the perils and the opportunities of this situation. An entire "Christian people" needed the sharp *words
of the Law*, and the Greeks, with proud insouciance, took the "soft" option:
they offered their charges the trivial medium of "little pictures."

> You, who claim to have preserved the purity of the faith by means of
> images, go and stand before them with your incense. We will search out
> the commands of our Lord by eager scrutiny, in the bound books – the
> *codices* – of God's own Law.[56]

Behind the contemptuous tone adopted by Theodulph toward Byzantine
piety there lay a great fear. Incorrect Christian worship might erode the boundary between the sacred and the profane. This boundary had been put in
place, only recently and with considerable effort, in many newly converted
areas of the Latin West. The stark contrast between a world of profane objects and a small cluster of "sacred things" was basic to Theodulph's arguments. In Byzantium, he claimed, far too many things were treated as "holy."
Theodulph showed no sensitivity to the central argument of John of Damascus. As we saw in chapter 17, this was that God's mercy had suffused the
entire created order with a generalized sacrality. The world was filled with
visible tokens which led the worshipper to the invisible God. Such argu-

ments did not impress Theodulph. They struck him as opening the way for a dangerous blurring of the sacred and the profane. In his opinion, Byzantine Christians had blurred the distinction between mere paintings and the truly "holy" tombs of the saints. Byzantine emperors had blurred the distinction between the human and the divine. They claimed to be "colleagues" and "co-rulers" with Christ. Charlemagne claimed to be never more than "a sinner" and the "servant" of Christ. Petitions by Byzantine holy men to the Byzantine court, so Theodulph noted, had even dared to speak of the emperor's "divine ears"! Such expressions struck him as close to paganism.[57]

In Theodulph's opinion, Charles' empire was superior to Byzantium because, in the Latin Church, the profane and the sacred had been held apart. Neither was allowed to invade the other. Each had its proper place. Because of this, each enjoyed a certain merciful freedom from the other. Condemned by Theodulph to a humble profanity, Latin artists could feel free to "do their own thing." They did not have to strain, as did the later painters of icons in the Orthodox world, to catch the exact likenesses of holy figures and to freeze in paint an unchanging vision preserved for them, since time immemorial, by the Orthodox tradition. Latin church-painters were free to change their minds. They could fill the churches with new creations. They could even make sculptures – a practice that remained deeply disturbing to Orthodox Christians. By the end of the Middle Ages, the free flow of western art had rendered the Christian iconography of Latin churches virtually unrecognizable to Byzantine visitors.[58]

In an analogous manner, French, Italian, and Spanish were declared to be "profane" languages, compared with the sacred quality of Latin. This set them free to evolve, as they rapidly slipped out of the control of a Latin now deemed to be a perfect, but safely dead, language.

Altogether, the sharp separation of the sacred from the profane had opened up a neutral space. In that space, the entire pre-Christian past of northern Europe might find its niche. For the pre-Christian past could be allowed to flank the Christian present, provided that it remained resolutely profane. Memories of the pre-Christian world must not be allowed to rival, in their fascination, the high, true, sacrality of the "Christian Law." They must also be shorn of the sinister, negative sacrality associated with true pagan practice – with sacrifice and divination. But, given these conditions, the ancestral cultures of western Europe were free to contribute to the creation of vernacular literatures and of ethnic histories which could be shared by Christian clergymen and by lay persons. Such a literature gave the Christians of many areas of northern Europe access to a "deep" past that was not that of the Church. It is to this development that we must turn in our last chapter.

Map 10 The Atlantic world

CHAPTER 20

In geār dagum, "In Days of Yore": Northern Christendom and its Past

The World of the Northmen

In the 820s and 830s Dorestad was the greatest port in western Europe. During the reign of Charlemagne's successor, Louis the Pious (814–840), four and a half million silver coins were struck at its mint. They showed a cross placed in the middle of the façade of a classical temple, and bore the inscription *Religio Christiana*.[1] An ostentatiously Christian empire lay at the southern end of the trade routes which led across the North Sea. North of Dorestad and Frisia stretched non-Christian lands, characterized by fragile chiefdoms. In Denmark, along the fjords of Norway, and in the lowlands of southern Sweden, small kings rose and fell according to their ability to gain access to wealth, through plunder on the waters of the North Atlantic and the Baltic. But they were also traders. In this period, Hedeby in Denmark and Birka (Björkö) in southern Sweden became the Dorestads of the North. They were *emporia*, ringed by fortified ditches. It was there that the merchants of the Christian south purchased the products of the wild lands of the north – all manner of sumptuous furs from the Baltic and precious walrus-tusk ivory from the Arctic seas.[2] The Franks referred to the varied inhabitants of Scandinavia as "Northmen." (What is now called Normandy, on the coast of France, was the "land of the Northmen": it was the only permanent Scandinavian settlement in Continental Europe.)

The Northmen were pagans. They had remained fiercely loyal to their gods. Only gods could impart to their worshippers the suprahuman vigor and good luck which gave to individuals and to groups a competitive edge over their many rivals. Thus, in around the year 800, two religious systems faced each other at either end of the North Sea. In true Carolingian style, the "Christian Religion" coinage of Dorestad conveyed a message of imperial solidity, protected by the power of Christ. Such confidence was met,

SCANDINAVIA, EUROPE, AND THE ATLANTIC ca. 800–ca. 1000

Offa, king of Mercia 757–796
Beowulf written down ca.780

Baptism of Harald Klak 826
Anskar 801–865
mission to Sweden 830/1

Period of Viking Raids in Western
Europe 850+

Rus' (Scandinavian) attack on
Constantinople 860

Settlement of Iceland 870

Settlement of Greenland 930

Harald Bluetooth, king of Denmark
958–987

Settlement at Anse-les-Meadows,
Labrador 982

Conversion of Kiev 987

Olaf Tryggvason of Norway 995–1000
Conversion of Iceland 1000

Snorri Sturluson 1179–1241

in Scandinavia, by a very different set of beliefs. As we saw in chapter 14, thousands of golden amulets associated with good fortune and the protection of the gods have been discovered in Denmark and southern Sweden. They were dedicated to shrines or worn on the persons of leaders so as to increase their numinous good fortune in war. In the fifth and sixth centuries, late Roman gold coins had reached as far as Denmark, where they were promptly transformed into images of victory-bringing gods.

In the ninth century, the Frankish kingdom was far closer to Scandinavia than Rome had ever been. Francia and the lands of the Northmen were close neighbors. Only a few hundred miles of the North Sea lay between them. Frankish goods poured into Denmark and southern Sweden. Not surprisingly, these goods included high-quality Frankish swords. Even the swords spoke of the power of a distant God. The hilt of a Frankish sword, found in Sweden, bears a verse from the Psalms:

> *Blessed be the Lord my strength, which teacheth my*
> *hands to war and my fingers to fight.* (Psalm 144:1)

For Franks and Northmen alike, war was a matter of truly religious seriousness. Sacred words – Latin Psalms or, in Scandinavia, arcane runes – showed that the gods were close to hand, to enhance the efficacy of a warrior's weapons. Christ was the Frankish god. It was possible that he might find acceptance in Scandinavia, provided that he lived up to the expectations of a society of brittle warriors and enterprising pirates and traders.[3]

Scandinavia itself consisted of a band of coastal settlements, caught between a North Sea whose southern end was ringed by Christian kingdoms and a vast hinterland which stretched as far as the Arctic Circle. But Scandinavia did not only look south. To the east, along the Baltic, the "Northmen" were in contact with a world which reached, through modern Finland, as far as the Siberian forest zone. This was a world of hunters and pastoralists, of Lapps and Finns. Their shamanistic rites, performed in animal costumes, implied an open frontier between the human and the animal and between the spirit and the human world. Shamanistic practices were partly adopted by the Northmen. Performed in southern Sweden, they struck observers from the distant Christian south. In around 850 an abbot in northern Francia wrote to a missionary in Birka to ask about the manner in which the Northmen transformed themselves through wearing animal masks. He wished to bring the *Etymologies* of Isidore of Seville up to date. Was it really true, he asked the missionary, that a race of dog-headed men lived at the far edge of the earth?[4]

As this letter shows, contact with Scandinavia had intensified by 850. It had been fed by Frankish imperial policy and by trading relations between the Northmen and Dorestad. But, with this contact, Continental Christians found themselves confronted by a far wider world than they had expected. With the pagan Northmen, it seemed as if they had truly reached the edge of the world, where humans merged with the beasts.

Between the years 800 and 1000, the entire North Sea area – Scandinavia, Britain, Ireland, and the shores of Continental Europe – was an immense "middle ground," in which Christians and pagans met, much as barbarians and Romans had once met in the "middle ground" of the Roman frontier regions. It was an infinitely more extensive "middle ground" than the frontiers of the Roman empire had ever been. Compared with the highly localized and slow-moving kingdoms of Continental Europe, the distances across which the Northmen moved with ease in their superb ships were unimaginable.

The expeditions of the Northmen reached both eastward and westward. Scandinavian long-ships reached far to the east along the Baltic as far as Lake Ladoga, behind modern Saint Petersburg. Then they turned south, edging down the great river systems of what are now Russia and the Ukraine, to reach Kiev on the Dnieper. These small bands of warriors and slave-traders from distant Sweden came to be known to the local populations as the *Rus'*. They have left their name on what we now call Russia. Once at Kiev, the way to the southeast lay open – contact could be made both with Baghdad and with Constantinople. A memorial stone set up in Sweden, carved with runic letters in the shape of a great snake, told the story of one such expedition to unimaginably distant lands:

> They fared like men
> far after gold
> and in the east
> gave the eagle food
> [by the slaughter of battle].
> They died southward
> in Serkland
> [the Land of Silk].[5]

The Dnieper flowed straight into the Black Sea where Constantinople lay, at its southern end. In 860, a fleet of Northmen (already known to Byzantines as the *Rôs*) even attempted without success to attack the city. Later, these warriors from the far north were employed as special guards for the emperor. One such guard may have scratched the runic inscription which can still be seen on the balustrade of the gallery of the Hagia Sophia.[6]

A century later, when the Scandinavian colonists of Kiev, the *Rus'*, decided to accept Christianity, they did it with characteristic canniness. They sent embassies to observe the various religions of Europe and the Middle East. It was the Byzantine, Orthodox Christianity, whose glory was made plain in Justinian's Hagia Sophia, which won the competition:

> We went among the Germans [the Latin Christians] and saw them performing many ceremonies in the churches. But we saw no glory there. Then we went to the Greeks . . . and they led us to the edifices where they worship their God, and we knew not whether we were on heaven or on earth. For on earth there is no such splendor or such beauty. We only know that God dwells there among men . . . For we cannot forget that beauty.[7]

The conversion of Kiev took place 987. Kiev lay at the easternmost end of the immense world which had been opened up by the ships of the Northmen. Kiev and Constantinople were as far away from southern Sweden to the southeast as Iceland and the coasts of Greenland were to the northwest. The Northmen had sailed there also. Iceland was settled in 870, a decade after the raid of the *Rus'* on Constantinople. Greenland was reached around 930. In 982, five years, that is, before the conversion of Kiev, Scandinavians landed at "Vinland" on the American mainland. An impressive outpost, plainly intended for permanent settlement, has been discovered at Anse-les-Meadows on the coast of Labrador.[8]

The conversion of Kiev was not an isolated event. It was part of a wave of official conversions to Christianity in Scandinavia and all over eastern Europe which took place in the decades before the year 1000. By A.D. 1000 the "middle ground" where pagans and Christians had once met was closed. From Iceland to the Dnieper, the Northmen became Christian.

The Viking Raids in Western Europe

It is not the purpose of this chapter to follow the story of the conversion of the Northmen in detail. Briefly, it began with the presence of the Carolingian empire. The new wealth generated in northern Europe under this empire drew the Northmen ever further south. They came first as traders and, soon after, as raiders. After 850, what we call the "Viking raids" gathered momentum. They inflicted great damage on Ireland and England. On the Continent, the "Vikings" intervened, in increasing numbers and with great ferocity, in the civil wars which eventually destroyed the unity of the proud Christian empire of Charlemagne and Louis the Pious. Like the barbarians of the last centuries of the Roman empire, the Vikings did not come as invaders as if from outer space. Often they intervened, ruthlessly, as the nominal allies of competing factions within the Frankish empire itself.

But they came with one overwhelming advantage. The small and mobile fleets of the Vikings could strike anywhere along the Atlantic coastline of Europe and the British Isles. Thus, the Viking incursions were never massive. Rather, they generated the sort of terror which is inspired by a ruthless sharpshooter. An account of a slightly later series of raids shows how the Vikings broke the morale of their Anglo-Saxon opponents:

> And when they went to the east, the English army was in the west, and when they were in the south, our army was in the north . . . Finally there was no leader who would collect an army, but each fled as best he could, and in the end no shire would even help the next.[9]

By a bitter irony of history, the greatest Christian shrines of northern Europe were easy prey to Viking raiders. The great centers of the golden age of Northumbria, Iona and the Holy Island of Lindisfarne, were offshore islands. Viking fleets edged up the great rivers, the Rhine and the Seine, which flowed through the very heart of the Frankish kingdom. They found churches and monasteries which the kings and aristocracies of Europe had filled with golden objects of devotion. An account in the *Anglo-Saxon Chronicle*, from a slightly later period, catches a Viking band at work in Peterborough, a major shrine in the Fenlands, beside the river Ouse:

> They went into the church, climbed up to the Holy Rood [the great Crucifix] and took the crown off the Lord's head – all of pure gold – and then took the footrest that was under his feet, which was all of red gold. They climbed up to the steeple and brought down the altar-frontal that was hidden there – it was all of gold and silver – and took there two golden shrines and nine of silver, and they took fifteen great crucifixes, both of gold and silver.[10]

The Viking incursions of the late ninth century were a terrible moment. But, seen against the overall background of the history of Scandinavia and the North Atlantic, they were over as quickly as an ocean squall. They were only part of the story. For we must remember what "Viking" meant. A "Viking" was an "entrepreneurial" king on the warpath, on the *vík*. He was in search of tribute and prestige.

> Better for you to bestride steed, draw sword, fell a host. Your brothers have fine halls and better lands than you. You should go *vík*-ing. Let men feel your blade.

In many ways, the Vikings were an unwelcome throwback to the untidy origins of the Christian kingdoms of Europe and the British Isles. They were what the warrior kings of Saxon Britain had been. Clovis and Charles Martel had once acted as they did, when they plundered the lands of southern Gaul. Though they now came in ships with terrifying range and mobility, the Vikings were warriors in the old style. They aimed to gather plunder, to exact tribute, and, if possible, to assert overlordship.[11]

But, as happened in earlier centuries, conquest meant contact. As a result of the Viking raids, Scandinavia filled up with Christian wealth, with Christian slaves, and with Christian ideas. The fleets of the Northmen bridged the North Atlantic in a single network which linked Dublin to Denmark and Iceland, and Sweden to Kiev and Constantinople. As a result, the Scandinavian world was sucked inexorably into the political and social structures of the Christian south by the very success of its pirate kings.

This happened in both east and west at roughly the same time. As we saw in chapter 17, the conversion of Kiev to Orthodox Christianity, in 987, represented a diplomatic triumph of the Byzantine empire which changed the face of eastern Europe. But in the west, also, the Latin Christianity of the lands to the south of Scandinavia came to penetrate the settlements of the Northmen wherever they were. By the year 1000, Christianity had spread to the furthest corners of a newly created North Atlantic world. Christian crosses marked the headland burial of a Scandinavian adventurer from Greenland, shot by Eskimo on the coast of Labrador. "'Call it Krossanes [Cross Headland] for ever more,' [he said] 'For Greenland was at that time Christian.'"[12] The runic grave-inscription of the chieftain Ulvljot, set up west of Trondheim in northern Norway in 1008, dated his death by the coming of the new religion. "Twelve winters had Christendom been in Norway."[13] Even in the distant north, *Kristintumr*, "Christendom," a word recently coined in Saxon England and now adopted in Norway, had come to stay.

"Let us enquire whether Christ will be on our side": Christianity in Denmark and Sweden

Let us look for a moment at the stages of the process by which this happened. We begin, in the ninth century, with the southern waters of the North Sea dominated by the Carolingian empire. The son of Charlemagne, Louis the Pious, was by no means a pale shadow of his father. He ruled an empire whose ideological ambitions were at their height. In 826, Harald Klak, an exiled Danish king, came south to be baptized. He hoped to return with Frankish support to assert hegemonial power over his fellow-chieftains. The emperor Louis himself acted as his godfather. Klak was brought to the palace at Ingelheim.

The frescoes in the main hall of the palace of Ingelheim conjured up the huge confidence of the Franks that their empire represented nothing less than the culmination of Christian history. Founders of pagan empires – Alexander the Great and the ancient Romans – were placed at the back of the hall. Near the apse, where Louis stood with his newly baptized Danish sub-king, were the emperors of a more advanced and yet greater age. These were "true" emperors, because they were Christian emperors, Roman and Frankish alike. Constantine and Theodosius I faced their equals, Charles Martel, shown conquering the Frisians, and Charles, as he "drew the Saxons under his [Christian] laws." Harald Klak, now dressed in a purple cloak, was to join the family of Christian kings. He was to establish in Denmark a more forceful style of kingship, linked to Frankish wealth and to Frankish Christianity.[14]

What seemed possible at Ingelheim, however, was by no means practicable in Denmark and southern Sweden. Harald Klak proved an immediate failure. Over-mighty kings were not welcome in Denmark. We can follow this tale of failed mission in the remarkable *Life of Anskar* written around 870 by his disciple, Rimbert, who was himself a converted Dane. Anskar was a Frank. He had been a monk of Corbie on the Somme. He first attached himself to Harald's retinue, and was later made bishop of Hamburg and Bremen. He visited Birka, in southern Sweden, in 830 and 852. Until his death in 865, he enjoyed a commission to evangelize the north which was as wide as that once held by Boniface in Germany. But he was a long way from home. Unlike Boniface, he did not have the support of Frankish armies. Anskar could never be a confident consolidator of previous, looser allegiances to Christianity, as Boniface had once been. The heroic Frankish bishop remained very much a peripheral figure to the chieftains he visited.[15]

Anskar faced a society that was quite prepared to accept Christ. But it was prepared to do so only if Christ was treated as one god among many, and provided that his usefulness was first indicated to them through traditional forms of divination. To take one example. A raiding party of Swedes stranded in Kurland discussed their dilemma.

> "The God of the Christians frequently helps those who cry to Him [they said] . . . Let us enquire whether He will be on our side." Accordingly . . . lots were cast and it was found that Christ was willing to help them.

They later learned from Christian merchants that a 40-day fast from meat (the Christian fast of Lent) would count as an acceptable return to Christ for his help.

> After this, many . . . began to lay stress upon the fasts observed by Christians and upon almsgiving . . . because they had learned that this was pleasing to Christ.[16]

Rimbert, Anskar's disciple, was a man of Danish origin. He knew what Scandinavians wanted and how they made up their minds on matters of religion. In his *Life of Anskar*, every successful contact between Christianity and the local population was framed by such a scene of divination, testing, and partial acceptance of Christ as a new god. We have come a long way from the triumphal narratives of supernatural confrontation and dramatic conversions of rulers, such as had fed the Christian imagination of the Mediterranean and northwestern Europe. In retrospect at least, Scandinavian societies chose to associate their adoption of "Christendom" with solemn moments of decision-making, in which the new religion was subjected to traditional divinatory techniques. Only when Christianity passed that test could it expect to gain public approval.

Narratives of this kind, which made the acceptance of Christianity dependent on local religious practices, effectively cut down to size the efforts of missionaries from the Christian south.[17] But it also cut down the role of local kings. After 900, kings could be overbearing in Scandinavia, especially when they enjoyed the plundered wealth of England and Francia. Harald Bluetooth of Denmark (958–987) was typical of a new style of strong kingship. This new kingship owed more to the Christian countries which he had once terrorized as a raider than to older Scandinavian traditions of consensual chieftainship. Harald Bluetooth was in a position to do what Harald Klak had failed to do. He declared the Danes Christian. And he did this without so much as consulting a missionary. He then built a large church at Jelling, near the graves of his ancestors. He flanked the church with a great rock, that showed a fiercely bearded Christ whose outstretched arms were lost in a tangle of snake-like ornament. The runic inscription declared that Harald had "won all Denmark to himself and made the Danes Christian." He even made his father a Christian in retrospect. Gorm, the old pagan, was taken from the neighboring royal burial mound and was placed in the church close to the altar. Altogether, Harald Bluetooth showed what a strong king could do.[18]

"Let us all have one law and one faith": The Conversion of Iceland, A.D. 1000

The high-handed activities of kings such as Harald Bluetooth were watched with disquiet by other Scandinavians, settled in Iceland, in the middle of the North Atlantic. The settlers of Iceland were proud of the fact that they had come to their island precisely so as to escape the rising power of kings.[19] Settled since the 870s at a safe distance from Scandinavia, they did not wish to be overshadowed once again by kings. They were disturbed by what they saw of the forceful Christian rule of Olaf Tryggvason (995–1000), who had established himself as king of Norway at Trondheim, 750 miles across the sea. Converted to Christianity through his contacts with Anglo-Saxon England, Olaf had imposed Christianity with great violence on the Trondelag, the region around Trondheim. The Trondelag was a prosperous fjord. It was the northernmost oasis of agrarian land in Europe, only 200 miles beneath the Arctic Circle. To impose his views, Olaf had broken the will of an entire society of independent farmers.[20]

Not surprisingly, with such an example just over the water, the Icelanders decided that, if they were to become Christians, it should be entirely on their own terms. They would not appear to succumb to pressure from a powerful Christian neighbor. For Iceland was a resolutely kingless society. The population lived in isolated farmsteads scattered over an immense landscape divided by steep fjords, lava flows, and lowering glaciers. Agreement to follow a common "law" was the only thing that Icelanders shared. The yearly meeting of the chief men of every district at Thingvellir – the Vale of the Assembly – was what knit the island together. A division between pagan and Christian families, each of them following a different religious law, would have destroyed what little consensus existed in these fragile settlements. So, in the Assembly of 1000, the Icelanders authorized their "Law Speaker," Thorgeir of Ljosvatn, to decide for them whether they should accept Christianity as the sole "law" of the island. "Let us all have one law and one faith. For it will prove that, if we sunder the law, we will also sunder the peace." An old-fashioned pagan, Thorgeir knew what to do. He could only "speak the law" with authority after he had "gone under the cloak." "He lay down and spread his cloak over himself, and lay all that day and the next night, nor did he speak a word."[21] It is possible that this was a shamanistic séance. It employed a form of divination, through sensory deprivation, which was common to Gaelic Scotland, Scandinavia, and Finland.[22] If that is so, then it was by the summoning of spirit powers, in a pan-North Atlantic ritual, that Christ was declared, next morning, at the Law Rock, to be the new god of the Icelanders:

> all people should be Christian and those be baptized who were still
> unbaptized in this land: but as for infanticide, the old law [which al-
> lowed it] should stand, as also the eating of horseflesh.

Even sacrifice was allowed for a time, provided that it was not seen by outside witnesses. We have every reason to believe that infanticide (especially the killing of female babies) continued.[23]

We must remember that this was how an influential group of Icelanders deliberately chose to remember their conversion. At the time, the situation may well have been more complex. The conversion to Christianity owed much to other factors. One factor was a massive influx of Irish slaves, which threatened to alter Icelandic society as drastically as the influx of British slaves to Ireland in the time of Saint Patrick had once threatened to undermine the Irish nobility. Another factor was the presence of important women, such as Aud the Deep-Minded. Aud was an influential landowner. When Aud settled in the Breidafjord, she brought with her the Christianity which she had adopted when she lived at Howth (the *Hofd*, the "headland," in Icelandic) which overlooked the Bay of Dublin. Dublin Bay was an open bay similar to that of the Breidafjord. It was a mere 1,600 miles south of her new home in Iceland – such was the size of the world of the Scandinavian settlements of the Atlantic! But, compared with the tale of Thorgeir the Law-Speaker, slaves and women did not make a good story.[24]

What is truly remarkable about the story is those who told it. The tale of the conversion of the Icelanders was written down over a century later, in the *Book of the Icelanders* of Ari Thorgilsson the Wise, at the behest of the Christian bishop of Skalholt.[25] This was in 1122–1133 – the age of Saint Bernard and of the Crusades. Yet, far to the north, the decision of Thorgeir "under the cloak" constituted the only narrative of Christianization worth remembering for the clergymen of Iceland. If the Icelanders had become Christian, what needed to be remembered about the process was that they had done so by following the wise procedures of decision-making laid down in their pagan laws.

The Past in the Present: Pre-Christian Gods and a Christian Social Order

The Icelanders were remarkable for their intense attachment to their own pre-Christian past. Many Icelandic clergymen were widely travelled persons. Some had been to the Schools of Paris. Yet, throughout the Middle Ages, they continued to patronize poets and writers of *Sagas* who drew, without a trace of embarrassment, on a frankly pre-Christian cultural inheritance. In Continental Europe, by this time, the only pagan past which attracted the attention of learned persons was the dreamlike paganism of Greece and Rome. They read of it in classical authors, as of a distant world, discontinuous with their own. But the pre-Christian past of Scandinavia was still very much a part of the present in Iceland, Norway, and Sweden. The only systematic account of what we have come to call "Nordic" paganism, the *Edda*, was written in the thirteenth century by the great Icelandic antiquarian, Snorri Sturluson (1179–1241).[26]

But Iceland was not unique. Icelandic literature was not the product of a romantic and exotic periphery. Though written at a later time, it brings into sharp focus a dilemma which had, in fact, dogged the Christian elites of northern Europe since the days of their conversion in the sixth and seventh centuries. It was this: how much of the pre-Christian past could be allowed to linger in the Christian present?

This would not have been so urgent an issue if Christianity had not come to be established in the British Isles and in much of northern Europe by persons who depended on the pre-Christian past for their own authority. The sinews of power in northern Europe reached back to a past which had known nothing of Christianity. This past could not be declared irrelevant, much less could it be declared to have been noxious and deluded. For the authority of kings, the codes of honor which determined the behavior of noble men and women, indeed, law and order itself, were rooted in that pre-Christian past.

The tension between past and present existed all over northern Europe. It is not well documented. It was pushed to one side by more articulate, more stridently Christian texts. Hence we can approach it only through chosen examples, taken at different times and from different regions. But such examples (though they involve skipping between Ireland, Anglo-Saxon Britain, Scandinavia, and the Continent) reveal a muffled debate which was going on all over Christian northern Europe.

Let us begin with the Anglo-Saxon kingdoms. As we saw in chapter 15, kings played a crucial role in the conversion of the pagan Saxons. Contemporary clergymen knew very well that the remarkable Christian culture of the island would not have happened if it had not been for the support of Christian kings. But then, what supported the kings? It was their genealogy. And this genealogy reached back, far beyond the coming of Christianity, to ancient gods.

We see one example of this dilemma. In the late eighth century, a priest in Northumbria (a contemporary of Alcuin) faced this problem when he edited the genealogies of the kings of the *Angli* – of the Saxon dynasties established in Britain. Nobody doubted (least of all our author, the priest) that these kings were men whose vigor and good fortune could be ascribed to their royal lineage. As kings, they were, somehow, a little "larger than life." And they were "larger than life" because they were descended from ancestors who were larger than human. They were descended from gods. A good Christian, the priest did not hesitate to impose his own, up-to-date Christian views upon these genealogies. He was careful to exclude all sons born out of Christian wedlock. The sons of royal concubines were not mentioned in his list. But he could not bring himself to exclude the gods. The genealogies would not provide a title to power if they did not reach back to their root. And at that root, heading the priest's list of the ancestors of every Anglian kingdom, stood the god Woden. They had all come from a god.[27]

As long as power based upon genealogies was taken seriously, the gods were taken seriously all over northern Europe. In this, northern Christianity differed sharply from the Christianity of the late Roman Mediterranean. Around the Mediterranean, Christian apologists had lingered with scorn on the gods of classical mythology. They were trivial and laughable beings, given to love-affairs and to inconstant emotions. But, as we saw in chapter 2, behind the showy façade of the gods of classical mythology, there lurked the real enemy – the Devil himself and his ministers, the wily demons who sought to trap mankind through sinister illusions.

The gods of northern Europe could not be treated in this manner. They were neither trivial nor malignant. They were seen as part of a glorious past. This past still gave a charge to the present. Hence the gods remained. Solemn figures even in their decline, they were like an ancient dynasty which had once ruled the earth until forced to abdicate in favor of the Christ of modern times.[28] Without a touch of such gods "in the blood," as it were, modern kings could not be great. And, if they could not be great, they could not act as effective defenders of the Church.

But it was not only power which came from the gods. The skills of the settled world reached back to the age of the gods. They belonged to a deep past, which could not be disowned. This was a problem which exercised a learned Irish clergyman in around the year 700. The Irish Church, like any other aspect of Irish society, depended on the activity of persons endowed with almost uncanny skills – on lawyers who controlled intricate tribal law and on poets who were known to depend on inspiration. But what sort of skill and inspiration was involved? It certainly did not come from Christianity. Knowledge of "the white Scriptures" of the Church was a phenomenon of recent times. And mere books (even Christian books) could not contain all the arts of life. The clergyman agreed that these skills had come from an earlier age when gods and men had lived side by side. The skills of poetry and law had been taught to the men of Ireland by their invisible neighbors, "the tribe of the gods." The gods could not possibly be dismissed as demons. They were the source of the high skills on which Irish society depended: "And though the faith came later, these arts were not put away, for they are good and no demons ever did good."[29]

All over northern Europe, the clergy took such matters seriously. Indeed, the fact that we know anything at all about the past of pre-Christian northern Europe depended on a process which is extraordinary in itself.

We know about the pagan past of Greece and Rome from pagan writers writing in pagan times – from Homer, Vergil, and similar classical authors. But (with the exception of a few runic inscriptions) there is not a word which was written about northern paganism that did not pass through the pens of Christian monks and clergymen. Apart from writers of runes (who were common enough, but whose activities do not appear to have extended to the creation of long written texts), the clergy remained the only literate class in northern Europe. And yet it was the clergy who went out of their way to consign to writing – and so have made available to us – all that we know of the pre-Christian narratives, the poetry, and the laws of Ireland, England, Scandinavia, and Germany.

They did this, of course, on their own terms. The act of writing, in itself, was an act of discreet censorship. But write they did. And they wrote because knowledge of such things was considered to be essential to law and order and to their own status in society. Those who wrote down the legends and poetry of the pre-Christian past in Ireland, Anglo-Saxon England, and Iceland were not grudging recorders, catching in written words the last vestiges of a pagan mythology doomed to extinction by the coming of the Christian Church. The situation was not like that at all. Rather, Christian monks and clergymen should be seen as the last great myth-makers of northern Europe. They transformed a living pagan past, so as to use it in their own, Christian present.[30]

"In days of yore": Epic and Social Status: The World of *Beowulf*

We must never forget what we saw, in chapter 16, in the case of Bede's Northumbria. Monasteries were never enclosed worlds, totally cut off from the society around them. Monks shared the values of their lay protectors and clients, many of whom were, in any case, their relatives. Abbots and abbesses came from the kin of kings and aristocrats. The central institutions of the Church were microcosms of local society. Many monks, nuns, royal chaplains, bishops, and their clerical dependents were noblemen and noblewomen. They continued to think of themselves as such in their new roles as religious leaders.[31]

They knew very well what it was to be noble. They grew up in an overwhelmingly oral culture which was awash with stories and maxims. These told them how to behave as noble men and noble women. To be noble was to stand out. It was to live well and to be seen by others to live well. It was to foster with gusto the memory of a past which lay on the edge of the Christian present. This was a past which was always a little larger than life. It was a past where human glory, human tragedy, and the working out of human obligations were so much more vivid and so much more clear-cut, so much more brimming over with magnificent lack of measure, than was the grey, Christian present.[32] To be noble was to toast one's companions with great drinking-horns that carried as much liquor as a present-day bottle of Moselle; to engage in high talk and loud laughter; to listen to the ancient sound of the harpist. To be a noble bishop (noted Alcuin, a prim scholar and a self-made man with little sympathy for his well-born colleagues) was to allow one's clergy to "gallop bawling over the fields after the fox" and to boast a retinue complete with minstrels, hawks, and performing bears. Most shocking of all, to a "career clergyman" such as Alcuin, was for a noble bishop or priest to appear in church and to conduct worship wearing elegant trousers! The custom was condemned at a council of the English Church in 747.[33]

All these attributes of aristocratic swagger were regularly adopted, at one time or other, by the upper-class clergy and monasteries of Saxon England and Francia. They were just as regularly condemned, at the same time, by "reforming" episcopal councils in both regions. Yet those members of the clergy who were close to the lay elites were never altogether disapproving. They knew very well that, in an overwhelmingly oral society, epic memories were far more than entertainment. They were more, even, than titles to rule. They were the unwritten law codes of an entire warrior class.

Even the great Charlemagne himself, for all his "Roman" title, felt that he could not do without epic poems. He knew that the cultivation of such memories was an essential strand in his power. He caused

> the unwritten laws of all the tribes that came under his rule to be compiled and reduced to writing. He also [Einhard added] directed that the age-old, non-Latin poems in which were celebrated the warlike deeds of the kings of ancient times should be written out and preserved.[34]

In his mind, epic and law went together.

It is significant that Frankish epics have not survived. Charlemagne's son, Louis the Pious, was brought up in Aquitaine and surrounded by "Romans" of the South. He did not share his father's old-fashioned pride in the achievements of the Franks. Louis could also afford to be pious because he felt so powerful. He was the head of a "Christian empire." He did not need that extra magical charge which came from the ability to invoke an epic past which lay beyond the Christian present.

In neighboring Britain, by contrast, king Offa of Mercia (757–796) was also a very strong king. He called himself "emperor of Britain" with some justice. Like Charles, he could organize the labor of his subjects to create titanic earthworks. Offa's Dyke stretches for 150 miles (longer than all the Roman walls of Britain put together) between the Saxon Midlands and Wales. But Offa's power still deployed, with gusto, an epic, Saxon style, tenacious of the past. The royal mausoleum church at Repton flanked ancient burial mounds. Offa's pedigree ascended into a galaxy of figures known from legend. It may well be that the Anglo-Saxon epic of *Beowulf* was committed to writing at his court.[35]

Though it was probably written down around A.D. 780, either in East Anglia or the Midlands, *Beowulf* was a record of events larger than life which had taken place *in geār dagum*, "in days of yore" – in fact, as far as we can see, around 520, a quarter of a millennium previously. We must remember that, impressive and complete though the existing text may seem to modern readers, *Beowulf* was only the tip of an iceberg. It was a mere drop, preserved for us by the accident of writing, from a vast reservoir of memories. The text, as it now stands, assumed a reader's knowledge of at least 20 similar legends.

Beowulf was very much a moral handbook. It was made up of gripping tableaux of loyalty and courage, of tragic conflict and of ceremonious good cheer in a well-ordered royal hall. All that was worst and best in the life of a Saxon nobleman was seen played out magnificently, in ancient times and in a distant homeland. Epics such as those which went to make up the text of *Beowulf* were constantly remembered and recited in differing versions, spliced and respliced like genes, to meet the needs of every occasion. Long after their conversion to Christianity, epic tales such as those which came together to make *Beowulf* constituted nothing less than the moral gene-pool of a warrior aristocracy.[36]

A Past for Germany

The accident of the preservation of texts leads us to highlight the epic poetry of Anglo-Saxon England. We treat it, much as we treat the Icelandic *Sagas*, as a glimpse into an exotic world. But it did not stand alone. The problems which produced such literature were common to much of northern Europe. In ninth-century Germany, for instance, we see similar attempts to heal the gap between the Christian present and the pre-Christian past. Again, it was an attempt made by those whose own standing in society depended on maintaining their links with the past. But in a manner which was characteristic of the Carolingian learned elite, the recuperation of the past of Germany was expressed as much through Latin literature as through patronage of the vernacular.[37]

The Carolingian "discovery of Germany" took place in Latin. It depended on decisions made in the *scriptoria* of monasteries founded by Boniface and later set up in Saxony, after Charlemagne's slow and murderous absorption of the region. To take one example. The *Histories* of Ammianus Marcellinus, written around 395, contain a uniquely vivid and circumstantial record of fourth-century frontier warfare along the Rhine and the Danube. They describe the sudden appearance of the Huns and the catastrophic defeat of the emperor Valens at Adrianople in 378. They survive in one manuscript only, copied in the ninth century at the monastery founded by Boniface at Fulda. Without the decision made in a German monastery to divert efforts usually spent on copying the "Christian Law" to copying the work of a fourth-century military man and evident pagan, simply because he had so much to say about the German world of his time, we would know next to nothing about the early stages of what we have come to know as the "barbarian invasions." Whole chapters of this book could not have been written.

The linking of past to present in Germany could take surprising forms, and would be used by unexpected persons. Thus, Tacitus' famous work *On Germany* (written in A.D. 98) was used again, for the first time in 300 years. Tacitus was cited in a preface to a book recording the miracles associated with the transfer of the relics of a little-known saint (Saint Alexander) all the way from Rome to Wildeshausen in Saxony. The founder of Wildeshausen was Walbert. And Walbert was none other than the grandson of the great Widukind, the stubborn leader of the last pagan resistance to Charlemagne. Now ensconced in his home territory as abbot of the monastery which he himself had founded – with the further provision that only members of his kin should succeed him – Walbert was not prepared to believe that the coming of Christianity to Saxony had created a break with the noble past of his own tribe. It had merely added further luster to their pre-existing natural excellence. In the words of the *Preface* to his book of miracles, Walbert wrote, in around 860:

> The Saxons of old went out of their way to maintain many effective customs and high moral standards, as far as the law of nature was concerned. Such a way of life would have gained them the true blessedness of Heaven if only they had not suffered from lack of knowledge of the Creator.[38]

A tolerant view of the pre-Christian past, first created in Ireland, now gave meaning to the rediscovery of Tacitus in Germany.

Keeping the Past in the Past

Faced by a past which had by no means lost its solemnity, the solution favored by the clergy was to treat it simply, for the first time, as the past. Woden was a glorious ancestor, greater in some indefinable manner than his modern descendants. But he was not a god. That meant, in effect, that he could not come into the present. He was part of the past. He and the other gods had been condemned to history. What the gods could not be for Christians was what they always had been for pagans – creatures out of time, who, as it were, lived alongside the present and who were instantly accessible to their worshippers. The gods were an ever-present source of supra-human energy and blessing. They were always there. They were brought into the present through sacrifice, through spells, and even through the heavy workings of strong liquor. The power of the gods could bubble up at solemn feasts. They stepped into the present through the inspiration which welled up in poets once they had drunk, in the name of the gods, the mead – the honey drink – of memory and had chewed on the heavy lumps of horseflesh in a stew consecrated to the gods.[39]

But it was never easy to keep the past in the past. In Iceland and Norway, the god Odin (the Northmen's Woden) remained for centuries far more present than any long-dead king could ever hope to be. Odin was a "culture hero" and a powerful ego-ideal. He would manifest himself with uncanny ease to people and even in people. A small but vivid detail shows this. The father of the great recorder of the *Sagas* and the author of the *Edda*, Snorri Sturluson, was Sturla, a wily Christian priest from Hvamm on the Breidafjord in western Iceland. At the height of a dispute, in which Sturla had shown his trickery to full advantage in a legal argument, the wife of his opponent attempted with a knife to blind him in one eye: "Why should I not make you look like him [the one-eyed Odin] whom you most want to resemble?"[40] At a time when Gothic cathedrals were beginning to arise all over Continental Europe, a clergymen in Iceland could still be thought of as, in some way, the avatar of an ancient trickster god.

When Snorri himself came to write down the *Saga* of Olaf Tryggvason's violent imposition of Christianity in the fjords around Trondheim, he was careful to record that Odin had appeared to the king. For Odin was the guardian of the past of Norway. One night, as Olaf rested at Ogvaldsness,

> an old and very wise-spoken man came in. He wore a hood coming down over his face and he was one-eyed. He had things to tell of every land . . . The king found much pleasure in his talk. [The stranger knew, for instance all about Ogvald, the king whose ancient burial mound gave its name to the headland.] He told the king those tales and many others about the ancient kings and other stories of olden times.

It was all that Olaf's bishop could do to persuade the fascinated king to go to bed. Only next morning, when the stranger had vanished, did Olaf realize that his moment of spell-bound access to the past had come from Odin, "the god heathen men had long worshipped."[41]

In many ways, the gods could never be put entirely in the past, unless that past itself was appropriated on Christian terms. All over Europe, and even in Scandinavia, sacrifice to the gods – the most clearly visible gesture of pagan worship – was forbidden. Sacrifice appears to have died out. But, in an overwhelmingly non-literate culture, words carried from the past were quite as dangerous as was sacrifice. In Germany, Saxon converts were expected to renounce not only the "works" of Woden, Thunor, and Saxnote but their "words" – that is, the spells recited in their names.[42]

Words might indeed bring back into the present certain powers that were by no means believed, by Christians, to be nonexistent. They were still there. But Christians had sworn not to turn to them. We can only glimpse, in scattered incidents, how powerful such pre-Christian words were thought to be, and how close to the Christian present they could come. We can see this happening, in around A.D. 1000, at the farthest edge of the European world. When famine struck the Icelandic settlements in Greenland, the prophetess Thorbjorg called for an assistant to recite, at the appropriate moment, the "Spirit Locking" spell. Gudrid had been taught the spell in Iceland by her foster-mother.

> "But this is a kind of lore and proceeding I feel I cannot assist in . . . For I am a Christian woman."
>
> "Yet it might happen [Thorbjorg reminded her] that you could prove helpful to people in this affair." [So] Gudrid recited the chant so beautifully that no one present could say that he had heard the chant recited in a lovelier voice.[43]

What occurred all over northern Europe, therefore, was a competition of words, between pre-Christian and Christian spells. Christian authors of the *Penitentials* commended those who set about the serious things of life – such as the gathering of healing herbs – with Christian prayers.[44] A spell was thought to work because it drew into the present the great moments of misadventure and of healing which had occurred in the glorious past. If the past was to be drawn into the present in this way, then it must be a past linked to the beginnings of Christian time. These were spells which evoked a time when Christian figures, and not Woden and Baldur, were imagined to have trod the woods of Germany. Despite the strictures of the Carolingian elite, clergymen were quite prepared to act as "ritual practitioners" for their flocks. They did so by copying out spells in High German, for themselves and for their clients. Some of the very earliest vernacular texts contained lists of such spells:

> Christ was born before wolf and thief were, and Saint Martin was Christ's shepherd. May Christ and Saint Martin take care of these dogs so that no wolf nor she-wolf should cause them harm, wherever they may run in wood or way or heath.[45]

It was the same in Anglo-Saxon England. To take one example. In the tenth century, the priest on an estate in England was expected to "heal" an infertile field by saying Mass over four sods taken from its four corners. By this Christian ritual, he revived the tired soil. The Mass brought back to the dry sods a touch of the abundance associated with God's first creation of the ever-fertile garden of Eden.

> Then let the plough be driven forwards and the first furrow opened up, then say:
> "Hale may thou be, earth, mother of mortals! Grow pregnant in the embrace of God, filled with food for mortals' use."[46]

"The paths where outcasts go": Monsters, Marginals, and the Triumph of Christianity

The beings of the past were expected to continue to ring the Christian present. What mattered was that they should be held at bay. Here the experience of northern Christians differed significantly from that of Mediterranean persons. Mediterranean Christians had inherited from ancient times a model of the demonic that was, basically, a "cosmic", vertical model. Demons filled the air with their subtle bodies. They did this because they were, quite literally, "fallen" angels. Thrust out of a heaven identified with the stars above, they swept around the earth in the space beneath the moon. There was something particularly threatening about their chill, ethereal nature: they were truly "spirits," evil spirits.

What we meet in the north, by contrast, was a more horizontal model. Evil did not come from the sky. It was not "demonic" in that strict sense. It came across the open land, and it was utterly concrete. We are dealing with a patterning of the social imagination which saw settled human society as surrounded, on every side, by the encroaching wild. A "middle world" of human order was forever hemmed in by an "outer world," whose grim or alluring denizens were quite as palpable as were human beings.[47]

This belief took many forms in different regions. We have seen (in chapter 14) how, in Ireland, the human and the nonhuman were placed in concentric rings. There was room, in such a map of the world, for innumerable categories of beings. Settled human life lay at the center, domesticated animals in the middle, and, along the edges, there flitted the grey shapes of wolves. In the same way, monks were ringed by tame, penitent lay persons, who, in turn, were hemmed in by the dread bands of outlaws and brigands. Celtic lore made much of the belief that the settled land of human beings was ringed by an entire, alternative population of the *Síde*, "the Other Side." The notion of an alternative population survived up to modern times in beliefs about the fairy kingdom. An entire world, untouched by sadness, was believed to exist alongside the Christian present:

> Sweet mild streams . . . matchless people without blemish, love and conception without sin, without guilt. We see everyone on all sides, and no one sees us.[48]

The ancestors also lived in such an alternative world, next door to the living. In the great barrow-mounds which studded the Irish landscape, the ancient heroes of Ireland were still present, locked forever in a glorious past which knew nothing of the coming of the "White Scriptures." They could still be visited. It was at the grave-rock of Fergus mac Roich in Connacht that the scholar in search of the full version of the *Táin*, the Tale of the Cattle Raid of Cooley, was taken into the mist for three days and three nights, to be told the full version of the story by Fergus himself, who appeared to the scholar "in fierce majesty, with a head of brown hair, in a green cloak . . . with gold hilted sword."[49]

We know this, of course, because, in around 800, an Irish cleric wrote it all down. He was in two minds about why he was doing so – or, rather, felt that he should present himself as being in two minds. In the Old Irish colophon to the Old Irish text, he presented himself, without a trace of embarrassment, as the proud transmitter of a glorious past:

> A blessing on everyone who shall faithfully memorize the *Táin* as it is written here and shall not add any other form to it.

In the Latin note that he added to the same Old Irish text, he adopted a more distanced tone:

> But I who have written out this history, or rather this fable, give no credence to the various incidents related in it. For some things in it are the deceptions of demons, others are flights of poetic fancy; some are probable, others are improbable; while others are intended for the amusement of foolish people.[50]

In Ireland, the people of "the Other Side" and the ancestors appeared rarely to humans. This was not so with the creatures of the wild who flanked the

human race in Saxon England, Germany, and Scandinavia. There was nothing elusive or insubstantial about them. Their being drew substance from the
inhuman landscapes which were known to be their appropriate haunts.
Monsters haunted the eery coastal marshlands of Britain. Entire riding-par-
ties of dethroned gods crashed deep in the woods of Saxony. Trolls wandered across the black lava-fields and misty glacier snouts of Iceland. In the
epic of *Beowulf* there was nothing insubstantial about Grendel, the monster
slain by Beowulf, nor about his mother. They had been seen:

> huge prowlers of the marshes, patrolling the moors, alien intruders . . .
> an ill-formed creature stalking the paths where outcasts go.[51]

Grendel and his mother were the primal outlaws. They were the all too concrete, menacing counterparts of the heroic human figures who were believed
to have been capable of holding them at bay in the distant past. Such heroes
were built for the task. Take, for instance, Hygelac, a sea-king mentioned
both in *Beowulf* and, surprisingly, also (as a failed pirate) in the works of
Gregory of Tours. Hygelac was so large that from the age of 12 no horse
could carry him.

> His bones are preserved in an island in the Rhine, where it flows into the
> ocean, and are shown to those who come from afar as a miracle.[52]

This information was included in a Latin handbook written around 800,
entitled *The Book of Monsters*. The larger-than-life Hygelac – and, by implication, the baleful Grendel – were not misty beings. For the clergy who set
their pens to work to record them in writing, they were an unquestioned part
of the topography of Europe.

   As late as the twelfth century, an Icelandic clergyman on pilgrimage to
Rome made a travel diary of his journey. He noted only his visits to Christian shrines, except on one occasion: travelling up the Rhine, having seen the
relics of Saint Ursula in Cologne, he made one detour to the Drachensberg.
For there he went to visit the place where Siegfried (the Icelandic Sigurd) had
slain the dragon Fafnir. Even for this pious pilgrim, the encounter between
human and dragon had been a real event at a real place that was as well-
known as any Christian shrine.[53]

   We are dealing with a moral topography which could be fitted with relative ease on to a sharp, Christian patterning of the world. We are even told
Grendel's pedigree. It reached back, not to respectable, old-world gods, as
did the pedigrees of Saxon Christian kings, but to the primal outcast of the
Old Testament – to Cain, the slayer of Abel, his own brother and kin. Mon-

sters such as Grendel continued into the present a past where, as the Old Testament showed, human beings, subject to human restraints on pride and violence, had been flanked by a "race of the giants" – by menacing outsiders who were the tyrannical embodiments of power and ambition unrestrained by human law. Far from being ethereal beings, or mere fictions, these creatures were still around. And they were spoken about often and with real art, because it was through them that northern persons grappled, in their own way, with the boundary between civilization and the brute violence which lurked along its margins.[54]

We should see the coming of Christianity to much of western Europe against this distinctive imaginative landscape. It was not a patterning unique to that region. But some regions lingered with greater intensity than did others on the thought of great, marginal creatures from a distant past ringing the present. Armenia of around the year 700 was a similar non-Mediterranean, clan-based society. The learned Armenian clergyman, Ananias of Shirak, viewing the storms which whipped across the surface of Lake Van, noted that many of his fellow-countrymen believed that the fierce white waves were caused by the struggle of a primal hero to remove from the lake the dragons which lurked in its depths.[55] Throughout the Middle Ages, in Armenia, blacksmiths would begin the week by striking their anvils so as to strengthen the chains which bound the giant Artavazd in his mountain prison.[56]

Whether in Christian Armenia or in Christian northern Europe, we meet a patterning of the imagination which implied a sharp distinction between center and periphery, between settled life and a murmurous population of outcasts who inhabited its margins. These beings existed but they did not belong. It was a pattern which gave imaginative weight and concreteness to the Christian claim to possess the center and to stand now for settled life against ever-threatening alternatives.

Seen in this light, the establishment of the Church may well have done no more than complete a process which had characterized religious change in Europe since prehistoric times. Europe has always had a religious history. As far as the prehistorian can reconstruct it, from the time of the spread of Bell-Beaker culture in the second millennium B.C., much of this history seems to have consisted in pushing to the margins beliefs, practices, and even social groups, to make room for new, differently organized and more prestigious conglomerations of power, culture, and religious expertise.[57]

What happened in early medieval Europe was, in many ways, a continuation of that age-old process. In a process which lasted over half a millennium, from around A.D. 400 to around 1000, Christianity came to hold the center. It came to stand for the world of order. It came to be identified with the world of human settlement as defined in sharp contrast to the wild. It blessed the world of the nobility, linked in epic to the radiant halls of the chieftains. On a humbler level, it protected the tilled fields and even helped to assert (through Christian spells) that most astonishing example of all of the far reach of human control over the natural world – the mysterious loyalty of the swarming bees as they returned, every year, to their owner's hive.[58] All of this now lay under the protection of Christ. Christian rituals upheld that world. Christian kings ruled it.

Around the fringes of a brightly lit Christian center, of which we know so much, beliefs from the deepest past of Europe still clustered. Let us end with one example which is calculated to make us ponder. As we saw in the last chapter, the great monastery of San Vicenzo in Volturno was a triumph of the "corrected" religion of the Carolingian empire. It was filled with solemn Latin inscriptions. Yet, in the humble cottages which abutted its stone walls, neolithic axe-heads (exquisite products of the Stone Age) have been found. They were fitted into the rafters. Gathered from caves and cemeteries, such flints were charged with meaning. They were spoken of as "thunderstones." They were preserved as charms to protect buildings from lightning. "Thunderstones" are found all over medieval Europe, from Lund, in Sweden, to southern Italy. Many found their way into church treasuries. In Utrecht, which formed the center of Willibrord's mission to the Frisians (as we saw in chapter 18), a large polished stone axe from neolithic times was kept as a relic in the cathedral. It was known, appropriately, as "Saint Martin's Axe." It was believed to have been the axe with which Martin had felled pagan holy trees all over Gaul.[59]

These flint-stones were mute presences. There is no reason to believe that they spoke directly to the Christians of the early medieval west of rituals which reached back to the stone age. Explicit continuities of belief and practice did not exist between medieval Europe and so distant an age. Yet the carefully honed flints were still there. Whatever they had meant to their first users, at some time in the pre-Christian past they achieved their magical connection with thunder and lightning. As "thunderstones" they carried a barely articulate message from an unimaginably older Europe. Under the shadow of a great Christian monastery, they added their own, subdued note to the texture of "Christian times." Scholars are condemned by the nature of the evidence to concentrate almost exclusively on Christian texts when writing a history of the early Middle Ages. But they should, nonetheless, attempt to develop a wide field of "peripheral vision." The "thunderstones," collected from the ground near stone age sites and still solemnly installed by Christians in their buildings give us a glimpse, out of the corner of the eye, of the sheer age and complexity of the European landscape in which the Christian Church was placed.

And so we end the story of a slow revolution. After many centuries, "Christendom" and the idea of permanence had come to coalesce. This had come to be the case even around the uncertain shores of the North Atlantic. By the year 1000, Christendom was a notion which carried with it the charge of perpetuity. It was thought to be something that would last forever. Times had changed. In A.D. 95. (while Tacitus wrote on the wild lands of Germany), Titus Praxias, in Phrygia in western Asia Minor (southwest of Ankara in modern Turkey) made a testamentary bequest. The bequest has survived, engraved in Greek on his stone tomb. Titus Praxias wished to ensure that his memory would survive in his home town. Every year roses would be placed on his tomb, and the town councillors would gather for a memorial banquet. These arrangements were to remain in force, he said, "for as long an age as the rule of the Romans shall be maintained."[60]

Paradoxically, if Titus Praxias had returned to his native Phrygia in the year 1000, he would still have found it ruled by "Roman" emperors. Though greatly changed and frequently ravaged by Muslim armies, Phrygia had never been ruled by any other power than that of emperors who were the direct successors of the emperor Augustus. The Christian populations of Phrygia (whom we Westerners insist mistakenly on calling "Byzantines") still spoke Greek. They called themselves "Romans." (Indeed, up to the present, Muslims call Orthodox Christians *Rûmi.*) In the year 1000, they were as convinced as ever Titus Praxias had been in A.D. 95, that the "Roman" empire was a God-given institution, destined to last forever. Parts of the old order with which we began our account, looking at the world from the Edessa of Bardaisan in the early third century, were still there. The "Roman" empire of the east (though greatly reduced in size) was a sizable fragment of that old order.

But other parts of Bardaisan's world had changed beyond recognition. In Western Europe, it was the Catholic Church, and not the Roman empire, which now stood for all that was most permanent. In around 871/889, a Kentish nobleman, the earldorman Alfred, granted 200 pence in alms to the church at Canterbury, to be rendered for Masses for his soul. Like Titus Praxias, he wished his gift to last forever. So he wrote that it should last "as long as baptism should last and money can be raised from the land."[61]

Fulwiht was the Anglo-Saxon term which the earldorman Alfred used for "baptism." The term echoed the Early Christian practice by which the newly baptized wore full white robes. In England as elsewhere all over Western Europe, "baptism" was what every Christian inhabitant had in common. "Baptism" had come slowly, over the centuries, to a world characterized throughout by remarkable diversities in landscape, in social structure, in culture, and in the nature of the religious past of each region. But "baptism" was now thought to have come forever.

This book has tried to convey, however briefly, something of the complexity of the process by which Christianity rose to dominance in Western Europe. It has attempted to delineate the very different forms which Christianity took in the regions in which it gained a foothold. It is for other books to take up the story, by describing the many forms which Christianity would continue to take in coming centuries, in the Middle Ages and in modern times. But we must remember that, whatever the achievements and the tragedies associated with the later history of Christianity in Europe, these represent the playing out of a Western Christendom which took on its first, distinctive face in the centuries described in this book.

Notes

Introduction

1. Among the collective volumes to appear after 1995, I am particularly indebted to the publications sponsored by the European Science Foundation on the theme of *The Transformation of the Roman World* under the general editorship of Ian Wood: W. Pohl and H. Reimitz (eds.), *Strategies of Distinction: The Construction of Ethnic Communities*, Leiden, 1998; R. Hodges and W. Bowden (eds.), *The Sixth Century: Production, Distribution and Demand*, Leiden, 1998; G. P. Brogiolo and B. Ward-Perkins (eds.), *The Idea and Ideal of the Town between Late Antiquity and the Early Middle Ages*, Leiden, 1999; E. Chrysos and I. Wood (eds.), *East and West: Modes of Communication*, Leiden, 1999; M. de Jong, F. Theuws, and C. van Rhijn (eds.), *Topographies of Power in the Early Middle Ages*, Leiden, 2001; F. Theuws and J. Nelson (eds.), *Rituals of Power: From Late Antiquity to the Early Middle Ages*, Leiden, 2000; G. P. Brogiolo, N. Gauthier, and N. Christie (eds.), *Towns and their Territories between Late Antiquity and the Early Middle Ages*, Leiden, 2000; W. Pohl, H. Reimitz, and I. Wood (eds.), *The Transformation of Frontiers: From Late Antiquity to the Carolingians*, Leiden, 2001; I. L. Hansen and C. Wickham, *The Long Eighth Century: Production, Distribution and Demand*, Leiden, 2001. Of equal importance for the earlier period are A. Cameron and P. Garnsey (eds.), *The Cambridge Ancient History 13: The Late Empire* A.D. *337–425*, Cambridge, 1998, and A. Cameron, B. Ward-Perkins, and M. Whitby (eds.), *The Cambridge Ancient History 14: Late Antiquity. Empire and Successors* A.D. *425–600*, Cambridge, 2000, with G. W. Bowersock, P. Brown, and O. Grabar, *Late Antiquity. A Guide to the Postclassical World*, Cambridge, MA, 1999. See now R. McKitterick (ed.), *The Early Middle Ages*, Oxford, 2001.

2. See now H. Inglebert, *Interpretatio Christiana. Les mutations des savoirs (cosmographie, géographie, histoire) dans l'Antiquité tardive*, Paris, 2001, pp. 48–73.

3. F. Haverfield, *The Romanization of Roman Britain*, Oxford, 1912, p. 10.

4. C. Dawson, *The Making of Europe. An Introduction to the History of European Unity*, London, 1932, p. 234.

5. J. Bryce, *The Holy Roman Empire*, London, 1904, p. 40.

6. P. Brown, Gibbon's views on culture and society in the fifth and sixth centuries, *Daedalus*, 104 (1976): 73–88, now in *Society and the Holy in Late Antiquity*, Berkeley, CA, 1982, pp. 22–48.

7. A fine example can be seen on the dustjacket of P. Geary, *The Myth of Nations: The Medieval Origins of Europe*, Princeton, NJ, 2002.

8. M. Carver, Conversion and politics on the eastern seaboard of Britain: some archaeological indications, in B. E. Crawford (ed.), *Conversion and Christianization in the North Sea*, St. Andrews, 1998, p. 14.

9. H. Pirenne, *Mohammed and Charlemagne*, transl. B. Miall, London, 1937. See P. Brown, Henri Pirenne, *Mohammed and Charlemagne*, *Daedalus*, 103 (1974): 25–33, now in *Society and the Holy in Late Antiquity*, Berkeley, CA, 1982, pp. 63–79, and P. Delogu, Reading Pirenne again, in R. Hodges and W. Bowden (eds.), *The Sixth Century: Production, Distribution and Demand*, Leiden, 1998, pp. 15–40.

10. Pirenne, *Mohammed and Charlemagne*, p. 234.

11. F. Braudel, *The Mediterranean and the Mediterranean World in the Age of Philip II*, transl. S. Reynolds, London, 1972.

12. R. Hodges and D. Whitehouse, *Mohammed, Charlemagne and the Origins of Europe. Archaeology and the Pirenne Thesis*, Ithaca, NY, 1983.

13. C. Wickham, The other transition: from the ancient world to feudalism, in *Land and Power: Studies in Italian and European Social History 400–1200*, London, 1994, pp. 7–42.

14. M. de Jong, Rethinking early medieval Christianity: a view from the Netherlands, *Early Medieval Europe*, 7 (1998): 261–76, at p. 270.

15. M. W. Helms, *Craft and the Kingly Ideal. Art, Trade and Power*, Austin, TX, 1993, p. 96.

16. Summarized by G. Woolf, World-systems analysis and the Roman Empire, *Journal of Roman Archaeology*, 3 (1990): 44–58, at p. 55.

17. M. de Jong, Religion, in R. McKitterick (ed.), *The Early Middle Ages*, Oxford, 2001, pp. 131–64, at p. 131.

18. De Jong, Rethinking early medieval Christianity, p. 270.

19. R. W. Southern, *Western Society and the Church in the Middle Ages*, Harmondsworth, 1970, pp. 27–33.

20. J. P. Devroey, Economy, in R. McKitterick (ed.), *The Early Middle Ages*, Oxford, 2001, pp. 97–129, at p. 100.

21. A. Angenendt, *Das Frühmittelalter: die abendländische Christenheit von 400 bis 800*, Stuttgart, 1996, 2nd edn., pp. 147–59.

22. P. Brown, *The Cult of Saints. Its Rise and Function in Latin Christianity*, Chicago, 1981, pp. 12–22.

23. A. F. Walls, African Christianity in the history of religions, in C. Fyfe and A. F. Walls (eds.), *Christianity in Africa in the 1990s*, Edinburgh, 1996, pp. 1–15, at p. 8.

24. P. Horden and N. Purcell, *The Corrupting Sea. A Study of Mediterranean History*, Oxford, 2000. See B. Shaw, Challenging Braudel: a new vision of the Mediterranean, *Journal of Roman Archaeology*, 14 (2001): 419–53.

25. Horden and Purcell, *The Corrupting Sea*, pp. 172 and 366. See M. McCormick,

Origins of the European Economy: Communications and Commerce A.D *300*, Cambridge, 2001.

26. M. Richter, *Ireland and its Neighbors in the Seventh Century*, Dublin, 1999, p. 235.
27. Richter, *Ireland and its Neighbors*, p. 184.
28. A. Declercq, *Anno Domini: The Origins of the Christian Era*, Turnhout, 2000.
29. A. Harding, Reformation in Barbarian Europe, 1300–600 B.C., in B. Cunliffe (ed.), *The Oxford Illustrated Prehistory of Europe*, Oxford, 1994, pp. 304–35, at p. 304. See also B. Cunliffe, *Facing the Ocean: The Atlantic and its Peoples 8000 BC–AD 1500*, Oxford, 2001, p. 187.
30. C. Treffort, *L'Eglise carolingienne et la mort*, Lyons, 1996, p. 189.
31. J. J. O'Donnell, The authority of Augustine, *Augustinian Studies*, 22 (1991): 7–35.
32. Julian of Toledo, *Prognosticon*, Preface, J. N. Hillgarth (ed.), *Corpus Christianorum* 115, Turnhout, 1975, p. 14.
33. T. O'Loughlin, *Teachers and Code-Breakers. The Latin Genesis Tradition 430–800.* Turnhout, 1998, p. 10.
34. C. Straw, *Gregory the Great. Perfection in Imperfection*, Berkeley, CA, 1988.
35. A. Kazhdan, *A History of Byzantine Literature (650–800)*, Athens, 1999, p. 142. On Sant'Agnese see M. Visser, *The Geometry of Love: Space, Time, Mystery and Meaning in an Ordinary Church*, New York, 2001, pp. 96–124.
36. G. Henderson, *Vision and Image in Early Christian England*, Cambridge, 1999, p. 228. The theological sophistication which went into the making of many images is strikingly illustrated by C. Chazelle, *The Crucified God in the Carolingian Era. Theology and the Art of Christ's Passion*, Cambridge, 2001.
37. *Life of Desiderius of Cahors* 16, B. Krusch (ed.), *Corpus Christianorum*, 117, Turnhout, 1957, p. 362.
38. C. Wickham, Italy and the early Middle Ages, in *Land and Power. Studies in Italian and European Social History 400–1200*, London, 1994, pp. 99–118, at p. 116, and Society, in R. McKitterick (ed.), *The Early Middle Ages*, Oxford, 2001, pp. 59–94.
39. Wickham, Society, in McKitterick (ed.), *The Early Middle Ages*, pp. 64–72.
40. C. R. Dodwell, *Anglo-Saxon Art: A New Perspective*, Manchester, 1984, pp. 24–43.
41. I. Silber, *Virtuosity, Charisma and Social Order. A Comparative Study of Theravada Buddhism and Medieval Catholicism*, Cambridge, 1995, p. 254.
42. Silber, *Virtuosity, Charisma and Social Order*, p. 254.
43. M. de Jong, *In Samuel's Image. Child Oblation in the Early Medieval West*, Leiden, 1996, p. 273.
44. De Jong, Religion, in McKitterick (ed.), *The Early Middle Ages*, pp. 160–1.
45. C. Cubitt, Sites and sacrality: revisiting the cult of murdered and martyred Anglo-Saxon royal saints, *Early Medieval Europe*, 9 (2000): 58–83.
46. Treffort, *L'Eglise carolingienne et la mort*, p. 188.
47. R. Faith, *The English Peasantry and the Growth of Lordship*, London, 1997, pp. 164–7.

Chapter 1: "The Laws of Countries"

1. Bardaisan, *Book of the Laws and Countries*, 583–9 and 607: transl. H. J. W. Drijvers, Assen, 1965, pp. 41–53 and 59–61.

2. A. V. Paykova, The Syrian Ostracon from Panjikent, *Le Mouséon*, 92 (1979): 159–69; E. C. R. Armstrong and R. A. S. Macalister, Wooden book found near Springmount Bog, Co. Antrim, *Journal of the Royal Society of Antiquaries of Ireland*, 50 (1920): 160–6.

3. Boniface, *Letter* 26 [35]: transl. E. Emerton, *The Letters of Saint Boniface*, New York, 1976 and 2000, p. 65.

4. Thomas of Marga, *The Book of the Governors* 5.4: transl. E. A. Wallis Budge, London, 1893, p. 480.

5. G. Schlegel, *Die chinesische Inschrift von Kara Balgassun*, Helsinki, 1896, pp. 57–61; I. Gillman and H. J. Klimkeit, *Christians in Asia before 1500*, Richmond, Surrey, 1999, pp. 109–281.

6. Bardaisan, *Book of Laws*, 595, Drijvers, p. 51.

7. Theophylact Simocatta, *Histories* 4.11.2–3: transl. M. and M. Whitby, Oxford, 1986, p. 117.

8. B. Shaw, "Eaters of Flesh, Drinkers of Milk": the Ancient Mediterranean ideology of the pastoral nomad, *Ancient Society*, 14/4 (1982/3): 5–31.

9. A. M. Khazanov, *Nomads and the Outside World*, Cambridge, 1983; P. Crone, Tribes and states: the nomadic exception, in J. A. Hall (ed.), *States in History*, Oxford, 1986, pp. 68–77.

10. *The Epic Histories attributed to P'awstos Buzand* 3.7: transl. N. Garsoian, Cambridge, MA., 1989, p. 73.

11. E. A. Thompson, *The Huns*, Oxford, 1996; P. Heather, The Huns and the end of the empire in Western Europe, *English Historical Review*, 110 (1995): 4–41; I. Bóna, *Das Hunnenreich*, Budapest, 1991.

12. W. Pohl, *Die Awaren. Ein Steppenvolk in Mitteleuropa, 567–822 n.Chr.*, Munich, 1988, pp. 163–236 and 288–331.

13. P. S. Wells, *The Barbarians Speak. How the Conquered Peoples Shaped the Roman Empire*, Princeton, NJ, 1999.

14. M. Tod, *The Early Germans*, Oxford, 1992, pp. 125–44.

15. Vegetius, *Epitome of Military Science* 1.2: transl. N. P. Milner, Liverpool, 1993, p. 3.

16. P. Heather and J. F. Matthews, *The Goths in the Fourth Century*, Liverpool, 1991, pp. 51–101.

17. Galen, *De sanitate tuenda* 1.10, C. G. Kühn (ed.), *Galeni Opera*, 6, Leipzig, 1825, p. 51.

18. B. Shaw, War and violence, in G. W. Bowersock, P. Brown, and O. Grabar (eds.), *Late Antiquity. A Guide to the Postclassical World*, Cambridge, MA, 1999, pp. 130–69 at pp.157–63; P. Heather, The late Roman art of client management: imperial defence in the fourth century West, in W. Pohl, I. Wood, and H. Reimitz (eds.), *The Transformation of Frontiers. From Late Antiquity to the Carolingians*, Leiden, 2001, pp. 15–68.

19. W. Groenman-van Waateringe, Food for soldiers, food for thought, in J. C.

Barrett (ed.), *Barbarians and Romans in North West Europe*, Oxford, 1989, pp. 96–107.

20. L. Hedeager, *Iron Age Societies*, Oxford, 1992; Wells, *The Barbarian Speaks*, pp. 224–58; T. M. Charles-Edwards, *Early Medieval Ireland*, Cambridge, 2001, pp. 145–81.
21. C. R. Whittaker, *Frontiers of the Roman Empire. A Social and Economic Study*, Baltimore, MD, 1994. I take the apposite term, "middle ground," from R. White, *The Middle Ground. Indians, Empires and Republics in the Great Lakes Region 1650–1815*, Cambridge, 1991.

Chapter 2: Christianity and Empire

1. P. Brown, *The World of Late Antiquity: From Marcus Aurelius to Muhammad*, London, 1971 and 1989, pp. 11–33; K. Strobel, *Das Imperium Romanum im "3. Jahrhundert". Modell einer historischen Krise*, Stuttgart, 1993; J. M. Carrié and A. Rousselle, *L'Empire romain en mutation des Sévères à Constantin 192–337*, Paris, 1999.
2. R. MacMullen, *Romanization in the Time of Augustus*, New Haven, CT, 2000; G. Woolf, *Becoming Roman: The Origins of Provincial Civilization in Gaul*, Cambridge, 1998; B. Jones and D. Mattingly, *An Atlas of Roman Britain*, Oxford, 1990; F. Jacques, *Privilegium Libertatis*, Rome, 1984.
3. R. Bagnall, *Egypt in Late Antiquity*, Princeton, NJ, 1993, pp. 45–77 and 133–72; P. Garnsey and R. Saller, *The Roman Empire. Economy, Society, Culture*, London, 1987, pp. 20–40.
4. J. Lendon, *Empire of Honour. The Art of Government in the Roman World*, Oxford, 1997.
5. J. Drinkwater, *The Gallic Empire. Separation and Continuity in the North-Western Provinces of the Roman Empire*, A.D. 260–274, Stuttgart, 1987; D. Potter, *Prophecy and History in the Crisis of the Roman Empire*, Oxford, 1990 (for Syria); A. Watson, *Aurelian and the Third Century*, London, 1999.
6. S. Williams, *Diocletian and the Roman Recovery*, London, 1985; J. M. Carrié, Dioclétien et la fiscalité, *Antiquité tardive*, 2 (1994): 33–64; S. Corcoran, *The Empire of the Tetrarchs: Imperial Pronouncements and Government*, A.D. 284–324, Oxford, 1996.
7. C. Kelly, Emperors, Government and Bureaucracy, and B. Ward-Perkins, The Cities, in Averil Cameron and P. Garnsey (eds.), *Cambridge Ancient History 13. The Late Empire*, Cambridge, 1999, pp. 138–53 and 371–410; C. Ando, *Imperial Ideology and Provincial Loyalty in the Roman Empire*, Berkeley, CA, 2000, pp. 285–398.
8. K. Hopkins, Conquest by book, in J. H. Humphreys (ed.), *Literacy in the Roman World*, *Journal of Roman Archaeology*, Supplement 3, Ann Arbor, MI, 1991, pp. 133–58.
9. R. Lane-Fox, *Pagans and Christians*, New York, 1987, pp. 64–261.
10. Lane-Fox, *Pagans and Christians*, pp. 27–63; K. Harl, *Civic Coins and Civic Politics in the Roman East* A.D.180–275, Berkeley, CA, 1987.
11. Symmachus, *Relatio* 3.8: transl. R. H. Barrow, *Prefect and Emperor*, Oxford, 1973, pp. 39–41.

12. M. Frede, Monotheism and pagan philosophy in Late Antiquity, in M. Frede and P. Athanassiadi (eds.), *Pagan Monotheism in Late Antiquity*, Oxford, 1999, pp. 41–64.
13. *Pap.Oxy* 2782, *Oxyrhynchus Papyri* 36, London, 1970, p. 79.
14. *Collatio Legum Romanarum et Mosaicarum* 15.3: transl. M. Dodgeon and S. N. C. Lieu, *The Roman Eastern Frontier and the Persian Wars (AD 226–362)*, London, 1991, p. 135.
15. J. R. Curran, *Pagan City and Christian Capital. Rome in the Fourth Century*, Oxford, 2000, pp. 70–90.
16. Eusebius, *Life of Constantine* 4.10: transl. (with an outstanding commentary) Averil Cameron and S. Hall, Oxford, 1999, p. 157.
17. H. A. Drake, *Constantine and the Bishops*, Baltimore, MD, 2000, pp. 250–72; T. D. Barnes, *Constantine and Eusebius*, Cambridge, MA, 1981, pp. 208–23.
18. J. B. Rives, The decree of Decius and the religion of empire, *Journal of Roman Studies*, 89 (1999): 135–54; Barnes, *Constantine and Eusebius*, pp. 3–27 and 148–63.
19. G. W. Clarke, *The Letters of St. Cyprian, Ancient Christian Writers*, 43–4 and 46–7, New York, 1984–9, provides transl. and an unequalled commentary.
20. C. H. Roberts and T. C. Skeat, *The Birth of the Codex*, London, 1983; R. Lane-Fox, Literacy and power in early Christianity, in A. K. Bowman and G. Woolf (eds.), *Literacy and Power in the Ancient World*, Cambridge, 1994, pp. 128–48.
21. G. F. Snyder, *Ante Pacem. Archaeological Evidence for Church Life before Constantine*, Macon, GA, 1985.
22. K. Hopkins, Christian number and its implications, *Journal of Early Christian Studies*, 6 (1998): 185–226.
23. R. Lane-Fox, *Pagans and Christians*, pp. 265–335; S. Mitchell, *Anatolia. Land, Men and Gods 2: The Rise of the Church*, Oxford, 1993, pp. 37–64.
24. *Council of Elvira* (306), canons 2, 5, 40, and 57: E. J. Jonkers (ed.), Leiden, 1974, pp. 5–23.
25. Lane-Fox, *Pagans and Christians*, pp. 493–608.
26. *Didascalia Apostolorum* 12 [2.57]: transl. R. H. Connolly, Oxford, 1929, p. 119.
27. s.v. baptism, in E. Ferguson (ed.), *Encyclopedia of Early Christianity*, New York, 1990, pp. 131–4.
28. *Didascalia Apostolorum* 3.5.4, pp. 132–3.
29. F. Brenk, *In Mist Apparelled. Religious Themes in Plutarch's Moralia and Lives*, Leiden, 1977, pp. 145–83.
30. E. Ferguson, *Demonology of the Early Christian World*, New York, 1984.
31. s.v. exorcism, in Ferguson (ed.), *Encyclopedia of Early Christianity*, pp. 333–4.
32. G. Bowersock, *Martyrdom and Rome*, Cambridge, 1995, pp. 41–57; s.v. martyrdom, in E. Ferguson (ed.), *Encyclopedia of Early Christianity*, New York, 2nd edn., 1997, pp. 724–8.
33. *Didascalia Apostolorum* 19 [5.1], p. 161.
34. Eusebius, *Ecclesiastical History* 8.7.4: transl. A. C. McGiffert, *Nicene and Post-Nicene Fathers* 1, Grand Rapids, MI, 1979, p. 329 and G. A. Williamson, Harmondsworth, 1965, p. 336.

35. s.v. *refrigerium*, in Ferguson (ed.), *Encyclopedia of Early Christianity*, 2nd edn., pp. 975–6.

36. P. Hadot, *Philosophy as a Way of Life*, Oxford, 1995, pp. 81–125.

37. Lactantius, *Divine Institutes* 3.26: transl. M. F. McDonald, *Fathers of the Church*, 49, Washington, DC, 1964, p. 234.

38. Tertullian, *On Purity* 13: transl. W. Le Saint, *Ancient Christian Writers*, 28, London, 1959, pp. 86–7.

39. *Didascalia Apostolorum* 2 [2.16], pp. 52–3.

40. *Didache* 1: transl. J. B. Lightfoot, London, 1891, p. 123.

41. *Baba Bathra* 9a: transl. I. Epstein, *Babylonian Talmud*, London, 1935, p. 42.

42. G. Schöllgen, *Die Anfänge der Professionalisierung des Klerus*, Münster, 1998; P. Brown, *Poverty and Leadership in the Later Roman Empire*, Hanover, NH, 2002, pp. 17–26; on collections by pagans, G. W. Bowersock, Les *Euémeroi* et les confréries joyeuses, *Comptes-Rendus de l'Académie des Inscriptions et Belles Lettres 1999*, pp. 1241–56.

43. Lactantius, *Divine Institutes* 6.11, p. 423.

44. Eusebius, *Ecclesiastical History* 6.43.11, McGiffert, p. 288, Williamson, p. 282.

45. *Gesta apud Zenophilum*: transl. M. Edwards, *Optatus. Against the Donatists*, Liverpool, 1997, p. 154.

Chapter 3: "Tempora Christiana"

1. Isidore of Pelusium, *Letter* 1270: *Patrologia Graeca* 78: 344A.

2. P. Brown, Christianization and religious conflict, in Averil Cameron and P. Garnsey (eds.), *The Cambridge Ancient History 13. The Late Empire* A.D. 337–425, Cambridge, 1998, pp. 632–64 at pp. 633–6 and *Authority and the Sacred. Aspects of the Christianization of the Roman World*, Cambridge, 1995, pp. 1–7.

3. Augustine, [Newly discovered] *Sermon Mayence 61/Dolbeau 25.25*, in F. Dolbeau (ed.), *Vingt-six sermons au peuple d'Afrique*, Paris, 1996, p. 266: transl. E. Hill, *The Complete Works of Saint Augustine: A Translation for the Twenty-First Century. Sermons III/1: Newly Discovered Sermons*, Hyde Park, NY, 1997, p. 382.

4. R. MacMullen, *Christianizing the Roman Empire* A.D.*100–400*, New Haven, CT, 1984, pp. 86–101, and *Christianity and Paganism in the Fourth to Eighth Centuries*, New Haven, CT, 1997, pp. 1–73; B. Caseau, Sacred landscapes, in G. W. Bowersock, P. Brown, and O. Grabar, *Late Antiquity. A Guide to the Postclassical World*, Cambridge, MA, 1999, pp. 21–59.

5. G. Fowden, Polytheist religion and philosophy, in Cameron and Garnsey (eds.), *Cambridge Ancient History 13*, pp. 538–60; F. Thélamon, *Païens et chrétiens au IVe. siècle*, Paris, 1981, pp. 157–279.

6. *Codex Theodosianus* 9.16.2: transl. C. Pharr, Princeton, NJ, 1952, p. 237.

7. Orosius, *History against the Pagans*, preface: transl. I. W. Raymond, New York, 1936, p. 30; s.v. Pagan, *Late Antiquity*, p. 625.

8. J. Harries, *Law and Empire in Late Antiquity*, Cambridge, 1999.

9. J. Evans-Grubbs, *Law and Family in Late Antiquity. The Emperor Constantine's Marriage Legislation*, Oxford, 1995; J. Beaucamp, *Le statut de la femme à*

Byzance (4e–7e siècle) 1: Le droit impérial, Paris, 1990; R. Bagnall, Women, law and social relations in Late Antiquity, *Bulletin of the American Society of Papyrologists*, 32 (1995): 65–86.

10. M. T. Fögen, *Die Enteignung der Wahrsager. Studien zur kaiserlichen Wissenschaftsmonopol in der Spätantike*, Frankfurt-am-Main, 1993.

11. J. F. Matthews, *Laying Down the Law: A Study of the Theodosian Code*, New Haven, CT, 2000.

12. *Codex Theodosianus* 15.5.5, p. 433. C. Humfress, Roman law, forensic argument and the formation of Christian orthodoxy, in E. Rebillard and A. Romano (eds.), *Orthodoxy, Christianity, History*, Collection de l'École française de Rome, 270, Rome, 2000, pp. 125–47.

13. Brown, *Authority and the Sacred*, pp. 29–54.

14. R. S. O. Tomlin, The Curse Tablets, in B. Cunliffe (ed.), *The Temple of Sulis Minerva at Bath 2*, Oxford, 1988, pp. 323–4.

15. Augustine, *Ennaration in Psalm 34* 7: transl. S. Hebgin and F. Corrigan, *Ancient Christian Writers* 30, London, 1961, pp. 193–4.

16. Augustine, *Sermon Mayence 60/Dolbeau* 24.10, ed. Dolbeau, p. 240; transl. Hill, p. 362.

17. P. Brown, Conversion and Christianization in Late Antiquity: the case of Augustine, in R. Lim and C. Straw (eds.), *The World of Late Antiquity: The Challenge of New Historioraphies*, Berkeley, CA (forthcoming).

18. Egeria, *Travels* 25.8: transl. J. Wilkinson, London, 1971, p. 127; R. Krautheimer, *Early Christian and Byzantine Architecture*, Harmondsworth, 1986, pp. 39–67; J. R. Curran, *Pagan City and Christian Capital. Rome in the Fourth Century*, Oxford, 2000, pp. 90–115.

19. J. C. Picard, L'Atrium dans les églises paléochrétiennes d'Occident, in N. Duval (ed.), *Actes du XIe Congrès international d'archéologie chrétienne*, vol. 1, Rome, 1986, pp. 503–58; S. Lancel, *Saint Augustin*, Paris, 1999, pp. 331–46.

20. P. Garnsey and C. Humfress, *The Evolution of the Late Antique World*, Cambridge, 2000, pp. 72–7; P. Brown, *Poverty and Leadership in the Later Roman Empire*, Hanover, NH, 2002, pp. 26–73.

21. P. Brown, *Power and Persuasion in Late Antiquity. Towards a Christian Empire*, Madison, WI, 1992, pp. 71–117; E. Rebillard and C. Sotinel (eds.), *L'évêque dans la cité du VIe et Ve siècle. Image et autorité*, Collection de l'École française de Rome, 248, Rome, 1998.

22. J. P. Caillet, *L'évergétisme monumental chrétien en Italie*, Rome, 1993.

23. K. S. Painter, *The Water Newton Early Christian Silver*, London, 1977.

24. T. D. Barnes, *Athanasius and Constantius. Theology and Politics in the Constantinian Empire*, Cambridge, MA, 1993.

25. Athanasius, *Apology to Constantius* 30.41: transl. *A Library of Fathers*, Oxford, 1873, p. 180.

26. N. B. McLynn, *Ambrose of Milan. Church and Court in a Christian Capital*, Berkeley, CA, 1994.

27. P. Brown, *Body and Society. Men, Women and Sexual Renunciation in Early Christianity*, New York, 1988, pp. 191–284; P. Rousseau, Monasticism, in Averil Cameron, B. Ward-Perkins, and M. Whitby (eds.), *The Cambridge Ancient His-*

tory 14. Late Antiquity: Empire and Successors A.D. *425–600,* Cambridge, 2000, pp. 745–80. A. de Vogüé, *Histoire littéraire du mouvement monastique dans l'antiquité. Première partie: le monachisme latin,* 5 vols., Paris, 1991–8, now provides an unequalled survey of the impact of monasticism on the Latin West.

28. M. Tardieu, La diffusion du Bouddhisme dans l'empire kouchan, l'Iran et la Chine d'après un Kepahalaion manichéen inédit, *Studia Iranica,* 17 (1988): 153–80.

29. S. N. C. Lieu, *Manichaeism in the Later Roman Empire and in Medieval China,* Manchester, 1985, Tübingen, 2nd edn., 1992.

30. *The Cologne Mani-Codex:* transl. R. Cameron and R. J. Dewey, Missoula, MT, 1979; on yet further discoveries, see M. F. Gardner and S. N. C. Lieu, From Narmouthis (Medinet Madi) to Kellis (Ismant al-Kharab), *Journal of Roman Studies,* 86 (1996): 146–69.

31. Augustine, *Confessions* 8.6.15 and 8.19.

32. Sulpicius Severus, *Life of Martin, Letters and Dialogues:* transl. F. R. Hoare, *The Western Fathers,* New York, 1954; the *Life of Martin* is now in T. Head and T. F. X. Noble, *Soldiers of Christ,* University Park, PA, 1995, pp. 1–29; C. Stancliffe, *St. Martin and his Hagiographer. History and Miracle in Sulpicius Severus,* Oxford, 1983.

33. Paulinus of Nola, *Letter* 29.12: transl. P. G. Walsh, *Ancient Christian Writers,* 36, New York, 1966, p. 115.

34. P. Heather, Senates and senators, *in Cambridge Ancient History 13,* pp. 184–210.

35. M. Mundell and A. Bennett, *The Sevso Treasure, Journal of Roman Archaeology.* Supplementary Volume 12, Ann Arbor, MI, 1994, pp. 55–97.

36. C. Dagron, *Naissance d'une capitale,* Paris, 1974; S. Bassett, Antiquities in the Hippodrome of Constantinople, *Dumbarton Oaks Papers,* 45 (1991): 87–96, and *Historiae Custos:* sculpture and tradition in the Baths of Zeuxippos, *American Journal of Archaeology,* 100 (1996): 491–506.

37. M. Meslin, *La fête des Kalendes de Janvier dans l'empire romain,* Brussels, 1970.

38. Augustine, *Sermon Mayence 62/Dolbeau 25,* ed. Dolbeau, pp. 345–417; transl. Hill, pp. 180–237.

39. H. R. Idris, Fêtes chrétiennes en Ifriqiya à l'époque ziride, *Revue africaine,* 98 (1954): 261–76.

40. P. Heather, Goths and Huns, and I. N. Wood, The Barbarian Invasions and the first settlements, in Cameron and Garnsey (eds.), *Cambridge Ancient History 13,* pp. 487–515 and 516–37.

41. Paulinus of Nola in Ausonius, *Letter* 31.63: transl. H. G. Evelyn-White, *Ausonius* 2, Loeb Classical Library, London, 1949, p. 128.

42. D. Trout, *Paulinus of Nola,* Berkeley, CA, 1999; H. Sivan, *Ausonius of Bordeaux. Genesis of a Gallic Aristocracy,* London, 1993.

43. Augustine, *Letter* 231.6. The best transl. of the *Confessions* are H. Chadwick, Oxford, 1991, and F. J. Sheed, Indianapolis, reprint 1992. J. J. O'Donnell, *Augustine: Confessions,* Oxford, 1992, is an outstanding commentary.

44. P. Brown, *Augustine of Hippo. New Edition with an Epilogue,* London and Berkeley, CA, 2000, pp. 505–13.

45. Brown, *Augustine of Hippo*, pp. 340–53; Pelagius, *Commentary on Saint Paul's Epistle to the Romans*, transl. T. de Bruyn, Oxford, 1993; *The Letters of Pelagius and his Followers*, transl. B. Rees, Woodbridge, Suffolk, 1991.
46. Eusebius of Caesarea, *Tricennial Orations* 18: transl. H. A. Drake, *In Praise of Constantine*, Berkeley, CA, 1976, p. 127.
47. Prosper of Aquitaine, *The Call of All Nations* 2.35: transl. P. De Letter, *Ancient Christian Writers*, 14, Westminster, MD, 1963, pp. 149–51.
48. P. Brown, Enjoying the saints in late antiquity, *Early Medieval Europe*, 9 (2000): 1–24 at pp. 1–14.
49. Augustine, *On Rebuke and Grace* 12.35: trans. P. Holmes and R. E. Wallis, *Nicene and Post-Nicene Fathers 5*, Grand Rapids, MI, 1975, p. 486.
50. S. Thier, *Kirche bei Pelagius*, Patristische Texte und Studien 50, Berlin, 1999.
51. Augustine, *On Virginity* 44.45: transl. C. I. Cornish, *Nicene and Post-Nicene Fathers 3*, p. 434.
52. Augustine, *Against the Letters of the Pelagians* 3.5.14: transl. Holmes and Wallis, p. 408.
53. Brown, *Augustine of Hippo*, pp. 459–61.
54. Brown, *Augustine of Hippo*, pp. 285–329.
55. Augustine [Newly discovered] *Letter* 2*.3, ed. *Bibliothèque augustinienne 46B: Lettres 1*–29**, Paris, 1987, p. 20: transl. R. Eno, *Fathers of the Church* 81, Washington, DC, 1989, p. 20.
56. Augustine, *City of God* 14.1: transl. H. Bettenson, Harmondsworth, 1976, p. 547.

Chapter 4: "Virtutes sanctorum . . ."

1. Augustine, *Letter* 199.35 and 45: transl. W. Parsons, *Fathers of the Church* 30, New York, 1955, pp. 384 and 394.
2. P. Heather, The western empire, 425–476, in Averil Cameron, B. Ward-Perkins and M. Whitby (eds.), *The Cambridge Ancient History 14. Late Antiquity: Empire and Successors A.D.425–600*, Cambridge, 2000, pp. 1–32; R. Collins, *Early Medieval Europe 300–1000*, New York, 1991, pp. 75–93.
3. S. Muhlberger, *Fifth-Century Chronicles*, Liverpool, 1990, pp. 193–266.
4. Hydatius, *Chronicle*, preface 1–6: transl. R. W. Burgess, Oxford, 1993, pp. 73–5.
5. Hydatius, *Chronicle*, Olympiad 309, p. 107.
6. J. Harries, *Sidonius Apollinaris and the Fall of Rome, A.D. 407–485*, Oxford, 1994.
7. Sidonius Apollinaris, *Letter* 4.20.2–3: transl. W. B. Anderson, Loeb Classical Library, London, 1965, pp. 137–9. See also A. C. Murray, *From Roman to Merovingian Gaul: A Reader*, Peterborough, Ontario, 2000, pp. 193–258.
8. Vegetius, *Epitome of Military Science* 2.5: transl. N. P. Milner, Liverpool, 1993, p. 35.
9. D. Janes, The golden clasp of the late Roman state, *Early Medieval Europe*, 5 (1996): 127–53; B. Arrhenius, *Merovingian Garnet Jewelry. Origins and Social Implications*, Stockholm, 1985.
10. G. Halsall, Movers and Shakers; the barbarians and the fall of Rome, *Early*

Medieval Europe, 8 (1999): 131–45; E. A. Thompson, *Romans and Barbarians*, Madison, WI, 1982, pp. 23–37 and 251–6.

11. W. Goffart, *Romans and Barbarians: Techniques of Accommodation* A.D. 418–584, Princeton, NJ, 1980 offers an enticingly elegant but oversimplified solution (the "settlers" simply took a share of the taxes, not of the land): see A. M. Jiménez Garnica, The settlement of the Visigoths in the fifth century, in P. Heather (ed.), *The Visigoths from the Migration Period to the Seventh Century: An Ethnographic Perspective*, Woodbridge, Suffolk, 1999, pp. 93–115 with the discussion on pp. 115–28.

12. *Anonymus Valesianus* 12.61: transl. J. C. Rolfe, *Ammianus Marcellinus*, Loeb Classical Library, London, 1952, p. 547; P. Amory, *People and Identity in Ostrogothic Italy 489–554*, Cambridge, 1997.

13. W. Pohl, Introduction and telling the difference: signs of ethnic identity, in W. Pohl and H. Reimitz, *Strategies of Distinction. The Construction of Ethnic Communities, 300–800*, Leiden, 1998, pp. 1–15 and 16–69; P. Geary, *The Myths of Nations. The Peoples of Europe in the Early Middle Ages*, Princeton, NJ, 2002. See W. Pohl, *Die Völkerwanderung: Eroberung und Integration*, Stuttgart, 2002.

14. *Book of Constitutions* 97: transl. K. F. Drew, *The Burgundian Code*, Philadelphia, 1949, p. 84. P. Heather, The creation of the Visigoths, in *The Visigoths*, pp. 43–73 makes a strong case for the importance of such a class.

15. P. Brown, The study of elites in Late Antiquity, *Arethusa*, 33 (2000): 321–46 at pp. 333–6; J. Harries, Sidonius Apollinaris, Rome and the barbarians: a climate of treason?, in J. Drinkwater and H. Elton (eds.), *Fifth-Century Gaul: A Crisis of Identity?*, Cambridge, 1992, pp. 298–308.

16. Amory, *People and Identity in Ostrogothic Italy*, pp. 195–276.

17. Victor of Vita, *History of the Vandal Persecution* 3.3–14: transl. J. Moorhead, Liverpool, 1992, pp. 64–9; F. Modéran, La chronologie de la Vie de Saint Fulgence de Ruspe et ses incidences sur l'histoire de l'Afrique vandale, *Mélanges de l'école française de Rome: Antiquité*, 105 (1993): 135–88.

18. Gregory of Tours, *History* 2, preface: transl. L. Thorpe, Harmondsworth, 1974, p. 103.

19. L. Maurin, Remparts et cités dans les trois provinces du Sud-Ouest de la Gaule au bas-empire, *Villes et agglomérations urbaines antiques du Sud-Ouest de la Gaule*, Aquitania: Supplément 6, Bordeaux, 1992, pp. 365–89; E. M. Butler, Late Roman town walls in Gaul, *Archaeological Journal*, 126 (1959): 25–50.

20. R. Samson, The Merovingian nobleman's hall: castle or villa? *Journal of Medieval History*, 13 (1987): 287–315.

21. Gregory of Tours, *History* 2.7, p. 116.

22. Gregory of Tours, *History* 2.32, p. 147.

23. *Life of Caesarius of Arles* 1.32: transl. W. Klingshirn, Liverpool, 1994, p. 25; W. Klingshirn, Charity and power: the ransoming of captives in sub-Roman Gaul, *Journal of Roman Studies*, 75 (1985): 95–102.

24. Gregory of Tours, *History* 2.16, p. 131; S. T. Loseby, Bishops and cathedrals: order and diversity in the fifth-century urban landscape of southern Gaul, in Drinkwater and Elton (eds.), *Fifth Century Gaul*, pp. 144–55.

25. Sidonius Apollinaris, *Letters* 5–14 and 7.1, pp. 217–19 and 287–93; G. Nathan,

Rogation ceremonies in Late Antique Gaul, *Classica et Medievalia*, 21 (1998): 276–303.

26. *Life of Genovefa* 3.11: transl. J. A. McNamara and J. Hallborg, *Sainted Women of the Dark Ages*, Durham, NC, 1992, pp. 23–4.

27. P. Brown, *The Cult of the Saints. Its Rise and Function in Latin Christianity*, Chicago, 1981; B. Beaujard, *Le culte des saints en Gaule*, Paris, 2000.

28. Paulinus of Perigueux, *Life of Martin* 6.93, *Corpus Scriptorum Ecclesiasticorum Latinorum* 16, Vienna, 1888, p. 143; R. Van Dam, *Leadership and Community in Late Antique Gaul*, Berkeley, CA, 1985, pp. 157–76.

29. M. Heinzelmann, *Die Bischofsherrschaften in Gallien*, Munich, 1976, remains the classic study.

30. Sidonius Apollinaris, *Letter* 7.9, pp. 335–9.

31. P'awstos Buzand, *Epic Histories* 6.2: transl. N. Garsoian, Cambridge, MA, 1989, p. 234.

32. S. Loseby, Marseilles: a late antique success story?, *Journal of Roman Studies*, 82 (1992): 165–85.

33. R. A. Markus, *The End of Ancient Christianity*, Cambridge, 1990, pp. 181–94; P. Rousseau, Cassian: monastery and world, in M. Fairburn and W. H. Oliver (eds.), *The Certainty of Doubt. Tributes to Peter Munz*, Wellington, New Zealand, 1995, pp. 68–89; C. Stewart, *Cassian the Monk*, New York, 1998.

34. Cassian, *Conferences* 18, preface: trans. E. C. S. Giles, *Library of the Nicene and Post-Nicene Fathers*, 11, Grand Rapids, MI, 1986, p. 471, also translated by C. Luibheid, New York, 1985, and B. Ramsey, Ancient Christian Writers, 57, New York, 1997; C. Leyser, *Authority and Asceticism from Augustine to Gregory the Great*, Oxford, 2000, pp. 33–61.

35. S. Pricoco, *L'Isola dei santi. Il cenobio di Lerino e le origini del monachesimo in Gallia*, Rome, 1978; C. Leyser, "This Sainted Isle": Panegyric, nostalgia and the invention of a "Lerinian monasticism", in W. Klingshirn and M. Vessey (eds.), *The Limits of Ancient Christianity. Essays on Late Antique Thought and Culture in Honor of R. A. Markus*, Ann Arbor, MI, 1999, pp. 188–206.

36. Hilary of Arles, *Life of Saint Honoratus* 1.8: trans., F. R. Hoare, *The Western Fathers*, New York, 1954, pp. 253–4.

37. Constantius, *Life of Germanus* 1: trans. Hoare, *The Western Fathers*, p. 286, reprinted in Noble and Head, *Soldiers of Christ*, pp. 75–106.

38. Constantius, *Life of Germanus* 12–18, 25–7, and 28–39, pp. 295–302, 306–7 and 308–17.

39. Ennodius, *Life of Epiphanius* 1.14: transl. G. M. Cook, Washington, DC, 1942, p. 9.

40. Leo, *Letter* 10.2: transl. C. L. Feltoe, *Library of the Nicene and Post-Nicene Fathers*, 12, Oxford, 1895, p. 9; R. W. Mathisen, *Ecclesiastical Factionalism and Religious Controversy in Fifth-Century Gaul*, Washington, DC, 1989, pp. 141–72.

41. F. Marazzi, Rome in transition: economic and political change in the fourth and fifth centuries, in J. M. H. Smith (ed.), *Early Medieval Rome and the Christian West. Essays in Honour of Donald A. Bullough*, Leiden, 2000, pp. 21–41; A. Gillett, Rome, Ravenna and the last Western emperors, *Papers of the British School at Rome*, 69 (2001): 131–67.

42. s.v. papa and Papacy, in G. W. Bowersock, P. Brown, and O. Grabar (eds.), *Late Antiquity. A Guide to the Postclassical World*, Cambridge, MA, 1999, pp. 633–5; C. Pietri, *Roma christiana*, 2 vols., Rome, 1976.

43. Pope Celestine, *Letter* 21.2: *Patrologia Latina*, 50: 529A.

44. Augustine [Newly discovered] *Letter* 20*.31: transl. R. Eno, *Fathers of the Church*, 81, Washington DC, 1989, p. 148.

45. C. Mango, The development of Constantinople as an urban center, *Studies in Constantinople*, Aldershot, 1993; B. Ward-Perkins, Constantinople: imperial capital of the fifth and sixth centuries, in G. Ripoll and J. M. Gurt (eds.), *Sedes Regiae (ann. 400–800)*, Barcelona, 2000, pp. 63–81.

46. N. H. Baynes, Alexandria and Constantinople: a study in ecclesiastical diplomacy, in *Byzantine Studies and Other Essays*, London, 1955, pp. 97–115.

47. Cyril of Alexandria, *Letter* 96: transl. J. I. McEnerney, *Fathers of the Church*, 77, Washington, DC, 1985, pp. 151–2.

48. W. H. C. Frend, *The Rise of the Monophysite Movement*, Cambridge, 1972, pp. 39–43.

49. Leo, *Sermon* 24.2, Feltoe, p. 135.

50. Eusebius, *In Praise of Constantine* 3.6: transl. H. A. Drake, Berkeley, CA, 1978, p. 81.

51. J. R. Lyman, *Christology and Cosmology*, Oxford, 1993, pp. 82–123.

52. *Synod of Alexandria of 362*, M. Tetz (ed.), *Zeitschrift der neutestamentlichen Wissenschaft*, 79 (1988): 272. Lyman, *Christology and Cosmology*, pp. 124–59.

53. J. A. McGuckin, *St. Cyril of Alexandria: The Christological Controversy, its History, Theology and Texts*, 1994; B. Meunier, *Le Christ de Cyrille d'Alexandrie*, Paris, 1997; N. Russell, *Cyril of Alexandria*, London, 2000.

54. Shenoute of Atripe, *Contra Origenistas* 821, T. Orlandi (ed.), Rome, 1985, pp. 62–3.

55. Nestorius, *The Bazaar of Heracleides* 2. 495–521: transl. G. Driver and L. Hodgson, Oxford, 1925, pp. 363–79; McGuckin, *Cyril of Alexandria*, pp. 126–74.

56. s.v. Monophysites, in *Late Antiquity. A Guide*, pp. 586–8.

57. Isaac of Antioch, *Memra 8. On the Bird that Sung at Antioch* 149–450, G. Bickell (ed.), Giessen, 1873, pp. 91–105.

58. P. Brown, *Poverty and Leadership in the Later Roman Empire*, Hanover, NH, 2001, pp. 97–111.

59. John Moschus, *The Spiritual Meadow* 147: transl. J. Wortley, Kalamazoo, MI, 1992, p. 120.

60. H. E. Chadwick, Preface, *Actes du Concile de Chalcédoine. Sessions III–VI*: transl. A. J. Festugière, Geneva, 1982, pp. 7–16, and Eucharist and Christology in the Nestorian controversy, *Journal of Theological Studies*, NS 2 (1951): 145–64.

61. s.v. Chalcedon, Council of, in *Late Antiquity. A Guide*, pp. 369–70; Frend, *The Rise of the Monophysite Movement*, pp. 50–142.

Chapter 5: On the Frontiers

1. Eugippius, *Life of Severinus* 20.1: transl. L. Bieler, *Fathers of the Church*, 55, Washington, DC, 1965, p. 78.
2. E. A. Thompson, *Romans and Barbarians*, Madison, WI, 1980, pp. 113–33; R. Bratož, *Severinus von Noricum und seine Zeit*, Vienna, 1983; W. Pohl and M. Diesenberger (eds.), *Eugippius und Severin. Der Autor, der Text und der Heilige*, Forschungen zur Geschichte des Mittelalters 2, Vienna, 2001.
3. A. Jenny, *Forschungen in Lauriacum 1*, Linz, 1954; K. Genser, *Der österreichische Donaulimes in der Römerzeit*, Vienna, 1986.
4. Eugippius, *Life of Severinus* 1, p. 1.
5. Eugippius, *Life of Severinus* 19.2, p. 77.
6. Eugippius, *Life of Severinus* 7.1, pp. 65–6.
7. Eugippius, *Life of Severinus* 8.3, pp. 65–6.
8. C. Leyser, *Asceticism and Authority from Augustine to Gregory the Great*, Oxford, 2000, pp. 108–17.
9. Bratož, *Severinus von Noricum*, p. 30.
10. F. Glaser, *Das frühchristliche Pilgerheiligtum auf dem Hemmaberg*, Klagenfurt, 1991 and Eine weitere Doppelkirchenanlage auf dem Hemmaberg, *Carinthia I*, 183 (1993): 163–86.
11. R. Bland and C. Johns, *The Hoxne Treasure*, London, 1993.
12. A. S. Esmonde-Cleary, *The Ending of Roman Britain*, London, 1989; B. Ward-Perkins, Specialized production and exchange, in Averil Cameron, B. Ward-Perkins, and M. Whitby, *The Cambridge Ancient History 14. Late Antiquity: Empire and Successors A.D. 425–600*, Cambridge, 2000, pp. 346–91. K. R. Dark, *Civitas to Kingdom. British Political Continuity 300–800*, Leicester, 1994, is the best of many, inevitably speculative, reconstructions of this period.
13. *The Exeter Book: The Ruin* 21: transl. S. A. J. Bradley, *Anglo-Saxon Poetry*, London, 1982, p. 402.
14. B. Ward-Perkins, Why did the Saxons not become more British?, *English Historical Review*, 115 (2000): 513–33.
15. C. Thomas, *Christianity in Roman Britain to A.D. 400*, Berkeley, CA, 1981; M. Lapidge and D. Dumville (eds.), *Gildas: New Approaches*, Woodbridge, Suffolk, 1984.
16. R. Sharpe, Martyrs and local saints in late antique Britain, in R. Sharpe and A. T. Thacker (eds.), *Local Saints and Local Churches in the Early Medieval West*, Oxford, 2002, pp. 75–154.
17. Aneurin, *Y Goddodin* 102 and 840: transl. A. O. H. Jarman, Llandysal, 1990, pp. 8 and 56.
18. Aneurin, *Y Goddodin* 286 and 362, pp. 20 and 24; Gildas, *On the Ruin of Britain* 28.1: transl. M. Winterbottom, London, 1978, p. 29.
19. D. Dumville, The idea of government in sub-Roman Britain, in G. Ausenda (ed.), *After Empire. Towards an Ethnography of Europe's Barbarians*, Woodbridge, Suffolk, 1995, pp. 177–216.
20. T. Charles-Edwards, *Early Christian Ireland*, Cambridge, 2000, pp. 145–81.
21. Charles-Edwards, *Early Christian Ireland*, pp. 202–14 and 233–40.
22. Patricius, *Confessio* 16: translation A. B. E. Hood, *St. Patrick*, London, 1978,

p. 44. See also the translation and commentary of D. R. Howlett, *The Book of Letters of Saint Patrick*, Dublin, 1994.

23. Patricius, *Letter to Coroticus* 2–3, p. 55.
24. Patricius, *Confessio* 49, p. 51.
25. Patricius, *Confessio* 12, 34, and 35, pp. 43, 48, and 49.
26. Charles-Edwards, *Early Christian Ireland*, pp. 8–123 and 182–202.
27. *The First Synod of Saint Patrick*, canon 6: transl. L. Bieler, *The Irish Penitentials*, Dublin, 1975, p. 55.
28. C. Donahue, *Beowulf*, Ireland and the natural good, *Traditio*, 7 (1949/51): 262–77.
29. Muirchú, *Life of Patrick* 25, in Hood, *St. Patrick*, pp. 95–6.
30. M. McNeill, *The Lughnasa*, Dublin, 1982.
31. S. Lebecq, *Les origines francques, Ve–IXe siècle*, Paris, 1990, pp. 9–60; E. James, *The Franks*, Oxford, 1988, pp. 34–161; I. N. Wood, *The Merovingian Kingdoms, 450–752*, London, 1994, pp. 33–54. The sources for the rise and conversion of Clovis are translated in J. Hillgarth, *Christianity and Paganism, 350–750*, Philadelphia, 1985, pp. 72–83 and A.C. Murray, *From Roman to Merovingian Gaul: A Reader*, Peterborough, Ontario, 2000, pp. 259–86.
32. G. Halsall, The origins of the Reihengräberzivilisation: forty years on, in J. Drinkwater and H. Elton, *Fifth-Century Gaul: A Crisis of Identity?*, Cambridge, 1992, pp. 196–207, and F. Theuws and J. Alkemade, A kind of mirror of men: sword deposits in Late Antique northern Gaul, in F. Theuws and J. L. Nelson (eds.), *Rituals of Power. From Late Antiquity to the Early Middle Ages*, Leiden, 2000, pp. 401–76.
33. Fredegar, *Chronicle* 2.4–6 and *Liber Historiae Francorum* 1: transl. Murray, *From Roman to Merovingian Gaul*, pp. 591–5; R. A. Geberding, *The Rise of the Carolingians and the Liber Historiae Francorum*, Oxford, 1987, pp. 11–30.
34. A. C. Murray, Post vocantur Merohingii. Fredegar, Merovech and "sacral kingship", in A. C. Murray (ed.), *After Rome's Fall. Narrators and Sources of Early Medieval History. Essays presented to Walter Goffart*, Toronto, 1998, pp. 121–52.
35. James, *The Franks*, pp. 58–64.
36. Remigius to Clovis in Hillgarth, p. 76 and Murray, p. 260
37. Gregory of Tours, *History* 2.27: transl. L. Thorpe, Harmondsworth, 1974, pp. 139–40.
38. Transl. K. F. Drew, *The Laws of the Salian Franks*, Philadelphia, 1991; Wood, *The Merovingian Kingdoms*, pp. 108–15.
39. Gregory of Tours, *History* 2.42, p. 157.
40. Gregory of Tours, *History* 2.42, p. 158.
41. *Council of Agde*, *Concilia Galliae*, C. Munier (ed.), *Corpus Christianorum*, 148, Turnhout, 1963, p. 192.
42. Gregory of Tours, *History* 2.37, p. 152.
43. Gregory of Tours, *History* 2.37, pp. 153–4.
44. The date of the baptism of Clovis remains hotly disputed. The reader should note that in this account I accept the arguments for a late date advanced by D. Shanzer, Dating the baptism of Clovis: the bishop of Vienne vs. the bishop of

Tours, *Early Medieval Europe*, 7 (1988): 29–57. An earlier date would mean a different story, especially of Clovis' relations with the Visigoths.

45. Gregory of Tours, *History* 2.31, p. 144.
46. Gregory of Tours, *History* 2.38, p. 154; M. McCormick, Clovis at Tours: Byzantine public rituals and the origin of medieval ruler symbolism, in E. Chrysos and A. Schwarcz (eds.), *Das Reich und die Barbaren*, Vienna, 1989, pp. 155–80.
47. G. Camps, Rex Gentium Maurorum et Romanorum. Recherches sur les royaumes de Maurétanie des VIe et VIIe siècles, *Antiquités africaines* 20 (1984): 183–218.
48. S. C. Munro-Hay, *Aksum. An African Civilization of Late Antiquity*, Edinburgh, 1991.
49. *Kaleb Inscription*, in Munro, *Aksum*, p. 230.
50. I. Shahid, The *Kebra Nagast* in the light of recent research, *Le Mouséon*, 89 (1976): 133–78.
51. Gregory of Tours, *History* 2.40, p. 156.
52. Gildas, *On the Ruin of Britain* 26.1, p. 28; N. J. Higham, *The English Conquest. Gildas and Britain in the Fifth Century*, Manchester, 1994, pp. 67–89.
53 Gildas, *On the Ruin of Britain* 4–6 and 13–20, pp. 17–18 and 20–4.
54. Charles-Edwards, *Early Christian Ireland*, pp. 231–3.

Chapter 6: *Reverentia, rusticitas*

1. G. Pomarès, *Gélase 1er: Lettre contre les Lupercales*, Sources chrétiennes, 65, Paris, 1959.
2. Leo, *Sermon* 27.4: transl. C. L. Feltoe, *Nicene and Post-Nicene Fathers*, 12, Oxford, 1895, p. 140.
3. N. Purcell, The population of Rome in late antiquity: problems of classification and historical description, in W. V. Harris (ed.), *The Transformations of Vrbs Roma in Late Antiquity, Journal of Roman Archaeology*: Supplementary Series 33, Portsmouth, RI, 1999, pp. 135–61 at pp. 135–7.
4. B. Beaujard, *Le culte des saints en Gaule. Les premiers temps. D'Hilaire de Poitiers à la fin du VIe siècle*, Paris, 2000, pp. 333–98.
5. R. Fletcher, *The Conversion of Europe. From Paganism to Christianity 371– 1386 A.D.*, London, 1998, pp. 34–65; P. Pergola (ed.), *Alle origini della parrocchia rurale (IV–VIII secolo)*, Rome: Vatican City, 1999.
6. G. Volpe, *San Giusto: la villa, le ecclesiae*, Bari, 1998 (a spectacular site in southern Italy); K. Bowes, "Nec sedere in villam." Villa-churches, rural piety and the Priscillianist controversy, in T. S. Burns and J. W. Eadie (eds.), *Urban Functions and Rural Contexts in Late Antiquity*, East Lansing, MI, 2001, pp. 323–48.
7. S. Barnish, Christians and countrymen at San Vicenzo c. A.D. 400–550, in R. Hodges (ed.), *San Vicenzo al Volturno* 2, Oxford, 1995, pp. 131–7, and *Religio in stagno*: nature, divinity and the Christianization of the countryside in Late Antique Italy, *Journal of Early Christian Studies*, 9 (2001): 387–402.
8. J. N. Hillgarth, Modes of evangelization of Western Europe in the seventh century, in P. Ní Chatháin and M. Richter (eds.), *Irland und die Christenheit*, Stuttgart, 1987, pp. 311–31.

9. V. Flint, *The Rise of Magic in Early Medieval Europe*, Princeton, NJ, 1991, pp. 108–15.

10. Gildas, *On the Ruin of Britain* 4.2: transl. M. Winterbottom, London, 1978, p. 17.

11. *Sixteenth Council of Toledo* (693), canon 2: J. Vives (ed.), *Concilios visigóticos*, Madrid, 1963, pp. 498–500; J. Hillgarth, Popular religion in Visigothic Spain, in E. James (ed.), *Visigothic Spain: New Approaches*, Oxford, 1980, pp. 3–60 (now in J. N. Hillgarth, *Visigothic Spain, Byzantium and the Irish*, London, 1985).

12. A. Rousselle, *Croire et guérir. La foi en Gaule dans l'Antiquité tardive*, Paris, 1990, pp. 31–52 and 65–75.

13. D. Frankfurter, *Religion in Egypt. Assimilation and Resistance*, Princeton, NJ, 1998, pp. 37–197.

14. Besa, *Life of Shenoute* 151–2: transl. D. N. Bell, Kalamazoo, MI, 1983, p. 84.

15. Shenoute, *Letter* 24, J. Leipoldt (ed.), *Corpus Scriptorum Orientalium Christianorum* 96: *Scriptores coptici* 8, Louvain, 1953, p. 45.

16. Theodoret of Cyrrhus, *A Cure for Hellenic Illnesses* 8.67–69, P. Canivet (ed.), Sources chrétiennes 57, Paris, 1958, vol. 2, p. 335. For the spectacular recent discovery of a Mithraeum underneath a church at Huarte (Syria): M. Gawlikowski, Un nouveau mithraeum récemment découvert à Huarte près d'Apamée, *Comptes rendus de l'Académie d'Inscriptions et Belles Lettres*, janvier–mars 2000, pp. 161–71.

17. *Corpus Inscriptionum Graecarum* 4, no. 8027, Berlin, 1877, p. 295.

18. Peter Brown, *Authority and the Sacred*, Cambridge, 1995, pp. 95–6.

19. P. Chuvin, *A Chronicle of the Last Pagans*, Cambridge, MA, 1990, pp. 101–18; P. Athanassiadi, Persecution and response in late paganism: the evidence of Damascius, *Journal of Hellenic Studies*, 113 (1993): 1–29.

20. Chuvin, *Chronicle of the Last Pagans*, pp. 131–48; F. Trombley, *Hellenic Religion and Christianization c.370–529*, Leiden, 1994; R. MacMullen, *Christianity and Paganism in the Fourth to Eighth Centuries*, New Haven, CT, 1997, pp. 1–73.

21. J. N. Hillgarth, *Christianity and Paganism. The Conversion of Western Europe, 350–750*, Philadelphia, 1986, pp. 105–10.

22. W. E. Klingshirn, *Caesarius of Arles. The Making of a Christian Community in Late Antique Gaul*, Cambridge, 1994, pp. 146–243.

23. *Life of Caesarius* 2.48: transl. W. E. Klingshirn, Liverpool, 1994, p. 65.

24. *Life of Caesarius* 1.54, p. 36.

25. Caesarius, *Sermons* 13.4 and 54.6: transl. M. Mueller, Fathers of the Church 31, New York, 1956, pp. 78 and 270.

26. *Council of Tours* (567), canon 23, J. de Clercq (ed.), *Concilia Galliae A.511–A.695*, Corpus Christianorum 148A, Turnhout, 1963, p. 191.

27. *Life of Caesarius* 1.27, p. 22, and 2.32, p. 58.

28. Caesarius, *Sermon* 52.3: transl. M. Mueller, Fathers of the Church 31, New York, 1956, p. 260.

29. Caesarius, *Sermon* 44.7, p. 225.

30. Caesarius, *Sermon* 192: transl. M. Mueller, Fathers of the Church 66, Wash-

ington, DC, 1972, pp. 26–30.

31. Caesarius, *Sermon* 193.4, p. 34.
32. Caesarius, *Sermon* 52.3, Fathers of the Church 31, p. 260.
33. MacMullen, *Christianity and Paganism*, pp. 74–149.
34. Caesarius, *Sermons* 47.5 and 54.6, pp. 241 and 270.
35. Caesarius, *Sermon* 50.1, p. 354.
36. Caesarius, *Sermon* 33.4, p. 167.
37. *Fourth Council of Toledo* (633), canon 11, Vives, p. 195.
38. W. Goffart, *Narrators of Barbarian History*, Princeton, NJ, 1988, pp. 112–234; M. Heinzelmann, *Gregor von Tours "Zehn Bücher der Geschichte". Historiographie und Gesellschaftsmodell im 6. Jht.*, Darmstadt, 1994; K. Mitchell; transl. C. Carroll, *Gregory of Tours: History and Society in the Sixth Century*, Cambridge, 2001. and I. N. Wood, *The World of Gregory of Tours*, Leiden, 2002.
39. I. N. Wood, *The Merovingian Kingdoms 450–751*, London, 1994, pp. 55–101, and *Gregory of Tours*, Bangor, 1994; E. James, Gregory of Tours and the Franks, in A. C. Murray (ed.), *After Rome's Fall. Narrators and Sources of Early Medieval History. Essays presented to Walter Goffart*, Toronto, 1998, pp. 51–66. See the material collected in A. C. Murray, *From Roman to Merovingian Gaul: A Reader*, Peterborough, Ontario, 2000, pp. 287–445.
40. Gregory of Tours, *History* 5, preface: transl. L. Thorpe, Harmondsworth, 1974, p. 253.
41. P. Fouracre, "Placita" and the settlement of disputes in later Merovingian Francia, in W. Davies and P. Fouracre (eds.), *The Settlement of Disputes in Early Medieval Europe*, Cambridge, 1986, pp. 23–44.
42. P. Fouracre, Attitudes towards violence in seventh and eighth century Francia, in G. Halsall (ed.), *Violence and Society in the Early Medieval West*, Woodbridge, Suffolk, 1998, pp. 60–75.
43. N. Pancer, *Sans peur et sans vergogne. De l'honneur et des femmes aux premiers temps mérovingiens*, Paris, 2001.
44. J. W. George, *Venantius Fortunatus. A Poet in Merovingian Gaul*, Oxford, 1997, and *Venantius Fortunatus: Personal and Political Poems*, Liverpool, 1995; S. Coates, Venantius Fortunatus and the image of episcopal authority in late antique and early medieval Gaul, *English Historical Review*, 115 (2000): 1109–37.
45. M. Roberts, The description of landscape in the poems of Venantius Fortunatus: the Moselle poems, *Traditio*, 49 (1994): 1–22.
46. C. Wickham, Overview, in R. Hodges and W. Bowden (eds.), *The Sixth Century: Production, Distribution and Demand*, Leiden, 1998, pp. 279–92.
47. M. Heinzelmann, Bischof und Herrschaft vom spätantiken Gallien bis zu den karolingischen Hausmeiern, in F. Prinz (ed.), *Herrschaft und Kirche*, Stuttgart, 1988, pp. 23–82; B. Jussen, Liturgy and legitimation, or How the Gallo-Romans ended the Roman empire, in B. Jussen (ed.), *Ordering Medieval Society*, Philadelphia, 2000, pp. 147–99.
48. M. Weidemann, *Das Testament des Bischofs Bertram von Le Mans von 27. März 616*, Mainz, 1986.

49. D. Janes, *God and Gold in Late Antiquity*, Cambridge, 1998, pp. 84–164.

50. Venantius Fortunatus, *Poem* 1.15: *Patrologia Latina* 88:79B.

51. Audoenus, *Life of Eligius* 2.41–42: B. Krusch (ed.), *Monumenta Germaniae Historica: Scriptores rerum merowingicarum* 4, Hanover, 1902, p. 725.

52. Beaujard, *Le culte des saints en Gaule*, pp. 455–510 and figs. 11–15, pp. 542–6; S. Lebecq, *Les origines franques, Ve-IXe siècle*, Paris, 1990, pp. 142–7. N. Gauthier, Le réseau de pouvoirs de l'évêque dans la Gaule du haut moyen âge, in G. P. Brogiolo, N. Gauthier, and N. Christie (eds.), *Towns and their Territories between Late Antiquity and the Early Middle Ages*, Leiden, 2000, pp. 173–207; S. Loseby, Gregory's cities: urban functions in sixth-century Gaul, in I. Wood (ed.), *Franks and Alemanni in the Merovingian Period. An Ethnographic Perspective*, San Marino, CA, 1998, pp. 239–84; I. N. Wood, Topographies of holy power in sixth-century Gaul, in M. de Jong and F. Theuws with C. van Rhijn (eds.), *Topographies of Power in the Early Middle Ages*, Leiden, 2001, pp.137–54.

53. Brown, *Poverty and Leadership*, pp. 45–73.

54. *Historical Memoirs of the Duc de Saint-Simon* 2: transl. L. Norton, London, 1967, p. 155.

55. Gregory of Tours, *Glory of the Martyrs* 83: transl. R. Van Dam, Liverpool, 1988, p. 108.

56. Gregory of Tours, *Glory of the Confessors* 39: transl. R. Van Dam, Liverpool, 1988, p. 51; *Miracles of Saint Julian* 45: transl. R. Van Dam, *Saints and their Miracles in Late Antique Gaul*, Princeton, NJ, 1993, p. 192.

57. Gregory of Tours, *Miracles of Saint Martin* 3.1: transl. Van Dam, *Saints and their Miracles*, p. 260.

58. Gregory of Tours, *History* 9.10, Thorpe, p. 493.

59. Gregory of Tours, *History* 2.24, p. 218.

60. G. de Nie, *Views from a Many-Windowed Tower. Studies of Imagination in the Works of Gregory of Tours*, Amsterdam, 1987.

61. Y. Hen, *Culture and Religion in Merovingian Gaul, A.D. 481–751*, Leiden, 1995, pp. 154–206.

62. Gregory of Tours, *History* 9.6 and 10.25, pp. 483–5 and 584–6.

63. Gregory of Tours, *History* 7.4, pp. 426–7.

64. Gregory of Tours, *Lives of the Fathers* 9.2: transl. E. James, Liverpool, 1985, p. 80.

65. S. Boesch-Gajano, Uso e abuso del miracolo nella cultura altomedioevale, *Les fonctions des saints dans le monde occidental (IIIe-XIIIe siècle)*, Collection de l'École française de Rome, 149, Rome, 1991, pp. 109–22.

66. Gregory of Tours, *Miracles of Saint Julian* 41, Van Dam, *Saints and their Miracles*, p. 189.

67. Gregory of Tours, *History* 6.29, p. 357.

68. *Life of Desiderius of Cahors* 16, B. Krusch (ed), *Corpus Christianorum*, 117, Turnhout, 1957, p. 362.

69. P. Fouracre, Eternal light and earthly needs: practical aspects of the development of Frankish immunities, in W. Davies and P. Fouracre (eds.), *Property and Power in the Early Middle Ages*, Cambridge, 1995, pp. 53–81.

70. Gregory of Tours, *Miracles of Saint Julian* 46b, p. 193.

71. Gregory of Tours, *Miracles of Saint Martin* 2.43 and 55, pp. 251 and 255.
72. Gregory of Tours, *Glory of the Confessors* 21, p. 26.
73. Gregory of Tours, *Lives of the Fathers* 2.3, p. 38.
74. Gregory of Tours, *Glory of the Confessors* 72, p. 76.
75. Gregory of Tours, *Glory of the Confessors* 21, p. 36.
76. Gregory of Tours, *Miracles of Saint Martin* 4.31, p. 298.
77. Gregory of Tours, *Glory of the Confessors* 7, p. 25.
78. Gregory of Tours, *Glory of the Confessors* 50, p. 60.

Chapter 7: Bishops, City, and Desert

1. *Life of Peter the Iberian*: transl. R. Raabe, Leipzig, 1895, p. 57.
2. G. Khoury-Sarkis, Réception d'un évêque syrien au VIe siècle, *L'Orient syrien*, 2 (1957): 137–84.
3. Leontius, *Life of John the Almsgiver* 9 and 45: transl. N. H. Baynes and E. Dawes, *Three Byzantine Saints*, Oxford, 1948, pp. 217–18 and 256; V. Déroche, *Études sur Léontios de Néapolis*, Uppsala, 1995, pp. 146–53; C. Haas, *Alexandria in Late Antiquity*, Baltimore, MD, 1997, pp. 249–58.
4. M. Whittow, Ruling the late Roman and early Byzantine city: a continuous history, *Past and Present*, 129 (1990): 3–39; J. H. W. G. Liebeschuetz, *The Decline and Fall of the Roman City*, Oxford, 2001.
5. Severus of Antioch, *Letter* 1.8: transl. E. W. Brooks, *Select Letters of Severus*, London, 1903, p. 43.
6. Piccirillo, *The Mosaics of Jordan*, Baltimore, MD, 1994; P. Donceel-Voûte, *Les pavements des églises byzantines de Syrie et du Liban*, Louvain, 1988; R. Schick, *The Christian Communities of Palestine from Byzantine to Islamic Rule. A Historical and Archaeological Survey*, Princeton, NJ, 1995, pp. 225–484.
7. M. Mundell Mango, *Silver From Early Byzantium*, Baltimore, Maryland, 1986.
8. Averil Cameron, *Christianity and the Rhetoric of Empire. The Development of Christian Discourse*, Berkeley, CA, 1991, pp. 189–202; P. Brown, *Power and Persuasion in Late Antiquity. Towards a Christian Empire*, Madison, WI, 1992, pp. 118–52.
9. *Codex Justinianus* 1.4.26 (530): transl. P. R. Coleman-Norton, *Roman State and Christian Church* 3, London, 1966, pp. 1058–61; D. Claude, *Die byzantinische Stadt im 6. Jht.* Munich, 1969, pp. 195–229.
10. D. Feissel and I. Kaygusuz, Un Mandement impérial du VIème siècle dans une inscription d'Hadrianoupolis d'Honoriade, *Travaux et Mémoires*, 9 (1985): 397–419.
11. P. L. Gatier, Nouvelles inscriptions de Gérasa: la prison de l'évêque Paul, *Syria*, 62 (1982): 297–305.
12. Theodoret of Cyrrhus, *Ecclesiastical History* 5.36: transl. B. Jackson, *Library of the Nicene and Post-Nicene Fathers* 3, Oxford, 1893, p. 156.
13. Severus of Antioch, *Letter* 1.9, p. 46.
14. J. Meyendorff, *Imperial Unity and Christian Division. The Church 450–680*, Crestwood, NY, 1989.
15. *Life of Peter the Iberian*, p. 72.
16. R. Webb, Salome's sisters: the rhetoric and reality of dancers in Late Antiquity

and Byzantium, in Liz James (ed.), *Women, Men and Eunuchs. Gender in Byzantium*, London, 1997, pp. 119–48; R. Lim, Consensus and dissensus in public spectacles in early Byzantium, *Byzantinische Forschungen*, 24 (1997): 159–79.

17. Jacob of Sarug, *On the Spectacles of the Theater* 5: transl. C. Moss, *Le Mouséon*, 48 (1935), p. 108.

18. *The Chronicle of Joshua the Stylite* 30: transl. W. Wright, Cambridge, 1882, pp. 20–1.

19. John of Ephesus, *Ecclesiastical History* 5.17: transl. R. Payne Smith, Oxford, 1860, p. 226.

20. C. Roueché, *Performers and Partisans at Aphrodisias in the Roman and Late Roman Periods*, London, 1993, pp. 129–56.

21. Alan Cameron, *Circus Factions. Blues and Greens at Rome and Byzantium*, Oxford, 1976; G. Dagron, L'organisation et le déroulement des courses d'après le *Livre des Cérémonies*, *Travaux et Mémoires*, 13 (2000): 3–180.

22. H. Kennedy, Syria, Palestine and Mesopotamia, in Averil Cameron, B. Ward-Perkins, and M. Whitby (eds.), *The Cambridge Ancient History 14. Late Antiquity: Empire and Sucessors* AD *425–600*, Cambridge, 2000, pp. 588–611; J. G. Keenan, Egypt, in *Cambridge Ancient History 14*, pp. 612–37; S. Brock, Syriac Culture, and M. Smith, Coptic Literature, in Averil Cameron and Peter Garnsey, *Cambridge Ancient History 13: The Late Empire*, Cambridge, 1998, pp. 708–19 and 720–35.

23. G. Tate, *Les campagnes de la Syrie du nord du IIe au VIIe siècle*, Paris, 1992.

24. R. Doran, *The Lives of Simeon Stylites*, Kalamazoo, MI, 1992; P. Brown, Holy Men, in *Cambridge Ancient History 14*, pp. 781–810, and The Rise and Function of the Holy Man in Late Antiquity: 1971–1997, *Journal of Early Christian Studies*, 6 (1998): 353–76; S. Harvey, The Stylite's liturgy, *Journal of Early Christian Studies*, 6 (1998): 523–39.

25. D. Chitty, *The Desert a City*, Oxford, 1966, pp. 82–142; Y. Hirschfeld, *The Judaean Monasteries in the Byzantine Period*, New Haven, CT, 1992; J. Patrich, *Sabas, Leader of Palestinian Monasticism: A Comparative Study of Eastern Monasticism in the Fourth to Seventh Centuries*, Washington, DC, 1995; E. Wipszycka, *Études sur le christianisme dans l'Égypte de l'antiquité tardive*, Rome, 1996.

26. B. Flusin, *Miracle et histoire dans l'oeuvre de Cyrille de Scythopolis*, Paris, 1983, pp. 125–8.

27. *Historia Monachorum* 11: *Patrologia Latina* 21: 431D.

28. *Life of Symeon the Younger*, 15: P. Van den Ven (ed.), *La Vie ancienne de S. Syméon le Jeune*, Brussels, 1970, pp. 13–14 and Evagrius, *Ecclesiastical History* 6.23 cited in Van den Ven, p. 93*.

29. Pseudo-Ephraim, *On Hermits and Desert-Dwellers* 497–505: transl. J. G. Amar, in V. Wimbush (ed.), *Ascetic Behavior in Greco-Roman Antiquity*, Minneapolis, 1990, p. 79.

30. W. E. Crum and H. G. Evelyn-White, *The Monastery of Epiphanius* 2, New York, 1926, pp. 194–5.

31. *Barsanuphe et Jean de Gaza: Correspondance* 686: transl. L. Regnault, Solesmes, 1972, p. 441.

32. C. Rapp, "For next to God you are my salvation": reflections on the rise of the holy man in late antiquity, in J. Howard-Johnston and P. A. Hayward (eds.), *The Cult of Saints in Late Antiquity and the Early Middle Ages*, Oxford, 1999, pp. 63–81; P. Escolan, *Monachisme et église: le monachisme syrien du IVe au VIIe siècle: un ministère charismatique*, Paris, 1999.

33. Zosimus, *Historia Nova* 4.59: transl. R. T. Ridley, Brisbane, 1982, p. 98; John Rufus, *Plerophoriae* 89: *Patrologia Orientalis* 8, p. 150.

34. *Confirmation of the Codex Justinianus* (529), in Coleman-Norton, *Roman State and Christian Church*, p. 1035.

35. John Lydus, *On the Magistracies of the Roman State* 1.2: transl. A. C. Bandy, Philadelphia, 1983, p. 25; M. Maas, *John Lydus and the Roman Past*, London, 1992.

36. W. Treadgold, *A History of the Byzantine State and Society*, Stanford, CA, 1997, pp. 276–7.

37. Averil Cameron, Justin I and Justinian, in *Cambridge Ancient History 14*, pp. 63–85; R. Browning, *Justinian and Theodora*, London, 1987; J. Moorhead, *Justinian*, London, 1994.

38. *Codex Justinianus* 1.11.102, p. 1049.

39. T. Honoré, *Tribonian*, London, 1978.

40. *Constitution "Deo Auctore"* 2 (530): transl. A. Watson, Philadelphia, 1985, p. xlv.

41. G. Greatrex, The Nika Riot: a reappraisal, *Journal of Hellenic Studies*, 117 (1997): 60–86; A. Chekalova, *Konstantinopol' v vi veke. Vosstanie Nika*, Moscow, 1986.

42. R. J. Mainstone, *Hagia Sophia: Architecture, Structure and Liturgy of Justinian's Great Church*, London, 1997.

43. Procopius, *On the Buildings* 1.1.21–78: transl. H. Dewing, *Procopius 6*, Loeb Classical Library, London, 1954, pp. 10–32. This and other materials are translated in C. Mango, *The Art of the Byzantine Empire*, Englewood Cliffs, NJ, 1972, pp. 72–102.

44. Justinian, *Novella* 30.11.2 (536).

45. T. S. Brown, *Gentlemen and Officers. Imperial Administration and Aristocratic Power in Byzantine Italy*, A.D. *554–800*, London, 1984; J. Durliat, *Les dédicaces d'ouvrages de défense dans l'Afrique byzantine*, Collection de l'École française de Rome, 49, Rome, 1981; A. Cameron, Gelimer's laughter: the case of Byzantine Africa, in F. M. Clover and R. S. Humphreys (eds.), *Tradition and Innovation in Late Antiquity*, Madison, WI, 1989, pp. 153–65.

46. Procopius, *The Wars*: transl. Dewing, *Procopius 1–5*, Loeb Classical Library, London, 1954; Averil Cameron, *Procopius and the Sixth Century*, Berkeley, CA, 1985.

47. Procopius, *Buildings* 1.10.15–19, pp. 85–7; Mango, *Art of the Byzantine Empire*, pp. 109–10.

48. Cosmas Indicopleustes, *Christian Topography* 11: transl. J. MacCrindle, Hakluyt Society 98, London, 1897, pp. 369–70.

49. C. Panella, Merci e scambi nel Mediterraneo tardo antico, in A. Schiavone (ed.), *Storia di Roma 3*, part 2, Turin, 1993, pp. 613–97; L. Conrad (ed.), *Trade and*

Exchange in the Late Antique and Early Islamic Near East, Princeton, NJ (forthcoming); S. Kingsley and M. Decker (eds.), *Economy and Exchange in the Eastern Mediterranean during Late Antiquity*, Oxford, 2001.

50. Procopius, *Wars* 2.22–3, Dewing 1, pp. 451–73; Pseudo-Dionysius of Tell-Mahre, *Chronicle III. Part III*: transl. A. Witakowski, Liverpool, 1996, pp. 74–98.

51. L. Conrad, Epidemic disease in central Syria in the late sixth century, *Modern Greek and Byzantine Studies*, 18 (1994): 12–58; M. McCormick, Bateaux de vie, bateaux de mort. Maladie, commerce et le passage économique du bas-empire au moyen âge, in *Morfologie sociali e culturali in Europa tra Tarda Antichità e Alto Medio Evo*, Settimane di Studi sull'Alto Medio Evo 45, Spoleto, 1998, pp. 35–118.

52. J. D. Howard-Johnston, The two great powers in Late Antiquity: a comparison, in Averil Cameron, (ed.), *The Byzantine and Early Islamic Near East 3: States, Resources, Armies*, Princeton, NJ, 1995, pp. 157–226; M. Whittow, *The Making of Byzantium, 600–1025*, London, 1996, pp. 15–81.

53. C. Wickham, *Early Medieval Italy. Central Power and Local Society 400–1000*, London, 1981, pp. 28–79; E. Zanini, *Le Italie bizantine. Territorio, insediamenti ed economia nella provincia bizantina d'Italia (VI–VIII secolo)*, San Spirito, 1998.

54. M. Whitby, The Balkans and Greece, 420–600, in *Cambridge Ancient History 14*, pp. 701–30; W. Pohl, *Die Awaren. Ein Steppenvolk in Mitteleuropa, 567–822*, Munich, 1988, pp. 94–127.

55. K. H. Uthemann, Kaiser Justinian als Kirchenpolitiker und Theologe, *Augustinianum*, 39 (1999): 5–83; *On the Person of Christ. The Christology of the Emperor Justinian*: transl. K. P. Wesche, Crestwood, NY, 1991; P. Allen, The definition and imposition of orthodoxy, *Cambridge Ancient History 14*, pp. 811–34; M. Maas, Junilius Africanus' *Instituta Regularia Divinae Legis* in its Justinianic context, in P. Allen and E. Jeffreys (eds.), *The Sixth Century. End or Beginning?*, Brisbane, 1996, pp. 131–44.

56. Procopius, *Wars* 7.32–39, Dewing 4, p. 423.

57. J. Herrin, *The Formation of Christendom*, Princeton, NJ, 1987, pp. 90–127; C. Sotinel, s.v. Vigilio, in *Enciclopedia dei Papi*, Rome, 2000, pp. 512–29.

58. John of Ephesus, *Lives of the Eastern Saints* 13: transl. E. W. Brooks, *Patrologia Orientalis* 17, p. 189.

59. Procopius, *The Secret History* 9–10, Dewing 6, pp. 103–29, and G. A. Williamson, Harmondsworth, 1966, pp. 83–93.

60. Severus of Antioch, *Letter* 1.63, p. 198.

61. C. Pazdernik, Our most pious consort given to us by God: dissident reactions to the partnership of Justinian and Theodora, *Classical Antiquity*, 13 (1994): 256–81.

62. John of Ephesus, *Lives of the Eastern Saints* 5, pp. 102–3.

63. H. Kennedy, The last century of Byzantine Syria: a reconsideration, *Byzantinische Forschungen* 10 (1986): 141–83.

64. John of Ephesus, *Lives of the Eastern Saints* 59, *Patrologia Orientalis* 18, p. 696.

65. Susan Ashbrook Harvey, *Asceticism and Society in Crisis. John of Ephesus and his "Lives of the Eastern Saints"*, Berkeley, CA, 1990.

66. G. Fowden, *Empire to Commonwealth. Consequences of Monotheism in Late Antiquity*, Princeton, NJ, 1993, pp. 100–37.

67. J. Grosdidier de Matons, *Romanos le Mélode et les origines de la poésie religieuse à Byzance*, Paris, 1977; *The Kontakia of Romanos*: transl. M. Carpenter, 2 vols, Columbia, MO, 1970.

68. P. Allen, Severus of Antioch and the homily: the end of the beginning?, in Allen and Jeffreys (eds.), *The Sixth Century*, pp. 163–75.

69. John Moschus, *The Spiritual Meadow*: transl. J. Wortley, Kalamazoo, MI, 1992; V. Déroche, *Études sur Léontios de Néapolis*, pp. 270–96; D. Krueger, *Symeon the Holy Fool*, Berkeley, CA, 1996.

70. John of Ephesus, *Lives of the Eastern Saints* 12, p. 179.

71. *Les Sentences des Pères du désert. Nouveau recueil* 442: transl. L. Regnault, Solesmes, 1970, p. 64.

Chapter 8: *Regimen animarum*

1. G. B. de Rossi, *Inscriptiones christianae urbis Romae* 2:1, Rome, 1888, p. 146.

2. P. Llewellyn, *Rome in the Dark Ages*, London, 1971, pp. 78–108.

3. Gregory I, *Letter* 5.38, D. Norberg (ed.), *Corpus Christianorum* 140–140A, Turnhout, 1982, p. 313.

4. Gregory I, *Dialogues* 3.27–8, 37.10–15, and 38.3: transl. O. J. Zimmerman, Fathers of the Church 39, New York, 1959, pp. 161–3, 181–2, and 186.

5. C. Wickham, *Early Medieval Italy. Central Power and Local Society 400–1000*, London, 1981, pp. 28–49 and 64–79; T. S. Brown, *Gentlemen and Officers. Imperial Administration and Aristocratic Power in Byzantine Italy*, A.D. 554–800, London, 1984, pp. 1–60; W. Pohl, L'armée romaine et les Lombards: stratégies militaires et politiques, in F. Valet and M. Kazanski (eds.), *L'armée romaine et les barbares du IIIe au VIIe siècle*, Rouen, 1993, pp. 291–6.

6. O. G. von Simson, *Sacred Fortress. Byzantine Art and Statecraft in Ravenna*, Princeton, NJ, 1987.

7. Brown, *Gentlemen and Officers*, pp. 144–59.

8. Bede, *Ecclesiastical History* 4.1, B. Colgrave and R. A. B. Mynors (eds.), Oxford, 1969, p. 332.

9. J. N. Hillgarth, Coins and chronicles: propaganda in sixth-century Spain and the Byzantine background, *Historia*, 15 (1966): 483–508, now in *Visigothic Spain, Byzantium and Ireland*, London, 1985; R. Collins, *Early Medieval Spain. Unity in Diversity, 400–1000*, London, 1983, pp. 32–87.

10. S. J. B. Barnish, Pigs, plebeians and *potentes*: Rome's economic hinterland, c.350–500 A.D., *Papers of the British School at Rome*, 65 (1987): 157–85, and Transformation and survival in the western senatorial aristocracy, c.A.D. 400–700, *Papers of the British School at Rome*, 66 (1988): 120–55.

11. Brown, *Gentlemen and Officers*, pp. 21–81.

12. Boethius, *Consolation of Philosophy*: transl. P. G. Walsh, Oxford, 1999; H. Chadwick, *Boethius. The Consolations of Music, Logic, Theology, and Philosophy*, Oxford, 1981; M. Gibson (ed.), *Boethius. His Life, Thought and In-*

fluence, Oxford, 1981.

13. J. J. O'Donnell, *Cassiodorus*, Berkeley, CA, 1979, with Averil Cameron, Cassiodorus deflated, *Journal of Roman Studies*, 71 (1981): 183–6.

14. S. J. B. Barnish, *Cassiodorus: Variae*, Liverpool, 1992.

15. Cassiodorus, *Institutes* 1.29.1: transl. L. W. Jones, *An Introduction to Divine and Human Readings*, New York, 1946, p. 131.

16. S. J. B. Barnish, The work of Cassiodorus after his conversion, *Latomus*, 48 (1989): 157–87.

17. Cassiodorus, *Institutes* 1.30.1, Jones, p. 133; F. Troncarelli, *Vivarium. I Libri, il Destino*, Turnhout, 1998, pp. 38–66; M. Stansbury, Early medieval Biblical commentaries. their writers and readers, *Frühmittelalterliche Studien, 33* (1999): 49–82 at pp. 59–68.

18. Cassiodorus, *Institutes* 1.8.16, Jones, p. 93.

19. Troncarelli, *Vivarium*, pp. 21–37.

20. R. A. Markus, *Gregory the Great and His World*, Cambridge, 1997; C. Straw, *Gregory the Great*, P. Geary (ed.), Authors of the Middle Ages 12, Aldershot, 1996; S. Boesch-Gajano, Gregorio I, *Enciclopedia dei Papi 1*, Rome, 2000, pp. 546–74.

21. C. Pavolini, Le *domus* del Celio, in S. Ernesti and E. La Rosa (eds.), *Aurea Roma. Dalla città pagana alla città cristiana*, Rome, 2000, pp. 147–8.

22. E. Giuliani and C. Pavolini, La "Biblioteca di Agapito", in W. V. Harris (ed.), *The Transformations of Vrbs Roma in Late Antiquity, Journal of Roman Archaeology*, Supplement 33, Portsmouth, RI, 1999, pp. 85–107.

23. Gregory I, *Dialogues* 2.15, Zimmerman, p. 81; A. Augenti, *Il Palatino nel Medio Evo: Archeologia e topografia (secoli VI–XIII)*, Rome, 1996.

24. Cassiodorus, *Institutes* 1. Pref. 1, Jones, p. 67; H. I. Marrou, Autour de la Bibliothèque du pape Agapit, *Mélanges d'archéologie et d'histoire*, 48 (1931): 124–212, now in *Christiana Tempora*, Collection de l'École française de Rome 35, Rome, 1978. The building itself has not yet been identified.

25. H. Brandenburg, L'edificio monumentale sotto la chiesa di San Stefano Rotondo, *Aurea Roma*, pp. 200–3.

26. B. Brenk, La cristianizzazione della Domus dei Valerii, *The Transformations of Vrbs Roma*, pp. 69–84.

27. Gregorius 9, *Prosopographie chrétienne du Bas-Empire: Prosopographie de l'Italie chrétienne (313–604)*, part 1, Rome, 1999, pp. 945–9.

28. Gregory I, *Letter* 5.46, p. 340.

29. Gregory I, *Forty Gospel Homilies* 38: transl. D. Hurst, Kalamazoo, MI, 1990, pp. 352–3, and *Dialogues* 4.17, Zimmerman, p 211.

30. Gregory I, *Moralia. Dedication to Leander of Seville* 1, M. Adriaen (ed.), *Corpus Christianorum* 143, 143A, 143B, Turnhout, 1979–85, pp. 1–2: transl., *Library of the Fathers*, Oxford, 1844–7, vol. 1, pp. 1–5 and *Letter* 5.53, p. 348.

31. John the Deacon, *Life of Gregory* 1.9–10: *Patrologia Latina* 75: 66–7.

32. Eustratius, *Life of Eutychius* 8.80: *Patrologia Graeca* 86: 2365B.

33. John of Ephesus, *Ecclesiastical History* 2.42: transl. J. Payne Smith, Oxford, 1860, p. 148.

34. Eustratius, *Life of Eutychius* 9.89: 2373D.

35. Y. M. Duval, La dissension entre l'apocrisaire Grégoire et le patriarche Eutychius

au sujet de la résurrection de la chair: arrière-plan doctrinal oriental et occidental, in J. Fontaine, R. Gillet, and S. Pellistrandi (eds.), *Grégoire le Grand*, Paris, 1986, pp. 347–66.

36. C. Dagens, *Grégoire le Grand. Culture et expérience chrétienne*, Paris, 1977; C. Straw, *Gregory the Great. Perfection in Imperfection*, Berkeley, CA, 1988.
37. Gregory I, *Moralia in Job* 8.30.49, p. 421, transl., vol. 1, p. 456.
38. Gregory I, *Moralia in Job* 9.33.50, p. 491, transl., p. 531.
39. Gregory I, *Moralia in Job* 10.9.15 and 10.10.17, pp. 548 and 550, transl., pp. 590–1 and 592–3.
40. Straw, *Gregory the Great. Perfection in Imperfection*, pp. 8–12 and 47–65.
41. Gregory I, *Moralia in Job* 5.29.52, p. 254, transl., p. 280.
42. Straw, *Gregory the Great. Perfection in Imperfection*, pp. 107–27.
43. Gregory I, *Moralia* 35.1.1., p. 1774, transl., vol. 3.2, p. 662
44. Gregory I, *Moralia* 34.3.7, pp. 1727–8, transl., pp. 623–4; H. Savon, L'Antéchrist dans l'oeuvre de Grégoire le Grand, *Grégoire le Grand*, pp. 389–405.
45. Dagens, *Grégoire le Grand*, pp. 98–116; R. Gillet, *Grégoire le Grand: Morales sur Job*, Sources chrétiennes, 32 bis, Paris, 1975, pp. 89–102.
46. Dagens, *Grégoire le Grand*, pp. 55–75, and Markus, *Gregory the Great and his World*, pp. 41–50.
47. Gregory I, *Moralia* 4.1.1, p. 158, transl., vol. 1, pp. 177–8.
48. Marrou, Autour de la bibliothèque du pape Agapit, pp. 125–6.
49. Dagens, *Grégoire le Grand*, pp. 77–81.
50. J. Fontaine, *Isidore de Séville et la culture classique dans l'Espagne wisigothique*, Paris, 2nd edn., 1983, pp. 5–9.
51. Gregory I, *Letter* 1.5, p. 5.
52. Gregory I, *Letter* 7.5, p. 449.
53. Markus, *Gregory the Great and his World*, pp. 112–24.
54. Gregory I, *Letter* 1.30; Markus, *Gregory the Great and his World*, pp. 97–107.
55. Evagrius, *Ecclesiastical History* 6.12: *Patrologia Graeca* 86: 2861A.
56. C. Leyser, *Authority and Asceticism from Augustine to Gregory the Great*, Oxford, 2000, pp. 143–50; P. Llewellyn, The Roman Church in the seventh century: the legacy of Gregory I, *Journal of Ecclesiastical History*, 25 (1974): 363–80.
57. *Roman Synod of 595*, can. 2: *Patrologia Latina* 77:1335B.
58. C. Pietri, Clercs et serviteurs laïcs de l'église romaine au temps de Grégoire le Grand, *Grégoire le Grand*, pp. 107–22, now in *Respublica Christiana*, Collection de l'École françcaise de Rome 234, Rome, 1997, vol. 1, pp. 110–16.
59. Gregory I, *Letter* 5.53, p. 348.
60. Zachariah of Mitylene, *Chronicle* 8.5: transl. F. J. Hamilton and E. W. Brooks, London, 1899, p. 211.
61. Gregory I, *Pastoral Care [Regula Pastoralis]*, 1.1: transl. H. Davis, Ancient Christian Writers 11. Westminster, MD, 1950, p. 21. See also R. Judic, *Grégoire le Grand: Règle pastorale*, Sources chrétiennes 381–2, Paris, 1992.
62. *Laws of Recceswinth* 8.5.6, K. Zeumer (ed.), Hanover, 1894, p. 257.
63. Pope Honorius, *Letter* 14: *Patrologia Latina* 80:841.
64. Gregory I, *Letter* 1.24, pp. 27–8.

65. Gregory I, *Letter* 1.24, p. 28; G. Cracco, Grégoire le Grand, un christianisme renouvelé, *Antiquité tardive*, 7 (1999): 215–29 at pp. 228–9.
66. Gregory I, *Regula Pastoralis* 2.5, Davis, p. 58.
67. Gregory I, *Regula Pastoralis* 3.1–35, Davis, pp. 90–226.
68. Gregory I, *Regula Pastoralis* 2.10, Davis, pp. 80–2.
69. Gregory I, *Regula Pastoralis* 3.13, Davis, p. 129.
70. Leyser, *Authority and Asceticism*, pp. 160–7.
71. Gregory I, *Letter* 1.5, p. 7.
72. Gregory I, *Regula Pastoralis* 1.1, Davis, p. 22.
73. Gregory I, *Dialogues* 4.57, Zimmerman, p. 267–70.
74. Gregory I, *Dialogues* 2.36, Zimmerman, p. 107. The entire Book 2 of the *Dialogues* (Zimmerman, pp. 55–110) is a *Life of Benedict*.
75. *The Rule of Saint Benedict* 5: transl. T. G. Kardong, Collegeville, MN, 1996, p. 103; Leyser, *Authority and Asceticism*, pp. 101–28.
76. G. Jenal, *Italia Ascetica atque Monastica. Das Asketen- und Mönchtum in Italien von den Anfängen bis zur Zeit der Langobarden*, Stuttgart, 1995, pp. 266–314.
77. Fructuosus of Braga, *Rule for the Monastery of Compludo* 3: transl. C. W. Barlow, Fathers of the Church 63, Washington, DC, 1969, p. 157.
78. *Rule of Benedict* 2.31–32, pp. 48–9.
79. S. Teillet, *Des Goths à la nation gothique*, Paris, 1984, pp. 346–63, with modifications by J. N. Hillgarth, Eschatological and political concepts in the seventh century, in J. Fontaine and J. N. Hillgarth (eds.), *The Seventh Century. Change and Continuity*, London, 1992, pp. 212–31.
80. P. O'Leary, The foreseeing driver of an old chariot: royal moderation in early Irish literature, *Cambridge Medieval Celtic Studies*, 11 (1986): 1–16.
81. C. Straw, *Gregory the Great. Perfection in Imperfection*, p. 22.
82. Leyser, *Authority and Asceticism*, p. 134.
83. John Moschus, *The Spiritual Meadow* 151: transl. J. Wortley, Kalamazoo, MI, 1992, p. 124.
84. E. Pitz, *Papstreskripte im frühen Mittelalter. Diplomatische und rechtsgeschichtliche Studien zum Brief-Corpus Gregors des Grossen*, Sigmaringen, 1990, p. 251. But see Markus, *Gregory the Great and his World*, pp. 206–8.
85. Gregory I, *Letter* 2.17, p. 102.
86. Gregory I, *Homilies on the Gospels* 28, Hurst, p. 224.
87. A. de Vogüé, *Grégoire le Grand: Les Dialogues*, Sources chrétiennes 251, 260 and 265, Paris, 1978, esp. 251, pp. 25–154.
88. Gregory I, *Homilies on the Gospels* 12, Hurst, p. 91, also in *Dialogues* 4.15, Zimmerman, p. 208.
89. Gregory I, *Homilies on the Gospels* 36, Hurst, pp. 324–5, also in *Dialogues* 4.27, Zimmerman, p. 224.
90. Gregory I, *Homilies on the Gospels* 3, Hurst, p. 19.
91. Gregory I, *Dialogues* 3.15, Zimmerman, p. 136.
92. C. Straw, *Gregory the Great*, Authors of the Middle Ages, p. 44.
93. Gregory I, *Letter* 9.229, p. 806.
94. Gregory I, *Letter* 5.36, p. 306.

95. Gregory I, *Letter* 6.10, p. 378.
96. Gregory I, *Letter* 8.29, p. 551.
97. *The Earliest Life of Gregory the Great*, B. Colgrave (ed.), Cambridge, 1985.

Chapter 9: Powerhouses of Prayer

1.   I take this title from a fundamental study, R. A. Markus, *The End of Ancient Christianity*, Cambridge, 1990.
2.   F. Prinz, *Frühes Mönchtum im Frankenreich*, 2nd edn., Munich, 1988; M. Dunn, *The Emergence of Monasticism: From the Desert Fathers to the Early Middle Ages*, Oxford, 2000, now provides an overview.
3.   G. Jenal, *Italia Ascetica atque Monastica*, Stuttgart, 1995.
4.   B. Rosenwein, *Negotiating Space. Power, Restraint and Privileges of Immunity in Early Medieval Europe*, Ithaca, NY, 1999, pp. 32–5.
5.   M. dell'Omo, *Montecassino. Un'abbazia nella storia*, Monte Cassino, 1999, p. 187 and figs. 30, 60, and 86.
6.   Gregory the Great, *Letter* 8.5.
7.   Benedict, *Rule* 48.7: transl. T. G. Kardong, Collegeville, MN, 1996, p. 382.
8.   A. de Vogüé, *La règle de Saint Benoît* 6, Sources chrétiennes 186, Paris, 1971, p. 967.
9.   Fortunatus of Braga, *General Rule* 9: transl. C. W. Barlow, Fathers of the Church 63, Washington, DC, 1969, p. 190.
10. H. Lutterbach, *Monachus factus est. Die Mönchwerdung im frühen Mittelalter*, Münster, 1995, pp. 90–105 and 120–3.
11. A. de Vogüé, *La règle de Saint Benoît* 6, pp. 1355–67; M. de Jong, *In Samuel's Image. Child Oblation in the Early Medieval West*, Leiden, 1996.
12. P. Brown, *Body and Society. Men, Women and Sexual Renunciation in Early Christianity*, New York, 1988, pp. 260–1; J. Boswell, *Expositio* and *Oblatio*: the abandonment of children and the ancient and medieval family, *American Historical Review*, 89 (1984): 10–33.
13. Gregory, *Letter* 3.61.
14. A. de Vogüé, *La règle de Saint Benoît* 1, Sources chrétiennes 181, Paris, 1972, pp. 41–3.
15. Benedict, *Rule* Prologue 45 and 73.8, pp. 3 and 603.
16. Gregory, *Dialogues* 2.20: transl. O. J. Zimmermann, Fathers of the Church 39, New York, 1959, p. 87.
17. Benedict, *Rule* 55.7, p. 440.
18. A. Diem, *Keusch und Rein*, Amsterdam, 2000.
19. G. Muschiol, *Famula Dei. Zur Liturgie in merowingischen Frauenklöstern*, Münster, 1994.
20. Brown, *Body and Society*, pp. 259–84.
21. Muschiol, *Famula Dei*, pp. 43–63; C. Peyroux, Canonists construct the nun? Church law and women's monastic practice in Merovingian Gaul, in R. W. Mathisen (ed.), *Law, Society, and Authority in Late Antiquity*, Oxford, 2001, pp. 242–55.
22. G. Lawless, *Augustine of Hippo and his Monastic Rule*, Oxford, 1987, pp. 135–48.

23. W. Klingshirn, *Caesarius of Arles*, Cambridge, 1994, pp. 117–24.
24. *Life of Caesarius* 1.35: transl. W. Klingshirn, Liverpool, 1994, pp. 26–7.
25. Caesarius, *Letter* 21.2 (to Caesaria), p. 130.
26. Caesarius, *Rule for Nuns* 56: transl. M. C. McCarthy, Catholic University of America, Washington, DC,1960, p. 189.
27. Diem, *Keusch und Rein*, pp. 132–61.
28. *Life of Caesarius* 2. 26, p. 56.
29. E. Diehl, *Inscriptiones latinae christianae veteres*, no. 46, Zurich, 1970, p. 13.
30. I. N. Wood, *The Merovingian Kingdoms 450–751*, London, 1994, pp. 136–9.
31. Venantius Fortunatus, *Life of Radegund* [1].2: transl. J. A. McNamara with J. Halborg and E. Whatley, *Sainted Women of the Dark Ages*, Durham, NC, 1992, p. 71. The *Life of Radegund* is in two parts, the first written by Venantius Fortunatus and the second by Baudovinia, a nun from Radegund's own convent: B. Brennan, St. Radegund and the early development of her cult at Poitiers, *Journal of Religious History*, 13 (1984/5): 340–54.
32. Venantius Fortunatus, *Life of Radegund* [1].6, p. 73.
33. Venantius Fortunatus, *Life of Radegund* [1].12, p. 75.
34. Venantius Fortunatus, *Life of Radegund* [1].13–14, pp. 75–6.
35. Venantius Fortunatus, *Life of Radegund* [1].19 and 25, pp. 78 and 81.
36. Venantius Fortunatus, *Life of Radegund* [1].17, p. 77.
37. Baudovinia, *Life of Radegund* [2].16, p. 97.
38. Baudovinia, *Life of Radegund* [2].1, p. 87.
39. Venantius Fortunatus, *Poems* 2.1–7: *Patrologia Latina* 88: 87B–96A.
40. Venantius Fortunatus, *Life of Radegund* [1].1, p. 70.
41. B. Rosenwein, *Negotiating Space*, pp. 52–8; J. M. H. Smith, Women at the tomb: access to relic shrines in the early Middle Ages, in K. Mitchell and I. N. Wood (eds.), *The World of Gregory of Tours*, Leiden, 2002, pp. 163–80.
42. Baudovinia, *Life of Radegund* [2].14, p. 95.
43. Gregory of Tours, *Lives of the Fathers* 8.6: transl. E. James, Liverpool, 1985, p. 71.
44. Venantius Fortunatus, *Poems*, book 11: transl. J. George, Liverpool, 1995, pp. 103–10.
45. Baudovinia, *Life of Radegund* [2].33 and 36, pp. 83–4.
46. Baudovinia, *Life of Radegund* [2].10, p. 93.

Chapter 10: The Making of a *Sapiens*

1. S. Lancel, La survie et la fin de la latinité en Afrique du Nord, *Revue des études latines*, 59 (1981): 269–97.
2. R. Wright, *Late Latin and Early Romance in Spain and Carolingian Francia*, Liverpool, 1982.
3. P. Riché, *Education and Culture in the Barbarian West*, Columbus, SC, 1976.
4. R. Kaster, *Guardians of Language*, Berkeley, CA,1988, pp. 3–8 and 11–70; H. I. Marrou, *A History of Education in Antiquity*, Madison, WI, 1982, pp. 299–339.
5. Cassiodorus, *Variae* 9.21.4: transl. S. J. B. Barnish, Liverpool, 1992, p. 122.
6. P, Heather, Literacy and power in the migration period, in A. K. Bowman and

G. Woolf (eds.), *Literacy and Power in the Ancient World*, Cambridge, 1994, pp. 177–97.

7. Kaster, *Guardians of Language*, pp. 70–95; J. Fontaine, *Isidore de Séville et la culture classique dans l'Espagne wisigothique*, 2nd edn., Paris, 1983, pp. 785–806.

8. G. Dagens, *Grégoire le Grand: culture et expérience*, Paris, 1977, pp. 38–50.

9. R.A. Markus, *The End of Ancient Christianity*, Cambridge, 1990, pp. 213–28.

10. Fontaine, *Isidore de Séville*, pp. 786–8.

11. Marrou, *History of Education*, p. 209.

12. P. Hadot, *Philosophy as a Way of Life*, Oxford, 1995; M. Nussbaum, *The Therapy of Desire. Theory and Practice in Hellenistic Ethics*, Princeton, NJ, 1994; R. Sorabji, *Emotion and Peace of Mind. From Stoic Agitation to Christian Temptation*, Oxford, 2000.

13. Dagens, *Grégoire le Grand*, pp. 75–81.

14. Fontaine, *Isidore de Séville*, pp. 277–337.

15. *Epistulae Austriacae* 13, 16, and 22, W. Gundlach (ed.), *Corpus Christianorum* 117, Turnhout, 1957, pp. 431–41.

16. *Life of Audoin, Bishop of Rouen* 1: transl. P. Fouracre and R. A. Geberding, *Late Merovingian France: History and Hagiography 640–720*, Manchester, 1996, p. 154.

17. P. D. King, *Law and Society in the Visigothic Kingdom*, Cambridge, 1972.

18. I. N. Wood, Administration, law and culture in Merovingian Gaul, in R. McKitterick (ed.), *The Uses of Literacy in Early Medieval Europe*, Cambridge, 1990, pp. 63–81.

19. C. Courtois and L. Leschi, *Les Tablettes Albertini*, Paris, 1952.

20. I. Velázquez Soriano, *Documentos de época visigoda escritos en pizarra (siglos VI–VIII)*, 2 vols., Turnhout, 2000.

21. B. Effros, Monuments and memory: repossessing ancient ruins in early medieval Gaul, in M. de Jong and F. Theuws with C. van Rhijn (eds.), *Topographies of Power in the Early Middle Ages*, Leiden, 2001, pp. 93–118. D. Kinney, Rape or restitution of the past? Integrating spolia, in S. C. Scott (ed.), *Art and Interpreting. Papers in Art History from the Pennsylvania State University*, 9, University Park, PA, 1995, pp. 56–67; J. Poeschke (ed.), *Antike Spolien in der Architektur des Mittelalters und der Renaissance*, Munich, 1996.

22. T. M. Charles-Edwards, *Early Christian Ireland*, Cambridge, 2000, pp. 170–6.

23. *The Martryrology of Oengus*: transl. W. Stokes, London, 1905, p. 193.

24. T. J. Brown, The oldest Irish manuscripts and their Late Antique background, in P. Ní Chatháin and M. Richter (eds.), *Irland und Europa*, Stuttgart, 1984, pp. 311–27.

25. For example T. Cahill, *How the Irish Saved Civilization*, New York, 1995.

26. N. Wright, Columbanus' *Epistolae*, in M. Lapidge (ed.), *Columbanus: Studies on the Latin Writings*, Woodbridge, Suffolk, 1997, pp. 29–92.

27. Charles-Edwards, *Early Christian Ireland*, pp. 176–81.

28. P. Harbison, *Pilgrimage in Ireland. The Monuments and the People*, Syracuse, NY, 1992, pp. 71–110.

29. M. W. Herren, Gildas and early British monasticism, in A. Bammesberger and

A. Wollman (eds.), *Britain 400–600: Language and History*, Heidelberg, 1990, pp. 65–78.

30. C. Vogel, Composition légale et commutation dans le système de la pénitence tarifiée, *Revue de droit canonique* 8 (1958): 285–318 and 9 (1959): 1–38 and 341–59.

31. P. Sims-Williams, Thought, word and deed: an Irish triad, *Ériu*, 29 (1978): 78–111.

32. C. Stancliffe, Red, white and blue martyrdom, in D. Whitelock, R. McKitterick, and D. Dumville (eds.), *Ireland in Early Medieval Europe*, Cambridge, 1982, pp. 21–46; C. Etchingham, *Church Organization in Ireland* A.D. *650–1000*, Maynooth, 1999, pp. 291–318.

33. L. Bieler, *The Irish Penitentials*, Dublin, 1963; J. T. McNeill and H. Gamer, *Medieval Handbooks of Penance*, New York, 1938 and 1990, pp. 75–178; K. Hughes, *Early Christian Ireland: Introduction to the Sources*, London, 1972, pp. 82–9.

34. *The Penitential of Cummian*: transl. Bieler, pp. 108–35; McNeill and Gamer, pp. 99–117.

35. *Penitential of Cummian* 2.18, Bieler, p. 117; McNeill and Gamer, p. 104.

36. P. Payer, *Sex and the Pentitentials*, Toronto, 1984; H. Lutterbach, *Sexualität im Mittelalter*, Cologne, 1999, pp. 64–214.

37. R. Kottje, *Studien zum Einfluss des Alten Testaments auf Recht und Liturgie des frühen Mittelalters*, Bonn, 1970; B. Jaski, Early Irish kingship and the Old Testament, *Early Medieval Europe*, 7 (1998): 329–44.

38. Charles-Edwards, *Early Christian Ireland*, pp. 136–44. F. Kelly, *A Guide to Early Irish Law*, Dublin, 1988, pp. 125–34.

39. Charles-Edwards, *Early Christian Ireland*, p. 107

40. *Bretha Déin Chécht* 26, D. Binchy (ed.), *Ériu*, 20 (1966): 1–65 at p. 39.

41. R. Stacey, *The Road to Judgement. From Custom to Court in medieval Ireland and Wales*, Philadelphia, 1994, pp. 27–81.

42. *Penitential of Finnian* 23, Bieler, pp. 81–2.

43. Charles-Edwards, *Early Christian Ireland*, pp. 344–90.

44. T. M. Charles-Edwards, The penitential of Columbanus, in Lapidge (ed.), *Columbanus*, pp. 217–39.

45. Charles-Edwards, *Early Christian Ireland*, pp. 291–3.

46. C. Stancliffe, Venantius Fortunatus, Ireland, Jerome: the Evidence of *Precamur Patrem*, *Peritia*, 10 (1996): 91–7.

47. T. M. Charles-Edwards, The social background to Irish *Peregrinatio*, *Celtica*, 11 (1976): 43–59.

Chapter 11: *Medicamenta paenitentiae*

1. Columbanus, *Letter* 1.9: transl. G. S. M. Walker, *Sancti Columbani Opera*, Dublin, 1960, p. 11.

2. H. B. Clarke and M. Brennan, *Columbanus and Merovingian Monasticism*, Oxford, 1981; D. Bullough, The career of Columbanus, in M. Lapidge (ed.), *Columbanus. Studies on the Latin Writings*, Woodbridge, Suffolk, 1997, pp. 1–28; T. M. Charles-Edwards, *Early Christian Ireland*, Cambridge, 2000, pp.

344–90.
3. Columbanus, *Letter* 1.4, p. 5.
4. Columbanus, *Letter* 5.8, p. 45; P. T. Gray and M. Herren, Columbanus and the three chapters controversy, *Journal of Theological Studies*, NS 45 (1994): 160–70.
5. Columbanus, *Instruction [Sermon]* 1.3, p. 63; C. Stancliffe, The thirteen sermons attributed to Columbanus, in Lapidge (ed.), *Columbanus*, pp. 93–202.
6. Columbanus. *Instruction* 7.1, p. 91.
7. Columbanus, *Instruction* 3.3, p. 77.
8. Columbanus, *Instruction* 4.1, p. 79.
9. Jonas, *Life of Columbanus* 1.12: transl. E. Peters, *Monks, Bishops, and Pagans*, Philadelphia, 1981, p. 81–2.
10. J. Stevenson, The monastic rules of Columbanus, in Lapidge (ed.), *Columbanus*, pp. 202–16.
11. Columbanus, *Rule for Monks* 10, p. 141.
12. Columbanus, *Instruction* 12.3, p. 115.
13. Jonas, *Life of Columbanus* 2.13: transl. J. A. McNamara with J. Halborg and E. G. Whatley, *Sainted Women of the Dark Ages*, Durham, NC, 1992, p. 166.
14. Jonas, *Life of Columbanus* 2.19, p. 171.
15. G. Muschiol, *Famula Dei*, Münster, 1994, pp. 222–63.
16. T. M. Charles-Edwards, The penitential of Columbanus, in Lapidge (ed.), *Columbanus*, pp 217–39.
17. H. Atsma (ed.), *La Neustrie. Les pays au nord de la Loire de 650 à 850*, Sigmaringen, 1989; I. N. Wood, *The Merovingian Kingdoms 450–751*, London, 1994, pp. 181–220; P. Fouracre and R. A. Geberding, *Late Merovingian France. History and Hagiography 640–720*, Manchester, 1996.
18. Jonas, *Life of Columbanus* 1.11, Peters, p. 80.
19. Jonas, *Life of Columbanus* 1.32–33, Peters, pp. 94–6.
20. D. Ganz, Bureaucratic shorthand and Merovingian learning, in P. Wormald (ed.), *Ideal and Reality in Frankish and Anglo-Saxon Society*, Oxford, 1983, pp. 58–75.
21. E. James, Archaeology and the Merovingian monastery, in Clarke and Brennan (eds.), *Columbanus and Merovingian Monasticism*, pp. 33–55.
22. R. Le Jan, Convents, violence and competition for power in seventh-century Francia, in M. de Jong and F. Theuws with C. van Rhijn (eds.), *Topographies of Power in the Early Middle Ages*, Leiden 2001, pp. 243–69.
23. Jonas, *Life of Columbanus* 1.50, Peters, p. 106.
24. B. Rosenwein, *Negotiating Space. Power, Restraint and Privileges of Immunity in Early Medieval Europe*, Ithaca, NY, 1999, pp. 74–96.
25. *Diploma* of Chlothar III cited in Rosenwein, *Negotiating Space*, pp. 79–80.
26. Wood, *The Merovingian Kingdoms*, pp. 215–16.
27. Y. Hen, Les authentiques des reliques de la Terre Sainte en Gaule franque, *Le Moyen Age*, 105 (1999): 71–90.
28. P. Brown, The rise and function of the holy man, *Journal of Roman Studies*, 61 (1971): 80–101, now in *Society and the Holy in Late Antiquity*, Berkeley, CA, 1982, pp. 103–52 at pp. 145–6.

29. M. de Jong, Transformations of penance, in F. Theuws and J. L. Nelson, *Rituals of Power. From Late Antiquity to the Early Middle Ages*, Leiden, 2000, pp. 185–224, which substantially revises accepted views, for which see: C. Vogel, *La discipline pénitentielle en Gaule des origines à la fin du VIIe siècle*, Paris, 1952, and B. Poschmann, *Penance and Anointing of the Sick*, New York, 1964.

30. Éric Rebillard, *In hora mortis. L'évolution de la pastorale chrétienne de la mort au IVe et Ve siècles dans l'Occident latin*, Bibliothèque des écoles françaises d'Athènes et de Rome 283, Rome, 1994, pp. 160–7.

31. Gregory the Great, *Moralia in Job* 8.6.8–9 and 24.41: M. Adriaen (ed.), *Corpus Christianorum* 143, Turnhout, 1979, pp. 385–8 and 412; transl. *Library of the Fathers*, vol.1, Oxford, 1844, pp. 418–19 and 447–8.

32. Gregory the Great, *Dialogues* 4.46.9: transl. J. O. Zimmermann, Fathers of the Church 39, New York, 1959, p. 257.

33. C. Etchingham, *Church Organization in Ireland* A.D. *650–1000*, Maynooth, 1999, pp. 291–318; R. Meens, The frequency and nature of early medieval penance, in P. Biller and A. Minns (eds.), *Handling Sin: Confession in the Middle Ages*, Woodbridge, Suffolk, 1998, pp. 35–61.

34. P. Brown, *Gloriosus obitus*: the end of the ancient other world, in W. Klingshirn and M. Vessey (eds.), *The Limits of Ancient Christianity*, Ann Arbor, MI, 1999, pp. 289–314 at pp. 296–9.

35. Jonas, *Life of Columbanus* 2.11, McNamara, *Sainted Women*, pp. 162–3.

36. Gregory, *Dialogues* 4.43.2, p. 250.

37. Gregory, *Dialogues* 4.42.1–5, pp. 248–9.

38. P. Brown, The decline of the Empire of God: amnesty, penance and the afterlife from Late Antiquity to the Early Middle Ages, in C. W. Bynum and P. Freedman (eds.), *Last Things. Death and Apocalyptic in the Middle Ages*, Philadelphia, 2000, pp. 41–59.

39. C. Carozzi, *Le voyage de l'âme dans l'au-delà*, Collection de l'École française de Rome, 189, Rome, 1994.

40. Carozzi, *Le voyage de l'âme*, pp. 99–138.

41. *Vision of Fursa [Fursey]* 7.1 and 9.9, Carozzi, *Le voyage de l'âme*, pp. 683–4.

42. *Vision of Fursa* 8.16, p. 683.

43. *Vision of Fursa* 16.5, p. 691.

44. Bede, *Ecclesiastical History* 3.19.

45. Carozzi, *Le voyage de l'âme*, pp. 139–86; Y. Hen, The structure and aims of the Visio Baronti, *Journal of Theological Studies*, NS 47 (1996): 477–97.

46. *Vision of Barontus* 12: transl. J. N. Hillgarth, *Christianity and Paganism 350–750. The Conversion of Western Europe*, Philadelphia, 1986, p. 199.

47. *Vision of Barontus* 22, p. 204.

48. Brown, *Gloriosus obitus*, pp. 302–3.

49. Brown, *Gloriosus obitus*, pp. 296–301.

50. Brown, *Gloriosus obitus*, pp. 312–13, and Decline of the Empire of God, pp. 58–9.

51. Carozzi, *Le voyage de l'âme*, p. 638.

52. F. Paxton, *Christianizing Death. The Creation of a Ritual Process in Early Medieval Europe*, Ithaca, NY, 1990; P.A Février, La mort chrétienne, *Segni e*

riti nella chiesa altomedievale occidentale, Settimane di Studio sull'Alto Medioevo 33, Spoleto, 1987, pp. 881–942.

53. E. Rebillard, Les formes d'assistance funéraire dans l'empire romain et leur évolution dans l'antiquité tardive, *Antiquité tardive* 7 (1999): 269–82.

54. E. Rebillard, Église et sépulture dans l'antiquité tardive (Occident latin, 3e–6e siècles), *Annales*, 54 (1999): 1027–46.

55. Y. Duval, *Auprès des saints corps et âme. L'inhumation ad sanctos dans la chrétienté d'Orient et d'Occident du IIIe au VIe siècle*, Paris, 1988.

56. D. Bullough, Burial, community and belief in the early medieval west, in P. Wormald (ed.), *Ideal and Reality in Frankish and Anglo-Saxon Society*, pp. 177–201.

57. G. Ripoll Lopez and I. Velázquez Soriano, El epitafio de Trasemirus, *Espacio, Tiempo y Forma, Prehistória y Arqueología*, 3 (1990): 273–87.

58. Gregory of Tours, *The Glory of the Confessors* 64: transl. R. Van Dam, Liverpool, 1988, p. 70–1

59. A. Angenendt, Theologie und Liturgie in der mittelalterlichen Toten-Memoria, in K. Schmid and J. Wollasch (eds.), *Memoria*, Munich, 1984, pp. 70–199.

60. *The Rule of Patrick*: transl. *Ériu*,1 (1904): 216–24.

61. G. Dagron, La perception d'une différence: les débuts de la "Querelle du purgatoire", *15e Congrès international des Études byzantines: Actes* 4, Athens, 1976, pp. 84–92; H. G. Beck, *Die Byzantiner und ihr Jenseits*, Sitzungsberichte der bayerischen Akademie der Wissenschaften. Philos.-hist. Klasse 1979 no. 6, Munich, 1979.

62. *Life of Gertrude* 6: transl. McNamara, *Sainted Women of the Dark Ages*, p. 227.

63. *Life of Gertrude*, Preface, p. 223.

Chapter 12: Christianity in Asia and the Rise of Islam

1. Theophylact Simocatta, *Histories* 5.10.15: transl. M. and M. Whitby, Oxford, 1986, pp. 146–7.

2. W. Wolska, *La Topographie chrétienne de Cosmas Indicopleustes*, Paris, 1962, and Stéphanos d'Athènes et Stéphanos d'Alexandrie, *Revue des études byzantines*, 47 (1989): 5–89.

3. Cosmas Indicopleustes, *Christian Topography* 2.1: transl. J. W. McCrindle, Hakluyt Society 98, London, 1897, p. 70.

4. Cosmas Indicopleustes, *Christian Topography* 2.1, p. 72; U. Monneret de Villard, *Le Leggende orientali dei Magi evangelici*, Rome, 1952.

5. M. Mikawaya and A. Kollautz, Ein Dokument zum Fernhandel zwischen Byzanz und China, *Byzantinische Zeitschrift*, 77 (1984): 6–19; P. Schreiner, Eine chinesische Beschreibung Konstantinopels, *Istanbuler Mitteilungen*, 39 (1989): 493–505; D. D. Leslie and K. H. J. Gardiner, *The Roman Empire in Chinese Sources*, Rome, 1996; F. Thierry and C. Morrison, Sur les monnaies byzantines trouvées en Chine, *Revue numismatique*, 6 ser. 36 (1994): 109–45.

6. A. Palmer, Une chronique contemporaine de la conquête arabe, in P. Canivet and J. P. Rey-Coquais, *La Syrie de Byzance à l'Islam*, Damascus, 1992, pp. 31–46 at p. 37.

7. Theophylact Simocatta, *Histories* 4.11.2–3, p. 117.

8. *Dialogue between the Calif al-Mahdi and the Catholicos Timothy* 167: transl. H. Putman, *L'Église et l'Islam sous Timothée I (780–823)*, Beirut, 1975, p. 249.

9. M. Whitby, Recruitment in Roman armies from Justinian to Heraclius (ca.565–615), and J. Howard-Johnston, The two great powers in Late Antiquity, in A. Cameron (ed.), *The Byzantine and Early Islamic Near East 3: States, Resources, and Armies*, Princeton, NJ, 1995, pp. 61–124 and 157–226.

10. H. Kennedy, From polis to madina: urban change in Late Antique and Early Islamic Syria, *Past and Present*, 106 (1985): 3–27; C. Foss, Syria in transition, A.D. 550–750: an archaeological approach, *Dumbarton Oaks Papers*, 51, (1997): 189–269; D. Kennedy, The identity of Roman Gerasa: an archaeological approach, *Mediterranean Archaeology*, 11 (1998): 39–70.

11. P. L. Gatier, Les villages du Proche-Orient protobyzantin (4ème–7ème s.): Étude régionale, and H. McAdam, Settlement and settlement patterns in northern and central Transjordania, ca.550–ca.750, in G. R. D. King and Averil Cameron (eds.), *The Byzantine and Early Islamic Near East 2: Land Use and Settlement Patterns*, Princeton, NJ, 1994, pp. 17–48 and 49–93; M. Piccirillo, *The Mosaics of Jordan*, Baltimore, MD, 1994; C. Foss, The Near Eastern countryside in Late Antiquity: a review article, *Journal of Roman Archaeology*, Supplement 14, Portsmouth, RI, 1995, pp. 213–34.

12. Sergius of Resh'aina, cited in S. Brock, The Syrian background, in M. Lapidge (ed.), *Archbishop Theodore*, Cambridge, 1995, pp. 30–53 at p. 43.

13. Severus of Sebokht, cited in Brock, Syrian background, p. 48.

14. G. Fowden, *From Empire to Commonwealth. Consequences of Monotheism in Late Antiquity*, Cambridge, 1993, pp. 14–19; M. Whittow, *The Making of Byzantium 600–1025*, Berkeley, CA, 1996, pp. 25–37.

15. A. Palmer, *Monk and Mason on the Tigris Frontier. The Early History of Tur 'Abdin*, Cambridge, 1990.

16. C. Robin, *L'Arabie antique de Karb'îl à Mahomet: nouvelles données sur l'histoire arabe grâce aux inscriptions*, Aix-en-Provence, 1991; s.v. Himyar and s.v. Yemen, in G. W. Bowersock, P. Brown, and O. Grabar (eds.), *Late Antiquity. A Guide to the Postclassical World*, Cambridge, MA, 1999, pp. 492–3 and 752–3; K. Schippmann, *Geschichte der alt-südarabischen Reiche*, Darmstadt, 1999.

17. J. Mahé, Quadrivium et cursus d'études au VIIe siècle en Arménie, *Travaux et Mémoires*, 10 (1987): 159–206, at p. 196.

18. A. E. Redgate, *The Armenians*, Oxford, 1998, pp. 116–22.

19. N. Garsoian, *Armenia between Byzantium and the Sasanians*, Aldershot, 1985 and The two voices of Armenian historiography: the Iranian Index, *Studia Iranica*, 25 (1996): 7–43, now in *Church and Culture in Early Medieval Armenia*, Aldershot, 1999.

20. P'awstos Buzand, *The Epic Histories* 3.3: transl. N. Garsoian, Cambridge, MA, 1989, p. 84.

21. P'awstos Buzand, *Epic Histories* 6.10, pp. 237–8.

22. J. R. Russell, *Zoroastrianism in Armenia*, Cambridge, MA, 1987.

23. Elishe Vardapet, *History of Vardan and the Armenian War* 3: transl. R. W.

Thomson, Cambridge, MA, 1982, pp. 105–9.

24. N. Garsoian, *L'Église arménienne et le grand schisme d'Orient*, Corpus Scriptorum Christianorum Orientalium 574, Louvain, 1999.

25. R. W. Thomson, The formation of the Armenian literary tradition, in N. Garsoian, T. F. Mathews, and R. W. Thomson (eds.), *East of Byzantium: Syria and Armenia in the Formative Period*, Washington, DC, 1980, pp. 135–50.

26. S. Brock, The "Nestorian Church": a lamentable misnomer, *Bulletin of the John Rylands Library*, 79 (1996): 23–35.

27. *Synod of Ctesiphon* (605), cited in S. Brock, The Christology of the Church of the East in the Synods of the fifth to early seventh centuries, in G. Dragas (ed.), *Thyateira-Aksum. A Festschrift for Archbishop Methodios*, London, 1985, pp. 125–42 at p. 129; also in *Studies in Syrian Christianity*, London, Aldergate, 1992.

28. H. J. W Drijvers, The School of Edessa. Greek learning and local culture, in J. W. Drijvers and A. A. MacDonald (eds.), *Centres of Learning. Learning and Location in Pre-Modern Europe and the Near East*, Leiden, 1995, pp. 49–59.

29. S. Gero, *Barsauma of Nisibis and Persian Christianity in the Fifth Century*, Corpus Scriptorum Christianorum Orientalium 426, Louvain, 1981.

30. G. Gropp, Die Pahlavi-Inschrift auf dem Thomas-Kreuz in Madras, *Archäologische Mitteilungen aus Iran*, 3 (1970): 267–71.

31. J. M. Fiey, *Les communautés chrétiennes en Irak et Iran*, London, 1979; P. Gignoux, Sceaux chrétiens d'époque sasanide, *Iranica Antiqua*, 15 (1980): 299–314; s.v. "Christianity," in E. Yarshater (ed.), *Encyclopaedia Iranica*, vol. 5, Costa Mesa, CA, 1991, pp. 523–44.

32. G. J. Reinink, "Edessa grew dim and Nisibis shone forth." The Schools of Nisibis at the transition of the sixth–seventh century, in Drijvers and MacDonald (eds.), *Centres of Learning*, pp. 77–89; A. Vööbus, *Statutes of the Schools of Nisibis*, Stockholm, 1965.

33. Thomas of Marga, *The Book of Governors* 2.2: transl. E. A. W. Budge, London, 1893, p. 120.

34. D. Chwolson, Syrische Grabinschriften aus Semirjetschie, *Mémoires de l'Académie impériale de Saint Pétersbourg*, 7 ser. 34 (1886), no. 4, pp. 14–15; W. Klein, Christliche Reliefgrabsteine des 14. Jahrhunderts aus der Seidenstrasse, in R. Lavenant (ed.), *VI Symposium Syriacum*, Orientalia Christiana Analecta 247, Rome, 1994, pp. 419–42.

35. M. Morony, *Iraq after the Muslim Conquest*, Princeton, NJ, 1984, pp. 27–164; Howard-Johnston, The two great powers, in Cameron (ed.), *States, Resources and Armies*, pp. 198–203.

36. S. Brock, Christians in the Sasanian empire: a case of divided loyalties, in S. Meens (ed.), *Religion and National Identity*, Studies in Church History, 18, Oxford, 1982, pp. 1–19; Morony, *Iraq*, pp. 332–42.

37. B. Flusin, *Anastase le Perse*, vol. 2, Paris, 1992, pp. 95–127 and 170–2.

38. E. Hunter, The Church of the East in Central Asia, *Bulletin of the John Rylands Library*, 78 (1996): 129–42.

39. *Mongolian–English Dictionary*, F. D. Lessing (ed.), Bloomington, IN, 1973, p. 59.

40. S. N. C. Lieu, *Manichaeism in the Later Roman Empire and in Medieval China*, Manchester, 1985, Tübingen, 2nd edn., 1992, pp. 219–304.

41. O. Hansen, Berliner soghdische Texte 2, *Mainz: Akademie der Wissenschaften 1954*, no. 15, pp. 830–1.

42. P. Pelliot, *L'inscription nestorienne de Si-ngan-fou*, with A. Forte, Paris/Kyoto, 1996; N. Standaert (ed.), *Handbook of Christianity in China. Volume One: 635–1800*, Leiden, 2001, pp. 1–42; F. S. Drake, Nestorian monasteries of the T'ang Dynasty, *Monumenta Serica*, 2 (1936/7): 293–340; S. Moffett, *A History of Christianity in Asia*, vol. 1, San Francisco, 1992, pp. 91–360.

43. W. Kaegi, *Byzantium and the Islamic Conquests*, Cambridge, 1992, pp. 26–65; Whittow, *The Making of Byzantium*, pp. 69–82.

44. *Life of Ahudemmeh: Patrologia Orientalis* 3:1, pp. 21–6.

45. *Story of 'Adî ibn Zayd, the Poet of Hira*: transl. I. Lichtenstadter, *Introduction to Classical Arabic Literature*, New York, 1976, p. 174.

46. P. Pentz, *The Inivisible Conquest. The Ontogenesis of Sixth and Seventh Century Syria*, Copenhagen, 1992; A. Shboul and A. Walmsley, Identity and self-image in Syria–Palestine in the transition from Byzantine to early Islamic rule, *Mediterranean Archaeology*, 11 (1998): 255–87.

47. L. I. Conrad, The Arabs, in Averil Cameron, B. Ward-Perkins, and M. Whitby (eds.), *The Cambridge Ancient History 14*, Cambridge, 2000, pp. 678–700, at p. 694.

48. Yaqût cited in G. Troupeau, Les couvents chrétiens dans la littérature arabe, *La Nouvelle Revue du Caire*, 1 (1975): 265–79, at p. 267.

49. E. Key Fowden, *The Barbarian Plain. Saint Sergius between Rome and Iran*, Berkeley, CA, 1999.

50. E. Key Fowden, An Arab building at Rusâfa-Sergiopolis, *Damaszener Mitteilungen*, 12 (2000): 303–24.

51. M. J. Kister, Al-Hîra: some notes on its relations with Arabia, *Arabica*, 15 (1968): 143–69; E. C. D. Hunter, Syriac inscriptions from al-Hîra, *Oriens christianus*, 80 (1996): 66–81.

52. I. Shahid, *The Martyrs of Najrân*, Brussels, 1971.

53. M. van Esbroeck, Le manuscrit hébreu Paris 755 et l'Histoire des Martyrs du Nedjran, in Canivet and Rey-Coquais (eds.), *La Syrie de Byzance à l'Islam*, pp. 25–30, at p .28.

54. M. Lings, *Muhammad: His Life based on the Earliest Sources*, London, 1991 (Muhammad as seen by Muslims); M. Rodinson, *Mohammed*, New York, 1971; s.v. Muhammad, in Bowersock, Brown, and Grabar (eds.), *Late Antiquity*, pp. 595–8.

55. G. R. D. King, Settlement in Western and Central Arabia and the Gulf in the sixth–eighth centuries A.D., in King and Cameron (eds.), *Land Use and Settlement Patterns*, pp. 181–212.

56. P. Crone, *The Meccan Trade and the Rise of Islam*, Oxford, 1987.

57. R. Bell, *A Commentary on the Qur'ân*, 2 vols., Manchester, 1991; M. A. Draz, *Introduction to the Qur'ân*, London, 2000; s.v. Qur'ân, in Bowersock, Brown, and Grabar (eds.), *Late Antiquity*, pp. 659–60.

58. Ibn Ishaq, *Sîrat Rasûl Allâh: The Life of Muhammad* 171 and 228: transl. A.

Guillaume, Oxford/Lahore, 1955, pp. 121 and 158.

59. U. Rubin, *Hanîfiyya* and Ka'aba: an inquiry into the Arabian pre-Islamic background of Dîn Ibrâhîm, *Jerusalem Studies in Arabic and Islam*, 8 (1990): 85–113; M. J. Kister, *Studies in Jahiliyya and Early Islam*, London, 1980.

60. F. M. Donner, *Narratives of Islamic Origins: The Beginnings of Islamic Historical Traditions*, Princeton, NJ, 1999, pp. 64–97.

61. E. Landau-Tasseron, Features of the pre-conquest Muslim army in the time of Muhammad, in Cameron (ed.), *States, Resources, Armies*, pp. 299–336; M. Bonner, *Aristocratic Violence and Holy War: Studies in the Jihad and the Arab–Byzantine Frontier*, New Haven, CT, 1996.

62. Ibn Ishaq, *Life of Muhammad* 821, pp. 552–3.

63. Kaegi, *Byzantium and the Islamic Conquests*, p. 74.

64. *The Armenian History attributed to Sebeos* 42: transl. R. W. Thomson, Liverpool, 1999, p. 97.

65. *Chronicle of Séert* 106: *Patrologia Orientalis* 13, p. 626.

Chapter 13: "The Changing of the Kingdoms"

1. *Doctrina Jacobi* 3.10: transl. V. Déroche, *Travaux et Mémoires*, 11 (1991): 47–229, at p. 168.

2. *Doctrina Jacobi* 5.16, p. 208; R. Hoyland, *Seeing Islam as Others Saw It: A Survey and Evaluation of Christian, Jewish, and Zoroastrian Writings on Early Islam*, Princeton, NJ, 1997, p. 57.

3. *The Armenian History attributed to Sebeos* 42: transl. R.W. Thomson, Liverpool, 1999, p. 105; R. W. Thomson, Biblical themes in the Armenian Histories of Sebeos, in G. J. Reinink and A. C. Klugkist, *After Bardaisan. Studies in Continuity and Change in Syriac Christianity in Honour of H. J. W. Drijvers*, Louvain, 1999, pp. 295–302.

4. F. M. Donner, *The Early Islamic Conquests*, Princeton, NJ, 1981; W. Kaegi, *Byzantium and the Early Islamic Conquests*, Cambridge, 1992.

5. S. Bashear, Apocalyptic and other materials on early Muslim–Byzantine wars, *Journal of the Royal Asiatic Society*, 3 ser. 1 (1991): 173–207.

6. al-Tabarî, *History* 2312: transl. Y. Friedmann, *The History of al-Tabarî* 12, Albany, NY, 1991, pp. 103–4.

7. G. R. Hawting, *The First Dynasty of Islam: The Umayyad Caliphate A.D. 661–750*, London, 1986.

8. S. Brock, Northern Mesopotamia in the late seventh century: Book XV of John bar Penkâye's *Rish Mellê*, *Jerusalem Studies in Arabic and Islam*, 9 (1987): 51–75, at p. 60.

9. Brock, Northern Mesopotamia in the late seventh century, p. 61.

10. R. Ettinghausen, *From Byzantium to Sasanian Iran and the Islamic World*, London, 1972; O. Grabar, *The Formation of Islamic Art*, New Haven, CT, 1973, pp. 145–78 and 188–205; R. Hillenbrand, The dolce vita in Early Islamic Syria, *Art History*, 5 (1982): 1–35.

11. A. A. Duri, *The Rise of Historical Writing among the Arabs*, Princeton, NJ, 1983; F. M. Donner, *Narratives of Islamic Origins. The Beginnings of Islamic Historical Traditions*, Princeton, NJ, 1999.

12. S. Bashear, *Arabs and Others in Early Islam*, Princeton, NJ, 1997, p. 8.
13. Bashear, *Arabs and Others in Early Islam*, pp. 32 and 44–66.
14. Grabar, *The Formation of Islamic Art*, pp. 93–6.
15. M. Sharon, An Arabic inscription from the time of the Caliph 'Abd al-Malik, *Bulletin of the School of Oriental and African Studies*, 29 (1966): 367–72.
16. S. H. Griffith, Images, Islam and Christian icons. a moment in the Christian–Muslim encounter in early Islamic times, in P. Canivet and J. P. Rey-Coquais (eds.), *La Syrie de Byzance à l'Islam*, Damascus, 1992, pp. 121–38.
17. Muqaddasi cited in Grabar, *The Formation of Islamic Art*, pp. 64–5.
18. S. Bashear, Qibla Musharriqa and early Moslem prayer in Christian churches, *The Muslim World*, 81 (1991): 268–82.
19. K. A. Cresswell, *Early Muslim Architecture*, Harmondsworth, 1958, pp. 44–81; O. Grabar, *The Formation of Early Islamic Art*, pp. 104–38; B. Caseau, Sacred landscapes, in Bowersock, Brown, and Grabar (eds.), *Late Antiquity*, pp. 21–59, at pp. 47–9.
20. J. Raby and J. Johns, *Bayt al-Makdis. 'Abd al-Malik's Jerusalem*, Oxford, 1992; O. Grabar, *The Shape of the Holy. Early Islamic Jerusalem*, Princeton, NJ, 1996.
21. Cited in A. Palmer, *The Seventh Century in West Syrian Chronicles*, Liverpool, 1993, p. xxi.
22. F. Décobert, *Le Mendiant et le combattant. L'Institution de l'Islam*, Paris, 1991.
23. R. Hillenbrand, 'Anjar and Early Islamic Urbanism, in G. P. Brogiolo and B. Ward-Perkins (eds.), *The Idea and the Ideal of the Town in Late Antiquity and the Early Middle Ages*, Leiden, 1999, pp. 59–98.
24. G. Dagron, Commentary to Déroche (ed.), *Doctrina Jacobi, Travaux et Mémoires*, 11 (1991): 230–73; Hoyland, *Seeing Islam as Others Saw It*, pp. 55–61 and 76–87.
25. D. Dennett, *Conversion and the Poll Tax in Early Islam*, Cambridge, MA, 1950; M. Gervers and R. J. Bikhazi (eds.), *Conversion and Continuity. Indigenous Christian Communities in Islamic Lands*, Toronto, 1990.
26. *History of Rabban Hormizd* 23: transl. E. A. W. Budge, London, 1902, p. 150; C. F. Robinson, *Empire and Elites after the Muslim Conquest. The Transformation of Northern Mesopotamia*, Cambridge, 2000, pp. 90–108; *History of the Patriarchs of Alexandria*: transl. B. Evetts, *Patrologia Orientalis* 5, p. 156.
27. R. Hoyland, Jacob of Edessa on Islam, in Reinink and Klugkist (eds.), *After Bardaisan*, pp. 149–60.
28. N. Robinson, *Christ in Islam and Christianity. The Representation of Jesus in the Qur'ān and the Classical Muslim Commentaries*, London, 1991.
29. R. Schick, *The Christian Communities of Palestine from Byzantine to Islamic Rule. An Historical and Archaeological Study*, Princeton, NJ, 1995, pp. 315–22, at p. 321.
30. M. F. Auzépy, De la Palestine à Constantinople (VIIe–IXe siècles): Étienne le Sabaïte et Jean Damascène, *Travaux et Mémoires*, 12 (1994): 183–218, at pp. 193–204.
31. R. Haddad, La phonétique de l'arabe chrétien vers 700, in Canivet and Rey-Coquais (eds.), *De la Syrie à Byzance*, pp. 159–64.

32. A. F. L. Beeston, T. M. Johnstone, R. B. Serjeant, and G. R. Smith (eds.), *Arabic Literature to the End of the Umayyad Period*, Cambridge, 1983, pp. 396–401.

33. Averil Cameron, Disputations, polemical literature and the formation of opinion in the early Byzantine period, in G. J. Reinink and H. L. J. Vanstiphout, *Dispute Poems and Dialogues in the Ancient and Medieval Near East*, Louvain, 1991, pp. 91–108.

34. B. Flusin, Démons et sarrasins, *Travaux et Mémoires*, 11 (1991): 381–409.

35. Dionysius of Tell-Mahre, *Chronicle*: transl., Palmer, *The Seventh Century in West Syrian Chronicles*, p. 141.

36. *History of the Patriarchs of Alexandria*, pp. 122–5.

37. S. Brock, From antagonism to assimilation: Syriac attitudes to Greek learning, in N. Garsoian, T. F. Mathews, and R. W. Thomson (eds.), *East of Byzantium: Syria and Armenia in the Formative Period*, Washington, DC, 1982, pp. 17–34; L. I. Conrad, Varietas Syriaca: secular and scientific culture in the christian communities after the Arab conquest, in Reinink and Klugkist (eds.), *After Bardaisan*, pp. 85–105.

38. A. Kazhdan, *A History of Byzantine Literature (650–850)*, Athens, 1999, p. 1.

39. Anthony of Tagrit, *The Fifth Book of Rhetoric*, Corpus Scriptorum Christianorum Orientalium 480/1, Louvain, 1986, cited in J. W. Watt, Grammar, rhetoric and the Enkyklios Paideia in Syria, *Zeitschrift der deutschen morgenländischen Gesellschaft*, 143 (1993): 45–71; see also J. W. Watt, Eastward and westward transmission of classical rhetoric, in J. W. Drijvers and A. A. MacDonald (eds.), *Centres of Learning. Learning and Location in Pre-Modern Europe and the Near East*, Leiden, 1995, pp. 63–75.

40. *The Chronicle of Zuqnîn: Parts III and IV, A.D. 485–775*: transl. A. Harrak, Toronto, 1999, p. 168.

41. Conrad, Varietas Syriaca, in Reinink and Klugkist (eds.), *After Bardaisan*, p. 88.

42. Bar Hebraeus, *Chronography* [413]: transl. E. A. W. Budge, Oxford, 1932, p. 356.

43. *Pahlavi Ballad of the End of Times*, cited in Hoyland, *Islam as Others Saw It*, pp. 531–2.

44. John bar Penkâye, *Rish Mellê*, cited in Brock, Northern Mesopotamia in the late seventh century, p. 58.

45. Thomas of Marga, *Book of Governors* 5.11: transl. E. A. W. Budge, London, 1893, p. 508.

46. Timothy, *Letter* 13: Corpus Scriptorum Christianorum Orientalium 75: Scriptores Syri 31, Rome, 1915, p. 70.

47. *Chronicle of Zuqnîn*, pp. 260 and 323–6.

48. S. Goitein, A plea for the periodization of Islamic history, *Journal of the American Oriental Society*, 88 (1968): 224–8, at p. 227.

49. Alvarus, *Indiculus luminosus* 35: J. Gil (ed.), *Corpus Scriptorum Muzarabicorum* 1, Madrid, 1973, pp. 314–15.

50. S. H. Griffith, Theodore abu Qurrah's Arabic text on the Christian practice of venerating images, *Journal of the American Oriental Society*, 105 (1985): 53–73.

51. Al-Jâhiz, *Refutation of the Christians* 136: transl. C.. Pellat, London, 1969, p. 88.

52. D. Gutas, *Greek Thought, Arabic Culture. The Greco-Arabic Translation Movement in Baghdad and Early Abbasid Society*, London, 1998; F. Rosenthal, *The Classical Heritage in Islam*, Berkeley, CA, 1975.

53. S. H. Griffith, Habib ibn Hidmah al Ra'itah, a Christian mutakallim, *Oriens Christianus*, 64 (1980): 161–201 at p. 171.

54. A. Miquel, *La géographie humaine du monde musulman*, vol. 2, Paris, 1975, pp. 381–481.

55. Theophanes, *Chronographia* A.D. 629/30: transl. C. Mango, Oxford, 1997, pp. 464–5; Hoyland, *Seeing Islam as Others Saw It*, pp. 427–34.

56. J. F. Haldon and M. Byrne, A possible solution to the problem of Greek fire, *Byzantinische Zeitschrift*, 70 (1977): 91–9.

57. Theophanes, *Chronographia* A.D.716/17, p. 546.

58. Miquel, *La géographie humaine du monde musulman*, vol 2, pp. 343–80.

59. Adomnán, *de locis sanctis* 2.12: transl. D. Mcchan, Dublin, 1983, p. 83.

60. Adomnán, *de locis sanctis* 1.23.11, p. 67.

61. Adomnán, *de locis sanctis* 3.3, p. 111.

62. Boniface, *Letter* 19 (27): transl. E. Emerton, New York, 1976 and 2000, p. 56.

63. *Hodoeporicon of Willibald* 4: transl. C. H. Talbot, *Anglo-Saxon Missionaries in Germany*, London, 1954, p. 162, and T. F. X. Noble and T. Head, *Soliders of Christ*, Philadelphia, 1995, p. 153.

64. *Hodoeporicon of Willibald* 4, Talbot, p. 170, Noble and Head, p. 159.

Chapter 14: Christianities of the North: Ireland

1. J. Werner, Das Grabfund von Malaja Pereščepina und Kuvrat, Kagan der Bulgaren, *Bayerische Akademie der Wissenschaften: Abhandlungen*, NF 91, Munich, 1984.

2. M. Carver, *The Age of Sutton Hoo. The Seventh Century in Northwestern Europe*, Woodbridge, Suffolk, 1982.

3. L. Hedeager, *Asgard* reconstructed? Gudme – a central place in the North, in M. de Jong and F. Theuws with C. Van Rijn (eds.), *Topographies of Power in the Early Middle Ages*, Leiden, 2000, pp. 467–507.

4. K. Hauck, *Die Goldbrakteaten der Völkerwanderungzeit*, Munich,1985.

5. Audoenus, *Life of Eligius* 2.3: B. Krusch (ed.), *Monumenta Germaniae Historica: Scriptores rerum merowingicarum* 4, Hanover, 1902, p. 696.

6. T. M. Charles-Edwards, *Early Christian Ireland*, Cambridge, 2000, pp. 145–58

7. Charles-Edwards, *Early Christian Ireland*, pp. 68–70.

8. *Córus Béscnai*, cited in F. Kelly, *Early Irish Law*, Dublin, 1998, p. 96.

9. This happened in the case of the Visigoths: R. Fletcher, *The Conversion of Europe. From Paganism to Christianity 371–1386 A.D.*, London, 1997, pp. 68–77.

10. D. O'Sullivan, The plan of the early Christian monastery at Lindisfarne, in G. Bonner, D. Rollason, and C. Stancliffe, *St. Cuthbert, his Cult and his Community to A.D.1200*, Woodbridge, Suffolk, 1989, pp. 125–42; Charles-Edwards, *Early Christian Ireland*, pp. 282–308.

11. T. M. Charles-Edwards, The social background of Irish *peregrinatio, Celtica*,

11 (1976): 43–59.

12. Cited in R. Sharpe, Introduction, Adomnán, *Life of Columba*, Harmondsworth, 1995, p. 90.
13. Adomnán, *Life of Columba* 1.8: transl. R. Sharpe, p. 150.
14. Adomnán, *Life of Columba* 2.29, p. 178.
15. Adomnán, *Life of Columba* 1.12, p. 121.
16. Charles-Edwards, *Early Christian Ireland*, pp. 308–26.
17. Adomnán, *Life of Columba* 1.1, p. 110.
18. Adomnán. *Life of Columba* 1.1, p. 111.
19. Sharpe, Introduction, Adomnán, *Life of Columba*, pp. 43–65.
20. *The Law of Innocents*: transl. J. N. Hillgarth, *Christianity and Paganism 350–750. The Conversion of Western Europe*, Philadelphia, 1986, pp. 125–31.
21. N. Delierneux, Arculfe, *sanctus episcopus gente Gallus*: une existence historique discutable, *Revue belge de philologie et d'histoire*, 75 (1995): 911–41.
22. R. Sharpe, Church and communities in early Ireland: towards a pastoral model, in J. Blair and R. Sharpe (eds.), *Pastoral Care before the Parish*, Leicester, 1992, pp. 81–109.
23. K. Hughes, *The Church in Early Irish Society*, London, 1966, pp. 79–90 and 111–20; Charles-Edwards, *Early Christian Ireland*, pp. 416–40.
24. C. Doherty, The monastic town in early medieval Ireland, in H. B. Clarke and A. Simms (eds.), *Comparative History of Urban Origins in Non-Roman Europe*, Oxford, 1985, pp. 45–75; M. Valante, Reassessing the Irish monastic towns, *Irish Historical Studies*, 31 (1999): 1–18.
25. *The Martyrology of Oengus*, Prologue 105–9: transl. W. Stokes, London, 1905, pp. 125–31.
26. *Poem of Aed dub mac Colmáin*, cited in Charles-Edwards, *Early Christian Ireland*, p. 95.
27. Cogitosus, *Life of Brigit* 32: transl. S. Conolly and J. M. Picard, *Journal of the Royal Society of Antiquaries of Ireland*, 117 (1982): 25–6, also in O. Davies, *Celtic Spirituality*, New York, 1999, pp. 137–8.
28. Muirchú, *Life of Patrick* 13: transl. A. B. E. Hood, London, 1978, p. 88.
29. Muirchú, *Life of Patrick* 29, p. 98.
30. F. Kelly, *Early Irish Farming*, Dublin, 1998.
31. Charles-Edwards, *Early Christian Ireland*, p. 526; *Seventh Council of Toledo* (646), canon 4: J. Vives (ed.), *Concilios Visigóticos*, Madrid, 1963, p. 255.
32. C. Etchingham, *Church Organization in Ireland AD 650–1000*, Maynooth, 1999, pp. 244–52.
33. Charles-Edwards, *Early Christian Ireland*, p. 24.
34. L. M. Bitel, *Isle of Saints. Monastic Settlement and Christian Community in Early Ireland*, Ithaca, NY, 1990, pp. 124–8; Charles-Edwards, *Early Christian Ireland*, pp. 118–19.
35. Etchingham, *Church Organization in Ireland*, pp. 291–318.
36. Stokes, *The Martyrology of Oengus*, pp. 65 and 183.
37. Etchingham, *Church Organization in Ireland*, p. 76.
38. Adomnán, *Life of Columba* 2.41, p. 195.
39. A. MacDonald, Aspects of the monastery and of monastic life in Adomnán's

Life of Columba, *Peritia*, 3 (1984): 271–302, cited at pp. 295–6.

40. K. McCone, Werewolves, Cyclopes, *Diberga* and *Fiánna*: juvenile delinquency in early Ireland, *Cambridge Medieval Celtic Studies*, 12 (1986): 1–22.

41. R. Sharpe, Hiberno-Latin *laicus*, Irish *láech* and the Devil's Men, *Ériu*, 30 (1973): 75–92.

42. J. N. Radner, *Fragmentary Annals of Ireland*, Dublin, 1978, pp. 60–3

43. *Life of Enda* 2 and *Life of Colman* 8, C. Plummer (ed.), *Vitae Sanctorum Hiberniae*, vol. 1, Oxford, 1910, pp. 60 and 261.

44. D. Binchy, The pseudo-historical prologue to the *Senchas Már*, *Studia Celtica*, 10–11 (1975–6): 15–28.

45. J. Stevenson, The beginnings of literacy in Ireland, *Proceedings of the Royal Irish Academy*, 100 (1982): 127–65.

46. Tirechán, *Collectanea* 2.3.1–2: transl. L. Bieler, *The Patrician Texts in the Book of Armagh*, Dublin, 1979, p. 123.

47. Tirechán, *Collectanea* 2.3.5, p. 123.

48. *Tripartite Life of Saint Patrick*: transl. W. Stokes, Rolls Series 89, London, 1887, p. 453.

49. C. Donahue, Beowulf, Ireland and the natural good, *Traditio*, 7 (1949–51): 263–77.

50. *Córus Béscnai* cited in Donahue, Beowulf, Ireland and the natural good, p. 268.

51. D. O'Cróinín, *Early Medieval Ireland 400–1000*, London, 1995, pp. 183–95.

52. A. Ahlqvist, *The Early Irish Linguist*, Helsinki, 1982, pp. 97–8.

53. W. Stokes and J. Strachan, *Thesaurus Palaeohibenicus: A Collection of Old Irish Glosses*, vol. 2, Cambridge, 1903, p. 224, cited in O'Cróinín, *Early Medieval Ireland*, p. 204.

54. K. McCone, *Pagan Past and Christian Present in Early Irish Literature*, Maynooth, 1990, pp. 1–28 and 54–83 is a challenging if extreme statement of this view; see also D. O'Cróinín, Creating the past. The early Irish genealogical tradition, *Peritia*, 12 (1998): 177–208.

55. J. Stevenson, Literacy and orality in early medieval Ireland, in D. Edel (ed.), *Cultural Identity and Cultural Integration: Ireland and Europe in the Early Middle Ages*, Dublin, 1995, pp. 11–23 at pp. 12–16.

56. Kelly, *Early Irish Law*, pp. 225–41.

57. *Bretha Crólige* 57, D. Binchy (ed.), *Ériu*, 12 (1934): 1–77 at p. 44.

Chapter 15: Christianities of the North: the Saxons of Britain

1. Bede, *Ecclesiastical History of the English People* 1.23: transl. B. Colgrave and R. A. B. Mynors, Oxford, 1969, p. 69. Other transl.s are L. Sherley-Price, Harmondsworth, 1955 and R. Collins and J. Mc Clure, Oxford, 1994.

2. I. N. Wood, Pagans and holy men 600–800, in P. Ní Chatháin and M. Richter (eds.), *Irland und die Christenheit*, Stuttgart, 1987, pp. 347–61.

3. Nennius, *British History* 64: transl. J. Morris, London, 1980, p. 28.

4. W. Davies, *Wales in the Early Middle Ages*, Leicester, 1982, pp. 90–102 and 141–93.

5. Adomnán, *Life of Columba* 1.1: transl. R. Sharpe, Harmondsworth, 1995, p. 111.

6   C. Stancliffe, The British Church and the mission of Augustine, in R. Gameson
    (ed.), *St Augustine and the Conversion of England*, Stroud, Gloucestershire,
    1999, pp. 107–51.
7.   Illustrated in L. Webster and M. Brown, *The Transformation of the Roman
    World*, London, 1997, fig. 48 and pp. 117 and 237; S. Bassett (ed.), *The Ori-
    gins of the Anglo-Saxon Kingdoms*, Leicester, 1989.
8.   Dado/Audoenus, *Life of Eligius* 1.10, T. Head (ed.), *Medieval Hagiography*,
    New York, 2000, p. 144; S. Lebecq, England and the Continent in the sixth and
    seventh centuries: the question of logistics, in Gameson (ed.,) *St Augustine and
    the Conversion of England*, pp. 50–67.
9.   C. Behr, The origins of kingship in early medieval Kent, *Early Medieval Eu-
    rope*, 9 (2000): 25–52; C. Stancliffe, Kings and conversion: some comparisons
    between the Roman mission to England and Patrick's to Ireland,
    Frühmittelalterliche Studien, 14 (1980): 59–94.
10.   P. Sims-Williams, *Religion and Literature in Western England, 600–800*, Cam-
    bridge, 1990, pp. 16–86.
11.   H. Mayr-Harting, *The Coming of Christianity to Anglo-Saxon England*, 2nd
    edn., University Park, PA, 1991, pp. 51–77; I. N. Wood, The mission of Augus-
    tine of Canterbury to the English, *Speculum*, 69 (1994): 1–17; N. J. Higham,
    *The Convert Kings: Power and Religious Affiliation in Early Anglo-Saxon Eng-
    land*, Manchester, 1997, pp. 53–131.
12.   Bede, *Ecclesiastical History* 1.32, p. 113.
13.   Bede, *Ecclesiastical History* 1.25, p. 75.
14.   Bede, *Ecclesiastical History* 1.29, pp. 105–7; Higham, *The Convert Kings*, pp.
    93–6.
15.   Bede, *Ecclesiastical History* 1.32, p. 113.
16.   R. A. Markus, Gregory the Great and a missionary strategy, in J. Cuming (ed.),
    The Mission of the Church and the Propagation of the Faith, Studies in Church
    History 6, Cambridge, 1970, pp. 29–38; I. N. Wood, Some historical
    reinterpretations and the Christianization of Kent, in G. Armstrong and I. N.
    Wood (eds.), *Christianizing Peoples and Converting Individuals*, Turnhout,
    2000, pp. 27–35.
17.   Bede, *Ecclesiastical History* 1.30, p. 109.
18.   Bede, *The Reckoning of Time* 15: transl. F. Wallis, Liverpool, 1999, pp. 54 and
    285–7.
19.   *Laws of Ethelbert*: transl. D. Whitelock, *English Historical Documents* 1, Ox-
    ford, 1955, pp. 357–61; S. Kelly, Anglo-Saxon lay society and the written word,
    in R. McKitterick (ed.), *The Uses of Literacy in Early Medieval Europe*, Cam-
    bridge, 1990, pp. 36–62; P. Wormald, *The Making of English Law 1: Legisla-
    tion and its Limits*, Oxford, 1999, pp. 29–108.
20.   Bede, *Ecclesiastical History* 2.5, p. 153.
21.   Bede, *Ecclesiastical History* 2.15, p. 191.
22.   M. Carver, Conversion and politics on the eastern seaboard of Britain: some
    archaeological indications, in B. E. Crawford (ed.), *Conversion and Christiani-
    zation in the North Sea*, St. Andrews, 1998, pp. 11–40.
23.   Bede, *Ecclesiastical History* 2.13, pp. 183–5.

24. Bede, *Ecclesiastical History* 2.13, p. 185.
25. Higham, *The Convert Kings*, pp. 146–8.
26. Bede, *Ecclesiastical History* 2.16, p. 193.
27. T. M. Charles-Edwards, *Early Christian Ireland*, Cambridge, 2000, pp. 308–26; A. T. Thacker, Bede and the Irish, in L. A. J. R. Houwen and A. MacDonald (eds.), *Beda Venerabilis. Historian, Monk and Northumbrian*, Groningen, 1996, pp. 31–59.
28. J. Campbell, Elements in the background to the Life of St. Cuthbert and his early cult, G. Bonner, D. Rollason, and C. Stancliffe (eds.), *St. Cuthbert, his Cult and his Community to* A.D.*1200*, Woodbridge, Suffolk, 1989, pp. 3–19.
29. I. N. Wood, *The Most Holy Abbot Ceolfrid*, Jarrow Lecture, 1995.
30. G. Bonner, *Famulus Christi*, London, 1976.
31. Bede, *Ecclesiastical History* 5.23, p. 561.
32. P. Wormald, Bede, *Bretwaldas* and the origin of the *Gens Anglorum*, in P. Wormald (ed.), *Ideal and Reality in Frankish and Anglo-Saxon Society*, Oxford, 1983, pp. 99–129.
33. J. McClure, Bede's Old Testament Kings, in Wormald (ed.), *Ideal and Reality in Frankish and Anglo-Saxon Society*, pp. 76–98.
34. Bede, *Ecclesiastical History* 3.2, pp. 217–19.
35. Bede, *Ecclesiastical History* 3.14, p. 259.
36. Bede, *Ecclesiastical History* 3.6, p. 231.
37. Bede, *Ecclesiastical History* 3.12, p. 252.

Chapter 16: Micro-Christendoms

1. Bede, *Life of Cuthbert* 8: transl. J. F. Webb, *Lives of the Saints*, Harmondsworth, 1965, p. 83.
2. Cuthbert, *Letter on the Death of Bede*: transl. B. Colgrave and R. A. B. Mynors, *Bede: Ecclesiastical History of the English People*, Oxford, 1969, p. 585.
3. Cuthbert, *Death of Bede*, p. 583.
4. Bede, *Ecclesiastical History* 5.25, p. 567.
5. P. Wormald, Bede and Benedict Biscop, in G. Bonner (ed.), *Famulus Christi*, London, 1976, pp. 141–69.
6. Bede, *Lives of the Abbots of Wearmouth and Jarrow*: transl. D. Farmer, *The Age of Bede*, Harmondsworth, 1983, p. 183.
7. Well illustrated in P. Wormald, The Age of Bede and Aethelbald, in J. Campbell (ed.), *The Anglo-Saxons*, Harmondsworth, 1991, pp. 70–100 at pp. 74–5; H. Mayr-Harting, *The Coming of Christianity to Anglo-Saxon England*, 2nd edn., University Park, PA, 1991, pp. 148–219; P. Meyvaert, Bede and the church paintings at Wearmouth-Jarrow, *Anglo-Saxon England* 8 (1979): 63–77.
8. I. N. Wood, *The Most Holy Abbot Ceolfrid*, Jarrow Lecture, 1995.
9. D. Dumville, The importation of Mediterranean manuscripts into Theodore's England, in M. Lapidge (ed.), *Archbishop Theodore. Commemorative Studies on his Life and Influence*, Cambridge, 1994, pp. 96–119.
10. T. O'Neill, Book-making in early Christian Ireland, *Archaeology in Ireland*, 2 (1988): 96–100.
11. P. Meyvaert, Bede, Cassiodorus and the *Codex Amiatinus*, *Speculum*, 71 (1996):

827–83.

12. Meyvaert, Bede, Cassiodorus and the *Codex Amiatinus*, pp. 828–30.
13. Mayr-Harting, *The Coming of Christianity*, pp. 129–47.
14. Bede, *Ecclesiastical History* 4.2, p. 335; Eddius Stephanus, *Life of Wilfrid* 47: transl. Webb, *Lives of the Saints*, p. 181.
15. Eddius Stephanus, *Life of Wilfrid* 5, pp. 137–8.
16. Eddius Stephanus, *Life of Wilfrid* 6, p. 138; compare Bede, *Ecclesiastical History* 5.21, pp. 547–51 (a discussion on the topic with Adomnán of Iona).
17. Mayr-Harting, *The Coming of Christianity*, pp. 103–13; N. Higham, *The Convert Kings*, Manchester, 1997, pp. 250–67.
18. E. James, Bede and the tonsure question, *Peritia*, 3 (1984): 85–98.
19. Bede, *Opera de Temporibus*, C. W. Jones (ed.), Cambridge, MA, 1943; T. M. Charles-Edwards, *Early Christian Ireland*, Cambridge, 2000, pp. 381–415.
20. Eddius Stephanus, *Life of Wilfrid* 10, p.142; Bede, *Ecclesiastical History* 3.25, p. 307.
21. Bede, *Ecclesiastical History* 3.25, p. 301.
22. Cummian, *On the Paschal Controversy* 107–10: transl. M. Walsh and D. O'Cróinín, Toronto, 1988, p. 72.
23. Eddius Stephanus, *Life of Wilfrid* 24, p. 156.
24. Mayr-Harting, *The Coming of Christianity*, pp. 130–9; Charles-Edwards, *Early Christian Ireland*, pp. 416–40.
25. Eddius Stephanus, *Life of Wilfrid* 21, 26–8, and 41, pp. 154, 158–60, and 174.
26. Eddius Stephanus, *Life of Wilfrid* 17, pp. 149–50.
27. Eddius Stephanus, *Life of Wilfrid* 22, pp. 154–5.
29. Illustrated in Wormald, The age of Bede, in Campbell (ed.), *The Anglo-Saxons*, fig. 82, p. 84.
30. Bede, *Ecclesiastical History* 3.5, pp. 227–9; W. Goffart, *The Narrators of Barbarian History*, Princeton, NJ, 1988, ch. 4: "Bede and the ghost of Bishop Wilfrid," pp. 235–328.
31. Barhadbshaba, *The Foundation of the Schools*, Patrologia Orientalis 4, p .64.
32. J. Mahé, Quadrivium et cursus d'études au VIIe siècle en Arménie, *Travaux et Mémoires*, 10 (1987): 159–206 at pp. 159 and 166–70.
33. J. Fontaine, *Isidore de Séville et la culture classique dans l'Espagne wisigothique*, 2nd edn., Paris, 1983.
34. Braulio of Saragossa, *Renotatio*, Patrologia Latina 81:61D
35. R. Collins, *Early Medieval Spain: Unity in Diversity*, London, 1983, pp. 59–145; J. Herrin, *The Formation of Christendom*, Princeton, NJ, 1987, pp. 220–47; G. Ripoll and Isabel Velázquez, *La Hispania visigoda*, Madrid, 1997; P. Diaz and M. R. Valverde, The theoretical strength and practical weakness of the Visigothic monarchy of Toledo, in F. Theuws and J. L. Nelson (eds.), *Rituals of Power. From Late Antiquity to the Early Middle Ages*, Leiden, 2000, pp. 59–94.
36. *Laws of Receswinth* 12.2.3: J. Zeumer (ed.), *Leges Visigothorum Antiquiorum*, Leipzig, 1894, p. 301; H. Sivan, The invisible Jews of Visigothic Spain, *Revue des études juives*, 159 (2001): 369–85.
37. *Laws of Receswinth* 8.4.16, p. 248.

38. I. Velázquez and G. Ripoll, Toletum, la construcción de una *sedes regia*, in G. Ripoll and J. M. Gurt (eds.), *Sedes Regiae (ann. 400–800)*, Barcelona, 2000, pp. 521–78.

39. *Tenth Council of Toledo* (655), J. Vives (ed.), *Los Concilios visigóticos*, Madrid, 1963, p. 309.

40. *Fourth Council of Toledo* (633), canon 3, p. 188.

41. *Fourth Council of Toledo*, canon 41, p. 207.

42. *Fourth Council of Toledo*, canon 75, p. 218.

43. *Chronicle of 754*: transl. K. Wolf, *Conquerors and Chroniclers in Early Medieval Spain*, Liverpool, 1990, p. 130.

44. Bede, *On Genesis* 4, C. W. Jones (ed.), *Corpus Christianorum* 118A, Turnhout, 1967, p. 201.

45. *The Táin*: transl. T. Kinsella, Oxford, 1970, p. 2.

46. M. Lapidge, The career of archbishop Theodore, in Lapidge (ed.), *Archbishop Theodore*, pp. 1–29.

47. Herrin, *The Formation of Christendom*, pp. 210–11.

48. Herrin, *The Formation of Christendom*, pp. 206–19 and 250–84; H. Chadwick, Theodore, the English Church and the Monothelite controversy, in Lapidge (ed.), *Archbishop Theodore*, pp. 88–95.

49. *Third Council of Constantinople*, cited in Lapidge, The career of archbishop Theodore, p. 23.

50. Bede, *Ecclesiastical History* 3.25, p. 295.

51. Bede, *Ecclesiastical History* 4.3, p. 337.

52. B. Bischoff and M. Lapidge, *Biblical Commentaries from the Canterbury School of Theodore and Hadrian*, Cambridge, 1994, pp. 133–89.

53. T. M. Charles-Edwards, The Penitentials of Theodore and the *Iudicia Theodori*, in Lapidge (ed.), *Archbishop Theodore*, pp. 141–74.

54. Bischoff and Lapidge, *Biblical Commentaries*.

55. Bischoff and Lapidge, *Biblical Commentaries*, pp. 243–66.

56. *Commentary on the Pentateuch* I 413, in Bischoff and Lapidge, *Biblical Commentaries*, pp. 374–5.

57. G. Henderson, *Vision and Image in Early Christian England*, Oxford, 1999.

58. Aethelwulf, *de abbatibus* 8.210–15: transl. A. Campbell, Oxford, 1967, p. 18.

59. G. Henderson, *From Durrow to Kells: The Insular Gospel Books*, New York, 1987, pp. 131–98; D. O'Corráin, The historical and cultural background to the Book of Kells, in F. O'Mahoney (ed.), *The Book of Kells*, Aldershot, 1994, pp. 1–32; M. Werner, Works on the Book of Kells, *Peritia*, 11 (1997): 250–326.

60. Gerald of Wales, *Topography of Ireland* 2.71: transl. J. O'Meara, Harmondsworth, 1982, p. 84.

61. Bede, *Letter to Egbert*: transl. J. McClure and R. Collins, Oxford, 1994, p. 352.

62. A. Thacker, Monks, preaching and pastoral care in early Anglo-Saxon England, and J. Blair, Anglo-Saxon minsters: a topographical review, in J. Blair and R. Sharpe (eds.), *Pastoral Care before the Parish*, Leicester, 1992, pp. 136–70 and 226–66, and the ensuing debate in *Early Medieval Europe*, 4 (1995): 87–104 and 193–212.

63. P. Wormald, Bede, "Beowulf," and the conversion of the Anglo-Saxon aristocracy, in R. T. Farrell (ed.), *Bede and Anglo-Saxon England*, Oxford, 1978, pp.

32–95, at pp. 49–58.

64. Boniface, *Letter* 2 [10]: transl. E. Emerton, *Letters of Boniface*, New York, 1976 and 2000, p. 27.
65. Bede, *Ecclesiastical History* 4.11, p. 364.
66. Cuthbert, *Letter on the Death of Bede*, p. 583.
67. Bede, *Ecclesiastical History* 5.12, pp. 489–99.
68. Bede, *Ecclesiastical History* 4.24, pp. 415–19.
69. Mayr-Harting, *The Coming of Christianity*, pp. 149–52.
70. Bede, *Ecclesiastical History* 4.23, pp. 409–11.
71. Bede, *Ecclesiastical History* 4.24, p. 417.
72. *The Dream of the Rood*: transl. S. A. J. Bradley, *Anglo-Saxon Poetry*, London, 1982, pp. 160–3.
73. B. Cassiday (ed.), *The Ruthwell Cross*, Princeton, NJ, 1992; É. O'Carragáin, The necessary distance: *Imitatio Romae* and the Ruthwell Cross, in J. Hawks and S. Mills (eds.), *The Golden Age of Northumbria*, Stroud, Gloucestershire, 1999, pp. 191–203.
74. R. I. Page, The Bewcastle Cross, *Nottingham Medieval Studies*, 4 (1960): 36–57.
75. Adomnán, *de locis sanctis* 3.3.7–8, D. Meehan (ed.), Dublin, 1983, p. 111.
76. É. O'Carragáin, The Ruthwell Crucifixion in its iconographic and liturgical context, *Peritia*, 6–7 (1987–8): 1–71.
77. M. and N. Thierry, La cathédrale de Mrèn et sa décoration, *Cahiers archéologiques*, 21 (1971): 43–77.

Chapter 17: The Crisis of the Image

1. *The Regions of the World* 42: transl. V. Minorsky, Oxford, 1937, p. 157.
2. J. F. Haldon, *Byzantium in the Seventh Century. The Transformation of a Culture*, Cambridge, 1990; M. Whittow, *The Making of Byzantium, 600–1025*, London and Berkeley, CA, 1993, pp. 96–193; A. P. Kazhdan, *A History of Byzantine Literature (650–850)*, Athens, 1999, pp. 137–65; see also L. Brubaker and J. Haldon, *Byzantium in the Iconoclast Era (ca. 680–850): The Sources, an Analytic Survey*, Aldershot, 2001.
3. Averil Cameron and J. Herrin, *Constantinople in the Early Eighth Century*, Leiden, 1984.
4. Averil Cameron, The language of images: the rise of icons and Christian representation, in D. Wood, (ed.), *The Church and the Arts*. Studies in Church History 28, Oxford, 1992, pp. 1–42.
5. T. F. Mathews, *The Clash of Gods: A Reinterpretation of Early Christian Art*, Princeton, NJ, 1999, 2nd edn., pp. 177–90; L. Robert, Le serpent Glycon d'Abônoutheichos à Athènes et Artémis d'Ephèse à Rome, *Opera Minora Selecta*, 5, Amsterdam, 1989, pp. 747–69.
6. *Life of Symeon the Younger* 118: transl. C. Mango, *The Art of the Byzantine Empire*, Englewood Cliffs, NJ, 1972, p. 134.
7. H. Belting, *Bild und Kunst. Eine Geschichte des Bildes vor der Zeitalter der Kunst*, Munich, 1990: transl. *Likeness and Presence. A History of the Image before the Era of Art*, Chicago, 1994, p. 38 with fig. 38 and pp. 115–43; Averil

Cameron, Images of authority: elites and icons in late sixth-century Byzantium, *Past and Present*, 84 (1979): 3–35.

8. V. Déroche, Léontios de Néapolis, *Apologie contre les Juifs, Travaux et Mémoires*, 12 (1994): 43–104.

9. O. Grabar, *Mediation of Ornament*, Princeton, NJ, 1992; R. Schick, *The Christian Communities of Palestine from Byzantine to Islamic Rule*, Princeton, NJ, 1995, pp. 180–224.

10. *Horos* (Definition) of the Council at Hiereia (754), cited in *Second Council of Nicaea*, G. D. Mansi, *Sacrorum conciliorum nova collectio* 13: 345A: transl. D. J. Sahas, *Icon and Logos*, Toronto, 1988, p. 161.

11. *The Chronicle of Theophanes the Confessor*, A.M. 6218: transl. C. Mango, Oxford, 1997, p. 560 and in *Art of the Byzantine Empire*, p. 152.

12. J. Moorhead, Iconoclasm, the Cross and the imperial image, *Byzantion*, 55 (1985): 165–79.

13. G. Dagron, *Empereur et Prêtre. Etudes sur le "césaropapisme" byzantin*, Paris, 1996, pp. 169–200.

14. The *Horos* (Definition) of the Council of Hiereia is partially translated in Mango, *Art of the Byzantine Empire*, pp. 165–8; *Vie d'Etienne le Jeune par Etienne le diacre*: transl. M. F. Auzépy, Aldershot, Hampshire, 1997, pp. 21–42.

15. A. Grabar, *L'iconoclasme byzantin. Le dossier archéologique*, Paris, 1984, pp. 175–6.

16. F. Boespflug and N. Lossky, *Nicée II*, Paris, 1987; J. Herrin, *Women in Purple*, London, 2001, pp. 51–129.

17. Whittow, *The Making of Byzantium*, pp. 262–98.

18. *Life of Leo V, Patrologia Graeca* 108:1028 and 1032: transl. Mango, *Art of the Byzantine Empire*, p. 157.

19. Mango, *Art of the Byzantine Empire*, pp. 157–65 and 168–9; W. Treadgold, *The Byzantine Revival, 780–842*, Stanford, CA, 1988; D. E. Afinogenov, *Konstantinopol'ski Patriarkhat i ikonoborcheskii krizis v Vizantij*, Moscow, 1997.

20. P. Lemerle, *Le premier humanisme byzantin*, Paris, 1971: transl. *Byzantine Humanism, the First Phase*, Canberra, 1986.

21. Mango, *Art of the Byzantine Empire*, pp. 169–77; *Byzantine Defenders of Images. Eight Saints' Lives*: transl. A. M. Talbot, Washington, DC, 1998; *St. Theodore the Studite on the Holy Icons*: transl. C. P. Roth, Crestwood, NY, 1981; *Nicéphorus. Discours contre les iconoclastes*: transl. M. J. Mondzain-Baudinet, Paris, 1989; K. Parry, *Depicting the Word. Byzantine Iconophile Thought in the Eighth and Ninth Centuries*, Leiden, 1996; L. Brubaker, *Vision and Meaning in Ninth-Century Byzantium*, Cambridge, 1999, pp. 19–58; Kazhdan, *History of Byzantine Literature (650–850)*, pp. 169–259 and 381–407.

22. John of Damascus, *On Divine Images*: transl. D. Anderson, Crestwood, NY, 1980; M. F. Auzépy, De la Palestine à Constantinople (VIIIe–IXe siècle): Etienne le Sabaïte et Jean Damascène, *Travaux et Mémoires*, 12 (1994): 183–218; A. Louth, Palestine under the Arabs 650–750: the crucible of Byzantine orthodoxy, in S. N. Swanson (ed.), *The Holy Land, Holy Lands and Christian His-*

tory, Studies in Church History 36, Woodbridge, Suffolk, 2000, pp. 67–77.

23. John of Damascus, *On Divine Images* 3.17, Anderson, p. 74.
24. John of Damascus, *On Divine Images* [1.32], Testimonies, Anderson, p. 34, citing Pseudo-Dionysius, *The Ecclesiastical Hierarchy* 1.2: transl. C. Luibheid, London, 1987, p. 197.
25. *Second Council of Nicaea*, ed. Mansi, 240C and 252C: transl., Sahas, pp. 75 and 84.
26. Photius, *Homily* 17.6: transl. C. Mango, Washington, DC, 1958, p. 295, and *Art of the Byzantine Empire*, p. 190.
27. John of Damascus, *On Images* [1.47], Testimonies, Anderson, p. 39.
28. H. Maguire, *Earth and Ocean. The Terrestrial World in Early Byzantine Art*, University Park, PA, 1987; B. Caseau, Christian bodies: the senses and early Byzantine Christianity, in Liz James (ed.), *Desire and Denial in Byzantium*, Aldershot, 1999, pp. 101–9.
29. H. Maguire, *The Icons of their Bodies. Saints and their Images in Byzantium*, Princeton, NJ, 1996, pp. 137–45.
30. Belting, *Likeness and Presence*, pp. 164–83; L. Brubaker, Icons before iconoclasm?, *in Morfologie sociali e culturali in Europa tra Tarda Antichità e Alto Medio Evo*, Settimane di Studio sull'Alto Medio Evo 45, Spoleto, 1998, pp. 1215–54.
31. Maguire, *The Icons of their Bodies*, pp. 100–45.
32. Steven of Novgorod: transl. G. P. Majeska, *Russian Travellers to Constantinople in the Fourteenth and Fifteenth Centuries*, Washington, DC, 1984, p. 36; R. Cormack, *Painting the Soul*, London, 1997, pp. 59–61; A. Lidov (ed.), *Chudotvornaia Ikona v Vizantii i drevneï Rusi*, Moscow, 1996.
33. Zosima the Deacon, Majeska, *Russian Travellers*, p. 182.
34. D. Obolensky, *The Byzantine Commonwealth*, London, 1971; I. Ševčeko, *Byzantium and the Slavs*, Cambridge, MA, 1991; S. Franklin and J. Shepard, *The Emergence of Rus 750–1200*, London, 1996.
35. Epifanij the Wise, cited in Cormack, *Painting the Soul*, p. 188.
36. J. Herrin, *The Formation of Christendom*, Princeton, NJ, 1987, pp. 344–444.
37. *Libri Carolini*, A. Freeman and P. Meyvaert (eds.), *Monumenta Germaniae Historica. Concilia 2: Supplement 1*, Hanover, 1998: selected transl. C. Davis-Weyer, *Early Medieval Art*, Toronto, 1986, pp. 99–103, reprinted in P. Dutton, *Carolingian Civilization: A Reader*, Peterborough, Ontario, 1993, pp. 84–87.
38. W. von Steinen, Karl der Grosse und die *Libri Carolini*, *Neues Archiv*, 39 (1931): 207–80, at pp. 250–1.
39. *Capitulary of Frankfurt* (794), 2: transl. P. King, *Charlemagne. Translated Sources*, Kendal, Cumbria, 1987, p. 224; *Das Frankfurter Konzil von 794*, R. Berndt (ed.), Mainz, 1997.
40. John C. Cavadini, *The Last Christology of the West. Adoptionism in Spain and Gaul, 785–820*, Philadelphia, 1993.

Chapter 18: The Closing of the Frontier

1. P. Fouracre, *The Age of Charles Martel*, Harlow, Essex, 2000; Shoichi Sato, The Merovingian accounting documents of Tours: form and function, *Early*

Medieval Europe, 9 (2000): 141–61.

2. Gottschalk, *Responsa* 168–9, C. Lambot (ed.), Louvain, 1945, p. 168.

3. Fouracre, *The Age of Charles Martel*, pp. 99–120; J. L. Nelson, *The Frankish World*, London, 1996, pp. xviii–xxxi; I. Wood, Before or after mission: social relations across the middle and lower Rhine in the seventh and eighth centuries, in I. L. Hansen and C. Wickham (eds.) *The Long Eighth Century. Production, Distribution and Demand*, Leiden, 2001, pp. 149–66.

4. Arbeo of Freising, *Life of Saint Emmeran* 41, *Monumenta Germaniae Historica: Scriptores rerum Merovingicarum* 6, Hanover, 1913, p. 518.

5. J. Werner, *Das alemannische Fürstengrab in Wittislingen*, Munich, 1960; F. Damminger, Dwellings, settlements and settlement patterns in Merovingian south-west Germany and adjacent areas, in I. Wood (ed.), *Franks and Alemanni in the Merovingian Period. An Ethnographic Perspective*, San Marino, CA, 1998, pp. 33–106; S. Burnell and E. James, The archaeology of conversion in the sixth and seventh centuries, in R. Gameson (ed.), *St. Augustine and the Conversion of England*, Stroud, Gloucestershire, 1999, pp. 83–106 at pp. 96–102.

6. *Life of Saint Corbinian* 16 and 29, *M.G.H.: Scriptores rerum Merovingicarum* 6, pp. 579 and 595.

7. Aethicus Ister, *Cosmographia* 2, O. Prinz (ed.), Munich, 1993, pp. 115–16.

8. R. Fletcher, *The Conversion of Europe. From Paganism to Christianity 371–1386 A.D.*, London, 1998, pp. 1–33; I. Wood, *The Missionary Life. Saints and Evangelization of Europe 400–1050*, London, 2001, pp. 25–53, and Missionaries and the Christian frontier, in W. Pohl, I. Wood, and H. Reimitz (eds.), *The Transformation of Frontiers. From Late Antiquity to the Carolingians*, Leiden, 2001, pp. 209–18.

9. Alcuin, *Life of Willibrord*: transl. T. F. X. Noble and T. Head, *Soldiers of Christ*, University Park, PA, 1995, pp. 191–211, and C. H. Talbot, *The Anglo-Saxon Missionaries in Germany*, London, 1954, pp. 3–22; Wood, *The Missionary Life*, pp. 79–99.

10. J. Herrin, *The Formation of Christendom*, Princeton, NJ, 1987, pp. 3–6.

11. S. Lebecq, *Marchands et navigateurs du Haut Moyen-Age*, Lille, 1983.

12. *Life of Wulfram of Sens* 8–9, *M. G. H.: Scriptores rerum Merovingicarum* 5, p. 607, and *Annals of Xanten*, anno 718, B. De Simson (ed.), Hanover, 1909, p. 36; S. Lebecq, Les Frisons entre Paganisme et Christianisme, *Christianisation et Déchristianisation*, Angers, 1986, pp. 19–45.

13. F. Theuws, Landed property and manorial organization in North Austrasia, in W. Roymans and F. Theuws (eds.), *Images of the Past*, Amsterdam, 1991, pp. 299–401; M. Costambeys, An Austrasian aristocracy on the northern Frankish frontier, *Early Medieval Europe*, 3 (1994): 39–62.

14. Boniface, *de grammatica*, R. Rau (ed.), Darmstadt, 1968, pp. 360–8. On Boniface, see especially: J. M. Wallace-Hadrill, *The Frankish Church*, Oxford, 1983, pp. 150–61; Fletcher, *The Conversion of Europe*, pp. 193–227; Fouracre, *The Age of Charles Martel*, pp. 126–37; Wood, *The Missionary Life*, pp. 55–78; T. F. X. Noble, Introduction to E. Emerton, *The Letters of Saint Boniface*, New York, 1976, reprint 2000, pp. vii–xxxv.

15. Boniface, *Letters* 22 [30], 53 [65] and 62 [78]: transl. E. Emerton, *The Letters*

of Saint Boniface, New York, 1976, pp. 60, 121, and 136; many, but not all, of Boniface's letters are also translated in Talbot, *Anglo-Saxon Missionaries*.

16. Boniface, *Letter* 36 [46], p.76. The citation echoes the plea of Israel to be reunited to Judah, after the victories of king David – 2 Samuel 5:1. Significantly, the Saxon appeal also followed a punitive raid by Charles Martel in 738.

17. Boniface, *Letter* 85 [105], p. 178.

18. Boniface, *Letter* 15 [23], pp. 48–50.

19. N. Brooks, Canterbury, Rome and the construction of English identity, in J. M. H. Smith (ed.), *Early Medieval Rome and the Christian West. Essays in Honor of Donald Bullough*, Leiden, 2000, pp. 221–46.

20. Boniface, *Letter* 70 [86]. pp. 158–9.

21. Boniface, *Letter* 16 [24], p. 120.

22. Boniface, *Letter* 54 [68] and 64 [80], pp. 122 and 144.

23. Willibald, *Life of Boniface* 6, Noble and Head, *Soldiers of Christ*, p. 134, and Talbot, *Anglo-Saxon Missionaries*, p. 42.

24. Boniface, *Letter* 64 [80], p. 147; J. Carey, Ireland and the Antipodes, *Speculum*, 64 (1989): 1–10.

25. Boniface, *Letter* 54 [68], p. 122.

26. *Roman Synod of 745*, in Boniface *Letter* 47 [59], pp. 101–2; M. de Jong, An unresolved riddle: early medieval incest legislation, in Wood (ed.), *Franks and Alemanni*, pp. 107–40.

27. *Roman Synod of 745*, p. 103; Jonas, *Life of Columbanus* 1.6: transl. E. Peters, *Monks, Bishops and Pagans*, Philadelphia, 1981, p. 75.

28. *Roman Synod of 745*, pp. 103–4.

29. *Roman Synod of 745*, p. 101; *Hodoeporicon of Willibald* 1, Noble and Head, *Soldiers of Christ*, p. 146, and Talbot, *Anglo-Saxon Missionaries*, p. 155.

30. *Roman Synod of 745*, p.101; Bede, *Life of Cuthbert* 9: transl. J. Webb, Harmondsworth, 1965, p. 84.

31. *Roman Synod of 745*, p. 101.

32. Boniface, *Letter* 40 [50], p. 82.

33. Boniface, *Letter* 51 [63], p. 115.

34. Boniface, *Letter* 51 [63], p. 116.

35. Boniface, *Letter* 52 [62], p. 120.

36. Willibald, *Life of Boniface* 8, Noble and Head, *Soldiers of Christ*, p. 136, and Talbot, *Anglo-Saxon Missionaries*, pp. 57–8.

37. Rudolf of Fulda, *Life of Leoba* 12, Noble and Head, *Soldiers of Christ*, pp. 267–9, and Talbot, *Anglo-Saxon Missionaries*, pp. 216–18.

38. Rudolf of Fulda, *Life of Leoba* 16, Noble and Head, *Soldiers of Christ*, p. 272, and Talbot, *Anglo-Saxon Missionaries*, p. 221.

39. R. McKitterick, Nuns' scriptoria in England and France in the 8th century, *Francia*, 19/1 (1992): 1–35; R. A. Markus, From Caesarius to Boniface: Christianity and Paganism in Gaul, in J. Fontaine and J. N. Hillgarth (eds.), *The Seventh Century: Change and Continuity*, London, 1992, pp. 154–72.

40. *Index Superstitionum*: transl. J. T. McNeill and H. A. Gamer, *Medieval Handbooks of Penance*, New York, 1990, pp. 419–21.

41. D. Harmening, *Superstitio*, Munich, 1979, is the most thorough treatment of

this theme.

42. R. Meens, Willibrords boeteboek?, *Tijdschrift voor Geschiedenis*, 106 (1993): 163–78.
43. E. von Steinmeyer (ed.), *Die kleinen althochdeutschen Sprachdenkmäler*, Berlin, 1916.
44. M. Garrison, The Collectanea and medieval florilegia, in M. Bayless and M. Lapidge (eds.), *Collectanea Pseudo-Bedae*, Dublin, 1998, pp. 42–83.
45. *Hodoeporicon of Willibald*, pref., Noble and Head, *Soldiers of Christ*, p. 44, and Talbot, *Anglo-Saxon Missionaries*, p. 153.
46. J. Nelson, The Lord's anointed and the people's choice, in D. Cannadine and S. Price (eds.), *Rituals of Royalty. Power and Ceremonial in Traditional Societies*, Cambridge, 1987, pp. 137–80, now in *The Frankish World*, pp. 99–132; M. Garrison, The Franks as the new Israel? Education for an identity from Pippin to Charlemagne, in Y. Hen and M. Innes (eds.), *The Uses of the Past in the Early Middle Ages*, Cambridge, 2000, pp. 114–61.
47. P. Delogu, The papacy, Rome and the wider world in the seventh and eighth centuries, in J. M. H. Smith (ed.), *Early Medieval Rome and the Christian West*, pp. 197–220, and La storia economica di Roma nell'alto Medio Evo, in L. Paroli and P. Delogu (eds.), *La storia economica di Roma nell'alto Medio Evo alla luce dei recenti scavi archeologici*, Florence, 1993, pp. 11–29, with R. Hodges, The riddle of St. Peter's Republic, pp. 353–63; R. Krautheimer, *Rome. Profile of a City*, Princeton, NJ, 1980, pp. 89–142.
48. R. S. Valenzani, Residential building in early medieval Rome, in J. M. H. Smith (ed.), *Early Medieval Rome and the Christian West*, pp. 101–12; Pope Hadrian to Charles (776), *Codex Carolinus* no. 59, *Monumenta Germaniae Historica. Epistolae* 3, Berlin, 1892, p. 585: transl. P. D. King, *Charlemagne*, Kendal, Cumbria, 1987, p. 286.
49. N. Purcell, The population of Rome in late antiquity: problems of classification and historical description, in W. V. Harris (ed.), *The Transformations of Vrbs Roma in Late Antiquity, Journal of Roman Archaeology*, Supplementary Series 33, Portsmouth, RI, 1999, pp. 135–61, at pp. 135–7.
50. *Inscriptiones christianae urbis Romae*, NS 4, Rome, 1964, no. 9524; A. Thacker, In search of saints. The English Church and the cult of Roman apostles and martyrs in the seventh and eighth centuries, and J. M. H. Smith, Old saints, new cults: Roman relics in Carolingian Francia, in Smith (ed.), *Early Medieval Rome and the Christian West*, pp. 247–77 and 317–39.
51. Willibald, *Life of Boniface* 6, Noble and Head, *Soldiers of Christ*, p. 125, and Talbot, *Anglo-Saxon Missionaries*, pp. 43–4.
52. A. Angenendt, *Das Frühmittelalter*, Stuttgart, 2nd edn., 1995, pp. 327–36; Y. Hen, Unity and diversity: the liturgy of Frankish Gaul before the Carolingians, in R. Swanson (ed.), *Unity and Diversity in the Church*, Studies in Church History 32, Oxford, 1996, pp. 19–29.
53. M. Enright, *Iona, Tara and Soissons*, Berlin, 1985.
54. H. Mayr-Harting, Charlemagne, the Saxons and the Imperial Coronation of 800, *English Historical Review*, 111 (1996): 1113–33.
55. *Liber Pontificalis* 97.35–44: transl. R. Davis, Liverpool, 1992, pp. 138–42; R. Schieffer, Charlemagne and Rome, in Smith (ed.), *Early Medieval Rome and*

the Christian West, pp. 279–95; T. F .X. Noble, The making of papal Rome, in M. de Jong and F. Theuws with C. Van Rhijn (eds.), *Topographies of Power in the Early Middle Ages*, Leiden, 2001, pp. 45–91.

56. W. Lammers (ed.), *Die Eingliederung der Sachsen in das Frankenreich*, Wege der Forschung 185, Darmstadt, 1970; M. Becher, *Rex, Dux und Gens: Untersuchungen zur Entstehung des sächsischen Herzogtums im 9. und 10. Jahrhundert*, Husum, 1996.

57. *Capitulary concerning the Parts of Saxony* 7, 8, and 11: transl. H. R. Loyn and J. Percival, *The Reign of Charlemagne*, London, 1975, p. 52; B. Effros, *De partibus Saxoniae* and the regulation of mortuary custom: a Carolingian campaign of Christianization or the suppression of Saxon identity?, *Revue belge de philologie et d'histoire*, 75 (1995): 267–86.

58. Wood, *The Missionary Life*, pp. 83–90.

59. *Translatio Sancti Liborii* 5, G. H. Pertz (ed.), *Monumenta Germaniae Historica: Scriptores* 4, Hanover, 1841, p. 151.

Chapter 19: "To rule the Christian people": Charlemagne

1. P. Fouracre, Frankish Gaul to 814, in R. McKitterick (ed.), *The New Cambridge Medieval History 2: c.700–c.900*, Cambridge, 1995, pp. 85–109; R. Collins, *Charlemagne*, London, 1998, pp. 43–101.

2. Einhard, *Life of Charlemagne* 13: transl. L. Thorpe, Harmondsworth, 1969, p. 67.

3. Alcuin, *Letter* 8 [121]: transl. S. Allott, *Alcuin of York*, York, 1974, p. 11; J. L. Nelson, Aachen as a place of power, in M. de Jong and F. Theuws, *Topographies of Power in the Early Middle Ages*, Leiden, 2001, pp. 217–41.

4. *Liber Pontificalis* 98.23–24: transl. R. Davis, Liverpool, 1992, pp. 190–1, and H. R. Loyn and J. Percival, *The Reign of Charlemagne*, London, 1975, pp. 24–6; *Royal Annals*, in Loyn and Percival, pp. 41–4. R. Folz, *The Coronation of Charlemagne*, London, 1974.

5. P. E. Dutton, *Charlemagne's Courtier. The Complete Einhard*, Peterborough, Ontario, 1998, pp. xvii–xxiv; M. Innes, The Classical tradition in the Carolingian Renaissance: ninth-century encounters with Suetonius, *International Journal of the Classical Tradition*, 3 (1997): 265–82.

6. Einhard, *Life of Charlemagne* 22 and 31, Thorpe, pp. 76–7 and 84.

7. M. McCormick, The liturgy of war in the early Middle Ages: crisis, liturgies and the Carolingian monarchy, *Viator*, 15 (1984): 1–23 at p. 4; R. Hodges, *Light in the Dark Ages. The Rise and Fall of San Vicenzo al Volturno*, London, 1997, pp. 29–34.

8. *Capitulary of Herstal* (779) c.16, *Monumenta Germaniae Historica: Legum Sectio 2: Capitularia* 1, Hanover, 1883, p. 51: transl. P. D. King, *Charlemagne*, Kendal, Cumbria, 1987, p. 204; *Capitulary of the Missi at Aachen* (810), cc.11 and 17, *Capitularia* 1, p. 153.

9. J. Nelson, Kingship and empire in the Carolingian world, in R. McKitterick (ed.), *Carolingian Culture: Emulation and Innovation*, Cambridge, 1994, pp. 88–107.

10. Alcuin, *Letter* 26 [20], Allott, p. 37.

11. *Royal Annals (Vienna Manuscript)* Ad 802, in Loyn and Percival, p. 45.
12. *Admonitio Generalis* (789), praef., *Capitularia* 1, p. 54, King, p. 209.
13. R. McKitterick, Introduction, *New Cambridge Medieval History*, pp. 3–17, at pp. 14–17.
14. J. Fleckenstein, *Die Hofkapelle der deutschen Königen 1*, Stuttgart, 1959; C. Hammer, Country churches, clerical inventories and the Carolingian Renaissance in Bavaria, *Church History*, 49 (1980): 5–17; Y. Hen, Knowledge of canon law among rural priests: the evidence of two Carolingian manuscripts of around 800, *Journal of Theological Studies*, NS 50 (1999): 117–34.
15. M. Innes, *State and Society in the Early Middle Ages. The Middle Rhine Valley, 400–1000*, Cambridge, 2000, pp. 42–3; M. de Jong, Carolingian monasticism: the power of prayer, in R. McKitterick (ed.), *New Cambridge Medieval History 2*, pp. 622–53.
16. Alcuin, *Letter* 29 [19] and 128 [295], Allott, pp. 40 and 134.
17. M. Driscoll, *Alcuin et la pénitence à l'époque carolingienne*, Münster in Westfalen, 1999.
18. M. Garrison, The social world of Alcuin: nicknames at York and at the Carolingian Court, in L. Houwen and A. MacDonald (eds.), *Alcuin of York. Scholar at the Carolingian Court*, Groningen, 1998, pp. 59–79.
19. D. Ganz, The preconditions of Carolingian minuscule, *Viator*, 18 (1987): 23–43.
20. Alcuin, *On Scribes*: transl. P. Godman, *Poetry of the Carolingian Renaissance*, London, 1985, p. 139.
21. D. Ganz, Book production in the Carolingian empire and the spread of Caroline minuscule, in McKitterick (ed.), *New Cambridge Medieval History 2*, pp. 786–808.
22. S. Rankin, Carolingian music, in McKitterick (ed.), *Carolingian Culture: Emulation and Innovation*, pp. 274–316; K. Levy, *Gregorian Chant and the Carolingians*, Princeton, NJ, 1998.
23. J, Mitchell, Literacy displayed: the uses of inscriptions at the monastery of San Vicenzo al Volturno in the early ninth century, in R. McKitterick (ed.), *The Uses of Literacy in the Early Middle Ages*, Cambridge, 1990, pp. 186–222.
24. R. Wright, *Late Latin and Early Romance in Spain and Carolingian France*, Liverpool, 1982, pp. 104–22; M. Banniard, *Viva voce. Communication écrite et communication orale du IVe au IXe siècle en Occident latin*, Paris, 1992, pp. 305–422.
25. Dutton, *Charlemagne's Courtier*, pp. xxv–xli, 68–130 and 168–71; R. McKitterick, *The Carolingians and the Written Word*, Cambridge, 1989, pp 211–70; J. Nelson, Literacy in Carolingian government, in McKitterick (ed.), *The Uses of Literacy*, pp. 258–96; M. Garrison, "Send more socks." On mentalities and the preservation context of medieval letters, in M. Mostert (ed.), *New Approaches to Medieval Communication*, Turnhout, 1999, pp. 69–99.
26. Dhuoda, *Liber Manualis*, P. Riche (ed.), Sources chrétiennes 225b, Paris, 1991: transl. C. Neel, *Handbook for William. A Carolingian Noblewoman's Counsel for her Son*, Lincoln, NE, 1991, and M. Thiébaux, *Dhuoda: Handbook for her Warrior Son*, Cambridge, 1998; J. M. H. Smith, Gender and ideology in the

early Middle Ages, in R. Swanson (ed.), *Gender and Christianity*, Studies in Church History 34, Woodbridge, Suffolk, 1998, pp. 51–71.

27. *Admonitio Generalis* (789), c.72, *Capitularia* 1, p. 59, King, p. 217.
28. *Admonitio Generalis*, pref., *Capitularia* 1, p. 54, King, p. 209.
29. *Admonitio Generalis*, pref., *Capitularia* 1, p. 54, King, p. 209.
30. *Admonitio Generalis* c.78, *Capitularia* 1, p. 60, King, p. 218. The letter enjoyed a very different fate outside the Carolingian empire in Ireland: J. G. O'Keefe, Cáin Domnaig, *Ériu*, 2 (1905): 189–214.
31. *Annals of Fulda* A.D. 847: transl. T. Reuter, Manchester, 1992, pp. 26–7.
32. *Council of Tours* (813) c.17, *Monumenta Germaniae Historica: Concilia* 2, Hanover, 1906, p. 288.
33. D. H. Green, *Medieval Literacy and Reading. The Primary Reception of German Literature 800–1300*, Cambridge, 1994, p. 43.
34. *General Capitulary of the Missi* (802) c.3, Loyn and Percival, p. 75.
35. *Frankish and Old Saxon Baptismal Oaths*, H. D. Schlosser (ed.), *Althochdeutsche Literatur*, Frankfurt am Main, 1970, p. 212.
36. D. H. Green, *The Carolingian Lord*, Cambridge, 1965; C. Edwards, German vernacular literature: a survey, in McKitterick (ed.), *Carolingian Culture: Emulation and Innovation*, pp. 141–70; A. Angenendt, *Das Frühmittelalter*, 2nd edn., Stuttgart, 1995, pp. 438–40.
37. E. J. Goldberg, The *Stellinga* revisited, *Speculum*, 70 (1995): 467–501; C. Carroll, The bishops in Saxony in the first century after Christianization, *Early Medieval Europe*, 8 (1999): 219–45.
38. G. Constable, *Monastic Tithes from their Origins to the Twelfth Century*, Cambridge, MA, 1964, p. 2.
39. Ghaerbald of Liège, *Capitula* 5, P. Brommer (ed.), *Monumenta Germaniae Historica: Capitula Episcoporum* 1, Hanover, 1984, p. 16; A. Dierkens, La christianisation des campagnes dans l'empire de Louis le Pieux. L'exemple du diocèse de Liège sous l'épiscopat de Walcaud (c.809–c.831), in P. Godman and R. Collins (eds.), *Charlemagne's Heir. New Perspectives on the Reign of Louis the Pious (814–830)*, Oxford, 1990, pp. 309–29.
40. Ghaerbald of Liège, *Second Diocesan Statute*, C. de Clercq (ed.), Louvain, 1936, pp. 357–62.
41. *Council on the Danube* (796), *Concilia* 2, pp. 172–6 (on the Avars); Alcuin, *Letter* 56 [99], Allott, pp. 72–4 (on the Saxons).
42. Charlemagne to Ghaerbald of Liège, *Capitularia* 1, p. 241.
43. J. H. Lynch, *Godparents and Kinship in Early Medieval Europe*, Princeton, NJ, 1986, pp. 285–332; B. Jussen, *Patenschaft und Adoption im frühen Mittelalter*, Göttingen, 1991.
44. Agobard of Lyons, *On Hail and Thunder*, *Patrologia Latina* 104: 147–58, and L. Van Acker (ed.), *Corpus Christianorum: series medievalis* 52, Turnhout, 1981: transl. P. E. Dutton, *Carolingian Civilization: A Reader*, Peterborough, Ontario, 1993, pp.189–91; P. E. Dutton, Thunder and Hail over the Carolingian countryside, in D. Sweeney (ed.), *Agriculture in the Middle Ages*, Philadelphia, 1995, pp. 111–37.
45. Agobard, *On the Illusion of Certain Miracles* 11, Van Acker (ed.), p. 242.

46. C. Chazelle, Matter, spirit and image in the *Libri Carolini, Recherches augustiniennes,* 21 (1986): 163–84; T. F. X. Noble, Tradition and learning in search of an ideology, R. E. Sullivan (ed.), *"The Gentle Voices of Teachers." Aspects of Learning in the Carolingian Age,* Columbus, OH, 1995, pp. 227–60, and *Images and the Carolingians: Discourses on Tradition, Order and Worship* (forthcoming); M. McCormick, Textes, images et iconoclasme dans le cadre des relations entre Byzance et l'Occident carolingien, *Testo e Immagine nell'Alto Medio Evo,* Settimane di Studi sull'Alto Medio Evo 41, Spoleto, 1994, pp. 95–162; C. Chazelle, *The Crucified God in the Carolingian Era. Theology and Art of Christ's Passion,* Cambridge, 2001, pp. 39–52.

47. H. von Steinen, Karl der Grosse und die *Libri Carolini, Neues Archiv,* 39 (1931): 246.

48. *Libri Carolini* 1.15, A. Freeman with P. Meyvaert (eds.), *Monumenta Germaniae Historica: Concilia 2: Supplementum* 1, Hanover, 1998, pp. 169–75.

49. *Libri Carolini* 4.21, Freeman (ed.), p. 540.

50. V. R. Jeck, Die frühmittelterliche Rezeption der Zeittheorie Augustins in den "Libri Carolini" und die Temporalität des Kultbildes, in R. Berndt (ed.), *Das Konzil von Frankfurt 794,* Mainz, 1997, vol. 2, pp. 861–84.

51. Theodulph, *First Capitulary* cc.5, 6, 8, 18, and 23, Brommer (ed.), *Capitula Episcoporum,* pp. 107–8, 115, and 120: transl. Dutton, *Carolingian Civilization,* pp. 94–105; see also A. Freeman and P. Meyvaert, The meaning of Theodulph's apse at Germigny-des-Prés, *Gesta,* 40 (2001): 125–39.

52. *Libri Carolini* 3.16 and 4.3, Freeman (ed.), pp. 409 and 495.

53. P. Brown, Images as a substitute for writing, in E. Chrysos and I. Wood (eds.), *East and West: Modes of Communication,* Leiden, 1999, pp. 15–34.

54. *Libri Carolini* 2.30, Freeman (ed.), p. 305.

55. *The Wish of Manchán of Liath*: transl. K. Jackson, *A Celtic Miscellany,* Harmondsworth, 1971, p. 280.

56. *Libri Carolini* 1.1, Freeman (ed.), p. 105.

57. *Libri Carolini* 4.5, Freeman (ed.), p. 497.

58. H. Maguire, *The Icons of their Bodies. Saints and their Images in Byzantium,* Princeton, NJ, 1996, p. 46: the reaction of Gregory Melissenos in 1438.

Chapter 20: In gear dagum: "In Days of Yore"

1. S. Coupland, Money and coinage under Louis the Pious, *Francia,* 17:1 (1990): 23–34.

2. P. Sawyer, *Kings and Vikings,* London, 1982, pp. 39–77; R. Hodges, *Towns and Trade in the Age of Charlemagne,* London, 2000.

3. K. Hauck, Zum Problem der "Götter" im Horizont der völkerwanderungzeitlichen Brakteaten, in G. Althoff (ed.), *Person und Gemeinschaft im Mittelalter,* Sigmaringen, 1988, pp. 73–98.

4. I. N. Wood, *The Missionary Life. Saints and the Evangelization of Europe 400–1050,* London, 2001, pp. 250–3, and in P. Sawyer, B. Sawyer and I. Wood (eds.), *The Christianization of Scandinavia,* Alingsås, 1987, pp. 64–6.

5. Sawyer, *Kings and Vikings,* plate IV.

6. S. Franklin and J. Shepard, *The Emergence of Rus 750–1250,* London, 1996.

7. *The Russian Primary Chronicle*: transl. S. H. Cross and O. P. Sherbowitz-Wetzor, Cambridge, MA, p.111; I. Ševčenko, Religious missions seen from Byzantium, *Harvard Ukrainian Studies*, 22/3 (1988/9): 6–27.

8. G. Jones, *The Norse Atlantic Saga*, Oxford, 1986, pp. 115–38; C. Keller, Vikings in the West Atlantic: a model of Norse Greenland medieval society, *Acta Archeologica*, 61 (1991): 126–41.

9. *The Anglo-Saxon Chronicle* A.D. 1010: transl. D. Whitelock, London, 1965, p. 90.

10. *Anglo-Saxon Chronicle* A.D. 1070, p. 151.

11. P. Wormald, Viking studies: whence and whither?, in R. T. Farrell (ed.), *The Vikings*, London, 1982, pp. 128–53; Sawyer, *Kings and Vikings*, pp. 113–30; G. Jones, *The Vikings*, Oxford, 1984, pp. 204–40; S. S. Hansen and K. Randsborg (eds.), *The Vikings in the West*, Acta Archaeologica, 71: Supplement 2, Copenhagen, 2000.

12. *Greenlanders' Saga* 4: transl. Jones, *Norse Atlantic Saga*, p. 196.

13. *Norges Inskrifter* 6, no. 449, Oslo, 1960, cited in Sawyer (ed.), *Christianization of Scandinavia*, pp. 73–4.

14. Ermold Nigellus, *On the Paintings at Ingelheim*: transl. P. Godman, *Poetry of the Carolingian Renaissance*, London, 1985, p. 225; K. Hauck, Der Missionsauftrag Christi und das Kaisertum Ludwigs des Frommen, in R. Collins and P. Godman (eds.), *Charlemagne's Heir*, Oxford, 1990, pp. 275–96.

15. Wood, *The Missionary Life*, pp. 123–4.

16. Rimbert, *Life of Anskar* 30: transl. C. H. Robinson, London, 1921, pp. 98–100.

17. R. Fletcher, *The Conversion of Europe. From Paganism to Christianity 371–1386 A.D.*, London, 1998, pp. 369–416.

18. Fletcher, *Conversion of Europe*, pp. 404–7.

19. K. Hastrup, *Culture and History in Medieval Iceland*, Oxford, 1985.

20. Snorri Sturluson, *Saga of Olaf Tryggvason 53–69: Heimskringla*: transl. L. M. Hollander, Austin, TX, 1964, pp. 195–208; S. Bagge, *Society and Politics in Snorri Sturluson's Heimskringla*, Berkeley, CA 1991.

21. Ari Thorgilsson, *Book of the Icelanders* 7: transl. Viking Society of America, Ithaca, NY, 1930, p. 66.

22. Jón Hnefill Adalsteinsson, *Under the Cloak*, Uppsala, 1978.

23. N. L. Wicker, Selective female infanticide as a potential explanation of the dearth of women in Viking Age Scandinavia, in G. Halsall (ed.), *Violence and Society in the Early Medieval West*, Woodbridge, Suffolk, 1998, pp .205–21.

24. J. Jochens, Late and peaceful: Iceland's Conversion through Arbitration in 1000, *Speculum*, 74 (1999): 621–55; R. Karras, God and man in medieval Scandinavia. Writing – and gendering – the conversion, in J. Muldoon (ed.), *Varieties of Religious Conversion in the Middle Ages*, Gainesville, FL, 1997, pp. 100–14.

25. O. Vésteinsson, *The Christianization of Iceland. Priests, Power and Social Change 1000–1300*, Oxford, 2000, pp. 17–57.

26. Snorri Sturluson, *The Prose Edda*: transl. A. Faulkes, London, 1987.

27. D. Dumville, The Anglian Collection of royal genealogies, *Anglo-Saxon England*, 5 (1976): 23–50.

28. A. Gurevich, Saga and history: the "historical concept" of Snorri Sturluson, *Historical Anthropology of the Middle Ages*, Chicago, 1992, pp. 103–15.

29. *Lebor Gabála Erenn*: The Book of the Taking of Ireland: transl. R. A .S. McAlister, Dublin, 1970, p. 165.

30. K. McCone, *Pagan Past and Christian Present in Early Irish Literature*, Maynooth, 1991, pp. 54–83; J. Carey, Native elements in Irish pseudo-history, in D. Edel (ed.), *Cultural Identity and Cultural Integration. Ireland and Europe in the Early Middle Ages*, Dublin, 1995, pp. 45–60.

31. P. Wormald, Bede, "Beowulf," and the conversion of the Anglo-Saxon aristocracy, in R. T. Farrell (ed.), *Bede and Anglo-Saxon England*, Oxford, 1978, pp. 32–95.

32. Gurevich, *Historical Anthropology of the Middle Ages*, pp. 124–73.

33. D. Bullough, *Friends, Neighbours and Fellow-Drinkers. Aspects of Community and Conflict in the Early Medieval West*, H. M. Chadwick Lectures 1, Cambridge, 1990; Alcuin, *Letters* 5 and 125: transl. I. Allott, York, 1974, pp. 8 and 132; *Council of Clovesho* (747), canon 28, A. W. Haddon and W. Stubbs, *Councils and Ecclesiastical Documents relating to Great Britain and Ireland* 3, Oxford, 1964, p. 374.

34. Einhard, *Life of Charlemagne* 29: transl. L. Thorpe, Harmondsworth, 1969, p. 82.

35. D. Whitelock, *The Audience of Beowulf*, Oxford, 1951.

36. Wormald, Bede, "Beowulf," and the conversion of the Anglo-Saxon aristocracy, pp. 49–58; P. A. Booth, King Alfred vs. Beowulf: the re-education of the Anglo-Saxon aristocracy, *Bulletin of the John Rylands Library*, 99 (1997): 41–66.

37. R. Frank, Germanic legend in Old English literature, in M. Godden and M. Lapidge (eds.), *Cambridge Companion to Old English Literature*, Cambridge, 1991, pp. 88–106; M. Innes, Memory, orality and history in an early medieval society, *Past and Present*, 158 (1998): 3–36, and Teutons or Trojans? The Carolingians and the Germanic past, in Y.Hen and M. Innes (eds.), *The Uses of the Past in the Early Middle Ages*, Cambridge, 2000, pp. 227–49.

38. Rudolf of Fulda, *Translatio Sancti Alexandri, Monumenta Germaniae Historica: Scriptores* 2, Berlin, 1829, p. 673.

39. M. Enright, *The Lady with a Mead Cup. Ritual, Prophecy and Lordship in the European Warband from La Tène to the Vikings*, Dublin, 1996, pp. 68–168.

40. *Sturlunga Saga* 31: transl. J. McGrew, New York, 1970, p. 108.

41. Snorri Sturluson, *Saga of Olaf Tryggvason* 64: *Heimskringla*, p. 204.

42. *Merseburg Spells*: H. D. Schlosser (ed.), *Althochdeutsche Literatur*, Frankfurt, 1970, pp. 251–60.

43. *Erik the Red's Saga* 3, Jones, *Norse Atlantic Saga*, p. 214.

44. Burchard of Worms, *The Corrector* 5.65: transl. J. T. McNeill and H. Gamer, *Medieval Handbooks of Penance*, New York, 1938, p. 330.

45. *Vienna Spell*, Schlosser, p. 260.

46. *Aecerbot: For Unfruitful Land*: transl. S.A.J. Bradley, London, 1982, pp. 545–7.

47. Gurevich, *Historical Anthropology of the Middle Ages*, pp. 200–9; Hastrup,

Culture and History in Medieval Iceland, pp. 140–51.

48. *Midhir's [the lord of the Fairies'] Invitation to the Earthly Paradise*: transl. K. H. Jackson, *A Celtic Miscellany*, Harmondsworth, 1987, p. 172.
49. *The Táin*: transl. T. Kinsella, Oxford, 1970, p. 2
50. *Táin Bó Cuailnge from the Book of Leinster*, C. O'Rahilly (ed.), Dublin, 1970, p. 272.
51. *Beowulf* 1347–52: transl. M. Alexander, Harmondsworth, 1973, p. 93. See also the new bilingual transl. of Seamus Heaney, New York, 2000.
52. *Book of Monsters*, M. Haupt (ed.), *Opuscula*, Leipzig, 1879, p. 223, cited in Whitelock, *The Audience of Beowulf*, p. 46.
53. F. P. Magoun, The pilgrim's diary of Nicholas of Munkathvera, *Medieval Studies*, 6 (1944): 314–54, at p. 347.
54. *Beowulf* 104–10, p. 54; J. R. R. Tolkien, Beowulf: the monsters and the critics, *Proceedings of the British Academy*, 22 (1936): 1–53; R. Mellinkoff, Cain's monstrous progeny in "Beowulf," *Anglo-Saxon England*, 8 (1979): 143–62 and 9 (1980): 183–97.
55. Ananias of Shirak in J. R. Russell, Dragons in Armenia, *Journal of Armenian Studies*, 5 (1990/1): 3–19.
56. Moses Korenats'i, *History of the Armenians* 1.61: transl. R. W. Thomson, Cambridge, MA, 1978, p. 204.
57. A. Sheratt, The emergence of elites: earlier Bronze Age Europe, 2500–1300 B.C., in B. Cunliffe (ed.), *Oxford Illustrated Prehistory of Europe*, Oxford, 1994, pp. 244–70.
58. *Lorsch Bee Spell*: Schlosser, *Althochdeutsche Literatur*, p. 260.
59. P. Carelli, Thunder and lightning, magical miracles. On the popular myth of thunderbolts and the presence of Stone Age artifacts in medieval deposits, in *Visions of the Past. Trends and Traditions in Swedish Medieval Archaeology*, Lund Studies in Medieval Archaeology 19, Lund, 1997, pp. 393–417 (I owe this reference and information on San Vicenzo in Volturno to the kindness of Professor R. Hodges); M. van Vlierden, *Willibrord en het begin van Nederland*, Utrecht, 1995, pp. 93 and 102.
60. *Revue des études anciennes*, 3 (1901): 273.
61. F. Harmer, *Documents of the Ninth and Tenth Centuries*, Cambridge, 1914, pp. 13–15.

Coordinated Chronological Tables

WEST

EAST

Bardaisan 154–ca.224
224 Rise of Sasanian empire

284–305 Diocletian
303 Great Persecution

306–337 Constantine
312 Battle of Milvian Bridge

324 Foundation of
   Constantinople
325 Council of Nicaea
Anthony, hermit in Egypt
   250–356
Athanasius of Alexandria
   296–373

Martin of Tours 335–397

378 Battle of Adrianople
379–395 Theodosius I
Augustine of Hippo 354–430
   writes *Confessions* 397/400
   writes *City of God* 413+
   Pelagian controversy 413+
406 Barbarian invasion of Gaul
410 Sack of Rome
418 Settlement of the Visigoths.
Beginning of "barbarian
   settlements"
John Cassian 360–435

WEST

EAST

408–450 Theodosius II as
    Eastern emperor
438 issues *Theodosian Code*
Cyril of Alexandria, patriarch
    412–444

Palladius' mission to Irish ca.431

431 Council of Ephesus

434–453 Empire of Attila the
    Hun

Leo I, pope 440–461

451 Council of Chalcedon

Severinus of Noricum, died 482
Patricius of Ireland, died ca.490
Sidonius Apollinaris 431–489

Resignation of Romulus
    Augustulus: end of Western
    empire 476
Odoacer rules in Italy 476–493

Caesarius of Arles 470–543

Theodoric the Ostrogoth rules
    in Italy 493–526

Clovis king of the Franks
    481–511

Ella Asbeha, king of Axum
    ca.519–ca.531

Gildas writes *On the Ruin of
    Britain* ca.520
Boethius 480–524 writes
    Consolation of Philosophy 524

Justinian 527–565
    Issues *Codex Justinianus* 529
    Building of Hagia Sophia 533
    Issues *Digest* and *Institutes*
        533
    Reconquest of Africa and
        Italy 533–540

Benedict of Nursia 480–547

WEST	BRITISH ISLES	EAST
		Plague 543–570
Cassiodorus 490–583		
		Khusro I Anoshirwan 530–579
Gregory of Tours 538–594 writes *Histories* 576–590		
Radegund 520–587 Convent of Holy Cross at Poitiers 561		
Lombard invasion of Italy 568		
Venantius Fortunatus ca.540– ca.600		
Gregory the Great, pope 590–604		
	Columba ca.520–597 founds Iona 565	
	Conversion of Kent 597	
		Khusro II, King of Kings 590–628
Isidore of Seville ca. 560–636		Heraclius, emperor 610–641 defeats Khusro II 627
Columbanus 543–615		
		Muhammad 570–632 Battle of Yarmuk 636 Battle of Qâdesiyya 637 Eastern Christians at Hsian-fu 638
Jonas of Bobbio, *Life of Columbanus* ca.640		
		Ummayad califate 661–750
	Synod of Whitby 664	

WEST	BRITISH ISLES	EAST
	Theodore of Tarsus, archbishop of Canterbury 668–690 Muirchú, *Life of Saint Patrick* 695	
	Bede 672–735 writes *Ecclesiastical History of the English People*	
		Calif 'Abd al-Malik 685–705 builds Dome of the Rock in Jerusalem 691/2
Muslim conquest of Spain 711		
		Defeat of Muslims at Constantinople 717 Leo II, emperor 717–741
Charles Martel, mayor of the palace 715–741 Willibrord 658–739		
Battle of Poitiers 733		
		John of Damascus ca.665– ca.749
Boniface 675–754		writes *Defence of Holy Images* 726/733
		Constantine V 741–775
Lombards conquer Ravenna 751		
	Book of Kells ca.750	
		Foundation of Baghdad 762
Charlemagne 768–814 conquers Lombards 774 *Capitulary on Saxony* 785 commissions *Libri Carolini* 793 Council of Frankfurt 794 Palace at Aachen 794 Crowned emperor at Rome 800 Alcuin of York 735–804		Iconophile Council of Nicaea 787
		Calif Harûn al-Rashid 786–809

WEST	SCANDINAVIA	EAST
Theodulph of Orléans 798–818		
Louis the Pious 814–840		
Einhard, *Life of Charlemagne* 824/836		
		"Triumph of Orthodoxy" 843
	Settlement of Iceland 870	
		Conversion of Kiev 987
	Conversion of Iceland 1000	

Bibliography

Primary Sources

(The reader should note that many of the transl. are attached to editions of the original text.)

Admonitio Generalis (789), *Monumenta Germaniae Historica: Legum Sectio 2: Capitularia* 1, Hanover, 1883: transl. P. King, *Charlemagne. Translated Sources*, Kendal, Cumbria, 1987.

Adomnán, *De locis sanctis*: transl. D. Meehan, Dublin, 1983.

—— *Life of Columba*: transl. R. Sharpe, Harmondsworth, 1995.

Aecerbot: For Unfruitful Land: transl. S. A. J. Bradley, *Anglo-Saxon Poetry*, London, 1982.

Aethelwulf, *De abbatibus*: transl. A. Campbell, Oxford, 1967.

Aethicus Ister, *Cosmographia*, O. Prinz (ed.), Munich, 1993.

Agobard of Lyons, *On Hail and Thunder*, *Patrologia Latina* 104 and L. Van Acker (ed.), *Corpus Christianorum: series medievalis* 52, Turnhout, 1981: transl. P. E. Dutton, *Carolingian Civilization. A Reader*, Peterborough, Ontario, 1993.

—— *On the Illusion of Certain Miracles*, L. Van Acker (ed.), *Corpus Christianorum: series medievalis* 52, Turnhout, 1981.

Alcuin, *Letters*: transl. S. Allott, *Alcuin of York*, York, 1974.

—— *Life of Willibrord*: transl. T. F. X. Noble and T. Head, *Soldiers of Christ*, University Park, PA, 1995, and C. H. Talbot, *The Anglo-Saxon Missionaries in Germany*, London, 1954.

—— *On Scribes*: transl. P. Godman, *Poetry of the Carolingian Renaissance*, London, 1985.

al-Jâhiz, *Refutation of the Christians*: transl. C. Pellat, London, 1969.

al-Tabarî, *History*: transl. Y. Friedmann, *The History of al-Tabarî*, Albany, NY, 1991.

Alvarus, *Indiculus luminosus*, J. Gil (ed.), *Corpus Scriptorum Muzarabicorum* 1, Madrid, 1973.

Aneurin, *Y Gododdin*: transl. A. O. H. Jarman, Llandysal, 1988.

Anglo-Saxon Chronicle, The: transl. D. Whitelock, London, 1965.

Annals of Fulda: transl. T. Reuter, Manchester, 1992.

Annals of Xanten, B. De Simson (ed.), Hanover, 1909.

Anonymus Valesianus: transl. J. C. Rolfe, *Ammianus Marcellinus*, Loeb Classical Library, London, 1952.

Anthony of Tagrit, *The Fifth Book of Rhetoric, Corpus Scriptorum Christianorum Orientalium* 480/1, Louvain, 1986.

Apophthegmata Patrum: transl. L. Regnault, *Les Sentences des Pères du désert. Nouveau recueil*, Solesmes, 1970.

Arbeo of Freising, *Life of Saint Emmeran, Monumenta Germaniae Historica: Scriptores rerum Merovingicarum* 6, Hanover, 1913.

Ari Thorgilsson, *Book of the Icelanders*: transl. Viking Society of America, Ithaca, NY, 1930.

Armenian History attributed to Sebeos, The: transl. R. W. Thomson, Liverpool, 1999.

Athanasius, *Apology to Constantius*: transl. *A Library of Fathers*, Oxford, 1873.

Audoenus, *Life of Eligius*, B. Krusch (ed.), *Monumenta Germaniae Historica: Scriptores rerum Merovingicarum* 4, Hanover, 1902, and T. Head (transl.), *Medieval Hagiography*, New York, 2000.

Augustine, *Against the Letters of the Pelagians*: transl. P. Holmes and R. E. Wallis, *Library of the Nicene and Post-Nicene Fathers* 5, Grand Rapids, MI, 1975.

—— *City of God*: transl. H. Bettenson, Harmondsworth, 1976.

—— *Confessions*: transl. H. Chadwick, Oxford, 1991 and F.J. Sheed, Indianapolis, reprint 1992.

—— *Ennaration in Psalm 34*: transl. S. Hebgin and F. Corrigan, *Ancient Christian Writers* 30, London, 1961.

—— *Letters*: transl. W. Parsons, *Fathers of the Church*, 30, New York, 1955.

—— *Newly Discovered Letters*, J. Divjak (ed.), *Bibliothèque augustinienne 46B: Lettres 1*–29**, Paris, 1987: transl. R. Eno, *Fathers of the Church* 81, Washington, DC, 1989.

—— *Newly Discovered Sermons*, F. Dolbeau (ed.), *Vingt-six sermons au peuple d'Afrique*, Paris, 1996: transl. E. Hill, *The Complete Works of Saint Augustine: A Translation for the Twenty-First Century. Sermons III/1: Newly Discovered Sermons*, Hyde Park, NY, 1997.

—— *On Rebuke and Grace*: transl. P. Holmes and R. E. Wallis, *Library of the Nicene and Post-Nicene Fathers* 5, Grand Rapids, MI, 1975.

—— *On Virginity*: transl. C. I. Cornish, *Library of the Nicene and Post-Nicene Fathers* 3, Grand Rapids, MI, 1980.

Baba Bathra: transl. I. Epstein, *Babylonian Talmud*, London, 1935.

Bardaisan, *Book of the Laws and Countries*: transl. H. J. W. Drijvers, Assen, 1965.

Barhadbshaba, *The Foundation of the Schools, Patrologia Orientalis* 4

Bar Hebraeus, *Chronography*: transl. E. A. W. Budge, Oxford, 1932.

Barsanuphius and John of Gaza, *Correspondence*: transl. L. Regnault, *Barsanuphe et Jean de Gaza: Correspondence*, Solesmes, 1972.

Baudovinia, *Life of Radegund*: transl. J. A. McNamara with J. Halborg and E. Whatley, *Sainted Women of the Dark Ages*, Durham, NC, 1992.

Bede, *Ecclesiastical History of the English People*: transl. B. Colgrave and R. A. B. Mynors, Oxford, 1969; L. Sherley-Price, Harmondsworth, 1955 and R. Collins and J. McClure, Oxford, 1994.

—— *Letter to Egbert*: transl. J. McClure and R. Collins, Oxford, 1994.

—— *Life of Cuthbert*: transl. J. F. Webb, *Lives of the Saints*, Harmondsworth, 1965.

—— *Lives of the Abbots of Wearmouth and Jarrow*: transl. D. Farmer, *The Age of Bede*, Harmondsworth, 1983.

—— *On Genesis*, C. W. Jones (ed.), *Corpus Christianorum* 118A, Turnhout, 1967.

—— *Opera de Temporibus*, C. W. Jones (ed.), Cambridge, MA, 1943: transl. F. Wallis, *The Reckoning of Time*, Liverpool, 1999.

Benedict of Monte Cassino, *Rule of Benedict*, A. de Vogüé (ed.), *La règle de Saint Benoît*, Sources chrétiennes 181–6, Paris, 1971–2: transl. T. Kardong, *The Rule of Saint Benedict*, Collegeville, MI, 1996.

Beowulf: transl. M. Alexander, Harmondsworth, 1973, and Seamus Heaney, New York, 2000.

Besa, *Life of Shenoute*: transl. D. N. Bell, Kalamazoo, MI, 1983.

Boethius, *Consolation of Philosophy*: transl. P.G. Walsh, Oxford, 1999.

Boniface, *De grammatica*, R. Rau (ed.), Darmstadt, 1968.

—— *Letters*: transl. E. Emerton, *The Letters of Saint Boniface*, New York, 1976 and 2000.

Book of Constitutions: transl. K. F. Drew, *The Burgundian Code*, Philadelphia, 1949.

Book of Monsters, M. Haupt (ed.), *Opuscula*, Leipzig, 1879.

Braulio of Saragossa, *Renotatio*, *Patrologia Latina* 81.

Bretha Crólige, D. Binchy (ed.), *Ériu*, 12 (1934): 1–77.

Bretha Déin Chécht, D. Binchy (ed.), *Ériu*, 20 (1966): 1–65.

Burchard of Worms, *The Corrector*: transl. J. T.McNeill and H. Gamer, *Medieval Handbooks of Penance*, New York, 1938.

Byzantine Defenders of Images. Eight Saints' Lives: transl. A. M. Talbot, Washington, DC, 1998.

Caesarius of Arles, *Letters*: transl. W. Klingshirn, Liverpool, 1994.

—— *Rule for Nuns*: transl. M. C. McCarthy, Washington, DC,1960.

—— *Sermons*: transl. M. Mueller, *Fathers of the Church* 31, New York, 1956.

Capitulary concerning the Parts of Saxony: transl. H. R. Loyn and J. Percival, *The Reign of Charlemagne*, London, 1975.

Capitulary of Frankfurt (794), R. Berndt (ed.), *Das Frankfurter Konzil von 794*, Mainz, 1997: transl. P. King, *Charlemagne. Translated Sources*, Kendal, Cumbria, 1987.

Capitulary of Herstal (779), *Monumenta Germaniae Historica: Legum Sectio 2: Capitularia* 1, Hanover, 1883: transl. P. D. King, *Charlemagne. Translated Sources*, Kendal, Cumbria, 1987.

Capitulary of the Missi at Aachen (810), *Monumenta Germaniae Historica: Legum Sectio 2: Capitularia* 1, Hanover, 1883.

Cassian, *Conferences*: transl. E. C. S. Giles, *Library of the Nicene and Post-Nicene Fathers* 13, Grand Rapids, MI, 1986; C. Luibheid, New York, 1985 and B. Ramsey, *Ancient Christian Writers* 57, New York, 1997.

Cassiodorus, *Institutes*: transl. L. W. Jones, *An Introduction to Divine and Human Readings*, New York, 1946.

—— *Variae*: transl. S. J. B. Barnish, Liverpool, 1992.

Celestine, Pope, *Letters*: *Patrologia Latina* 50.

Chronicle of Joshua the Stylite, The: transl. W. Wright, Cambridge, 1882.

Chronicle of Séert, Patrologia Orientalis 13.

Chronicle of 754: transl. K. Wolf, *Conquerors and Chroniclers in Early Medieval Spain*, Liverpool, 1990.

Chronicle of Zuqnîn: Parts III and IV, A.D. 485–775: transl. A. Harrak, Toronto, 1999.

Codex Carolinus, Monumenta Germaniae Historica. Epistolae 3, Berlin,1892: transl. P. D. King, *Charlemagne. Translated Sources*, Kendal, Cumbria, 1987.

Codex Justinianus: transl. (extracts) in P. R. Coleman-Norton, *Roman State and Christian Church: A Collection of Legal Documents to A.D. 535*, London, 1966.

Codex Theodosianus: transl. C. Pharr, Princeton, NJ, 1952.

Cogitosus, *Life of Brigit*: transl. S. Conolly and J. M. Picard, *Journal of the Royal Society of Antiquaries of Ireland*, 117 (1982) and O. Davies, *Celtic Spirituality*, New York, 1999.

Collatio Legum Romanarum et Mosaicarum: transl. M. Dodgeon and S. N. C. Lieu, *The Roman Eastern Frontier and the Persian Wars (A.D. 226–362)*, London, 1991.

Collectio Casinensis: transl. J. I. McEnerney, *Fathers of the Church* 77, Washington, DC, 1985.

Cologne Mani-Codex, The: transl. R. Cameron and R. J. Dewey, Missoula, MT, 1979.

Columbanus, *Instruction*: transl. G. S. M. Walker, *Sancti Columbani Opera*, Dublin, 1960.

—— *Letters*: transl. G. S. M. Walker, *Sancti Columbani Opera*, Dublin, 1960.

—— *Rule for Monks*: transl. G. S. M. Walker, *Sancti Columbani Opera*, Dublin, 1960.

Concilia Galliae a.314–a.506, C. Munier (ed.), *Corpus Christianorum* 148, Turnhout, 1963.

Concilia Galliae a.511–a.695, C. de Clercq (ed.), *Corpus Christianorum* 148A, Turnhout, 1963.

Concilios visigóticos e hispano-romanos, J. Vives (ed.), Madrid, 1963.

Confirmation of the Codex Justinianus (529): transl. P. R. Coleman-Norton, *Roman State and Christian Church: A Collection of Legal Documents to A.D. 535*, London, 1966.

Constantius, *Life of Germanus*: transl. F. R. Hoare, *The Western Fathers*, reprinted in T. Head and T. F. X. Noble, *Soldiers of Christ*, University Park, PA, 1995.

Constitution "Deo Auctore" (530): transl. A. Watson, Philadelphia, 1985.

Corpus Inscriptionum Graecarum, Berlin, 1877.

Cosmas Indicopleustes, *Christian Topography*: transl. J. W. MacCrindle, Hakluyt Society, 98, London, 1897.

Council of Clovesho (747), A. W. Haddon and W. Stubbs, *Councils and Ecclesiastical Documents relating to Great Britain and Ireland* 3, Oxford, 1964.

Council of Elvira (306), E. J. Jonkers (ed.), Leiden, 1974.

Council of Tours (813), *Monumenta Germaniae Historica: Concilia* 2, Hanover, 1906.

Council on the Danube (796), *Monumenta Germaniae Historica: Concilia* 2, Hanover, 1906.

Cummian, *On the Paschal Controversy*: transl. M. Walsh and D. O'Cróinín, Toronto, 1988.

Cuthbert, *Letter on the Death of Bede*: transl. B. Colgrave and R. A. B. Mynors, *Bede: Ecclesiastical History of the English People*, Oxford, 1969.

Cyprian, *Letters*: transl. G. W. Clarke, *The Letters of St. Cyprian, Ancient Christian Writers* 43–4 and 46–7, New York 1984–89.

Cyril of Alexandria, *Letters*: transl. J. I. McEnerney, *Fathers of the Church* 77, Washington, DC, 1985.

Dhuoda, *Liber Manualis*, P. Riché (ed.), *Sources chrétiennes* 225b, Paris, 1991: transl. C. Neel, *Handbook for William. A Carolingian Noblewoman's Counsel for her Son*, Lincoln, NE, 1991 and M. Thiébaux, *Liber Manualis: Handbook for her Warrior Son*, Cambridge, 1998.

Dialogue between the Calif al-Mahdi and the Catholicos Timothy: transl. H. Putman, *L'Église et l'Islam sous Timothée I (780–823)*, Beirut, 1975.

Didache: transl. J. B. Lightfoot, London, 1891.

Didascalia Apostolorum: transl. R. H. Connolly, Oxford, 1929.

Doctrina Jacobi: transl. V. Déroche, *Travaux et Mémoires*, 11 (1991): 47–229.

Dream of the Rood, The: transl. S. A. J. Bradley, *Anglo-Saxon Poetry*, London, 1982.

Eddius Stephanus, *Life of Wilfrid*: transl. J. F. Webb, *Lives of the Saints*, Harmondsworth, 1965.

Egeria, *Travels*: transl. J. Wilkinson, London, 1971.

Einhard, *Life of Charlemagne*: transl. L. Thorpe, Harmondsworth, 1969.

Elishe Vardapet, *History of Vardan and the Armenian War*: transl. R. W. Thomson, Cambridge, MA, 1982.

Ennodius, *Life of Epiphanius*: transl. G. M. Cook, Washington, DC, 1942.

Epistulae Austriacae, W. Grundlach (ed.), *Corpus Christianorum* 117, Turnhout, 1957.

Erik the Red's Saga: transl. G. Jones, *The Norse Atlantic Saga*, Oxford, 1986.

Ermold Nigellus, *On the Paintings at Ingelheim*: transl. P. Godman, *Poetry of the Carolingian Renaissance*, London, 1985.

Eugippius, *Life of Severinus*: transl. L. Bieler, *Fathers of the Church* 55, Washington, DC, 1965.

Eusebius of Caesarea, *Ecclesiastical History*: transl. A. C. McGiffert, *Library of the Nicene and Post-Nicene Fathers* 1, Grand Rapids, 1979, and G. A. Williamson, Harmondsworth, 1965.

—— *In Praise of Constantine*: transl. H. A. Drake, Berkeley, CA, 1978.

—— *Life of Constantine*: transl. Averil Cameron and S. Hall, Oxford, 1999.

—— *Tricennial Orations*: transl. H. A. Drake, *In Praise of Constantine*, Berkeley, CA, 1976.

Eustratius, *Life of Eutychius*: *Patrologia Graeca* 86.

Evagrius, *Ecclesiastical History*: *Patrologia Graeca* 86.

Exeter Book: The Ruin, The: transl. S. A. J. Bradley, *Anglo-Saxon Poetry*, London, 1982.

First Synod of Saint Patrick, The: transl. L. Bieler, *The Irish Penitentials*, Dublin, 1975.

Frankish and Old Saxon Baptismal Oaths, H. D. Schlosser (ed.), *Althochdeutsche*

Literatur, Frankfurt am Main, 1970.

Fredegar, *Chronicle*: transl. A. C. Murray, *From Roman to Merovingian Gaul. A Reader*, Peterborough, Ontario, 2000.

Fructuosus of Braga, *General Rule*: transl. C. W. Barlow, *Fathers of the Church* 63, Washington, DC, 1969.

—— *Rule for the Monastery of Compludo*: transl. C. W. Barlow, *Fathers of the Church* 63, Washington, DC, 1969.

Galen, *De sanitate tuenda*, C. G. Kühn (ed.), *Galeni Opera* 6, Leipzig, 1825.

Gelasius I, *Letter against the Lupercalia*, G. Pomares (ed.), *Lettre contre les Lupercales, Sources chrétiennes* 65, Paris, 1959.

General Capitulary of the Missi (802), H.R. Loyn and J. Percival, *The Reign of Charlemagne. Documents on Carolingian Government and Administration*, New York, 1976.

Gerald of Wales, *Topography of Ireland*: transl. J. O'Meara, Harmondsworth, 1982.

Gesta apud Zenophilum: transl. M. Edwards, *Optatus. Against the Donatists*, Liverpool, 1997.

Ghaerbald of Liège, *Capitula*, P. Brommer (ed.), *Monumenta Germaniae Historica: Capitula Episcoporum* I, Hanover, 1984.

—— *Second Diocesan Statute*, C. de Clercq (ed.), Louvain, 1936.

Gildas, *On the Ruin of Britain*: transl. M. Winterbottom, London, 1978.

Gottschalk, *Responsa*, C. Lambot (ed.), Louvain, 1945.

Greenlanders' Saga: transl. G. Jones, *The Norse Atlantic Saga*, Oxford, 1986.

Gregory I, *Dialogues*, A. de Vogüé (ed.), *Grégoire le Grand: Les Dialogues, Sources chrétiennes* 251, 260, and 265, Paris, 1978: transl. O. J. Zimmerman, *Fathers of the Church* 39, New York, 1959.

—— *Forty Gospel Homilies*: transl. D. Hurst, Kalamazoo, MI, 1990.

—— *Letters*, D. Norberg (ed.), *Corpus Christianorum* 140–140A, Turnhout, 1982.

—— *Moralia in Job*, M. Adriaen (ed.), *Corpus Christianorum* 143, 143A, 143B, Turnhout, 1979–85 and R. Gillet (ed.) *Grégoire le Grand: Morales sur Job, Sources chrétiennes*, 32 bis, Paris, 1975: transl., *Library of the Fathers*, Oxford, 1844–7.

—— *Pastoral Care* [*Regula Pastoralis*]: transl. H. Davis, *Ancient Christian Writers* 11. Westminster, MD, 1950 and R. Judic, *Grégoire le Grand: Règle pastorale, Sources chrétiennes* 381–2, Paris, 1992.

Gregory of Tours, *Glory of the Confessors*: transl. R. Van Dam, Liverpool, 1988

—— *Glory of the Martyrs*: transl. R. Van Dam, Liverpool, 1988.

—— *History*: transl. L. Thorpe, Harmondsworth, 1974.

—— *Lives of the Fathers*: transl. E. James, Liverpool, 1985.

—— *Miracles of Saint Julian*: transl. R. Van Dam, *Saints and their Miracles in Late Antique Gaul*, Princeton, NJ, 1993.

—— *Miracles of Saint Martin*: transl. R. Van Dam, *Saints and their Miracles in Late Antique Gaul*, Princeton, NJ, 1993.

Hilary of Arles, *Life of Saint Honoratus*: transl. F. R. Hoare, *The Western Fathers*, New York, 1954.

Historia Monachorum, Patrologia Latina 21.

History of Rabban Hormizd: transl. E. A. W. Budge, London, 1902.

History of the Patriarchs of Alexandria: transl. B. Evetts, *Patrologia Orientalis* 5.

Hodoeporicon of Willibald: transl. C. H. Talbot, *The Anglo-Saxon Missionaries in Germany*, London, 1954, and T. Head and T. F. X. Noble, *Soldiers of Christ*, University Park, PA, 1995.

Honorius, Pope, *Letters*: *Patrologia Latina* 80.

Hydatius, *Chronicle*: transl. R. W. Burgess, Oxford, 1993.

Ibn Ishaq, *Sîrat Rasûl Allâh: The Life of Muhammad*: transl. A. Guillaume, Oxford/ Lahore, 1955.

Index Superstitionum: transl. J. T. McNeill and H. A. Gamer, *Medieval Handbooks of Penance*, New York, 1990.

Inscriptiones christianae urbis Romae, Rome, 1964.

Isidore of Pelusium, *Letters*: *Patrologia Graeca* 78.

Isaac of Antioch, *Memra 8. On the Bird that Sung at Antioch*, G. Bickell (ed.), Giessen, 1873.

Jacob of Sarug, *On the Spectacles of the Theater*: transl. C. Moss, *Le Mouséon*, 48 (1935): 87–112.

John Lydus, *On the Magistracies of the Roman State*: transl. A. C. Bandy, Philadelphia, 1983.

John Moschus, *The Spiritual Meadow*: transl. J. Wortley, Kalamazoo, MI, 1992.

John of Damascus, *On Divine Images*: transl. D. Anderson, Crestwood, NY, 1980.

John of Ephesus, *Ecclesiastical History*: transl. R. Payne Smith, Oxford, 1860.

—— *Lives of the Eastern Saints*: transl. E. W. Brooks, *Patrologia Orientalis* 17.

John Rufus, *Plerophoriae*: *Patrologia Orientalis* 8.

John the Deacon, *Life of Gregory*: *Patrologia Latina* 75.

Jonas, *Life of Columbanus*: transl. E. Peters, *Monks, Bishops, and Pagans*, Philadelphia, 1981.

Julian of Toledo, *Prognosticon*, J. N. Hillgarth (ed.), *Corpus Christianorum* 115, Turnhout, 1975.

Justinian, *Novella* (536): R. Schöll and W. Kroll (eds.), Zurich, 1972.

—— *On the Person of Christ. The Christology of the Emperor Justinian*: transl. K. P. Wesche, Crestwood, NY, 1991.

Kontakia of Romanos, The: transl. M. Carpenter, 2 vols., Columbia, MO, 1970.

Lactantius, *Divine Institutes*: transl. M. F. McDonald, *Fathers of the Church* 49, Washington, DC, 1964.

Law of Innocents: transl. J. N. Hillgarth, *Christianity and Paganism 350–750. The Conversion of Western Europe*, Philadelphia, 1986.

Laws of Ethelbert: transl. D. Whitelock, *English Historical Documents* 1, Oxford, 1955.

Laws of Recceswinth: K. Zeumer (ed.), *Leges Visigothorum Antiquiores*, Hanover, 1894.

Laws of the Salian Franks, The: transl. K. F. Drew, Philadelphia, 1991.

Lebor Gabála Érenn: The Book of the Taking of Ireland: transl. R. A. S. McAlister, Dublin, 1970.

Leo, *Letters*: transl. C. L. Feltoe, *Library of the Nicene and Post-Nicene Fathers* 12, Oxford, 1895.

—— *Sermons*: transl. C. L. Feltoe, *Library of the Nicene and Post-Nicene Fathers* 12, Oxford, 1895.

Leontius, *Life of John the Almsgiver*: transl. N. H. Baynes and E. Dawes, *Three Byzantine Saints*, Oxford, 1948.

Letters of Pelagius and his Followers, transl. B. Rees, Woodbridge, Suffolk, 1991.

Liber Historiae Francorum: transl. A. C. Murray, *From Roman to Merovingian Gaul: A Reader*, Peterborough, Ontario, 2000.

Liber Pontificalis: transl. R. Davis, Liverpool, 1992.

Libri Carolini, A. Freeman and P. Meyvaert (eds.), *Monumenta Germaniae Historica. Concilia 2: Supplement 1*, Hanover, 1998; selected transl. C. Davis-Weyer, *Early Medieval Art*, Toronto, 1986, reprinted in P. Dutton, *Carolingian Civilization: A Reader*, Peterborough, Ontario, 1993.

Life of Ahudemmeh, *Patrologia Orientalis* 3.

Life of Audoin, Bishop of Rouen: transl. P. Fouracre and R. A. Geberding, *Late Merovingian France: History and Hagiography 640–720*, Manchester, 1996.

Life of Caesarius of Arles: transl. W. Klingshirn, Liverpool, 1994.

Life of Colman, C. Plummer (ed.), *Vitae Sanctorum Hiberniae*, vol. 1, Oxford, 1910.

Life of Corbinian, *Monumenta Germaniae Historica: Scriptores rerum Merovingicarum* 6, Hanover, 1977.

Life of Desiderius of Cahors, B. Krusch (ed), *Corpus Christianorum* 117, Turnhout, 1957.

Life of Enda, C. Plummer (ed.), *Vitae Sanctorum Hiberniae*, vol. 1, Oxford, 1910.

Life of Genovefa: transl. J. A. McNamara and J. Halborg, *Sainted Women of the Dark Ages*, Durham, NC, 1992.

Life of Gertrude: transl. J. A. McNamara and J. Halborg, *Sainted Women of the Dark Ages*, Durham, NC, 1992.

Life of Gregory the Great, The Earliest, B. Colgrave (ed.), Cambridge, 1985.

Life of Leo V, Patrologia Graeca 108: transl. C. Mango, *The Art of the Byzantine Empire*, Englewood Cliffs, NJ, 1972.

Life of Peter the Iberian: transl. R. Raabe, Leipzig, 1895.

Life of Symeon the Younger, P. Van den Ven (ed.), *La Vie ancienne de S. Syméon le Jeune*, Brussels, 1970: extracts transl. C. Mango, *The Art of the Byzantine Empire*, Englewood Cliffs, NJ, 1972.

Life of Wulfram of Sens, *Monumenta Germaniae Historica: Scriptores rerum Merovingicarum* 5, Hanover, 1977.

Lives of Simeon Stylites, The: transl. R. Doran, Kalamazoo, MI, 1992.

Lorsch Bee Spell, H. D. Schlosser (ed.), *Althochdeutsche Literatur*, Frankfurt, 1970.

Martryrology of Oengus, The: transl. W. Stokes, London, 1905.

Merseburg Spells, H. D. Schlosser (ed.), *Althochdeutsche Literatur*, Frankfurt, 1970.

Moses Korenats'i, *History of the Armenians*: transl. R. W. Thomson, Cambridge, MA, 1978.

Muirchú, *Life of Patrick*: transl. A .B. E. Hood, London, 1978.

Nennius, *British History*: transl. J. Morris, London, 1980.

Nestorius, *The Bazaar of Heracleides*: transl. G. Driver and L. Hodgson, Oxford, 1925.

Nicephorus of Constantinople, *Adversus iconomachos*: transl. M. J. Mondzain-Baudinet, *Nicéphorus. Discours contre les iconoclastes*, Paris, 1989.

Orosius, *History against the Pagans*: transl. I. W. Raymond, New York, 1936.

Oxyrhynchus Papyri, London, 1970.

Patricius, *Confessio*: transl. A. B. E. Hood, *St. Patrick: his writings and Muirchú's Life*, London, 1978 and D. R. Howlett, *The Book of Letters of Saint Patrick*, Dublin, 1994.

—— *Letter to Coroticus*: transl. A. B. E. Hood, *St. Patrick: His Writings and Muirchú's Life*, London, 1978.

Paulinus of Nola, *Letters*: transl. P. G. Walsh, *Ancient Christian Writers* 36, New York, 1966.

—— *Poems to Ausonius*: transl. H. G. Evelyn-White, *Ausonius* 2, Loeb Classical Library, London 1949.

Paulinus of Périgueux, *Life of Martin*, *Corpus Scriptorum Ecclesiasticorum Latinorum* 16, Vienna, 1888.

P'awstos Buzand, *The Epic Histories attributed to P'awstos Buzand*: transl. N. Garsoian, Cambridge, MA 1989.

Pelagius, *Commentary on Saint Paul's Epistle to the Romans*: transl. T. de Bruyn, Oxford, 1993.

Penitential of Cummian: transl. L. Bieler, *The Irish Penitentials*, Dublin, 1975.

Penitential of Finnian, transl. L. Bieler, *The Irish Penitentials*, Dublin, 1975.

Photius, *Homilies*: transl. C. Mango, Washington, DC, 1958, and C. Mango, *The Art of the Byzantine Empire*, Englewood Cliffs, NJ 1972.

Procopius, *On the Buildings*: transl. H. Dewing, *Procopius* 6, Loeb Classical Library, London, 1954, and C. Mango, *The Art of the Byzantine Empire*, Englewood Cliffs, NJ 1972.

—— *The Secret History*: transl. H. Dewing, *Procopius* 6, Loeb Classical Library, London, 1954, and G. A. Williamson, Harmondsworth, 1966.

—— *The Wars*: transl. H. Dewing, *Procopius* 1–5, Loeb Classical Library, London, 1954.

Prosper of Aquitaine, *The Call of All Nations*: transl. P. De Letter, *Ancient Christian Writers* 14, Westminster, MD, 1963.

Pseudo-Dionysius, *The Ecclesiastical Hierarchy*: transl. C. Luibheid, London, 1987.

Pseudo-Dionysius of Tell-Mahre, *Chronicle III, Part III*: transl. W. Witakowski, Liverpool, 1996 and A. Palmer, *The Seventh Century in the West Syrian Chronicles*, Liverpool, 1993.

Pseudo-Ephraim, *On Hermits and Desert-Dwellers*: transl. J. G. Amar and V. Wimbush (ed.), *Ascetic Behavior in Greco-Roman Antiquity*, Minneapolis, 1990.

Regions of the World, The: transl. V. Minorsky, Oxford, 1937.

Rimbert, *Life of Anskar*: transl. C. H. Robinson, London, 1921.

Roman Synod of 595, *Patrologia Latina* 77.

Royal Annals (Vienna Manuscript): transl. H. R. Loyn and J. Percival, *The Reign of Charlemagne*, London, 1975.

Rudolf of Fulda, *Life of Leoba*: transl. T. Head and T. F. X. Noble, *Soldiers of Christ*, University Park, PA, 1995, and C. H. Talbot, *The Anglo-Saxon Missionaries in Germany*, London, 1954.

—— *Translatio Sancti Alexandri*, *Monumenta Germaniae Historica: Scriptores* 2, Berlin, 1829.

Rule of Patrick, The: transl. *Ériu*, 1 (1904): 216–24.

Russian Primary Chronicle, The: transl. S. H. Cross and O. P. Sherbowitz-Wetzor, Cambridge, MA, 1953.

Saint-Simon, Duc de, *Historical Memoirs*: transl. L. Norton, London, 1967.

Second Council of Nicaea, G. D. Mansi (ed.), *Sacrorum conciliorum nova collectio* 13: transl. D. J. Sahas, *Icon and Logos: Sources in Eighth-Century Iconoclasm*, Toronto, 1988.

Senchas Már: transl. *Ancient Laws of Ireland*, vol. 3, Dublin, 1873.

Severus of Antioch, *Letters*: transl. E. W. Brooks, *Select Letters of Severus*, London, 1903.

Shenoute of Atripe, *Contra Origenistas*, T. Orlandi (ed.), Rome, 1985.

Shenoute of Atripe, *Letters*, J. Leipoldt (ed.), *Corpus Scriptorum Orientalium Christianorum*, 96 and *Scriptores Coptici* 8, Louvain, 1953.

Sidonius Apollinaris, *Letters*: transl. W. B. Anderson, Loeb Classical Library, London, 1965.

Snorri Sturluson, *The Prose Edda*: transl. A. Faulkes, London, 1987.

—— *Saga of Olaf Tryggvason: Heimskringla*: transl. L. M. Hollander, Austin, TX, 1964.

Stephen the Deacon, *Life of Stephen the Younger*: transl. M. F. Auzépy, *Vie d'Etienne le jeune par Etienne le diacre*, Aldershot, Hampshire, 1997.

Steven of Novgorod, *The Wanderer*: transl. G. P. Majeska, *Russian Travellers to Constantinople in the Fourteenth and Fifteenth Centuries*, Washington, DC, 1984.

Story of 'Adî ibn Zayd, the Poet of Hira: transl. I. Lichtenstadter, *Introduction to Classical Arabic Literature*, New York, 1976.

Sturlunga Saga: transl. J. McGrew, New York, 1970.

Sulpicius Severus, *Life of Martin, Letters and Dialogues*: transl. F. R. Hoare, *The Western Fathers*, New York, 1954, and T. Head and T. F. X. Noble, *Soldiers of Christ*, University Park, PA, 1995.

Symmachus, *Relatio*: transl. R. H. Barrow, *Prefect and Emperor*, Oxford, 1973.

Synod of Alexandria of 362, M. Tetz (ed.), *Zeitschrift für die neutestamentlichen Wissenschaft*, 79 (1988): 262–81.

Táin Bó Cúalnge from the Book of Leinster, C. O'Rahilly (ed.), Dublin, 1970: transl. T. Kinsella, Oxford, 1970.

Tertullian, *On Purity*: transl. W. Le Saint, *Ancient Christian Writers* 28, London, 1959.

Theodore Studites, *St. Theodore the Studite on the Holy Icons*: transl. C. P. Roth, Crestwood, NY, 1981.

Theodoret of Cyrrhus, *A Cure for Hellenic Illnesses*, P. Canivet (ed.), *Sources chrétiennes* 57, vol. 2, Paris, 1958.

—— *Ecclesiastical History*: transl. B. Jackson, *Library of the Nicene and Post-Nicene Fathers* 3, Oxford, 1893.

Theodulph, *First Capitulary*, P. Brommer (ed.), *Monumenta Germaniae Historica: Capitula Episcoporum*, Hanover, 1984: transl. P. E. Dutton, *Carolingian Civilization: A Reader*, Peterborough, Ontario, 1993.

Theophanes the Confessor, *Chronicle*: transl. C. Mango, Oxford, 1997, and extracts in his *Art of the Byzantine Empire 312–1453: Sources and Documents*, Englewood Cliffs, NJ, 1972.

Theophylact Simocatta, *Histories*: transl. M. and M. Whitby, Oxford, 1986.

Thomas of Marga, *The Book of the Governors*: transl. E. A. Wallis Budge, London, 1893.

Timothy, *Letters, Corpus Scriptorum Christianorum Orientalium 75: Scriptores Syrici* 31, Rome, 1915.

Tirechán, *Collectanea*: transl. L.Bieler, *The Patrician Texts in the Book of Armagh*, Dublin, 1979.

Translatio Sancti Liborii, G. H. Pertz (ed.), *Monumenta Germaniae Historica: Scriptores* 4, Hanover, 1841.

Tripartite Life of Saint Patrick: transl. W. Stokes, Rolls Series 89, London, 1887.

Vegetius, *Epitome of Military Science*: transl. N. P. Milner, Liverpool, 1993.

Venantius Fortunatus, *Life of Radegund*: transl. J. A. McNamara with J. Halborg and E. Whatley, *Sainted Women of the Dark Ages*, Durham, NC, 1992.

—— *Poems, Patrologia Latina* 88: transl. J. George, Liverpool, 1995.

Victor of Vita, *History of the Vandal Persecution*: transl. J. Moorhead, Liverpool, 1992.

Vienna Spell: H. D. Schlosser (ed.), *Althochdeutsche Literatur*, Frankfurt, 1970.

Vision of Barontus: transl. J. N. Hillgarth, *Christianity and Paganism 350–750. The Conversion of Western Europe*, Philadelphia, 1986.

Vision of Fursa [Fursey], C. Carozzi (ed.), *Le voyage de l'âme dans l'au-delà*, Collection de l'École française de Rome, 189, Rome, 1994.

Willibald, *Life of Boniface*: transl. T. F. X. Noble and T. Head, *Soldiers of Christ*, University Park, PA, 1995, and C. H. Talbot, *The Anglo-Saxon Missionaries in Germany*, London, 1954.

Zachariah of Mitylene, *Chronicle*: transl. F. J. Hamilton and E. W. Brooks, London, 1899.

Zosima the Deacon, *Xenos*: transl. G. P. Majeska, *Russian Travellers to Constantinople in the Fourteenth and Fifteenth Centuries*, Washington, DC, 1984.

Zosimus, *Historia Nova*: transl. R. T. Ridley, Brisbane, 1982.

Secondary Sources

Adalsteinsson, Jón Hnefill *Under the Cloak*, Uppsala, 1978.

Afinogenov, D. E., *Konstantinopol'ski Patriarkhat i ikonoborcheskii krizis v Vizantij*, Moscow, 1997.

Ahlqvist, A., *The Early Irish Linguist: An Edition of the Canonical Part of the Auraicept na néces*, Helsinki, 1983.

Allen, P., The definition and imposition of orthodoxy, in Averil Cameron, B. Ward-Perkins and M. Whitby (eds.), *The Cambridge Ancient History 14. Late Antiquity: Empire and Successors* A.D. *425–600*, Cambridge, 2000, pp. 811–34.

—— Severus of Antioch and the Homily: The end of the beginning?, in P. Allen and E. Jeffreys (eds.), *The Sixth Century. End or Beginning?*, Brisbane, 1996, pp. 163–75.

Amory, P., *People and Identity in Ostrogothic Italy 489–554*, Cambridge, 1997.

Ando, C., *Imperial Ideology and Provincial Loyalty in the Roman Empire*, Berkeley, CA, 2000.

Angenendt, A., *Das Frühmittelalter: die abendländische Christenheit von 400 bis 800*, 2nd edn., Stuttgart, 1995.
—— Theologie und Liturgie in der mittelalterlichen Toten-Memoria, in K. Schmid and J. Wollasch (eds.), *Memoria*, Munich, 1984, pp. 70–199.
Arrhenius, B., *Merovingian Garnet Jewelry. Origins and Social Implications*, Stockholm, 1985.
Armstrong, E. C. R. and Macalister, R. A. S., Wooden book found near Springmount Bog, Co. Antrim, *Journal of the Royal Society of Antiquaries of Ireland*, 50 (1920): 160–6.
Ashbrook Harvey, S., The Stylite's liturgy, *Journal of Early Christian Studies*, 6 (1998): 523–39.
—— *Asceticism and Society in Crisis. John of Ephesus and his "Lives of the Eastern Saints,"* Berkeley, CA, 1990.
Athanassiadi, P., Persecution and response in late paganism: the evidence of Damascius, *Journal of Hellenic Studies*, 113 (1993): 1–29.
Atsma, H. (ed.), *La Neustrie. Les pays au nord de la Loire de 650 à 850*, Sigmaringen, 1989.
Augenti, A., *Il Palatino nel Medio Evo: Archeologia e topografia (secoli VI–XIII)*, Rome, 1996.
Auzépy, M. F., De la Palestine à Constantinople (VIIIe–IXe siècles): Étienne le Sabaïte et Jean Damascène, *Travaux et Mémoires*, 12 (1994): 183–218.
Bagnall, R., Women, law, and social relations in Late Antiquity, *Bulletin of the American Society of Papyrologists*, 32 (1995): 65–86.
—— *Egypt in Late Antiquity*, Princeton, NJ, 1993.
Banniard, M., *Viva voce. Communication écrite et communication orale du IVe au IXe siècle en Occident latin*, Paris, 1992.
Barnes, T. D., *Athanasius and Constantius. Theology and Politics in the Constantinian Empire*, Cambridge, MA, 1993.
—— *Constantine and Eusebius*, Cambridge, MA, 1981.
Barnish, S. J. B., *Religio in Stagno*: Nature, Divinity and the Christianization of the countryside in Late Antique Italy, *Journal of Early Christian Studies*, 9 (2001): 387–402.
—— Christians and countrymen at San Vicenzo c.A.D. 400–550, in R. Hodges (ed.), *San Vicenzo al Volturno 2*, Oxford, 1995, pp. 131–7.
—— *Cassiodorus: Variae*, Liverpool, 1992.
—— The work of Cassiodorus after his conversion, *Latomus*, 48 (1989): 157–87.
—— Transformation and survival in the Western senatorial aristocracy, c.A.D. 400–700, *Papers of the British School at Rome*, 66 (1988): 120–55.
—— Pigs, plebeians and *potentes*: Rome's economic hinterland, c.350–500 A.D., *Papers of the British School at Rome* 65 (1987): 157–85
Bashear, S., *Arabs and Others in Early Islam*, Princeton, NJ, 1997.
—— Apocalyptic and other materials on early Muslim–Byzantine wars, *Journal of the Royal Asiatic Society*, ser. 3, 1 (1991): 173–207.
—— Qibla Musharriqa and Early Moslem Prayer in Christian Churches, *Muslim World*, 81 (1991): 268–82.
Bassett, S., *Historiae Custos*: sculpture and tradition in the Baths of Zeuxippos, *Ameri-*

can Journal of Archaeology,100 (1996): 491–506.

—— Antiquities in the Hippodrome of Constantinople, *Dumbarton Oaks Papers*, 45 (1991): 87–96.

Bassett, Steven (ed.),*The Origins of the Anglo-Saxon Kingdoms*, Leicester, 1989.

Baynes, N. H., Alexandria and Constantinople: a study in ecclesiastical diplomacy, in *Byzantine Studies and Other Essays*, London, 1955, pp. 97–115.

Beaucamp, J., *Le statut de la femme à Byzance (4e–7e siècle) 1: Le droit impérial*, Paris, 1990.

Beaujard, B., *Le culte des saints en Gaule. Les premiers temps. D'Hilaire de Poitiers à la fin du VIe siècle*, Paris, 2000.

Becher, M., *Rex, Dux und Gens: Untersuchungen zur Entstehung des sächsischen Herzogtums im 9. und 10. Jahrhundert*, Husum, 1996.

Beck, H. G., *Die Byzantiner und ihr Jenseits*, Sitzungsberichte der bayerischen Akademie der Wissenschaften, Philos.-hist. Klasse no.6, Munich, 1979.

Beeston, A. F. L., Johnstone, T. M., Serjeant, R. B., and Smith, G. R. (eds.), *Arabic Literature to the End of the Umayyad Period*, Cambridge, 1983.

Behr, C., The origins of kingship in early medieval Kent, *Early Medieval Europe*, 9 (2000): 25–52.

Bell, R., *A Commentary on the Qur'ân*, 2 vols., Manchester, 1991.

Belting, H., *Bild und Kunst. Eine Geschichte des Bildes vor der Zeitalter der Kunst*, Munich, 1990: transl. *Likeness and Presence. A History of the Image before the Era of Art*, Chicago, 1994.

Bieler, L., *The Irish Penitentials*, Dublin, 1975.

Binchy, D., The pseudo-historical prologue to the *Senchas Már*, *Studia Celtica*, 10–11 (1975–6): 15–28.

Bischoff, B. and Lapidge, M., *Biblical Commentaries from the Canterbury School of Theodore and Hadrian*, Cambridge, 1994.

Bitel, L. M., *Isle of Saints. Monastic Settlement and Christian Community in Early Ireland*, Ithaca, NY, 1990.

Blair, J., Anglo-Saxon minsters: a topographical review, in J. Blair and R. Sharpe (eds.), *Pastoral Care before the Parish*, Leicester, 1992, pp. 226–66.

Bland, R., and Johns, C., *The Hoxne Treasure*, London, 1993.

Boesch-Gajano, S., Gregorio I, in *Enciclopedia dei Papi 1*, Rome, 2000, pp.546–74.

—— Uso e abuso del miracolo nella cultura altomedievale, *Les fonctions des saints dans le monde occidental (IIIe–XIIIe siècle)*, Collection de l'École française de Rome 149, Rome, 1991, pp. 1109–22.

Boespflug, F. and Lossky, N., *Nicée II*, Paris, 1987.

Bóna, I., *Das Hunnenreich*, Budapest, 1991.

Bonner, G., *Famulus Christi*, London, 1976.

Bonner, M., *Aristocratic Violence and Holy War: Studies in the Jihad and the Arab–Byzantine frontier*, New Haven, CT, 1996.

Booth, P. A., King Alfred vs. Beowulf: the re-education of the Anglo-Saxon aristocracy, *Bulletin of the John Rylands Library*, 99 (1997): 41–66.

Boswell, J., *Expositio* and *Oblatio*: the abandonment of children and the ancient and medieval family, *American Historical Review*, 89 (1984): 10–33.

Bowersock, G. W., Les *Euémeroi* et les confréries joyeuses, *Comptes-Rendus de l'Académie des Inscriptions et Belles Lettres 1999*, pp. 1241–56.

—— *Martyrdom and Rome*, Cambridge, 1995.

Bowersock, G. W., Brown, P., and Grabar, O. (eds.), *Late Antiquity. A Guide to the Postclassical World*, Cambridge, MA, 1999.

Bowes, K., "Nec sedere in villam." Villa-churches, rural piety and the Priscillianist controversy, in T. S. Burns and J. W. Eadie (eds.), *Urban Functions and Rural Contexts in Late Antiquity*, East Lansing, MI, 2001, pp. 323–48.

Brandenburg, H., L'edificio monumentale sotto la chiesa di San Stefano Rotondo, in *Aurea Roma: dalla città pagana alla città cristiana: guida alla mostra*, Rome, 2001, pp. 200–3.

Bratož, R., *Severinus von Noricum und seine Zeit: geschichtliche Anmerkungen*, Vienna, 1983.

Braudel, F., *The Mediterranean and the Mediterranean World in the Age of Philip II*, transl. S. Reynolds, London, 1972.

Brenk, B., La cristianizzazione della Domus dei Valerii, in W. V. Harris (ed.), *The Transformations of Vrbs Roma in Late Antiquity, Journal of Roman Archaeology*, Supplement 33, Portsmouth, RI, 1999, pp. 69–84.

Brenk, F., *In Mist Apparelled. Religious Themes in Plutarch's Moralia and Lives*, Leiden, 1977.

Brennan, B., St. Radegund and the early development of her cult at Poitiers, *Journal of Religious History*, 13 (1984/5): 340–54.

Brock, S., Syriac culture, in Averil Cameron and Peter Garnsey (eds.), *The Cambridge Ancient History 13: The Late Empire* A.D. *337–425*, Cambridge, 1998, pp. 708–19.

—— The "Nestorian Church": a lamentable misnomer, *Bulletin of the John Rylands Library*, 79 (1996): 23–35.

—— The Syrian background, in M. Lapidge (ed.), *Archbishop Theodore*, Cambridge, 1995, pp. 30–53.

—— The Christology of the Church of the East in the Synods of the fifth to early seventh centuries, in G. Dagras (ed.), *Thyateira-Aksum. A Festschrift for Archbishop Methodios*, London, 1985, pp. 125–42, now in *Studies in Syrian Christianity*, London, 1992.

—— Northern Mesopotamia in the late seventh century: Book XV of John bar Penkâye's *Rish Mellê, Jerusalem Studies in Arabic and Islam*, 9 (1987): 51–75.

—— Christians in the Sasanian empire: a case of divided loyalties, in S. Meens (ed.), *Religion and National Identity*, Studies in Church History 18, Oxford, 1982, pp. 1–19.

—— From antagonism to assimilation: Syriac attitudes to Greek learning, in N. Garsoian, T. F. Mathews, and R. W. Thomson (eds.), *East of Byzantium: Syria and Armenia in the Formative Period*, Washington, DC, 1982, pp. 17–34.

Brooks, N., Canterbury, Rome and the construction of English identity, in J. M. H. Smith (ed.), *Early Medieval Rome and the Christian West. Essays in Honor of Donald Bullough*, Leiden, 2000, pp. 221–46.

Brown, P., *Augustine of Hippo. New Edition with an Epilogue*, London and Berkeley, CA, 2000.

—— *Authority and the Sacred. Aspects of the Christianization of the Roman World*,

Cambridge, 1995.

—— *Body and Society. Men, Women and Sexual Renunciation in Early Christianity*, New York, 1988.

—— Christianization and religious conflict, in Averil Cameron and P. Garnsey (eds.), *The Cambridge Ancient History 13. The Late Empire* A.D. *37–425*, Cambridge, 1998, pp. 632–64.

—— Conversion and Christianization in Late Antiquity: the case of Augustine, in R. Lim and C. Straw (eds.), *The World of Late Antiquity: The Challenge of New Historiographies*, Berkeley, CA, (forthcoming).

—— *The Cult of the Saints. Its Rise and Function in Latin Christianity*, Chicago, 1981.

—— The decline of the Empire of God: amnesty, penance and the afterlife from Late Antiquity to the early Middle Ages, in C. W. Bynum and P. Freedman (eds.), *Last Things. Death and Apocalyptic in the Middle Ages*, Philadelphia, 2000, pp. 41–59.

—— Enjoying the saints in Late Antiquity, *Early Medieval Europe*, 9 (2000): 1–24.

—— Gibbon's views on culture and society in the fifth and sixth centuries, *Daedalus*, 104 (1976): 73–88, now in *Society and the Holy in Late Antiquity*, Berkeley, CA, 1982, pp. 22–48.

—— *Gloriosus obitus*: the end of the ancient other world, in W. Klingshirn and M. Vessey (eds.), *The Limits of Ancient Christianity*, Ann Arbor, MI, 1999, pp. 289–314.

—— Henri Pirenne, *Mohammed and Charlemagne, Daedalus*, 103 (1974): 25–33, now in *Society and the Holy in Late Antiquity*, Berkeley, CA, 1982, pp. 63–79.

—— Holy Men, in Averil Cameron, B. Ward-Perkins, and M. Whitby (eds.), *The Cambridge Ancient History 14. Late Antiquity: Empire and Successors* A.D. *425–600*, Cambridge, 2000, pp. 781–810.

—— Images as a substitute for writing, in E. Chrysos and I. Wood, (eds.), *East and West: Modes of Communication*, Leiden, 1999, pp.15–34.

—— *Poverty and Leadership in the Later Roman Empire*, Hanover, NH, 2002.

—— *Power and Persuasion in Late Antiquity. Towards a Christian Empire*, Madison, WI, 1992.

—— The rise and function of the Holy Man, *Journal of Roman Studies*, 61 (1971): 80–101; now in *Society and the Holy in Late Antiquity*, Berkeley, CA, 1982, pp. 103–52.

—— The rise and function of the Holy Man in Late Antiquity: 1971–1997, *Journal of Early Christian Studies*, 6 (1998): 353–76.

—— The study of elites in Late Antiquity, *Arethusa*, 33 (2000): 321–46.

—— *The World of Late Antiquity: From Marcus Aurelius to Muhammad*, London, 1971 and 1989.

Brown, T. J., The oldest Irish manuscripts and their Late Antique background, in P. Ní Chatháin and M. Richter (eds.), *Irland und Europa*, Stuttgart, 1984, pp. 311–27.

Brown, T. S., *Gentlemen and Officers. Imperial Administration and Aristocratic Power in Byzantine Italy*, A.D. *554–800*, London, 1984.

Browning, R., *Justinian and Theodora*, London, 1987.

Brubaker, L., *Vision and Meaning in Ninth-Century Byzantium*, Cambridge, 1999.
—— Icons before Iconoclasm?, in *Morfologie sociali e culturali in Europa tra Tarda Antichità e Alto Medio Evo*, Settimane di Studio sull'Alto Medio Evo 45, Spoleto, 1998, pp. 1215–54.
Brubaker, L. amd Haldon, J., *Byzantium in the Iconoclast Era (ca. 680–850): The Sources, an Analytic Survey*. Aldershot, 2001.
Bryce, J., *The Holy Roman Empire*, London, 1904.
Bullough, D., The career of Columbanus, in M. Lapidge (ed.), *Columbanus. Studies on the Latin Writings*, Woodbridge, Suffolk, 1997, pp. 1–28.
—— *Friends, Neighbours and Fellow-Drinkers. Aspects of Community and Conflict in the Early Medieval West*, H. M. Chadwick Lectures 1, Cambridge, 1990.
—— Burial, community and belief in the Early Medieval West, in P. Wormald (ed.), *Ideal and Reality in Frankish and Anglo-Saxon Society*, Oxford, 1983, pp. 177–201.
Burnell, S. and James, E., The archaeology of conversion in the sixth and seventh centuries, in R. Gameson (ed.), *St. Augustine and the Conversion of England*, Stroud, Gloucestershire, 1999, pp. 83–106.
Butler, E. M., Late Roman Town walls in Gaul, *Archaeological Journal*, 126 (1959): 25–50.
Cahill, T., *How the Irish Saved Civilisation*, New York, 1995.
Caillet, J. P., *L'évergétisme monumental chrétien en Italie*, Rome, 1993.
Cameron, Alan, *Circus Factions. Blues and Greens at Rome and Byzantium*, Oxford, 1976.
Cameron, Averil, Cassiodorus deflated, *Journal of Roman Studies*, 71 (1981): 183–6.
—— *Christianity and the Rhetoric of Empire. The Development of Christian Discourse*, Berkeley, CA, 1991.
—— Disputations, polemical literature and the formation of opinion in the early Byzantine period, in G. J. Reinink and H. L. J. Vanstiphout (eds.), *Dispute Poems and Dialogues in the Ancient and Medieval Near East*, Louvain, 1991, pp. 91–108.
—— Gelimer's laughter: the case of Byzantine Africa, in F. M. Clover and R. S. Humphreys (eds.), *Tradition and Innovation in Late Antiquity*, Madison, WI, 1989, pp. 171–90.
—— Images of authority: elites and icons in late sixth-century Byzantium, *Past and Present*, 84 (1979): 3–35.
—— Justin I and Justinian, in Averil Cameron, B. Ward-Perkins, and M. Whitby (eds.), *The Cambridge Ancient History 14. Late Antiquity: Empire and Successors* A.D. *425–600*, Cambridge, 2000, pp. 63–85.
—— The language of images: the rise of icons and Christian representation, in D. Wood (ed.), *The Church and the Arts*, Studies in Church History 28, Oxford, 1992, pp. 1–42.
—— *Procopius and the Sixth Century*, Berkeley, CA, 1985.
Cameron, Averil and Herrin, J., *Constantinople in the Early Eighth Century*, Leiden, 1984.
Campbell, J., Elements in the background to the Life of St. Cuthbert and his early cult, in G. Bonner, D. Rollason, and C. Stancliffe (eds.), *St. Cuthbert, his Cult and*

his Community to A.D. *1200*, Woodbridge, Suffolk, 1989, pp. 3–19.

Camps, G., Rex Gentium Maurorum et Romanorum. Recherches sur les royaumes de Maurétanie des VIe et VIIe siècles, *Antiquités africaines*, 20 (1984): 183–218.

Carelli, P., Thunder and lightning, magical miracles. On the popular myth of thunderbolts and the presence of Stone-Age artifacts in medieval deposits, in *Visions of the Past. Trends and Traditions in Swedish Medieval Archaeology*, Lund Studies in Medieval Archaeology 19, Lund, 1997, pp. 393–417.

Carey, J., Native elements in Irish pseudo-history, in D. Edel (ed.), *Cultural Identity and Cultural Integration. Ireland and Europe in the Early Middle Ages*, Dublin, 1995, pp. 45–60.

—— Ireland and the Antipodes, *Speculum*, 64 (1989): 1–10.

Carozzi, C., *Le voyage de l'âme dans l'au-delà*, Collection de l'École française de Rome, 189, Rome, 1994.

Carrié, J. M., Dioclétien et la fiscalité, *Antiquité tardive*, 2 (1994): 33–64.

Carrié, J. M. and Rousselle, A., *L'Empire romain en mutation des Sévères à Constantin 192–337*, Paris, 1999.

Carroll, C., The bishops in Saxony in the first century after Christianization, *Early Medieval Europe*, 8 (1999): 219–45.

Carver, M., Conversion and politics on the eastern seaboard of Britain: some archaeological indications, in B. E. Crawford (ed.), *Conversion and Christianization in the North Sea*, St. Andrews, 1998, pp. 11–40.

Carver, M. (ed.), *The Age of Sutton Hoo. The Seventh Century in Northwestern Europe*, Woodbridge, Suffolk, 1982.

Caseau, B., Christian bodies: the senses and early Byzantine Christianity, in Liz James (ed.), *Desire and Denial in Byzantium*, Aldershot, 1999, pp. 101–9.

—— Sacred landscapes, in G. W. Bowersock, P. Brown, and O. Grabar (eds.), *Late Antiquity. A Guide to the Postclassical World*, Cambridge, MA, 1999, pp. 21–59.

Cassiday B. (ed.), *The Ruthwell Cross*, Princeton, NJ, 1992.

Cavadini, John C., *The Last Christology of the West. Adoptionism in Spain and Gaul, 785–820*, Philadelphia, 1993.

Chadwick, H., *Boethius. The Consolations of Music, Logic, Theology, and Philosophy*, Oxford, 1981.

—— Eucharist and Christology in the Nestorian controversy, *Journal of Theological Studies*, NS 2 (1951): 145–64.

—— Preface, *Actes du Concile de Chalcédoine. Sessions III–VI*: transl. A. J. Festugière, Geneva, 1982, pp. 7–16.

—— Theodore, the English Church and the Monothelite controversy, in M. Lapidge (ed.), *Archbishop Theodore. Commemorative Studies on his Life and Influence*, Cambridge, 1994, pp. 88–95.

Charles-Edwards, T. M., *Early Christian Ireland*, Cambridge, 2000.

—— The penitential of Columbanus, in M. Lapidge (ed.), *Columbanus: Studies on the Latin Writings*, Woodbridge, Suffolk, 1997, pp. 217–39.

—— The Penitentials of Theodore and the *Iudicia Theodori*, in M. Lapidge (ed.), *Archbishop Theodore. Commemorative Studies on his Life and Influence*, Cambridge, 1994, pp. 141–74.

—— The social background to Irish *Peregrinatio*, *Celtica*, 11 (1976): 43–59.

Chazelle, C., *The Crucified God in the Carolingian Era. Theology and Art of Christ's Passion*, Cambridge, 2001.

—— Matter, Spirit and image in the *Libri Carolini*, *Recherches augustiniennes*, 21 (1986): 163–84.

Chekalova, A., *Konstantinopol' v vi veke. Vosstanie Nika*, Moscow, 1986.

Chitty, D., *The Desert a City*, Oxford, 1966.

Chuvin, P., *A Chronicle of the Last Pagans*, Cambridge, MA, 1990.

Chwolson, Syrische Grabinschriften aus Semirjetschie, *Mémoires de l'Académie impériale de Saint Pétersbourg*, 7 ser. 34 (1886), no. 4, pp. 14–15.

Clarke, H. B. and Brennan, M. (eds.), *Columbanus and Merovingian Monasticism*, Oxford, 1981.

Claude, D., *Die byzantinische Stadt im 6. Jht.* Munich, 1969.

Coates, S., Venantius Fortunatus and the image of episcopal authority in Late Antique and early medieval Gaul, *English Historical Review*, 115 (2000): 1109–37.

Collins, R., *Charlemagne*, London, 1998.

—— *Early Medieval Europe 300–1000*, New York, 1991.

—— *Early Medieval Spain. Unity in Diversity, 400–1000*, London, 1983.

Conrad, L., The Arabs, in Averil Cameron, B. Ward-Perkins, and M. Whitby (eds.), *The Cambridge Ancient History 14. Late Antiquity: Empire and Successors* A.D.*425–600*, Cambridge, 2000, pp. 678–700.

—— Epidemic disease in central Syria in the late sixth century, *Modern Greek and Byzantine Studies*, 18 (1994): 12–58.

—— Varietas Syriaca: secular and scientific culture in the Christian communities after the Arab conquest, in G. J. Reinink and A. C. Klugkist (eds.), *After Bardaisan. Studies in Continuity and Change in Syriac Christianity in Honour of H. J. W. Drijvers*, Louvain, 1999, pp. 85–105.

Conrad, L. (ed.), *Trade and Exchange in the Late Antique and Early Islamic Near East*, Princeton, NJ (forthcoming).

Constable, G., *Monastic Tithes from their Origins to the Twelfth Century*, Cambridge, MA, 1964.

Corcoran, S., *The Empire of the Tetrarchs: Imperial Pronouncements and Government, A.D. 284–324*, Oxford, 1996.

Cormack, R., *Painting the Soul: Icons, Death Masks and Shrouds*, London, 1997.

Costambeys, M., An Austrasian aristocracy on the northern Frankish frontier, *Early Medieval Europe*, 3 (1994): 39–62.

Coupland, S., Money and coinage under Louis the Pious, *Francia*, 17:1 (1990): 23–34.

Courtois C., and Leschi, L., *Les Tablettes Albertini*, Paris, 1952.

Cracco, G., Grégoire le Grand, un christianisme renouvelé, *Antiquité tardive*, 7, (1999): 215–29.

Cresswell, K. A., *Early Muslim Architecture*, Harmondsworth, 1958.

Crone, P., *The Meccan Trade and the Rise of Islam*, Oxford, 1987.

—— Tribes and states: the nomadic exception, in J. A. Hall (ed.), *States in History*, Oxford, 1986, pp. 68–77.

Crum, W. E. and Evelyn-White, H. G., *The Monastery of Epiphanius 2*, New York, 1926.

Cubitt, C., Sites and sacrality: revisiting the cult of murdered and martyred Anglo-Saxon royal saints, *Early Medieval Europe*, 9 (2000): 58–83.

Cunliffe, B., *Facing the Ocean: The Atlantic and its Peoples 8000 BC–AD 1500*, Oxford, 2001.

Curran, J. R., *Pagan City and Christian Capital. Rome in the Fourth Century*, Oxford, 2000.

Dagens, C., *Grégoire le Grand. Culture et expérience chrétienne*, Paris, 1977.

Dagron, G., *Empereur et Prêtre. Etudes sur le "césaropapisme" byzantin*, Paris, 1996.

—— *Naissance d'une capitale: Constantinople et ses institutions de 330 à 451*, Paris, 1974.

—— L'organisation et le déroulement des courses d'après le *Livre des Cérémonies*, *Travaux et Mémoires* 13 (2000): 3–180.

—— La perception d'une différence: les débuts de la "Querelle du purgatoire," in *15e Congrès international des Études byzantines: Actes* 4, Athens, 1976, pp. 84–92.

Damminger, F., Dwellings, settlements and settlement patterns in Merovingian southwest Germany and adjacent areas, in I. Wood (ed.), *Franks and Alemanni in the Merovingian Period. An Ethnographic Perspective*, San Marino, CA, 1998, pp. 33–106.

Dark, K. R., *Civitas to Kingdom. British Political Continuity 300–800*, Leicester, 1994.

Davies, W., *Wales in the Early Middle Ages*, Leicester, 1982.

Dawson, C., *The Making of Europe. An Introduction to the History of European Unity*, London, 1932.

Décobert, F., *Le Mendiant et le combattant. L'Institution de l'Islam*, Paris, 1991.

De Jong, M., Carolingian monasticism: the power of prayer, in R. McKitterick (ed.), *The New Cambridge Medieval History 2: c.700–c.900*, Cambridge, 1995, pp. 622–53.

—— *In Samuel's Image. Child Oblation in the Early Medieval West*, Leiden, 1996.

—— Religion, R. McKitterick (ed.), *The Early Middle Ages*, Oxford, 2001, pp.131–64.

—— Rethinking early medieval Christianity: a view from the Netherlands, *Early Medieval Europe*, 7 (1998): 261–76.

—— Transformations of Penance, in F. Theuws and J.L. Nelson, *Rituals of Power. From Late Antiquity to the Early Middle Ages*, Leiden, 2000, pp.185–224.

—— An unresolved riddle: early medieval incest legislation, in I. Wood (ed.), *Franks and Alemanni in the Merovingian Period. An Ethnographic Perspective*, San Marino, CA, 1998, pp.107–40.

Delierneux, N., Arculfe, *sanctus episcopus gente Gallus*: une existence historique discutable, *Revue belge de philologie et d'histoire*, 75 (1995): 911–41.

Dell'Omo, M., *Montecassino. Un'abbazia nella storia*, Monte Cassino, 1999.

Delogu, P., The papacy, Rome and the wider world in the seventh and eighth centuries, in J. M. H. Smith (ed.), *Early Medieval Rome and the Christian West. Essays in Honour of Donald A. Bullough*, Leiden, 2000, pp. 197–220.

—— Reading Pirenne again, in R. Hodges and W. Bowden (eds.), *The Sixth Century. Production, Distribution and Demand*, Leiden, 1998, pp. 15–40.

—— La storia economica di Roma nell'alto Medio Evo, in L. Paroli and P. Delogu (eds.), *La storia economica di Roma nell'alto Medio Evo alla luce dei recenti scavi archeologici*, Florence, 1993, pp. 11–29.

De Nie, G., *Views from a Many-Windowed Tower. Studies of Imagination in the Works of Gregory of Tours*, Amsterdam, 1987.

Dennett, D., *Conversion and the Poll-Tax in Early Islam*, Cambridge, MA, 1950.

Déroche, V., *Études sur Léontios de Néapolis*, Uppsala, 1995.

—— Léontios de Néapolis, *Apologie contre les Juifs, Travaux et Mémoires*, 12 (1994): 43–104.

Devroey, J. P., Economy, in R. McKitterick (ed.), *The Early Middle Ages*, Oxford, 2001, pp. 97–129.

Diaz, P. and Valverde, M. R., The theoretial strength and practical weakness of the Visigothic monarchy of Toledo, in F. Theuws and J. L. Nelson (eds.), *Rituals of Power. From Late Antiquity to the Early Middle Ages*, Leiden, 2000, pp. 59–94.

Diehl, E., *Inscriptiones latinae christianae veteres*, 3 vols., Zurich, 1970.

Diem, A., *Keusch und Rein*, Amsterdam, 2000.

Dierkens, A., La christianisation des campagnes dans l'empire de Louis le Pieux. L'exemple du diocèse de Liège sous l'épiscopat de Walcaud (*c*.809–*c*.831), in P. Godman and R. Collins (eds.), *Charlemagne's Heir. New Perspectives on the Reign of Louis the Pious (814–830)*, Oxford, 1990, pp. 309–329.

Dodwell, C. R., *Anglo-Saxon Art: A New Perspective*, Manchester, 1984.

Doherty, C., The monastic town in early medieval Ireland, in H. B. Clarke and A. Simms (eds.), *Comparative History of Urban Origins in Non-Roman Europe*, Oxford, 1985, pp. 45–75

Donahue, C., Beowulf, Ireland and the natural good, *Traditio*, 7 (1949–51): 263–77.

Donceel-Voûte, P., *Les pavements des églises byzantines de Syrie et du Liban*, Louvain, 1988.

Donner, F. M., *The Early Islamic Conquests*, Princeton, NJ, 1981.

—— *Narratives of Islamic Origins. The Beginnings of Islamic Historical Traditions*, Princeton, NJ, 1999.

Drake, F. S., Nestorian monasteries of the T'ang dynasty, *Monumenta Serica*, 2 (1936/7): 293–340.

Drake, H. A., *Constantine and the Bishops*, Baltimore, MD, 2000.

Draz, M. A., *Introduction to the Qur'ân*, London, 2000.

Drijvers, H. J. W., The School of Edessa. in Greek learning and local culture, in J. W. Drijvers and A. A. MacDonald (eds.), *Centres of Learning. Learning and Location in Pre-Modern Europe and the Near East*, Leiden, 1995, pp. 49–59.

Drinkwater, J., *The Gallic Empire. Separation and Continuity in the North-Western Provinces of the Roman Empire*, A.D. 260–274, Stuttgart, 1987.

Driscoll, M., *Alcuin et la pénitence à l'époque carolingienne*, Münster in Westfalen, 1999.

Dumville, D., The Anglian collection of royal genealogies, *Anglo-Saxon England*, 5 (1976): 23–50.

—— The idea of government in sub-Roman Britain, in G. Ausenda (ed.), *After Empire. Towards an Ethnography of Europe's Barbarians*, Woodbridge, Suffolk, 1995, pp. 177–216.

—— The importation of Mediterranean manuscripts into Theodore's England, in M. Lapidge (ed.), *Archbishop Theodore. Commemorative Studies on his Life and Influence*, Cambridge, 1994, pp.96–119.

Dunn, M., *The Emergence of Monasticism: From the Desert Fathers to the Early Middle Ages*, Oxford, 2000.

Duri, A. A., *The Rise of Historical Writing among the Arabs*, Princeton, NJ, 1983.

Durliat, J., *Les dédicaces d'ouvrages de défense dans l'Afrique byzantine*, Collection de l'École française de Rome, 49, Rome, 1981.

Dutton, P. E., *Charlemagne's Courtier. The Complete Einhard*, Peterborough, Ontario, 1998.

—— Thunder and hail over the Carolingian countryside, in D. Sweeney (ed.), *Agriculture in the Middle Ages*, Philadelphia, 1995, pp. 111–37.

Duval, Y., *Auprès des saints corps et âme. L'inhumation ad sanctos dans la chrétienté d'Orient et d'Occident du IIIe au VIIe siècle*, Paris, 1988.

Duval, Y. M., La dissension entre l'apocrisaire Grégoire et le patriarche Eutychius au sujet de la résurrection de la chair: arrière-plan doctrinal oriental et occidental, in J. Fontaine, R. Gillet, and S. Pellistrandi (eds.), *Grégoire le Grand*, Paris, 1986, pp. 347–66.

Edwards, C., German vernacular literature: a survey, in R. McKitterick (ed.), *Carolingian Culture: Emulation and Innovation*, Cambridge, 1994, pp. 141–70.

Effros, B., *De partibus Saxoniae* and the regulation of mortuary custom. A Carolingian campaign of Christianization or the suppression of Saxon identity?, *Revue belge de philologie et d'histoire*, 75 (1995): 267–86.

—— Monuments and memory: repossessing ancient ruins in early medieval Gaul, in M. de Jong and F. Theuws with C. van Rhijn (eds.), *Topographies of Power in the Early Middle Ages*, Leiden, 2001, pp. 93–118.

Enright, M., *Iona, Tara and Soissons*, Berlin, 1985.

—— *The Lady with the Mead Cup. Ritual, Prophecy and Lordship in the European Warband from La Tène to the Vikings*, Dublin, 1996, pp. 68–168.

Esbroeck, M. van, Le manuscrit hébreu Paris 755 et l'Histoire des Martyrs du Nedjran, in P. Canivet and J. P. Rey-Coquais (eds.), *La Syrie de Byzance à l'Islam*, Damascus, 1992, pp. 25–30.

Escolan, P., *Monachisme et église: le monachisme syrien du IVe au VIIe siècle: un ministère charismatique*, Paris, 1999.

Esmonde-Cleary, A. S., *The Ending of Roman Britain*, London, 1989.

Etchingham, C., *Church Organization in Ireland* A.D. *650–1000*, Maynooth, 1999.

Ettinghausen, R., *From Byzantium to Sasanian Iran and the Islamic World*, London, 1972.

Evans-Grubbs, J., *Law and Family in Late Antiquity. The Emperor Constantine's Marriage Legislation*, Oxford, 1995.

Faith, R., *The English Peasantry and the Growth of Lordship*, London, 1997.

Feissel D., and Kaygusuz, I., Un Mandement impérial du VIème siècle dans une inscription d'Hadrianoupolis d'Honoriade, *Travaux et Mémoires*, 9 (1985): 397–419.

Ferguson, E., *Demonology of the Early Christian World*, New York, 1984.

Ferguson, E. (ed.), *Encyclopedia of Early Christianity*, New York, 1990.

Février, P. A., La mort chrétienne, in *Segni e riti nella chiesa altomedievale occidentale*, Settimane di Studio sull'Alto Medioevo 33, Spoleto, 1987, pp. 881–942.

Fiey, J.M., *Les communautés chrétiennes en Irak et Iran*, London, 1979.

Fleckenstein, J., *Die Hofkapelle der deutschen Königen 1*, Stuttgart, 1959.

Fletcher, R., *The Conversion of Europe. From Paganism to Christianity 371–1386 A.D.* , London, 1998.

Flint, V., *The Rise of Magic in Early Medieval Europe*, Princeton, NJ, 1991.

Flusin, B., *Anastase le Perse*, vol. 2, Paris, 1992.

—— Démons et sarrasins, *Travaux et Mémoires*, 11 (1991): 381–409.

—— *Miracle et histoire dans l'oeuvre de Cyrille de Scythopolis*, Paris, 1983.

Fögen, M.T., *Die Enteignung der Wahrsager. Studien zur kaiserlichen Wissenschaftsmonopol in der Spätantike*, Frankfurt-am-Main, 1993.

Folz, R., *The Coronation of Charlemagne*, London, 1974.

Fontaine, J., *Isidore de Séville et la culture classique dans l'Espagne wisigothique*, 2nd edn., Paris, 1983.

Foss, C., The Near Eastern countryside in late antiquity: a review article, *Journal of Roman Archaeology*, Supplement 14, Portsmouth, RI, 1995, pp. 213–34.

—— Syria in transition, A.D. 550–750: an archeological approach, *Dumbarton Oaks Papers*, 51 (1997): 189–269.

Fouracre, P., *The Age of Charles Martel*, Harlow, Essex, 2000.

—— Attitudes towards violence in seventh and eighth century Francia, in G. Halsall (ed.), *Violence and Society in the Early Medieval West*, Woodbridge, Suffolk, 1998, pp. 60–75.

—— Eternal light and earthly needs: practical aspects of the development of Frankish immunities, in W. Davies and P. Fouracre (eds.), *Property and Power in the Early Middle Ages*, Cambridge, 1995, pp. 53–81.

—— Frankish Gaul to 814, in R. McKitterick (ed.), *The New Cambridge Medieval History 2: c.700–c.900*, Cambridge, 1995, pp. 85–109.

—— "Placita" and the settlement of disputes in later Merovingian Francia, in W. Davies and P. Fouracre (eds.), *The Settlement of Disputes in Early Medieval Europe*, Cambridge, 1986, pp. 23–44.

Fouracre, P. and Geberding, R. A., *Late Merovingian France: History and Hagiography, 640–720*, Manchester, 1996.

Fowden, G., *Empire to Commonwealth. Consequences of Monotheism in Late Antiquity*, Princeton, NJ, 1993.

—— Polytheist religion and philosophy, in Averil Cameron and Peter Garnsey (eds.), *The Cambridge Ancient History 13. The Late Empire A.D. 337–425*, Cambridge, 1998, pp. 538–60.

Frank, R., Germanic legend in Old English literature, in M. Godden and M. Lapidge (eds.), *Cambridge Companion to Old English Literature*, Cambridge, 1991, pp. 88–106

Frankfurter, D., *Religion in Egypt. Assimilation and Resistance*, Princeton, NJ, 1998.

Franklin, S., and Shepard, J., *The Emergence of Rus 750–1200*, London, 1996.

Frede, M., Monotheism and pagan philosophy in Late Antiquity, in M. Frede and P. Athanassiadi (eds.), *Pagan Monotheism in Late Antiquity*, Oxford, 1999, pp. 41–64.

Freeman, A. and Meyvaert, P., The meaning of Theodulph's apse at Germigny-des-Prés, *Gesta*, 40 (2001): 125–39.

Frend, W. H. C., *The Rise of the Monophysite Movement*, Cambridge, 1972.

Ganz, D., Book production in the Carolingian empire and the spread of Caroline minuscule, in R. McKitterick (ed.), *The New Cambridge Medieval History 2: c.700–c.900*, Cambridge, 1995, pp. 786–808.

―― Bureaucratic shorthand and merovingian learning, in P. Wormald (ed.), *Ideal and Reality in Frankish and Anglo-Saxon Society*, Oxford, 1983, pp. 58–75.

―― The preconditions of Carolingian minuscule, *Viator*, 18 (1987): 23–43.

Gardner, M. F., and Lieu, S. N. C., From Narmouthis (Medinet Madi) to Kellis (Ismant al-Kharab), *Journal of Roman Studies*, 86 (1996): 146–69.

Garnsey, P. and Humfress, C., *The Evolution of the Late Antique World*, Cambridge, 2000.

Garnsey, P. and Saller, R., *The Roman Empire. Economy, Society, Culture*, London, 1987.

Garrison, M., The Collectanea and medieval florilegia, in M. Bayless and M. Lapidge (eds.), *Collectanea Pseudo-Bedae*, Dublin, 1998, pp. 42–83.

―― The Franks as the New Israel? Education for an identity from Pippin to Charlemagne, in Y.Hen and M. Innes (eds.), *The Uses of the Past in the Early Middle Ages*, Cambridge, 2000, pp. 114–61.

―― "Send more socks." On mentalities and the preservation context of medieval letters, in M. Mostert (ed.), *New Approaches to Medieval Communication*, Turnhout, 1999, pp. 69–99.

―― The social world of Alcuin. Nicknames at York and at the Carolingian court, in L. Houwen and A. MacDonald (eds.), *Alcuin of York. Scholar at the Carolingian Court*, Groningen, 1998, pp. 59–79.

Garsoian, N., *Armenia between Byzantium and the Sasanians*, Aldershot, 1985.

―― *L'Église arménienne et le grand schisme d'Orient*, Corpus Scriptorum Christianorum Orientalium 574, Louvain, 1999.

―― The two voices of Armenian historiography: the Iranian Index, *Studia Iranica*, 25 (1996): 7–43, now in *Church and Culture in Medieval Armenia*, Aldershot, 1999.

Gatier, P. L., Nouvelles inscriptions de Gérasa: la prison de l'évêque Paul, *Syria*, 62 (1982): 297–305.

―― Les villages du Proche-Orient protobyzantin (4ème–7ème s.). Étude régionale, in G. R. D. King and Averil Cameron (eds.), *The Byzantine and Early Islamic Near East 2: Land Use and Settlement Patterns*, Princeton, NJ, 1994, pp. 17–48.

Gauthier, N., Le réseau de pouvoirs de l'évêque dans la Gaule du haut moyen âge, in G. P. Brogiolo. N. Gauthier, and N. Christie (eds.), *Towns and their Territories between Late Antiquity and the Early Middle Ages*, Leiden, 2000, pp. 173–207.

Gawlikowski, M., Un nouveau mithraeum récemment découvert à Huarte près d'Apamée, *Comptes rendus de l'Académie d'Inscriptions et Belles Lettres*, janvier–mars 2000, pp. 161–71.

Geary, P., *The Myth of Nations. The Peoples of Europe in the Early Middle Ages*, Princeton, NJ, 2001.

Geberding, R. A., *The Rise of the Carolingians and the Liber Historiae Francorum*,

Oxford, 1987.

Genser, K., *Der österreichische Donaulimes in der Römerzeit*, Vienna, 1986.

George, J. W., *Venantius Fortunatus: Personal and Political Poems*, Liverpool, 1995.

—— *Venantius Fortunatus. A Poet in Merovingian Gaul*, Oxford, 1997.

Gero, S., *Barsauma of Nisibis and Persian Christianity in the Fifth Century*, Corpus Scriptorum Christianorum Orientalium 426, Louvain, 1981.

Gervers, M. and Bikhazi, R. J. (eds.), *Conversion and Continuity. Indigenous Christian Communities in Islamic Lands*, Toronto, 1990.

Gibson, M. (ed.), *Boethius. His Life, Thought and Influence*, Oxford, 1981.

Gignoux, P., Sceaux chrétiens d'époque sasanide, *Iranica Antiqua*, 15 (1980): 299–314.

Gillett, A., Rome, Ravenna and the last Western emperors, *Papers of the British School at Rome*, 69 (2001): 131–67.

Gillman, I. and Klimkeit, H. J., *Christians in Asia before 1500*, Richmond, Surrey, 1999.

Giuliani, E. and Pavolini, C., La "Biblioteca di Agapito", in W. V. Harris (ed.), *The Transformations of Vrbs Roma in Late Antiquity*, Journal of Roman Archaeology, Supplement 33, Portsmouth, RI, 1999, pp. 85–107.

Glaser, F., Eine weitere Doppelkirchenanlage auf dem Hemmaberg, *Carinthia I*, 183 (1993): 165–86.

—— *Das frühchristliche Pilgerheiligtum auf dem Hemmaberg*, Klagenfurt, 1991.

Goffart, W., *The Narrators of Barbarian History*, Princeton, NJ, 1988.

—— *Romans and Barbarians: Techniques of Accommodation* A.D. *418–584*, Princeton, NJ, 1980.

Goitein, S., A plea for the periodization of Islamic history, *Journal of the American Oriental Society*, 88 (1968): 224–8.

Goldberg, E. J., The *Stellinga* Revisited, *Speculum*, 70 (1995): 467–501.

Grabar, A., *L'iconoclasme byzantin. Le dossier archéologique*, Paris, 1984.

Grabar, O., *The Formation of Islamic Art*, New Haven, CT, 1973.

—— *Mediation of Ornament*, Princeton, NJ, 1992.

—— *The Shape of the Holy. Early Islamic Jerusalem*, Princeton, NJ, 1996.

Gray, P. T. and Herren, M., Columbanus and the Three Chapters controversy, *Journal of Theological Studies*, NS 45 (1994): 160–70.

Greatrex, G., The Nika riot. a reappraisal, *Journal of Hellenic Studies*, 117 (1997): 60–86.

Green, D. H., *The Carolingian Lord*, Cambridge, 1965.

—— *Medieval Literacy and Reading. The Primary Reception of German Literature 800–1300*, Cambridge, 1994.

Griffith, S. H., Habib ibn Hidmah al Ra'itah, a Christian mutakallim, *Oriens Christianus*, 64 (1980): 161–201.

—— Images, Islam and Christian Icons. A moment in the Christian-Muslim encounter in early Islamic times, in P. Canivet and J. P. Rey-Coquais (eds.), *La Syrie de Byzance à l'Islam*, Damascus, 1992, pp. 121–38.

—— Theodore abu Qurrah's Arabic text on the Christian practice of venerating images, *Journal of the American Oriental Society*, 105 (1985): 53–73.

Groenman-van Waateringe, W., Food for soldiers, food for thought, in J. C. Barrett (ed.), *Barbarians and Romans in North West Europe*, Oxford, 1989, pp. 96–107.

Gropp, G., Die Pahlavi-Inschrift auf dem Thomas-Kreuz in Madras, *Archäologische Mitteilungen aus Iran*, 3 (1970): 267–71.

Grosdidier de Matons, J., *Romanos le Mélode et les origines de la poésie religieuse à Byzance*, Paris, 1977.

Gurevich, A., *Historical Anthropology of the Middle Ages*, Cambridge, 1992.

Gutas, D., *Greek Thought, Arabic Culture. The Greco-Arabic Translation Movement in Baghdad and Early Abassid Society*, London, 1998.

Haas, C., *Alexandria in Late Antiquity: Topography and Social Conflict*, Baltimore, MD, 1997.

Haddad, R., La phonétique de l'arabe chrétien vers 700, in P. Canivet and J. P. Rey-Coquais, (eds.), *La Syrie de Byzance à l'Islam*, Damascus, 1992, pp. 159–64.

Hadot, P., *Philosophy as a Way of Life: Spiritual Exercises from Socrates to Foucault*, Oxford, 1995.

Haldon, J. F., *Byzantium in the Seventh Century. The Transformation of a Culture*, Cambridge 1990.

Haldon, J. F., and Byrne, M., A possible solution to the problem of Greek fire, *Byzantinische Zeitschrift*, 70 (1977): 91–9.

Halsall, G., Movers and shakers; the barbarians and the fall of Rome, *Early Medieval Europe*, 8 (1999): 131–45.

—— The origins of the Reihengräberzivilisation: forty years on, in J. Drinkwater and H. Elton (eds.), *Fifth-Century Gaul: A Crisis of Identity?*, Cambridge, 1992, pp. 196–207.

Hammer, C., Country churches, clerical inventories and the Carolingian Renaissance in Bavaria, *Church History*, 49 (1980): 5–17.

Hansen, O., Berliner soghdische Texte 2, *Mainz: Akademie der Wissenschaften 1954*, no. 15, pp. 830–1.

Hansen, S. S. and Randsborg, K. (eds.), *The Vikings in the West*, Acta Archaeologica 71: Supplement 2, Copenhagen, 2000.

Harbison, P., *Pilgrimage in Ireland. The Monuments and the People*, Syracuse, NY, 1992.

Harding, A., Reformation in barbarian Europe, 1300–600 B.C., in B. Cunliffe (ed.), *The Oxford Illustrated Prehistory of Europe*, Oxford, 1994, pp. 304–35,.

Harl, K., *Civic Coins and Civic Politics in the Roman East A.D.180–275*, Berkeley, CA, 1987.

Harmening, D., *Superstitio: überlieferungs- und theoriegeschichtliche Untersuchungen zur kirchlich-theologischen Aberglaubensliteratur des Mittelalters*, Berlin, 1979.

Harmer, F., *Documents of the Ninth and Tenth Centuries*, Cambridge, 1914.

Harries, J., *Law and Empire in Late Antiquity*, Cambridge, 1999.

—— *Sidonius Apollinaris and the Fall of Rome, A.D. 407–485*, Oxford, 1994.

—— Sidonius Apollinaris, Rome and the Barbarians: a climate of treason?, in J. Drinkwater and H. Elton (eds.), *Fifth-Century Gaul: A Crisis of Identity?*, Cambridge, 1992, pp. 298–308.

Hastrup, K., *Culture and History in Medieval Iceland*, Oxford, 1985.

Hauck, K., *Die Goldbrakteaten der Völkerwanderungzeit*, Munich, 1985.

—— Zum Problem der "Götter" im Horizont der völkerwanderungzeitlichen

Brakteaten, in G. Althoff (ed.), *Person und Gemeinschaft im Mittelalter*, Sigmaringen, 1988, pp. 73–98.

Haverfield, F., *The Romanization of Roman Britain*, Oxford, 1912.

Hawting, G.R., *The First Dynasty of Islam: The Umayyad Caliphate* A.D. 661–750, London, 1986.

Head, T. (ed.), *Medieval Hagiography*, New York, 2000.

Heather, P., The Creation of the Visigoths, in P. Heather (ed.), *The Visigoths from the Migration Period to the Seventh Century: An Ethnographic Perspective*, Woodbridge, Suffolk, 1999, pp. 43–73.

—— Goths and Huns, in Averil Cameron and Peter Garnsey (eds.), *The Cambridge Ancient History 13. The Late Empire* A.D. 337–425, Cambridge, 1998, pp.487–515.

—— The Huns and the end of the empire in western Europe, *English Historical Review*, 110 (1995): 4–41.

—— The late Roman art of client management: imperial defence in the fourth-century West, in W. Pohl, I. Wood, and H. Reimitz (eds.), *The Transformation of Frontiers. From Late Antiquity to the Carolingians*, Leiden, 2001, pp. 15–68.

—— Literacy and power in the migration period, in A.K. Bowman and G. Woolf (eds.), *Literacy and Power in the Ancient World*, Cambridge, 1994, pp. 177–97.

—— Senates and senators, in Averil Cameron and Peter Garnsey (eds.), *The Cambridge Ancient History 13: The Late Empire* A.D. 337–425, Cambridge, 1998, pp. 184–210.

—— The western empire, 425–476, in Averil Cameron, B. Ward-Perkins, and M. Whitby (eds.), *The Cambridge Ancient History 14. Late Antiquity: Empire and Successors* A.D. 425–600, Cambridge, 2000, pp. 1–32

Heather, P. and Matthews, J. F., *The Goths in the Fourth Century*, Liverpool, 1991.

Hedeager, L., *Asgard* reconstructed? Gudme – a central place in the North, in M. de Jong and F. Theuws with C. Van Rijn (eds.), *Topographies of Power in the Early Middle Ages*, Leiden, 2000, pp. 467–507.

—— *Iron Age Societies*, Oxford, 1992.

Heinzelmann, M., Bischof und Herrschaft vom spätantiken Gallien bis zu den karolingischen Hausmeiern, in F. Prinz, (ed.), *Herrschaft und Kirche: Beitrage zur Entstehung und Wirkungsweise episkopaler und monastischer Organisationsformen*, Stuttgart, 1988, pp. 23–82.

—— *Die Bischofsherrschaften in Gallien. Zur Kontinuität römischer Führungsschichten vom 4. bis 7. Jahrhundert: soziale, prosopographische und bildungsgeschichtliche Aspekte*, Munich, 1976.

—— *Gregor von Tours "Zehn Bücher der Geschichte". Historiographie und Gesellschaftsmodell im 6. Jht.*, Darmstadt, 1994.

—— *Gregory of Tours: History and Society in the Sixth Century*, transl. C. Carroll, Cambridge, 2001.

Helms, M. W., *Craft and the Kingly Ideal. Art, Trade and Power*, Austin, TX, 1993.

Hen, Y., Les authentiques des reliques de la Terre Sainte en Gaule franque, *Le Moyen Age*, 105 (1999): 71–90.

—— *Culture and Religion in Merovingian Gaul*, A.D. 481–751, Leiden, 1995.

—— Knowledge of canon law among rural priests: the evidence of two Carolingian manuscripts of around 800, *Journal of Theological Studies*, NS 50 (1999): 117–34.

—— The structure and aims of the *Visio Baronti*, *Journal of Theological Studies*, NS 47 (1996): 477–97.

—— Unity and diversity: the liturgy of Frankish Gaul before the Carolingians, in R. Swanson (ed.), *Unity and Diversity in the Church*, Studies in Church History 32, Oxford, 1996, pp. 19–29.

Henderson, G., *From Durrow to Kells: The Insular Gospel Books*, New York, 1987.

—— *Vision and Image in Early Christian England*, Oxford, 1999.

Herren, M. W., Gildas and early British monasticism, in A. Bammesberger and A. Wollman (eds.), *Britain 400–600: Language and History*, Heidelberg, 1990, pp. 65–78.

Herrin, J., *The Formation of Christendom*, Princeton, NJ, 1987.

—— *Women in Purple*, London, 2001.

Higham, N. J., *The Convert Kings: Power and Religious Affiliation in Early Anglo-Saxon England*, Manchester, 1997.

—— *The English Conquest. Gildas and Britain in the Fifth Century*, Manchester, 1994.

Hillenbrand, R., 'Anjar and early Islamic urbanism, in G. P. Brogiolo and B. Ward-Perkins (eds.), *The Idea and the Ideal of the Town in Late Antiquity and the Early Middle Ages*, Leiden, 1999, pp. 59–98.

—— The dolce vita in early Islamic Syria, *Art History* 5 (1982): 1–35.

Hillgarth, J. N., *Christianity and Paganism. The Conversion of Western Europe, 350–750*, Philadelphia, 1986.

—— Coins and chronicles: propaganda in sixth-century Spain and the Byzantine background, *Historia*, 15 (1966): 483–508; now in J. N. Hillgarth, *Visigothic Spain, Byzantium and Ireland*, London, 1985.

—— Eschatological and political concepts in the seventh century, in J. Fontaine and J. N. Hillgarth (eds.), *The Seventh Century. Change and Continuity*, London, 1992, pp. 212–31.

—— Modes of evangelization of Western Europe in the seventh century, in P. Ní Chatháin and M. Richter (eds.), *Irland und die Christenheit*, Stuttgart, 1987, pp. 311–31.

—— Popular religion in Visigothic Spain, in E. James (ed.), *Visigothic Spain: New Approaches*, Oxford, 1980, pp. 3–60; now in J. N. Hillgarth, *Visigothic Spain, Byzantium and the Irish*, London, 1985.

Hirschfeld, Y., *The Judean Monasteries in the Byzantine Period*, New Haven, CT, 1992.

Hodges, R., *Light in the Dark Ages. The Rise and Fall of San Vicenzo al Volturno*. London, 1997.

—— The riddle of St. Peter's Republic, in L. Paroli and P. Delogu (eds.), *La storia economica di Roma nell'alto Medio Evo alla luce dei recenti scavi archeologici*, Florence, 1993, pp. 353–363.

—— *Towns and Trade in the Age of Charlemagne*, London, 2000.

Hodges, R., and Whitehouse, D., *Mohammed, Charlemagne and the Origins of Europe. Archaeology and the Pirenne Thesis*, Ithaca, NY, 1983.

Honoré, T., *Tribonian*, London, 1978.

Hopkins, K., Christian number and its implications, *Journal of Early Christian Studies*, 6 (1998): 185–226.

—— Conquest by book, in J. H. Humphreys (ed.), *Literacy in the Roman World*, *Journal of Roman Archaeology*, Supplement 3, Ann Arbor, MI, 1991, pp. 133–58.

Horden, P., and Purcell, N. *The Corrupting Sea. A Study of Mediterranean History*, Oxford, 2000.

Howard-Johnston, J. D., The two great powers in Late Antiquity: a comparison, in Averil Cameron, (ed.), *The Byzantine and Early Islamic Near East 3: States, Resources, Armies*, Princeton, NJ, 1995, pp. 157–226.

Howlett, D. R., *The Book of Letters of Saint Patrick*, Dublin, 1994.

Hoyland, R., Jacob of Edessa on Islam, in G. J. Reinink and A. C. Klugkist (eds.), *After Bardaisan. Studies in Continuity and Change in Syriac Christianity in Honour of H. J. W. Drijvers*, Louvain, 1999, pp. 149–60.

—— *Seeing Islam as Others Saw It: A Survey and Evaluation of Christian, Jewish and Zoroastrian Writings on Early Islam*, Princeton, NJ, 1997.

Hughes, K., *The Church in Early Irish Society*, London, 1966.

—— *Early Christian Ireland: Introduction to the Sources*, London, 1972.

Humfress, C., Roman law, forensic argument and the formation of Christian orthodoxy, in E. Rebillard and A. Romano (eds.), *Orthodoxy, Christianity, History*, Collection de l'École française de Rome, 270, Rome, 2000, pp. 125–47.

Hunter, E., The Church of the East in Central Asia, *Bulletin of the John Rylands Library*, 78 (1996): 129–42.

—— Syriac inscriptions from al-Hîra, *Oriens Christianus*, 80 (1996): 66–81.

Idris, H. R., Fêtes chrétiennes en Ifriqiya à l'époque ziride, *Revue africaine*, 98 (1954): 261–76.

Inglebert, H., *Interpretatio Christiana. Les mutations des savoirs (cosmographie, géographie, histoire) dans l'Antiquité tardive*, Paris, 2001.

Innes, M., The Classical tradition in the Carolingian Renaissance: ninth-century encounters with Suetonius, *International Journal of the Classical Tradition*, 3 (1997): 265–82.

—— Memory, orality and history in an early medieval society, *Past and Present*, 158 (1998): 3–36.

—— *State and Society in the Early Middle Ages. The Middle Rhine Valley, 400–1000*, Cambridge, 2000.

—— Teutons or Trojans? The Carolingians and the Germanic past, in Y. Hen and M. Innes (eds.), *The Uses of the Past in the Early Middle Ages*, Cambridge, 2000, pp. 227–49.

Jackson, K., *A Celtic Miscellany*, Harmondsworth, 1971.

Jacques, F., *Privilegium Libertatis*, Rome, 1984.

James, E., Archaeology and the Merovingian Monastery, in H. B. Clarke and M. Brennan (eds.), *Columbanus and Merovingian Monasticism*, Oxford, 1981, pp. 33–55.

—— Bede and the tonsure question, *Peritia*, 3 (1984): 85–98.

—— *The Franks*, Oxford, 1988.

—— Gregory of Tours and the Franks, in A. C. Murray (ed.), *After Rome's Fall. Narrators and Sources of Early Medieval History. Essays presented to Walter*

Goffart, Toronto, 1998, pp. 51–66.

Janes, D., *God and Gold in Late Antiquity*, Cambridge, 1998.

—— The golden clasp of the late Roman state, *Early Medieval Europe*, 5 (1996): 127–53.

Jaski, B., Early Irish kingship and the Old Testament, *Early Medieval Europe*, 7 (1998): 329–44.

Jeck, V. R., Die frühmittelalterliche Rezeption der Zeittheorie Augustins in den "Libri Carolini" und die Temporalität des Kultbildes, in R. Berndt (ed.), *Das Konzil von Frankfurt 794*, Mainz, 1997, vol. 2, pp. 861–84.

Jenal, G., *Italia Ascetica atque Monastica. Das Asketen- und Mönchtum in Italien von den Anfängen bis zur Zeit der Langobarden*, 2 vols., Stuttgart, 1995.

Jenny, A., *Forschungen in Lauriacum 1*, Linz, 1954.

Jiménez Garnica, A. M., The settlement of the Visigoths in the fifth century, in P. Heather (ed.), *The Visigoths from the Migration Period to the Seventh Century: An Ethnographic Perspective*, Woodbridge, Suffolk, 1999, pp. 93–115.

Jochens, J., Late and peaceful: Iceland's conversion through arbitration in 1000, *Speculum*, 74 (1999): 621–55.

Jones, B. and Mattingly, D., *An Atlas of Roman Britain*, Oxford, 1990.

Jones, G., *The Norse Atlantic Saga*, Oxford, 1986.

—— *The Vikings*, Oxford, 1984.

Jussen, B., Liturgy and legitimation, or how the Gallo-Romans ended the Roman empire, in B. Jussen (ed.), *Ordering Medieval Society*. Philadelphia, 2000, pp. 147–99.

—— *Patenschaft und Adoption im frühen Mittelalter*, Göttingen, 1991.

Kaegi, W., *Byzantium and the Early Islamic Conquests*, Cambridge, 1992.

Karras, R., God and man in medieval Scandinavia: writing – and gendering – the conversion, in J. Muldoon (ed.), *Varieties of Religious Conversion in the Middle Ages*, Gainesville, FL, 1997, pp. 100–14.

Kaster, R., *Guardians of Language: The Grammarian and Society in Late Antiquity*, Berkeley, CA, 1988.

Kazhdan, A., *A History of Byzantine Literature (650–850)*, Athens, 1999.

Keenan, J. G., Egypt, in Averil Cameron, B. Ward-Perkins, and M. Whitby (eds.), *The Cambridge Ancient History 14. Late Antiquity: Empire and Sucessors* A.D. *425–600*, Cambridge, 2000, pp. 612–637.

Keller, C., Vikings in the West Atlantic: a model of Norse Greenland medieval society, *Acta Archeologica*, 61 (1991): 126–41.

Kelly, C., Emperors, government and bureaucracy, in Averil Cameron and P. Garnsey (eds.), *Cambridge Ancient History 13. The Late Empire* A.D. *337–425*, Cambridge, 1999, pp. 138–53.

Kelly, F., *Early Irish Farming*, Dublin, 1998.

—— *A Guide to Early Irish Law*, Dublin, 1988.

Kelly, S., Anglo-Saxon lay society and the written word, in R. McKitterick (ed.), *The Uses of Literacy in Early Medieval Europe*, Cambridge, 1990, pp. 36–62.

Kennedy, D. H., The identity of Roman Gerasa: an archaeological approach, *Mediterranean Archaeology*, 11 (1998): 39–70.

Kennedy, H., From polis to madina: urban change in late antique and Early Islamic

Syria, *Past and Present*, 106 (1985): 3–27.

—— The last century of Byzantine Syria: a reconsideration, *Byzantinische Forschungen*, 10 (1986): 141–83.

—— Syria, Palestine and Mesopotamia, in Averil Cameron, B. Ward-Perkins, and M. Whitby (eds.), *The Cambridge Ancient History 14. Late Antiquity: Empire and Successors* A.D. *425–600*, Cambridge, 2000, pp. 588–611.

Key Fowden, E., An Arab building at Rusâfa-Sergiopolis, *Damaszener Mitteilungen*, 12 (2000): 303–24.

—— *The Barbarian Plain. Saint Sergius between Rome and Iran*, Berkeley, CA, 1999.

Khazanov, A.M., *Nomads and the Outside World*, Cambridge, 1984.

Khoury-Sarkis, G., Réception d'un évêque syrien au VIe siècle, *L'Orient syrien*, 2 (1957): 137–84.

King, G. R. D., Settlement in western and central Arabia and the Gulf in the sixth–eighth centuries A.D., in G. R. D. King and Averil Cameron (eds.), *The Byzantine and Early Islamic Near East 2: Land Use and Settlement Patterns*, Princeton, NJ, 1994, pp. 181–212.

King, P. D., *Law and Society in the Visigothic Kingdom*, Cambridge, 1972.

Kingsley, S. and Decker, M. (eds.), *Economy and Exchange in the Eastern Mediterranean during Late Antiquity*, Oxford, 2001.

Kinney, D., Rape or restitution of the past? Integrating spolia, in S. C. Scott (ed.), *Art and Interpreting. Papers in Art History from the Pennsylvania State University 9*, University Park, PA, 1995, pp. 56–67.

Kister, M. J., Al-Hira: some notes on its relations with Arabia, *Arabica*, 15 (1968): 143–69.

—— *Studies in Jahiliyya and Early Islam*, London, 1980.

Klein, W., Christliche Reliefsgrabsteine des 14. Jahrhunderts aus der Seidenstrasse, in *VI Symposium Syriacum*, R. Lavenant (ed.), *Orientalia Christiana Analecta 247*, Rome, 1994, pp. 419–42.

Klingshirn, W. E., *Caesarius of Arles. The Making of a Christian Community in Late Antique Gaul*, Cambridge, 1994.

—— Charity and power: the ransoming of captives in sub-Roman Gaul, *Journal of Roman Studies*, 75 (1985): 95–102.

Kottje, R., *Studien zum Einfluss des Alten Testaments auf Recht und Liturgie des frühen Mittelalters*, Bonn, 1970.

Krautheimer, R., *Early Christian and Byzantine Architecture*, Harmondsworth, 1986.

—— *Rome. Profile of a City*, Princeton, NJ, 1980.

Krueger, D., *Symeon the Holy Fool*, Berkeley, CA, 1996.

Lammers, W., (ed.), *Die Eingliederung der Sachsen in das Frankenreich*, Wege der Forschung 185, Darmstadt, 1970.

Lancel, S., *Saint Augustin*, Paris, 1999.

—— La survie et la fin de la latinité en Afrique du Nord, *Revue des études latines*, 59 (1981): 269–97.

Landau-Tasseron, E., Features of the pre-conquest Muslim army in the time of Muhammed, in A. Cameron (ed.), *The Byzantine and Early Islamic Near East 3: States, Resources and Armies*, Princeton, NJ, 1995, pp. 299–336.

Lane-Fox, R., *Pagans and Christians*, New York, 1987.

—— Literacy and power in early Christianity, in A. K. Bowman and G. Woolf (eds.) *Literacy and Power in the Ancient World*, Cambridge, 1994, pp. 128–48.

Lapidge, M., The career of archbishop Theodore, in M. Lapidge (ed.), *Archbishop Theodore. Commemorative Studies on his Life and Influence*, Cambridge, 1994, pp. 1–29.

Lapidge, M., and Dumville, D. (eds.), *Gildas: New Approaches*, Woodbridge, Suffolk, 1984.

Lawless, G., *Augustine of Hippo and his Monastic Rule*, Oxford, 1987.

Lebecq, S., England and the Continent in the sixth and seventh centuries: the question of logistics, in R. Gameson (ed.), *St Augustine and the Conversion of England*, Stroud, Gloucestershire, 1999, pp. 50–67.

—— Les Frisons entre paganisme et christianisme, *Christianisation et déchristianisation*, Angers, 1986, pp. 19–45.

—— *Marchands et navigateurs du haut moyen-âge*, Lille, 1983.

—— *Les origines francques, Ve–IXe siècle*, Paris, 1990.

Le Jan, R., Convents, violence and competition for power in seventh-century Francia, in M. de Jong and F. Theuws with C. van Rhijn (eds.), *Topographies of Power in the Early Middle Ages*, Leiden 2001, pp. 243–69.

Lemerle, P., *Le premier humanisme byzantin*, Paris, 1971: transl. *Byzantine Humanism, the First Phase*, Canberra 1986.

Lendon, J., *Empire of Honour. The Art of Government in the Roman World*, Oxford, 1997.

Leslie, D. D. and Gardiner, K. H. J., *The Roman Empire in Chinese Sources*, Rome, 1996.

Levy, K., *Gregorian Chant and the Carolingians*, Princeton, NJ, 1998.

Leyser, C., *Authority and Asceticism from Augustine to Gregory the Great*, Oxford, 2000.

—— "This Sainted Isle": panegyric, nostalgia, and the invention of a "Lerinian Monasticism", in W. E. Klingshirn and M. Vessey (eds.), *The Limits of Ancient Christianity. Essays on Late Antique Thought and Culture in Honor of R. A. Markus*, Ann Arbor, MI, 1999, pp. 188–206.

Lidov, A. (ed.), *Chudotvornaia Ikona v Vizantii i drevneï Rusi*, Moscow, 1996.

Liebeschuetz, J. H. W. G., Administration and politics in the cities of the fifth to the mid-seventh century, in Averil Cameron, B. Ward-Perkins, and M. Whitby (eds.), *The Cambridge Ancient History 14. Late Antiquity: Empire and Successors A.D. 425–600*, Cambridge, 2000, pp. 207–37.

—— *The Decline and Fall of the Roman City*, Oxford, 2001.

Lieu, S. N. C., *Manichaeism in the Later Roman Empire and in Medieval China*, Manchester, 1985, 2nd edn., Tübingen, 1992.

Lim, R., Consensus and Dissensus in public spectacles in early Byzantium, *Byzantinische Forschungen*, 24 (1997): 159–79.

Lings, M., *Muhammed: His Life based on the Earliest Sources*, London, 1991.

Llewellyn, P., The Roman Church in the seventh century: the legacy of Gregory I, *Journal of Ecclesiastical History*, 25 (1974): 363–80.

—— *Rome in the Dark Ages*, London, 1971.

Loseby, S.T., Bishops and cathedrals: order and diversity in the fifth-century urban landscape of southern Gaul, in J. Drinkwater and H. Elton (eds.), *Fifth Century Gaul: A Crisis of Identity?*, Cambridge, 1992, pp.144–55.

—— Gregory's cities: urban functions in sixth-century Gaul, in I. Wood (ed.), *Franks and Alemanni in the Merovingian Period. An Ethnographic Perspective*, San Marino, CA, 1998, pp. 239–84.

—— Marseilles: a late antique success story?, *Journal of Roman Studies*, 82 (1992): 165–85.

Louth, A., Palestine under the Arabs 650–750: the crucible of Byzantine Orthodoxy, in S. N. Swanson (ed.), *The Holy Land, Holy Lands and Christian History*, Studies in Church History 36, Woodbridge, Suffolk, 2000, pp. 67–77.

Loyn, H. R., and Percival, J., *The Reign of Charlemagne*, London, 1975.

Lutterbach, H., *Monachus factus est. Die Mönchwerdung im frühen Mittelalter*, Münster, 1995.

—— *Sexualität im Mittelalter*, Cologne, 1999.

Lyman, J. R., *Christology and Cosmology*, Oxford, 1993.

Lynch, J. H., *Godparents and Kinship in Early Medieval Europe*, Princeton, NJ, 1986.

Maas, M., *John Lydus and the Roman Past*, London, 1992.

—— Junilius Africanus' *Instituta Regularia Divinae Legis* in its Justinianic context, in P. Allen and E. Jeffreys (eds.), *The Sixth Century. End or Beginning?*, Brisbane, 1996, pp. 131–44.

MacDonald, A., Aspects of the monastery and of monastic life in Adomnán's Life of Columba, *Peritia*, 3 (1984): 271–302.

MacMullen, R., *Christianity and Paganism in the Fourth to Eighth Centuries*, New Haven, CT, 1997.

—— *Christianizing the Roman Empire* A.D. *100–400*, New Haven, CT, 1984.

—— *Romanization in the Time of the Augustus*, New Haven, CT, 2000.

Magoun, F. P., The Pilgrim's Diary of Nicholas of Munkathvera, *Medieval Studies*, 6 (1944): 314–54.

Maguire, H., *Earth and Ocean. The Terrestrial World in Early Byzantine Art*, University Park, PA, 1987.

—— *The Icons of their Bodies. Saints and their Images in Byzantium*, Princeton, NJ, 1996.

Mahé, J., Quadrivium et cursus d'études au VIIe siècle en Arménie, *Travaux et Mémoires*, 10 (1987): 159–206.

Mainstone, R. J., *Hagia Sophia: Architecture, Structure and Liturgy of Justinian's Great Church*, London, 1997.

Mango, C., *The Art of the Byzantine Empire, 312–1453: Sources and Documents*, Englewood Cliffs, NJ, 1972.

—— The development of Constantinople as an urban center, *Studies in Constantinople*, Aldershot, 1993.

Marazzi, F., Rome in transition: economic and political change in the fourth and fifth centuries, in J. M. H. Smith (ed.), *Early Medieval Rome and the Christian West. Essays in Honour of Donald A. Bullough*, Leiden, 2000, pp. 21–41.

Markus, R. A., *The End of Ancient Christianity*, Cambridge, 1990.

—— From Caesarius to Boniface: Christianity and Paganism in Gaul, in J. Fontaine and J. N. Hillgarth (eds.), *The Seventh Century: Change and Continuity*, London, 1992, pp. 154–72.

—— Gregory the Great and a missionary strategy, in J. Cuming (ed.), *The Mission of the Church and the Propagation of the Faith*, Studies in Church History 6, Cambridge, 1970, pp. 29–38.

—— *Gregory the Great and his World*, Cambridge, 1997.

Marrou, H. I., Autour de la bibliothèque du pape Agapit, *Mélanges d'archéologie et d'histoire*, 48 (1931): 124–212; now in *Christiana Tempora*, Collection de l'École française de Rome, 35, Rome, 1978.

—— *A History of Education in Antiquity*, Madison, WI, 1982.

Mathews, T. F., *The Clash of Gods: A Reinterpretation of Early Christian Art*, 2nd edn., Princeton, NJ, 1999.

Mathisen, R. W., *Ecclesiastical Factionalism and Religious Controversy in Fifth-Century Gaul*, Washington, DC, 1989.

Matthews, J. F., *Laying Down the Law: A Study of the Theodosian Code*, New Haven, CT, 2000.

Maurin, L., Remparts et cités dans le trois provinces du Sud-Ouest de la Gaule au bas-empire, *Villes et agglomérations urbaines antiques du Sud-Ouest de la Gaule, Aquitania*: Supplément 6, Bordeaux, 1992, pp. 365–89.

Mayr-Harting, H., Charlemagne, the Saxons and the imperial coronation of 800, *English Historical Review*, 111 (1996): 1113–33.

—— *The Coming of Christianity to Anglo-Saxon England*, 2nd edn., University Park, PA, 1991.

McAdam, H., Settlement and settlement patterns in northern and central Transjordania, ca.550–ca.750, in G. R. D. King and Averil Cameron (eds.), *The Byzantine and Early Islamic Near East 2: Land Use and Settlement Patterns*, Princeton, NJ, 1994, pp. 49–93.

McClure, J., Bede's Old Testament kings, in P. Wormald (ed.), *Ideal and Reality in Frankish and Anglo-Saxon Society*, Oxford, 1983, pp. 76–98.

McCone, K., *Pagan Past and Christian Present in Early Irish Literature*, Maynooth, 1990.

—— Werewolves, Cyclopes, *Diberga* and *Fiánna*: juvenile delinquency in early Ireland, *Cambridge Medieval Celtic Studies*, 12 (1986): 1–22.

McCormick, M., Bateaux de vie, bateaux de mort. Maladie, commerce et le passage économique du bas-empire au moyen âge, in *Morfologie sociali e culturali in Europa tra Tarda Antichità e Alto Medio Evo*, Settimane di Studi sull'Alto Medio Evo 45, Spoleto, 1998, pp. 35–118.

—— Clovis at Tours: Byzantine public rituals and the origin of medieval ruler symbolism, in E. Chrysos and A. Schwarcz (eds.), *Das Reich und die Barbaren*, Vienna, 1989, pp. 155–80.

—— The liturgy of war in the early Middle Ages: crisis, liturgies and the Carolingian monarchy, *Viator*, 15 (1984): 1–23.

—— Textes, Images et Iconoclasme dans le cadre des relations entre Byzance et l'Occident carolingien, in *Testo e Immagine nell'Alto Medio Evo*, Settimane di Studi sull'Alto Medio Evo 41, Spoleto, 1994, pp. 95–162.

—— *Origins of the European Economy Economy: Communications and Commerce AD 300–900*, Cambridgr, 2001.

McGuckin, J. A., *St. Cyril of Alexandria: The Christological Controversy, its History, Theology and Texts*, 1994.

McKitterick, R., *The Carolingians and the Written Word*, Cambridge, 1989.

—— Introduction, in R. McKitterick (ed.), *The New Cambridge Medieval History 2: c.700–c.900*, Cambridge, 1995, pp. 3–17.

—— Nuns' scriptoria in England and Francia in the 8th century, *Francia*, 19/1 (1992): 1–35.

McKitterick, R. (ed.), *The Early Middle Ages*, Oxford, 2001.

McLynn, N. B., *Ambrose of Milan. Church and Court in a Christian Capital*, Berkeley, CA, 1994.

McNeill, J. T. and Gamer, H., *Medieval Handbooks of Penance*, New York 1938 and 1990.

McNeill, M., *The Lughnasa*, Dublin, 1982.

Meens, R., The frequency and nature of early medieval penance, in P. Biller and A. Minns, (eds.), *Handling Sin: Confession in the Middle Ages*, Woodbridge, Suffolk, 1998, pp. 35–61.

—— Willibrords boeteboek?, *Tijdschrift voor Geschiednis*, 106 (1993): 163–78.

Mellinkoff, R., Cain's monstrous progeny in "Beowulf," *Anglo-Saxon England*, 8 (1979): 143–62 and 9 (1980): 183–97.

Meslin, M., *La fête des Kalendes de Janvier dans l'empire romain*, Brussels, 1970.

Meunier, B., *Le Christ de Cyrille d'Alexandrie*, Paris, 1997.

Meyendorff, J., *Imperial Unity and Christian Division. The Church 450–680*, Crestwood, New York, 1989.

Meyvaert, P., Bede and the church paintings at Wearmouth-Jarrow, *Anglo-Saxon England*, 8 (1979): 63–77.

—— Bede, Cassiodorus and the *Codex Amiatinus*, *Speculum*, 71 (1996): 827–83.

Mikawaya. M. and Kollautz, A., Ein Dokument zum Fernhandel zwischen Byzanz und China, *Byzantinische Zeitschrift*, 77 (1984): 6–19.

Miquel, A., *La géographie humaine du monde musulman*, vol. 2, Paris, 1975.

Mitchell, J., Literacy displayed: the uses of inscriptions at the monastery of San Vicenzo al Volturno in the early ninth century, in R. McKitterick (ed.), *The Uses of Literacy in the Early Middle Ages*, Cambridge, 1990, pp. 186–222.

Mitchell, K. and Wood, I. N. (eds.), *The World of Gregory of Tours*, Leiden, 2002.

Mitchell, S., *Anatolia. Land, Men and Gods 2: The Rise of the Church*, Oxford, 1993.

Modéran, F., La chronologie de la Vie de Saint Fulgence de Ruspe et ses incidences sur l'histoire de l'Afrique vandale, *Mélanges de l'École française de Rome: Antiquité*, 105 (1993): 135–88.

Moffett, S., *A History of Christianity in Asia*, vol. 1, San Fransisco, 1992.

Monneret de Villard, U., *Le Leggende orientali dei Magi evangelici*, Rome, 1952.

Moorhead, J., Iconoclasm, the Cross and the imperial image, *Byzantion*, 55 (1985): 165–79.

—— *Justinian*, London, 1994.

Morony, M., *Iraq after the Muslim Conquest*, Princeton, NJ, 1984.

Muhlberger, S., *The Fifth-Century Chroniclers: Prosper, Hydatius and the Gallic Chronicler of 452*, Leeds, 1990.

Mundell, M. and Bennett, A. The Sevso Treasure, *Journal of Roman Archaeology*, Supplementary volume 12, Ann Arbor, MI, 1994, pp. 55–97.

Mundell Mango, M., *Silver from Early Byzantium: The Kaper Koraon and Related Treasures*, Baltimore, MD, 1986.

Munro-Hay, S. C., *Aksum. An African Civilization of Late Antiquity*, Edinburgh, 1991.

Murray, A. C., *From Roman to Merovingian Gaul: A Reader*, Peterborough, Ontario, 2000.

—— Post vocantur Merohingii. Fredegar, Merovech and "sacral kingship," in A. C. Murray (ed.), *After Rome's Fall. Narrators and Sources of Early Medieval History. Essays presented to Walter Goffart*, Toronto, 1998, pp. 121–52.

Muschiol, G., *Famula Dei. Zur Liturgie in merowingischen Frauenklöstern*, Münster, 1994.

Nathan, G., Rogation ceremonies in Late Antique Gaul, *Classica et Medievalia*, 21 (1998): 276–303

Nelson, J., Kingship and empire in the Carolingian world, in R. McKitterick (ed.), *Carolingian Culture: Emulation and Innovation*, Cambridge, 1994, pp. 88–107.

—— Literacy in Carolingian government, in R. McKitterick (ed.), *The Uses of Literacy in Early Medieval Europe*, Cambridge, 1990, pp. 258–96.

—— The Lord's Anointed and the people's choice, in D. Cannadine and S. Price (eds.), *Rituals of Royalty. Power and Ceremonial in Traditional Societies*, Cambridge, 1987, pp. 137–80.

—— Aachen as a place of power, in M. de Jong and F. Theuws with C. van Rhijn (eds.), *Topographies of Power in the Early Middle Ages*, Leiden, 2001, pp. 217–41.

—— *The Frankish World*, London, 1996.

Noble, T. F. X., *Images and the Carolingians: Discourses on Tradition, Order and Worship* (forthcoming).

—— The making of papal Rome, in M. de Jong and F. Theuws with C. Van Rhijn (eds.), *Topographies of Power in the Early Middle Ages*, Leiden, 2001, pp. 45–91.

—— Tradition and learning in search of an ideology, in R. E. Sullivan (ed.), *"The Gentle Voices of Teachers." Aspects of Learning in the Carolingian Age*, Columbus, OH, 1995, pp. 227–60.

Nussbaum, M., *The Therapy of Desire. Theory and Practice in Hellenistic Ethics*, Princeton, NJ, 1994.

Obolensky, D., *The Byzantine Commonwealth*, London, 1971.

O'Carragáin, É., The necessary distance: *Imitatio Romae* and the Ruthwell Cross, in J. Hawks and S. Mills (eds.), *The Golden Age of Northumbria*, Stroud, Gloucestershire, 1999, pp. 191–203.

—— The Ruthwell Crucifixion in its iconographic and liturgical context, *Peritia*, 6–7 (1987–8): 1–71.

O'Corráin, D., The historical and cultural background to the Book of Kells, in F. O'Mahoney (ed.), *The Book of Kells*, Aldershot, 1994, pp. 1–32.

O'Cróinín, D., Creating the past: the early Irish genealogical tradition, *Peritia*, 12 (1998): 177–208.

—— *Early Medieval Ireland 400–1000*, London, 1995.

O'Donnell, J. J., The Authority of Augustine, *Augustinian Studies*, 22 (1991): 7–35.

—— *Cassiodorus*, Berkeley, CA, 1979.

O'Keefe, J. G., Cáin Domnaig, *Ériu*, 2 (1905): 189–214.

O'Leary, P., The foreseeing driver of an old chariot: royal moderation in early Irish literature, *Cambridge Medieval Celtic Studies*, 11 (1986): 1–16.

O'Loughlin, T., *Teachers and Code-Breakers. The Latin Genesis Tradition 430–800.* Turnhout, 1998.

O'Neill, T., Book-making in early Christian Ireland, *Archaeology in Ireland*, 2 (1988): 96–100.

O'Sullivan, D., The plan of the early Christian monastery at Lindisfarne, in G. Bonner, D. Rollason, and C. Stancliffe (eds.), *St. Cuthbert, his Cult and his Community to* A.D. *1200*, Woodbridge, Suffolk, 1989, pp. 125–42.

Page, R. I., The Bewcastle Cross, *Nottingham Medieval Studies*, 4 (1960): 36–57.

Painter, K. S., *The Water Newton Early Christian Silver*, London, 1977.

Palmer, A., Une chronique contemporaine de la conquête arabe, in P. Canivet and J. P. Rey-Coquais (eds.), *La Syrie de Byzance à l'Islam*, Damascus, 1992, pp. 31–46.

—— *Monk and Mason on the Tigris Frontier. The Early History of Tur 'Abdin*, Cambridge, 1990.

—— *The Seventh Century in West Syrian Chronicles*, Liverpool, 1993.

Pancer, N., *Sans peur et sans vergogne. De l'honneur et des femmes aux premiers temps mérovingiens*, Paris, 2001.

Panella, C., Merci e scambi nel Mediterraneo tardo antico, in A. Schiavone (ed.), *Storia di Roma* 3, part 2, Turin, 1993, pp. 613–97.

Paret, R., *Der Koran: Kommentar und Konkordanz*, Stuttgart, 1971.

Parry, K., *Depicting the Word. Byzantine Iconophile Thought in the Eighth and Ninth Centuries*, Leiden, 1996.

Patrich, J., *Sabas, Leader of Palestinian Monasticism: A Comparative Study of Eastern Monasticism in the Fourth to Seventh Centuries*, Washington, DC, 1995.

Pavolini, C., Le *domus* del Celio, in S. Ernesti and E. La Rosa (eds.), *Aurea Roma. Dalla città pagana alla città cristiana*, Rome, 2000, pp.147–8.

Paxton, F., *Christianizing Death. The Creation of a Ritual Process in Early Medieval Europe*, Ithaca, NY, 1990.

Payer, P., *Sex and the Pentitentials*, Toronto, 1984.

Paykova, A.V., The Syrian Ostracon from Panjikent, *Le Mouséon*, 92 (1979): 159–69.

Pazdernik, C., Our most pious consort given to us by God: dissident reactions to the partnership of Justinian and Theodora, *Classical Antiquity*, 13 (1994): 256–81.

Pelliot, P., *L'inscription nestorienne de Si-ngan-fou*, with A. Forte, Paris/Kyoto, 1996.

Pentz, P. *The Invisible Conquest. The Ontogenesis of Sixth and Seventh Century Syria*, Copenhagen, 1992.

Pergola, P. (ed.), *Alle origini della parrocchia rurale (IV–VIII secolo)*, Rome: Vatican City, 1999.

Peyroux, C., Canonists construct the nun? Church law and women's monastic practice in Merovingian Gaul, in R. W. Mathisen (ed.), *Law, Society and Authority in Late Antiquity*, Oxford, 2001, pp. 242–55.

Picard, J. C., L'Atrium dans les églises paléochrétiennes d'Occident, in N. Duval (ed.), *Actes du XIe Congrès international d'archéologie chrétienne*, vol. 1, Rome, 1986, pp. 503–58.

Piccirillo, *The Mosaics of Jordan*, Baltimore, MD, 1994.

Pietri, C., Clercs et serviteurs laïcs de l'église romaine au temps de Grégoire le Grand, in J. Fontaine, R. Gillet, and S. Pellistrandi (eds.), *Grégoire le Grand*, Paris, 1986, pp. 107–22, now in *Respublica Christiana*, Collection de l'École française de Rome, 234, Rome, 1997, vol. 1, pp. 110–16.

—— *Roma christiana*, 2 vols., Rome, 1976.

Pirenne, H., *Mohammed and Charlemagne*, transl. B. Miall, London, 1937.

Pitz, E., *Papstreskripte im frühen Mittelalter. Diplomatische und rechtsgeschichtliche Studien zum Brief-Corpus Gregors des Grossen*, Sigmaringen, 1990.

Poeschke, J. (ed.), *Antike Spolien in der Architektur des Mittelalters und der Renaissance*, Munich, 1996.

Pohl, W., L'armée romaine et les Lombards: stratégies militaires et politiques, in F. Valet and M. Kazanski (eds.), *L'armée romaine et les barbares du IIIe au VIIe siècle*, Rouen, 1993, pp. 291–6.

—— *Die Awaren. Ein Steppenvolk in Mitteleuropa, 567–822 n.Chr.*, Munich, 1988.

—— Introduction and Telling the difference: signs of ethnic identity, in W. Pohl and H. Reimitz (eds.), *Strategies of Distinction. The Construction of Ethnic Communities, 300–800*, Leiden, 1998, pp. 1–15 and 16–69.

—— *Die Völkerwanderung. Eroberung und Integration*. Stuttgart, 2002.

Pohl, W., and Disenberger, M. (eds.), *Eugippius und Severin. Der Autor, der Text und der Heilige*. Forschungen zur Geschichte des Mittelalters 2, Vienna, 2001.

Poschmann, B., *Penance and Anointing of the Sick*, New York, 1964.

Potter, D., *Prophecy and History in the Crisis of the Roman Empire*, Oxford, 1990.

Pricocco, S., *L'Isola dei santi. Il cenobio di Lerino e le origini del monachesimo in Gallia*, Rome, 1978.

Prinz, F., *Frühes Mönchtum im Frankenreich: Kultur und Gesellschaft in Gallien, dem Rheinland und Bayern am Beispiel der monastichen Entwicklung (4. bis 8. Jahrhunderts)*, 2nd edn., Munich, 1988.

Prosopographie chrétienne du Bas-Empire: Prosopographie de l'Italie chrétienne (313–604), part 1, Rome, 1999.

Purcell, N., The population of Rome in late antiquity: problems of classification and historical description, in W. V. Harris (ed.), *The Transformations of Vrbs Roma in Late Antiquity*, *Journal of Roman Archaeology*: Supplementary Series 33, Portsmouth, RI, 1999, pp.135–161.

Raby, J. and Johns, J. (eds.), *Bayt al-Makdis. 'Abd al-Malik's Jerusalem*, Oxford, 1992.

Radner, J. N., *Fragmentary Annals of Ireland*, Dublin, 1978.

Ramsey, W. M., Deux jours en Phrygie, *Revue des études anciennes*, 3 (1901): 269–75.

Rankin, S., Carolingian music, in R. McKitterick (ed.), *Carolingian Culture: Emulation and Innovation*, Cambridge, 1994, pp. 274–316.

Rapp, C., "For next to God you are my salvation": reflections on the rise of the holy man in late antiquity, in J. Howard-Johnston and P. A. Hayward (eds.), *The Cult of Saints in Late Antiquity and the early Middle Ages*, Oxford, 1999, pp. 63–81.

Rebillard, E., Église et sépulture dans l'Antiquité tardive (Occident latin, 3e–6e siècles), *Annales*, 54 (1999): 1027–46.

―― Les formes d'assistance funéraire dans l'empire romain et leur évolution dans l'antiquité tardive, *Antiquité tardive*, 7 (1999): 269–82.

―― *In hora mortis. L'évolution de la pastorale chrétienne de la mort au IVe et Ve siècles dans l'Occident latin*, Bibliothèque des Écoles françaises d'Athènes et de Rome, 283, Rome, 1994.

Rebillard, E. and Sotinel, C. (eds.), *L'évêque dans la cité du VIe et Ve siècle. Image et autorité*, Collection de l'École française de Rome, 248, Rome, 1998.

Redgate, A. E., *The Armenians*, Oxford, 1998.

Reinink, G. J., "Edessa grew dim and Nisibis shone forth." The Schools of Nisibis at the transition of the sixth–seventh century, in J. W. Drijvers and A. A. MacDonald (eds.), *Centres of Learning. Learning and Location in Pre-Modern Europe and the Near East*, Leiden, 1995, pp. 77–89.

Riché, P., *Education and Culture in the Barbarian West: Sixth through Eighth Centuries*, Columbus, SC, 1976.

Richter, M., *Ireland and its Neighbors in the Seventh Century*, Dublin, 1999.

Ripoll, G. and Velázquez, I., *La Hispania visigoda: del rey Ataúlfo a Don Rodrigo*, Madrid, 1997.

Ripoll Lopez, G., and Velázquez Soriano, I., El epitafio de Trasemirus, *Espacio, Tiempo y Forma, Prehistória y Arqueología*, 3 (1990): 273–87.

Rives, J. B., The decree of Decius and the religion of empire, *Journal of Roman Studies*, 89 (1999): 135–54.

Robert, L., Le serpent Glycon d'Abônoutheichos à Athènes et Artémis d'Ephèse à Rome, *Opera Minora Selecta 5*, Amsterdam, 1989, pp. 747–69.

Roberts, C. H. and Skeat, T. C., *The Birth of the Codex*, London, 1983.

Roberts, M., The description of landscape in the poems of Venantius Fortunatus: the Moselle poems, *Traditio*, 49 (1994): 1–22.

Robin, C., *L'Arabie antique de Karb'îl à Mahomet: nouvelles données sur l'histoire arabe grâce aux inscriptions*, Aix-en-Provence, 1991.

Robinson, C. F., *Empire and Elites after the Muslim Conquest. The Transformation of Northern Mesopotamia*, Cambridge, 2000.

Robinson, N., *Christ in Islam and Christianity. The Representation of Jesus in the Qur'ân and the Classical Muslim Commentaries*, London, 1991.

Rodinson, M., *Mohammed*, New York, 1971.

Rosenwein, B., *Negotiating Space. Power, Restraint and Privileges of Immunity in Early Medieval Europe*, Ithaca, NY, 1999.

Rosenthal, F., *The Classical Heritage in Islam*, Berkeley, CA, 1975.

Rossi, G. B. de, *Inscriptiones christianae urbis Romae*, Rome, 1888.

Roueché, C., *Performers and Partisans at Aphrodisias in the Roman and Late Roman Periods*, London, 1993.

Rousseau, P., Cassian: monastery and world, in M. Fairburn and W. H. Oliver (eds.), *The Certainty of Doubt. Tributes to Peter Munz*, Wellington, New Zealand, 1995, pp. 68–89.

—— Monasticism, in Averil Cameron, B. Ward-Perkins, and M. Whitby (eds.), *The Cambridge Ancient History 14. Late Antiquity: Empire and Successors* A.D. *425–600*, Cambridge, 2000, pp. 745–80.

Rousselle, A., *Croire et guérir. La foi en Gaule dans l'Antiquité tardive*, Paris, 1990.

Rubin, U., *Hanîfiyya* and Ka'aba: an inquiry into the Arabian pre-Islamic background of Dîn Ibrâhîm, *Jerusalem Studies in Arabic and Islam*, 8 (1990): 85–113.

Russell, J. R., Dragons in Armenia, *Journal of Armenian Studies*, 5 (1990/1): 3–19.

—— *Zoroastrianism in Armenia*, Cambridge, MA, 1987.

Russell, N., *Cyril of Alexandria*, London, 2000.

Sahas, D. J., *Icon and Logos: Sources in Eighth-Century Iconoclasm*, Toronto, 1988.

Samson, R., The Merovingian nobleman's hall: castle or villa? *Journal of Medieval History*, 13 (1987): 287–315.

Sato, S., The Merovingian accounting documents of Tours: form and function, *Early Medieval Europe*, 9 (2000): 141–61.

Savon, H., L'Antéchrist dans l'oeuvre de Grégoire le Grand, in J. Fontaine, R. Gillet, and S. Pellistrandi (eds.), *Grégoire le Grand*, Paris, 1986, pp. 389–405.

Sawyer, P., *Kings and Vikings*, London, 1982.

Schick, R., *The Christian Communities of Palestine from Byzantine to Islamic Rule. A Historical and Archeological Study*, Princeton, NJ, 1995.

Schieffer, R., Charlemagne and Rome, in J. M. H. Smith (ed.), *Early Medieval Rome and the Christian West. Essays in Honor of Donald Bullough*, Leiden, 2000, pp. 279–95.

Schippman, K., *Geschichte der alt-südarabischen Reiche*, Darmstadt, 1999.

Schlegel, G., *Die chinesische Inschrift von Kara Balgassun*, Helsinki, 1896.

Schöllgen, G., *Die Anfänge der Professionalisierung des Klerus*, Münster, 1998.

Schreiner, P., Eine chinesische Beschreibung Konstantinopels, *Istanbuler Mitteilungen*, 39 (1989): 493–505.

Ševčenko, I., *Byzantium and the Slavs*, Cambridge, MA., 1991.

—— Religious missions seen from Byzantium, *Harvard Ukrainian Studies*, 22/3 (1988/9): 6–27.

Shahid, I., The *Kebra Nagast* in the light of recent research, *Le Mouséon*, 89 (1976): 133–78.

—— *The Martyrs of Najrân*, Brussels, 1971.

Shanzer, D., Dating the baptism of Clovis: the bishop of Vienne vs. the bishop of Tours, *Early Medieval Europe*, 7 (1988): 29–57.

Sharon, M., An Arabic inscription from the time of the Caliph 'Abd al-Malik, *Bulletin of the School of Oriental and African Studies*, 29 (1966): 367–72.

Sharpe, R., Church and communities in early Ireland: towards a pastoral model, in J. Blair and R. Sharpe (eds.), *Pastoral Care before the Parish*, Leicester, 1992, pp.81–109.

—— Hiberno-Latin *laicus*, Irish *láech* and the Devil's Men, *Ériu*, 30 (1973): 75–92.

—— Martyrs and local saints in late antique Britain, in A. T. Thacker and R. Sharpe (eds.), *Local Saints and Local Churches in the Early Medieval West*, Oxford, 2002, pp. 75–154.

Shaw, B., Challenging Braudel: a new vision of the Mediterranean, *Journal of Roman Archaeology*, 14 (2001): 419–53.

—— "Eaters of flesh, drinkers of milk": the ancient Mediterranean ideology of the pastoral nomad, *Ancient Society*, 14/4 (1982/3): 5–31.

—— War and violence, in G. W. Bowersock, P. Brown, and O. Grabar (eds.), *Late Antiquity. A Guide to the Postclassical World*, Cambridge, MA, 1999, pp. 130–69.

Shboul, A. and Walmsley, A., Identity and self-image in Syria-Palestine in the Transition from Byzantine to early Islamic rule, *Mediterranean Archaeology*,11 (1998): 255–87.

Shcratt, A., The emergence of elites: earlier Bronze Age Europe, 2500–1300 B.C., in B. Cunliffe (ed.), *Oxford Illustrated Prehistory of Europe*, Oxford, 1994, pp. 244–70.

Silber, I., *Virtuosity, Charisma and Social Order. A Comparative Study of Theravada Buddhism and Medieval Catholicism*, Cambridge, 1995.

Simson, O. G. von, *Sacred Fortress. Byzantine Art and Statecraft in Ravenna*, Princeton, NJ, 1987.

Sims-Williams, P., *Religion and Literature in Western England, 600–800*, Cambridge, 1990.

—— Thought, word and deed: an Irish triad, *Ériu*, 29 (1978): 78–111.

Sivan, H., *Ausonius of Bordeaux. Genesis of a Gallic Aristocracy*, London, 1993.

—— The invisible Jews of Visigothic Spain, *Revue des études juives*, 159 (2000): 369–85.

Smith, J. M. H., Gender and ideology in the early Middle Ages, in R. Swanson (ed.), *Gender and Christianity*, Studies in Church History 34, Woodbridge, Suffolk, 1998, pp. 51–71.

—— Old saints, new cults: Roman relics in Carolingian Francia, in J. M. H. Smith (ed.), *Early Medieval Rome and the Christian West. Essays in Honor of Donald Bullough*, Leiden, 2000, pp. 317–39.

—— Women at the tomb: access to relic shrines in the early Middle Ages, in K. Mitchell and I. N. Wood (eds.), *The World of Gregory of Tours*, Leiden, 2002, pp. 163–80.

Smith, M., Coptic Literature, in Averil Cameron and Peter Garnsey (eds.), *The Cambridge Ancient History 13: The Late Empire A.D. 337–425*, Cambridge, 1998, pp. 720–35.

Snyder, G. F., *Ante Pacem. Archaeological Evidence for Church Life before Constantine*, Macon, GA, 1985.

Sorabji, R., *Emotion and Peace of Mind. From Stoic Agitation to Christian Temptation*, Oxford, 2000.

Southern, R. W., *Western Society and the Church in the Middle Ages*, Harmondsworth, 1970.

Stacey, R., *The Road to Judgement. From Custom to Court in medieval Ireland and Wales*, Philadelphia, 1994.

Stancliffe, C., The British Church and the mission of Augustine, in R. Gameson (ed.), *St Augustine and the Conversion of England*, Stroud, Glouccestershire, 1999, pp. 107–51.

—— Kings and conversion: some comparisons between the Roman mission to England and Patrick's to Ireland, *Frühmittelalterliche Studien*, 14 (1980): 59–94.

—— Red, white and blue martyrdom, in D. Whitelock, R. McKitterick, and D. Dumville (eds.), *Ireland in Early Medieval Europe*, Cambridge, 1982, pp. 21–46.

—— *St. Martin and his Hagiographer. History and Miracle in Sulpicius Severus*, Oxford, 1983.

—— The thirteen sermons attributed to Columbanus, in M. Lapidge (ed.), *Columbanus: Studies on the Latin Writings*, Woodbridge, Suffolk, 1997, pp.93–202.

—— Venantius Fortunatus, Ireland, Jerome: the evidence of *Precamur Patrem*, *Peritia*, 10 (1996): 91–7.

Standaert, N. (ed.), *Handbook of Christianity in China. Volume One: 635–1800*, Leiden, 2001.

Stansbury, M., Early medieval Biblical commentaries: their writers and readers, *Frühmittelalterliche Studien*, 33 (1999): 49–82.

Steinen, W. von, Karl der Grosse und die *Libri Carolini*, *Neues Archiv*, 49 (1931): 207–80.

Steinmeyer E. von (ed.), *Die kleinen althochdeutschen Sprachdenkmäler*, Berlin, 1916.

Stevenson, J., The beginnings of literacy in Ireland, *Proceedings of the Royal Irish Academy*, 100 (1982): 127–65.

—— Literacy and orality in early medieval Ireland, in D. Edel (ed.), *Cultural Identity and Cultural Integration: Ireland and Europe in the Early Middle Ages*, Dublin, 1995, pp. 11–23.

—— The monastic rules of Columbanus, in M. Lapidge (ed.), *Columbanus: Studies on the Latin Writings*, Woodbridge, Suffolk, 1997, pp. 202–16.

Stewart, C., *Cassian the Monk*, New York, 1998.

Stokes, W. and Strachan, J., *Thesaurus Paleohibernicus: A Collection of Old Irish Glosses*, vol. 2, Cambridge, 1903.

Straw, C., *Gregory the Great*, in P. Geary (ed.), Authors of the Middle Ages 12, Aldershot, 1996.

—— *Gregory the Great. Perfection in Imperfection*, Berkeley, CA, 1988.

Strobel, K., *Das Imperium Romanum im "3. Jahrhundert." Modell einer historischen Krise*, Stuttgart, 1993.

Talbot, C. H., *The Anglo-Saxon Missionaries in Germany*, London, 1954.

Tardieu, M., La diffusion du Bouddhisme dans l'empire kouchan, L'Iran et la Chine d'après un Kephalaion manichéen inédit, *Studia Iranica*, 17 (1988): 153–80.

Tate, G., *Les campagnes de la Syrie du Nord du IIe au VIIe siècle*, Paris, 1992.

Teillet, S., *Des Goths à la nation gothique*, Paris, 1984.

Thacker, A., Bede and the Irish, in L. A. J. R. Houwen and A. MacDonald (eds.), *Beda Venerabilis. Historian, Monk and Northumbrian*, Groningen, 1996, pp. 31–59.

—— In search of saints. The English Church and the cult of Roman Apostles and martyrs in the seventh and eighth centuries, in J. M. H. Smith (ed.), *Early Medieval Rome and the Christian West. Essays in Honor of Donald Bullough*, Leiden, 2000, pp. 247–77.

—— Monks, preaching and pastoral care in early Anglo-Saxon England, in J. Blair and R. Sharpe (eds.), *Pastoral Care before the Parish*, Leicester, 1992, pp. 136–70.

Thélamon, F., *Païens et chrétiens au IVe. siècle*, Paris, 1981.

Theuws, F., Landed property and manorial organization in North Austrasia, in W. Roymans and F. Theuws (eds.), *Images of the Past*, Amsterdam, 1991, pp. 299–401.

Theuws, F. and Alkemade, J., A kind of mirror of men: sword deposits in Late Antique northern Gaul, in F. Theuws and J. L. Nelson (eds.), *Rituals of Power. From Late Antiquity to the Early Middle Ages*, Leiden, 2000, pp. 401–76.

Thier, S., *Kirche bei Pelagius*, Patristische Texte und Studien 50, Berlin 1999.

Thierry, F. and Morrison, C., Sur les monnaines byzantines trouvées en Chine, *Revue numismatique*, 6 ser., 36 (1994): 109–45.

Thierry, M. and N., La cathédrale de Mrèn et sa décoration, *Cahiers archéologiques*, 21 (1971): 43–77.

Thomas, C., *Christianity in Roman Britain to A.D. 400*, Berkeley, CA, 1981.

Thompson, E. A., *The Huns*, Oxford, 1996.

—— *Romans and Barbarians*, Madison, WI, 1982.

Thomson, R. W., Biblical themes in the Armenian histories of Sebeos, in G. J. Reinink and A .C. Klugkist (eds.), *After Bardaisan. Studies in Continuity and Change in Syriac Christianity in Honour of H. J. W. Drijvers*, Louvain, 1999, pp. 295–302.

—— The formation of the Armenian literary tradition, in N. Garsoian, T. F. Mathews, and R. W. Thomson (eds.), *East of Byzantium: Syria and Armenia in the Formative Period*, Washington, DC, 1980, pp. 135–50.

Tod, M., *The Early Germans*, Oxford, 1992.

Tolkien, J. R. R., Beowulf: the monsters and the critics, *Proceedings of the British Academy*, 22 (1936): 1–53.

Tomlin, R. S. O., The Curse Tablets, in B. Cunliffe (ed.),*The Temple of Sulis Minerva at Bath 2*, Oxford, 1988, pp. 323–4.

Treadgold, W., *The Byzantine Revival, 780–842*, Stanford, CA, 1988.

—— *A History of the Byzantine State and Society*, Stanford, CA, 1997.

Treffort, C., *L'Eglise carolingienne et la mort*, Lyons, 1996.

Trombley, F., *Hellenic Religion and Christianization c.370–529*, Leiden, 1994.

Troncarelli, F., *Vivarium. I Libri, il Destino*, Turnhout, 1998.

Troupeau, G., Les couvents chrétiens dans la littérature arabe, *La Nouvelle Revue du Caire*, 1 (1975): 265–79.

Trout, D., *Paulinus of Nola*, Berkeley, CA, 1999.

Uthemann, K.H., Kaiser Justinian als Kirchenpolitiker und Theologe, *Augustinianum*, 39 (1999): 5–83.

Valante, M., Reassessing the Irish monastic towns, *Irish Historical Studies*, 31 (1999): 1 18.

Valenzani, R. S., Residential building in early medieval Rome, in J. M. H. Smith (ed.), *Early Medieval Rome and the Christian West. Essays in Honor of Donald Bullough*, Leiden, 2000, pp. 101–12.

Van Dam, R., *Leadership and Community in Late Antique Gaul*, Berkeley, CA, 1985.

Velázquez, I. and Ripoll, G., Toletum, la construcción de una *sedes regia*, in G. Ripoll and J. M. Gurt (eds.), *Sedes Regiae (ann. 400–800)*, Barcelona, 2000, pp. 521–78.

Velázquez Soriano, I., *Documentos de época visigoda escritos en pizarra (siglos VI–*

VIII), 2 vols., Turnhout, 2000.

Vésteinsson, O., The Christianization of Iceland. Priests, Power and Social Change 1000–1300, Oxford, 2000.

Visser, M., The Geometry of Love: Space, Time, Mystery and Meaning in an Ordinary Church, New York, 2001.

Vlierden, M. van, Willibrord en het begin van Nederland, Utrecht, 1995.

Vogel, C., Composition légale et commutation dans le système de la pénitence tarifiée, Revue de droit canonique, 8 (1958): 285–318 and 9 (1959): 1–38 and 341–59.

—— La discipline pénitentielle en Gaule des origines à la fin du VIIe siècle, Paris, 1952.

Vogüé, A. de, Histoire littéraire du mouvement monastique dans l'antiquité. Première partie: le monachisme latin, 5 vols., Paris, 1991–8.

Volpe, G., San Giusto: la villa, le ecclesiae, Bari, 1998.

Vööbus, A., Statutes of the Schools of Nisibis, Stockholm, 1965.

Wallace-Hadrill, J. M., The Frankish Church, Oxford, 1983.

Walls, A. F., African Christianity in the history of religions, in C. Fyfe and A. F. Walls (eds.), Christianity in Africa in the 1990s, Edinburgh, 1996, pp. 1–15.

Ward-Perkins, B., The cities, in Averil Cameron and P. Garnsey (eds.), Cambridge Ancient History 13. The Late Empire A.D. 337–425, Cambridge, 1999, pp. 371–410.

—— Constantinople: imperial capital of the fifth and sixth centuries, in G. Ripoll and J. M. Gurt (eds.), Sedes Regiae (ann. 400–800), Barcelona, 2000, pp. 63–81.

—— Specialized production and exchange, in Averil Cameron, B. Ward-Perkins, and M. Whitby (eds.), The Cambridge Ancient History 14. Late Antiquity: Empire and Successors A.D. 425–600, Cambridge, 2000, pp. 346–91.

—— Why did the Saxons not become more British?, English Historical Review, 115 (2000): 513–33.

Watson, A., Aurelian and the Third Century, London, 1999.

Watt., J. W., Eastward and westward transmission of Classical rhetoric, in J. W. Drijvers and A. A. MacDonald (eds.), Centres of Learning. Learning and Location in Pre-Modern Europe and the Near East, Leiden, 1995, pp. 63–75.

—— Grammar, rhetoric and the Enkyklios Paideia in Syria, Zeitschrift der deutschen morgenländischen Gesellschaft, 143 (1993): 45–71.

Webb, R., Salome's sisters: the rhetoric and reality of dancers in Late Antiquity and Byzantium, in Liz James (ed.), Women, Men and Eunuchs. Gender in Byzantium, London, 1997, pp. 119–8.

Webster, L., and Brown, M. (eds.), The Transformation of the Roman World, London, 1997.

Weidemann, M., Das Testament des Bischofs Bertram von Le Mans von 27. März 616, Mainz, 1986.

Wells, P. S., The Barbarians Speak. How the Conquered Peoples Shaped the Roman Empire, Princeton, NJ, 1999.

Werner, J., Das alemannische Fürstengrab in Wittislingen, Munich, 1960.

—— Das Grabfund von Malaja Pereščepina und Kuvrat, Kagan der Bulgaren, Bayerische Akademie der Wissenschaften: Abhandlungen, NF 91, Munich, 1984.

Werner, M., Works on the Book of Kells, Peritia, 11 (1997): 250–326.

Whitby, M., The Balkans and Greece, 420–600, in Averil Cameron, B. Ward-Perkins, and M. Whitby (eds.), *The Cambridge Ancient History 14. Late Antiquity: Empire and Successors* A.D. *425–600*, Cambridge, 2000, pp. 701–30.

—— Recruitment in Roman armies from Justinian to Heraclius (ca.565–615), in A. Cameron (ed.), *The Byzantine and Early Islamic Near East 3: States, Resources and Armies*, Princeton, NJ, 1995, pp. 61–124.

White, R., *The Middle Ground. Indians, Empires and Republics in the Great Lakes Region 1650–1815*, Cambridge, 1991.

Whitelock, D., *The Audience of Beowulf*, Oxford, 1951.

Whittaker, C. R., *Frontiers of the Roman Empire. A Social and Economic Study*, Baltimore, MD, 1994.

Whittow, M., *The Making of Byzantium, 600–1025*, London, 1996.

—— Ruling the late Roman and early Byzantine city: a continuous history, *Past and Present*, 129 (1990): 3–39.

Wicker, N. L., Selective female infanticide as a potential explanation of the dearth of women in Viking Age Scandinavia, in G. Halsall (ed.), *Violence and Society in the Early Medieval West*, Woodbridge, Suffolk, 1998, pp. 205–21.

Wickham, C., Italy and the early Middle Ages, in *Land and Power. Studies in Italian and European Social History 400–1200*, London, 1994, pp. 99–118.

—— The other transition: from the ancient world to feudalism, in *Land and Power. Studies in Italian and European Social History 400–1200*, London, 1994, pp. 7–42.

—— Overview, in R. Hodges and W. Bowden (eds.), *The Sixth Century: Production, Distribution and Demand*, Leiden, 1998, pp. 279–92.

—— Society, in R. McKitterick (ed.), *The Early Middle Ages*, Oxford, 2001, pp. 59–94.

Williams, S., *Diocletian and the Roman Recovery*, London, 1985.

Wipszycka, E., *Études sur le christianisme dans l'Éygpte de l'antiquité tardive*, Rome, 1996.

Wolska, W., Stéphanos d'Athènes et Stéphanos d'Alexandrie, *Revue des études byzantines*, 47 (1989): 5–89.

—— *La topographie chrétienne de Cosmas Indicopleustes*, Paris, 1962.

Wood, I., Christians and pagans in ninth-century Scandinavia, in P. Sawyer, B. Sawyer, and I. Wood (eds.), *The Christianization of Scandinavia*, Alingsås, 1987, pp. 36–67.

—— Missionaries and the Christian frontier, in W. Pohl, I. Wood and H. Reimitz (eds.), *The Transformation of Frontiers. From Late Antiquity to the Carolingians*, Leiden, 2001, pp. 209–18.

—— *The Missionary Life. Saints and Evangelization of Europe 400–1050*, London, 2001.

—— Administration, law and culture in Merovingian Gaul, in R. McKitterick (ed.), *The Uses of Literacy in Early Medieval Europe*, Cambridge, 1990, pp. 63–81.

—— The barbarian invasions and the first settlements, in Averil Cameron and Peter Garnsey (eds.), *The Cambridge Ancient History 13: The Late Empire* A.D. *337–425*, Cambridge, 1998, pp. 487–515.

—— Before or after mission: social relations across the middle and lower Rhine in the seventh and eighth centuries, in I. L. Hansen and C. Wickham (eds.), *The Long Eighth Century. Production, Distribution and Demand*, Leiden, 2001, pp. 149–66.

—— *Gregory of Tours*, Bangor, 1994.

—— *The Merovingian Kingdoms, 450–751*, London, 1994.

—— The mission of Augustine of Canterbury to the English, *Speculum*, 69 (1994): 1–17.

—— *The Most Holy Abbot Ceolfrid*, Jarrow Lecture, 1995.

—— Pagans and holy men 600–800, in P. Ní Chatháin and M. Richter (eds.), *Irland und die Christenheit*, Stuttgart, 1987, pp. 347–61.

—— Some historical reinterpretations and the Christianization of Kent, in G. Armstrong and I. N. Wood (eds.), *Christianizing Peoples and Converting Individuals*, Turnhout, 2000, pp. 27–35.

—— Topographies of holy power in sixth-century Gaul, in M. de Jong and F. Theuws with C. van Rhijn (eds.), *Topographies of Power in the Early Middle Ages*, Leiden, 2001, pp. 137–54.

Woolf, G., *Becoming Roman: The Origins of Provincial Civilisation in Gaul*, Cambridge, 1998.

—— World-systems analysis and the Roman empire, *Journal of Roman Archaeology*, 3 (1990): 44–58

Wormald, P., The age of Bede and Aethelbald, in J. Campbell (ed.), *The Anglo-Saxons*, Harmondsworth, 1991, pp. 70–100.

—— Bede and Benedict Biscop, in G. Bonner (ed.), *Famulus Christi*, London, 1976, pp. 141–69.

—— Bede, "Beowulf," and the conversion of the Anglo-Saxon aristocracy, in R. T. Farrell (ed.), *Bede and Anglo-Saxon England*, Oxford, 1978, pp. 32–95.

—— *Bretwaldas* and the origin of the *Gens Anglorum*, in P. Wormald (ed.), *Ideal and Reality in Frankish and Anglo-Saxon Society*, Oxford, 1983, pp. 99–129.

——*The Making of English Law 1: Legislation and its Limits*, Oxford, 1999.

—— Viking studies: whence and whither?, in R. T. Farrell (ed.), *The Vikings*, London, 1982, pp. 128–53.

Wright, N., Columbanus' *Epistolae*, in M. Lapidge (ed.), *Columbanus: Studies on the Latin Writings*, Woodbridge, Suffolk, 1997, pp. 29–92.

Wright, R., *Late Latin and Early Romance in Spain and Carolingian France*, Liverpool, 1982.

Yarshater, E. (ed.), *Encyclopaedia Iranica*, Costa Mesa, CA, 1991.

Zanini, E., *Le Italie bizantine. Territorio, insediamenti ed economia nella provincia bizantina d'Italia (VI–VIII secolo)*, San Spirito, 1998.

Index

Aachen (Aix-la-Chapelle) 435, 437, 443
abbesses 373, 476
abbots 210–11, 415, 476
  British 353
  Carolingian 442
  Irish 330–1, 333
  social status 330–1
Abd al-Malik, calif 301, 303, 309
Abd al-Walid, calif 301, 302, 303
Abgar VIII of Osrhoene 63
Abraham 37, 293
A.D. dating system 23, 416
Admonitio Generalis (Charlemagne)
  441, 450
Adomnán, abbot of Iona 329, 362
Adrianople 48, 86, 479
áes dana 372
Africa
  churches 114
  see also North Africa; the names of
    individual countries
afterlife *see* death and the afterlife
Agapetus, Pope 199
Agde, council of (506) 136
Agilulf, king of the Lombards 250
Agobard, archbishop of Lyons 455,
  456
agrarian rites 154
agrarian society 43, 46, 47, 48, 50,
  147, 172
Aï Qanum 27
Aistulf, king of the Lombards 405
Aix-la-Chapelle *see* Aachen

al-Akhtal (Arab poet) 308
Alans 102
Alaric I, king of the Visigoths 48, 86
Alaric II, king of the Visigoths 136, 137
  Breviarium Alaricianum 136
Alban, Saint 125
Alcuin of York 433, 439, 440, 443–4,
  446, 447, 453–4, 477
Aldebert (heretic) 421, 422–3, 450
Alemanni 413
Alexander, Saint 479
Alexandria 2, 50, 54, 115
  patriarchs 115, 116, 118, 172
  population 54
  Serapeum 74
almsgiving 69–70, 71, 157, 158, 222
alphabet, Armenian 277
Ambrose, bishop of Milan 80, 87, 105,
  256
Amida 185, 188
Ammianus Marcellinus, *Histories*
  478–9
amsâr 305
amulets 77, 153, 159, 324, 464
Ananias of Shirak 365, 485
  K'nnikon 365
Anastasius, emperor 137–8, 177
Anastasius of Sinai 309
  Stories to Strengthen the Faith 309
Anatolia 57, 390
  Christianization 390
Aneirin 128
  Y Gododdin 128

Anglo-Saxon Chronicle 468
Anglo-Saxon language 346, 373, 374
Anglo-Saxon verse 373, 377–8
Anglo-Saxons 378
'Anjar 305
anmcharae ("soul friend") 333
Annianus, bishop of Orléans 107
Anskar (Frankish missionary) 470
Anthony the hermit 81, 82
Anthony of Tagrit 311–12
Antichrist 203, 295
Antioch 2, 50, 54, 77, 115, 119–20,
    171, 206, 272, 273, 370
  patriarchs 115–16, 119, 171
  population 54
Antirrheticus (Evagrius) 284–5
Antirrhetikos (Nicephorus) 397
Antrim, County 41
Apamea 273
Apennines 182, 192
Apollos, Apa 174
"applied culture" 27–8
Aquileia 63
Arab culture 316
Arabian peninsula 286–8, 289
Arabic language 289–90, 301, 308,
    337, 386, 449
  spread 315–16
Arcadius, emperor 134
Arculf, bishop 318–19, 377–8
"arguments in stone" 29, 30, 32, 55,
    108
Ari Thorgilsson the Wise 473
  Book of the Icelanders 473
Arianism 79, 80, 105, 106, 136, 137,
    425
aristocracy 84–5
  aristocratic swagger 476–7
  bishops 110–11, 477
  early medieval Europe 30–1
  Frankish 31, 253, 354, 378, 410,
    411, 412, 442, 447, 448
  land ownership and wealth 56, 98
  literate 448, 452
  urban 56
aristocratization of the Church
    110–11
Aristotle 274
Arius 79, 117

Ark of the Covenant 457, 458
Arles 112, 151, 153, 154, 227–8
Armagh monastery 330
Armenia 9, 44, 187, 276–9, 485
  alphabet 277
  Christianity 276–9
  division between Rome and Persia
    277
  literature 277
  national identity 9, 278
  warrior aristocracy 277–8
Armenian Church 111, 277, 278
  Katholikos 111, 277, 288
  Monophysitism 278
armies
  Arab 296, 298, 315
  barbarian militias 102, 103–4, 105
  barbarian recruits 49, 101
  ethnic specificity 104
  German 47
  Roman 49, 101
  Themes 386
art
  early medieval 459, 461
  frescoes 204–5, 469
  Islamic 300
  mosaics 162, 168, 180, 190, 193,
    271, 300, 390, 400
  Muslim 390
  see also crafts; icons
asceticism 81, 87, 173, 200, 242,
    252
  ascetic missionaries 81, 82
  ascetic sensibility 199
  desert saints 173, 174, 175
  monastic discipline 112
  penitential asceticism 374
Asia
  Christianity in 40, 41, 267–94
  Islam in 289–94
Athanasius, patriarch of Alexandria
    79–80, 82, 105, 117, 118
Athens 58, 149, 178
atonement 220, 242
  see also penance
Attila the Hun 44, 45, 107
Aud the Deep-Minded 476
Augustine of Canterbury
  at Canterbury 345

conversion of Britain 215, 340, 342, 344–7
Augustine of Hippo, Saint 27, 73, 76, 82–3, 85, 87, 93, 129, 150, 151, 202, 204–5, 233, 235, 256
on baptism 91, 92
City of God 91–2
Confessions 28, 87–8, 204
death 93
doctrine of election 89, 90
and the Pelagian controversy 88–9
theology of grace 88–9
Aurelius Isidore 57–8
Ausonius of Bordeaux 86–7
Austrasia 408, 410–11
Autun 164
Auvergne 137
Avarayr, battle of (451) 278
Avars 44, 45, 183, 394, 434, 453–4
Axum 138–9, 187, 276
Aya Sofya *see* Hagia Sophia basilica

Baghdad 316, 317
Balkans
conversion of 404
crisis 394–5
Balthild, queen 255
Bamburgh 353
Bangor 246–7
Banu Ghassân 287, 290
baptism 65, 68, 91, 92, 344–5, 453
adult 453
baptismal vows 427, 451, 453
enforced 305, 366, 453
fulwiht 487
godparents 453, 454
infant 453
mass baptisms 349, 361
potency 154
preparation for 453–4
transformative rite 68, 88
barbarians 6, 43–8
absorption of Roman frontier zone 51, 100
"barbarian invasions" 4, 44, 48, 86, 93, 438
Christianity 105–6
definitions 43
farmers 43, 46, 47, 48

image of 6, 7, 45, 99–100
nomads 43–4
oral culture 48
para-Roman world 49, 50, 100
Pirenne thesis 9–10
pre-Christian past 8
in Roman armies 49, 101
Roman attitudes to 45, 46–7, 48, 49, 99–100
Roman collaboration with 99, 100–1, 102
settlements 7, 101–6
warrior society 48–9
Bardaisan 40, 42, 43, 48, 54, 63
The Book of the Laws of Countries 40, 54
Barhebraeus (Gregory Abu al-Farâj) 313
Barontus (monk) 259–60, 262, 374
Barsanuphius of Gaza 175–6, 203
Questions and Answers 175
Barsauma, bishop of Nisibis 280
basilicas 30, 63, 77, 78, 108, 125, 458, 459
Gallic 162
"sacred theater" 187
Basra 305
Bath 76, 127
Bauto (Frankish chieftain) 134
Bavaria 412, 421
Bede, the Venerable 30, 33, 52, 350–4, 355–6, 358, 363–4, 367, 373, 374
death 355
Ecclesiastical History of the English Nation 9, 351, 352, 416, 419
Life of Cuthbert 355
Belisarius 180
Bell-Beaker culture 485
Benedict, Saint 210, 221, 222, 250
Rule 210, 225, 441
Benedict Biscop 356, 359, 364
Benevento 192
Beowulf 478, 484
Berbers 138
Berry 161
Bertha (wife of Ethelbert) 344, 345
Bertram, bishop of Le Mans 157
Bewcastle 377

Bible 370–1, 460
  allegorical interpretation 204, 370
  copying and meditation on 41, 460
  explanation 27, 282, 370–1
  Ten Commandments 389
  Vulgate 199
  see also Old Testament; Scriptures
Birka (Björkö) 463
bishops 68, 78, 80, 107–8, 415
  arbiters of sin and repentance 68
  aristocrats 110–11, 477
  Chalcedonian 185
  church-building 168
  city "fathers" 158
  civic and episcopal power and
    activities 78, 80, 107, 157, 166,
    168–9, 208, 209, 211
  convergence of holiness and
    ecclesiastical office 173
  entry into their cities 166–7
  founders of monasteries 223
  Frankish 414, 423–4
  Gallic 110, 112, 113, 114, 116,
    157–8
  Gregory's guidance for 209, 211,
    212, 237
  Irish 330–1
  judges in civil litigation 78
  monk-bishops 111–13, 207
  Monophysites 186
  and the pagan past 149–50
  retinues 332, 362
  of Rome 114–15, 116
  and rural Christianity 146, 147
  social status 330–1
  tools of imperial government 168–9
  wealth 157
blood-money 245
boars 135
Bobbio 248
Boethius 195, 275
  Consolation of Philosophy 195
Bogu Qaghan 41–2
Boisil, prior 355
Boniface, Pope 249
Boniface, Saint 4, 41, 418–21, 423–5,
  430, 449
Book of Daniel 296
Book of History (Gregory of Tours)

139, 160, 161, 163
Book of the Icelanders (Air Thorgilsson
  the Wise) 473
Book of Job 204, 205
Book of Kells 30, 372–3, 377, 459
The Book of the Laws of Countries
  (Bardaisan) 40, 54
Book of Leviticus 244
The Book of Monsters 484
Book of Tobit 159
books
  centers of book production 22
  codices 23, 62–3, 82, 111
  copying 357, 372, 430
  encyclopedic works 364–5, 387
  illuminated 372–3, 459
  Manichaean texts 82
  material production 23, 25, 357, 445
  of penance *see Penitentials*
  of rituals 427
  treated as gifts 357
  "wisdom literature" 427
  see also libraries; translations
Boseth 73
Bostra 169
Bourges 110
Braga 99
Braudel, Fernand 11
Breviarium Alaricianum 136
Brigit, Saint 330, 331
Brioude 162
Britain
  Angli 214–15, 352, 474
  Anglo-Saxons 378
  Augustinian mission 4, 215, 219,
    340, 341, 344–7
  burial hoards 126
  Celtic hill-shrines 127
  Christian language 346
  Christianity 7, 8, 76, 127–8, 129,
    242, 341, 342, 344–64, 373–8
  churches 79
  civil wars 126
  economic collapse 12, 13
  "folk Christianity" 341
  gens Anglorum 351
  gift-giving relationship 31, 129, 344,
    347, 350
  hill-forts 129

kings/kingdoms 342, 343, 352, 474
Latin Christian culture 239, 241
metropolitan bishops 345
"micro-Christendoms" 15, 358–9, 368, 378
monasteries/monasticism 128, 373–4
overlordship 343
post-imperial Britain 12, 125–9
Roman economy 126
Roman garrisons 49–50
Romano-Britons 126–7, 128–9, 140
Saxons 7, 8, 15, 127, 242, 301, 341, 342–54
single "English nation" 9, 351
warrior elite 348, 353
written histories 1, 9, 140, 351, 352, 416, 419
see also Northumbria
British language 239
bubonic plague 155, 161, 180–3, 394
Buddha 82
Buddhism 32, 285
Bulayiq 284
Bulgars 394
Burdona' *see* Jacob Baradaeus
Burgundians 101, 102, 104, 228
Burgundofara 251, 254
burial hoards 126, 321, 324
burial practices
  burial beside saints and shrines 263
  Christian 67, 262–5
  Frankish 418
  Gallic 133, 134
  grave inscriptions 264, 282
  ship burials 321, 324, 343, 347
Byzantine Church 386–7, 404
  theology of images 395–9
  see also Orthodox Church
Byzantine empire 2, 177, 379, 386
  centralized 443
  Iconoclast Controversy 26–7, 387–406, 408, 457
  "orthodox" belief systems 387
  pressure of Muslim invasions 394, 395
  simplified society 386
  see also east Roman empire

Caecilius (Berber ruler) 138
Caedmon 376, 377
Caesarius, bishop of Arles 107, 112, 116, 150–4, 227–8, 426, 427, 451
  and paganism 151–3
  problem of the *mundus* 152–3
  sermons 151, 445
  weekday naming 152
calendar
  A.D. dating system 23, 416
  regnal years 416
  Roman "provincial era" 416
canon law 370
Canterbury 215, 345, 369, 370
Capitulary on the Region of Saxony (Charlemagne) 432
Caratene, queen of the Burgundians 228
Caroline minuscule 444, 445
Carolingian empire 378, 406, 431, 437–40
  Carolingian myth 438
  court 435, 437, 443, 444
  instruction and control system 451
  intense religious curiosity 450
  program of *correctio* 439, 440, 442–3, 447, 454
  technocrats 455
"Carolingian Renaissance" 22, 23, 31, 220, 438, 440
Carthage 62, 85, 105, 179, 296
  fall 10, 296
Cassian *see* John Cassian
Cassiodorus 27, 196–8, 199, 233, 240, 274, 358
  Institutes of Christian Culture 196
  Variae 196
Castile 238
Catholic Church 4, 91, 92, 106, 129, 130, 487
Celestial Hierarchies (Pseudo-Dionysius) 398
Celestine, Pope 114
celibacy
  clerical 81
  see also virgins
Celsus 160
Celtic language 232, 239
  British 239
  Old Irish 239

"Celtic Mediterranean" 16, 51, 129, 132
cemeteries 24–5, 33, 262, 263
Ceolfrith, abbot of Wearmouth 356, 358
ceramics 180–1
Chad, bishop 369–70
Chalcedon 120
　Council of (451) 116, 120, 121, 166, 169, 177, 183–4, 279, 310
Chalcedonians 166, 187, 189, 308, 309, 310
　bishops 185
charismatic preachers 81
Charlemagne, emperor 5, 6, 41, 378, 405, 406, 428, 431–2, 433, 434–7, 440–1, 442, 461, 477
　Admonitio Generalis 441, 449–50
　on baptism 453–4
　Capitulary on the Region of Saxony 432
　concept of loyalty 437, 451
　conquest of the Lombards 431, 436
　coronation 435
　death 436
　invasion of Saxony 432
　Life (Einhard) 435–6
　new imperial order 434–5, 437
　program of *correctio* 440–1
Charles Martel (the Hammer) 319, 378, 408, 410, 420, 428
Childeric, king of the Franks 134, 321
Chinese empire 272
Chlothar III, king of the Franks 255
Chlothar, king of Neustria 228, 229
Chlothild, queen 136
"Christian Law" 441–2, 444, 446, 448, 451, 455, 456, 461, 479
Christian Topography (Cosmas) 271
Christian visual imagination 399–400
Christianity
　applied 25–9
　aristocratic preoccupation 33
　in Asia 40, 41, 267–94
　in Britain 7, 8, 76, 127–8, 129, 242, 341, 342, 344–64, 373–8
　Dark Age 17–20
　democracy 65

early Church 62–71, 439
early medieval 17–20, 29, 30, 52
East Roman empire 2, 168, 265, 267–94, 365
Egypt 81, 82, 111, 118, 172, 174, 183, 241, 242, 250
emphasis on Christ-like nature of common man 188
"folk Christianity" 125, 341, 411, 413, 420–1, 455
"frontier Christianity" 421
in Gaul 99–101, 106–7, 146–7, 150–65, 252–5
Germany 413, 420–1, 481
Golden Age 17
grassroots movement 78–9
Great Persecution 62
Greek 2, 25, 26, 149, 183, 387
interconnectivity 13–14, 16
in Ireland 132, 326, 330–5, 344
late antique 24–5, 29
Latin 83
localization and diversity 14–16, 17
as a minority religion 132
oral 420, 449, 450
Primitive Church 18
public welfare system 69–70, 78, 158
Roman empire 54–92
rural 81, 146–7
salvation 65
in Scandinavia 7, 467, 469–84
spread 7–8, 61–4, 469
Syria 3, 82, 172, 173, 174, 183, 186, 310–11
"top-down" view of establishment of Christian Church 375
universal religion 14, 15, 40–1, 62, 91, 169, 414
"vernacular" 449, 450
Western 265
Christogram 84
Christological controversy 116–22, 291
chronicle tradition 312–13
Chronicle of Zuqnîn 314, 315
Church councils
　Agde (506) 136

Chalcedon (451) (Great
Prevarication) 116, 120, 121, 166,
169, 177, 183–4, 279, 310
Ephesus (431) 116, 119, 120, 149
Frankfurt (794) 406
Hiereia (754) 392
Nicaea (325) 61, 79
Nicaea (787) 393, 396, 405, 406,
457
Toledo (589–694) 366
Tours (813) 450
Whitby (664) 361
Church of the Ascension, Jerusalem
318–19
Church of the Holy Sepulcher,
Jerusalem 77
"Church of Satan" 170, 187
churches 77–8
building complexes 78
church building 79, 108, 168
destruction 63
disendowment of rival churches 91
iconography of Latin churches 461
on pagan sites 146, 149
visual magnificence 77, 157–8, 388,
400, 401
see also basilicas
Church–State conflict 80
cingulum militiae 101
Cirta 70
cities
councils 55, 78
decay of post-Roman cities 21, 22
East Roman empire 273
fortified 106–7
and imperial centralization 57
inner cities 158
Islamic garrison cities 305
local gods 58
local militia power bases 104
pagan monuments 170
populations 54–5
repeated sackings 99
Roman cities 21, 49, 54–5
trade associations and cultic
brotherhoods 64
urban aristocracies 54, 80
City of God (Saint Augustine) 91–2
civil wars 86, 93

Britain 126
Germany 452
Islamic empire 299, 300
Spain 193
Clement (heretic) 421, 422
Clermont 106, 108, 113
climate 17–18
clothing
"barbarian" 6, 100, 103
Irish clergy 132
monks 223, 225
and status 223
Clovis, king of the Franks 6, 133,
134–5, 136–8, 156
baptism 137
Gregory's account 139
Lex Salica 135
Cluain Melsige (Clonmelsh) 415
Codex Amiatinus 357, 358, 371–2
Codex Grandior 357–8
Codex Justinianus 178
codices 23, 62–3, 82, 111
see also books
Cogitosus, *Life* (of Saint Brigit) 331
Coifi (pagan high priest) 348
coinage 130, 463
Arabic 302
Axum 138
Merovingian 416
Roman 464
solidi 180
colloquia 203
Cologne 50, 54
Colum *see* Columbanus
Columba (of Iona), Saint 327–9, 334,
361
at Iona 327–9
Life of Columba 329
Columbanus, Saint 4, 165, 219, 220,
246–50, 257, 327
asceticism 252
in the Frankish world 248, 252–5
and Gregory the Great 248, 249
Letters 249
Life of Columbanus (Jonas) 251,
252, 258
Monastic Instructions 249
column saints 173, 174, 310–11
Comgall, abbot 246, 247

commerce 12, 22
  and Christianity 11, 146–7, 284
  decline of western Mediterranean
    trading networks 364
  Frisian 416–17
Companions of Muhammad 292, 293
Compludo 210
concubinage 305
confession 24, 243, 244, 251, 257, 333,
    422
  auricular 24
Confession (Saint Patrick) 131, 331
Confessions (Saint Augustine) 28, 87–8,
    204
Consolation of Philosophy (Boethius)
    195
Constantine, emperor 67, 74, 77, 80,
    86
  benefactions to the Church 77
  conversion 60–1, 73
  death 61
  rise to power 3
  sense of imperial mission 89
  suppression of paganism 74
Constantine IV, emperor 319
Constantine V, emperor 390, 392, 393,
    397
Constantine VI, emperor 393
Constantinople 2, 21, 50, 57, 85, 177,
    201–2, 267, 297, 317, 318, 386,
    392, 404
  Blue and Green factions 178, 187
  church of Saint Irene 393
  fall (1453) 318
  Haghia Sophia 178–9, 377, 386,
    395, 400, 403, 404
  Hippodrome 171–2, 178, 386
  library 386
  "New Rome" 57, 97, 115, 201
  Nika riot (532) 178
  plague (543) 181
  population 57, 115, 386
  rise 21, 115–16
Constantius II, emperor 74, 79, 324
convents
  of Caesaria (Arles) 227–8
  child novices 223
  family foundations 373
  Faremoutiers 251–2, 254, 258

Frankish 254–5
Gallic 221
  powerhouses of atonement 252
  powerhouses of prayer 226, 230, 425
  of Radegund of Poitiers 229
  "rules" 227, 229
  Spain 221
  Tauberbischofsheim 425–6
  wealth 254–5
conversion 67, 68, 225
  forced 306
  personal transformation through 68
conversion narratives 6, 86–7, 88
Coptic language 172
Corbie monastery 255
Cornwall 130
Coroticus (British warlord) 131, 332,
    334
correctio 439, 440, 442–3, 447, 454
Cosmas Indicopleustes (the India-
    Sailor) 267, 271, 296
  Christian Topography 271
cosmological works 365
countryside, Christianization of 81,
    146–7
crafts
  ceramics 180–1
  frescoes 204–5, 269
  jewelry 45, 101, 372, 459
  metalworking 46–7
  silverware 84, 172
"the Creeper" (Christian wrestler) 64
Cross 302
  relics of 229–30, 284, 285, 319, 377
  sign of the Cross 72, 153, 391, 392,
    393, 395
  victorious power 72
  victory-bringing sign 378, 391
Ctesiphon 37
Cúl Drebene, battle of (561) 327
culture
  Arab 316
  creativity and retrenchment 236
  ecclesiastical 236
  Latin Christian 239–41
  Latin secular 237, 238
  narrowing down 235–6
  secular culture in "barbarian" West
    237–9

"culture of wisdom" 203–5, 236–7, 241, 261
Cummian (Cumméne the Tall) 361–2
Cunorix MacCullen 126
curse-tablets 76
Cuthbert, Saint 355, 422
Cyprian, bishop of Carthage 62, 138
Cyril, patriarch of Alexandria 116, 118, 183

daemones 65, 76
    see also demonic world
Dalriada Irish 129
Damascus 307, 308
    Great Mosque 302, 303, 401
dancers 170–1
Daniel 67
Daniel, bishop of Winchester 419, 424
Danube valley 47, 123, 124, 182, 183
Dark Ages 5, 9, 17, 22
    Christianity 17–20
    visual and artistic achievements 30, 31
Dastkart 284
dating systems
    A.D. 23, 415–16
    Muslim system 416
    Roman "provincial era" 416
Dawson, Christopher 11, 13, 14
days of the week 152
deacons 64
death and the afterlife
    Christianization of death 262–5
    preoccupation with 257–62
    triumph over death 67
    Voyage of the Soul 259–60
    see also Heaven; Hell
Defense of Holy Images (John of Damascus) 398
Demetrius, Saint 389
demonic world 65, 73, 147, 455–6, 475, 482
    Christian attitudes to 65
    exorcism 66, 72, 83
Denmark 324, 463, 464, 470, 471
"depaganization" of Christians 423
Dermot mac Cerball 327
desert 173–4, 175
Desert Christians/Fathers 24, 81, 203, 256

    see also hermits
Dhû Nuwâs 288
Dhuoda 448
Dialogues (Gregory the Great) 213–14, 258, 259, 264
Digest (Tribonian) 178
Diocletian, emperor 56, 60, 62
Dionysius the Areopagite *see* Pseudo-Dionysius
Dioscorus, patriarch of Alexandria 116, 118
divide and rule policy 102–3, 432
divination 410, 472
doctrinal unity 169, 170
    failure to impose 170, 176
Dokkum 424
Dome of the Rock, Jerusalem 303, 309
Dorestad (Duurstede) 416–17, 463
Drachensberg 484
Dream of the Rood 377–8
druids 336
Drythelm 375
Dublin Bay 473
Dubtach maccu Lugair 336
Dura Europos 63

Eanbald 347
Eanfled, queen 359
East Roman empire 2, 97, 115, 165, 378
    annual budget 177
    Christianity 2, 168, 265, 267–94, 365
    cities 273
    collapse 297, 308
    crisis of identity 379
    desert/world divide 173
    destabilization of barbarian kingdoms 193
    diminished state 383
    government 56
    Islamic attacks 296–7, 298, 378, 383
    Monophysites 274
    remnants of paganism 149
    territorial area 168, 181
    war with Persian empire 272–3, 285–6, 287

Easter
  date calculations 61, 248–9, 360,
    361, 365
  etymology 346
  "Roman" Easter 363, 371
Ecclesiastical Hierarchies (Pseudo-
    Dionysius) 398
*Ecclesiastical History of the English
    Nation* (Bede) 9, 351, 352, 416,
    419
Echternach 417, 418
eclipses of the moon 153
Edda 473
Edessa 14, 37, 40, 170–1, 280, 313,
    371
education
  classical education 197, 234–7
  private education 235
  uniformity 233
Edwin, king of Northumbria 348, 349
Egfrith, king of Northumbria 350, 351
Egypt 55, 81, 82, 172
  Christianity 81, 82, 111, 118, 172,
    174, 183, 241, 242, 250
  government 55
  monasteries/monasticism 81, 82, 111,
    174, 241, 242, 250
  Monophysite province 183
  monotheism 118
  remnants of paganism 148
Einhard 435–6, 448
  Life of Charlemagne 435–6
the elect 89, 90
Eligius, Saint 158
Elipandus, archbishop of Toledo 406
Elishe Vardapet 9, 278
Ella Atsbeha 139, 288
Eloi *see* Eligius, Saint
Elvira 64
Emmanuel 118
"End of Ancient Christianity" 221
end of the world 93
  see also Last Days/Last Judgment
Ephesus 58, 149
  council of (431) 116, 119, 120, 149
Epic Histories (P'awst'os Buzand) 9
epic poetry 477, 478
  Frankish epics 477
Epifanij the Wise 404

Epiphanius, Apa 175–6
Epiphanius, bishop 113, 203
Ercantrudis (nun) 251, 252
Escomb 373
Ethelbert, king of Kent 215, 344–5
  Laws 346–7
Ethelburga (daughter of Ethelbert) 348,
    349
Ethiopia 138, 139
Etymologies (Isidore of Seville) 365,
    367, 465
Eucharist 166, 187, 264, 458
Eugippius 125, 357
  Life of Severinus 125
Euphemia (Monophysite) 188
Eusebius, bishop of Caesarea 117
Eutychius, patriarch of Constantinople
    202
Evagrius of Pontos 284–5
  Antirrheticus 284–5
execution, public 66
exiles 247, 334
  "exiles of God" 415, 421
  religious exiles 415
exorcism 66, 72, 83

fairy kingdom 421, 483
Faremoutiers monastery 251–2, 254,
    258
farming 43, 46, 47, 48, 50, 147
fasting 470
Fathers of the Church 17, 19, 24, 26
feasting 48
Feddersen Wierde 46
feis Temro 327
Felix III, Pope 199
Fénelon, François, bishop of Cambrai
    159
Feofan (Theophanes) the Greek 404
Ferghil, abbot of Aghaboe *see* Vergil,
    bishop of Salzburg
Fergus mac Roich 483
Fertile Crescent 37, 276, 285, 299, 300
Finns 465
Firmus (of Carthage) 92
flint-stones 486
Florentius, abbot 214
"folk Christianity" 125, 341, 411, 413,
    420–1, 455

Fossa Carolina 434
Francia/Franks 5, 7, 51, 104, 133–8,
  194, 234, 252–5, 378, 405, 408,
  410
  aristocracy 31, 253, 354, 378, 410,
    411, 412, 442, 447, 448
  bishops 414, 423–4
  chieftainship 135
  clergy 442
  formation of the Frankish kingdom
    411
  gift-giving relationship 253–4
  international elite 411
  landowning system 411
  military ethos 155–6
  mixed aristocracy 234
  monasticism 253–5
  warfare 410
Frankfurt, council of (794) 406
free will 88, 89
Freising 413
French language 447, 451
frescoes 204–5, 469
Friderichus (of the Rugians) 124–5
Friesland 417
Frisia 46, 412, 414, 415, 416–17, 427
"frontier" Christianity 421
Fulda 420, 424, 442, 479
Fursa, abbot 259, 350, 375

Gafsa 232
Galen of Ephesus 48
Garonne valley 102, 103
Gaul 7, 97, 133–8
  aristocratization of the Church
    110–11
  barbarian raids 86
  basilicas 108
  bishops 110, 112, 113, 114, 116,
    157–8
  burial practices 133, 134
  Christianity 99–101, 106–7, 146–7,
    150–65, 252–5
  convents 221
  erosion of Latin culture 233
  holy springs 148
  Merovingian Gaul 12, 13, 158, 162,
    163
  monasteries 221

new aristocracy 157
  potentes 157, 160
  religious experimentation 161
  stability 156
  veneration of the martyrs 109
  warfare 107
  see also Francia/Franks
Gaza 166
Geismar, sacred oak at 41, 421
General Warning see *Admonitio
  Generalis* (Charlemagne)
Genovefa, Saint 109
gentes 104–5
Gerald of Wales 372–3
German language 451
Germanus, bishop of Auxerre 112–13
  Life of Germanus 113
Germany 451, 481
  "Apostle of Germany" (Saint
    Boniface) 418–19
  armies 47
  Carolingian "discovery" of 478
  Carolingian instruction and control
    451
  Carolingian invasion of Saxony 432
  cattle-tributes 47
  Christianity 413, 420–1, 481
  "Conversion of Germany" 412
  Frankish landowning system 411–12
  local chieftains, power of 413
  monasteries 442
  Old Saxons 413
  paganism 413, 420
  peripheral Roman economy 46
  program of *correctio* 442–3
  recuperation of the past 478, 479
  tribal warfare 47
  warrior society 413
Germia 181
Gertrude, abbess of Nivelles 265–6,
  408
Ghaerbald, bishop of Liège 452, 453,
  454
Gibbon, Edward 5–6
Gibuldus, king of the Alemanni 124
gift-giving relationship 31, 32–3, 129
  Britain 31, 129, 344, 347, 350
  churches and monasteries 32
  Franks 253–4

gift-giving relationship (*cont'd*)
   Ireland 31, 133, 326, 332–3
   popes and emperors 31
   reciprocity 333
Gildas 128, 140, 240, 242, 351
   On the Ruin of Britain 140
Giso, Queen of the Rugians 124
Glorious Raven *see* Bertram, bishop of Le Mans
Goar, king of the Alans 113
God
   Allah 290
   grace of 88, 89, 173, 187
   see also Jesus Christ
godparents 453, 454
gods 58–60, 65
   classical mythology 475
   and genealogies 474
   local gods 58
   lower gods 59, 65, 76
   power of 480
   sacrifice to 481
   Scandinavian 475, 479–80
   source of energy 480
   source of high skills 475
   see also God
Gogo (*referendarius*) 237
Goodmanham 348
Gospel Harmony 452
Gospel of Saint Luke 399
Gothic age 17
Goths 47–8, 104, 194
   see also Visigoths
Gottschalk (theologian) 410
grace of God 88, 89, 173, 187
Grand Narrative of European history 4–5
Great Liturgy 166, 167
Great Mosque, Damascus 302, 303, 401
Great Persecution (303–14) 62, 66, 73, 74
Great Prevarication (Council of Chalcedon) 116, 120, 121, 166, 169, 177, 183–4, 279, 310
Greek Christianity 2, 25, 26, 149, 183, 387
Greek Fathers 183, 387
"Greek fire" 318, 392

Greek scholarship 3, 311, 317, 368, 395
Greenland 467, 469, 481
Gregorius, Georgius Florentius *see* Gregory, bishop of Tours
Gregory I, pope (Gregory the Great) 4, 28, 120, 165, 198–215, 219, 224, 234, 345, 346, 351, 357
   at Constantinople 201–2
   and biblical allegory 370
   "care of souls" 28, 203–4, 205, 208–9, 246, 346
   and Columbanus 248, 249
   correspondence 212–13
   "culture of wisdom" 203–5, 236
   death 205, 215
   Dialogues 213–14, 258, 259, 264
   on exercise of spiritual power 207–12
   Homilies on the Gospels 214, 258, 260
   Life 215, 377
   mission to Britain 4, 345, 346
   monk 200–1, 209–10
   Moralia on Job 205, 207, 236
   papal office 205–7
   praedicator 213
   Prefect of Rome 200
   Regestum 212
   Regula Pastoralis 207–12, 236–7, 248
   on sin and penance 256–7, 258, 261
   on "worldly wisdom" 235
Gregory, bishop of Tours 7, 106, 108, 139, 155–65, 174, 187, 208, 260, 264, 376
   Book of History 139, 160, 161, 163
   books of *Wonders* 161
Gregory Nazianzen 207, 311
Grigor ("Gregory the Illuminator") 277
Groningen 417
Gudme 324
Guntram Boso 160

hack silver 134–5, 353
Hadiths 297
Hadrian, pope 405
Hadrian's Wall 129, 363
Hagia Sophia basilica 178–9, 377, 386, 395, 400, 403, 404

hagiography 187
  Irish 331
hair shirts 228, 229
hairstyles
  declaration of identity 223, 361
  see also tonsure
Harald Bluetooth of Denmark 471
Harald Klak, king of Denmark 469–70
Harran 37
Harun al-Rashid 314, 316
healing 159, 163, 181
Heaven 258, 375
Heavenfield, battle of (635) 352
Hedeby 463
Helena (mother of Constantine) 229
Heliand, The Savior 452
Hell 258, 260–1, 375, 422
"Hellenes" 149
Hellenism, eastern 310
Hemmaberg 125
Hengist and Horsa 127
Heraclius, emperor 285, 293–4, 305
heretics 91, 176, 184
hermits 81, 123
  stylite 173, 310–11
Hesse 420
Hesychius, bishop of Salona 93
Hexham abbey 363
Hezekiah of Israel 393
hijra 293, 304, 416
Hilary, bishop of Arles 112, 113
Hild, abbess 215, 376
Hippo 78, 87, 91
Hira 288
Hisham Palace 299, 300
Histories (Ammianus Marcellinus) 478–9
Histories (Monophysite) 312, 313
History against the Pagans (Orosius) 74
Hlodovech *see* Clovis, king of the Franks
Holland 4
Holy Commonwealth 194, 211
Holy Island *see* Lindisfarne
holy men and women 173, 174, 175, 200, 203, 388, 422, 455
  ascetics 173, 174, 175
  icons 388
  Monophysites 185

spiritual guides 176, 200, 203
  see also saints
holy pictures *see* icons
Holy Spirit 173–4
holy war (*jihâd*) 292
homilies 450–1
Homilies on the Gospels (Gregory) 214, 258, 260
honor 245–6, 253, 361
  clerical 346–7
  codes 156
  compensation for damaged honor 245–6
Honoratus, Saint 111
horse-archers 179
horses
  horse-sacrifice 134
  horseflesh, eating 370, 472
  stirrups 45
  in warfare 44, 410
Hoxne hoard 126
Hsian-fu 267, 272, 285, 314
Hunayn ibn Ishaq 317
Huneberc (Anglo-Saxon nun) 427–8
Huns 44, 47, 107, 119, 124, 479
hunting 45, 103
Hydatius, bishop of Chaves 98–9
  Chronicle 99
hymns 187, 188, 281

Ibas of Edessa 184
Iceland 467, 480
  conversion of 471–3
  literature 473–4
  Sagas 478, 480
Iconoclast Controversy 2, 26–7, 387–406, 408
  First Iconoclasm 391–3
  Iconoclasts 389, 390, 391, 457
  Iconophiles/Iconodules 387–8, 389, 392, 393, 395, 396–7, 402, 403
  Second Iconoclasm 393–5
  theology of images 395–9
icons 25, 26, 387–8, 389, 457, 458, 461
  "clericalized" devotion 402
  enkolpia 403
  link to Christ and the Apostles 399
  miraculous 388, 402, 403

icons (*cont'd*)
  protective function 389, 401–2, 403
  sense of privacy 403
  veneration 388, 399, 403
Iliad (Homer) 311
Illerup 47
images
  cult of 405–6, 456–7
  talismans 402
  theology of 395–9
  see also icons
imaginative landscape 485
incest 421
Index of Superstitions and Pagan Practices 426
infanticide 472
Ingelheim 469
Institutes of Christian Culture (Cassiodorus) 196
Institutions of the Monastic Life (Cassian) 111
Iona 30, 320, 327–9, 330, 341, 349, 350, 353, 361, 362, 371, 372, 468
Iraq 313
Ireland 6, 129–33, 325–39
  áes dana 372
  anmcharae ("soul friend") 333
  base clients 325–6, 332
  brithemain 335
  British Christian slaves 130
  cattle raids 47
  Celtic 325
  centers of learning 22
  Christian communities 332–5
  Christianity 132, 326, 330–5, 344
  clergy 330–1, 332, 333
  "conversion" of 326, 335
  cultural riches 240
  Dalriada Irish 129
  druids 336
  First Synod of Saint Patrick 132
  gift-giving relationship 31, 133, 326, 332–3
  hagiography 331
  introduction of literacy 335–6, 337
  Irish literature 337, 338
  kings/kingdoms 342, 343
  laech 335

Latin Christian culture 239–41, 335–6
law of damages 245
laws 335, 336, 337–9, 475
legal texts 337–9
Lughnasa festival 133
manaig 333
Mass priests 265
"micro-Christendoms" 15
monasteries/monasticism 128, 330, 332–3
ogham script 50, 130, 335
Old Irish 50, 130, 239, 277, 337, 374
paganism 335
Palladius' mission 130
penitential practices 333–4
poetry 335, 336, 475
pre-Christian Ireland 338
sapientes 20
Síde ("the Other Side") 421, 455, 483
sixth-century 325–6
slaves 326
stratified society 325–6
taboos, codification of 20
túath 132, 325, 330
warrior elite 335
Isidore, bishop of Seville 365, 367
  Etymologies 365, 367, 465
Isidore of Pelusium 72
Islam 3, 9, 219, 291–2, 294, 305
  Christian attitudes to 307–9, 317–18
  Christians under 295–320
  conversions 304, 315
  criticism of contemporary Christian practice 390
  and the debate on images 390
  Eastern Church under 3, 313–14
  emergence 3, 289–94
  Islamization of Near East 314–17
  Jews under 3, 309
  Muslim art and architecture 390
Islamic empire 383
  Arab conquests 296, 297, 299
  attacks on East Roman empire 296–7, 298, 378, 383
  civil wars 299, 300
  creation of Arabic historical tradition

301
  feuds 298
  garrison cities 305
  public face 301–4
Italy
  economic depression 156
  Frankish invasion 431
  "geographical expression" 192
  Lombard invasion 182, 184, 192,
    430–1
  new "Roman" empire 194, 195
  reconquest by Justinian 179

Jacob Baradaeus, bishop of Edessa 186
Jacobites *see* Monophysites
Jafnid family 287
Jarrow 51–2, 351, 356, 374
Jebel Sem'an 173
Jelling 471
Jerash 307
Jericho 299
Jerome, Saint 99, 199, 235, 246–7, 248
Jerusalem
  Church of the Ascension 318–19
  Church of the Holy Sepulcher 77
  Dome of the Rock 303, 309
  fall (618) 284
  Heavenly Jerusalem 92
  Temple 393
Jesus Christ
  Christological Controversy 116–22,
    291
  Crucifixion 72, 119, 369, 377
  divine and human nature 116–22,
    188, 369
  icons 388
  Incarnation 117, 118, 119
  Islamic attitudes to 307
  "Monothelite" controversy 369, 378
jewelry 101, 459
  barbarian 45
  Irish 372
Jews
  enforced baptism 305, 366
  and the Messiah 295
  under Islamic empire 3, 306
  and the worship of images 389–90
jihâd 292
jizya tax 306

Joazeira 14
John bar Penkâye 299
John, bishop of Ephesus 186, 188
  Lives of the Eastern Saints 186
John Cassian 111, 203, 242
  Conferences 111
  Institutions of the Monastic Life 111
John of Damascus (John Damascene)
  307–8, 397–8, 399, 401, 404, 457,
  460
  Defense of Holy Images 398
John Lydus 177
John Moschus 188, 212
John the Persian 212
John of Tella 311
Jonas (biographer of Columbanus) 251,
  252, 258
Jordan 273, 390
Judaism 70, 289, 290
  almsgiving 69
Julian, Saint 162
Julian the Apostate, emperor 86, 170
Julian, archbishop of Toledo 26
Julius Africanus 63–4
Justin, Emperor 177
Justinian, emperor 2, 122, 155, 165,
  169, 176–80, 193, 249, 400
  Codex Justinianus 178
  condemnation of Three Chapters
    184, 249
  death 181
  invasion of southern Spain 366
  orthodoxy 193
  Procopius' account 180
  quest for religious unity 183–5
  reconquest of Italy and Africa 179
  suppression of paganism 178
Jutland 50

Ka'ba, Mecca 291, 293
Kalends of January (Roman festival)
  85, 152, 154, 423
Karabalghasun 41
Katholikoi (of Armenia) 111, 277, 288
Kebra Nagast 139
Kerala 271
Kerkuk 284, 285
Khan Krum 394
Khirbet al-Mafjar 299

Khusro I Anoshirwan, king of Persia 182, 283, 287
Khusro II Aparwez, king of Persia 283, 285
Kiev 404, 466
  conversion 467, 469
Kildare monastery 330, 372
kingship
  genealogy 474–5
  identification with civilization 413–14
  sacral 343
  see also gift-giving relationship
Kirgizstan 267
K'nnikon (Ananaias of Shirak) 365
kontakion 187
Kufa 305

laech 335
laity 14, 173, 335
  Ireland 332–3
  monastic endowments 224, 254, 357, 373
  pursuit of piety 199, 200
languages
  linguistic boundaries of Europe 447
  liturgical 172
  "profane" languages 461
  see also the names of individual languages
laos 14
Lapps 465
Last Days/Last Judgment 203, 235, 237, 292, 304
Latin culture 198, 233
  Christian 239–41, 335–6, 439
  erosion 233, 235
  oral transmission 197
Latin language 116, 177, 232, 237, 446–7, 461
  consolidation 232
  "correct" Latin 449
  fixed pronunciation 447
  legal 116, 177, 238
  loan words 50
  Roman 430
  "rustic" 160, 232, 233, 238, 448
  sub-Latin 447
law

canon 370
"Christian Law" 441–2, 444, 446, 448, 451, 455, 456, 461, 479
  Irish 335, 336
  Mongol 313
  natural 336
  Roman 97, 178, 183, 238
  Scriptural 336
  Visigothic codes 237–8
"law of the face" 245, 246
Law of Innocents 329
Laws (Ethelbert, king of Kent) 346–7
Lazar of Pharp (or P'arp) 9, 278
Le Mans 158
Leander, bishop of Seville 205, 365
Leeuwarden 50
Leo I, pope (Leo the Great) 113, 115, 116, 130, 145
  and the Christological controversy 117, 120–1
  Tome 120–1, 184
Leo III, pope 435
Leo III, emperor 318, 390, 392
Leo V, emperor 394–5
Leoba (Anglo-Saxon nun) 425
Leontius of Neapolis 188
Lérins 111–12
Letter from Heaven 422, 450
Letter to Coroticus (Saint Patrick) 131, 331
Leubella (prophetess) 161
Lex Salica 135
libraries 195, 357
  assembling 357
  Constantinople 386
  monastic 52
  Rome 64, 195, 199
  Vivarium 196–7
  Wearmouth 356
Libri Carolini 457
Liège 452
Life of Anskar (Rimbert) 470
Life of Anthony (Athanasius) 82
Life of Charlemagne (Einhard) 435–6
Life of Mani 82
Life of Martin (Severus) 83
Life of Severinus (Eugippius) 125
limes 156, 411, 412, 414, 431

Lindisfarne (Holy Island) 328, 353, 357, 360, 369, 372, 468
literacy 22, 446
  active 447
  grammar 418
  historical narratives 8–9
  introduction into Ireland 335–6, 337
  passive 448
  practical 22
literature
  Armenian 277
  chronicle tradition 312–13
  Greek Church 26
  Irish 337, 338
  Latin 478
  Latin Christian 26, 198
  Patristic Age 22–3
  see also poetry
Lives of the Eastern Saints (John of Ephesus) 186
livestock 47
Loire valley 102
Lombards 182, 192–3, 206, 429, 430, 431, 436
  invasion of Italy 182, 405, 430–1
London 50, 54
Lorch 123, 125
Louis the Pious, emperor 440, 442, 463, 469, 477
loyalty 13, 361
  and autonomy 15
  Charlemagne and 437, 451
  local loyalties 98
  oaths of 451
  and *pietas* 87
  soldier's oath of 101
  to the Roman state 101
Lughnasa festival 133
Luni 222
Lupercalia ceremony 145
Luxeuil monastery 248, 250, 253, 254
Lyons 100, 108, 455

Maccabees 278, 279
Madaura 233
Magi 271
magic 48, 75, 481–2
Mainz 411, 417
Maiouma 166

Malaia Pereščepina 321
Mamertus, bishop of Vienne 108
manaig 333
Mani 81
Manichaean psalm book 82
Manichaeism 41, 81–2, 284
Mansûr (of Damascus) 307
Mansûr bar Sarjûn *see* John of Damascus
Marburg 426
Marcia (Christian concubine) 63
Marcian, emperor 120
Marcus Aurelius, *Meditations* 205
marriage
  marital intercourse 208, 243, 334
  polygamy 305, 339
  prohibited degrees of 421–2
  widows 422
Marseilles 111
Martel, Charles *see* Charles Martel (the Hammer)
Martin I, pope 369
Martin of Tours, Saint 83, 109–10, 125, 164, 261
  Life of Martin (Severus) 83
  tomb 109–10, 125, 137, 154, 159, 163, 261
martyrdom 66–7, 89, 90
  festivals of martyrs 89, 109, 346
  holy war martyrs 309
  sign of power of Christ 66, 73, 89
  women 90
Mass 264, 265, 458, 482
  see also Eucharist
Mass priests 265
Maurice, emperor 224
Maxentius 60
Maximus the Confessor 369
Mecca 289, 290, 291, 293
Medina 293
The Mediterranean and the Mediterranean World in the Age of Philip II (Braudel) 11
Mediterranean region
  intensification patterns 20–1
  Pirenne unity thesis 9–12
megalithic culture 23
Melania the Elder 83, 87, 284
Melkites *see* Chalcedonians

Melrose 355, 375
Menas, Saint 125
Menelik (son of Solomon) 139
menhirs 23
Merovingians 134, 155, 159, 229, 255,
    411, 428
Merv 275, 284
Mesopotamia 3, 37, 81, 86, 272, 274,
    275–6, 283, 285–6, 314
  monasteries 275
Mesrop Mashtots 277
metalworking 46–7
Metz 411
Michael, Archangel 181
Michael II, emperor 395
Michael the Syrian 313
"micro-Christendoms" 15, 364, 367,
    368, 378, 387, 406, 430
  Britain 15, 358–9, 376, 378
  Ireland 15
  Spain 367, 406
"middle ground" 51, 465
Milan 78
milestones 302
Milvian Bridge, battle of (312) 60, 84
Mimar Sinan 179
minuscule script 312
miracles 161, 163, 214, 388
mission civilisatrice 427
missionaries 4, 6, 324–5, 414, 427
  ascetic missionaries 81, 82
  exchange of "symbolic goods" 16
  image of 6, 7
  Manichaeans 41, 82
  Monophysites 186–7
  Nestorians 41
Mohammed and Charlemagne (Pirenne)
    9–10
Moldavia 47
monachos 81
monasteries 209–10
  amelioration of sinners 224, 225
  Arabian peninsula 287
  association with shrines 23
  competition 330
  "desert" monasteries 174
  double monasteries 376
  endowments 224, 253, 254, 357, 373
  episcopal founders 221

family foundations 373
Frankish 253–5, 373, 410
Gallic 221
Germany 442
gift-giving relationship 32, 332–3
grants of immunity 254–5
Ireland 330
Italy 210, 221
landholdings 222
Latin scholarship 51–2
Mesopotamia 275
microcosms of local society 374, 476
otherworldly self-image 374
poverty 222
powerhouses of atonement 252, 374
powerhouses of prayer 226, 255, 264
retired warriors in 374
sacred spaces 334
symbiosis with laity 224
Syriac 173, 174, 310–11
wealth 254–5, 332
monasticism 81–4, 220–31
  changing role 220, 226
  Egyptian 242, 250
  Frankish 253–5
  geographical shift 253
  identification with stability and
      political success 231
  increasing prominence 220
  low-profile early monasticism 222
  in Mediterranean western Europe
      221–4
  monastic discipline 112
  monastic "Rules" 210, 227, 250
  oblation 223–4
  see also monasteries; monks
Mongolia 284
monks 81
  and alms 222
  child novices 223–4
  dress 223, 225
  education 374
  exiles 247
  last great myth-makers 476
  self-mortification 225
  shared values with lay protectors
      476
  tonsure 223, 224
Monkwearmouth *see* Wearmouth

Monophysites 119, 172, 176, 177, 183, 184, 185, 186–7, 189, 274, 278, 279, 280, 288, 308, 309, 310, 368, 369
  Armenia 278
  East Roman empire 274, 279
  Histories 312, 313
  holy men 185
  missionaries 186–7
  opposition to Council of Chalcedon 183–4
  radical Christology 279
  region-wide networks 186–7
  theology 119, 120
monotheism 76, 117, 118
"Monothelite" controversy 369, 378
Monte Cassino monastery 201, 210, 221–2, 225
Moorish kings 138
Moralia on Job (Gregory) 205, 207, 236
moralitas 236
mosaics 162, 168, 180, 190, 193, 271, 300, 390, 400
Moses 459–60
mosques 302–3
Mren 378
Mu'awiya, calif 299
Much Wenlock 374
Muhammad 219, 289–94, 295, 300–1, 304, 318, 376
  Companions of 292, 293
  death 293
  hijra to Medina 293
Muirchú moccu Machtheni 331, 352
  Life (of Patricius) 331–2
al-Mundhîr 288
mundus (natural world) 145, 146, 147, 152, 153, 154, 162
musical notation 445–6
Muslims *see* Islam
myth-making 8, 438, 476

Najrân 288
Narsai 281
Nestorians 41, 279, 280, 288, 365
Nestorius, patriarch of Constantinople 119, 280
Neuillé-le-Lierre 164

Neustria 16, 253, 410, 430
New Grange 23, 130
New Hellenism 310–13
"New Rome" *see* Constantinople
Nicaea 61, 391
  council of (325) 61, 79
  council of (787) (Iconophile Council) 393, 396, 405, 406, 459
Nicene Creed 80
Nicephorus, emperor 394
Nicephorus, patriarch 397
  Antirrhetikos 397
Nieul-les-Saintes 164
Nihâwand 296
Nika riot, Constantinople (532) 178
Nisibis (Nusaybin) 267, 274, 281, 365
nodfyr ("fire of need") 426
nomads 43–4, 284, 286–7, 289, 301
Noricum 123, 125
Normandy 463
North Africa
  ceramics 180–1
  Christian states 138–9
  reconquest by Justinian 179
Northmen 463, 465, 469
  conversion 467
  expeditions 466, 467
  Viking raids 467–8
  see also Scandinavia
Northumbria 328, 349, 368
  Christianization 350, 356, 373
  diversity of local ecclesiastical cultures 371
  "Golden Age of Northumbria" 350
  "micro-Christendoms" 359
  vernacular visionary culture 375, 376
Norway 463, 469, 471–2, 480
Novgorod 403
Nubia 187
numerals
  Arabic 275
  Roman 275
nuns 90, 223, 226, 227, 476
  see also convents

Oak of Thunor 41, 421
oblation 223–4
Odin 481
Odoacer 124, 194

Offa, king of Mercia 477, 478
Offa's Dyke 477
ogham script 50, 130, 335
Olaf Tryggvason, king of Norway
    471–2, 480–1
Old Irish 50, 130, 239, 277, 337, 374
Old Saxons 413, 414, 419, 431, 432,
    451
Old Testament
    appeal to Old Testament models 279
    justification of pre-Christian practices
        339, 422
    Latin translations 140
    as model for Christian piety 18
On Germany (Tacitus) 479
On the Ruin of Britain (Gildas) 140
O'Neill dynasty (Ireland) 327, 342, 360
oracles 73, 76, 77, 137
oral Christianity 420, 449, 450
oral culture 48, 476, 477
ordo see town councils
Origen of Alexandria 64
Orléans 107
Orosius 74
    History against the Pagans 74
Orthodox Church 387, 403
Osrhoene 40
Ostbornholm 324
ostraka 175
Ostrogoths 104, 105, 136, 179, 182,
    196
Oswald of Northumbria 349, 350,
    352–3, 378
Oswy, king of Northumbria 350, 360,
    361
outlaws 334–5, 484
Oxyrhynchus 170

paganism 146, 148, 340–1
    Germany 413, 420
    Ireland 335
    northern 463, 473, 475
    suppression of 41, 73, 74, 146
    survivals 148, 149, 150, 151, 153
Palestine 174, 272, 390
    monasticism 82, 174
Palladius 130
Panjikent 41, 284
Pannonia 84, 86

papacy 114
    appeals/petitions to 114, 212
    patronage and administration
        network 212
    subject to East Roman empire 179–80
    see also entries for individual popes
Paradise
    artistic representation 401
    Christian 162, 163, 174, 260, 261,
        303, 401
    desire for 202
    on earth 163, 164, 187
    Muslim 303
    visions of 162
Paris 50, 54, 109
    churches and shrines 158
    parishes 33
Parthian kingdom 54
Pascha *see* Easter
Passover 346
past and present, tension between 474
pastoralists 43, 44, 47, 182
Patricius *see* Patrick, Saint
Patrick, Saint 51, 130–2, 133, 140,
        265–6, 325, 331–2, 334, 336, 352
    Confession 131, 331
    Letter to Coroticus 131, 331
    Life (Muirchú moccu Machtheni)
        331–2
Patristic Age 22–3
Patroclus (hermit) 161
Paul, Saint 208
Paulinus, archbishop of York 348, 349
Paulinus, bishop of Nola 86–7, 235,
        415
Pavia 206
P'awstos Buzanderan (Faustus the Bard)
        9, 277, 278
    Epic Histories 9
peasantry
    control of 102, 107
    Dark Ages 31
    farming economy 43, 46, 47, 48
    runaway serfs 107
    seigneurial system 410
Pehlevi language 281
Pelagian Controversy 88–90, 127–8
Pelagianism 130
Pelagius 88, 89–90, 127

Pelusium 72, 181
penance 242, 245
    Augustinian view 256
    elective element 243, 257, 333
    Gregorian view 256–7, 261
    group penance 108
    Irish penitential practices 333
    medicamenta paenitentiae 252, 255,
        257
    perpetual penance 256
    public penance 68, 80, 125, 256
    restoring the honor of God 245,
        246
    "tariffed penance" 242, 243–4, 252,
        257, 326, 370
    in the Western Church 255–7
Penitentials 19, 24, 243–4, 245, 246,
        334, 481
peregrinatio 414–15
perfection, attainment of 199
Perpetuus, bishop of Tours 109
Persia
    Church in 279–82
    Sasanian dynasty 37, 54, 283
Persian empire 181–2, 272–3
    war with East Roman empire 272–3,
        285–6, 287
    Zoroastrianism 271, 278, 283, 313
Peter the Iberian, bishop of Maiouma
        166
Peterborough 468
philosophy 67, 70, 236
    Christian 68
    and morality 70–1
Phrygia 383, 487
pietas 87
piety 199–200
    lay pursuit of 199, 200
pilgrimage 125, 154, 319, 449
Pippin of Herstal 408, 415, 417, 420,
        428, 430–1
pirates
    Greeks 193
    Saxons 102, 126
Pirenne, Henri 9–12, 14
Platonic mysticism 250
Po valley 182, 192
poetry 480
    Anglo-Saxon 373, 377–8

Arabic 308
    Christian 330, 373, 377
    epic 477, 478
    Irish 330, 331
Poitiers
    battle of (733) 319, 410
    Holy Cross convent 255
polygamy 305, 339
polytheism 58–60, 65, 73, 74, 77
    coexistence with Christianity 76–7
    see also paganism
Portugal 152
Potho, abbot of San Vicenzo 436
poverty, and Christian charity 69–70,
        78, 158
power
    condescensio 208, 212
    spiritual 208, 209, 211
praedicatio 213, 214, 215
prayer
    communal 108
    frequency 458
    spiritual guides 176, 226
predestination 89
Procopius of Caesarea 180, 185
    Secret History 185
prophetesses 160, 161, 450, 481
Prosper of Aquitaine 89, 130
Provence 97, 151
Psalms of David 41, 82
Pseudo-Dionysius 29, 398, 457
    Celestial Hierarchies 398
    Ecclesiastical Hierarchies 398
public building traditions 32, 55,
        302
purgatory 24, 258–9, 265, 375

Qâdisiyya 296
Qenneshre 272
qeryana 281–2, 290
Questions and Answers 175, 308–9,
        387
Qur'ân 290, 291, 292, 300, 302, 303,
        304, 337, 390, 449
Quryash family 290

Radbod (Frisian chieftain) 417
Radegund of Poitiers 228–31, 255
Ragnachar of Cambrai 135

Ravenna 97, 136, 179, 192, 193, 196, 430
  fall 405
  Lombard occupation 430
  San Vitale 193, 401, 405
  Sant'Apollinare Nuovo 271
ravens 148
Reccared, king of the Visigoths 193, 214
rectores 236
Redwald, king of East Anglia 347
Regensburg 411
Regestum (Gregory) 212
Regula Pastoralis (Gregory) 207–12, 236–7, 248
Reichenau monastery 442
relics 162, 255, 429, 430, 458
  Holy Cross 229–30, 284, 285, 319, 377
religiones 58–60, 61, 63, 70, 74, 75
reliquaries 458
Remigius, bishop of Rheims 134, 137
repentance 67, 68, 69
  and almsgiving 69, 71
  see also atonement; penance
Repton 477–8
res sacratae 458
Resafa 287
Resh'aina 274
reverentia 154–5, 159
Rhine valley 49, 50
Rhône valley 102, 228
Rihab 273
Rimbert, *Life of Anskar* 470
Ripon 363
ritual 18
  Adoration of the Cross 377
  agrarian rites 154
  books of 427
  borrowing between pagans and Christians 153
  consolidation 366–7
  Great Liturgy 166, 167
  healing rituals 77
  "high" liturgical language 449
  lay rituals 454
  see also burial practices
Rogation processions 108, 281
Roma Invicta 194

Romagna 179
Roman empire
  aristocratic collaboration with non-Roman warlords 98, 100–1
  barbarian invasions 4, 44, 48, 86, 93, 438
  centralization 57
  Christianity 54–92
  collapse of Western empire 21, 50–1, 56, 97, 98, 149, 177
  command economy 12–13
  "downsizing" 12, 20, 102, 128
  economic collapse 12–13
  end of Roman peace 99
  frontiers 50–1
  "Golden Age" 56
  government 55
  imperial court 57
  indirect rule 55–6
  provinces 57
  religion 58–60
  religiously neutral public culture 85–6
  taxation 31, 55, 56, 57
  Tetrarchy 56
  see also East Roman empire
Romance languages 232, 447
Romani 98, 103, 123, 124, 125
Romanos Melodes 187
Rome
  archaic pagan ceremonies 145, 194
  bankruptcy 429
  basilicas 77, 114
  bishops of 114–15, 116
  Christian 199
  Christian relics 429, 430
  emptying and neglect of 21, 190, 198, 429
  falls to Justinian 179
  frontier city of East Roman empire 2
  libraries 64, 195, 199
  monuments 60
  new social order 195
  patrimony of Saint Peter 206
  population 21, 50, 54, 114, 190, 429
  re-creation 429–30
  Roman clergy 114, 206–7
  sack of (410) 48, 86, 91
  Saint Peter's 77

San Cosmà e Damiano 199
San Giovanni in Laterano 77
San Stefano Rotondo 199
Santa Constanza 29
Sant'Agnese 29
senatorial aristocracy 194–5
Romulus and Remus 177, 194
Romulus Augustulus, emperor 97,
    121–2, 125, 194
Rugi 124
Rule (Saint Benedict) 210, 225, 441
Rûm 297, 317, 318, 383
    see also East Roman empire
Rûmi 487
runes 48, 377, 475–6
rural Church 81, 146–7
Rus' 466
Russia 466
Russian Orthodoxy 403
rustici 152, 159
Ruthwell 377

"Sacramentary of King Pippin" 430
sacraments 395, 398
sacred and profane
    bridged by gift-giving 32
    separation 460, 461
sacred landscapes 147–8, 164, 426
"sacred theater" 187
sacrifice 60, 64, 74, 85, 472, 481
    animal 60, 309
    horse 134
    human 324, 417
Sa'd bar Abî Waqqâs 298
saeculum 82
Sagas 473, 478, 480
St. Gall, monastery 442
Saint Germigny-des-Prés 458
Saint Sabas monastery 397
Saint Thomas' Christians 271
saints 109
    column saints 173, 174, 310–11
    continued presence of 163–4
    cult of 19
    deathbeds 258
    desert saints 173, 174, 175
    icons 388
    intercessors 154–5
    patron saints 109, 110

veneration of 109, 154, 159
    see also hagiography
Salic Law 346
Salona, bishop of 213
salvation 65
Salzburg 421
San Vicenzo monastery 436, 446, 486
San Vitale church, Ravenna 193, 401,
    405
sancta respublica 193
Saône valley 102
sapientes 20, 24, 241–2, 246, 252, 329,
    368
sarcophagi 238
Sardis 63
Sarjûn (of Damascus) 307
Sasanian dynasty 37, 54, 283
Saxons 101, 102, 126, 127, 319
    in Britain 7, 8, 15, 126, 127, 301,
        341, 342–54
    ideas of the sacred 348
    pirates 102, 126
Saxony 412, 431, 451, 452
    "frontier" province 452
Sayings of the Fathers 188–9
Scandinavia 465, 468–9
    Christ as Frankish god 465
    Christianity 7, 467, 469–84
    Northmen 463, 465, 466, 467–8,
        469
    paganism 463, 473, 475
    territorial reach 465
    see also the names of individual
        countries
schismatics 91
Scotland 51, 129
scotti (sea-rovers) 129, 327
scriptoria 22
scripts 23
    Caroline minuscule 444, 445
    minuscule 312
    ogham 50, 130, 335
    punctuation 445
    runic 377
    uncial 363
Scriptures
    copying 372, 459
    divine law 62–3
    exegesis 282

Scriptures (*cont'd*)
    manifestation of the will of God 459
    qeryana ("reading aloud") 281–2,
        290
    textual community 14
    see also Bible; Old Testament
seasonal festivals 154
Sebbi, king of Essex 374
Seine valley 21
Semirechye 282
Senchas Már 338–9, 422
Seneca 205
Serapeum of Alexandria 74
Sergius (Christian martyr) 287, 288
Severinus of Noricum 123–4, 125
    Life of Severinus (Eugippius) 125
Severus of Antioch 185
Severus of Sebokht 275
Sevso 84
sexual codes and practices 152, 334
sexual sins 243
shamanism 465, 472
Shapur II, king of Persia 60
Shenoute of Atripe 118, 148
Shirin (wife of Khusro II) 283
shrines 458
    Christian 29, 109–10, 125, 154, 158,
        181, 331, 342, 458
    Islamic 291
    and monasteries 221
    pagan 146, 148, 345
Shubhhal-Isho', Mar 41
Sicily 179, 192, 206, 208, 405
Síde ("the Other Side") 483
Sidonius Apollinaris, bishop of
        Clermont-Ferrand 99–100,
        110–11, 113
Siegfried 484
sign of the Cross 72, 153, 267, 391,
        392, 393, 395
Silk Route 272
silverware 84, 172
sin
    atonement 242–3, 258
    calibration of 24, 242
    capital sins 256
    confession 257
    districtio 257, 258
    inner cross-examination 256

    new language of 67
    new view of 220
    and repentance 67, 68, 69
    retribution for 160
    unatoned sin 258
    in the Western Church 255–7
Sinkepha 59
Sinkiang 284
Sisetrudis (nun) 258
Sklaviniai 182–3, 192
slave trade 131, 214, 326, 416, 472
    British Christian slaves 130
    Christian slave-owners 64
    slave-raiding 124, 325
Slavs 182, 394, 404
Slovenia 125
Snorri Sturluson 473, 480
    Sagas 480
Soghdians 284
Soissons 134
Spain
    Arab conquest 296, 319, 367
    civil wars 193
    competition with East Roman empire
        366
    erosion of Latin culture 233
    imperial garrisons 179, 366
    Justinian's invasion 366
    "micro-Christendom" 367, 406
    monasteries 221, 222
    Visigothic 6, 193–4, 211, 214, 234,
        319, 365–8
spells 481–2, 486
spiritual guidance 176, 203–4, 205,
        208–9, 242
Spoleto 192
stelae 139
Stellinga 452
Stephen the Younger, Saint 392
Stephen II, pope 430, 431
Stoic sages 205
Stonehenge 23
Stories to Strengthen the Faith
        (Anastasius) 309
Streanaeshalch *see* Whitby
Sturla (father of Snorri Sturluson) 480
stylite hermits 173, 310–11
Subiaco 221
Sulpicius Severus 83, 87

supernatural, attitudes towards 76,
376, 421, 426, 455–6, 482–5
see also demonic world
superstitio 150
superstitious practices 426
Susanna (Monophysite) 188
*Sutra of the Causes and Effects of
Actions* 285
Sutton Hoo 321, 324, 347
Sweden 463, 464, 466
swords 464–5
"symbolic goods" 15–16, 22
"symbolic systems" 16
Symeon (hermit) 185–6
Symeon the Stylite, Saint 125, 173, 402
Symeon the Younger 174
Symmachus, prefect of Rome 59
synagogues 63, 80
Syria 3, 21, 81, 82, 172, 272, 273,
274–5
agrarian society 172
biculturalism 311
charismatic preachers 81
Christianity 3, 82, 172, 173, 174,
183, 186, 310–11
holy men 173
Justinian's theological politics 183
monasteries/monasticism 82, 173,
174, 310–11
Monophysite clergy 186
weakening of imperial control 186
Syriac language 40, 172, 274, 275,
281–2, 312, 317
Syriac literature 311

taboos 19–20
codification of 20
Tacitus, *On Germany* 479
Taín (Tale of the Cattle Raid of Cooley)
368, 483
talismans 402
Tara Brooch 372
Tarsus 368
Tauberbischofsheim 425–6
taxation 31, 55, 56, 57, 301, 314
administration 55, 56, 57–8, 75, 76
clerical immunity 78
jizya tax 306
Roman empire 31, 55, 56, 57

tithes 33, 452–3
Tembris valley 64
temples, closing and destruction of 74,
75–6, 91
temptation 203
Tetrarchy 56
Thagaste 233
theaters 170
Themes 386
Theodora (consort of Justinian/
empress) 185, 193
Theodore, abbot of Studios 396–7
Theodore abu Qurrah 316
Theodore of Mopsuestia 183–4, 280,
365
Theodore of Tarsus 368, 369–71
Theodoret, bishop of Cyrrhus 183–4
Theodoric, king of the Ostrogoths 103,
136, 194
Theodosian Code 75, 97, 178
Theodosiopolis 169
Theodosius I, emperor 74, 80, 130, 256
Theodosius II, emperor 75, 97, 134,
149, 177–8
Theodulph, bishop of Orléans 405–6,
456–7, 458, 460, 461
Theophilus of Edessa 311
Theophilus, emperor 395
Theotokos 120
Thessalonica 389
massacre at 80
Theuderic II, king of the Franks 253
Thiota (prophetess) 450
Thorbjorg (prophetess) 481
Thorgeir of Ljosvatn 472
Thrace 119, 394
Three Chapters 184, 249
"thunderstones" 486
Thuringia 420
Timothy I, Katholikos 314
Tintagel 130
tithes 33, 452–3
Titus Praxias 487
Toledo 366
Tome (Leo I) 120–1, 184
tonsure 223, 224
Celtic 360
Roman 360
Touareg language 138

Toulouse 103–4
Touraine 164
Tournai 134
Tours 108, 109–10, 146, 159, 164
    council of (813) 450
    tomb of Saint Martin of Tours
        109–10, 125, 137, 154, 159, 163,
        261
trade associations and cultic
        brotherhoods 64
translations
    of the Bible 199
    Greek texts 198, 311
    Syriac 3, 275, 311, 317
Travancore 281
Trdat III 277
trees
    Christian symbolism 164
    sacred 41, 314, 413, 421
Tribonian (lawyer) 178
Trier 50, 78
Triumph of Orthodoxy (843) 396, 398
Trondheim 471
túath 132, 325, 330
Tyché 171

Uighur empire 41, 284
Ukraine 47
Ultán (Irish monk) 372
Ummayad Empire 298–301, 319
    collapse 314
Undley, Suffolk 342
"unity" of Western Europe 9–12, 16
    commercial unity notion 12, 13
    and diversity 16
    evaporation 12
    Pirenne thesis 10–12
    "Roman" unity 10
upper class
    creation 84
    ethnic specificity 104
    fragile monopoly of Christianity 375
    militarization 234
    see also aristocracy
Urnfield Period 23, 24
Utrecht 417, 486

Valens, emperor 479
Vandals 97, 101, 104, 105–6, 136, 179

Vardan Mamikonian 278
Venantius Fortunatus 156–7, 230, 237,
    247
Verden 432
Vergil, bishop of Salzburg 421
"vernacular" Christianity 449, 450
vernacular visionary culture 375–6, 377
Vienne 104
Vigilius, Pope 184
Viking raids 467–8
villa, Roman 146
villages 46, 273–4
Vinniau (Saint Findbarr) 239, 246
violence 155–6, 163
    buying off 245
    regulation of 156
Virgin Mary
    cult of 120
    icons 388, 389, 457
virgins 90
    high value placed on 226
    sanctity 227
    see also nuns
Visigoths 48, 86, 99, 101, 102, 103,
        105, 106, 136, 234
    Arian Visigoths 136, 137
    Catholicism 193, 214
    legislators 237–8
    sack of Rome 48, 86, 91
    in Spain 6, 193–4, 211, 214, 234,
        319, 365–8
visionaries 450
visual imagination, schooling 399, 403
Vitalian, pope 369
Vivarium 196, 222
Volturno 446
Volubilis 138
votive offerings 324
Vouillé, battle of (507) 137
Voyage of the Soul 259–60, 313

Walbert (of Wildeshausen) 479
Walcaud, bishop of Liège 452
Wales 128, 129, 240
wandering preachers 161
warrior society
    Armenia 277–8
    barbarians 48–9
    Britain 348, 353

Germany 413
Ireland 335
Water Newton church 79
wealth
  bishops 157
  convents and monasteries 254–5, 332
  mobilization of 71, 126, 157–8
  Roman aristocracy 71
Wearmouth (later Monkwearmouth)
    monastery 51–2, 351, 355, 356,
    358, 372, 374
Welsh language 239
Whitby 215, 361, 376
  council of (664) 361
widows 422
Widukind (Saxon noble) 432, 479
Wildeshausen 479
Wilfrid, bishop of York 52, 359–64
  deposition 370
Willibald, bishop of Eichstätt 319–20,
    428
Willibrord 4, 415–16, 417–18, 427
  calendar 415–16
"wisdom literature" 427
Wittislingen 413
Woden 474, 479–80
women

abbesses 373, 476
in the Christian Church 64
cultic sisterhoods 64
martyrdom 90
and piety 200, 227, 228, 229, 231
prophetesses 160, 161, 450, 481
reclusiveness 200
virgins 90, 226, 227
widows 422
see also nuns; Virgin Mary
Wonders, books of (Gregory) 161
"worldly wisdom" 234, 235
written vernacular 374–5
Wroxeter 126
Wynfrith *see* Boniface, Saint

Y *Gododdin* (Aneirin) 128
Yazdin of Kerkuk 283
Yazdkart II, king of Persia 278, 283
Yazid II, calif 302
Yeavering 349
Yemen 138, 276, 288, 290
York 345, 359

Zacharias II, pope 430
Zoroastrianism 271, 278, 283, 313
Zuqnîn 314